The CIA and the Pursuit of S

Series editors: Richard J. Aldrich, Rory Cormac, Michael S. Goodman and Hugh Wilford

This series explores the full spectrum of spying and secret warfare in a globalised world.

Intelligence has changed. Secret service is no longer just about spying or passively watching a target. Espionage chiefs now command secret armies and legions of cyber warriors who can quietly shape international relations itself. Intelligence actively supports diplomacy, peacekeeping and warfare: the entire spectrum of security activities. As traditional inter-state wars become more costly, covert action, black propaganda and other forms of secret interventionism become more important. This ranges from proxy warfare to covert action; from targeted killing to disruption activity. Meanwhile, surveillance permeates communications to the point where many feel there is little privacy. Intelligence, and the accelerating technology that surrounds it, have never been more important for the citizen and the state.

Titles in the *Intelligence, Surveillance and Secret Warfare* series include:

Published:

The Arab World and Western Intelligence: Analysing the Middle East, 1956–1981
Dina Rezk

The Twilight of the British Empire: British Intelligence and Counter-Subversion in the Middle East, 1948–63
Chikara Hashimoto

Chile, the CIA and the Cold War: A Transatlantic Perspective
James Lockhart

The Clandestine Lives of Colonel David Smiley: Code Name 'Grin'
Clive Jones

The Problem of Secret Intelligence
Kjetil Anders Hatlebrekke

Outsourcing US Intelligence: Private Contractors and Government Accountability
Damien Van Puyvelde

The CIA and the Pursuit of Security: History, Documents and Contexts
Huw Dylan, David V. Gioe and Michael S. Goodman

Forthcoming:

The Snowden Era on Screen: Signals Intelligence and Digital Surveillance
James Smith

https://edinburghuniversitypress.com/series-intelligence-surveillance-and-secret-warfare.html

The CIA and the Pursuit of Security

History, Documents and Contexts

Huw Dylan
David V. Gioe and
Michael S. Goodman

EDINBURGH
University Press

Edinburgh University Press is one of the leading university presses in the UK. We publish academic books and journals in our selected subject areas across the humanities and social sciences, combining cutting-edge scholarship with high editorial and production values to produce academic works of lasting importance. For more information visit our website: edinburghuniversitypress.com

© Huw Dylan, David V. Gioe and Michael S. Goodman, 2020, 2022

Edinburgh University Press Ltd
The Tun – Holyrood Road, 12(2f) Jackson's Entry, Edinburgh EH8 8PJ

First published in hardback by Edinburgh University Press 2020

Typeset in 11/14 Sabon by
Servis Filmsetting Ltd, Stockport, Cheshire,

A CIP record for this book is available from the British Library

ISBN 978 1 4744 2884 2 (hardback)
ISBN 978 1 4744 2885 9 (paperback)
ISBN 978 1 4744 2886 6 (webready PDF)
ISBN 978 1 4744 2887 3 (epub)

The right of Huw Dylan, David V. Gioe and Michael S. Goodman to be identified as the authors of this work has been asserted in accordance with the Copyright, Designs and Patents Act 1988, and the Copyright and Related Rights Regulations 2003 (SI No. 2498).

Contents

Documents

Foreword

Intelligence matters. Good intelligence keeps us safe; it helps us understand our place in the world, and it fosters sound decisions. Inaccurate information matters too. It corrodes our ability to understand reality and stunts our progress towards a better, safer world. This push and pull – between truth and fiction, trust and distrust – shapes not only our understanding of the present but also our understanding of history.

As the world becomes more complex and connected – tweets that shift markets in seconds, political and social movements that rise in an instant – it's more important than ever to understand the path that brought us here. Accurate, dependable history is not just a concern for professors and curators. It's vital for every citizen, allowing us to not only disentangle the complications of the current day but to avoid repeating the mistakes of the past.

An appreciation of history is especially critical in matters of intelligence. While no set of historical facts is immune from reappraisal, the history created and recorded by covert organisations is, by definition, more irregular than much of the standard historical record. As years turn to decades, as classifications expire and redactions are lifted, we must constantly reconcile new information with old, measuring long-held assumptions against fresh facts. That, of course, makes writing a book like this especially difficult – but even more necessary.

Any accounting of the history of the Central Intelligence Agency is particularly challenging because this constant churn continuously adds nuance to our understanding, sometimes even uprooting narratives entirely. As such, it's incumbent on any volume of intelligence history to take a comprehensive, detailed look at the matters it examines. It requires both a wide lens and a zoom, as well as perspective that can allow the picture to come into clearer focus in the years ahead.

I believe the authors of this book accomplish that task. They tell an immersive story, spanning more than seven decades since the Agency was founded. David Gioe, Michael Goodman and Huw Dylan examine historical eras through declassified documents, and, like any experienced CIA analyst, tell us the unique context and crosswinds surrounding each time period. They spell out the contingencies considered, the consequences wrought. They place us inside the minds and consciences of the analysts and decision-makers of the day, laying bare the grey inside stories that may seem black or white today.

It's an approach worth applauding – and a style of scholarship and popular criticism that I wish we saw more of in the world, particularly in appraisals of the CIA. Secret organisations are easy to criticise. Citizens quickly grow sceptical, and often rightly so. And when information remains missing from the public record, observers tend to rush to the darkest corner, filling in any gaps with their worst assumptions.

This book is a useful corrective to that impulse. Gioe, Goodman and Dylan understand that if citizens are to have confidence in covert organisations, the history must be told honestly, unflinchingly and completely. It avoids the pitfalls of sycophancy to an agency that clearly has its flaws, while also avoiding the assumption that agents and analysts working in secret must be up to no good – an approach to criticism in no short supply when it comes to the CIA.

In this book, readers are trusted to decide for themselves. The authors understand their obligation to shed light on these once-held secrets responsibly rather than salaciously. It is written with the understanding that the vast majority of the tens of thousands of Americans who have served this agency have done so honourably and in service to a nation they love. I am one of those Americans. I am proud of my service – but it doesn't mean I agree with every decision made or every action taken by the Agency. That's true, I imagine, for most of my former colleagues, and the colleagues still hard at work today. But I also believe the CIA is a cornerstone in America's security. I believe our nation is safer because of the women and men who dedicate their lives to serving it. And I believe that the courage and quiet sacrifice of those humble servants is honoured by this book.

The CIA and the Pursuit of Security: History, Documents and Contexts is a worthy and necessary addition to the literature and scholarship on the CIA. You'll see how women and men grappled with the pursuit of American interests and values amid an evolving, complex and often dangerous world. When you're done, you'll see an agency not without its faults, but also not without its triumphs. And hopefully, you'll appreciate better that within the historical record, it's important to leave room for both.

Michael Morell,
Former Acting Director of the CIA

Acknowledgements

HD: His co-authors and the Department for the wonderful support as this project unfolded. And the girls, for their patience as it came together.

DVG: Thanks to my family for waiting for me for dinner. Donna Artusy and MAJ Jim Twist for invaluable research assistance and advice on the chapters dealing with CIA and technology. The Army Cyber Institute at West Point and Dr Edward Sobiesk for institutional support and professional encouragement to write this book. As a US government employee, David Gioe wishes to note that this analysis does not necessarily reflect that of the United States Military Academy, the US Army, the Department of Defense or the US government.

MSG: His lovely family for their patience and humour; Huw and Dave for their humour; and West Ham for their humour. One of these is not intentional . . .

Introduction

'The essential skill of a secret service is to get things done secretly and deniably.'[1]
John Bruce Lockhart, a former Deputy Chief
of the Secret Intelligence Service

Perhaps surprisingly for an organisation carapaced in secrecy, the Central Intelligence Agency (CIA) is one of the best-known institutions around the world. Its activities since its creation in 1947 have had a global resonance; they have occasionally generated internal controversy and strife in the US; they have left a substantial mark in popular culture. Famous (or infamous) though it is, however, the CIA is a profoundly misunderstood organisation. Myths and conspiracies have surrounded the agency since its earliest days, and these have blossomed over the decades. Fact and fiction coexist and are tightly interwoven in the public imagination concerning the CIA. The facts are often more fascinating than the myths.

What are the facts; what feeds the fiction? It is a global agency with a worldwide mission, chartered to prevent strategic surprise and support American policymaking by narrowing the cone of uncertainty for the president and the executive branch, and the armed forces they command. The CIA fulfils this responsibility by collecting, analysing, assessing and disseminating intelligence gathered though all sources to its customers in government. It recruits spies in foreign countries, it manages a substantial technical intelligence capacity, it processes publicly available information to supplement classified collection efforts; it is home to enough subject matter experts in the form of linguists, area studies specialists, psychologists and technical experts to staff a university; it maintains myriad liaison relationships with partner intelligence services all over the world; it maintains a paramilitary capability and undertakes disruptive, covert actions when ordered to do so. But, primarily, it is an agency concerned with gathering and processing secret intelligence and using it to enable US political and military leaders to make more effective policy choices. Despite its fame, it is a very secretive agency.

Myths and conspiracies feed upon secrecy, certainly. But the CIA's activities have also generated plenty of supplementary fodder. Intelligence services are more than mechanisms for intelligence collection and analysis; they also serve as foreign policy tools, undertaking deniable, yet often visible, action to influence world events on behalf of their governments. Indeed, no understanding of America's relationship with Cuba, its containment doctrine or rollback strategy can be found absent an appreciation of how successive policymakers attempted to use the paramilitary and covert action capacity of the CIA as a lever to exert pressure on their targets. Covert actions constitute a small percentage of the CIA's overall activities, but they are intrinsic to the agency, part of its DNA as a creature born of the early Cold War.

One need only read the text of US National Security Directive 10/2, promulgated in 1948, less than a year after the creation of the agency, to understand its pedigree in the field of covert actions. The directive authorised the CIA to engage in: 'Propaganda; economic warfare; preventive direct action, including sabotage, anti-sabotage, demolition and evacuation measures; subversion against hostile states, including assistance to underground resistance movements, guerrillas and refugee liberation groups, and support of indigenous anti-Communist elements in threatened countries of the free world.'[2] The mandate has changed only slightly over the years, but the CIA continues to enjoy a broad capacity to conduct operations designed to *influence* as well as to *understand* targets. It is these activities that receive the lion's share of media interest, and form the basis for most of Hollywood's engagement with the secret world. They also help propagate the myths surrounding CIA. In an environment of infotainment it has become ever more complicated to distil fact from fiction and understand CIA's role in international history, much less contemporary international affairs. This book aims to dispel some of the wilder notions about the agency and its activities, and replace them with historical analysis based upon properly declassified primary sources.

We have written this book with the aim of illuminating a broader cross-section of the CIA's history at several critical points in the twentieth century and on into the twenty-first. This book builds upon several excellent books on CIA, including by authors who are familiar names to any intelligence historian: Christopher Andrew, Richard Aldrich, Joe Trento and John Ranelagh, to name but four. But we write with the benefit of several recent documentary releases, concerning both historic and contemporary issues. Therefore, this book will complement earlier volumes through the reinterpretation of several key events in CIA's history, recent and more distant. We aim to bring to the fore certain understudied aspects of CIA's past, including an explicit emphasis on the role of technological innovation, disinformation and political warfare, but also the Anglo-American special intelligence relationship that has been a durable yet hidden feature of CIA's history. A focus on Anglo-American intelligence liaison in this volume is our attempt to shine a special light on the relationships between intelligence agencies, between intelligence officers and between Washington and Whitehall, who used their foreign intelligence services to undergird and manage the special political relationship.

We publish this volume at a time when the prominence of the CIA in the media and in general political debate is very pronounced. Rarely does a day pass without a commentary on the CIA in the news (or a former CIA officer commenting upon the news). This is part of a longer trend of publicising and, in so doing, attempting to weaponise the products and actions of the agency in support of one political cause or another. The 9/11 attacks and the later debate concerning Iraq's weapons programmes thrust the agency into the limelight at the turn of the century; the more recent discussions concerning Russian interference in the 2016 US election and the subsequent special counsel investigation conducted by Robert S. Mueller have ensured that it remained there. But much of the political discussion as well as media coverage of CIA is ahistorical in nature, and may leave the non-specialist wondering what the historical antecedents of these often-breathless headlines (or tweets) might be. We hope to offer such perspective with this book. For specialist or academic readers, we hope to offer a deeper understanding of how the various primary source documents fit together in the broad sweep of global history, and to pose a reminder that the hidden hand of intelligence has operated in the background, sometimes subtly, sometimes not so subtly, throughout the history of American international relations. Integrating intelligence work into our understanding of past and current events can yield a fuller and more nuanced perspective on military and diplomatic history in particular – a lantern for what has been, and a headlight for what might be.

Our approach is to illuminate CIA's past by featuring and contextualising primary source documents from CIA's archive, and to connect the modern reader with CIA's history. We aim to illustrate that many issues currently in the media spotlight actually have their roots in an earlier age, often under not totally dissimilar circumstances. Essentially, this is an effort then to re-historicise CIA's past with the benefit of time and additional documentary evidence. While not every signal event in CIA's history can be explored in a single volume, we hope that the twenty-five chapters in this volume, when taken together, will demonstrate and characterise CIA's place in the warp and woof of American and international history.

Intelligence history has come a long way since its inception as a serious topic for academic study in the 1980s. It is an established subject at a number of universities; there is a booming research and writing culture, particularly in the English-speaking world; and it is steadily becoming a more globalised academic topic. But we have barely scratched the surface of the role and influence of the hidden hand in international and domestic affairs – as the leading intelligence historian Christopher Andrew identified not too long ago, a wide intellectual space is still available for continued intelligence-based contributions.[3] He observed as early as 1984 that intelligence studies was the 'missing dimension'[4] of twentieth-century diplomatic history, and two decades later he could still lament: 'Intelligence is still denied its proper place in studies of the Cold War – and indeed of international relations in general.'[5] As he noted, and as any historian of intelligence will attest to, the secrecy surrounding intelligence agencies, their work, and their records is a fundamental reason for this. And in many official quarters attitudes have not changed that much since 1984, when British prime minister Margaret Thatcher rather bluntly stated her view that 'too much has been said and written about intelligence and less should be in future'.[6] Thankfully, this attitude does not enjoy universal support; more researchers are willing to concede that intelligence history is a valuable, occasionally key, ingredient in our understanding of contemporary and Cold War history, and the progress in researching intelligence agencies and their work has developed significantly. Indeed, the growing body of work continues to demonstrate that the neglect of intelligence history by previous generations led often to a skewed perspective on major political and military events.

Given the level of secrecy concerning the CIA and its work, locating reliable source material is a peculiar challenge for intelligence historians; the document declassification and release process presents historiographical challenges. The procedure and timeliness of document declassification, as well as the chronological order of revelations, has led to an availability bias for historians and journalists, and therefore distortions in the public understanding of international history. For instance, the role of signals intelligence and codebreaking has been underappreciated, whereas the role of special operations and human intelligence is more widely examined. This trend, holding true since the Second World War, is perhaps best illustrated by examining the relative trajectories of the histories concerning the wartime British Special Operations Executive (SOE) and the American Office of Strategic Services (OSS) compared with those of wartime sigint and codebreaking. The former dominated the latter for decades. But this was not because of its relative importance: it was because historians could access the files of the SOE and the OSS, whereas they could not access the files of Bletchley Park to write the history of Enigma and the Ultra secret. One must always bear in mind the advice of the historian Richard Aldrich to remember that the archive is not an analogue for reality; the researcher

4

needs to dig deep. The historian also must remember that the challenges posed by the relative paucity of official sources are not necessarily resolved by the availability of the materials that have been leaked *en masse* over recent years, but are, instead, often rather compounded by questions over the contextualisation and reliability of these revelations. Intelligence and secrecy, past and present: *plus ça change*.

We thus extend an invitation to both the lay and specialist audiences to read on and seek new insights and new interpretations for documents that tell us something consequential about CIA's history and its role in American politics and international affairs. We also welcome practitioners to reconnect with CIA's history in these pages, to draw linkages between the past and present, and to see how previous generations of intelligence officers faced an international system that they found challenging. Famed CIA analyst and historian Sherman Kent argued that 'the only reason for reconstructing the history of a government agency is to further the operational efficiency of that agency. This cannot be history for history's sake. It must be history for the improvement of today's and tomorrow's operations.'[7] We would certainly agree that the lessons of history need to be identified, lest mistakes or missteps be unnecessarily repeated. However, while Kent's rationale may be compelling for the official historians at CIA or in other intelligence communities, we wish to broaden the scope of resonance for readers from all professions and perspectives. Our purpose in writing this book is to explore newly available documents (and fresh practitioner insights), to recontextualise existing primary source documents in concert with scholarly literature and to reveal an updated interpretation of CIA's place both in the world and also *vis-à-vis* American policymakers. In that sense, it is in fact history for its own sake, a chronicle of the CIA and its activities during the turbulent decades of the Cold War and the early twenty-first century.

Issues of transparency are attendant with any contemporary discussion of intelligence agencies. While this was not always so, the 'right to know' what is being done in the public's name is a centrepiece of modern discourse concerning the CIA, leaving it and its sister agencies struggling with how to balance security and transparency. It is perhaps worth noting, however, that the CIA has travelled far further down the road of (relative) transparency than practically any other major intelligence agency. A global comparison may be best to illuminate the situation: no other intelligence agency releases so much material about its operations, its analytical assessments, and its structure and inner workings. Beyond declassification of material, CIA directors are public figures whose speeches and published statements give further details about CIA's positions. To be sure, overclassification is a major issue in the US intelligence community. CIA has resisted declassification mandates on several occasions and has been forced to release information in response to Freedom of Information Act requests, legal challenges and congressional oversight investigations. CIA will never declassify enough material to satisfy those who believe in total transparency; nor will any level of transparency satiate the die-hard conspiracy theorists who see the hidden hand of the CIA behind any and every significant global event. But in comparison with other global intelligence services, including those of its closest ally, the British intelligence community, the CIA leads by a wide margin. In fact, that a book on CIA using primary source documents can be written at all is a testament to how far CIA has come in declassification.

Since America developed a peacetime intelligence bureaucracy at the end of the Second World War, the CIA has been at the heart of the American pursuit of security. Like its foe the KGB, it has been both sword and shield – a hidden hand in pursuit of foreign policy objectives and the first line of defense against foreign threats. Former CIA Director, General Michael Hayden stated in 2007 that this has, by and large, been an honourable mission, noting that 'We can, and should, be proud of the many great things CIA has done, and will do, to defend the United States in a very dangerous world.'[8] Not everyone would agree, of course. Several of the subsequent chapters are concerned with instances of controversy, national and international, some of it profound. An agency operating for so long, so broadly, and at the cutting edge of US foreign policy will inevitably become entangled in moral hazard. No intelligence agency can avoid wrestling with difficult ethical dilemmas; nor can (or, at least, should) responsible policymakers. How to manage these risks is one of the big questions of our time. The answer, or, certainly, the debate, should be coloured by an understanding of the lessons of history. The following pages offer an insight into how the CIA developed over the past seven decades, and how it navigated the fraught international environment in its mission to keep the US secure. Reality can be more interesting than myth or fiction.

Notes

1. John Bruce Lockhart, 'Intelligence: A British View', in K. G. Robertson (ed.), *British and American Approaches to Intelligence* (Basingstoke: Macmillan, 1987), p. 46.
2. *Foreign Relations of the United States, 1945–1950, Emergence of the Intelligence Establishment*, US Department of State Document 292, Section 5.
3. Christopher Andrew, 'Intelligence, International Relations and "Under-Theorisation"', *Intelligence and National Security*, 19.2 (2004), p. 172.
4. Christopher M. Andrew and David Dilks, *The Missing Dimension: Governments*

and Intelligence Communities in the Twentieth Century (Urbana: University of Illinois Press, 1984).

5. Andrew, 'Intelligence, International Relations and "Under-Theorisation"', p. 174.

6. As quoted in Stephen S. Lander, 'International Intelligence Cooperation: An Inside Perspective', *Cambridge Review of International Affairs*, 17.3 (2004), p. 484. Lander cites a prime minister's file that, as of 2004, had not been released to the British National Archives.

7. 'The CIA Museum: Looking Back to See the Future', CIA website: *News & Information*, 20 November 2008, <https://www.cia.gov/news-information/featured-story-archive/2008-featured-story-archive/cia-museum.html> (last accessed 10 January 2020).

8. Michael V. Hayden, 'Director's Statement on the Release of the 9/11 IG Report Executive Summary', CIA website: *News & Information*, 21 August 2007, <https://www.cia.gov/news-information/press-releases-statements/press-release-archive-2007/911-ig-report-summary.html> (last accessed 10 January 2020).

1   Intelligence for an American Century: Creating the CIA

Successive US presidents, from George Washington to Franklin Roosevelt, did not prioritise establishing a peacetime foreign intelligence capability. For most, there was no need. The Republic was flanked by two vast oceans and had weak or friendly neighbours. It was prosperous and secure. Some presidents were naive about intelligence. President Woodrow Wilson attested to his own ignorance of the subject in 1919: 'Let me testify to this, my fellow citizens, I not only did not know it until we got into this war, but I did not believe it when I was told that it was true, that Germany was not the only country that maintained a secret service. Every country in Europe maintained it.'[1] And many senior American politicians considered the business of espionage ungentlemanly and un-American.[2] Secretary of State Henry Stimson noted in his autobiography that he closed America's 'Black Chamber' because 'gentlemen don't read each other's mail'.[3] Consequently, the US was the last of the great powers to establish a coordinated intelligence machinery.

Certainly, wars, foreign and civil, had prompted the creation of detective agencies, secret services and rudimentary intelligence organisations. The US was no stranger to intelligence *per se*. But the effort was haphazard and episodic. George Washington depended on espionage during the Revolutionary War; both Union and Confederate forces established sundry spying organisations during the Civil War. The Office of Naval Intelligence (ONI) was formed in 1882, and a Military Intelligence Division (MID) followed in 1885. Both were small, poorly resourced and under-utilised.[4] Both grew significantly with US involvement in the First World War.[5] Both were severely cut following the armistice.[6] The first US codebreaking office, MI-8, was founded in June 1917 under Herbert O. Yardley, and achieved the significant distinction of surviving into peacetime. MI-8 became the Cipher Bureau, and went on to attack Japanese, German and British ciphers[7] before having the rug pulled from beneath its feet by Secretary of State Stimson in 1929.[8] A rump sigint capability was preserved in the Army and Navy, which achieved some notable successes against Japanese cipher systems. But throughout the 1930s, the overall US intelligence effort was fragmented, often amateurish, and lacked a customer base in the armed forces or government who accorded it the priority it deserved, even as the threat of world war grew. When Japanese aircraft attacked US ships at Pearl Harbor on 7 December 1941, US intelligence lacked resources and was disastrously disorganised.

Pearl Harbor underlined the need for reforms to US intelligence. These reforms, ultimately, yielded a powerful, capable and global intelligence service, supporting practically all areas of America's war effort. The sigint effort was rationalised. The Army and Navy agreed that it be centralised under the Special Branch of the Army, with the Army responsible for diplomatic and military operations, the Navy responsible for naval operations, and domestic counter-intelligence and security becoming the responsibility of the FBI and Coast Guard.[9] This did not resolve all the problems that had plagued the pre-war organisations: inter-service rivalry, poor communication and liaison. But over the next four years of war, the number of personnel working in sigint grew from roughly 300 (mostly military) staff to over 37,000 military and civilian personnel. According to Matthew Aid, US sigint's pre-eminent historian, the effort yielded insight into 350 diplomatic systems, used by about sixty countries.[10] Cryptanalysts working at the Navy's sigint organisation, OP-20-G, managed to crack several variants of the Japanese Naval (JN-25) code system, yielding unparalleled insights into Japanese capabilities and intentions. Together, these breakthroughs allowed the US Army, Navy and Marine Corps to wage intelligence-led operations on a scale unlike anything previously witnessed in American history.[11]

The reforms to the sigint machinery were but one step on the road to a coordinated US intelligence community. Foreign intelligence, intelligence assessment and coordination, and covert operations remained underdeveloped and a low priority throughout most of Roosevelt's presidency. But the deteriorating international situation prompted reforms that, ultimately, paved the way for the Central Intelligence Agency, and peacetime foreign intelligence. The central figure in these developments was a decorated First World War veteran, William J. Donovan – a New York Republican, often known as 'Wild Bill'. President Roosevelt appointed Donovan to impose order on the squabbling and disordered intelligence organisations in the military and State Department. His solution was to create the office of the Coordinator of Information (COI); it set to work in July 1941 with a remit to coordinate the collection, dissemination and organisation of the intelligence that the US government produced.[12] As well as coordinating the government's information, in September 1941 it adopted the espionage functions of the Army and Navy's intelligence offices; it was permitted to use 'unvouchered funds' with minimal oversight, other than Donovan's signature; and it established a 'Research and Analysis' branch, staffed by civilian experts with the responsibility to produce intelligence assessments based on all sources.[13] Donovan developed what was identifiable as a modern intelligence organisation.

Donovan's energetic empire-building, and the developing intelligence requirements of a nation at war, soon prompted another round of organisational reform and bureaucratic squabbling. The COI was moved under the wing of the Chiefs of Staff, and on 13 June 1942 it became the Office of Strategic Services (OSS). It lost some functions, like the Foreign Information Service and the responsibility for 'white propaganda'. Donovan fought but failed to gain responsibility over sigint, leaving his organisation largely cut off from the most significant source of the war. Rival commanders in the Pacific, Admiral Chester Nimitz and General Douglas MacArthur, prevented the OSS from operating against Japan in their theatres. The FBI jealously guarded its responsibility over domestic counter-intelligence.[14] But the OSS continued to develop and expand. It built clandestine agent networks in the theatres it could operate; its Research and Analysis branch produced intelligence assessments to support operations and policy; it developed a foreign counter-intelligence branch, X-2; it conducted covert operations and secret warfare; it forged a good working relationship with Allied partners. By 1944, it employed close to 13,000 men and women.[15] Donovan created an organisation unlike any hitherto seen in US history.

There was no doubt in Donovan's mind that the intelligence machine he had developed should be preserved, in some form, for the post-war world. From 1944 he was lobbying President Roosevelt with his ideas for a national central intelligence agency. Following Roosevelt's death and the inauguration of Harry Truman, he redoubled his efforts. Truman, however, was unimpressed by Donovan and the OSS.[16] The fate of the OSS was sealed. Donovan's swashbuckling organisation was ended with Executive Order 9621, signed on 20 September 1945. Owing, reportedly, to an administrative error, it left Donovan with ten days to wind up the agency.[17] The Research and Analysis wing was moved to the State Department; the espionage (SI) and counter-intelligence wings were adopted by the Army, and became the Strategic Services Unit (SSU).[18] The dissolution of OSS was indicative more of what Truman did not want in a peacetime intelligence service, and his personal dislike of Donovan, than a defined alternative vision. The President did not want an American 'Gestapo', of that he was certain, but neither did he want a state of confusion and inter-service rivalry to persist between the various federal organisations that developed intelligence and supplied it to the White House. The result was, inevitably, a further series of reforms to the hastily constructed system built from the detritus of Donovan's empire.[19]

By the end of 1945 the US intelligence system was, again, in a state of disarray. It was plagued by interservice rivalry and consequent weaknesses in coordination, the same disease that had afflicted it before Pearl Harbor. Christopher Andrew noted that 'the Army, the Navy, the State Department, and the FBI were agreed only in a common desire to protect their departmental prerogatives from outside interference'.[20] The problems were particularly acute in the generation of coordinated intelligence assessments, which, during the war, had been coordinated in the White House Map Room.[21] Truman's solution was to centralise. In a Presidential Policy Directive on 22 January 1946 he ordered the creation of a National Intelligence Authority (NIA) to coordinate Federal intelligence activities; the establishment of the post of Director of Central Intelligence (DCI); and the creation of a Central Intelligence Group (CIG), with a responsibility to coordinate, plan, evaluate and disseminate intelligence. The CIG soon absorbed the SSU, and had its powers clarified and bolstered when the NIA produced document 'National Intelligence Authority 5', in July 1946. The CIG became not only an agency responsible for coordinating and evaluating intelligence, but also one that collected raw intelligence.[22] The first DCI was Rear Admiral Sidney W. Souers, whom Truman, tongue-in-cheek, described as the 'Director of centralized snooping'.[23]

Despite being a promising step on the road to centralised peacetime intelligence, the CIG remained tethered to the departments of State, War and the Navy.[24] This arrangement proved unsatisfactory, and by July 1946 CIG officials were already pressing for significant reforms – reforms that would yield a powerful, independent agency.[25] The fate of the CIG, and indeed the fate of central intelligence, became entangled with the debate concerning the centralisation of the US defence establishment. Air Force General Hoyt Vandenberg, the second DCI, succeeding Souers, pressed for legislation to untether the CIG from the departments of War, Navy and State.[26] But Truman's priority remained to establish a Department of Defense, with the objective of ensuring that 'we must never fight another war the way we fought the last two'.[27] The issue lingered throughout 1946 and the early months of 1947. But on 26 July 1947 the National Security Act became law. It created the Department of Defense, which would unify the services. It created the National Security Council, which would function as a forum to coordinate and guide US foreign and defence policy. It also created the Central Intelligence Agency (CIA), which would go on to become synonymous in the public consciousness with America's approach to peacetime intelligence.

The section of the National Security Act concerned with the CIA's creation, section 102, is relatively short. The outline of the CIA's duties is shorter still:

1) to advise the National Security Council in matters concerning such intelligence activities of the Government departments and agencies as relate to national security; (2) to make recommendations to the National Security Council for the coordination of such intelligence activities of the departments and agencies of the Government as relate to the national security; (3) to correlate and evaluate intelligence relating to the national security, and provide for the appropriate dissemination of such intelligence within the Government using where appropriate existing agencies and facilities: PROVIDED, That the Agency shall have no police, subpoena, law-enforcement powers, or internal-security functions: PROVIDED FURTHER, That the departments and other agencies of the Government shall continue to collect, evaluate, correlate, and disseminate departmental intelligence: AND PROVIDED FURTHER, That the Director of Central Intelligence shall be responsible for protecting intelligence sources and methods from unauthorized disclosure; (4) to perform, for the benefit of the existing intelligence agencies, such additional services of common concern as the National Security council determines can be more efficiently accomplished centrally; (5) to perform such other functions and duties related to intelligence affecting the national security as the National Security Council may from time to time direct.[28]

The agency that was created was one that had to balance several contrasting, even contradictory requirements. The agency needed to be competent, central and capable, but no 'Gestapo'. It needed to centralise, but not become overbearing nor too powerful. The consequence was an organisation that centralised the national intelligence mission but did not control it. The armed services retained control of their intelligence organisations; the CIA would draw upon their information and complement their work, but also replicate it; it would operate on foreign soil. The DCI, nominally head of the entire intelligence community, enjoyed only weak authority beyond the CIA. Indeed, DCIs could only control the budget and administration of the CIA. As noted by Michael Warner, then on the CIA's History Staff, 'this prescription of coordination without control guaranteed friction and duplication of intelligence efforts as the CIA and the departmental agencies pursued common targets, but it also fostered a potentially healthy competition of views and abilities.'[29] The matters of duplication, inter-service and agency competition, and the power of the DCI remained consistent features in discussions of the agency's performance for the next five decades and beyond.

Notwithstanding the structural issues inherent in its design, the CIA set to work gathering intelligence, producing assessments and conducting covert operations to disrupt foreign adversaries. But the matter of the organisation of national intelligence and the responsibilities of the CIA remained points for vigorous debate. The DCI, Rear Admiral Roscoe H. Hillenkoetter, was routinely the subject of criticism – much of it unfair – for the staff the agency hired, the standard of its reporting and its capacity to generate accurate warnings of significant events, like the Soviet atomic bomb test.[30] There was also pressure for the agency to become more active in psychological warfare to help prevent the spread of communism, although much of it was characterised more by ignorance of the agency's activities than robust analysis. So, in the early years of Cold War the agency was both a problem and the solution. In response to the criticism, on 13 January 1948 the NSC recommended to the President that the CIA be surveyed by individuals not then in government. Three individuals were nominated for the task: Allan W. Dulles (a future DCI), William H. Jackson and Mathias F. Correa.[31] They submitted their report on the CIA on 1 January 1949; it became known as the Dulles-Jackson-Correa report. It underlined the problems in coordinating the national intelligence mission, particularly in counter-intelligence, and criticised the CIA's leadership, particularly Hillenkoetter. It was received by the NSC, which in response issued NSC-50, concurring with a large proportion of the review's recommendations.[32] Historian Rhodri Jeffreys-Jones described this period as being characterised by 'expansion and obfuscation'.[33] The survey is substantial and detailed. But the summary and the fourth chapter, reproduced here, offer an intriguing perspective not only on the CIA after its first fifteen months, but more widely on the US intelligence machinery.

While Donovan's wartime intelligence apparatus was a victim of bureaucratic fratricide, the impetus for, and necessity of, intelligence had been proven in the crucible of combat; and, despite a hesitant appreciation for intelligence, Truman midwifed a peacetime Central Intelligence Agency that would quickly make its mark in the American popular imagination and the crystallising Cold War.

```
THE CENTRAL INTELLIGENCE AGENCY
and
NATIONAL ORGANIZATION
FOR INTELLIGENCE

NSC review(s) completed

                A Report to the
          NATIONAL SECURITY COUNCIL
```

```
              1 JANUARY 1949
```

THE CENTRAL INTELLIGENCE AGENCY
and
NATIONAL ORGANIZATION FOR INTELLIGENCE

A REPORT TO THE NATIONAL SECURITY COUNCIL
by
Allen W. Dulles, Chairman
William H. Jackson
Mathias F. Correa

1 January 1949

THIS DOCUMENT CONTAINS INFORMATION
AFFECTING THE NATIONAL DEFENSE OF THE
UNITED STATES WITHIN THE MEANING OF THE
ESPIONAGE ACT, 50 U.S.C., 31 AND 32 AS
AMENDED. ITS TRANSMISSION OR THE REVELATION
OF ITS CONTENTS IN ANY MANNER TO AN
UNAUTHORIZED PERSON IS PROHIBITED BY LAW.

LETTER OF TRANSMITTAL

January 15, 1949

National Security Council
Washington, D. C.

Attention: Mr. Sidney W. Souers
Executive Secretary

Gentlemen:

In accordance with the terms of the memorandum to
the undersigned from Mr. Sidney W. Souers, Executive
Secretary of the National Security Council, dated
February 13, 1948, as supplemented by his memorandum

of March 17, 1948,* we submit herewith our report on "The Central Intelligence Agency and National Organization for Intelligence."

On January 13, 1948, the National Security Council recommended to the President that a group comprising individuals not in Government service should make a "comprehensive, impartial, and objective survey of the organization, activities, and personnel of the Central Intelligence Agency." The group was asked to report to the Council its findings and recommendations on the following matters:

"(a) The adequacy and effectiveness of the present organizational structure of CIA.

"(b) The value and efficiency of existing CIA activities.

"(c) The relationship of these activities to those of other Departments and Agencies.

"(d) The utilization and qualifications of CIA personnel."

As a result of this action, the present Survey Group was created and the undersigned appointed by the National Security Council with the approval of the President. The terms of the resolution approved by the National Security Council were communicated to the Group on February 13, 1948.

Following discussions with the undersigned regarding the scope of the survey, the Executive Secretary of the National Security Council, with the approval of the Secretaries of State, Defense, Army, Navy and Air Force, sent to the Survey Group on March 17, 1948, a second memorandum which constituted an extension of the scope of the survey as originally set forth by the National Security Council. In particular, this memorandum included the following provisions:

"The survey will comprise primarily a thorough and comprehensive examination of the structure, administration, activities and inter-agency relationships of the Central Intelligence Agency as outlined in

---

* See Annexes No. 1 and 2 for the texts of these two memoranda which constitute the terms of reference for this survey.

the resolution of the National Security Council. It will also include an examination of such intelligence activities of other Government Departments and Agencies as relate to the national security, in order to make recommendations for their effective operation and over-all coordination, subject to the understanding that the Group will not engage in an actual physical examination of departmental intelligence operations (a) outside of Washington or (b) in the collection of communications intelligence. On behalf of the National Security Council, I will undertake to seek the cooperation in this survey of those Government Departments and Agencies not represented on the Council which have an interest in intelligence as relates to national security.

"It should be understood that the Survey of the Central Intelligence Agency and its relationship to other Departments and Agencies will be done for and with the authority of the National Security Council. The survey of the intelligence activities of the Departments of State, Army, the Navy, and the Air Force, however, will be for and with the authority of the respective heads of those Departments."

It was also provided that the Survey Group should submit from time to time recommendations on individuals problems, and that problems concerning the Central Intelligence Agency should be given priority over those involving other agencies.

The Survey Group has submitted two special reports to the National Security Council, each one in connection with particular problems being considered by the Council and its members. The first of these reports, dated May 3, 1948, dealt with ▮▮▮▮▮▮▮▮▮▮" The second interim report, dated May 13, 1948, dealt with the "Relations Between Secret Operations and Secret Intelligence."

The present report is based on an examination and appraisal of our national intelligence structure and operations as created by the National Security Act of 1947 and developed in the Central Intelligence Agency

and the individual departments and agencies concerned
with national security. In accordance with the directive from the National Security Council, emphasis has
been placed upon the Central Intelligence Agency,
but there has also been an examination of the principal departmental intelligence agencies in order to
determine their scope in the field of intelligence,
and their relations to each other and to the Central
Intelligence Agency. Our examination has been confined almost entirely to the over-all intelligence
organization and activities in the Washington headquarters of the Central Intelligence Agency and the
Departments of State, Army, Navy and Air Force.

We have met with members of the directorate and
personnel of the Central Intelligence Agency and with
representatives of other agencies. With the assistance of our staff, we have consulted approximately
300 persons who by virtue of their present position
or past experience are familiar with intelligence
problems. In addition, a series of conferences were
held at which officials of all of the intelligence
agencies were invited to submit their recommendations
and suggestions and discuss

ANNEXES

11. National Security Council Intelligence Directive No. 5: "Espionage and Counter-Espionage Operations"
12. ██████████████
13. National Security Council Intelligence Directive No. 7: "Domestic Exploitation"
14. National Security Council Intelligence Directive No. 8: "Biographical Data on Foreign Scientific and Technological Personalities"
15. ██████████████

CHAPTER IV
THE RESPONSIBILITY OF THE CENTRAL INTELLIGENCE AGENCY FOR THE COORDINATION OF INTELLIGENCE ACTIVITIES

The coordination of the intelligence activities of the several departments and agencies concerned with national security was a primary reason for establishing the Central Intelligence Agency. This is clear from the early discussions concerning the creation of a central agency and from the language of Section 102 of the National Security Act.

THE STATUTORY PROVISIONS

To achieve this purpose, the Central Intelligence Agency was assigned the duty of advising the National Security Council in matters concerning such intelligence activities as relate to the national security and of making recommendations to the National Security Council for their coordination. The Act does not give the Central Intelligence Agency independent authority to coordinate intelligence activities. Final responsibility to establish policies is vested in the National Security Council.

This duty of advising the National Security Council, together with the two other principal duties of correlating national intelligence and performing common services as determined by the National Security Council, all serve the general purpose of coordination. In fact, these three basic duties of the Central Intelligence Agency, although distinct in themselves, are necessarily inter-related and the performance of one function may involve another.

For example, in performing its duty of advising on the coordination, of intelligence activities, the Central Intelligence Agency may recommend to the National Security Council the means to be employed in the assembly of reports and estimates requisite for the performance by the Agency of its second duty, the correlation of national intelligence. As another example, the Central Intelligence Agency may recommend, in accordance with its duty to make recommendations for the coordination of intelligence activities, that a particular intelligence function be performed henceforth by the Agency itself under its third duty of providing services of common concern more efficiently accomplished centrally.

The statutory limitations upon the authority of the Central Intelligence Agency to coordinate intelligence activities without the approval of the National Security Council were obviously designed to protect the autonomy and internal arrangements of the various departments and agencies performing intelligence functions. The Secretaries of departments who are members of the National Security Council are in a position to review recommendations of the Central Intelligence Agency concerning their own departments, and provision is made that other departmental heads may be invited to attend meetings of the National Security Council when matters pertaining to their activities are under consideration. In spite of these calculated limitations on the authority of the Central Intelligence Agency, it is clear that the Agency was expected to provide the initiative and leadership in developing a coordinated intelligence system. In practice, the National Security Council has, almost without exception, approved the recommendations submitted to it by the Central Intelligence Agency for the coordination of intelligence activities.

The national Security Act does not define the "intelligence activities" which are to be coordinated under the direction of the National Security Council, or specify the departments whose activities are covered. Presumably all [2]intelligence activities relating to the national security are included, from collecting information in the first instance to the preparation and dissemination of finished intelligence reports and estimates. The criterion, a very broad one, is "such intelligence activities … as relate to the national security" and not the identity of the departments concerned or the nature or locale of the intelligence activity. Thus, practically no limitations are set upon the scope of the intelligence activities with which the Central Intelligence Agency is to concern itself.

THE ORGANIZATION AND OPERATION OF THE MACHINERY FOR COORDINATION

Three organizations assist the Director of Central Intelligence in discharging his responsibilities respecting the coordination of intelligence activities: the Intelligence Advisory Committee (IAC), with its Standing Committee; the Interdepartmental Coordinating and Planning Staff (ICAPS) of the Central Intelligence Agency and the Office of Collection and Dissemination (OCD), also in the Central Intelligence Agency.

INTELLIGENCE ADVISORY COMMITTEE

The membership of this Committee, created by National Security Council Intelligence Directive No. 1 of December 12, 1947 (See Annex No. 7), includes the Director of Central Intelligence, as chairman, the heads of the intelligence staffs of the Departments of State, Army, Navy and Air Force, the head of the Joint Intelligence Group of the Joint Staff and the Director of Intelligence of the Atomic Energy Commission. It is the direct successor to the Intelligence Advisory Board which was created by President Truman in his letter of January 22, 1946 setting up the Central Intelligence Group (See Annex No. 3).

Beginning with the discussions that preceded the creation of the Committee there have been two different concepts as to its proper mission. On the one hand was the view, held in the various departments, that the Committee should, in a sense, be a "governing board" for the Central Intelligence Agency. On the other hand, it was argued that Congress had set up the Agency autonomously and that any interdepartmental committee should serve merely in an advisory capacity at the discretion of the Director. The solution established in Intelligence Directive No. 1 lies between these views.

In practice, the role of the Committee has not been significant, and in our opinion, this has been one of the reasons for the weakness of the present arrangements for the coordination of intelligence. In this chapter and the next we will submit our recommendations for increasing the responsibility of the Intelligence Advisory Committee, both with respect to the coordination of intelligence activities and the preparation of intelligence estimates.

The members of the Intelligence Advisory Committee are authorized to pass upon recommendations of the Director of Central Intelligence to the National Security Council and upon directives proposed by the Director in implementation of National Security Council Intelligence Directives. Although it is incumbent upon the Director to transmit to the National Security Council dissents of members of the Committee to his recommendations, the Committee may not prevent the Director from making his recommendations to the National Security Council regardless of dissents. Where unanimity is not obtained on a proposed directive among the military department members of the Committee, the Director is required to refer the problem to the Secretary of Defense before presenting it to the National Security Council.

The activities of the Intelligence Advisory Committee have been largely confined to taking formal action, usually by voting slips, upon directives proposed by the Director of Central Intelligence to be submitted to the National Security Council or upon implementing directives. These actions are prepared for the Committee by the Interdepartmental Coordinating and Planning Staff and the Committee's own Standing Committee of departmental representatives. The Committee has met only infrequently and has had little to do with the continuing coordination of intelligence activities or with the preparation of coordinated intelligence estimates.* This situation is probably due to a combination of circumstances, including the failure of the Director to appreciate the responsibility of the Central Intelligence Agency for bringing about coordination, lack of mutual confidence among the departments and the Central Intelligence Agency and a general failure to understand how a coordinated intelligence system can be brought about.

The conception of the Intelligence Advisory Committee is sound. It is sound because interdepartmental coordination in such a complicated field as intelligence cannot be achieved solely by directives and without the fullest cooperation of the interested departments. It requires frequent consultation and continuing collaboration on all important questions. The Intelligence Advisory Committee should be the medium for accomplishing this, but it will not succeed if it continues to meet only infrequently, and avoids serious grappling with intelligence problems and continuous consultation on questions of common interest.

INTERDEPARTMENTAL COORDINATING AND PLANNING STAFF (ICAPS)

This was set up as a staff unit of the Director of Central Intelligence to assist him in his responsibilities for the coordination of intelligence activities. Its members are representatives nominated by the intelligence organizations of the State, Army, Navy and Air Force Departments; the senior State Department representative is the Chairman of the group.

The assigned task of ICAPS Is to review the Intelligence activities of the Government, and assist the Director in initiating measures of coordination for recommendation to the National Security Council. In order to accomplish this mission effectively,

---

* On this subject, see Chapter V and particularly page 75 where there is a discussion of the ad hoc committee set up In March, 1948.

it should have intimate knowledge of the organizations, responsibilities, activities and priorities
of the various intelligence agencies. Actually, its
achievements reflect inadequate knowledge of these
subjects and failure to appreciate the breadth of the
responsibility of the Central Intelligence Agency for
coordination of intelligence activities.

ICAPS has been largely concerned with the coordination of intelligence activities by assisting in the
preparation of the nine National Security Council
Intelligence Directives and the four implementing
directives of the Director of Central Intelligence.

It was originally expected that ICAPS would act as
the secretariat or working staff for the Intelligence
Advisory Committee, but owing in part to the infrequent meetings of the Committee, this has not happened. Moreover, there has been confusion between the
functions of ICAPS and those of the Standing Committee
comprising representatives from the staffs of the
members of the Intelligence Advisory Committee, with
the result that responsibilities are divided and
unclear. Moreover, the status of the members of ICAPS
has been ambiguous because it has never been entirely
clear whether the group was primarily a staff of
the Director of Central Intelligence or a committee
representing the member agencies. This has left the
group with divided loyalties and uncertainty as to
its mandate.

The position of ICAPS has been rendered more difficult because its members have been given operating responsibilities which are not only unrelated
to their primary task of assisting to formulate
plans for the coordinating of intelligence, but are
responsibilities which seem to belong more properly
to the operating branches of the Central Intelligence
Agency. Thus, one member of the staff serves as the
full-time liaison officer with the Joint Intelligence
Group of the Joint Staff. This is purely an intelligence research and reporting function in which the
Office of Reports and Estimates has almost exclusive
interest. Moreover, the official liaison officer
from the Central Intelligence Agency to the National

Security Council staff is the Chairman of ICAPS. This function also concerns matters affecting primarily the Office of Reports and Estimates and, in fact, a representative from that Office now also works with the National Security Council staff.

In these and other ways ICAPS has acquired operating rather than planning functions and has become, to some extent, a buffer between the operating parts of the Central Intelligence Agency and outside agencies. In carrying out both its planning and operating functions, it is not in close touch with the intelligence branches of the Central Intelligence Agency. There are numerous complaints that it is not only failing to carry out its own mission properly, but is actually impeding the other parts of the Central Intelligence Agency in carrying out theirs.

In general, we have found that ICAPS, staffed by individuals whose experience with problems of intelligence organization is not extensive, and lacking a clear and firm mandate, has failed to undertake a broad and effective program of coordination of intelligence activities. It has been allowed to dissipate its energies in activities for which it is not suited and to neglect its primary mission. It has not given the impression within the Central Intelligence Agency or outside that it grasps the nature of the responsibility for coordination of intelligence activities which is imposed upon the Central Intelligence Agency by the National Security Act.

OFFICE OF COLLECTION AND DISSEMINATION
The Office of Collection and Dissemination combines three functions, only one of which is directly related to the task of coordinating intelligence activities.

In the first place, it acts as a service organization for the other Offices of the Central Intelligence Agency by procuring intelligence data from other agencies and by disseminating to those agencies the intelligence collected or produced by these Offices. Its second task is the provision of certain services of common concern for the benefit of the Central Intelligence Agency and other agencies. These include the maintenance of an intelligence library and of certain central registers and indices.

Finally, the Office of Collection and Dissemination performs certain coordinating functions with respect to the collection of intelligence. It processes all intelligence requests received by the Central Intelligence Agency, whether these call merely for documentary material or require field collection. It canvasses the collection capabilities of the Agency and all other appropriate agencies in order to determine how best to meet these requests. Thus, if the Office of Naval Intelligence should request of the Central Intelligence Agency Information on the petroleum producing capabilities of various foreign countries, the Office of Collection and Dissemination would determine the intelligence resources which should be tapped in order to satisfy the request. If the request cannot be satisfied within the Central Intelligence Agency it will determine what outside agency is capable of procuring necessary information and will be responsible for forwarding the request to such agency. In the course of this action, the Office of Collection and Dissemination will attempt to discover whether any other agency has a similar requirement for information which might be combined with the original request. In this manner the Office assists in coordinating the requirements and collection requests received from within the Central Intelligence Agency and from outside agencies.

It is obvious that this function of coordination is designed to meet current requests and does not involve a broad responsibility continuously to monitor and coordinate the collection procedures and requirements of the various intelligence agencies, including the Central Intelligence Agency. Such a responsibility would force the Office of Collection and Dissemination into the position of a central clearing house for all collection requirements and requests of all agencies. It would be impractical to have such an arrangement due to the mass of administrative detail involved and the resulting delay in the satisfaction of the requests. In practice,

direct inter-agency requests, not requiring coordination, may by-pass the Central Intelligence Agency
completely.

NATIONAL SECURITY COUNCIL INTELLIGENCE DIRECTIVES
The formal accomplishment of over-all coordination is
represented mainly by nine Intelligence Directives
approved by the National Security Council upon recommendation of the Director of Central Intelligence in
consultation with the Intelligence Advisory Committee,
and four implementing directives which need not be
discussed here.

The National Security Council Intelligence Directives*
provide for the coordination of intelligence activities in various ways. The basic Directives, Nos. 1,
2, 3 and 4 seek to achieve coordination of intelligence activities by allocation of general areas of
responsibility to the several departments and to the
Central Intelligence Agency.

Directive No. 1, as we have pointed out, establishes the general arrangements for such coordination. It sets up the Intelligence Advisory Committee,
discussed above, to advise the Director of Central
Intelligence, specifies the procedures for the issu-
ance of Intelligence Directives and defines the duty
of the Central Intelligence Agency with respect to
the production of "national intelligence." Insofar
as practicable, the Central Intelligence Agency
"shall not duplicate the intelligence activities and
research of the various Departments and Agencies, but
shall make use of existing intelligence facilities."
The Directive provides for exchange of information
between the Central Intelligence Agency and the
departmental agencies, and authorizes the assignment
of officers to the Central Intelligence Agency by the
departmental organizations. It also includes provision for the Central Intelligence Agency to request
authority to inspect intelligence material in agencies of the Government.

Directive No. 2 allocates responsibility for the

* See Annexes No. 7-15 for the texts of the Directives.

collection abroad of overt intelligence among the Departments of State, Army, Navy and Air Force by establishing "certain broad categories of agency responsibility." Political, cultural and sociological intelligence are assigned to the State Department. Military, naval and air intelligence are assigned to the respective Services. The collection of economic, scientific and technological intelligence is allocated to each agency "in accordance with its respective needs." The Directive provides for coordination of these collection activities in the field by the senior United States representative.

Directive No. 3 is an elaborate definition of categories of intelligence production, i.e., basic, current, staff, departmental and national intelligence, and it assigns the responsibilities of the departmental agencies and the Central Intelligence Agency in intelligence production. The same areas of "dominant interest" are specified as for intelligence collection, and the production of "national intelligence" is reserved to the Central Intelligence Agency. However, the terms of the various definitions are broadly drawn, the exceptions are numerous, and confusion of intelligence functions has continued despite the effort to eliminate it by definition.

Directive No. 4 provides that the Central Intelligence Agency shall take the lead in preparing a comprehensive outline of national intelligence objectives, and from time to time shall indicate the priorities attaching to these objectives.

Four of the Directives, Nos. 5, 6, 7 and 8, assign certain "services of common concern" to the Central Intelligence Agency under the authority granted in the National Security Act (Section 102 (d)). These are coordinating actions in the sense that, by common agreement, they assign to the Central Intelligence Agency primary or exclusive responsibility for conducting certain intelligence activities of common concern. Directive No. 5 provides that the Central Intelligence Agency will conduct all espionage and counter-espionage operations abroad except for certain agreed activities and it also provides that the Central Intelligence Agency will coordinate covert and overt collection activities. (See Chapter VIII).

Directive No. 7 gives the Central Intelligence Agency authority for the exploitation of domestic sources of foreign intelligence, and provides for the participation of departmental agencies in this activity. (See Chapter VII).

A fourth "service of common concern" is provided in Directive No. 8 which assigns to the Central Intelligence Agency responsibility for maintaining a central file of biographical data on foreign scientific and technological personalities.

These Intelligence Directives allocate responsibilities to the Central Intelligence Agency in fields which have been conceded to be those of common concern where work can best be done centrally. This is also true of the allocation to the Central Intelligence Agency of responsibility for the conduct of secret operations (other than intelligence) abroad by the Office of Policy Coordination which was accomplished by direct National Security Council action (NSC 10/2) and not by Intelligence Directive submitted through the Intelligence Advisory Committee. (See Chapter IX). In all of these cases where particular functions of common concern have been assigned, the allocation of functions has been generally accepted as sound.

THE DEGREE OF COORDINATION ACHIEVED
In spite of these formal directives for the coordination of intelligence activities, it is probably correct to say that departmental intelligence activities are substantially unaffected by this program of coordination except where the Central Intelligence Agency has been given exclusive responsibility for certain activities.

In general, there is an absence of effective coordination under the leadership of the Central Intelligence Agency and there is virtually no supervision of the ways in which the various directives are carried out, except that the Central Intelligence Agency controls those common service activities assigned to it. Conflicts of jurisdiction and duplication of activities remain. In many cases they have not only been unresolved, which is hardly surprising after such - short time, but they remain unrecognized and unacknowledged.

Despite the provisions of Directives Nos. 2 and 3 in regard to the allocation of dominant interest, each department collects and produces the intelligence it chooses according to priorities it establishes. The very large loopholes in these directives and the absence of any continuously effective monitoring of their implementation makes this possible. The Central Intelligence Agency itself has become a competitive producer of intelligence on subjects of its own choosing which can by no stretch of the imagination be called national intelligence. (See Chapters V and VI). The amount of undesirable duplication among intelligence agencies is considerable and the absence of coordinated intelligence collection and production is serious.

In our opinion, certain essentials for the improvement of this situation would include: continuous examination on the initiative of the Central Intelligence Agency of instances of duplication and failure of coordination; directives which establish more precisely the responsibilities of the various departments; and the effective carrying out of plans through close inter-departmental consultation at all levels. To a greater or lesser degree, all of these essentials are lacking at the present time.

Clearly, as pointed out above, the authority of the Central Intelligence Agency to coordinate intelligence activities is subject to directives of the National Security Council. However, the responsibility to advise the National Security Council and to make recommendations for coordination is squarely placed on the Central Intelligence Agency. Therefore, lack of authority in a specific situation should not deter the Central Intelligence Agency from exercising its responsibility to submit recommendations so that proper coordination will result. If there are doubts as to how the coordination should be affected, it is the duty of the Agency to ask the National Security Council to resolve them.

The coordination of intelligence activities today is particularly important in three fields illustrative of the general problem, namely – scientific intelligence, domestic Intelligence and counter-intelligence affecting the national security, and communications intelligence.

SCIENTIFIC INTELLIGENCE[*]

The field of scientific and technological intelligence is obviously one which may overshadow all others in importance. At the present time there is no proper coordination of effort in this field, which is one in which there is a broad area of common interest. In fact, this diffusion of responsibility is confirmed in National Security Council Intelligence Directives Nos. 2 and 3 which allocate collection and production responsibilities for scientific and technological intelligence to "each agency in accordance with its respective needs."

Each of the military Services collects scientific and technological intelligence in accordance with its own program and produces such reports as it chooses. The Central Intelligence Agency performs certain central collecting services through its Office of Operations and Office of Special Operations. The Office of Special Operations also houses the Nuclear Energy Group which is the central governmental unit for interpreting atomic energy intelligence. Separate from it is a Scientific Branch in the Office of Reports and Estimates which was expected to become the central group for stimulating and coordinating scientific intelligence. It has not yet filled this role. The Research and Development Board does not itself actively engage in scientific intelligence but has an important interest in the field. Its needs

---

[*] Since this report was written, steps are being taken to create in the Central Intelligence Agency a separate Office of Scientific Intelligence and to transfer to it the Nuclear Energy Group now in the Office of Special Operations.

should therefore be given major consideration in plans and arrangements for coordination.

In summary, responsibilities are scattered, collection efforts are uncoordinated, atomic energy intelligence is divorced from scientific intelligence generally, and there is no recognized procedure for arriving at authoritative intelligence estimates in the scientific field, with the possible exception of atomic energy. Here is a situation which must have priority in coordination of intelligence activities. In Chapter VI we propose certain steps which come within the scope of this survey.

DOMESTIC INTELLIGENCE AND COUNTER-INTELLIGENCE AFFECTING THE NATIONAL SECURITY

Another broad field requiring coordination is that of foreign intelligence derived from domestic sources and the allied field of domestic counter-intelligence. ██████████████████████ responsibility for the other activities is scattered among the State Department, the Armed Services, the Federal Bureau of Investigation and the Central Intelligence Agency. There is little effective coordination among them, except on a case basis.

The Federal Bureau of Investigation, which has primarily security and law enforcement responsibilities, is concerned in fact with an important area of intelligence. This includes domestic counter-espionage and counter-sabotage, control of communist and other subversive activities and surveillance of alien individuals and groups. All of these functions are closely related to the comparable activities abroad of the Central Intelligence Agency. They all have an important Intelligence aspect, particularly today when intelligence from domestic and foreign sources is so closely related. The fact that the Federal Bureau of Investigation is primarily concerned with security and law enforcement may result in a failure to exploit the intelligence possibilities of a situation and may create difficulties in reconciling the intelligence with the security interests.

The Federal Bureau of Investigation is not part of

the existing machinery for coordination of intelligence through the Intelligence Advisory Committee
or otherwise. There is no continuing manner whereby
domestic intelligence and counter-intelligence are
related to over-all national intelligence in order to
serve the general purpose set forth in the National
Security Act "of coordinating the intelligence activities of the several Government departments and agencies in the interest of national security."

In our opinion, the Central Intelligence Agency
has the duty under the Act to concern itself with
the problem of coordinating those phases of domestic
intelligence and counter-intelligence which relate
to the national security and should submit recommendations on this subject to the National Security
Council. This is not inconsistent with the stipula-
tion of the National Security Act that the Central
Intelligence Agency "shall have no police, subpoena,
law-enforcement powers, or internal security functions." It would in fact serve to carry out the program
of coordination set forth in the Act in a broad field
which has hitherto been largely neglected.

A step toward bringing about the coordination we
recommend would be to provide for closer association of the Federal Bureau of Investigation with the
intelligence agencies by making it a member of the
Intelligence Advisory Committee.

COMMUNICATIONS INTELLIGENCE
A further problem in the field of coordination of
intelligence activities is that of communications
intelligence. We have referred above to Intelligence

We have not made an on-the-spot examination of communications intelligence and, in view of the necessarily stringent security restrictions, it seemed
un-wise that a non-governmental committee such as
ours, without specific mandate to go into the whole
subject, should press such an inquiry. Accordingly,
the Survey Group is not in a position to express
a judgement upon the efficiency of the present
arrangements for the production of communications

intelligence through the separate establishments of the Army and the Navy. We have, however, generally considered the problem of communications intelligence insofar as it relates to the over-all arrangements for the coordination of intelligence activities.

We consider that coordination of communications intelligence is of most vital concern not only to the Services but to the Department of State in the formulation of policy and to the Central Intelligence Agency in its operations and other activities. The procedure by which the United States Communications Intelligence Board was established conformed to what should be the normal functioning of the arrangements for the coordination of activities in that the Board was established by National Security Council Intelligence Directive adopted upon the recommendation of the Director of Central Intelligence and the Intelligence Advisory Committee.

To be effective, communications intelligence must be properly coordinated at all stages, from collection and production* to dissemination and use. One of the prime objectives of coordination in this field is to assure prompt receipt of the product of communications intelligence by its essential users in State Department and the Central Intelligence Agency, as well as in the Services. As we have pointed out in our subsequent chapter dealing with secret Intelligence operations (Chapter VIII), there is some reason to believe that these operations and communications intelligence activities are not at the present time sufficiently closely coordinated so as to provide for each the maximum support from the other's work.

We further believe that the recommendation we have made in this chapter for the coordination of intelligence activities could best be achieved with respect to communications intelligence by making the Director of Central Intelligence permanent chairman of the United States Communications Intelligence Board.

* We understand that, at the direction of the Secretary of Defense, a committee comprising representatives of the three Services is completing a study of the question of creating a joint organization for the production of communications intelligence.

PROPOSALS FOR IMPROVED COORDINATION
In order to remedy the existing situation in respect
of coordination of activities, several steps are
necessary. The Director of Central Intelligence must
show a much greater concern than hitherto with
the general problem of coordination of intelligence
activities which is one of his essential statutory duties. His is a responsibility to all of the
departments concerned with national security; it can
be properly discharged by leadership, imagination,
initiative and a realization that only a joining of
efforts can achieve the desired results.

The other members of the Intelligence Advisory
Committee must also share in the general responsibility for carrying out the intent of the National
Security Act by quickening their interest and exhib-
iting a spirit of active cooperation. No amendment to
the Committee's charter as set forth in Intelligence
Directive No. 1 appears necessary to bring about this
improvement.

In the next chapter where we deal with the question of national intelligence estimates we propose
that the Intelligence Advisory Committee assume a
more active role in producing these estimates. In
our opinion, this would not only improve the relevance and quality of the estimates but would give
the Committee the impetus and the background it needs
to deal effectively with the coordination of intelligence activities. More than any other stage in the
intelligence process, the consideration of estimates
should reveal the deficiencies and overlaps as well
as the accomplishments in intelligence.

We believe, as stated above, that the Federal Bureau
of Investigation should be added to the permanent
membership of the Intelligence Advisory Committee.
We also believe that the Atomic Energy Commission
and the Joint Staff might be dropped from the regular
membership. The role of the Atomic Energy Commission
in intelligence is a limited one and confined to a
highly specialized field. The representation of the
Joint Staff upon the Intelligence Advisory Committee
appears to be largely duplicative in view of the

predominantly Service membership of the Committee. However, they, together with other interested agencies such as the Departments of Treasury and Commerce, the Research and Development Board and the National Security Resources Board, should attend meetings whenever matters of direct concern to them are being considered.

Within the internal organization of the Central Intelligence Agency the Interdepartmental Coordinating and Planning Staff (ICAPS) should be set up clearly as an integral part of the Agency, charged with the task of seeking out, studying and developing, in consultation with the other parts of the Central Intelligence Agency and outside agencies, plans for the coordination of intelligence activities. It should have no responsibility for current operations, except that certain current tasks of coordination (such as some of those now performed by the Office of Collection and Dissemination) might be carried out under its direction. The reconstituted ICAPS which might appropriately be called "Coordination Division" should be small. Its members should be persons interested in, and qualified to deal with, problems of intelligence organization. Finally, and perhaps most important of all, the Director must look upon this reorganized and strengthened group as his major support in fulfilling one of his most difficult assignments under the National Security Act, that of advising the National Security Council on the intelligence activities of the Government and making recommendations for their coordination.

It is our belief that the relationship between certain of the functions presently performed by ICAPS and the Office of Collection and Dissemination should be considerably closer. ICAPS is responsible for the promulgation of plans and policy in relation to the coordination of collection activities. As one of its tasks, the Office of Collection and Dissemination coordinates actual collection and dissemination and in some respects is in a position to implement the general plans and policies for coordination. Constantly dealing with the day-to-day "working level" problems of collection, the Office of Collection and Dissemination is in a good position to make recommendations in regard to the improvement of collection procedures and the coordination of collection activities.

We, therefore, recommend that the collection and dissemination functions of this Office be placed under the new Coordination Division, subject to future determination of the extent to which individual Offices may conduct their own dissemination. (See Conclusions to Chapters VII and VIII). We further recommend that all of the library, index and register functions be separated from the Office of Collection and Dissemination and be placed in a centralized Research and Reports Division as described in Chapter VI.

Notes

1. Christopher Andrew, *For the President's Eyes Only: Secret Intelligence and the American Presidency from Washington to Bush* (New York: Harper Perennial, 1996), p. 30.
2. Henry Stimson, Herbert Hoover's secretary of state, was appalled to discover that the US intercepted and decrypted Japanese telegrams. In 1929 he ordered such activities to cease forthwith. The 'Black Chamber' was shut down. Reportedly, neither Stimson nor Hoover regretted the loss in capability. Andrew, *For the President's Eyes Only*, pp. 72–3.
3. Louis Kruh, 'Stimson, the Black Chamber, and the "Gentlemen's Mail" quote', *Cryptologia*, 12.2 (1988), pp. 65–89.
4. Andrew, *For the President's Eyes Only*, p. 25.
5. For a history of the origins of MID, see John Patrick Fennegan and Romana Danysh, *Military Intelligence* (Washington, DC: Center of Military History, 1998).
6. Andrew, *For the President's Eyes Only*, p. 69.
7. See Mark Stout, 'World War I and the Birth of American Intelligence Culture', *Intelligence and National Security*, 32.3 (2017), pp. 378–94; Andrew, *For the President's Eyes Only*, pp. 61–3.
8. Andrew, *For the President's Eyes Only*, pp. 72–3; Kruh, 'Stimson, the Black Chamber'.

9. Andrew, *For the President's Eyes Only*, p. 123.
10. Matthew Aid, *The Secret Sentry: The Untold Story of the National Security Agency* (London: Bloomsbury, 2010), p. 8.
11. For an insight into the US SIGINT war see John Prados, *Combined Fleet Decoded: The Secret History of American Intelligence and the Japanese Navy in World War II* (New York: Random House, 1995); and Edward J. Drea, *MacArthur's Ultra: Codebreaking and the War Against Japan* (Lawrence: University Press of Kansas, 1991).
12. See 'History of the CIA', CIA website: *About CIA*, 10 April 2007, <https://www.cia.gov/about-cia/history-of-the-cia> (last accessed 10 January 2020).
13. See the CIA's internal history: Michael Warner, 'COI Came First', in *The Office of Strategic Services: America's First Intelligence Agency* (Washington, DC: CIA, 2007), <https://www.cia.gov/library/publications/intelligence-history/oss/art02.htm> (last accessed 10 January 2020).
14. 'History of the CIA'.
15. Ibid.
16. There are several instances where the President's personal dislike of Donovan was displayed. Andrew, *For the President's Eyes Only*, p. 157 and pp. 158–9 present a number.
17. See Michael Warner, *The Office of Strategic Services: America's First Intelligence Agency* (Washington, DC: CIA, 2007), <https://www.cia.gov/library/publications/intelligence-history/oss/art10.htm> (last accessed 10 January 2020).
18. Andrew, *For the President's Eyes Only*, pp. 160–1; and Warner, *The Office of Strategic Services*.
19. See Douglas T. Stuart, *Creating the National Security State: A History of the Law that Transformed America* (Woodstock: Princeton University Press, 2008).
20. Andrew, *For the President's Eyes Only*, p. 164.
21. 'History of the CIA'; Andrew, *For the President's Eyes Only*, p. 165.
22. On the impact of NIAD-5 see Michael Warner, 'Central Intelligence: Origin and Evolution', in *The Creation of the Intelligence Community: Founding Documents* (Washington, DC: CIA, 2012), <https://www.cia.gov/library/publications/intelligence-history/creation-of-ic-founding-documents/creation-of-the-intelligence-community.pdf> (last accessed 10 January 2020).
23. Andrew, *For the President's Eyes Only*, p. 164.
24. Discussion of this in Stuart, *Creating the National Security State*, p. 259.
25. Andrew, *For the President's Eyes Only*, p. 169.
26. Ibid. p. 168.
27. Ibid. p. 169.
28. National Security Act 1947, at <https://www.cia.gov/library/readingroom/docs/1947-07-26.pdf> (last accessed 10 January 2020).
29. Warner, 'Central Intelligence', p. 8.
30. This is discussed in Appendix B, 'A Brief History of US Intelligence', in Loch Johnson's *Strategic Intelligence* (London: Prager Security International, 2007).
31. This was referenced NSC Action No. 25. See 'Survey of the Central Intelligence

Agency', Souers to Secretary of Defense, 27 February 1948, <https://www.cia.gov/library/readingroom/docs/CIA-RDP86B00269R000500030006-7.pdf> (last accessed 10 January 2020).

32. See 'NSC-50 Comments and Recommendations to the National Security Council on the Report of The Dulles-Jackson-Correa Committee Prepared by the Secretary of State and Secretary of Defense', 1 July 1949, <https://history.state.gov/historicaldocuments/frus1945-50Intel/d384> (last accessed 10 January 2020).

33. Rhodri Jeffreys-Jones, *The CIA and American Democracy* (London: Yale, 2003), p. 43.

2 The Development of CIA Covert Action

Throughout 1944 and 1945, 'Wild Bill' Donovan lobbied energetically for Presidents Roosevelt and Truman to act and establish the skeleton of a peacetime intelligence organisation. Truman gave him short shrift, declining even to thank him personally for his service after ordering the disbanding of the OSS.[1] But Donovan's legacy and impact on the CIA were profound. Upon its establishment in 1947, one third of the CIA's staff were OSS veterans:[2] 'Files, funds, procedures, and contacts assembled by the OSS found their way into the CIA more or less intact.'[3] Four of the CIA's future directors cut their teeth in the OSS.[4] To this day, a statue of Donovan stands in the lobby of the Original Headquarters building, and the CIA claims that it 'derives a significant institutional and spiritual legacy from the OSS'.[5] Donovan's OSS provided a model for the peacetime global intelligence agency that was incrementally rebuilt after 1945 – an agency that engaged in espionage, open-source intelligence, research and analysis, all-source strategic assessment, counter-intelligence and, significantly, covert action. Over the past seventy years, covert actions, with their legacies stretching back to the jungles of Burma or the beaches of Normandy, have become synonymous with the CIA in popular myth. But transferring the experience and skills of wartime into a peacetime agency, and establishing a functioning bureaucratic and doctrinal model for their employment, took time. The centralisation of America's covert action function in the CIA has a somewhat convoluted history.

It begins with Donovan and the OSS. Prior to its entry into the Second World War, the US had not engaged systematically in covert action. The more established intelligence powers, like Britain or the Soviet Union, had engaged in subversive and paramilitary activities for decades. For them, the Second World War was an opportunity to hone and expand their skills. For the US, the war was a new departure in the way it conducted statecraft; the OSS led the way. As Michael Warner has outlined in his internal history of the OSS, the organisation conducted a broad spectrum of operations across multiple theatres. The men and women of the OSS cooperated and coordinated with the British, the French Resistance, with partisans across occupied Europe and North Africa and in parts of the Asian theatre. These operations ranged from coordinating missions and delivering weapons and supplies to resistance partners, to more direct assault and sabotage operations, conducted by paramilitary units, to psychological operations, designed and managed by the Morale Operations Branch.[6] They rendered valuable support to conventional Allied forces. Some of their most notorious exploits included their work prior to Operation Torch and the Allied landings in North Africa, where they facilitated the landings and subsequent advance; while the exploits of Detachment 101 in Burma, which built and coordinated a powerful paramilitary force from the Kachin tribe, spied upon and harassed the Japanese forces in the area.[7] By the end of the war, the US had built a substantial stock of experience in designing and deploying all manner of covert operations.

The framers of the 1947 National Security Act believed that the US would break from its tradition and would hitherto be conducting covert action in peacetime. The realities of the post-war balance of power made it all but inevitable. But the precise nature of the capability and where in the national security bureaucracy it would rest was debated, as rival organisations jockeyed for influence on the matter. There can be little doubt that the wording of the National Security Act 1947 indicated that the CIA could be tasked with covert action (President Truman's later statements that he was opposed to peacetime covert actions notwithstanding). It was the stated duty of the CIA 'to perform such other functions and duties related to intelligence affecting the national security as the National Security Council may from time to time direct'.[8] The White House Counsel, Clark Clifford, later noted that this wording was designed to include covert actions in the CIA's mandate without having to define them explicitly and thus give notice to America's enemies.[9] Equally, however, it was not specifically stated that the CIA would be the sole agency responsible for this work; nor was it clear what precisely these 'other functions and duties' would be. So despite its founding charter, and it being tasked with designing and implementing covert operations in Europe almost from the moment of its creation, the CIA's responsibility over the matter was contested.

The growth in the mass appeal of communist parties in several key Western European states, and behind them, of course, the influence of the USSR and the newly formed Communist Information Bureau (Cominform), prompted a major escalation in US covert activities, particularly in the field of psychological warfare. It also underlined the lack of bureaucratic clarity over who would manage, design and implement them. President Truman approved NSC 1/1 in November 1947, with the aim of countering communist advances in Italy with all necessary means, including 'unvouchered funds'.[10] This policy was in line with what several advocates of increased covert operations were supporting, including 'Wild Bill' Donovan.[11] Originally, James Forrestal, the Secretary of Defense, pushed for the State Department to take charge.[12] But George C. Marshall, by now the Secretary of State, objected, noting that such activities could 'discredit American foreign policy both short-term and long-term'.[13] NSC 4/A transferred the responsibility for covert psychological operations to the CIA, with policy guidance being provided by the State Department.[14] The Italian operation was managed by a Special Procedures Group (SPG) within the CIA, which, under the supervision of James Jesus Angleton, went on to launder millions of dollars, and which it used to support various non-communist political parties and causes in the 1947 Italian election.[15] Non- or anti-communist parties went on to dominate the election; in Washington, the fledgling CIA believed that the covert actions had let to a major early Cold War victory.

The success, perceived or real, of the CIA's operations in Italy encouraged the advocates of Cold War covert action and its potential in aiding the policy of containment. The zeal of individuals like Allen Dulles and his brother John Foster was reinforced by a series of events that seemed to underline the urgency of adopting a more proactive approach to fighting communist propaganda and encroachment, notably the fallout from a series of riots that coincided with Secretary of State Marshall's visit to Bogota.[16] One of the fiercest advocates for covert action was George Kennan, the head of the Policy Planning Staff at Marshall's State Department. Despite Marshall's reticence over his department being linked to underhanded operations, Kennan did not wish for the CIA to have sole control and so, in May 1948, proposed that a special group be created in the State Department to manage covert action. DCI Hillenkoetter accepted the proposals, despite believing that the proposed arrangements were bureaucratically peculiar.[17] The idea was codified in NSC 10/2, on 17 June 1948, which supplanted NSC 4/A.

The NSC, 'taking cognizance of the vicious covert activities of the USSR ... determined that, in the interests of world peace and US national security, the overt foreign activities of the US Government must be supplemented by covert operations'.[18] These operations would be 'so planned and executed that any US Government responsibility for them is not evident to unauthorized persons and that if uncovered the US Government can plausibly disclaim any responsibility for them'. NSC 10/2 outlined what covert actions comprised, giving the CIA the responsibility over

> 'any covert activities related to: propaganda, economic warfare; preventive direct action, including sabotage, anti-sabotage, demolition and evacuation measures; subversion against hostile states, including assistance to underground resistance

movements, guerrillas and refugee liberation groups, and support of indigenous anti-communist elements in threatened countries of the free world.'[19]

These operations would be the responsibility of an Office of Special Projects, in the CIA. This soon became the Office of Policy Coordination (OPC), headed by OSS veteran Frank Wisner. The OPC started waging the covert Cold War, and grew spectacularly. Wisner controlled a staff of 302 personnel and had a budget of $4.7 million by the end of 1948. By mid-1950 his staff numbered closer to 1,500.[20] He built a concept for the OPC's mission, and a network that could implement his operations. The OPC started undertaking propaganda operations in Europe, set to with establishing a paramilitary training facility, and worked with the British with the objective of undermining communist rule in Albania.[21] Wisner was so energetic that he earned the OPC the moniker 'Wisner's Wurlitzer'. George Kennan, who had strongly advocated against a covert action capability, was reportedly horrified at the scale of the OPC's development and its activities.[22]

Despite its rapid growth, and the obvious appetite in Washington for more covert action, the OPC remained something of a bureaucratic anomaly. It was part of the CIA, but removed from the CIA's operations arm, the Office of Special Operations (OSO), who often viewed the new Office as over-moneyed, ill-disciplined and unregulated, unnecessary risk-takers.[23] It was distant also from its analysis wing, the Office of Reports and Estimates (ORE). NSC 10/2 gave the DCI nominal authority over OPC, but its head had been appointed by the NSC, and he reported to the Secretaries of State and Defense, as well as the DCI.[24] The NSC mandated that during peace the State Department should set policy for the OPC, while in war this responsibility should pass to Defense.[25] DCI Hillenkoetter lacked the authority to impose order on this particular Washington turf battle, so the OPC remained as if suspended between the three agencies.[26] Wisner used the confusion that this arrangement caused to his advantage as he built his empire, approaching the department most likely to approve a particular scheme. His star continued to rise for several years. But the situation became increasingly untenable as the OPC's expansion began to clash with the OSO's expansion, and as the domestic and international situation led to calls for more strategic deployment of covert action, on a greater scale. In January 1948 President Truman agreed that a panel be convened to consider the situation and the CIA in general. This panel wrote the Dulles-Jackson-Correa report (a section of which is reproduced in the previous chapter). Published in January 1949, the report recommended that the OPC and OSO be fused in one office, an 'operations division'.[27]

The fusion of the Offices took another three years and the efforts of Hillenkoetter's successor as DCI, the redoubtable Lieutenant General

Walter Bedell Smith. During these years the scope of the CIA's covert actions increased markedly, mostly owing to the Korean War. The OPC's staff numbered 2,812 by 1952, and its budget had ballooned to $82 million.[28] Smith cut through some of the bureaucratic confusion in the meantime. In 1950, one of his first acts as DCI was to inform the Intelligence Advisory Board, and the State and service Departments, that although the wording of NSC 10/2 was 'somewhat ambiguous', his reading of it clearly indicated that the DCI had authority over the OPC – and that henceforth Mr Wisner would certainly take advice from State and Defense, but would act under the authority and be under the control of the DCI.[29] Combined with the added authority over unvouchered funds granted by the CIA Act of 1949, and the subsequent reaffirmation of the CIA's covert mandate and its expanded powers over guerrilla warfare contained in NSC 10/5, there was little doubt over the CIA's authority with regard to covert action by late 1951.[30] However, Smith initially declined to implement the Dulles-Jackson-Correa report's recommendation concerning merging OPC and OSO. He changed his mind on this point by August 1952. By then the feuding between the OPC and the OSO had, in the words of Rhodri Jeffreys-Jones, 'become chronic'.[31] He ordered that the OPC and OSO be merged in the CIA in a new section, the euphemistically named Directorate of Plans (DP).[32] The DP was headed by Allen Dulles, who became the Deputy Director for Plans (DDP). Despite being characterised in the 1954 Doolittle Report as a 'shotgun marriage', the merger was the most significant step to rationalising the covert action machinery during the Truman administration.[33]

DCI Smith's motivation in merging the OPC and OSS was to protect the CIA's espionage and counter-espionage mission. Covert action was, in his opinion, 'subject to short-term variations in the prosecution of the Cold War'.[34] Despite his intention, the CIA's covert action wing continued to outgrow and overshadow its other business. The pace of its operations did not slow with the end of the Korean War; instead, it increased. Significant actions were undertaken in Guatemala and Iran, and in China. Psychological warfare against the USSR was increased. By the end of the Truman administration in January 1953, the CIA enjoyed substantial freedom of action with regard to covert action. As DDP, Allen Dulles was an unashamed advocate of covert action, and his activities, although nominally subject to the advice of the NSC and the Psychological Strategy Board, were in practice only limited by the authority of the DCI and the President.[35] With President Eisenhower's inauguration in January 1953, Dulles replaced Smith as DCI. His enthusiasm for covert action and relative lack of interest in the bureaucratic management of the CIA drew the attention of Congress, which in 1954 established a task force to investigate the issue. President Eisenhower countered by establishing his own investigation into the CIA's covert action, led by Air Force Lt Gen. Doolittle.[36] Eisenhower also began limiting the CIA's freedom of action by reigning in Dulles.

Between March 1954 and December 1955, three NSC directives clarified the management of CIA covert action. The first, NSC 5412, reiterated the CIA's responsibility and set out the methods by which the State Department, the Defense Department, the White House and the CIA would coordinate covert action policy, via an Operations Coordinating Board (OCB). The second, in March 1955, NSC 5412/1, clarified the responsibilities for supervising covert action, mandating that a Planning Coordination Group would be briefed in advance of major CIA covert programmes initiated, and would be the normal channel for giving policy approval for such programmes, and coordinating with the Departments of State and Defense. This was partly in response to criticisms of the CIA's management of covert actions in the Doolittle report.[37] The third directive, in December 1955, NSC 5412/2, gave the Coordination group more clout; members would now hold a rank of assistant secretary or above. This group became known as the '5412 Group', or sometimes the 'NSC 5412 Special Group', or simply 'Special Group'.[38] It became the main committee charged with reviewing the CIA's covert actions, for the CIA's 'golden age'. Its control remained limited, given the enthusiasm of the CIA and the President for covert action, and it could not constrain some of the more audacious ideas of the agency. It would take the very public failure at the Bay of Pigs in 1961 to reform the system again and impose more control on the agency.

```
NSC 5412/2                        Washington, undated.
                COVERT OPERATIONS
1. The National Security Council, taking cognizance
of the vicious covert activities of the USSR and
Communist China and the governments, parties and
groups dominated by them, (hereinafter collectively
referred to as "International Communism") to dis-
credit and defeat the aims and activities of the
United States and other powers of the free world,
```

determined, as set forth in NSC directives 10/2 and 10/5, that, in the interests of world peace and U.S. national security, the overt foreign activities of the U.S. Government should be supplemented by covert operations.

2. The Central Intelligence Agency had already been charged by the National Security Council with conducting espionage and counterespionage operations abroad. It therefore seemed desirable, for operational reasons, not to create a new agency for covert operations, but, subject to directives from the NSC, to place the responsibility for them on the Central Intelligence Agency and correlate them with espionage and counter-espionage operations under the over-all control of the Director of Central Intelligence.

3. The NSC has determined that such covert operations shall to the greatest extent practicable, in the light of U.S. and Soviet capabilities and taking into account the risk of war, be designed to:

   a.   Create and exploit troublesome problems for International Communism, impair relations between the USSR and Communist China and between them and their satellites, complicate control within the USSR, Communist China and their satellites, and retard the growth of the military and economic potential of the Soviet bloc.

   b.   Discredit the prestige and ideology of International Communism, and reduce the strength of its parties and other elements.

   c.   Counter any threat of a party or individuals directly or indirectly responsive to Communist control to achieve dominant power in a free world country.

   d.   Reduce International Communist control over any areas of the world.

   e.   Strengthen the orientation toward the United States of the peoples and nations of the free world, accentuate, wherever possible, the identity of interest between such peoples and nations and the United States as well as favoring, where appropriate, those groups genuinely advocating or believing in the advancement of such mutual interests, and increase the capacity and will of such peoples and nations to resist International Communism.

f.   In accordance with established policies and to the extent practicable in areas dominated or threatened by International Communism, develop underground resistance and facilitate covert and guerrilla operations and ensure availability of those forces in the event of war, including wherever practicable provision of a base upon which the military may expand these forces in time of war within active theaters of operations as well as provision for stay-behind assets and escape and evasion facilities.

4. Under the authority of Section 102(d)(5) of the National Security Act of 1947, the National Security Council hereby directs that the Director of Central Intelligence shall be responsible for:

a.   Ensuring, through designated representatives of the Secretary of State and of the Secretary of Defense, that covert operations are planned and conducted in a manner consistent with United States foreign and military policies and with overt activities, and consulting with and obtaining advice from the Operations Coordinating Board and other departments or agencies as appropriate.

b.   Informing, through appropriate channels and on a need-to-know basis, agencies of the U.S. Government, both at home and abroad (including diplomatic and military representatives), of such operations as will affect them.

5.   In addition to the provisions of paragraph 4, the following provisions shall apply to wartime covert operations:

a.   Plans for covert operations to be conducted in active theaters of war and any other areas in which U.S. forces are engaged in combat operations will be drawn up with the assistance of the

Department of Defense and will be in consonance with and complementary to approved war plans of the Joint Chiefs of Staff.

b.   Covert operations in active theaters of war and any other areas in which U.S. forces are engaged in combat operations will be conducted under such command and control relationships as have been or may in the future be approved by the Department of Defense.

6.   As used in this directive, "covert operations" shall be understood to be all activities conducted pursuant to this directive which are so planned and executed that any U.S. Government responsibility for them is not evident to unauthorized persons and that if uncovered the U.S. Government can plausibly disclaim any responsibility for them. Specifically, such operations shall include any covert activities related to: propaganda; political action; economic warfare; preventive direct action, including sabotage, anti-sabotage, demolition; escape and evasion and evacuation measures; subversion against hostile states or groups including assistance to underground resistance movements, guerrillas and refugee liberation groups; support of indigenous and anti-communist elements in threatened countries of the free world; deception plans and operations; and all activities compatible with this directive necessary to accomplish the foregoing. Such operations shall not include: armed conflict by recognized military forces, espionage and counterespionage, nor cover and deception for military operations.

7.   Except as the President otherwise directs, designated representatives of the Secretary of State and of the Secretary of Defense of the rank of Assistant Secretary or above, and a representative of the President designated for this purpose, shall hereafter be advised in advance of major covert programs initiated by CIA under this policy or as otherwise directed, and shall be the normal channel for giving policy approval for such programs as well as for securing coordination of support therefor among the Departments of State and Defense and the CIA.

8. This directive supersedes and rescinds NSC 10/2, NSC 10/5, NSC 5412, NSC 5412/1, and subparagraphs "a" and "b" under the heading "Additional Functions of the Operations Coordinating Board" on page 1 of the President's memorandum for the Executive Secretary, National Security Council, supplementing Executive Order 10483.

Notes

1. Some examples of President Truman's dislike of Donovan can be observed in Christopher Andrew, *For the President's Eyes Only: Secret Intelligence and the American Presidency from Washington to Bush* (New York: Harper Perennial, 1996), pp. 156–7.
2. 'History of the CIA', CIA website: *About CIA*, 10 April 2007, <https://www.cia.gov/about-cia/history-of-the-cia> (last accessed 10 January 2020).
3. 'The Office of Strategic Services: The Forerunner of Today's CIA', CIA website: *News & Information*, 3 April 2008, <https://www.cia.gov/news-information/featured-story-archive/2008-featured-story-archive/office-of-strategic-services.html> (last accessed 10 January 2020).
4. Douglas Waller, 'How the OSS Shaped the CIA and American Special Ops', *War on the Rocks*, <https://warontherocks.com/2015/09/how-the-oss-shaped-the-cia-and-american-special-ops/> (last accessed 10 January 2020).
5. 'The Office of Strategic Services Memorial: Honoring the Forerunner of Today's CIA', CIA website: *News & Information*, 21 January 2010, <https://www.cia.gov/news-information/featured-story-archive/2010-featured-story-archive/oss-memorial.html> (last accessed 10 January 2020).
6. Michael Warner, *The Office of Strategic Services: America's First Intelligence Agency* (Washington, DC: CIA, 2007), <https://www.cia.gov/library/publications/intelligence-history/oss/art05.htm> (last accessed 10 January 2020).
7. Andrew, *For the President's Eyes Only*, p. 134. For Detachment 101 see Troy J. Sacquety, *The OSS in Burma: Jungle War Against the Japanese* (Lawrence: University Press of Kansas, 2013).
8. National Security Act 1947, at <https://www.dni.gov/index.php/ic-legal-reference-book/national-security-act-of-1947> (last accessed 10 January 2020).
9. Andrew, *For the President's Eyes Only*, p. 171.
10. Ibid. pp. 171–2.
11. See Rhodri Jeffreys-Jones, *The CIA and American Democracy* (London: Yale, 2003), p. 49.

12. Ibid. p. 50.
13. Douglas T. Stuart, *Creating the National Security State: A History of the Law that Transformed America* (Woodstock: Princeton University Press, 2008), p. 268.
14. Andrew, *For the President's Eyes Only*, p. 172; Jeffreys-Jones, *The CIA and American Democracy*, p. 50.
15. Jeffreys-Jones, *The CIA and American Democracy*, p. 52.
16. Ibid. p. 53.
17. Stuart, *Creating the National Security State*, p. 269.
18. 'National Security Council Directive on Office of Special Projects', NSC 10/2, 18 June 1948, <https://history.state.gov/historicaldocuments/frus1945-50Intel/d292> (last accessed 10 January 2020).
19. Ibid.
20. John Prados, *Safe for Democracy: The Secret Wars of the CIA* (Chicago: Ivan R. Dee, 2006), p. 44.
21. Ibid. pp. 48–9; 58–9. See also the reports of the Church Committee, specifically Vol. 7, *Covert Action*, p. 146.
22. Prados, *Safe for Democracy*, p. 45.
23. Ibid. p. 65.
24. See Stuart, *Creating the National Security State*, p. 269; Prados, *Safe for Democracy*, p. 44.
25. Prados, *Safe for Democracy*, p. 46.
26. Jeffreys-Jones, *The CIA and American Democracy*, p. 56.
27. See Allen W. Dulles et al., *The Central Intelligence Agency and National Organization for Intelligence*, report to the NSC, 1 January 1949, p. 134, <https://www.cia.gov/library/readingroom/docs/CIA-RDP86B00269R001100090002-8.pdf> (last accessed 10 January 2020).
28. Andrew, *For the President's Eyes Only*, p. 193.
29. Minutes of the Intelligence Advisory Committee, IAC-M-1, 20 October 1950, <https://www.cia.gov/library/readingroom/docs/CIA-RDP82-00400R000100010001-4.pdf> (last accessed 10 January 2020).
30. See 'Appropriations' in 'CIA Act of 1949', 20 June 1949, <https://www.dni.gov/index.php/ic-legal-reference-book/central-intelligence-agency-act-of-1949> (last accessed 10 January 2020).
31. Jeffreys-Jones, *The CIA and American Democracy*, p. 70.
32. See the reports of the Church Committee, specifically Vol. 7, *Covert Action*, pp. 145–6.
33. The Doolittle Report was a classified and fairly comprehensive survey of the CIA. See the 'Doolittle Report', 'Report on the Covert Activities of the Central Intelligence Agency', 30 September 1954, <https://history.state.gov/historicaldocuments/frus1950-55Intel/d192> (last accessed 10 January 2020).
34. Reports of the Church Committee, specifically Vol. 7, *Covert Action*, p. 146.
35. See *Foreign Relations of the United States, 1964–1968, Volume XII, Western Europe* – 'Note on US Covert Actions', <https://history.state.gov/historicaldocuments/frus1964-68v12/actionsstatement> (last accessed 10 January 2020).

36. Stuart, *Creating the National Security State*, p. 270.
37. Ibid. p. 272.
38. Ibid. p. 272; Andrew, *For the President's Eyes Only*, p. 212; *Foreign Relations of the United States, 1964–1968, Volume XII, Western Europe* – 'Note on US Covert Actions'.

3 A 'Gangster Act': The Berlin Tunnel

Berlin has rightly been at the heart of every serious study of the Cold War. Germany's divided capital had strategic importance beyond any other foreign capital. Though military lines had ossified into a series of potential battlegrounds with border checkpoints, and a foreboding wall with watch towers sprouted where families once freely crossed, intelligence operations were much more fluid. As Richard Aldrich observed, 'the Cold War was fought, above all, by the intelligence services.'[1] Intelligence officers from many countries found themselves in both East and West Berlin attempting to discern the next move of the North Atlantic Treaty Organization (NATO) and the Warsaw Pact. David E. Murphy, a former Chief of CIA's Berlin Base, and his unlikely co-author, former KGB Officer Sergei Kondrashev, characterised the city as a 'battleground' of enormous importance.[2]

If the battleground was enormous, so were the audacity and scale of intelligence collection efforts within it. Between 1952 and 1956 the CIA and its partner, the British SIS, undertook the largest data exfiltration operation from a single point of presence in the pre-cyber era. The Berlin Tunnel, whose daring matched its logistical and technological complexity, was codenamed Operation Gold by the Americans and Stopwatch by the British. Its primary purpose was to discern indications and warning that would suggest the Soviets were planning a military invasion of Western Europe. The roots of the operation, however, were in the failure of another signals intelligence operation.

As world war turned to Cold War, both East and West refitted their intelligence machinery for the contest to come. In October 1948, the USSR clamped down on the poor information assurance practice of multiple uses of one-time pads to encrypt sensitive information before transmission thanks to the betrayal of William Weisband, a Soviet MGB (forerunner of the KGB) agent in the Russian section of the US Army's Security Agency (succeeding the Army Signals Intelligence Service) at Arlington Hall.[3] In the context of the national emergency in the Soviet Union during its so-called Great Patriotic War, this vulnerability created by the one-time pads was

perhaps understandable, but afterwards the Soviets readopted more systematic information security procedures to safeguard their most sensitive
global intelligence operations. This essentially halted the lifeblood of the
American Venona project, which exploited the wartime encryption vulnerability, although exploitation of Venona intelligence continued many years
hence. Compounding the problem, in the view of American cryptologist
Frank Rowlett, was the fact that Soviet communications were switching
from radio to cables, making communications interception itself much
more difficult.

However, the switch to cables and the loss of Venona material – which
had been so valuable to CIA for identification of both atom spies and
the Cambridge spy ring – were primary drivers towards other large-scale
interception operations, such as the Berlin Tunnel under the leadership of
colourful CIA officer Bill Harvey, an FBI Special Agent turned spook who
never seemed more than an arm's reach away from either a pistol or a cocktail. Harvey understood that a vast subterranean telephone and telegraph
network conducted Soviet military communications across the Warsaw
Pact from under the Soviet sector. In a time before satellites, sophisticated
cable-tapping operations were the cutting edge of technology.

The audacious Berlin Tunnel operation was essentially a large-scale
Communications Intelligence (COMINT) operation, and showed that
signals intelligence collection operations were not only left to the American
National Security Agency (NSA), founded the same year, and Britain's
Government Communications Headquarters (GCHQ); SIS and CIA would
also be involved in Cold War sigint collection. The joint plan was to dig a
shallow tunnel, beginning in a warehouse in the American sector of Berlin,
under the Soviet sector to tap a military telephone switch. SIS, under the
legendary Peter Lunn, had already undertaken a successful unilateral tunnelling operation, codenamed Silver, targeting the Soviet Military in Vienna
(another divided capital city along the front lines of the Cold War), which
lasted from 1949 until Austria regained its sovereignty in 1955.[4] When the
British learned that the Americans wished to undertake a similar tunnelling
operation whose intelligence product could be levels of magnitude greater
than Operation Silver, the British opted to declare Silver to the Americans
in exchange for full partnership in Gold.

After nearly two years of planning, actual construction began on the
tunnel in 1954 and the first intercepts arrived the following year. The
operation was characterised by transatlantic innovation and ingenuity with
a massive expenditure of agency resources in Berlin and also harnessed supporting elements from every other directorate. By the time it was complete,
the tunnel ran for nearly 1,500 feet and displaced 3,100 tonnes of earth.

That the endeavour was based on Anglo-American partnership is hinted at by one of its cryptonyms, PBJOINTLY, and it has been at the heart of competing hypotheses about the nature of the Anglo-American special intelligence relationship and its historiography. For instance, specialness-sceptic Alex Danchev attempted to characterise the relationship based solely on political directives by quoting a fictional passage, voiced by an imaginary American intelligence officer, from Ian McEwan's novel *The Innocent*, which bases itself in mid-1950s Berlin during the joint tunnelling and cable tapping operation:

> 'This operation is costing the government, the US government, millions of dollars. You guys are making a useful contribution, especially with the vertical tunnelling. You've also supplied the light bulbs. But do you know something? I'll tell you. It's all political. You think we couldn't lay those taps ourselves? You think we don't have amplifiers of our own? It's for politics that we're letting you in on this. We're supposed to have a special relationship with you guys, that's why.'[5]

McEwan's passage clearly seeks to satirise the perspective that the Anglo-American relationship was based on mutual benefit or synergistic outcomes. However, it is fortuitous that Danchev should choose this passage to caricature his estimation of the 'close approximation' of Anglo-American relations, based on inconvenient and distant political directives, because the actual basis for US–UK cooperation in Operation Gold was in fact anything but. In reality, the Americans could not 'lay those taps ourselves', according to OSS veteran and CIA officer Hugh Montgomery, who was serving in Berlin in the early 1950s.

Specifically, during the planning phase for Operation Gold, the Americans identified the Soviet communications cable that they wished to tap as a gas-filled variety with a lead sheath. The primary purpose of utilising gas in a cable is to insulate it and to keep moisture out, understandable concerns in the Berlin climate. But, from an intelligence and security perspective, using gas-filled cables has a bonus feature in that they may let the owner know if gas is escaping – a tell-tale sign that the cable has been damaged or compromised in some way. According to Montgomery's recollection, CIA did not have its own experts to handle a tap of a gas-filled cable and they initially sought advice from American companies such as AT&T on a way forward. Remarkably, no American company could claim expertise with gas-filled cables, so CIA turned to SIS, who could tap a lead-sheathed, gas-filled cable.[6] Thus, from the first, Operation Gold would have remained in the file of impossible good ideas had CIA not approached SIS on the basis of trust and mutual benefit, in this case seeking a skill that CIA was lacking.[7]

If the concept of an underground tap was sound in theory, the unsound personnel vetting practices of SIS would have significant ramifications in practice. Indeed, counter-intelligence failures – what might be called an insider threat in contemporary terms – would jeopardise the operation from the first. While the Anglo-American partners were busy digging and establishing a technically state-of-the-art telephone tap and recording operation, George Blake (codenamed Diomid), a Soviet agent in SIS, was betraying it. Thus, even before the first shovelful of earth was covertly removed under the Soviet sector, the KGB was aware of the operation.

Although understandably tempting, the KGB never used this opportunity to provide deceptive 'feed material' to the West through their knowledge of the operation, potentially calculating that the material was low-level order of battle material and thus opting to let it run for a while in order to protect Blake.[8] As David Stafford explained, 'Far from using the tunnel for misinformation and deception, the KGB's First Chief Directorate had taken a deliberate decision to conceal its existence from the Red Army and GRU, the main users of the cables being tapped. The reason for this extraordinary decision was to protect "Diomid", their rare and brilliant source George Blake.'[9] Still, like the Venona vulnerability, Moscow knew it needed to come to an end, so KGB ultimately orchestrated a dramatic 'accidental discovery' of the tunnel after nearly a year of interception operations in late April 1956.

If the Soviets made no attempt at information warfare via misleading 'feed material' during the course of the operation, they attempted to make up for it upon their 'discovery' of it under the guise of maintenance. The Soviets loudly labelled it a 'gangster act' in the international media, hoping it would reveal the underhanded nature of CIA. However, in the estimation of both CIA's official narrative as well as former DCI Allen Dulles' retirement memoir, Soviet attempts at milking their discovery of the tunnel backfired, at least in the American press. *Time* magazine concluded, 'It's the best publicity the US has had in Berlin for a long time.'[10] Instead of being understood as a 'gangster act', it was greeted with a degree of marvel at the project's audacity and perceived in the global commons as the feat of engineering that it was. As ever, audacity is expensive, costing the rough equivalent of two U-2 spy planes, which were under development at the same time. However – perhaps signifying the approval of the US government – after the operation ended, the audacious CIA was lavished with even more money to build its permanent headquarters in Langley.

The product of the operation suited its scale, and the king-sized expectations of Washington and Whitehall were presumably satisfied. According to CIA's calculations, Operation Gold netted 50,000 reels of tape, 443,000 fully transcribed conversations, 40,000 hours of telephone conversations and 6,000,000 hours of Teletype traffic. Out of this intelligence bonanza CIA published 1,750 intelligence reports on topics such as Soviet military leadership, order of battle and political-military relations (and tensions) with satellite militaries.[11] It took CIA and SIS two more years to conduct a comprehensive review of all the material that was recorded before the discovery, and in the end it was judged as a worthwhile undertaking despite Blake's treachery.[12] As the declassified chapter reference document avers: '[the] REGAL operation provided the United States and the British with a unique source of current intelligence on the Soviet Orbit of a kind and quality which had not been available since 1948. Responsible officials considered PBJOINTLY, during its productive phase, to be the prime source of early warning concerning Soviet intentions in Europe, if not world-wide.'[13]

While American and British ingenuity was on display, so was Soviet counter-intelligence prowess. The premature exposure of the Berlin Tunnel succeeded Venona's early compromise due to betrayal. With the end of the Venona code-breaking operation and the Berlin Tunnel cable-tapping operation, perhaps Soviets felt themselves finally free of American prying ears. If that feeling existed at all, it would prove to be short-lived. Two months after the 'discovery' of the tunnel, an even greater marvel of engineering and technological prowess took flight. In July 1956, the first U-2 flights ascended over Soviet airspace, replacing America's prying ears with prying eyes as a way of keeping tabs on Soviet military developments.

This operation again showcased the power of Anglo-American liaison synergy, the boldness and scope of Cold War intelligence collection and the ever-present risk of betrayal by counter-intelligence failures. Still, Allen Dulles judged the Berlin Tunnel as 'one of the most valuable and daring projects'[14] ever undertaken by the agency.

CS Historical Paper
No.150

CLANDESTINE SERVICES HISTORY

THE BERLIN TUNNEL OPERATION
1952–1956

Other copy held by: DDP Controlled by: FI/Division D
Copy No. 2 of 2   Date prepared: 25 August
                          1967
                          Date published: 24 June
                          1968
                          Written
by: ███████████████████

TABLE OF CONTENTS

Page

APPENDIX B

RECAPITULATION OF THE INTELLIGENCE DERIVED

Set forth below are a recapitulation of intelligence
derived from the REGAL material and some typical
consumer comments.

GENERAL

The REGAL operation provided the United States and
the British with a unique source of current intelligence on the Soviet Orbit of a kind and quality which
had not been available since 1948. Responsible U.S.
and British officials considered PBJOINTLY, during

its productive phase, to be the prime source of early warning concerning Soviet intentions in Europe, if not world-wide. Following are examples of items of intelligence for which REGAL was either a unique or most timely and reliable source.

POLITICAL

Throughout the life of source (11 May 1955 – 22 April 1956) we were kept currently informed of Soviet intentions in Berlin; REGAL provided the inside story of every "incident" occurring in Berlin during the period – a story which was in each case considerably at variance with accounts of the same incident as reported by other sources. REGAL showed that, contrary to estimates by other sources, the Soviets at that time did not intend to relinquish their prerogatives vis-a-vis the other three occupying powers despite continually increasing pressure from the East Germans to assert their sovereignty in East Berlin as well as in the rest of East Germany. REGAL provided a clear picture of the unpreparedness, confusion, and indecision among Soviet and East German officials whenever an incident occurred in East Berlin involving citizens of one of the Western powers.

The Soviet decision to implement the establishment of an East German Army was disclosed by REGAL in October 1955, in time to notify our representatives at the Foreign Ministers Conference in Geneva to that effect.

REGAL provided a detailed account of the Soviet program for implementation of the decisions of the 20th Party Congress, including measures to suppress unrest among Soviet nuclear scientists resulting from a too-literal interpretation of the new theory of collective leadership and the denigration of Stalin.

The progress of Marshal Zhukov's attempt to curtail the influence of the political officer in the Soviet Armed Forces (which led to his subsequent downfall) was traced in REGAL material from the autumn of 1955 to mid-April 1956.

REGAL provided considerable intelligence on the relationships between various key military and political figures of the Soviet hierarchy and on relations between the Poles and the Soviet military forces stationed in Poland.

MILITARY
General
a.   Reorganization of the Soviet Ministry of Defense.
b.   Soviet plans to implement the Warsaw Pact by increasing Soviet-Satellite military coordination.
c.   Implementation of the publicly announced intention to reduce the strength of the Soviet Armed Forces.
d.   Identification of several thousand Soviet officer personnel.
Air
a.   Development of an improved nuclear delivery capability in the Soviet Air Army in East Germany.
b.   Re-equipment of the Soviet Air Army in East Germany with new bombers and twin-jet interceptors having an airborne radar capability.
c.   Doubling of the Soviet bomber strength in Poland and the appearance there of a new fighter division.
d.   Identification and location of approximately 100 Soviet Air Force installations in the USSR, East Germany, and Poland, including a number of key aircraft factories.

Ground Forces
a.   Order of battle of Soviet ground forces within the USSR not previously identified or not located for several years by any other source.
b.   Soviet training plans for the spring and early summer of 1956 in East Germany and Poland.
c.   Identification of several thousand Soviet field post numbers (used by G-2 to produce Soviet order of battle intelligence).
Navy
a.   Reduction in the status and personnel strength of the Soviet Naval Forces.
b.   Organization and administrative procedures of the Headquarters of the Soviet Baltic Fleet and Soviet Naval Bases on the Baltic Coast.

SCIENTIFIC
Identification of several hundred personalities associated with the Soviet Atomic Energy (AE) Program.
Association of certain locations in the USSR with AE
activities.

Organization and activities of Wismuth SDAG (mining
uranium in the Aue area of East Germany).

OPERATIONAL
Organization, functions, and procedures of the Soviet
Intelligence Services in East Germany; identification
of several hundred Soviet Intelligence personalities
in East Germany and Moscow.

TYPICAL CONSUMER COMMENTS
March 1956
ACSI/Army - "REGAL has provided unique and highly
valuable current information on the order of battle,
training, organization, equipment, and operations of
the Soviet and East German Ground Forces. In addition, the scope and variety of the types of information found in REGAL have confirmed that it is our
best source of early warning of Soviet attack."
ACSI/Air - "The numerous productions received from
the REGAL project have been an extremely valuable
contribution to the Intelligence Community in our
common problems."

7 February 1958
CIA/OSI - "REGAL has provided valuable information on
atomic energy activities in East Germany, including
organizational relationships, personalities, procurement details, and uranium ore shipment data. The
number of hitherto unknown atomic energy localities,
personalities, and activities disclosed in REGAL
traffic is impressive."

CIA/ORR - "In referenced memorandum we indicated
our great interest in financial material of all kinds
which was available in REGAL material. Thanks to your
cooperation we are exploiting the material with great
success."

Notes

1. Richard J. Aldrich, *The Hidden Hand: Britain, America, and Cold War Secret Intelligence* (London: Allen Lane, 2001), p. 5.
2. David E. Murphy, Sergei A. Kondrashev and George Bailey, *Battleground Berlin: CIA Vs. KGB in the Cold War* (New Haven, CT: Yale University Press, 1997).
3. Christopher Andrew, *For the President's Eyes Only: Secret Intelligence and the American Presidency from Washington to Bush* (New York: Harper Perennial, 1996), pp. 180–1.
4. Author interview with former senior SIS officer, WT, 8 April 2014, London, UK. For further details on the role of Peter Lunn and the Vienna and Berlin tunnels, see David Stafford, *Spies Beneath Berlin* (New York: The Overlook Press, 2002).
5. As quoted in Alex Danchev, 'On Friendship: Anglo-America at fin de siècle', *International Affairs*, 73 (1997), p. 751.
6. Author interview with Hugh Montgomery, 11 April 2013, Langley, VA.
7. Interestingly, nine years hence, in light of information provided in David Stafford's *Spies Beneath Berlin*, Danchev corrects his 1997 argument in his 2006 article in *Diplomacy and Statecraft*, and states that the tap needed British expertise after all. His conclusions, however, remained the same.
8. David G. Coleman, '*Spies Beneath Berlin* (Review)', *Journal of Cold War Studies*, 7.1 (2005), pp. 200–2.
9. David Stafford, *Spies Beneath Berlin* (London: John Murray, 2002), p. 180.
10. As quoted in Paul Simpson, *A Brief History of the Spy: Modern Spying from the Cold War to the War on Terror* (Philadelphia: Running Press, 2013), p. 98.
11. 'The Berlin Tunnel', CIA website: *About CIA*, 23 July 2012, <https://www.cia.gov/about-cia/cia-museum/experience-the-collection/text-version/stories/the-berlin-tunnel.html> (last accessed 10 January 2020).
12. 'Clandestine Services History: The Berlin Tunnel Operation 1952–1956', CS Historical Paper No. 150, published in classified form (internally) 25 August 1967, declassified and released 15 February 2007, <https://www.cia.gov/library/readingroom/docs/DOC_0001459120.pdf> (last accessed 10 January 2020).
13. Ibid. section: 'Recapitulation of Intelligence Derived', Appendix B, p. 1.
14. Allen Dulles, *The Craft of Intelligence* (Guilfort, CT: The Lyons Press, 2006), p. 206.

4 The CIA and the USSR: The Challenge of Understanding the Soviet Threat

The CIA was created as relations between the Soviet Union and its erstwhile allied partners deteriorated markedly, from wartime cooperation to mutual, simmering hostility that occasionally threatened to boil over. This hostility determined the CIA's priorities for over four decades, which could be summarised quite simply as 'watching the bear'.[1] The agency's main target was the USSR. The agency's objectives were to observe, assess and determine Soviet capabilities and intentions. Its role was to provide the US policy and military community with information and analysis that would allow them to form effective policies and to avoid surprise. This was a big task. Several studies have delved into the scale of the challenges the CIA faced, and how it set out to resolve them. Many of these studies have been produced by the CIA or former officers to illustrate, and occasionally defend, their record.[2] The complexity and scale of the undertaking has often been understated by those who comment on the agency's record; this is a mistake. The CIA, and Western intelligence in general, faced an extremely difficult task in the early years of the Cold War, particularly in attempting to gain insights into the Soviet leadership, its deliberations, and what they intended to do. Joseph Stalin's Soviet Union was, in several if not most respects, a secret state.

In the absence of concrete intelligence from the Soviet Union, intelligence analysts needed to form judgements based on the best, although almost inevitably incomplete, information that they possessed at the time, as well as their expertise and key assumptions about Soviet policy. Observers often suspected that the conclusions of some assessments were more than a little reliant on a degree of Kremlinology (see the chapter in this volume on the end of the Cold War). But to assume so in general would be a disservice to the complicated work that underpinned the CIA's analyses. The analysts' task became a highly specialised one, requiring a large number of deep, specialist subject matter experts on all manner of Soviet weapons systems and doctrines, politics, industry, education and economics. The CIA probably amassed the greatest concentration of Soviet experts in the world. Generally, they were more successful at gauging Soviet capabilities than

Soviet intentions; but the record shows that they could be extremely perceptive, and could offer policymakers in Washington insights into developments in Moscow. However, the emergence of the CIA's analytical function took time, and there remained a question mark over the impact of CIA analyses on US policy for several years after 1947. This chapter examines the origin of the CIA's analysis function and its early assessments of the Soviet threat, and underlines the problems it faced in gathering intelligence on the USSR.

By 1946, the year that President Truman ordered the creation of the CIG, there was little doubt in Washington that the Soviet Union was the principal security concern and would remain so for the foreseeable future. Numerous indicators in Europe showed that the cooperation that had characterised the wartime Grand Alliance was faltering. These included concerning reports of Soviet behaviour in East Germany and Poland; the systematic and sometimes ruthless establishment of Soviet rule in Eastern Europe more broadly; and, later, reluctance to disengage from Iran and Turkey.[3] Such events reinforced the long-held view of many policy and military elites in Washington and London that the Second World War was something of an aberration, and, with Nazi Germany dealt with, the traditional enemy of Soviet Communism would once again be the priority.[4] These views were only reinforced in policymaking circles when the diplomat George Kennan outlined for the State Department what he believed to be driving Soviet policy in his February 1947 'Long Telegram'.[5] Similarly, Winston Churchill's 'iron curtain' speech at Westminster College in Missouri, on 5 March 1946, underlined for the Western world the challenge he saw presented in Soviet action. Washington's policymakers did not need intelligence analysis to help them make up their mind about the nature of the Soviet Union. Stalin's quest for security all but guaranteed a conflict with his former allies.[6]

Over the following year the division of Europe was crystallised, and the need for more nuanced intelligence analysis became clearer. Allied forces were being harassed by the Soviets in Berlin. The Cold War was being waged on the subterranean front by the secret services of both sides with vigour. Meanwhile, the scale and significance of Soviet espionage had also become clearer, particularly following the defection of the Soviet cipher clerk Igor Gouzenko in Ottawa in 1945. By 1948, American cryptanalysts were exploiting flaws in Soviet coding procedure to gain insights into theoretically unbreakable Soviet messages. As noted in Chapter 3, the Venona Project eventually led to the unmasking of some of Stalin's best-placed agents, deep in the heart of the British establishment.[7] But it was also becoming apparent that the Soviets had penetrated the deepest recesses of the military research establishments in the US and UK, Los Alamos and the 'Tube Alloys' project, the atomic weapons programmes. By 1947, with President Truman's speech setting containment as US policy, the US and its allies were faced with the prospect of what they perceived as an implacable foe, ideologically bent on spreading communism globally and on undermining the capitalist world, being armed with the most powerful weapons in existence. The need for nuanced analyses of Soviet actions and intentions based on the best possible intelligence became clearer.

This requirement notwithstanding, the development of the CIA's capability and authority over analyses of the USSR was protracted. Its legacy can be traced to the OSS Research and Analysis wing, elements of which had been absorbed by the State Department after the war. The successor of the OSS, the CIG, was given responsibility for estimates of significant foreign situations. But initially these were just collations of other departments' intelligence, and the departments did not necessarily feel obliged to share their information with the fledgling organisation; some refused outright.[8] The principle of centralised coordination gained support nevertheless, and the National Intelligence Authority mandated that the CIG was authorised to collect and assess intelligence if the task was not being done by an existing agency. It was awarded extra staff to fulfil this responsibility, and by October 1946 it had established an Office of Reports and Estimates (ORE).[9] Despite still being reliant on the Service and State Departments for some intelligence material, the CIG rapidly evolved into an organisation that developed its own intelligence, rather than merely coordinating it.

The ORE's first report concerned the USSR: 'ORE 1: Soviet Foreign and Military Policy'. In this paper they stressed that 'the Soviet government anticipates an inevitable conflict with the capitalist world', and will 'increase its relative power by building up its own strength and undermining that of its assumed antagonists.' The ORE underlined that a key component of this effort involved developing strategic air power and 'a maximum effort to develop as quickly as possible such special weapons as guided missiles and the atomic bomb'. The USSR's perceived insecurity, it argued, was not the product of a rational analysis of its geopolitical situation and of whether it was in reality threatened by an 'antagonistic capitalist encirclement'. Rather, it was 'deeply rooted in a haunting sense of internal and external insecurity inherited from the Russian past, is required by compelling internal necessity as a justification for the burdensome character of the Soviet police state and derived its authority from the doctrine of Marx and Lenin.'[10] Whilst this report highlighted crucial trends for policymakers, its impact, as with that of the CIG in general, was limited. The contemporaneous report on the same subject compiled by the short-lived US Joint Intelligence Committee and published by the Joint Chiefs of Staff as JIC 1696 – and described by the main author of ORE 1 as 'a hodge-podge' – seems to have achieved more prominence in Washington.[11] The ORE's assessment was a victim of the CIG's weakness in Washington bureaucratic battles.

The CIA was created, in part, to ensure that the US possessed a more powerful, better coordinated system for developing national intelligence. The NSA of 1947 mandates that one of the new agency's core functions was to 'to correlate and evaluate intelligence relating to the national security, and provide for the appropriate dissemination of such intelligence within the Government using where appropriate existing agencies and facilities'.[12] To achieve this aim, CIA maintained the ORE as its analysis body. The ORE, in turn, continued to publish reports on significant global developments until late in 1950, although only a small number concerned the USSR directly.[13] But the performance of the CIA in terms of fulfilling its 'national intelligence' mandate, and of the ORE's reports specifically, were the subjects of criticism in the Dulles-Jackson-Correa report of 1949.

In their judgement, a national intelligence estimate needed to meet certain criteria: it needed to be based on coordination of the best intelligence opinion; 'it should be based on all available information, including of the US's plans and policy requirements'; it should be compiled and assembled centrally, 'by an agency whose objectivity and disinterestedness are not open to question'; 'its ultimate approval should rest upon the collective responsibility of the highest officials in the various intelligence agencies'; and it should 'command recognition and respect throughout the Government as the best and presumably the most authoritative intelligence estimate'.[14] The CIA was producing reports that fulfilled these criteria only to a very limited degree. The ORE tended to draft reports itself, based on CIA-acquired intelligence, and then circulate them for broader consultation; the receiving departments were more reviewers than collaborators, and often did not share their own intelligence with the CIA. The net result was that, first, the CIA's papers were not necessarily relevant to policymakers' needs. Second, that there was a failure to develop truly coordinated national intelligence products that were recognised as superior to departmental reports. The Dulles group offered the stinging criticism that 'the position today of the Central Intelligence Agency is that of an independent producer of national intelligence, the quality of whose product is variable and the influence of which is questionable'.[15]

The main exception to this conclusion was the work of an ad-hoc committee that had been formed in March 1948 to report on Soviet capabilities and intentions. It was formed in response to a telegram penned by General Lucius D. Clay, the US military governor in Berlin. Clay had observed a hardening of the Soviet position in the city over the latter months of 1947 and early 1948, and on 5 March 1948 he felt compelled to telegram Washington outlining his concern – which was based not on hard intelligence but on his feeling that the change in atmosphere was palpable, that war 'may come with dramatic suddenness'.[16] It was, reportedly, received by the Joint Chiefs of Staff as a war warning.[17] But it was apparent that an assessment was needed of the Soviet position: was Governor Clay's feeling right?

The Intelligence Advisory Committee (examined in the previous chapters) directed that an ad-hoc committee be created under the CIA to examine the situation.[18] It comprised representatives from the Army, Navy, Air Force and State Department, and was chaired by a CIA official, the ORE's DeForest Van Slyck. He worked to marshal what he considered to be institutionally biased Army and Air Force estimates of the Soviets' intentions, and to provide President Truman with an agreed collective judgement: the Soviets were unlikely to initiate a war within the next sixty days.[19] In the midst of continued bureaucratic argument, the committee's conclusions on this point were delivered to the White House on 15 March 1948.[20] The sustained campaign of pressure on the Allies in Berlin mandated continued vigilance, so the Committee continued its work for the rest of 1948 and produced a number of reports underlining the unlikelihood of war, other than by miscalculation.[21] The estimates gave President Truman the confidence not to capitulate to the Soviets when they blocked ground access to Berlin in June 1948; he could maintain the airbridge without fear that it would escalate into war.[22] The Dulles group judged that this case demonstrated that, properly managed under CIA leadership, interdepartmental arrangements could provide 'the President and top policy-makers with an authoritative intelligence estimate'. They went on to recommend that an Estimates Division should be created in the CIA that would in future collate and review departmental intelligence reports and prepare coordinated national intelligence estimates, and that these should be reviewed by a revised Intelligence Advisory Committee whose members would be collectively responsible for the estimates.[23]

DCI Walter Bedell Smith used these recommendations as a basis for his reforms of the CIA. Over 1950 and 1951, he implemented sweeping changes to the way the CIA generated reports, centralising analysis by function.[24] Then in 1952 he brought all the CIA's analytical offices under the umbrella of the Directorate for Intelligence. Smith replaced the ORE with a Board of National Estimates (BNE); this in turn was supported by an Office of National Estimates (ONE), which was tasked with coordinating departmental intelligence products, although it soon developed the capability to conduct its own research.[25] The BNE and ONE reported to the Director of Central Intelligence, ensuring that the agency retained control of the national strategic intelligence product. And the CIA's influence was further enhanced with the determination that it would be responsible for the scientific intelligence and economic intelligence contributions to the ONE's deliberations. It took the economic intelligence officers of the CIA's Office of Research and Reports (ORR) little time to interpret their brief generously, and to conclude that it was impossible to consider economics apart from political and military considerations.[26] The ONE was headed first by Harvard historian and OSS veteran William L. Langer, and then by another Ivy League OSS veteran and author of *Strategic Intelligence for American World Policy*, Sherman Kent.[27] Under their leadership the National Intelligence Estimates of the ONE provided senior US policymakers with the national intelligence products that many considered so vital.

The range of questions they had to answer concerned all manner of subjects of varying levels of opacity, from the relatively open, like aspects of the Soviet economy, to the mysterious, like Soviet military strategy in the atomic age. The key challenge facing the officers of the ONE concerned the difficulty of gaining accurate intelligence on the broad swathe of subjects that they needed to understand if they were to accurately gauge Soviet capabilities and intentions. Rarely was it possible in the early Cold War to apply to an estimate an assumption that the Soviets' underlying intentions were anything but aggressive and expansionist.[28] Thus, estimates were often based on 'worst case' scenarios rather than 'most likely' ones, and it was only in January 1953 that the ONE judged that the Soviets were unlikely to deliberately start a war and would probably pursue their objectives by other means. It was not until the end of the decade that they could state that Soviet actions might be motivated by defensive concerns.[29] The longevity of worst-case thinking, and the assumption of offensiveness, were both related to ingrained views in Washington and the West more broadly, certainly. These were clearly stated in the most influential policy documents of the early Cold War, Kennan's 'Long Telegram' and NSC 68. But they were also related to the difficulty of gaining intelligence that could challenge key assumptions.

As the chapter reference document illustrates, the CIA was interested in a great many facets of the Soviet Union and its development, but with a limited number of exemptions they only had limited insight. It would take years of patient research and traditional intelligence work to redress this issue. This document, despite not discussing the specifics of the challenges posed by tight Soviet security, supported by outstanding penetration of the Western security apparatus, underlines clearly for the National Security Council the implication of the intelligence problem: the CIA's judgement in March 1953 that: 'In the event of a surprise attack we could not hope to obtain any detailed information of the Soviet military intentions.' With Pearl Harbor still fresh in the minds of politicians and officials, this constituted a very serious situation.

INTELLIGENCE ON THE SOVIET BLOC

The adequacy of intelligence on the Soviet bloc varies from firm and accurate in some categories to inadequate and practically nonexistent in others. We have no reliable inside intelligence on thinking in the Kremlin. Our estimates of Soviet long range plans and intentions are speculations drawn from inadequate evidence. At the other extreme, evidence confirming the existence of major surface vessels in the bloc naval forces is firm and accurate. Operational intelligence in support of current military operations in Korea is generally excellent. Other phases of Soviet bloc activities fall into intervening degrees of intelligence coverage.

SCIENTIFIC AND TECHNICAL INTELLIGENCE

In the field of atomic energy, our estimates of future Soviet stockpiles of fission weapons are reasonably adequate. The margin of error is such that the actual stockpile may be from 1/3 less to twice the estimate. However, gaps exist regarding production of U-235, and more important, their thermonuclear program.

Intelligence on Soviet biological and chemical warfare programs is extremely limited. On the other hand, we have a fairly good picture of Soviet capabilities in contributing scientific fields.

Knowledge of Soviet electronics has improved significantly in the last eighteen months. Intelligence on Soviet electromagnetic warfare capabilities is now very good. While our knowledge of the electronics aspects of Soviet air defense has improved, there are still serious gaps.

Knowledge of current Soviet guided missiles programs is poor, although certain projects based on German developments are fairly well known.

Technical intelligence on conventional military weapons and equipment is reasonably good as far as standardized items are concerned. However, there is little knowledge of important improvements in such fields as underwater and aerial warfare.

With respect to basic scientific research, present estimates of long-range developments are very weak, but our estimates of the current status are believed to be more nearly adequate.

ECONOMIC INTELLIGENCE

The adequacy of economic intelligence on the Soviet Bloc varies widely from one industry to another and from one country to another. The best intelligence is on the USSR.

Our intelligence is believed best on output of basic industries in the USSR – the primary metals, fuels and power, transportation, and some machinery and chemical industries. This intelligence is based in part on official Soviet announcements. Although contrary to what is usually regarded as Kremlin practice and not in keeping with Soviet character, such announcements have been shown to be reliable. The validity of official Soviet statistics has been confirmed by several independent studies based on intelligence materials. We believe, therefore, that official releases are not distributed for propaganda purposes. Nevertheless, there may be a margin of error due to faulty statistical practices and to falsification by the lower echelon. Thus our evidence on most major industries is probably within ten per cent of accuracy and, in the case of critical items such as steel, oil and electric power, within five per cent.

For other industries and for agriculture output estimates are built up from fragmentary intelligence. The techniques used include ███████████████████████ plant studies based on reports of prisoners of war, defectors, and returned scientists and technicians who were employed in the bloc in the postwar period; and crop-weather correlation analyses to estimate biological yields. Improvement in such estimates will depend in the future upon refinement of research techniques and upon improved collection of raw intelligence materials. To date, these techniques have given output estimates for all major agricultural commodities, and for several branches of industry which range from within ten per cent to within twenty-five per cent of accuracy.

There are still a large number of industries about which little is known. These include producers of certain machinery and equipment items and a few of the rare minerals.

By combining all available output statistics, annual growth rates for industry, agriculture, and gross national product are derived. We believe that they are probably within one percentage point of accuracy, that is, an estimated annual growth rate of six per cent for Soviet gross national product is probably no higher than seven per cent and no lower than five per cent.

Information for East Germany is the most complete, for Czechoslovakia and Poland it is fairly good, while that for China is the least adequate.

At present, intelligence is too fragmentary to permit estimates on strategic stockpiles and working inventories in all Bloc countries.

ARMED FORCES INTELLIGENCE

Military intelligence concerning the Soviet Bloc is considered from two points of view, tactical and strategic.

Tactical

Intelligence on the activities of the Soviet Bloc armed forces varies with the geographical area under consideration. Intelligence needed in support of ground military operations in Korea is generally excellent. Intelligence on the installations and on developments in Manchuria, such as the movement and activities of the Chinese Communist forces and North Korean units, is inadequate.

Order of battle and equipment intelligence on the USSR, Communist China and – to a lesser degree – the European Satellites, is partial and inadequate. Intelligence on the Communist Bloc units and equipment in most areas with which the US or nations friendly to the US are in contact is more nearly complete and reliable.

Intelligence concerning the strength of the Soviet Bloc and Satellite ground forces is believed to be of a fairly high order of reliability. Intelligence on the navies of the Soviet Bloc is, however, in general, satisfactory and adequate because of the greater accessibility of naval forces to observation.

Air
Estimates of Soviet air strength are derived from intelligence which is considered of acceptable reliability, but collection coverage is incomplete. Estimates of over-all size and composition of Soviet Air Forces are derived from identification of individual units and from estimated Table of Organization and Equipment strengths authorized for the various types of air regiments. Current estimates of jet fighter and medium bomber strength are considered reasonably valid.

Strategic
Reliable intelligence of the enemy's long-range plans and intentions is practically non-existent. Little improvement in these deficiencies can be expected in the near future despite our efforts.

Warning of Attack
The period of warning which the Western Powers might expect to receive if they were attacked by the Soviet Union vary according to the circumstances of the attack. There is no guarantee that intelligence will be able to give adequate warning of attack prior to actual detection of hostile formations. Opportunity for detection of indications of Soviet or Satellite attack varies from fair in the border areas of Germany and Korea to extremely poor in the Transcaucasus and Southeast Asia.

In the event of a surprise attack we could not hope to obtain any detailed information of the Soviet military intentions. There would be no detectable redeployment of forces. We could therefore expect at most a few hours warning of air attack and hostile action might well take place in Germany or other territories bordering the Soviet Orbit before any warning at all had been received.

In the event of Soviet strength being fully mobilized for war, we could expect from overt sources at least a month's warning, with confirmation of Soviet hostile intentions building up continuously thereafter.

The period of warning in the event of partial Soviet mobilization for war would vary from the few hours of the surprise attack to something less than the warning to be expected when the attack was delayed until the full strength of the Soviet forces had been mobilized.

Notes

1. This is the title of a very useful collection compiled by the CIA concerning the evolution of its estimates on the USSR. See Gerald K. Haines and Robert E. Legget, *Watching the Bear: Essays on CIA's Analysis of the Soviet Union* (Washington, DC: CIA, 2003), <https://www.cia.gov/library/center-for-the-study-of-intelligence/csi-publications/books-and-monographs/watching-the-bear-essays-on-cias-analysis-of-the-soviet-union/> (last accessed 10 January 2020).

2. See for example Haines and Legget, *Watching the Bear*; Gerald K. Haines and Robert E. Legget, *CIA's Analysis of the Soviet Union, 1947–1991* (Washington, DC: CIA, 2001), <https://www.cia.gov/library/center-for-the-study-of-intelligence/csi-publications/books-and-monographs/cias-analysis-of-the-soviet-union-1947-1991/index.html> (last accessed 10 January 2020); Gerald K. Haines, *At Cold War's End: US Intelligence on the Soviet Union and Eastern Europe, 1989–1991* (Washington, DC: CIA, 1999), <https://www.cia.gov/library/center-for-the-study-of-intelligence/csi-publications/books-and-monographs/at-cold-wars-end-us-intelligence-on-the-soviet-union-and-eastern-europe-1989-1991/art-1.html> (last accessed 10 January 2020).

3. See for instance Richard J. Aldrich, *The Hidden Hand: Britain, America, and Cold War Secret Intelligence* (London: Allen Lane, 2001), pp. 59–61; and broader histories like Melvyn Leffler and David S. Painter, *Origins of the Cold War: An International History* (1994).

4. Richard Aldrich presents several interesting perspectives from Western soldiers and intelligence officials who worked with their Soviet counterparts in *The Hidden Hand*; see chapters 1, 2.

5. The 'Long Telegram' is available online at <https://www.trumanlibrary.gov/library/research-files/telegram-george-kennan-james-byrnes-long-telegram> (last accessed 10 January 2020).

6. There are many excellent studies and collections concerning the early Cold War. Consider Melvyn P. Leffler and Odd Arne Westad (eds), *The Cambridge*

History of the Cold War: Vol 1: Origins (Cambridge: Cambridge University Press, 2005) as an introduction, or John Lewis Gaddis, *The Cold War* (London: Allen Lane, 2005).

7. The National Security Agency has published a significant amount of material concerning the Venona Programme; see <https://www.nsa.gov/news-features/declassified-documents/venona/> (last accessed 10 January 2020). See also the Wilson Center's *Cold War International History Project* section on the decrypts: <https://www.wilsoncenter.org/article/venona-project-and-vassiliev-notebooks-index-and-concordance> (last accessed 10 January 2020).

8. Rhodri Jeffreys-Jones, *The CIA and American Democracy* (London: Yale, 2003), pp. 45–6. See also Donald P. Steury, 'Origins of CIA's Analysis of the Soviet Union' in Haines and Legget, *Watching the Bear.*

9. Steury, 'Origins of CIA's Analysis of the Soviet Union'.

10. The US National Archives, College Park, ORE 1, 'Soviet Foreign and Military Policy', 23 July 1946, <https://catalog.archives.gov/id/6924242> (last accessed 10 January 2020).

11. On the US Joint Intelligence Committee see Larry A. Valero, 'The American Joint Intelligence Committee and Estimates of the Soviet Union, 1945–1947', *Studies in Intelligence*, 9 (Summer 2000), <https://www.cia.gov/library/center-for-the-study-of-intelligence/csi-publications/csi-studies/studies/summer00/art06.html> (last accessed 10 January 2020); see also Steury, 'Origins of CIA's Analysis of the Soviet Union'.

12. See the National Security Act, 1947, <https://www.dni.gov/index.php/ic-legal-reference-book/national-security-act-of-1947> (last accessed 10 January 2020).

13. See US TNA, 'List of ORE Documents by Number', 14 September 1993, <https://catalog.archives.gov/id/6924241> (last accessed 10 January 2020).

14. Allen W. Dulles et al., *The Central Intelligence Agency and National Organization for Intelligence*, report to the NSC, 1 January 1949, pp. 68–9, <https://www.cia.gov/library/readingroom/docs/CIA-RDP83-01034R000400110009-0.pdf> (last accessed 10 January 2020).

15. Ibid. pp. 72–3.

16. Steury, 'Origins of CIA's Analysis of the Soviet Union'.

17. Ibid.

18. Ibid.

19. Ibid.

20. Ibid.

21. Ibid.

22. See the CIA's note on this episode, 'Learning to Estimate', CIA website: *News & Information*, 12 March 2008, <https://www.cia.gov/news-information/featured-story-archive/2008-featured-story-archive/learning-to-estimate-1948.html> (last accessed 10 January 2020).

23. Dulles et al., 'A Report to the National Security Council', p. 81.

24. For further details on the reforms and reorganisation, see Nicholas Dujmovic, 'The Significance of Walter Bedell Smith as Director of Central Intelligence,

1950–1953', n.d., <https://www.cia.gov/library/readingroom/docs/Misc-009. pdf> (last accessed 10 January 2020).

25. Ibid.
26. Steury, 'Origins of CIA's Analysis of the Soviet Union'.
27. Kent is probably better remembered, but see here his note on the Directorship of Langer at the ONE, 'The First Year of the Office of National Estimates' (10 December 1970), <https://www.cia.gov/library/center-for-the-study-of-intelligence/csi-publications/books-and-monographs/sherman-kent-and-the-board-of-national-estimates-collected-essays/7year.html> (last accessed 10 January 2020).
28. For a discussion of this point see Raymond L. Garthoff, 'Estimating Soviet Military Intentions and Capabilities', in Haines and Legget, *Watching the Bear*.
29. Ibid.

5 Anglo-American Intelligence Liaison and the Outbreak of the Korean War

The 1946 UKUSA Agreement between the US and Britain, which later expanded to include Australia, Canada and New Zealand – consequently earning the moniker 'Five-Eyes' – provided for extensive liaison on sigint specifically. Close relations also existed between humint and military agencies, and between the CIA and Britain's Joint Intelligence Committee (JIC) on the exchange of intelligence assessments. By and large, these relationships existed separately from the political whims of those in charge of the White House or Downing Street, but during the Korean War, political differences had a direct effect on the quality and quantity of intelligence material shared across the Atlantic.

The problem was China. Since the 1930s there had raged a civil war fought by the nationalists, supported by the US, and the communists, propped up by the Soviet Union. As the late 1940s wore on the civil war continued, and it became increasingly clear that the tide was turning towards the communists and their leader, Mao Zedong. In late 1948 the State Department confirmed to the British that the US would maintain a presence in China whichever way the civil war was won – but within six months, that position was being reversed as the communists stood on the brink of victory. In August 1949 this change of position was clear, for as the British Foreign Secretary, Ernest Bevin, informed his Cabinet colleagues, the decision had now been taken that all US government nationals would be withdrawn from China. Bevin succinctly summed up the situation: '[W]e are faced with the dilemma that unless we can persuade the United States authorities to agree with us we must either agree to differ and pursue our own policy of keeping a foot in the door, or abandon the whole of our interests in China in order to follow in the American wake.'[1]

The divergence in opinion between Washington and London was based on different factors. For President Truman, one of the key issues was not to declare the civil war over and therefore not signal that it had been a communist success, the objective being to protect major allies and assets – particularly Japan, the largest and most significant American interest in the region. This was an early test of the logic that would become known as the domino theory a few years later. For Britain, the two concerns were to ensure the protection of its colonial interests in Hong Kong, and also to ensure that trade and economic relations were preserved. For these reasons, Mao's declaration of success in late September 1949 was a significant moment for Anglo-American relations in the region.

After discussion with his American counterparts, Bevin made the decision that Britain would maintain a consular presence in China, thereby offering *de facto* recognition of the communist government. There was a delay in this official notification reaching Washington and President Truman complained that the British had not informed him in advance of what had been planned. UK–US relations worsened shortly thereafter with the UK's *de jure* recognition of Mao's government in early 1950.[2]

Initially, at least, these political disagreements did not have a detrimental effect on intelligence relations. Indeed, liaison in the summer of 1949, just as the first political cracks were appearing, was strong, with joint lists of intelligence requirements being produced. This mood did not last long. In August, British intelligence expressed some concern about 'overloading' the existing liaison channels between both countries in the Far East, and just a few weeks later serious signs of a rift appeared.[3]

At a meeting of the JIC, the representative from Naval Intelligence informed colleagues that 'at present the official flow of information from the Americans, even in London and Washington, was far from complete . . . the problem was extremely delicate and therefore required careful handling',[4] as noted in the first chapter reference document. To redress the situation, it was decided that a joint intelligence summit be convened in Washington the following month. By all accounts it did not go well. The US Joint Chiefs of Staff (JCS) had decreed that no military assistance should be offered to the British in the case of an attack on Hong Kong because, put bluntly, its loss would not materially affect the spread of communism in the region and therefore it was not an American concern.[5] This difference of opinion and the disunity over the recognition of Mao's government were not the only areas of Anglo-American disagreement. On Formosa, for instance, the US showed a commitment to assist the Nationalist forces. In the UK, both the Foreign Office and Chiefs of Staff had agreed that 'strong representations' should be made to the US to stop this support.[6]

There were similar concerns over Korea. Following the Japanese surrender in 1945, Korea had been divided between the victors: North Korea was in the Soviet sphere of influence, with the South going to the United States. The leaders of both North and South shared a belief that the peninsula should be united, but differed as to who should control it: the communists wanted Kim II Sung, while the South wanted its leader, Syngman Rhee.

US forces had been based in the south of the country after the end of the Second World War, but had started to withdraw in 1948 following elections. Some British reports claimed these had been rigged. Many British officials complained in the late 1940s about the inconsistent policies that the Truman administration adopted towards Asia. For instance, in the Foreign Office one senior official declared that 'US policy in the Far East – or lack of policy – is a gift to the Russians'.[7]

In late December 1949 the US passed NSC 48, which called for a stronger US stance on communism in the Far East. For the US, Japan was a central aspect in its policy towards the region, both in terms of its strategic position and industrial potential. Despite an overwhelming concentration on Japan, the fate of Korea given its proximity to Japan would be of huge interest to Washington. For Britain, Korea was a lesser concern than the perceived increase in the threat to Hong Kong and the pace of the emergency in Malaya.

These diplomatic wrangles had a powerful impact on intelligence relations. Referring to the September 1949 Anglo-American meetings, the British military Directors of Intelligence subsequently briefed the Chiefs of Staff committee on the situation:

When the JIC Team visited Washington last year [i.e. September 1949] the Americans had been asked for information on Korea which had been refused . . . In discussion on sources of intelligence, the Directors of Intelligence confirmed that the Americans did not consider that Korea or Formosa could be covered as regards intelligence . . . in view of the political difference between us over China. Thus, no intelligence had been received from the Americans on either of these countries. Somewhat illogically, however, the Americans expected us to provide them with any such intelligence available, which, within limits, was being done.[8]

Anglo-American differences continued to affect intelligence sharing adversely in the Far East at all levels, from the exchange of intelligence assessments, to planning for 'special operations'. For the British, these instances of communication failure would have a direct impact on their ability to gauge developments in the Far East.

The political differences over China were, by now, so severe that they had resulted in the termination of the steady pattern of intelligence exchange across the Atlantic on Far East topics. Hence, as a 1951 retrospective British study made explicit, 'before the attack on South Korea the Americans had reports about military activity in North Korea which were not available to us. Had the JIC received these reports they might well have given some warning of the impending attack.'[9]

79

This view is difficult to support given what we now know about US intelligence prior to the attack by North Korea on its southern neighbour in June 1950. The CIA, just three years old at the time of the outbreak of hostilities, was still learning its trade. The outbreak of the Korean War and the surprise it generated has often been held up as a classic example of an intelligence failure – but how much did the CIA really know?[10] The CIA only had a small number of staff in Korea itself, and none of these were aligned to analytical efforts back in the US. Nonetheless, it still managed to produce a steady series of assessments on events in Korea. One prescient report in February 1949, for example, concluded that:

> In the absence of US troops, it is highly probable that northern Korea alone, or northern Koreans assisted by other Communists, would invade southern Korea and subsequently call upon the USSR for assistance. Soviet control or occupation of Southern Korea would be the result . . . withdrawal of US forces from Korea in the spring of 1949 would probably in time be followed by an invasion, timed to coincide with Communist-led South Korean revolts, by the North Korean People's Army possibly assisted by small battle-trained units from Communist Manchuria. . . . US troop withdrawal would probably result in a collapse of the US-supported Republic of Korea.[11]

Subsequent reports issued in the first half of 1950 highlighted the potential for something significant to happen, but there was no specific warning. Just a week before the invasion the CIA aired it as a possibility, commenting on the identification of tanks and heavy artillery along the border area, but there was no suggestion that war was imminent. Why was this? For the CIA analysts it was felt that without Soviet or Chinese support the North Koreans could not achieve a military victory and were therefore unlikely to attack.[12] Strategically, then, there was some awareness of the North Korean threat, but tactically there was no suggestion that war might occur in the near future, as the second chapter reference document details.[13]

The British also assessed the situation in the same way and despite the liaison difficulties, clearly must have had some access to US thinking: 'the Americans did not anticipate any actual frontier invasion from North Korea in the foreseeable future, though the North Korean forces are deployed in a fashion which is equally suitable for offence or defence . . . all the above information makes it clear . . . that no direct invasion is at present contemplated'.[14] All of these forecasts and assessments proved to be erroneous when, on 25 June 1950, the North Korean Army crossed the 38th Parallel, supposedly to repel an earlier cross-border raid by the South Koreans.

Anglo-American difficulties continued, not helped by military problems in coordinating the response. Intelligence liaison did improve to some extent but it did not reach the levels of cooperation achieved in other theatres. There was greater collaboration, but the UK still transmitted more intelligence to the US than it received in return. The situation had certainly not been resolved by March 1953, as the JIC Chairman could tell Committee members that 'whilst we were giving the Americans all the intelligence we possessed, the Americans were less forthcoming'. The difficulty, as the Director of Military Intelligence reported, 'was that we did not know how much intelligence the Americans possessed'.[15] For the British at least, these instances of communication failure would have a direct impact on its ability to gauge developments in the Far East, problems that would persist into the next decade with Vietnam.

THIS DOCUMENT IS THE PROPERTY OF HIS BRITANNIC
MAJESTY'S GOVERNMENT
The circulation of this paper has been strictly
limited.
It is issued for the personal use of Record.
TOP SECRET   Copy No. 44

J.I.C. (49) 82nd Meeting   GUARD
CHIEFS OF STAFF COMMITTEE
JOINT INTELLIGENCE COMMITTEE

MINUTES of the EIGHTY-SECOND Meeting of the
Committee (Deputy Directors) held in Conference
Room "G", at the Ministry of Defence, S.W. 1., on
WEDNESDAY, 24TH AUGUST, 1949, at 11.00 a.m.

PRESENT
Mr. H.N. Brain,
Foreign Office
(In the Chair)

Captain J.S.S. Litchfield-Speer, R.N., (Representing Director of Naval Intelligence), Admiralty.	Brigadier V. Boucher, (Representing Director of Military Intelligence), War Office.

Air Commodore A.J. Rankin, (Representing Assistant Chief of the Air Staff (Intelligence)), Air Ministry.	(Representing Major-General Sir Stewart Menzies).
Mr. M.F. Serpell, (Representing Sir Percy Sillitoe), Security Service. Mr. M.Y. Watson,	(Representing Major-General K.W.D. Strong), Joint Intelligence Bureau.

Sir Marston Logan,
Colonial Office.

THE FOLLOWING WERE ALSO PRESENT

Lieut.-Commander G.C. Crowley, Admiralty (For Items 1 & 2).	Major O.D. Le Feuvre, War Office (For Items 1 & 2).
Squadron Leader B.H. Worts, Air Ministry (For Items 1 & 2).	Mr. R.A. Burrows, Foreign Office(For Items 1 & 2).

Mr. A. Goodwill,
Joint Intelligence Bureau
(For Items 1 & 2).

SECRETARIAT
Squadron Leader I.S. Stockwell
Mrs. C.M. Warburton

5. INTELLIGENCE REQUIREMENTS FROM UNITED STATES SOURCES ON CHINA   TOP SECRET   GUARD
(Previous Reference: J.I.C. (49) 80th Meeting, Minute 8)

CAPTAIN LITCHFIELD-SPEER referred to a minute[+] by the Secretary circulating a draft telegram to the Chairman, Joint Intelligence Committee, Far East, on the exchange of intelligence with the Americans in the Far East, which had been prepared in accordance with their previous discussion. He said that, on reconsideration, the Admiralty had doubts regarding the desirability of endeavouring to arrange a formal channel for the exchange of intelligence with the Americans in the Far East. At present the official flow of information from the Americans, even in London and Washington, was far from complete. So far as the Admiralty was concerned there was no formal agreement for the exchange of information although a working arrangement existed with certain American representatives in London. The problem was extremely delicate and therefore required careful handling. It was possible that certain changes during the next three months might make it easier for the Admiralty to arrange a formal exchange of information, with the United States Office of Naval Intelligence and, in view of this, the present might not be an appropriate time to raise the question of establishing a formal channel of exchange of intelligence in the Far East.

In discussion, it was generally agreed that, in the light of Captain Litchfield-Speer's comments, the draft telegram should be re-worded to state that the committee accepted the view of the Joint Intelligence Committee, Far East, that to endeavour to increase formal exchange of intelligence at a high level would be undesirable. It should be pointed out, however, that since the exchange of information in London and Washington was incomplete, it was all the more important to develop informal exchange through local contacts. In addition, with the extension of communist influence to South China, the United States authorities in Tokyo might well become more interested in receiving intelligence from British sources, particularly Hong Kong, than had previously been the case.

THE COMMITTEE:-
Approved the draft telegram, as amended in discussion, and instructed the Secretary to arrange for its despatch to the Joint Intelligence Committee, Far East.

CURRENT CAPABILITIES OF THE
NORTHERN KOREAN REGIME

CENTRAL INTELLIGENCE AGENCY

CURRENT CAPABILITIES OF THE NORTHERN KOREAN REGIME
Estimate of Current Capabilities

The "Democratic People's Republic" of northern Korea is a firmly controlled Soviet Satellite that exercises no independent initiative and depends entirely on the support of the USSR for existence. At the present time there is no serious internal threat to the regime's stability, and, barring an outbreak of general hostilities, the Communists will continue to make progress toward their ultimate domestic goals. The Communist regime in northern Korea suffers from a shortage of skilled administrative personnel and from weaknesses in its economy and its official Party organizations. There is widespread, although passive, popular discontent with the Communist government. Despite these weaknesses, however, the regime has, with Soviet assistance, clearly demonstrated an ability to continue its control and development of northern Korea along predetermined political, economic, and social lines.

The northern Korean regime is also capable, in pursuit of its major external aim of extending control over southern Korea, of continuing and increasing its support of the present program of propaganda, infiltration, sabotage, subversion, and guerrilla operations against southern Korea. This program will not be sufficient in itself, however, to cause a collapse of the southern Korean regime and the extension of Communist control over the south so long as US economic and military aid to southern Korea is not substantially reduced or seriously dissipated.

At the same time the capability of the northern Korean armed forces for both short- and long-term overt military operations is being further developed.

Although the northern and southern forces are nearly equal in terms of combat effectives, training, and leadership, the northern Koreans possess a superiority in armor, heavy artillery, and aircraft. Thus, northern Korea's armed forces, even as presently constituted and supported, have a capability for attaining limited objectives in short-term military operations against southern Korea, including the capture of Seoul.

Northern Korea's capability for long-term military operations is dependent upon increased logistical support from the USSR. If the foreign supporters of each faction were called upon for increased assistance, there is no reason to believe that Soviet support would be withheld and considerations of proximity and availability of such assistance would greatly favor the northern Korean regime. Soviet assistance to northern Korea, however, probably would not be in the form of direct participation of regular Soviet or Chinese Communist military units except as a last resort. The USSR would be restrained from using its troops by the fear of general war; and its suspected desire to restrict and control Chinese influence in northern Korea would militate against sanctioning the use of regular Chinese Communist units in Korea.

Despite the apparent military superiority of northern over southern Korea, it is not certain that the northern regime, lacking the active participation of Soviet and Chinese Communist military units, would be able to gain effective control over all of southern Korea. The key factors which would hinder Communist attempts to extend effective control under these circumstances are: (1) the anti-Communist attitude of the southern Koreans; (2) a continuing will to resist on the part of southern troops; (3) the Communist regime's lack of popular support; and (4) the regime's lack of trained administrators and technicians.

Note: The intelligence organizations of the Departments of State, Army, Navy, and the Air Force have concurred in this report. It contains information available to CIA as of 15 May 1950.

ANNEX A

SOVIET POSITION IN NORTHERN KOREA

The USSR's fundamental strategic concern with Korea is positional. Northern Korea has a short common border with Soviet territory, flanks sea and land communication lines between Vladivostok and Port Arthur, and shares a long, common frontier with Manchuria. Control of northern Korea provides the USSR with an advance fringe of secondary air and naval bases beyond the boundaries of the Soviet Far East. In addition, northern Korea provides a base for eventual extension of Soviet control over southern Korea, which, if accomplished, would give the Soviet Union a further strategic advantage in its positional relationship with Japan and consequently enhance the position of the USSR vis-à-vis the US in the Far East. Of increasing importance at the present time is the area's economic potential, which, although limited, can make valuable contributions to the economy of the Soviet Far East.

To assure continued control and to protect and advance strategic and economic interests in northern Korea, the Soviet Union since 1945 has concentrated on the following objectives: (1) the establishment of a strong, effective, and obedient Communist government and society; (2) the exploitation of economic and human resources, with simultaneous development of a self-supporting, expanding economy within northern Korea; and (3) the exploitation of northern Korea as a base for the penetration and subversion of southern Korea.

Since the establishment of the "Democratic People's Republic" (September 1948) and the withdrawal of Soviet troops (December 1948), the Soviet Union has maintained the fiction of northern Korean independence and has exercised its control through the medium of the Communist-dominated Korean Government and associated political organizations. The Soviet Embassy at the "capital city" of Pyongyang is headquarters for the four- to five-thousand-man Soviet mission in northern Korea. The Soviet mission, infiltrated as advisers throughout the government, economy, and political organizations, serves as a guarantee of northern Korean subservience and a source of technical assistance.

ANNEX B
CURRENT POLITICAL SITUATION

1. Indigenous Leadership.

The "Democratic People's Republic" is under the immediate control of a small group of Korean Communist leaders whose primary qualification for high office is loyalty to the USSR and willingness to accept a subordinate role within the pattern of Soviet control. Thus, Koreans with a Soviet background appear to have been given positions superior to those held by either native-trained Communists or Koreans who received Communist indoctrination in Yenan and Manchuria, and this Soviet-trained leadership appears to be well knit. The intensity of Soviet control, the leaders' lack of strong personal followings among the Korean people, and the composition of the present southern Korean Government which makes it unpalatable to possible northern "nationalist deviationists" as an alternative prevents either significant deviations or disruptive factionalism.

Except for their loyalty and subservience to the USSR, northern Korea's leaders possess few qualifications for the responsibility of high government and party office. They have gained no popular support and despite four years in office they still lack requisite administrative and technical skills. Although these weaknesses lower the regime's efficiency and decrease its popular appeal, they do not materially affect the stability of the "People's Republic," since experienced Soviet advisers adequately maintain government efficiency at the top level and the police effectively control the populace.

2. Government Organization.

The Government of northern Korea closely resembles that of all other "people's democracies" and a democratic facade obscures its basic totalitarian pattern. Constitutional provisions for a popularly elected representative assembly, a responsible cabinet – actually the key organ in the government – civil liberties and other rights and institutions normally associated with democratic government, are intended to develop popular support for the "People's Republic" not only in northern Korea but in southern Korea as well. Changes gradually being made in the institutions established by the Constitution, however, point to the transformation of the "People's Democracy" into an "orthodox" socialist state of the Soviet type.

3. Party Organization.

The organization of the Communist Party (officially known as the North Korea Labor Party) (NKLP), which parallels the hierarchical government structure, is similar to the Party in the USSR. Top government positions are all held by NKLP members, and the Party's Politbureau is the regime's major policy-making body. Most of the government's bureaucrats are drawn from the Party ranks. The Party is intended to be the activist element among the politically passive northern Koreans, is responsible for political activities – including elections, demonstrations, and the dissemination of propaganda – and is the nucleus for what will eventually be a one-party system. In the interim, however, the fiction of a multi-party system is maintained. The Front and its organizations, manipulated and controlled by the NKLP leadership, and designed to include every segment of society, support and assist internal indoctrination and control programs and play an even more important role in operations against southern Korea.

Membership in the NKLP is estimated at between five and six hundred thousand, an unusually high percentage of the total population. The Party is controlled by a group of about a hundred, who provide the indigenous leadership in the state apparatus and who subject the several thousand petty officials, intellectuals, and professional men in the middle bracket of the Party (generally less thoroughly indoctrinated Marxists) to the most stringent Party discipline.

The remainder of the Party's membership is four-fifths peasant and one-fifth urban and industrial workers. The support of this vast majority of the Party's members is maintained through preferential treatment and strict discipline. Devotion and loyalty to the Party's leadership, rather than intellectual adherence to Marxism, is required from this Party majority that serves fundamentally as a large base with à vested interest in perpetuation of the regime, rather than as a mature activist element.

4. Methods of Control.

Both the state organization and the regimentation of Korean society depend on firm control of the people and the maintenance of internal security. The police force is the instrument of primary control. Exclusive of the para-military border constabulary which is still under the Minister of Interior, there are some thirty to forty thousand police agents and uniformed police. The former maintain a constant check on public attitudes and seek out dissident elements. Groups such as former landlords, business-men, property owners, intellectuals and Christians in the north Korean population are singled out by the police (as dissident or potentially dissident ele-ments) and are subject to particularly rigid police controls.

As a long-range source of stability, Korea's Communist regime has sought popular support through the use of persuasive techniques, principally prop-aganda and the conferring of material benefits. Propaganda, disseminated through a wide variety of media, reaches every element of the Korean popula-tion. Its main effort is directed at concealing the dictatorial nature of the government, the extent of Soviet domination and similar aspects of Communism in Korea, while creating, on the other hand, the illusion of national independence, representative government, equality with the Soviet Union, and other favorable stereotypes. Material benefits designed to recruit mass support include: reforms purported to correct deep-seated inequities in the Korean social and economic system; the provision of social and public services on much larger scale than under the Japanese; and specific state actions - such as the release of extra consumer goods – timed to counteract public discontent over new economic regulations.

5. Effectiveness of the Political System.

The "Democratic People's Republic" has established firm control over the northern Korean people. Despite weaknesses, the Communist regime is progressing toward its ultimate domestic objectives of establishing a stable, fully socialized state. Its strength and stability are mainly attributable to: (1) rigid direction exercised through Soviet advisers and loyal Korean Communists; (2) Soviet material aid and technical advice in all fields; (3) comprehensive and highly organized state regulation of political, economic, and social activity, maintained both through government controls and through the actions of Communist-controlled mass organizations; (4) effective police control, supplemented by techniques of persuasion and psychologically bolstered by the proximity of Soviet forces; (5) cohesiveness and loyalty to both the government and the Soviet Union on the part of northern Korea's indigenous leaders, the bureaucracy, the police, the North Korea Labor Party and the more skilled technicians and workers; and (6) the achievement, since 1946, of substantial increases in production, which have raised living standards in northern Korea to a minimum subsistence level.

Despite the strength and stability of the "People's Republic" the regime has a number of important weaknesses to overcome, major among them being: (1) a lack of experienced and competent leaders, administrators, technicians, and dynamic activist strength in the NKLP; (2) the regime's narrow base of popular support, which results from the relatively widespread popular discontent; (3) Soviet interference and exploitation, which offends Korean desires for complete independence and contributes to the low standard of living, which is a basic cause for popular discontent and a factor contributing to low labor productivity.

The Communist system, itself inherently incompatible with traditional social, economic, and political forms in Korea, assures the existence of discontented groups under the northern regime. In the brief period of Communist control, nearly two million northern Korean refugees have moved to the south; the great mass of the northerners have not yet appeared receptive to a Communist, Soviet-oriented state, and indoctrination in Marxian ideology remains extremely limited. There is believed to be widespread discontent and dissatisfaction among farmers, for example, particularly among those who formerly owned large or medium-sized farms. The forced labor required on community projects, as well as the government's collection of large special crop taxes, moreover, has incurred the resentment of former landless tenant farmers, whose support was actively solicited by means of the 1946 "land reform." The 100,000 or more Christians are strongly anti-Communist, and considerable discontent also exists among the pre-liberation middle classes. This popular discontent appears to be largely passive, however, and in the few known attempts to organize the opposition for action, the groups were quickly broken up by the police.

The low standard of living, although primarily an economic problem, has its political ramifications. The problem is a difficult one because the low standard arises directly and indirectly from other weaknesses in the system and cannot be resolved completely so long as the Soviet Union continues the economic exploitation of northern Korea.

None of these problems, however, is sufficiently critical at present either to threaten the USSR's control over northern Korea or to challenge the northern Korean regime's ability to maintain itself. Northern Korean internal security forces are fully capable of maintaining the regime in power during the period required for the reduction of current weaknesses in administration, leadership and production, and the progressive development of more advanced Communist political forms. Barring a period of internal disorganization, or crises arising from external military pressures, the Communist regime's present lack of popular support does not represent a serious problem. In the long run, living standards probably will be somewhat improved, and the regime's persuasive tactics are likely to gain additional recruits among the younger generation. On the other hand, while these weaknesses do not seriously impair the Communists' ability to control and develop northern Korea, they do materially reduce that regime's current ability to extend and maintain control over southern Korea.

ANNEX C

CURRENT ECONOMIC SITUATION

1. Organization of the Economy.

Koreans were almost completely excluded from ownership and management when Korea's economic system was under Japanese rule. As a consequence, the USSR's Introduction of a socialized economy in northern Korea after 1945 proceeded with little internal opposition. The principal Soviet economic objective in northern Korea has been the gearing of the economy to the requirements of the Soviet Far East while developing northern Korean resources to provide the maximum of self-support. The USSR has fostered the development of those industries producing exports required by its economy and has also sought to overcome the existing shortages in consumer goods production and other items presently obtained from external sources. These plans, if successful, would ensure a viable, although low level, economy in northern Korea and would also insure increasing returns to the USSR in their exploitation of the northern Korean economy.

Effective Soviet direction of the northern Korean economy is insured through: (1) the placement of Soviet advisers and Koreans loyal to the USSR in all key positions controlling the economy; (2) the use of Soviet advisers and engineers in all key Korean installations; and (3) the existence of "joint" Soviet-Korean control over northern Korea's foreign trade.

All major economic undertakings in northern Korea are planned, financed, and directed by the responsible government ministries, which are under intensive Soviet supervision. Private ownership is confined to

92

small commercial establishments and trading companies, some mining activities, and agriculture. Even
in agriculture, legal title to the land distributed
by the Communist regime in the Land Reform Program of
1946 still rests with the state, and there is a considerable degree of state control over agricultural
production.

2. Production and Trade.

By the end of 1946, a combination of Japan's wartime
abuses of Korea's arable land and industrial plant,
and subsequent Soviet looting and Korean neglect,
had reduced northern Korea's economy to a state of
near chaos. Recovery has been slow, but by 1949 the
industrial plant had achieved a significant level
of activity. Today, to judge by the northern Korean
regime's published two-year production plan (1949-
1950) and by scattered intelligence reports, heavy
industrial plant production, while it has increased
significantly over 1946, it is still 15-30 percent
below the peak 1944 level.

Postwar production plans have reflected a reduction
in the production of some finished heavy industrial
items, such as pig iron and aluminum, which formerly
was geared to Japanese rather than to domestic absorp-
tion capacity. Emphasis has been shifted, instead, to
the construction and expansion of plants producing
basic and end-use equipment and consumer goods.

The current production of iron and steel, non-
ferrous metals, fertilizers, industrial chemicals,
and cement is still in excess of the Korean economy's
capacity to process and absorb. The resultant surplus
is exported both to meet Soviet demands and to
obtain needed imports of basic equipment and consumer
goods. Although only spotty information is available
concerning the degree of recovery in the fields of
agriculture, forestry, and fisheries, these too have
apparently revived to such an extent that selected
exports are practicable. As a result of the possession
of some industrial and agricultural surplus, and the
need for basic and end-use equipment, a relatively
large volume of foreign trade is both possible and
necessary for the maintenance of the northern Korean

economy. Additionally, the area's lack of petroleum and bituminous coal forces the importation of both.

It is believed that northern Korea's balance of payments is unfavorable. This unfavorable balance probably arises largely from Soviet pricing policies which underprice Korean exports and overprice Soviet exports. Exports to the USSR, northern Korea's principal postwar trading partner, are, for the most part, iron and steel, non-ferrous metals and ores, chemicals, lumber, marine products, and grain. Imports are machinery, armaments, coal, and petroleum.

Hong Kong is northern Korea's principal non-Communist trading partner, and a wide variety of imports are sought on that market. Chief among these are textiles, basic machinery, pharmaceuticals, and selected industrial chemicals. Korean exports to Hong Kong consist of cattle fodder, marine products, grains, fats and oils, and chemicals. Less important trade relations are conducted directly with Manchuria, North China, Southeast Asia, and – clandestinely – with Japan and southern Korea.

3. Standards of Living.

The living standard of the great majority of northern Koreans has shown a significant increase from the below-subsistence level which immediately followed World War II. Rationing of all foods and basic necessities, which has ensured the meeting of the population's minimum requirements, has been a factor in preventing development of the widespread discontent into active resistance.

The shortage of housing in urban areas, harsh working conditions, low wages, the high cost of consumer goods, and the high taxes on agricultural production are all major problems which remain to be overcome before the present subsistence level of living can be raised. Attempts to this end are evident in the Communist regime's current plans for expansion of consumer goods industries, as well as in the volume of consumer goods imported from Hong Kong in 1949. While Soviet exploitation of the northern Korean economy continues, however, any substantial improvement in living standards will be inhibited.

4. Limitations on the Economy.
Several problems will continue to hamper the Communist regime's progress toward self-support. The most important among these arises from the fact that the USSR will continue to support and assist the development of the northern Korean economy only to the ultimate benefit of the Soviet economy. So long as the importation of bituminous coal and petroleum and the operation of the northern Korean merchant marine is under Soviet control, the operation of Korea's economy will remain almost completely dependent on the USSR. A further major problem faced by the northern Korean regime is the internal one of the Korean people's low level of productivity. Since there is a shortage of both skilled and unskilled manpower in the north, low productivity can be expected to continue despite the Communist regime's efforts to improve the situation.

ANNEX D
CURRENT MILITARY SITUATION
Northern Korea's military forces are still being expanded. So far as the ground forces are concerned, this process involves the integration into the "People's Army" of local recruits and of Korean troops that have seen service under the Chinese Communists in Manchuria, as well as the equipping of this force with small arms, artillery, vehicles, aircraft, and armor from the USSR.

Trained and equipped units of the Communist "People's Army" are being deployed southward in the area of the 38th Parallel. "People's Army" and Border Constabulary units there equal or surpass the strength of southern Korean army units similarly deployed. Tanks and heavy artillery have also been moved close to the Parallel in recent months.

1. Army.
Current estimates place the strength of the "People's Army" (PA) at 66,000 men (including 16,000 ex-Manchurian troops) organized into at least three infantry divisions and an independent brigade. The PA's critical arms include: (1) an armored unit,

estimated to possess 65 Soviet T-34 tanks; (2) divi-
sional artillery units equipped with 76 mm guns and
122 mm howitzers; and (3) anti-aircraft units in the
border regions. The 20,500-man Border Constabulary
(BC), which is also being expanded with ex-Manchurian
levies, is nominally a paramilitary police force and
was previously armed with Japanese weapons. The BC
has been trained to infantry standards, however, and
has now been re-equipped with Soviet weapons.

2. Air Force.

According to current accepted estimates, the "People's
Army Air Force" (PAAF) consists of an air regiment
of 1,500 men, including 150 pilots, equipped with 35
YAK-9 and/or IL-10 fighters, 3 twin-engine bombers,
2 twin-engine transports, and 35 Japanese or Soviet
training planes. This estimate may be subject to an
upward revision in the near future.

3. Navy.

The northern Korean navy performs mainly as a coast
guard force. Present navy strength is estimated at
5,100 men. A marine unit whose exact functions are
as yet undetermined, numbers approximately 5,400 men.
Northern Korean navy shore installations and ships
are of little consequence.

4. Logistics and Manpower.

The northern Korean armed forces depend almost wholly
on the USSR for logistic support. Recent reports
have indicated, however, that limited quantities of
Soviet-type small arms, munitions, and uniforms are
being locally manufactured.

A large segment of the domestic economy is as yet
uncommitted to the logistic support of the armed
forces and could provide further manpower for expansion of the military machine. However, the Communist
regime's military machine already constitutes a drain
on the undermanned northern Korean economy. An additional sixty to seventy thousand Koreans who have seen
service with the Chinese Communists, furthermore, are
believed to be available in Manchuria if needed for
integration in or loan to the "People's Army."

5. Training.

The northern Korean military forces are entirely the

product of Soviet planning, and depend heavily on the large Soviet military mission for training at higher command levels and for tactical advice down to the battalion level. The PA's state of training is comparable to that of the southern Korean Army. Air training is probably still in a basic stage, however, and there is no indication that the Air Regiment has attained operational status. The navy has received less Soviet attention.

There is evidence of a continuing program of sending small numbers of ground and air officers to the USSR for advanced training. Soviet advisers to the PA are believed to number at least 2,000; to the PAAF, 70; and to the Navy, 33. An additional 2,000 Soviet naval personnel are reported to be stationed in major northern Korean ports, to service Soviet naval units and to control port facilities.

6. Morale.

The morale of the northern Korean military forces generally appears to be good, and, although factions exist, factionalism is not a significant problem. Troops are subject to continuous indoctrination and surveillance, and their loyalty is further induced by above-average food rations, good wages, and special privileges. At the present time, the northern Korean armed forces are probably psychologically prepared to fight wholeheartedly against southern Korean troops. Their loyalty to the Communist regime and their fighting spirit, however, would vary inversely with the strength of the opposition and the duration of the struggle. In contrast, the ex-Manchurian Koreans, whose loyalty was indicated by the fact of their transfer to the PA, now form a significant percentage of that force. These troops possibly have less feeling of kinship for southern Koreans and therefore may provide a firm backbone for the PA in the event of military operations.

ANNEX E

CURRENT OPERATIONS AGAINST SOUTHERN KOREA

The ultimate local objective of the Soviet Union and of the northern Korean regime is the elimination of the southern Republic of Korea and the unification of the Korean peninsula under Communist domination. To this end, an open invasion of the Republic by northern Korean military forces has thus far been delayed in favor of a coordinated campaign involving political pressure within southern Korea, subversion, propaganda, intimidation, economic pressure, and military actions by infiltration of guerrilla forces.

To date, this campaign has succeeded in damaging south Korea's economy to a serious extent. The withholding of northern Korean power, fertilizer, coal, iron, and steel from the southern Republic has been offset only in part by large-scale US economic aid. In turn, the Communist-trained guerrillas operating in south Korea, while they have not been successful in developing large concentrations or seriously threatening the Republic's internal stability, have forced the Republic to expend large sums of money in "suppression campaigns," and thus have contributed materially to the dangerous inflationary situation in south Korea. Anti-guerrilla activity, moreover, has prevented the deployment of some Republican Army units along the strategic corridors adjacent to the 38th Parallel.

Communist propaganda, especially that which reiterates the theme of unification, probably has little present appeal to the southern Korean people, since they are basically anti-Communist. The Republic's anti-Communist program has also materially reduced the Communists' ability to infiltrate southern Korean governmental and political organizations.

Although Communist operations against the southern Republic of Korea have not thus far produced decisive results, the Republic has been forced to make serious political and economic sacrifices in order to counter the ever-present Communist threat. At the same time, the cost to the Communists has been relatively slight, and their ability to continue the campaign far exceeds the Republic's capability to continue effective resistance without US aid.

Notes

1. CP (49)180, 'Memorandum by Mr Bevin on China', 23 August 1949. TNA: CAB 129/36.
2. For more, see S. R. Ashton (ed.), *Documents on British Policy Overseas* [hereafter *DBPO*], *Series I, Volume VIII: Britain and China, 1945–1950* (London: Frank Cass, 2002); also R. Ovendale, 'Britain, the United States, and the Recognition of Communist China', *The Historical Journal*, 26.1 (1983).
3. For more details, see Michael S. Goodman, *The Official History of the Joint Intelligence Committee, Volume I: From the Approach of the Second World War to the Suez Crisis* (London: Routledge, 2014).
4. JIC (49) 82nd Meeting, 24 August 1949. TNA: CAB 159/6.
5. Memorandum by Mr Troy L. Perkins of the Office of Chinese Affairs, 5 November 1949, in *Foreign Relations of the United States, 1949: The Far East: China, Volume IX* (Washington, DC: CIA, 1974).
6. COS (49) 171st Meeting, 16 November 1949. TNA: DEFE 4/26.
7. Cited in M. L. Dockrill, 'The Foreign Office, Anglo-American Relations and the Korean War, June 1950–June 1951', *International Affairs*, 62.3 (1986), p. 459.
8. COS (50) 107th Meeting, 11 July 1950, Confidential Annex. TNA: DEFE 11/349.
9. JIC (51) 87(Final), 'Review of Assessments Made of Communist Intentions since January, 1947 by the Joint Intelligence Committee', 12 December 1951. TNA: CAB 158/13.
10. For an overview see Matthew Aid, 'US Humint and Comint in the Korean War: From the Approach of War to the Chinese Intervention', *Intelligence and National Security*, 14.4 (1999), pp. 17–63.
11. ORE 3-49, 'Consequences of US Troop Withdrawal from Korea in Spring, 1949', 28 February 1949, <https://www.cia.gov/library/readingroom/docs/DOC_0000258388.pdf> (last accessed 10 January 2020).
12. The subsequent failure to predict Chinese intervention has been identified as another classic intelligence failure. For the most recent review see A. Ovodenko, '(Mis)interpreting Threats: A Case Study of the Korean War', *Security Studies*, 16.2 (2007), pp. 254–86.
13. ORE 18-50, 'Current Capabilities of the Northern Korean Regime', 19 June 1950, <https://www.cia.gov/library/readingroom/docs/DOC_0000258828.pdf> (last accessed 10 January 2020).
14. Cited in Goodman, *Official History of the Joint Intelligence Committee*, p. 309.
15. Confidential Annex to JIC (53) 39th Meeting, 16 April 1953. Cited in Goodman, *Official History of the Joint Intelligence Committee*, p. 308.

6 The CIA and the Bomber and Missile Gap

Geography ensured the relative security of the United States for most of its early history. Unlike Britain, it had no pressing need to develop a foreign intelligence capacity because it faced no real, plausible foreign threats. Technology changed this in a limited way in the 1930s. The aircraft carrier, in the possession of competitor powers in Asia, afforded them the power to threaten American naval bases. In 1941 aircraft launched from six Japanese carriers attacked the US naval base at Pearl Harbor, Hawaii, drawing the US into the Second World War. But none of the enemy powers during the war possessed the capability to inflict significant damage to the US homeland. By the end of the war, however, it was clear that geography would not afford the US the same level of security it had historically enjoyed. Scientists and engineers in belligerent countries had developed new machines that, when perfected, would allow them to attack inter-continental targets with munitions of almost unimaginable destructive power. These technologies included long-range bombers, jet-engines, ballistic missiles and the atomic bomb. The German V-2 rocket attacks on London demonstrated the vulnerability of urban centres to ballistic missiles; the attacks on Hiroshima and Nagasaki demonstrated the revolutionary power of atomic bombs. It was obvious that sooner or later these technologies – long-range delivery systems and atomic bombs – would be combined, and that when they were the US homeland would be vulnerable like never before.

The exposure of elements of Soviet atomic espionage efforts left Western leaders in no doubt about Stalin's atomic ambitions. The scale of the Soviet Union's penetration of the Anglo-American atomic infrastructure was extensive. It included reports from several members of the Cambridge Five spy ring in the UK. John Cairncross, for instance, reported to his Soviet handler in September 1941 that the British were intent upon developing an explosive device that harnessed the power of the atom. This was but the first of many reports that reached Moscow through the latter half of 1941 and early 1942; ultimately they would convince Soviet scientists that the plans were feasible, and Stalin to start work on a Soviet bomb.[1]

But Stalin's sources also included Americans, including machinist David Greenglass and physicist Theodore Hall.[2] His spies were prolific, physicist Klaus Fuchs even securing and delivering the designs for the American bomb.[3] Determining how much of a boost the Soviet programme had gained from espionage was a tricky challenge for Western intelligence since it was a secretive programme in a police state. Consequently, spying on the Soviet atomic programme became a major priority for the CIA and allied intelligence services throughout the Cold War.[4] They were more successful in some areas than others; elements of the Soviet programme remained secret for decades.[5] But atomic bombs were only one element that needed to be considered when US intelligence officials worked to determine the development of the Soviet threat. Several other elements of the intelligence effort concerned the USSR's broader weapons of mass destruction programmes and, crucially, its development of modern delivery systems.

To spy on these programmes the Western Allies relied upon their position in Germany, especially their toehold in occupied Berlin. As the Red Army marched westward it raced to acquire the new technologies of war (indeed, securing German scientists and advanced technology – and, in turn, denying them to the others – was a priority for each Allied power). The Germans, generally, preferred to fall into the hands of the Western Allies rather than the USSR and moved to sectors under American, British or French control. But a significant amount of expertise and, equally importantly, industrial infrastructure was captured by the Red Army. This included most of the Nazi's guided weapons projects in Nordhausen and Bleicherode, and some 60 per cent of their aircraft industry.[6] The Soviets also secured a significant amount of German scientific expertise, which they had put to work on Soviet programmes, developing guided weapons, long-range aircraft and weapons of mass destruction. Stalin's Germans brought more cutting-edge technology to the already impressive brute power of the Red Army. Intelligence on these programmes filtered out to the occupying powers in the western sectors of Germany through a variety of channels following the war: through traditional espionage, large-scale intelligence programmes, induced defections, technical intelligence, sigint and allies.[7] This intelligence was used not only to determine the development of Soviet weapons programmes, but also to help the West physically locate Soviet military industries. Germany was a unique window through which the British and American intelligence agencies could observe Soviet developments. Nevertheless, understanding what they were developing, where, and how quickly was a challenging intelligence collection requirement and analytical puzzle.

By the early 1950s there had been some notable missteps in assessing the development of Soviet weapons systems. One concerned the underestimation of the speed of the Soviet atomic programme, which, under Lavrenti Beria's direction, made remarkable headway. The ORE, first under the CIG and then under the CIA, produced several estimates on the subject which later drew the ire of the Washington establishment. Their first, in October 1946, judged that the Soviets might develop a bomb between 1950 and 1953, and would be able to stockpile weapons by 1956.[8] The assessment was revisited several times over the following three years. Generally, as CIA historian Donald Steury noted, the assessment became 'more precise but less accurate'.[9] On 24 August 1949 the CIA's estimate was that the most probable date was mid-1953. The Soviets tested their first weapon, Joe-1, on 29 August 1949. But this shock was soon overtaken by other matters. Perhaps the most notable instances of controversy and failure concerning the Soviet strategic threat did not concern the bomb itself, but the means with which it could be delivered to the US. The controversies, which survived in one form or another from 1954 to 1961, brought several important factors into sharp relief: the limits of the CIA's capacity to gather intelligence; the danger of political prerogatives influencing the judgements produced by the ONE system; and that strategic intelligence and politics were more closely related than at any previous point in peacetime. These were the controversies of the 'bomber gap' and 'the missile gap'.

The bomber and missile 'gaps' have been thoroughly analysed over the decades. But, over half a century later, they still attract the attention of historians.[10] Both controversies concerned overestimation of the speed at which the Soviets could develop operational strategic weapons and then the rate at which they could be produced; it first concerned bombers then missiles. The root of the controversies concerned fears about the erosion, and possible complete undermining, of the US capacity to deter a Soviet attack.

The bomber gap's origins lay in efforts to penetrate the secretive Soviet strategic bomber programme. Western intelligence was aware of elements of the programme. They knew, for instance, that the Soviets had captured three more or less intact American B-29 bombers, which had crash-landed in the USSR during the war. These had been reverse engineered to produce the TU-4 'Bull' bomber.[11] But the intercontinental bomber programme was very secretive. The first aircraft associated with this project to be identified was the M-4 'Bison'. It was observed at a distance in July 1953, but not in flight until the rehearsals for the 1954 May Day parades.[12] A year later, at the June 1955 Aviation Day parade, US observers noted twenty-eight M-4s, as well as another long-range aircraft, the TU-20 'Bear'. The number of aircraft on display persuaded many in the US intelligence community that production must be far higher than had hitherto been considered, and that it had probably started earlier than they had previously assessed. This factored into the NIE on Soviet military power, which, in 1956, estimated that within four or five years the Soviets could build 500 bombers, perhaps even 800 according to the Air Force, which they could use against the US.[13] This number could overwhelm US air defences and, potentially, fatally undermine its ability to retaliate.

These numbers, however, were wrong. The CIA's economic analysis of Soviet production, and after June 1956 the intelligence gathered on the early flights of the CIA's U-2 aircraft, revealed the limited extent of Soviet intercontinental bomber production. Special National Intelligence Estimate (SNIE) 11-7-58, in June 1958, downgraded the inflated estimates, noting that by mid-1960 the Soviets could produce 100 to 200 heavy bombers.[14] It was an accurate assessment. The Soviets, by 1960, had produced 116 Bisons and 85 Bears.[15]

The bomber gap gave way to the missile gap. Western intelligence agencies had known for some time that the Soviets were developing ballistic missiles. Grigori Tokaev, who had defected to the British in Berlin in 1948, brought information about the 'transformation of Soviet armaments', including ballistic missile programmes.[16] But missiles had been overshadowed by the more immediate threat posed by bombers. This began to change as the CIA developed better intelligence on Soviet missiles through technical intelligence, and when Chairman Nikita Khrushchev began publicly drawing attention to the potency of the Soviet missile industry. Initially, estimates were conservative. But two shocks prompted a re-evaluation of the Soviet rocketry programme: the successful test of an intercontinental ballistic missile (ICBM) in August 1957, and the launch of Sputnik in October 1957. In the wake of these events, US NIEs consistently overestimated the speed at which the Soviets could reach an initial operating capacity (considered to be ten ICBMs), as well as their ability to produce missiles thereafter. Spanning late 1957 to mid-1961, the estimates of the missile gap suggested that the US could lose its capacity to deter the Soviets from launching a first strike by the early 1960s.[17] In November 1957, for instance, the NIE projected that the Soviets could have 500 ICBMs by late 1962, or a year earlier if they proceeded with all possible haste.[18] In August 1960 the NIE noted that there could be as many as 700 ICBMs by mid-1963, with estimates tempered slightly the following year.[19]

Not only did the missile gap NIEs point to a serious potential threat to national security, they also underlined fractures in the US intelligence community's perception of the USSR, and the ambiguity that could be generated by the possibility of adding dissenting footnotes in NIEs. The US Air Force (USAF) overestimated Soviet capacity the most, the Army and Navy the least, with the CIA's judgement resting between them. Thus, policymakers were faced with a wide range of estimates, and plenty of material with which to make political hay.[20] Just as with the bomber gap, better intelligence improved the assessment: U-2 imagery was supplemented by images from the satellites of the CORONA programme; the CIA and SIS recruited a spy with knowledge of Soviet rocketry, Colonel Oleg Penkovsky. NIE 11-8/1-61, published in August 1961, noted that 'new information, providing a much firmer base for estimates on Soviet long range ballistic missiles, has caused a sharp downward revision in our estimate of present Soviet ICBM strength'.[21] They adjusted their force level projection to between 75 and 125 operational missiles in 1963.[22] By September they adjusted their figures again, estimating that the Soviets had between ten and twenty-five launchers and that this number was unlikely to increase in the near future.[23] The Soviets deployed some sixteen first-generation missiles.[24]

The 'gaps' were the result of several factors that undermined the quality of intelligence assessments. One fundamental issue was the assumptions concerning the Soviet Union's behaviour that guided the defence, intelligence and political establishments at this point of the Cold War. The Soviet Union was viewed, generally, as hostile, expansionist and aggressive. This view had its roots in the key policy documents of America's Cold War, Kennan's 'Long Telegram' and NSC-68 in April 1950. As was illustrated in the previous chapter, the intelligence community found it very difficult to attribute any defensive motivations to the USSR's actions until very late in the 1950s. As Fred Kaplan wrote, 'there was no question in 1957, even among the sceptical economists in the CIA, that the Reds were out to clobber America'.[25] This assumption was combined with a tendency during the early days of the ONE's existence to generate assessments based on 'worst case' scenarios, rather than on 'most likely' alternatives.[26] Thus, ambiguous or thin intelligence tended to be interpreted in the most negative light in the NIEs.

A second identifiable factor in the inflated estimates concerns bias. Bias can be considered in several senses. One concerns the analytical pitfall of 'mirror imaging', and the likelihood that American intelligence officials, in the absence of better intelligence, transferred their assumptions and worldviews onto their Soviet targets rather than attempting to view the world from a Soviet perspective.[27] But another, more concerning and more sustained instance of bias concerns what could be considered the politicisation of the assessment and estimates process. The USAF contribution to the bomber and missile estimates was consistently the highest. NIEs and SNIEs are littered with dissenting footnotes from USAF noting their disagreement with the numbers offered in the body of the paper. For instance, in NIE 11-8-60, 'Soviet Capabilities for Long Range Attack through Mid-1965', published in August 1960, the Assistant Chief of Staff for Intelligence at USAF records his dissent from the main conclusions of the report, which indicated that the Soviets considered ICBMs primarily in terms of deterrence. He believed they would strive for superiority.[28] Several analyses have concluded that USAF's consistently high estimates of Soviet bomber and missile capability and capacity, and their general predisposition to interpret ambiguous or negative evidence in the most negative light, were institutionally biased. The logic was that a bigger Soviet threat justified a larger USAF budget.[29] This tendency was observed by the closest allies of the US in the British intelligence community. Britain's Joint Intelligence Committee was briefed on the matter in 1952 and told that there were 'powerful "vested interests" at work to ensure that the "intelligence threat" against the USA is not reduced'.[30] It was also a trend that the CIA had identified from its earliest days, and its work on the ad hoc committee in 1948 (discussed in the previous chapter) to estimate Soviet intentions in Berlin. In a memorandum for the DCI titled 'CIA Relations with the Air Force on Estimates of Soviet Intentions', the author, whose name is redacted but is probably the CIA chair of the ad hoc committee DeForest Van Slyck, noted:

> . . . It is quite true, however, that at the time of the preparation of the 60-day estimate for the second meeting of the IAC Directors and of ORE 22-48, the Air Force elements were far more alarmist than any of the others and would probably have preferred that the possibility of Soviet military action be more strongly emphasized.
>
> During a number of interviews with representatives of the Hoover and the Dulles-Jackson Committees, I made the following comments with reference to the necessity for an independent, top level agency such as CIA to make intelligence appreciations and estimates for the policymakers of the Government.
>
> a. I stated that it was virtually impossible under present circumstances to get a completely objective intelligence estimate from the Service departments, as they were unable to few themselves from the influences of departmental policy and budgetary interests.
>
> . . . I also told them that the Air Force was far more alarmist than the rest of the committee members and that everyone noted a marked change in their attitude after the 70 Group Air Force had been obtained . . . [31]

The persistence of the USAF's resistance to lowering the estimates of Soviet bombers and missiles and its influence on the ONE's NIEs underlined that not even the highest-level intelligence reports generated for policymakers could necessarily be considered objective.

However, the gaps were also a product of limited intelligence. The sustained, inflated and biased assessments could only flourish in the absence of reliable countervailing data. The record illustrates how open-source reporting and assessment contributed to the CIA's understanding of the

Soviet's rocketry and earth satellite programme, Sputnik. This programme was clearly intimately related to the Soviet ICBM threat and had to be watched as closely as possible. But the open sources were not enough, and they were soon supplemented by a host of secret intelligence approaches. Western intelligence agencies developed a number of sources on Soviet strategic weapons, including the well-placed agent Colonel Oleg Penkovsky.[32] But it was technical sources that were most influential in ending the 'gaps'. There were radar stations in Turkey and Iran monitoring Soviet missile test ranges; there were also crucial developments in imagery intelligence (imint), which are the subject of the chapter reference document. First, following its first operational flight over the USSR (4 July 1956), the U-2 spy-plane punctured the inflated bomber gap estimates;[33] second, the CORONA satellite programme illustrated clearly the limited extent of the Soviet ICBM programme in 1961. The imint they generated was far harder to dismiss than the reports provided by spies, and provided policymakers with reassurance: there was a bomber and missile gap, but it was in America's favour. The document concerns the establishment of these advanced imint capabilities, and the imperative importance in the CIA given to developing ways to peer over the iron curtain. Understanding the extent of the USSR's strategic development precisely was at a premium in the nuclear age.

AQUATONE BRIEFING PAPER FOR THE JOINT CHIEFS OF STAFF RE GUIDED MISSILES, ATOMIC ENERGY, AND LONG RANGE BOMBERS

Gentlemen,
We propose to define for you the unique role which AQUATONE-type photography plays in the production of National Intelligence estimates, which provide the basis for important decisions affecting the National Security. All of the principal objectives we will discuss fall into those strengths that have been determined by the National Intelligence Community to be the most significant in the Soviet ability to strike at the United States.

These are: The Soviet guided missile system, the Soviet nuclear weapons production program, and the Soviet long-range bomber force.

Our present intelligence on all of these critical Soviet capabilities still contains major areas of uncertainties. A significant quantity of our existing information on these strengths is fragmentary, and, consequently, our present estimates, in some cases, admit to significant margins of possible error.

US defense plans, and budgets to support them, involve vast sums of money and allocation of effort, and, admittedly, are at present based on information having these margins of possible error. Accordingly, such plans and budgets can be materially affected by reducing these margins. And we feel that in the AQUATONE system we have an important tool in reducing these possible errors.

In the critical field of Soviet guided missile development, we find some of our major intelligence gaps. Other intelligence sources have provided knowledge of at least 260 ballistic missile firings on the KAPUSTIN YAR range since 1953. We have never seen a Soviet ballistic missile. We have had only limited information regarding launching pads, erection and handling equipment, guidance installations and equipment, test stands, fuel storage, and other associated launching devices. Data on these items are essential for a firm statement as to the size, type, and pay load of missiles, guidance systems, and types of engines used for propulsion. This type of information is vital for the production of estimates of present and potential Soviet missile capabilities.

During AQUATONE operations in late July of 1956 two small probable missile facilities were photographed, but it was not until about two weeks ago that we had actually seen a major physical facility supporting the USSR ballistic missile test program.

Now, at TYURA TAM, we have photographed and can study in detail a relatively new rangehead still under construction. The overcast on the far oblique in this display obscures our ability to identify what is probably the actual launching area – with its associated equipment, and conceivably – actual long-range missiles. There is, however, considerable information on the rangehead support elements. The TYURA TAM photography is the first visual evidence of a facility bearing on the Soviet ICBM test program. A complete, unobscured coverage could have given indications not only of the status of the program but possibly the timing - a critical element in the guided missile estimates, and - at the moment - would be particularly useful in an evaluation of current Soviet claims on ICBM progress. We intend to go back as soon as operationally feasible to clarify the launching site at TYURA TAM.

MOZHAYSK - which we stumbled on in a 1956 mission - has us baffled at the moment. We cannot say conclusively that it is associated with the atomic energy or the guided missiles program. A canvass of outstanding engineers in both these fields has failed to resolve this question. Additional photographic coverage now or in the near future may allow us to find the answer. If it is associated with the guided missile program, it could make vital differences in our estimates of the Soviet missile program.

Our principal estimative problems with regard to the Soviet long-range bomber force relate to its capabilities for attack on the US, in numbers and types of delivery vehicles available to the force as well as the availability of nuclear weapons of various types. While our exploitation of a wide variety of intelligence data has permitted broad estimates of the strength and capabilities of the long-range bomber force, there are significant gaps which we believe could be narrowed by additional photographic coverage. Photography of MOSCOW/FILI, the only known producer of BISON jet heavy bombers, has enabled us to determine more precisely the production capacity of the plant. Similar photography of the aircraft factories at VORONEZH, KUYBYSHEV, KAZAN, and IRKUTSK, identified from other sources would enable us to measure their actual and potential production capabilities with a degree of precision not now possible.

Our knowledge of the true stature of the Soviet heavy bomber force has been limited not only by lack of precise information on production facilities but equally by the lack of first hand observation of the home bases of this force.

Analysis of various types of intelligence, ▮▮▮▮▮▮▮▮▮▮▮▮▮ SARATOV/ ENGELS in European Russia and VKRAINA in the Soviet Far East are major BISON bases and that CHEPELEVKA and BELAYA TSERKOV are major BEAR bases. Photography confirming this belief would provide bench marks enabling us to ascertain far more accurately than is now possible the size and deployment of Soviet heavy bomber forces.

Valuable intelligence by-products also can be anticipated as a result of the coverage of the primary systems we have discussed. Route photography can be expected to yield significant details of other Soviet air installations, transportation systems, industrial facilities, and other economic and military targets which could be of a significance only slightly less than the information we anticipate on primary objectives. One of the outstanding bonus effects that we know will be derived by future exercise of the AQUATONE capability will be an increase in our knowledge of Soviet air defense capabilities. ▮▮▮▮▮▮▮▮▮▮▮▮ This increase in knowledge will result in a firmer basis for operational plans that involve employment of our nuclear strike force. And it also must be noted that the exercise of the AQUATONE capability over otherwise largely inaccessible areas of the Soviet Union could reveal installations and activities of a completely unknown but highly significant nature. In the TASHKENT area of the Soviet Union, close to the Afghan border where we had previously known only of the deployment of Soviet tactical aircraft, photography has revealed an airstrip of approximately 15,000 feet in length is under construction. The establishment of such a facility in an area not normally considered to be the site of long-range air force operations opens up a new region of research into possible Soviet plans for employment of its long-range air-craft. As a specific by-product, AQUATONE photography yields terrain information from which accurate radar navigation and bombing charts can be construed.

Notes

1. Christopher Andrew and Vasili Mitrokhin, *The Mitrokhin Archive: The KGB in Europe and the West* (London: Penguin, 1999), pp. 150–5.
2. Ibid. p. 169.
3. See David Holloway, *Stalin and the Bomb: The Soviet Union and Atomic Energy, 1939–1956* (London: Yale University Press, 1994).
4. On this effort see, *inter alia*, Michael S. Goodman, *Spying on the Nuclear Bear: Anglo-American Intelligence and the Soviet Bomb* (Stanford: Stanford University Press, 2007); Jeffrey T. Richelson, *Spying on the Bomb: American Nuclear Intelligence from Nazi Germany to Iran and North Korea* (London: W. W. Norton, 2006).
5. See Oleg Bukharin, 'US Atomic Energy Intelligence against the Soviet Target, 1945–1970', *Intelligence and National Security*, 19.4 (2004), pp. 655–79.
6. See Paul Maddrell's excellent study of the West's efforts to gather intelligence on Soviet scientific development: *Spying on Science: Western Intelligence in Divided Germany, 1945–1961* (Oxford: Oxford University Press, 2006), pp. 24–5, for further details on the exploitation of German science.
7. See Maddrell, *Spying on Science*, especially chapter 5, 'Mass Espionage: Western Spying in Germany 1945–61'.
8. The issue of the CIA's estimates on the Soviet programme is discussed in several sources; the CIA has an interesting discussion on the matter: Donald P. Steury, 'How the CIA Missed Stalin's Bomb', *Studies in Intelligence*, 49.1 (2005), <https://www.cia.gov/library/center-for-the-study-of-intelligence/csi-publications/csi-studies/studies/vol49no1/html_files/stalins_bomb_3.html> (last accessed 10 January 2020).
9. Steury, 'How the CIA Missed Stalin's Bomb'.
10. Some of the most notable studies include Fred Kaplan, *The Wizards of Armageddon* (Stanford: Stanford University Press, 1983); John Prados, *The Soviet Estimate: US Analyses of the Soviet Union, 1947–1991* (Princeton: Princeton University Press, 1982); Peter J. Roman, *Eisenhower and the Missile Gap* (Ithaca: Cornell University Press, 1995). See also the CIA's internal study of the affair, Leonard F. Parkinson and Logan H. Potter, 'Closing the Missile Gap', in Joan Bird and John Bird (eds), *Penetrating the Iron Curtain: Closing the Missile Gap With Technology* (Washington, DC: CIA, 2011), <https://www.cia.gov/library/publications/cold-war/resolving-the-missile-gap-with-technology/missile-gap.pdf> (last accessed 10 January 2020).
11. Luke Benjamin Wells, 'The "Bomber Gap": British Intelligence and an American Delusion', *Journal of Strategic Studies*, 40.7 (2017), pp. 963–89.
12. Huw Dylan, *Defence Intelligence and the Cold War: Britain's Joint Intelligence Bureau, 1946–1964* (Oxford: Oxford University Press, 2014), p. 132.
13. Ibid. p. 133.
14. 'Strength and Composition of the Soviet Long Range Bomber Force', SNIE

11-7-58, 5 June 1958, <https://www.cia.gov/library/readingroom/docs/DOC_0000267654.pdf> (last accessed 10 January 2020).

15. See Steven J. Zaloga, *The Kremlin's Nuclear Sword: The Rise and Fall of Russia's Strategic Nuclear Forces, 1945–2000* (Washington, DC: Smithsonian Books, 2002), pp. 54–60.

16. Maddrell, *Spying on Science*, p. 71.

17. Raymond L. Garthoff, 'Estimating Soviet Military Intentions and Capabilities', in Haines and Legget, *Watching the Bear*.

18. For an interesting account of the years of the bomber and missile gaps, see Kaplan, *The Wizards of Armageddon*.

19. Garthoff, 'Estimating Soviet Military Intentions and Capabilities'.

20. Ibid.

21. 'Strength and Deployment of Soviet Long Range Ballistic Missile Forces', NIE 11-8/1-61, 4 August 1961, <https://www.cia.gov/library/readingroom/docs/DOC_0000267739.pdf> (last accessed 10 January 2020).

22. Ibid.

23. Parkinson and Potter, 'Closing the Missile Gap', pp. 131–2.

24. Zaloga, *The Kremlin's Nuclear Sword*, p. 76.

25. Kaplan, *The Wizards of Armageddon*, p. 161.

26. Garthoff, 'Estimating Soviet Military Intentions and Capabilities'.

27. Ibid.

28. See 'Soviet Capabilities for Long Range Attack Through Mid-1965', NIE 11-8-60, 1 August 1960, pp. 2, 4, <https://www.cia.gov/library/readingroom/docs/DOC_0000267734.pdf> (last accessed 10 January 2020).

29. Kaplan, *The Wizards of Armageddon*; Lawrence Freedman, *US Intelligence and the Soviet Strategic Threat* (Princeton: Princeton University Press, 1986).

30. Goodman, *Spying on the Nuclear Bear*, p. 162.

31. 'Memorandum for the Director of Central Intelligence. Subject: CIA Relations with Air Force on Estimates of Soviet Intentions', 23 December 1948, <https://www.cia.gov/library/readingroom/docs/CIA-RDP84-00022R000200040047-8.pdf> (last accessed 10 January 2020).

32. See Jerrold Schecter and Peter Deriabin, *The Spy Who Saved the World: How a Soviet Colonel Changed the Course of the Cold War* (New York: Scribner, 1992).

33. Christopher Andrew, *For the President's Eyes Only: Secret Intelligence and the American Presidency from Washington to Bush* (New York: Harper Perennial, 1996), p. 223. See also the CIA's released history of the U-2 programme: Gregory W. Pedlow and Donald E. Welzenbach, *The Central Intelligence Agency and Overhead Reconnaissance: The U-2 and OXCART Programs, 1954–1974* (New York: Skyhorse Publishing, 2016), <https://www.cia.gov/library/readingroom/docs/DOC_0000190094.pdf> (last accessed 10 January 2020).

7 The CIA and Cuba:
The Bay Of Pigs and the Cuban Missile Crisis

If the Berlin Tunnel operation was a career highlight in Allen Dulles' retire-ment rear-view mirror, an ill-fated landing on the shores of a nearer com-munist stronghold must be judged as his nadir, and it cost the long-serving DCI his job. Communist Cuba, floating menacingly in 'America's' own hemisphere', was perceived both at CIA and in Washington more gener-ally as the alligator nearest the boat, requiring constant attention. In fact, the CIA spent enormous amounts of time, money and effort to dislodge Cuba from its Soviet sponsor, but to no avail. Outrages from the Fidel Castro regime were not limited to leftist rhetoric; Castro expropriated and then nationalised several American assets, including oil refineries. American officials felt that left unchallenged, the communist contagion could spread from Cuba and infect other Latin American countries. Aside from various farcical assassination attempts,[1] the most notorious effort to 'liberate' the island from Fidel Castro, encrypted JMATE, was a failed small-scale inva-sion by CIA-trained and backed Cuban exiles at the Bay of Pigs on 17 April 1961.

Although it was most closely associated with the John F. Kennedy administration, planning for the Bay of Pigs invasion actually began in 1960, during the waning days of the Dwight D. Eisenhower administra-tion. Seen in global historical perspective, the Eisenhower administration did enjoy a relatively successful track record in the realm of covert action, having orchestrated the overthrow of several odious leaders such as Iranian Premier Mohammad Mossadeq in Iran in 1953 and Jacobo Arbenz nearer to home in Guatemala the following year.[2] It seemed like things were going Eisenhower's way in political subversion, but by his second term things were coming off the rails. Perhaps a harbinger of stormy subversion seas ahead, CIA's effort to topple Indonesian president Achmed Sukarno found-ered, as would the Bay of Pigs invasion, between the Scylla of operational insecurity and the Charybdis of wishful thinking.[3]

The failed coup in Indonesia would not be the last time that American policymakers confused nationalism with communism in Southeast Asia, but planning for the invasion of Cuba, under the direction of Deputy Director for Plans Richard M. Bissell Jr, was well under way by the time Eisenhower left office in January 1961. Conveniently, the earlier Guatemala coup, encrypted PBSUCCESS, continued to pay dividends for CIA because it, along with Nicaragua, was suitable as a training and staging base for the Cuban exile brigade.[4] Training areas were not the only legacy of that coup. Bissell's team included several agency veterans of PBSUCCESS,[5] including his deputy Tracy Barnes, possibly lending a degree of confidence in the experienced operational hands by the newly inaugurated and youthful Kennedy administration. At least national security advisor McGeorge Bundy was convinced, telling Kennedy on 15 March 1961 that '[CIA has] done a remarkable job of reframing the landing plan so as to make it unspectacular and quiet, and plausibly Cuban in its essentials. . . . I have been a skeptic of Bissell's operation, but I now think we are on the edge of a good answer.'[6]

Buoyed by Bundy's optimism, Kennedy, who had campaigned as a Cuba hawk,[7] green-lighted the landing by the unimaginatively named Brigade 2506, numbering some 1,450 rebels who quickly ran out of ammunition, never established air superiority, and were forced to surrender without sparking the popular uprising that CIA had hoped for. Aside from some notable accounts of battlefield heroism, the operation was an unmitigated disaster. The tinder at the Bay of Pigs failed to set any organic anti-Castro fire ablaze, the CIA having judged the popular zeitgeist in error. In fact, the Anglo-American special relationship did offer some corrective judgement, but it was not heeded.

According to the subsequent personal account of his time in the Kennedy administration, Arthur M. Schlesinger Jr stated that Her Majesty's Ambassador in Washington informed him that 'British intelligence estimates, which had been made available to CIA, showed that the Cuban people were still predominately behind Castro and that there was no likelihood at this point of mass defections or insurrections.'[8] This may not have been a revelation to Schlesinger, who was privately opposed to the invasion. Outside of the CIA's own echo chamber it seemed clear that the political environment in Cuba was not ripe for an uprising, and in any case CIA had done little by the way of psychological operations in the lead up to the invasion to influence the Cuban population in advance. Perhaps the British were more sensitive to interventions of hubris with wishful outcomes, having been humbled by President Gamal Abdel Nasser in Egypt in 1956.[9] If 'Suez' had become a byword for folly in British English, 'the Bay of Pigs' would assume that role in the American lexicon.

The Kennedy administration was savaged as international fallout was beyond salvaging. In the estimation of journalist Cyrus Sulzberger, writing in the *New York Times*, 'we looked like fools to our friends, rascals to our enemies, and incompetents to the rest'.[10] Kennedy was as furious as he was humiliated, reportedly telling an advisor he had a mind to 'scatter CIA to the winds'.[11] Instead, he settled for firing Allen Dulles as DCI and also removing his deputy, Air Force General Charles P. Cabell. On 29 November 1961, Kennedy formally installed Republican industrialist John A. McCone at the helm in Langley.

Unlike the British pullback after Suez, Kennedy ordered further efforts to topple Castro and reinvigorated Operation Mongoose, whose purpose was to turn the screws on Castro even further. His new DCI, however, proved to be a foil to continued aggressive impulses by Robert Kennedy, the president's brother and attorney general, who urged 'massive activity', especially in 'the sabotage field'. McCone's moderating voice warned the Kennedys that further covert action would be blamed on the United States no matter what and that deniability was implausible. Responding to Robert Kennedy's appeal for ever greater action and results from Mongoose, according to the minutes of a Special Group meeting held in early October 1962, McCone was under 'the impression that high levels of the government want to get on with activity but still wish to retain a low noise level, [but he] does not believe this will be possible ... Any sabotage would be blamed on the United States ... responsible officials [should] be prepared to accept a higher noise level if they want to get on with operations.'[12] McCone's honeymoon with both CIA and his new wife would be quickly interrupted by an even greater threat emanating from Cuba.

If the disappointing outcome of the Bay of Pigs invasion underscored Castro's depressing durability from the American perspective, that the Americans tried to overthrow him by naked use of military force (albeit via badly camouflaged proxies) at all signalled his vulnerability in Nikita Khrushchev's eyes. Given the undeniable ruckus of JMATE and Operation Mongoose, the Soviet Premier ordered his toehold in the western hemisphere to be reinforced with Soviet soldiers and hardware. Under the codename Operation Anadyr, the Red Army deployed over 50,000 troops, including anti-aircraft batteries, patrol boats, fighter jets, bombers and, most alarmingly, intermediate and medium-range missiles that were capable of carrying nuclear warheads. Such an array of Soviet power was intended to be a deterrent for further adventures such as the Bay of Pigs, and simultaneously a show of unwavering partnership for Castro.[13]

Like the Bay of Pigs invasion force, Operation Anadyr was too big to hide. In mid-October 1962, a CIA-piloted U-2 reconnaissance plane took pictures of Soviet missile bases on Cuba that revealed the existence of weapons that could strike nearly all of the United States, triggering the most dangerous period of the Cold War: the Cuban Missile Crisis.[14] With the establishment of the National Photographic Interpretation Center (NPIC) under Art Lundahl on 18 January 1961, the US intelligence community was actually rather well positioned to support its policymaking masters, specifically the Executive Committee of the National Security Council (EXCOMM), with a variety of finished intelligence products and briefings based on all-source intelligence analysis. This included imagery intelligence as well as human intelligence from CIA's prized source, Soviet military intelligence[15] Colonel Oleg Vladimirovich Penkovsky, who was run jointly with SIS.[16] Given the scope of the missile crisis and the existing wealth of literature on the subject, it is worth exploring an understudied aspect of an otherwise familiar event. The balance of this chapter will consider the Cuban Missile Crisis through the prism of the specific and unique contribution of Penkovsky to CIA's overall ability to narrow EXCOMM's cone of decision uncertainty during the crisis.

Many remarkable, even categorical, claims have been made about Penkovsky, tellingly codenamed Hero[17] by CIA and Yoga[18] by SIS. Jerrold Schecter and Peter Deriabin, authors of the definitive account to date, were not too far wide of the mark when they indulged in hyperbole to argue that Penkovsky was the 'Spy Who Saved the World', alluding to his crucial role in providing information on Soviet missile capabilities and field deployment doctrine and procedures during the Cuban Missile Crisis.[19] Penkovsky's timely intelligence provided the Kennedy administration with the breathing space to take a more measured approach to confronting the Soviets over Cuba. This sort of intelligence coup was a new frontier for the Americans. Christopher Andrew noted that Penkovsky's intelligence enabled Langley to give the White House a rare upper hand: 'In all previous Cold War crises Soviet intelligence had been better, often vastly better, than that available to the West. During the missile crisis in October 1962 American intelligence was for the first time as good as, if not better than, that supplied to the Kremlin.'[20]

Charles Cogan has correctly noted that Penkovsky was actually in KGB custody during the critical days of the crisis itself, having been arrested the previous month: 'He did not "save the world" in the Cuban missile crisis, as he had no real-time role.'[21] But it is not clear why a real-time role is required to 'save the world', or alternatively, why a lack of chronological congruence would somehow devalue the intelligence contribution of Penkovsky. He provided critical information about Soviet Medium and Intermediate-Range Ballistic Missiles *in advance* of their actual field deployment.[22] In this case the timeline, if anything, swings in Penkovsky's favour as intelligence, particularly indications and warning, is most desirable as far in advance as possible. In short, if real-time intelligence is good, foreknowledge is better. As Christopher Andrew observed: 'Despite Penkovsky's arrest by the KGB in September, his intelligence continued to be of *the first importance* during the thirteen days of the October Missile Crisis.'[23]

Penkovsky's documents, already disseminated to and digested by the US intelligence community by mid-1962, aided NPIC analysts to recognise the field deployment pattern of Soviet nuclear missiles in Cuba.[24] Richard Helms was Deputy Director for Plans (DDP) during the crisis, and he addressed the timeliness issue head on: 'I don't know of any single instance where intelligence was more immediately valuable than at this time. Penkovsky's material had a direct application because it came right in the middle of the decision-making process.'[25] Helms' account accords with the view in Whitehall as recorded by historian Peter Hennessy: 'Veterans of those days still describe Penkovsky in terms of pure gold and stress that "we had him at the crucial time" of hyper-anxiety about nuclear weapons . . .'[26]

Interestingly, the US policymakers – particularly those of EXCOMM – seemed to hold a different valuation of Penkovsky than the intelligence professionals. Richard Aldrich has framed the debate: 'Some have claimed that Penkovsky's intelligence played a dominant role in the Cuban missile crisis. . . . But those who sat with Kennedy on the Executive Committee of the National Security Council during the dark days of October 1962 recall that Penkovsky only provided general background information. It now seems that the latter view is correct.'[27] In contrast, according to Sidney Graybeal, Chief of CIA's analytical effort on missiles, Penkovsky provided the confirmation needed for the CIA's analysts to reach their conclusions with a high level of confidence that would be desired when the Commander in Chief was considering a menu of military options that quite possibly could have led to war with the USSR. Graybeal recalled: 'Penkovsky was providing extremely useful information which was filling a gap in our knowledge about the Soviet missile programme, specifically the data that he was acquiring from Soviet manuals was telling us how medium-range ballistic missiles were actually operated in the field, both the missiles' operational characteristics, nuclear warhead, where it was stored, did it move with the missile units or not?'[28] Although Penkovsky did not provide concrete indications that offensive Soviet nuclear missiles were headed to Cuba, the information he provided a year earlier about the missiles themselves is why he is rightly credited with a key role in the Cuban Missile Crisis. Schecter and Deriabin, amongst other practitioners such as Baroness Park of Monmouth, are correct to conclude that Penkovsky's information, properly analysed in CIA's National Intelligence Estimates (NIEs), enabled Kennedy to take a measured approach to resolving the conflict that stopped short of direct military intervention in Cuba.[29]

In the heat of the crisis Kennedy was receiving bellicose advice from his generals. An American invasion, or bombing, of Cuba may well have passed a Soviet 'red line' on retaliatory action and thus the CIA's human intelligence contribution, provided by Penkovsky, arguably 'saved the world' from a nuclear missile exchange.[30] Commentators on the impact of the Penkovsky case, even including practitioners such as Helms and Graybeal, often focus on the admittedly important role of the medium-range ballistic missile (MRBM) and intermediate-range ballistic missile (IRBM) capabilities and field deployment manuals as provided by Penkovsky, but they usually neglect Penkovsky's main message, not contained in the better-known IRONBARK (documentary) material he provided, that he repeatedly sought to drive home during personal meetings with his CIA and SIS case officers: Khrushchev, full of bluster and invective, was actually bluffing about his military strength from a position of relative weakness *vis-à-vis* American military might. In Penkovsky's view, a resolute posture and firm dealings with him would force him to back down. Penkovsky's words were intended in specific terms to relate to the ongoing Berlin Crisis and the future status of Germany, not a future Cuban crisis, but Kennedy may have recalled Penkovsky's advice, filtered through CIA's estimates, in broader terms for his calculations about the so-called naval 'quarantine' as an intermediate step toward confronting Khrushchev in the western hemisphere.

If Kennedy was well served by a GRU colonel on CIA's payroll, Khrushchev was alarmingly poorly served by GRU's intelligence collection and assessment in the run up to the missile crisis. In March 1962, the GRU erroneously warned Khrushchev that the Americans were already planning a nuclear first strike. According to Andrew: 'He was partly motivated by his desire to impress Washington with Soviet nuclear might and so deter it from further (non-existent) plans for a first strike.'[31] Although Soviet intelligence erroneously contributed to a climate of fear in the Kremlin, it also helped find a resolution in Washington through a journalist. KGB *rezident* (station chief) in Washington, Aleksandr Semyonovich Feklisov (alias Fomin) offered ABC news correspondent John Scali a deal for onward transmission to the White House. Feklisov suggested that the offensive weapons (including light bombers) could be removed from the island in exchange for a pledge that Cuba would not be invaded.[32]

In the end, Khrushchev agreed to remove the missiles from Cuba, and in exchange, the Americans also removed the outdated Jupiter missiles from Turkey (although this was not publicly acknowledged at the time) in addition to security guarantees.[33] While the missile crisis ended peacefully, Oleg Penkovsky, the man who helped the world avoid World War III, was found guilty of aiding CIA by a Soviet tribunal and executed for treason in the basement of KGB headquarters on 16 May 1963. The week before Penkovsky's execution, one of his CIA case officers, Joe Bulik, wrote an impassioned memo to CIA leadership [reference document 3] pleading for

CIA to 'grasp whatever slim opportunity there may be to save Penkovsky's life' and intercede with the Soviet government on Penkovsky's behalf.[34] Bulik waged a principled, if borderline insubordinate, internal battle on behalf of his agent, remarking in a formal memo to his immediate superior that 'not to consider ways and means of saving [Penkovsky's] life is to me a reflection of low moral level'.[35] If appealing to CIA's better angels would not work, Bulik also took a pragmatic view and noted that it would be good for future asset recruitment if it could be shown that CIA never rests while an agent remained alive. It was too late. Penkovsky's actions may have helped to save the world, but they doomed him.

That the Cuban Missile Crisis comes quickly on the heels of the Bay of Pigs invasion is not an accident of history. What is clear is that the conventional view of Soviet nuclear-capable missiles in Cuba as the proximate cause of the Cuban Missile Crisis requires a critical reappraisal, since they were not *ex nihilo*. While exporting the communist revolution was a consistent talking point in Soviet ideology, reinforcing Cuba can also be reviewed as at least partly defensive in nature thanks to CIA's covert action at the Bay of Pigs and continued pressure via Operation Mongoose. Although it is a counterfactual question, it is worth considering whether and how the missile crisis would have been precipitated if the Kennedy administration had not permitted the Bay of Pigs invasion in the first instance, or if CIA leaders had valued the implications of the failed coup in Indonesia as highly as the successes in Iran and Guatemala. Nevertheless, these episodes of CIA's history, when taken in tandem, illuminate several important discoveries.

For the Kennedy administration, the lesson of the Bay of Pigs fiasco (and indeed the Berlin Crisis of 1961) was to avoid half measures, vacillation and looking indecisive, which would be perceived by Khrushchev as weakness. These episodes underscored to John Kennedy, if not his brother, that there were limits to what *sub rosa* operations could usefully accomplish, at least without overt contributions from the US military, something Kennedy withheld in the event that appeared to come as a surprise to CIA officials when it became clear the invasion force would be overrun.[36] CIA disagreed within its own ranks on what the lessons were, but, over time, it became a touchstone for seeing the world as it really is instead of as an opportunity for half-baked freedom evangelism. Several of CIA's senior leaders were invited to retire, making room for a new generation of leaders.

In trying to apprehend some lessons learned, CIA's failure at the Bay of Pigs was subjected to unprecedented levels of scrutiny from both inside and outside the organisation. Kennedy invited General Maxwell Taylor to head a Presidential Commission into what went wrong. Amongst other failings, Taylor noted the operational insecurity leading to a lack of surprise when the invaders hit the beach. Echoing some of Taylor's findings, CIA's own

Inspector General Lyman Kirkpatrick also provided a report that he himself characterised as 'a fair report, even though highly critical'. He blamed bad planning and bad task management, poor staffing and training, and identified several other deficiencies, such as groupthink: 'the Agency became so wrapped up in the military operation that it failed to appraise the chances of success realistically'.[37] Part of the reason for this, the IG concluded, was that the intelligence analysts working on JMATE were too intimately involved with the operational planning, thereby short-circuiting the necessary distance between the operational and analytical functions of CIA.[38]

As chapter reference document 2 reveals, Deputy DCI Cabell was stung by Kirkpatrick's criticism, complaining that 'the report misses objectivity by a wide margin. In unfriendly hands it can become a weapon unjustifiably to attack the entire mission, organization, and functioning of the Agency ... and presents a picture of unmitigated and almost willful bumbling and disaster.'[39] Over two decades later, CIA's history staff also disputed the IG's findings of fault and suggested that continued political tinkering with operational plans contributed to the mission's failure. These feelings of political betrayal that lingered decades after the event are best described by an Agency historian who complained that CIA got a 'bum rap' for a 'political decision which insured the military defeat of the anti-Castro forces'.[40]

As is clear, Agency personnel from the Deputy Director down to the history staff were deeply wounded by Kirkpatrick's report, but one suggested lesson the IG identified proved to be well learned. Kirkpatrick's review stated: 'It is assumed that the Agency, because of its experience in this Cuban operation, will never again engage in an operation that is essentially an overt military effort.'[41] That CIA at least sought some level of plausible deniability for covert action would prove to be a truism from the Bay of Pigs until the advent of paramilitary operations in the post-11 September 2001 War on Terror.

If the Bay of Pigs provided ample lessons for Kennedy, so did the Cuban Missile Crisis. Kennedy and his advisors needed to thread the needle, given the stakes, between careful diplomacy, half-measures and incremental moves, while not giving over to hasty displays of military strength such as bombing or invading Cuba to deal with the missile crisis. Kennedy learned that he would have to trust his own instincts and not lose his own counsel in the competing voices of military brass or senior CIA officials. Kennedy found his footing, especially after the Vienna summit held two months after the ignominious landings in June 1961, appreciating that firm resolve was the best posture when dealing with Khrushchev. This key insight would serve Kennedy well during the missile crisis.

Beyond leadership lessons for Kennedy and rebalancing the connective sinews between Langley and the White House, there were other practical lessons as well. The use of back-channel negotiations in the ultimate resolution of the crisis pointed to the future need for direct communication between Moscow and Washington, and was a key driver for the immediate telephone link between Moscow and the White House. Across the Potomac River in Langley, although their prize agent was dead, CIA would continue to recruit several more significant Soviet sources as the Cold War continued, and it would learn to improve its clandestine tradecraft to handle agents like Penkovsky in more secure ways. Although covert action would remain a key tool in America's foreign policy arsenal from Iran to Angola to Chile, the days of freewheeling paramilitary undertakings would be rebalanced in favour of support for policymakers through all-source analytical fusion.

                                                    1 December 1961

MEMORANDUM FOR : Director of Central Intelligence
SUBJECT   : Report on the Cuban Operation

1. In our conversation on Friday morning, the first of December, you mentioned your concern that the Inspector General's Report on the Cuban Operation, taken alone, might give an erroneous impression as to the extent CIA is responsible for the failure of the operation. In my opinion the failure of the operation should be charged in order to the following factors.
    a. An over-all lack of recognition on the part of the U.S. Government as to the magnitude of the operation required to over-throw the Fidel Castro regime.
    b. The failure on the part of the U.S. Government to plan for all contingencies at the time of the Cuban operation including the necessity for using regular U.S. military forces in the event that the exiled Cubans could not do the job themselves.
    c. The failure on the part of the U.S. Government to be willing to commit to the Cuban operation, as planned and executed, those necessary resources required for its success.

                                        /s/ Lyman Kirkpatrick
                                        Lyman B. Kirkpatrick
                                            Inspector General
                                            15 December 1961

SUBJECT: The Inspector General's Survey of the Cuban
          Operation

To comment on the subject report in detail would
result in a paper approaching in length, that of the
survey itself. Such a commentary would have to deal
in depth with the aim of the survey, its scope, and
the method used in compiling it. Such a commentary
would, at a large number of pages, be required to
note inaccuracies, omissions, distortions, unsup-
ported allegations, and many erroneous conclusions.

A detailed inquiry on the Cuban operation on elements other than clandestine tradecraft, has already
been completed by the group headed by General Taylor.
General Taylor's report was based on testimony by all
the principal officers involved in the Cuban operation. The Inspector General's report is not based on
complete testimony; some of its conclusions are in
conflict with General Taylor's conclusions.

It is not clear what purpose the Inspector General's
report is intended to serve. If it is intended primarily as an evaluation of the Agency's role, it is
deficient. Neither Mr. Dulles nor I was consulted in
the preparation of the Inspector General's report.
As a result, there are many unnecessary inaccuracies.

The report tries to do both too much and too little.

On the one hand, it attempts to describe the processes of national security policy-making as though
this were a process in logical deduction like working
a problem in geometry. According to the Inspector
General's account, firm propositions should be laid
down in writing and in advance from which correct
conclusions as to proper actions must inevitably be
drawn. In this respect the report goes far beyond an
analysis of the Agency's role, and it is not accurate. It tries to do too much.

On the other hand, the report treats the preparations
for the April landings as if these were the only
activities directed against Castro and his influence
throughout the hemisphere and the world. It chooses
to ignore all other facets of the Agency's intelligence collection and covert actions program which

preceded, accompanied, and have followed the landings in April of 1961. Thus, it does too little.

The report misses objectivity by a wide margin. In unfriendly hands, it can become a weapon unjustifiably to attack the entire mission, organization, and functioning of the Agency. It fails to cite the specific achievements of persons associated with the operation and presents a picture of unmitigated and almost willful bumbling and disaster.

In its present form, this is not a useful report for anyone inside or outside the Agency. If complete analysis beyond that already accomplished by General Taylor and his group is still required, then a new kind of report is called for, - a report with clear terms of reference based on complete testimony. Such a report could concentrate on clandestine trade-craft, an asset for which the Agency remains uniquely responsible.

/s/ C. P. Cabell
C.P. Cabell
General, USAF
Deputy Director

10 May 1963

MEMORANDUM FOR: CHIEF, SR DIVISION
SUBJECT: Oleg V. Penkovskiy

1. This afternoon I handed you a draft plan designed not only to assure that word reaches many GRU and KGB ears that U.S. Intelligence is concerned about those who collaborate with us and who may be caught but also to grasp whatever slim opportunity there may be to save Penkovskiy's life.
2. On the first point, there is no doubt that many GRU and KGB officers realize that CIA was able to run a highly successful operation in a professional manner. Their respect for CIa must have gone up. They do not know what interest CIA has for the security and well-being of anyone who collaborates. If indeed word should be spread about that U.S. intelligence

is trying to save Penkovskiy's life, this is bound to have a tremendous impact on many in the ranks. The need for other Oleg Penkovskiys, as the Director expressed to you, is greater now than ever. We must do all we can to achieve this.

3. On the Second point, we all know of the tremendous contribution that Oleg Penkovskiy made to our Government and to our Agency. We were at one point prepared to give him an unusually large sum of money whenever it was feasible for him to defect. As a professional intelligence officer, he was well aware of the risks he was taking for himself and for us. I feel we owe him a tremendous debt. For us not to consider ways and means of saving his life is to me a reflection of low moral level. I do not suggest any reckless or ill-conceived means.

4. As you know, last November 1962, I proposed this plan in written form to C/CI who turned it down with a reason I could not then, and cannot now understand or accept. I am addressing you formally on this point with the view of obtaining a formal reply which would include, should the proposal or any variation of it be turned down, the reason or reasons for the turndown.

JOSEPH J. BULIK
Chief, SR Special Operations Branch

Notes

1. Calder Walton, *Empire of Secrets* (London: Harper Press, 2013), p. 296.
2. For treatment of the Guatemala operation, see Nicholas Cullather, *Operation PBSUCCESS: The United States and Guatemala, 1952–1954* (Washington, DC: CIA, 1994).
3. For a more detailed discussion on the CIA and Indonesia than is available here, see Andrew Roadnight, *United States Policy Towards Indonesia in the Truman and Eisenhower Years* (Basingstoke: Palgrave Macmillan, 2002).
4. Howard Jones, *Crucible of Power: A History of American Foreign Relations from 1897* (Lanham, MD: Rowman & Littlefield, 2008), p. 347.
5. Robert E. Quirk, *Fidel Castro* (New York: W. W. Norton and Co., 1993), p. 307.
6. McGeorge Bundy, 'Memorandum for the President: Meeting on Cuba, 4:00 PM, March 15, 1961', declassified 24 October 2014, <https://www.cia.gov/library/

readingroom/docs/CIA-RDP85-00664R000400050065-2.pdf> (last accessed 10 January 2020).

7. John F. Kennedy, 'Statement on Cuba by Senator John F. Kennedy', *The American Presidency Project*, <https://www.presidency.ucsb.edu/node/274373> (last accessed 10 January 2020).

8. Arthur M. Schlesinger, Jr, *A Thousand Days: John F. Kennedy in the White House* (Boston: Houghton Mifflin, 1965), p. 291.

9. On the British in Suez see Evelyn Shuckburgh and John Charmley, *Descent to Suez: Diaries, 1951–56* (New York: Norton, 1987), and Anthony Nutting, *No End of a Lesson: The Story of Suez* (New York: C. N. Potter, 1967). For a perspective from an American intelligence officer in London, see Chester L. Cooper, *The Lion's Last Roar: Suez, 1956* (New York: Harper & Row, 1978).

10. As quoted in Howard Jones, *Crucible of Power: A History of American Foreign Relations from 1897* (Lanham, MD: Rowman & Littlefield, 2008), p. 350.

11. As quoted in Randall B. Woods, *Shadow Warrior: William Egan Colby and the CIA* (New York: Basic Books, 2018), p. 158.

12. NSC Memorandum for Record, 'Minutes of Meeting of the Special Group (Augmented) on Operation MONGOOSE, 4 October 1962', Belin Report, Tab A, Gerald R. Ford Presidential Library, Ann Arbor, MI.

13. Anatoli I. Gribkov, William Y. Smith and Alfred Friendly, *Operation Anadyr: US and Soviet Generals Recount the Cuban Missile Crisis* (Chicago: Edition Q, 1994).

14. For a history of the Cuban Missile Crisis in broader international context, see David Gioe, Len Scott and Christopher Andrew (eds), *An International History of the Cuban Missile Crisis: A 50-year Retrospective* (Abingdon: Routledge, 2014).

15. *Glavnoye Razvedyvatel'noye Upravleniye* (GRU) Soviet military intelligence.

16. For a clinical assessment of Anglo-American tradecraft used in the Penkovsky case, see David Gioe, 'Handling HERO: Joint Anglo-American Tradecraft in the Case of Oleg Penkovsky', in Gioe et al., *An International History of the Cuban Missile Crisis*, pp. 135–75. See also Len Scott, 'Espionage and Cold War: Oleg Penkovsky and the Cuban Missile Crisis', *Intelligence and National Security*, 14.3 (1999), pp. 23–47.

17. See for instance Anne Karalekas, 'History of the Central Intelligence Agency', in *Book IV, Final Report of the Select Committee to Study Governmental Operations with Respect to Intelligence Activities. United States Senate* (Washington, DC: CIA, 1976), p. 58.

18. Declassified Memorandum for the Record, Subject: Discussion between SR/COP, CSR/9, DCSR/9 [redacted] re SR/COP's European Trip, 1–5 FEB 62, and SR/COP conversations with [redacted], dated 6 February 1962.

19. Jerrold Schecter and Peter Deriabin, *The Spy Who Saved the World: How a Soviet Colonel Changed the Course of the Cold War* (New York: Scribner, 1992). For another work which accords with the view that holds Penkovsky in

a special status above agents in importance, see Jeremy Duns, *Dead Drop: The True Story of Oleg Penkovsky and the Cold War's Most Dangerous Operation* (London, UK: Simon & Schuster, 2013).

20. Christopher Andrew and Oleg Gordievsky, *KGB: The Inside Story of its Foreign Operations from Lenin to Gorbachev* (New York: Harper Collins, 1990), p. 469.
21. Charles Cogen and Len Scott, 'The CIA and Oleg Penkovsky, 1961–63', in R. Gerald Hughes, Peter Jackson and Len Scott (eds), *Exploring Intelligence Archives* (London: Routledge, 2008), p. 143.
22. R-12 MRBMs, NATO Designation: SS-4 *Sandal* and R-14 IRBMs, NATO Designation: SS-5 *Skean*.
23. Christopher Andrew, *Defend the Realm* (New York: Vintage Books, 2010), p. 494. Emphasis added.
24. For a rather conspiratorial assessment, see Servando Gonzalez, *The Nuclear Deception: Nikita Khrushchev and the Cuban Missile Crisis* (Oakland, CA: Spooks Books, 2002), pp. 123–35.
25. Schecter and Deriabin, *Spy Who Saved the World*, p. 335.
26. Peter Hennessy, *The Secret State: Whitehall and the Cold War* (London: Allen Lane, 2002), p. 42.
27. Richard J. Aldrich, *The Hidden Hand: Britain, America, and Cold War Secret Intelligence* (London: Allen Lane, 2001), p. 619.
28. National Security Archive interview with Sidney Grayeal, 29 January 1998, <http://www.gwu.edu/~nsarchiv/coldwar/interviews/episode-21/graybeal1.html> (last accessed 10 January 2020).
29. 'Retired SIS Officer Says He "Averted War in Cuba",' letter from Baroness Park of Monmouth to *The Times*, 8 February 2004.
30. Schecter and Deriabin, *Spy Who Saved the World*, p. 110.
31. Christopher Andrew and Vasili Mitrokhin, *The Sword and the Shield: The Mitrokhin Archive and the Secret History of the KGB* (Basic Books: New York, 1999), p. 182.
32. Alexander Feklisov, *The Man Behind the Rosenbergs: Memoirs of the KGB Spymaster Who Also Controlled Klaus Fuchs and Helped Resolve the Cuban Missile Crisis* (New York: Enigma Books, 2001).
33. For an account of the diplomatic considerations and wrangling, see 'The Cuban Missile Crisis, October 1962', US Department of State Office of the Historian, <https://history.state.gov/milestones/1961-1968/cuban-missile-crisis> (last accessed 10 January 2020).
34. Joseph J. Bulik, Memorandum for Chief, SR Division, Subject 'Oleg V. Penkovskiy', 10 May 1963.
35. Ibid.
36. Piero Gleijeses, 'Ships in the Night: The CIA, the White House and the Bay of Pigs', *Journal of Latin American Studies*, 27.1 (1995), pp. 1–42.
37. See 'The Inspector General's Survey of the Cuban Operation', 15 December 1961, p. 143, <https://www.cia.gov/library/readingroom/docs/CIA-RDP80B01676R001900160013-3.pdf> (last accessed 10 January 2020).

38. Michael Warner, 'Lessons Unlearned: The CIA's Internal Probe of the Bay of Pigs Affair', *Studies in Intelligence*, 42.5 (2007).
39. 'The Inspector General's Survey of the Cuban Operation'.
40. Jack B. Pfeiffer, 'The Taylor Commission Investigation of the Bay of Pigs', 9 November 1984 (approved for public release 25 July 2011), <https://nsarchive2.gwu.edu/NSAEBB/NSAEBB355/bop-vol4.pdf> (last accessed 10 January 2020).
41. 'The Inspector General's Survey of the Cuban Operation', p. 145.

8 The CIA in Vietnam

The long war in Vietnam left an indelible mark on the fabric of innumerable elements of American life. It shaped elements of America's military and political debates for decades following the end of the war. Its divisiveness and polarising impact generated a profound cultural shift in some quarters, which subsequently bled over into literature, film and, more generally, the contested nature of the national memory. The nature of the fighting, and the general character of the war, was a harbinger for the types of challenges that would come to dominate America's wars in the late twentieth and early twenty-first centuries: asymmetric, both conventional and 'among the people', and to a greater or lesser extent, reliant upon good intelligence for their effective prosecution.[1] Just as with more contemporary wars, the intelligence war in Vietnam has generated several narrative strands that dominate the popular imagination: paramilitarism and violence, controversy and politicisation, and accusations of profound failure. Some of these narratives withstand historical scrutiny, others do not. But the scope of the intelligence war in Vietnam is both broader and deeper than credited in the popular imagination.

The historiography of US intelligence, and the CIA in particular, in Vietnam and South East Asia more broadly is well developed, and has continued to grow over recent years. Elements of it have been immortalised in fiction, most notably from the early days of US involvement in Indochina in Graham Greene's *The Quiet American*, published in 1955. And the intelligence element has, of course, been a staple feature of general histories of the war for decades owing, in no small part, to the very public controversies that surrounded it. More recent histories have benefited from greater perspective – for example, from the memoirs of key CIA individuals – and from access to declassified materials that have been published by the US government. These include John Prados' study of the war, published in 2009, which offers an illuminating perspective on the CIA's evolving role in the conflict.[2] These general histories of the war have also been supplemented with volumes focused on the CIA and its work more specifically;

some, such as Tim Weiner's *Legacy of Ashes*, offer a very critical perspective.[3] A particularly interesting section of this literature illuminates how the CIA came to develop its paramilitary capabilities in Indochina, particularly in the Laotian and Cambodian theatres. Joshua Kurlantzick, for example, traces the origins of what some consider the 'paramilitary CIA' to its operations in Laos.[4]

The general literature on the intelligence war in Vietnam is built upon, and supplemented by, a wealth of declassified material (indeed, the State Department's history office has noted that 'the Vietnam war is one of the best documented events in US history').[5] Innumerable pages of documents have been released by the US, including intelligence material. Researchers will find several volumes of *Foreign Relations of the United States* dedicated to Vietnam: seven volumes cover Vietnam-related issues from the Johnson administration alone, while another nine cover the Kennedy and Nixon administrations.[6] These collections are supplemented by several volumes of internal intelligence histories commissioned by the CIA and NSA, written in the 1980s and later by intelligence officers for an internal audience and previously highly classified. The NSA volumes offer fascinating insights into the challenges of managing sigint operations in the Indochina theatre and illuminate the stories behind some of the most contested episodes in the war, such as the intelligence picture behind the 1964 Gulf of Tonkin incident.[7] But they are overshadowed in volume by the CIA collections. Five volumes, written by veteran CIA officer Thomas Ahern, cover the agency's work in Vietnam and Indochina in excellent detail.[8] These are supplemented by several other relevant sources, including a separate collection of National Intelligence Council (NIC) documents focused on Vietnam; Bruce Palmer's study *US and Vietnam*, published in the CIA's in-house journal *Studies in Intelligence*; and a study of the CIA's interplay with policymakers during the war.[9] In short, as noted by Michael Warner, historian for the US Cyber Command and previously historian for the CIA, the official histories have rendered America's wars in Indochina, between the 1954 Geneva Accords and North Vietnamese forces taking Saigon in 1975, the 'best publicly documented intelligence struggle since World War II'.[10]

The scale of the historical record mirrors the scale of the CIA's operations in Vietnam, Laos and Cambodia. Langley's involvement in the conflict was significant, multi-faceted, and multi-dimensional. CIA officers were active in Vietnam before the escalation of US involvement; the OSS was there earlier still.[11] Its involvement could be categorised in a number of ways, but Michael Warner offers a useful analysis of the broad thrust of the CIA's involvement by describing it as concerning, first, attempts to bolster the political support for US allies in the South and undermine support for Hanoi and its forces and objectives; second, attempts to secure US and allied information and personnel, security and counter-intelligence; and third, intelligence operations to develop information for US political and military leaders concerning the enemy's capabilities and intentions, and the progress (or not) of the war.[12] These broad categories cover a multitude of activities, episodes and people. Within each one it is possible to identify vital lessons, significant controversies and telling episodes. But, regardless of its scale, intelligence could not make a decisive enough difference in any of the categories to affect conclusively the course of the war, either leading to a decisive military victory or by persuading US policymakers to cut their losses in the face of what many considered to be an unwinnable war.

Indeed, a strong case can be made that intelligence was peripheral to the matter of victory and defeat in Vietnam. Hanoi's forces, and North Vietnam in general, were willing to absorb more punishment and pain over a longer period of time than the US was willing to suffer or inflict.[13] CIA analysts came to understand this, and briefed policymakers on their judgements. It is unlikely that more or better intelligence from Hanoi, or more or better paramilitary operations, would have changed this fundamental dynamic. However, there are many good reasons for examining some of the key intelligence successes and failures of the war, as they provide valuable insights for the management of intelligence in subsequent and contemporary conflicts. After all, many of America's wars since 1975 have borne similar characteristics to Vietnam.

Several key instances, personalities or controversies occupy the foreground of the public imagination with regard to the war. These include the agency's early presence in South Vietnam, its attempts to bolster the country against the threat from the North, and the work of CIA officer Ed Lansdale (sometimes, and probably incorrectly, labelled as the influence behind the character Alden Pyle in *The Quiet American*). Tim Weiner, in his critical history *Legacy of Ashes*, considers Lansdale's mandate to be extraordinarily broad: 'It was literally, "Ed, do what you can to save South Vietnam".'[14] Lansdale was a key link between the US and the administration of Ngo Dinh Diem, facilitating the latter's rise as the US bulwark against communism. When Lansdale was withdrawn from Vietnam in 1956 his legacy ensured that the CIA would be a key conduit for relations between the US and South Vietnam, and that the agency has excellent sources from most sections of South Vietnamese politics. Indeed, the degree of the agency's contacts on all sides of South Vietnamese politics ensured that it had insight from both sides of the coup attempt in 1960, generating a good deal of controversy and friction.[15] And there is little doubt that the 1963 coup, where Diem was murdered, happened with the knowledge of many in the agency and in Washington (although DCI McCone opposed allowing the plotters to go ahead with their plan).[16] Lansdale's visits and reports on the deteriorating situation in the country would influence President Kennedy's decision to increase American unconventional warfare assets and covert action programmes, slowly escalating the CIA's role in the area into a broad-based effort to understand and influence its friends, and understand and disrupt its enemies.[17] Each of these missions generated challenges and controversies.

Many of the most notable controversies surround the CIA's own paramilitary programmes, or those with which it was linked. The agency undertook a number of such operations in support of US objectives, both in North and South Vietnam (with but a short interruption after 1961 and the Bay of Pigs, where President Kennedy ordered a retrenchment of CIA paramilitary activities. They were resumed within a year, having been managed in the interim by the military, which subsequently undertook a more active special operations posture in the conflict, with CIA intelligence support), as well as in neighbouring Laos and Cambodia.[18] These ranged from projects like Project Tiger, designed to infiltrate North Korea with trained paramilitaries in the late 1950s and early 1960s, to projects like the Village Defense Program, designed to train local commandos to protect areas of the South Vietnamese central highlands from communist-sponsored intimidation. The incursion-based programmes tended to be penetrated by Hanoi in short order; the more locally focused efforts in South Vietnam were often more successful.[19]

As the war escalated after 1965, so too did the CIA's paramilitary programmes, targeting communist influence, guerrillas, supply chains and morale. This escalation included an intensification of the CIA's paramilitary activity in Laos, Operation Momentum.[20] And it included, after 1968, the agency's involvement in the Phoenix programme, eventually managed by future CIA director William Colby and implemented in tandem with Civil Operations and Rural Development Support (CORDS), an interagency rural pacification outfit, and various branches of the South Vietnamese police and military forces. Thousands of National Liberation Front (NLF) guerrilla suspects were identified and either arrested or killed under the programme. The programme became notorious for abuse, human rights violations, its use as a mechanism of intimidation and score-settling by some South Vietnamese officials, and its failure to develop intelligence or informants in the senior echelons of the NLF.[21]

Operations to influence and disrupt the NLF were undertaken hand in hand with operations to develop intelligence on them and on Hanoi's broader political and military intentions. Just as with the paramilitary and covert action programmes, these efforts generated substantial controversies and, ultimately, showed the limits of the CIA's reach in Vietnam. As several studies and accounts have underlined, the agency's record in developing intelligence was mixed. It gathered some good local and tactical intelligence, but it struggled to glean high-level strategic intelligence from Hanoi. Some charged that many of the CIA officers who worked in Vietnam lacked the necessary deep understanding of the country and its people.[22] This charge in particular was repeated by former DCI Richard Helms, who described the Vietnam War as 'my nightmare for a good ten years'.[23]

Nevertheless, the CIA understood the limited impact that US actions were having on the North's will to continue the fight, retaining a higher degree of pessimism concerning the development of the war compared to the generally more positive military assessments.[24] Perhaps the most notorious controversy concerns the CIA's long-running debate with the Pentagon over the strength of North Vietnamese forces facing the South Vietnamese and their US allies. This debate pitted the intelligence analysts at Military Assistance Command Vietnam (MACV), who considered order of battle intelligence to be their territory, against the analysts at the CIA, who came to examine order of battle via a more circuitous route. There was relative agreement on the number of regular or uniformed North Vietnamese forces, but considerable disagreement on the number of irregular or guerrilla forces. CIA analysts came to judge that MACV consistently and considerably underplayed the North's irregular strength, by as much as 200,000 people in some estimates.[25] Some ascribed the differences to the pressure felt in the Pentagon to show results; others believed the differences resulted from methodological disagreements and the difficulty of assessing who, precisely, could be counted as an irregular. The fallout from the controversy lasted well beyond the end of the war itself.[26]

The order of battle controversy was closely related to the main intelligence collection and analysis controversy of the war, the debate over intelligence and the Tet Offensive of 30 January 1968. The Tet Offensive involved coordinated, simultaneous attacks against over one hundred South Vietnamese civilian and military targets, including the US Embassy in Saigon. It is estimated that some 80,000 North Vietnamese troops were involved, thousands of whom were killed or captured following the US and South Vietnamese forces regrouping and delivering an effective counterattack, recapturing most of the lost territory. General Vo Nguyen Giap did not achieve his objective of breaking the South Vietnamese army and prompting a popular rebellion. But, it is argued, the psychological impact of the offensive on America's will to continue the war was devastating: how could the US be achieving its objectives as the administration was claiming, if the North could mount such a large offensive?

The enemy that millions of US citizens saw on their television screens and read about in their newspapers was clearly motivated and capable, the significant losses they were sustaining notwithstanding. Despite the continued and sustained escalation over the previous years it was clear that victory was by no means imminent. This view was repeated by the respected television journalist Walter Cronkite, who reported that 'it seems now more certain that ever that the bloody experience of Vietnam is to end in a stalemate . . . it is increasingly clear to this reporter that the only rational way out then will be to negotiate, not as victors, but as an honorable people who lived up to their pledge to defend democracy, and did the best they could'.[27] The State Department Office of the Historian suggested that 'the Tet Offensive played an important role in weakening US public support for the war'.[28] The impact of the Offensive was such that the intelligence on any North Vietnamese preparations for attack would inevitably become a matter of controversy.

Several contemporaneous and subsequent analyses have labelled the surprise of the offensive as an extremely significant intelligence failure. Christopher Andrew cites a military textbook that labels it a failure to rank with Pearl Harbor.[29] But, as with the attacks of December 1941, the headline obscures a more nuanced history of intelligence collected and not, of warnings provided and not. The CIA certainly had great difficulty in penetrating the command structures of the North Vietnamese military. Richard Helms notes in his memoirs that 'on form, civil wars create an optimum espionage venue'. Factors including a common language, national family ties, and population movement generally generate an environment where approaching potential recruits is easier. 'In South Vietnam these factors proved to be a one-way street.'[30] He describes how, over ten years, the CIA's most experienced officers attempted to penetrate the leadership in Hanoi, but to no avail: 'What had worked successfully against the USSR and its Eastern European cohort failed in North Vietnam. It is little comfort to describe how hard we tried . . .'[31]

But the failure to penetrate the North's leadership circles or to attract senior enough defectors does not mean that there was no relevant information gathered concerning the Tet Offensive. On the contrary, the CIA and the broader US intelligence machinery gathered large amounts of relevant data; they also predicted some elements of the offensive. For instance, Joseph Hovey, a CIA officer in the Saigon station, assessed that the North Vietnamese intended to launch a general offensive – but his assessment was downplayed by Langley.[32] Nonetheless, as Helms noted, relevant intelligence was gathered in December 1967, and US forces were placed on high alert before the offensive.[33] So the intelligence failure was not total. James Wirtz, in his study of the event, offers a more nuanced judgement that US intelligence failed to anticipate the nature of the attack.[34] The attached document was written in the aftermath of the attack. It comprises the President's Foreign Intelligence Advisory Board's (PFIAB) investigation into the quality of US intelligence bearing on the Tet Offensive.[35] It illustrates the nature of the reports that the CIA and other US intelligence bodies received and processed before the Tet Offensive, and belies a simple explanation for the surprise. Indeed, General Maxwell Taylor, chairman of the PFIAB, noted in his commentary on the reports and the investigation that 'the intelligence bearing on the TET Offensive proved adequate in that it alerted US commanders in time to permit them to carry out their missions successfully and, therefore, there are no grounds to support the charge of a major intelligence failure'.[36] The document serves as a reminder of the complex task that intelligence agencies face in anticipating attacks. The focus on the relative difficulty of providing specific tactical warning, as opposed to the more general strategic warning, will resonate with many who studied the failures of Pearl Harbor and, indeed, September 11th. It reminds us too of one of the most important lessons of the CIA's war in Vietnam: that ultimately, intelligence is only as good as the policymakers who use it.

INTELLIGENCE WARNING OF THE TET OFFENSIVE IN SOUTH VIETNAM

Table of Contents

I. REPORT OF THE INTERAGENCY TEAM

II. COMMUNIST PREPARATIONS FOR THE OFFENSIVE IN RETROSPECT

III. CHRONOLOGY

IV. LIST OF PERSONS INTERVIEWED IN THE FIELD

V. BRIEFINGS IN THE FIELD ON INTELLIGENCE WARNING
    1. Countrywide
    2. I CTZ
    3. II CTZ
    4. III CTZ
    5. IV CTZ

VI. SELECTION OF SIGNIFICANT REPORTS
    1. Countrywide
    2. I CTZ
    3. II CTZ
    4. III CTZ
    5. IV CTZ

VII. INDICATIONS RECEIVED IN WASHINGTON, 15-30 JAN 1968
    1. Material Available in CIA
    2. Material Available in DIA

```
    3. Material Available in INR
    4. Material Available in NSA
VIII. TREATMENT OF INDICATIONS IN FINISHED
INTELLIGENCE
    1. CIA
    2. DIA
    3. INR
    4. NSA
IX. PROCEDURES FOR HANDLING CURRENT INTELLIGENCE
    1. CIA
    2. DIA
    3. INR
    4. NSA
```

INTELLIGENCE WARNING OF THE TET
OFFENSIVE IN SOUTH VIETNAM
(Interim Report)

A. Procedures
1. A working group has been formed under the chairmanship of R. J. Smith, on which CIA, DIA, INR, NSA,
and the Joint Staff are represented. This group has
compiled dossiers on the raw intelligence informa-
and intelligence summaries and judgments received in
various US headquarters before Tet, with emphasis on
the period 15-30 January 1968, and on the finished
intelligence disseminated to senior officers of the
government as a result.
2. Representatives of the group from CIA, DIA, and the
Joint Staff visited Vietnam from 16 to 23 March. They
were joined there by observers from CINCPAC, MACV, and
the CIA station in Saigon. In addition to collecting
a large quantity of pertinent documents, the delegation received briefings and conducted interviews,
both in Saigon and the field, with many senior officials, US and Vietnamese. On the US side, members of
the delegation talked to Ambassador Bunker, General
Westmoreland, General Abrams, Ambassador Komer, Lt.
General Cushman, Lt. General Rosson, Maj. General
Peers, Maj. General Eckhardt, and the commanding
generals of 1st Marine Division and 4th Infantry

Division. They also interviewed the G-2s of I and II Field Forces and the G-2 of III Marine Amphibious Force, and the G-2 advisers and the CIA Regional officers in all four Corps Tactical Zones (CTZs). They were briefed extensively by MACV J-2 and by the CIA station in Saigon, and contacted the Director of Intelligence, Seventh Air Force, ▇▇▇▇▇ Vietnam, and the Army Headquarters Area Command in Saigon. On the Vietnamese side, they interviewed the commanding generals of I and II Corps, J-2 of the Joint General Staff and his deputy, and the deputy director of ▇▇▇▇▇▇ In the course of these discussions members of the group visited Phu Bai, Da Nang, Pleiku, Camp Enari, Nha Trang, Bien Hoa, Long Binh, and Can Tho.

B. General Findings

3. As the DCI informed the President's Foreign Intelligence Advisory Board in February, there was evidence, both in Saigon and in Washington, that the enemy was engaging in his much-advertised "winter-spring campaign" and was preparing for a series of coordinated attacks, probably on a larger scale than ever before. There was evidence in January that some attacks in the highlands might be conducted during the Tet holiday. In the latter part of the month it was evident that other attacks were imminent, and some of the targets had been identified. Both in Saigon and in Washington this intelligence was communicated to senior military and political officers. As a result, a series of actions were taken in Vietnam which reduced the impact of the enemy offensive.

4. The warning thus provided represents no small achievement for the US intelligence apparatus in Vietnam. ▇▇▇▇▇▇▇▇ It must therefore rely on classic indications techniques. This is difficult under any circumstances. The intelligence organization itself, military and civil, US ▇▇▇, is complex and the volume of material it handles is large. Thus, the recognition of significant reports from human sources through the blare of background noise presents a major problem. Moreover, the very nature of the war leads to the "crying wolf" syndrome. We have

little doubt that at some level of the intelligence apparatus low-level reports could be found forecasting many of the attacks made at Tet; we have equally little doubt that similar reports could be found alluding to attacks on many other cities and on many other dates.

5. The enemy took great pains to conceal his intentions. Knowledge of his plans was fully compartmented and the actual attack order was disseminated to attacking units only in the final 24 to 72 hours. Although US and Vietnamese authorities received some reports of individual attack plans, probably no Communist officer below the level of COSVN, front, or military region was aware of the full scope of the offensive. General Westmoreland believes the Communists sacrificed coordination for security, and this is evident in the premature attacks by units of Military Region 5 (MR 5) on the night of 29-30 January, attacks which served to alert the US command to the much more extensive attacks on the following night.

6. Despite enemy security measures ▇▇▇ able to provide clear warning that attacks, probably on a larger scale than ever before, were in the offing. They included references to impending attacks, more widespread and numerous than seen before. Moreover, they indicated a sense of urgency, along with an emphasis on thorough planning and secrecy not previously seen ▇▇▇ served both to validate information from other sources ▇▇▇ and to provide warning to senior officials. The indicators, however, were not sufficient to predict the exact timing of the attack.

C. Impact of the Enemy Offensive

7. Although warning had thus been provided, the intensity, coordination, and timing of the enemy attack were not fully anticipated. Ambassador Bunker and General Westmoreland attest to this. The most important factor was timing. Few US or GVN officials believed the enemy would attack during Tet, nor did the Vietnamese public. There was good reason for this: Tet symbolizes the solidarity of the Vietnamese people. It is the most important holiday in Vietnam,

an occasion observed by all members of every family whether they are Buddhist, Christian, or Communist. The Communists evidently believed they could exploit this solidarity to produce an antigovernment, anti-foreign, antiwar uprising. This did not take place. The enemy therefore paid a price in the antagonisms he generated among the urban population, but he gained enormously in two ways: The GVN's army and police were generally far below their usual state of readiness, and the precedent of Tet made it possible for large numbers of VC to enter the cities without causing alarm. General Westmoreland expected heavy attacks either just before or just after Tet, and as Tet approached and major attacks had not materialized, the Vietnamese Joint General Staff had authorized 50 percent leaves. Evidence to upset this general belief did not come to hand until 24 hours or so before the attacks were launched, the most important being the premature initiatives in MR-5. The latter brought the intelligence already available into sharp focus and provided the missing element of timing. In the short time available, US and ARVN units could be alerted and were, but ARVN performance was reduced in many areas by Tet leaves.

8. A second major unexpected element was the number of simultaneous attacks mounted. US intelligence had given the enemy a capability of attacking virtually all of the points which he did in fact attack and of mounting coordinated attacks in a number of areas. He was not, however, granted a specific capability for coordinated attacks in all areas at once. More important, the nature of the targets was not anticipated. Washington and Saigon expected attacks on some cities, but they did not expect the offensive to have the cities, the civilian command and control centers, radio stations and police headquarters as primary objectives. Finally, the quantity of new, modern, weapons in the hands of Main and Local Force Viet Cong who engaged in the attacks was higher than expected. The AK-47 rifle and RPG-7 antitank grenade were particularly effective against ARVN units and the Regional and Popular Forces.

9. Underlying these specific problems was a more basic one: most commanders and intelligence officers, at all levels, did not visualize the enemy as capable of accomplishing his stated goals as they appeared in propaganda and in captured documents. Prevailing estimates of attrition, infiltration, and local recruitment, reports of low morale, and a long series of defeats had degraded our image of the enemy. The general picture presented was an enemy unable to conduct an offensive of such scope and intensity. Commanders and intelligence officers saw his generalized calls for a "general uprising" as merely exhortatory, and not as a blueprint for what was to follow. Moreover, in the past many "great offensives" had blossomed in Communist propaganda but had not materialized on the ground.

D. Response to Warnings
10. Nevertheless, Washington and Saigon were, as stated earlier, fully aware that the enemy planned a major offensive, probably coordinated attacks in northern I CTZ, at Dak To in the highlands of II CTZ, and toward Saigon from virtually all sides in III CTZ. As early as 10 January, General Westmoreland had canceled certain planned operations in northern III CTZ in order to reposition US forces nearer to Saigon. In subsequent days he issued a series of warnings to his commanders, and to the US Mission, that the enemy was preparing to attack. Although he had not originally expected attacks during Tet, he recognized the significance of the premature attacks in MR 5 and on 30 January notified all his commanders to expect attacks that night. As a result all US units were fully alerted, although in most cases they did not have time or information to take offensive measures against the enemy prior to the actual attack. All Seventh Air Force bases were put on a maximum state of alert, and 7th AF Director of Intelligence testifies that this step "saved Tan Son Nhut." Perhaps the best evidence that COMUSMACV's measures were effective and that the enemy's strategic intelligence was faulty is that, with the exception of Hue, the enemy

failed to hold any of his major military objectives for a significant period of time.

11. The urgency felt in Saigon was not, however, fully felt in Washington in the immediate pre-attack period. As a result, finished intelligence dissemi- nated in Washington did not contain the atmosphere of crisis present in Saigon. We do not believe this represents a failure on anyone's part. The informa- tion available was transmitted and duly analyzed, but atmosphere is not readily passed over a teletype circuit. Although senior officials in Washington received warnings in the period of 25-30 January, they did not receive the full sense of immediacy and intensity which was present in Saigon. On the other hand, with Saigon alerted, virtually nothing further could be done in Washington that late in the game which could affect the outcome.

12. Within this general picture, there were signifi- cant difference among the four corps areas. III MAF expected assaults on Khe Sanh and Quang Tri. It had received ████ the enemy attack plan for Da Nang, but not the date. General Cushman stated that he expected to be attacked during Tet, and enemy activi- ties in northeren I CTZ has prompted higher authority to cancel the Tet truce in I CTZ. As result both US and Vietnamese forces were better prepared here than elsewhere. Most Vietnamese units were at nearly full strength. The extent and coordination of the enemy's attacks, considerably exceeded expectations, as did his tenaciously held lodgement in Hue. In general, however, his assaults were easily thrown back.

13. In II CTZ, allied forces in the coastal lowlands were for the most part attacked on the night of 29-30 January by MR 5 units. They did not have the advantage of forewarning which these attacks provided units farther south, nor were they in the "alert" posture of Allied forces in I Corps. The Allied forces were on a higher than normal state of alert, which was, however, directed against the inevitable cease- fire violations rather than attacks on the cities. In the highlands, singularly unlike any other area, ████████████ prisoners, and documents reflecting

specific plans for attacks during Tet. For instance, Communist plans for attacking Dak To, Pleiku, and Kontum were known well in advance, and the US 4th Division was able to correlate them with enemy deployments. This provided one of the few opportunities for US forces to take active measures against the enemy; Pleiku was the most successful US operation of the offensive. Elsewhere in the highlands intelligence was not as good, but there was enough information to lead two of the three ARVN division commanders in II CTZ to cancel all leaves on their own initiative. We do not believe, however, that these orders were totally effective in recovering personnel who had already departed.

14. It has been noted above that US redeployments in III Corps began before mid-January. These movements were triggered by the concentration of three enemy divisions along the Cambodian border north and northwest of Saigon and by indications that these units were beginning to deploy southward toward the city. In addition, US and ARVN intelligence officers had earlier deduced from a reorganization of the enemy command structure in MR 4, which surrounds the Saigon area, that its purpose was to improve command and control for the coordination of an attack on that city III Corps and II Field Force were put on a general alert on 30 January (General Westmoreland's actions resulting from the attacks in MR 5 the previous night), and during the course of the day began to receive more specific information that Saigon was to be attacked that night. In most ARVN units in III Corps the troops appear to have been in their normal Tet condition.

15. In IV CTZ, the nature and extent of the enemy's attacks were almost totally unexpected. Allied forces were aware that Viet Cong capabilities had improved. ██████ The supply of modern weapons had increased and the VC had shown an ability to conduct a series of co-ordinated attacks throughout the Delta. To some degree however, this could be interpreted as reactions to a more aggressive allied posture in the area. In the Delta cities the presence of the VC during

Tet was so traditional as to be accepted as routine. General Eckhardt, Senior Adviser, stated that the only warning he received was General Westmoreland's alerting message of 30 January. General Eckhardt was able to alert the US support and logistic units in the Delta, but was unable in the time available to restore the readiness of ARVN units. The ARVN Corps commander and his three division commanders were present at their headquarters when the offensive struck, but their units were far below strength.

E. Responses to Specific Questions

16. The preceding paragraphs have been responsive to General Taylor's questions a, b, f, and g. Our preliminary findings on questions c, d, and e are as follows:

c. (Provision of information by civilians)

Prior to the offensive there were very few cases of civilians volunteering information on the impending attacks. This is not necessarily, however, a measure of the degree of civilian cooperation with the regime. The enemy's security measures, his rapid deployments through territory much of which was under his control, and the basic difficulty of rapid communication from countryside to city would have prevented friendly villages from passing warnings in many cases. As noted above the presence of infiltrators in the cities was unremarkable during Tet. During the Tet fighting, and since, there has been a marked increase in information volunteered from the populace.

e. (Identification of units)

Most of the units engaged in the offensive have been identified. In general, there was a close correlation between US order-of-battle holdings in a given area prior to the attacks and the units identified in the attacks, although not all units deployed in any given area were actually committed in most cases, and some new provisional units were identified in the attacks. As noted above, the enemy's facade of a "general uprising" required him to attack with his Viet Cong units wherever possible. Especially in III and IV CTZs he held back many Main Force and most NVN units for follow-up. Because of the failure of the initial attacks, in all but a few instances a follow-up never came.

COMMUNIST PREPARATIONS FOR THE TET OFFENSIVE IN RETROSPECT

1. The overall concept of a massive attack against South Vietnam's cities and towns was probably formulated by the High Command in Hanoi at least as early as last summer. Subsequently, the outline plan for the 1967-68 winter-spring campaign was ███████ to various headquarters in South Vietnam by September 1967.

2. From the beginning, extreme, precautions were taken to keep the Tet plans secret in order to preserve the all-important element of surprise. Need-to-know criteria were probably strictly enforced in disseminating battle plans. Possibly only the Communists' Central Office for South Vietnam (COSVN) and some elements of the Military Administrative Regions and major theatre commands were given a complete overview of the planned offensive.

3. At the other end of the Communist chain of command, battalion, commanders probably were given the specifics only of their own missions and those of cooperating units. The country-wide character of the effort apparently was described only in the most general terms to the command staffs even at the provincial and regional levels. Thus, only the highest echelons probably had clear knowledge that for the first time virtually every major city and town in South Vietnam was to be invaded in force.

4. The Communists began a new indoctrination program among all their party cadres and military officers in September, based on Resolution 13 of the Hanoi party central committee. The resolution called for a "general offensive" and "general uprising" which would prepare the way for a Communist-dominated coalition government.*

---

* A copy of the resolution itself has never been obtained; the reflections of it in captured documents and other sources have been so general as to preclude judgements on any specific changes in strategy that the resolution might have called for.

5. A wide variety of battle preparations for the Tet offensive had to be undertaken, many of them starting in November. Detailed operations planning commenced at each command level. Units had to be strengthened by replacements and augmented or reinforced with newly arrived units. Some effort apparently was made to infiltrate guerrillas into cities and towns to strengthen units there. Special local recruiting and new infiltrators provided some of the fresh personnel. Others were upgraded from irregular elements. Larger volumes of supplies had to be brought in and stockpiled.

6. Communist intelligence, security, and logistical elements probably began to reconnoiter approach routes toward each target city and town in order to assure that large forces would be able to march long distances in complete secrecy. Requirements for detailed city maps showing key control points were levied under some cover story, for example, to support stepped up terror operations, and arrangements for special communications were made to coordinate the attack.

7. Special training for newly organized sapper units presumably was under way by late November. All units needed special training in street fighting, but many apparently received relatively little so as to keep Hanoi's intentions well disguised.

8. By December, each command level was reviewing the tactical plans of subordinate commands and monitoring their implementation. Many coordination problems were solved along the way. By this time, all command levels of the Communist military apparatus must have had a clear idea that a major coordinated attack would be launched sometime around the turn of the lunar year.

9. By late December, preparations along the approach routes were almost certainly well advanced, since troops would begin to march in mid-January. Security arrangements were completed to assure that villagers living along the approach routes kept silent. Bivouac areas were selected, prepared and staffed. Guides were arranged. Boats were made available at water

crossings. Ammunitian and some of the heavier weapons were cached, and forward stations were prepared near the target cities and towns.

10. Briefings were given to commanding officers on their missions.

11. When Hanoi decided that preparations were satisfactorily advanced, attack plans presumably were given final approval for all command levels, the timing was set, and orders were issued to march at the appropriate time.

12. Thus, in mid and late January many Communist units began to converge on the cities and towns of South Vietnam, some making relatively long forced marches and all employing the tightest possible security precautions.

13. Meanwhile, more routine operations continued in the Khe Sanh and DMZ areas as well as further south. These operations probably were mounted partly to help screen the coming urban offensive.

14. As the troops neared their final pre-attack stations, rear services elements presumably supplied them with the previously cached weapons and ammunition. Final briefings were given to prepare the officers and troops to fight in a new environment.

15. Shortly before 30 January, Hanoi gave the attack order and the Tet offensive was launched.

```
        LIST OF PERSONS INTERVIEWED IN THE FIELD
SAIGON          Ambassador Bunker
                General Westmoreland
                General Abrams
                Ambassador Komer
CIA Officials   CIA Chief of station
                CIA
                CIA
                CIA
                CIA
                Leo Crampsey, Embassy Security
                  Officer
                Brig. Gen. Philip Davidson, J-2 MACV
                Col. Daniel Graham, J-2
                Brig. Gen. Irzyk, CG Headquarters
```

```
              Area Command
              Brig. Gen. Keegan, DI, 7th Air Force
              Col. Tarwater, 7th Air Force
              Col. Hutchins, 7th Air Force
              Col. Loi, J-2 JGS
              Lt. Col. Theip, Deputy J-2
              Bui Van Nhu, Deputy Director National
                Police
DANANG        Lt. Gen. Cushman, CG III MAF
              Major Gen. Roberton, CG I Marine
                Division
              Col. Beckington, G-2 III MAF
              Col. Beeson, Deputy Senior Adviser,
              I corps.
              ████ CIA
              LT. Gen. Lam, CG I Corps
PHU BAI       Lt. Gen. Rosson, CG, Province Corps,
                vietnam
PLEIKU        Major Gen. Stone, CG, 4th Infantry
                Division
              Col. Barnes, Deputy Senior Adviser,
                II Corps
              Lt. Col. Hindaven G-2 Adviser, II
                Corps
              Major Gen. Lam, CG II Corps
NHA TRANG     Major Gen. Peers, CG, I Field Force
              Col. Duchet, G-2, I Field Force
              Col. Ladd, CO. 5h Special Forces
                Corps
              ████ CIA
LONG BINH     Col. Foulks, G-2, II Field Force
BIEN HOA      Col. Peters, Deputy Senior Adviser,
                III Corps
              Lt. Col. Kizirian, G-2 Adviser
              ████ CIA
CAN THO       Major Gen. Eckhardt, Senior Adviser,
                IV Corps
              Lt. Col. Carey, G-2 Adviser ████ CIA
              Lt. Col. Conger, Senior Adviser,
                Phong Dinh Province
```

INDICATIONS RECEIVED IN CIA, 15-30 JANUARY 1968
Field reporting from South Vietnam during the few
weeks prior to Tet revealed that widespread, coordinated attacks were likely some time around the
holiday period. The attacks were expected to be large
scale and to include some cities and towns among the
targets.

The reporting did not, however, reflect the massive
character of the preparations under way all over
South Vietnam for simultaneous invasions of nearly
all major cities and towns. Nor did this reporting
impart a sense that "all hell" was about to break
loose. There were few hints, moreover, that the urban
attacks would be mass assaults in many cases, rather
than the tradition affairs in which only allied
facilities within the towns were hit and there was no
intent to hold a major urban center. ▮▮▮▮ provided
clear evidence of a developing nationwide Communist
campaign as well as specific threats to a number of
population centers and military bases. In addition
to giving a clear idea of the magnitude of the North
Vietnamese build-up in the DMZ area, ▮▮▮▮ indicated
significant pre-Tet deployments and concentrations
of enemy units near such areas as Quang Tri city,
Hue, Da Nang, targets in Pleiku and Kontum, certain
provincial capitals along the central coast. Threats
were also noted in III Corps provinces north of
Saigon. ▮▮▮▮ provided only tenuous indications,
however, of troop deployments toward Saigon.

▮▮▮▮ the enemy was making major improvements in his
command and control posture, including the improvement of tactical intelligence. ▮▮▮▮ suggested
combat preparations over wide areas of the country
hardly associated with a sevenday standdown.
▮▮▮▮ referred to a plan for a "final performance"
that had to be reported by 0600 hours on 26 January.
▮▮▮▮ and Communist interest in specific areas in
the Nam Bo region.

Some thirty provincial summaries covering December
1967 ▮▮▮▮ made frequent mention of increased
terrorist activity in the context of the winter-
spring campaign. The Dinh Tuong Province summary, for

example, reported the Viet Cong planning for attacks on district towns and on the province capital were continuing.

Captured documents also contributed to this picture. Some of these contained lecture notes which represented the winter-spring campaign as of "historical importance," designed to usher in the "general offensive and the general uprising," two concepts dating from Viet Minh days, and to achieve "a decisive victory," language applied to earlier winter-spring campaigns.

One fairly specific document, reported to Washington in mid-January, referred to attacks on urban areas. According to the notes, the Headquarters of Military Region 5, had pledged to liberate its entire area during the campaign. This was said to involve "very strong military attacks in conjunction with uprisings ... to take over towns and cities."

During the weeks immediately preceding the Tet offensive, the daily cable summary sent to Washington by the combined Documents Exploitation Center in Saigon included several allusions to planned actions against urban areas.

The 12 January cable summarized a top secret memorandum captured in Quang Da which stated that "the time is ripe for all units and agencies to make every effort to regain control of rural areas, and to launch attacks on American and Puppet units, logistical installations, district towns, key posts ..."

On 22 January the cable referenced a 20 November directive captured in Pleiku Province which revealed that: "All provincial and district concentrated units should maintain two-thirds of their forces in 'forward' areas for combat purposes ..."

References like those above had often been seen in past years in the usual exhortative style of Communist documents. The number of the references and their general format prior to Tet simply did not arouse extraordinary concern in the intelligence community and thus force attention on the possibility that something unique in enemy action was impending.

PROCEDURES FOR HANDLING CURRENT INTELLIGENCE MATERIAL
IN CIA

A. <u>Flow</u>

The Office of Current Intelligence in CIA receives
indications intelligence and other current information from all sources at regular intervals during
every day and night. Agency traffic is routed directly
from the Cable Secretariat; material from other agencies is received electrically and by regular courier
runs. The precedence of incoming traffic ranges from
CRITIC (the CIA Operations Center is the Washington
terminal for the Critical Communications System)
to the slowest pouched material. Classification of
the material ranges from codeword and other sensitive top secret traffic to unclassified press
ticker.

Cable traffic bearing on the situation in Vietnam
is routed directly to the Indochina Division of OCI's
Far East Area. Significant items are selected by the
Operations Center and sent to the command echelons
immediately on receipt, usually with appropriate
analyst comment. Non-cable traffic is also routed
directly to the regional division (e.g., captured
documents and dispatches processed both by CIA and
other intelligence agencies).

OCI has the principal responsibility within the
Agency for receiving, disseminating, and storing
codeword material.

B. <u>Analysis and Reporting</u>

The Indochina Division of OCI is responsible for
analyzing current information and producing finished
intelligence on Vietnam.

Material from all sources is screened, digested,
and filed or destroyed by desk analysts responsible
for various aspects of the situation. Significant
items are sifted from the large volume of daily take
and selected for use in briefing and in preparing
material for the daily and weekly publications.

Finished intelligence items are written for consumers at various levels of interest and are published
in several daily publications:

a. <u>The President's Daily Brief</u>, and supplements thereto;
b. <u>The Central Intelligence Bulletin</u>;
C. <u>The Situation in Vietnam</u>;
d. <u>The Current Intelligence Digest</u>;
  Weekly publications containing articles on Vietnam include:
a. <u>The Situation in South Vietnam</u> (Weekly);
b. <u>The weekly Review</u> (codeword);
c. <u>The Weekly Summary</u> (secret);
  In addition to articles prepared for the regular publications, assessments in greater depth and detail are published in the form of a Directorate of Intelligence Memorandum or Reports. These memos frequently are prepared at the request of a high-level policymaker, and are given single-addressee or limited distribution; they are also produced from time to time on the initiative of the division or at the direction of senior Agency chiefs.

  Informal spot reports and comments are prepared for the White House and sent by LDX.

  Current intelligence material is sent regularly to the Secretary of Defense and his deputies through the CIA liaison officer in OSD.

  The same range of material processed for use in the publications and informal written briefs is used in numerous verbal briefings inside and outside the Agency. The Director of Current Intelligence is briefed by his staff each weekday morning, with emphasis on the situation in Vietnam. He in turn attends a morning executive meeting in which he briefs the Director of Central Intelligence on significant developments overnight.

  Division and branch chiefs in the Far East Area participate in a variety of regular and ad hoc briefings on aspects of the Vietnam situation.

TREATMENT OF INDICATIONS IN FINISHED INTELLIGENCE CIA Finished intelligence produced and disseminated in Washington reflected in general terms the picture provided the field reporting described above. It warned of impending large-scale attacks, including some against cities and towns, and described the planned offensive as coordinated and widespread.

On the other hand, published intelligence, like the field reports, did not carry strong overtones of alarm. Although a powerful attack was forecast, it was not predicated to go beyond all precedent. Nor did the warning focus on the threat to the cities.

As to timing, the predicted offensive was described as likely to occur before or after the Tet holidays in intelligence items published during the two weeks before the attack. By the day before the offensive actually began, however, readers were warned that action might begin on 30 January.

The following excerpts are taken from CIA publications circulated during the weeks immediately preceding the urban offensive. They are representative of the type of warning provided. Limited circulation memoranda followed a similar line; they are mainly addressed to the situation developing around Khe Sanh.

"In recent months the intensity of enemy activity in the Mekong Delta has increased markedly. The initiation of widespread coordinated activity throughout the corps is in line with captured documents and interrogation reports which have provided information on the 1967-68 winter-spring campaign goals. In addition, the conduct of the enemy actions suggests that the Communists in the delta are becoming more sophisticated, receiving more modern weapons, and developing more effective command and control procedures." (The Situation in Vietnam, 11 January 1968)

"This phase of the Communist winter-spring campaign has been marked by unprecedented enemy losses – a record of 2,868 Communists were killed last week – as well as by an extremely high level Of enemy aggressiveness throughout South Vietnam. It is possible that the enemy is attempting a particularly heavy show of force to gain the maximum psychological advantage with the populace prior to the Tet holiday that begins on 30 January. Communist military preparations, however, appear to foreshadow a resumption of major offensive action after Tet." (Weekly Review, 12 January 1968)

150

"A series of significant developments noted in Communist Communications since early January in the northern area of III Corps suggest that a major shift of functions by high-level military entities may currently be under way." (<u>Ibid</u>.)

"In South Vietnam's III Corps, there appears to be a distinct chronological pattern in the enemy's current winter-spring campaign. The major attacks - against Loc Ninh, Bu Dop, and fire-support base Burt - have occurred at approximately one-month intervals. If this pattern continues, coordinated attacks - spearheaded by elements of the Viet Cong 5th, 9th, or North Vietnamese 7th divisions - could occur before the Tet holiday that begins in late January." (<u>Weekly Review</u>, 19 January 1968)

"Several recently captured documents add to evidence of impending enemy military action in the highlands. Many of the documents reflect an increased coordination between North Vietnamese main force units and Viet Cong forces on local levels. This closer coordination has also been observed ███████ Some of the captured documents include plans to attack specific-targets including an ambitious assault on Pleiku city, purportedly to be staged shortly after Tet. This attack would be preceded by a series of coordinated attacks against US and South Vietnamese defensive positions in the area surrounding the provincial capital 25-29 January." (<u>The Situation in Vietnam</u>, 22 January 1968)

"A new Communist headquaters complex in Binh Long Province, originally believed to be a new tactical front headquarters for enemy units in northen III Corps, may assume a bigger role. ███████ Although the precise role of the new front is still not clear, these developments suggest that it may be in the process of assuming command authority over all enemy forces south of the two northernmost provinces." (<u>Central Intelligence Bulletin</u>, 23 January 1968)

"... the 21st regiment ... just moved to a position some six miles southwest of Tam ky and reportedly is poised for a large scale assault on the provincial capital ifself" (<u>The Situation in Vietnam</u>, 23 January 1968)

"This increase in enemy activity further indicates that the Communist main forces together with local force units in this area are determined to initiate offensive action in central I Corps. Such an offensive may take place in conjunction with increased enemy military activity in the Hue area and possibly as part of countrywide series of large-scale actions just preceding or closely following the Tet holiday." (<u>Ibid.</u>)

"... in the Quang Nam – Quang Tin province-area, recent maneuvering by elements of the North Vietnamese 2nd Division and by headquarters elements of the Communist's Military Region 5 command has increased the threat to other allied coastal positions ranging from Da Nang to Tam Ky." (<u>Central Intelligence Bulletin</u>, 24 January 1968) ███████████ even a chance they will start before the conclusion of the holiday period." (<u>Central Intelligence Bulletin</u>, 27 January 1968.

"Although the bulk of this evidence indicates the most critical areas to be in the northern section of South Vietnam, there are strong indications that key Communist military units throughout most of the country may also be involved. The major target areas of enemy offensive planning include the western highlands, the coastal provinces of the Communist Military Region (MR 5), the provinces immediately north of Saigon that border on Cambodia, as well as the northern Quang Tri and Thua Thien provinces.

"While some of these signs point to the initiation of enemy activity of large magnitude in immediate future, it is not yet possible to determine if the enemy is indeed planning an all-out, country-wide offensive during, or just following, the Tet holiday period ..." (<u>The Situation in Vietnam</u>, 28 January 1968).

Battle preparations are being completed by North Vietnamese main force units in the western highlands of Pleiku and Kontum provinces and there are indications ██████ that the beginning of a well-coordinated series of large-scale attacks may be imminent. ████████ (<u>Central Intelligence Bulletin</u>, 29 January 1968)

Like the field reporting cited earlier, these selections were part of a large volume of tactical reporting and – when excerpted – perhaps convey a somewhat different impression than that conveyed by the finished intelligence publications at the time. They do, however, indicated the degree of prior warning given before the Tet offensive.

Notes

1. See Michael Warner's comments on this in Warner, 'US Intelligence and Vietnam: The Official Versions(s)', *Intelligence and National Security*, 25.5 (2010), pp. 611–37.
2. John Prados, *Vietnam: A History of an Unwinnable War, 1945–1975* (Lawrence: University Press of Kansas, 2009).
3. Tim Weiner, *Legacy of Ashes: The History of the CIA* (Penguin: London, 2007).
4. Joshua Kurlantzick, *A Great Place to Have a War: America in Laos and the Birth of a Military CIA* (New York: Simon and Schuster, 2016).
5. See the Office of the Historian, <https://history.state.gov/historicaldocuments/guide-to-sources-on-vietnam-1969-1975> (last accessed 10 January 2020).
6. See <https://history.state.gov/historicaldocuments/johnson> (last accessed 10 January 2020).
7. See Robert J. Hanyok, *Spartans in Darkness: American SIGINT and the Indochina War, 1945–1975*, <https://www.nsa.gov/news-features/declassified-documents/cryptologic-histories/assets/files/spartans_in_darkness.pdf> (last accessed 10 January 2020).
8. Thomas L. Ahern, Jr, *Vietnam Histories*, available at <https://www.cia.gov/library/readingroom/collection/vietnam-histories> (last accessed 10 January 2020).
9. See the NIC Vietnam collection at <https://www.cia.gov/library/readingroom/collection/vietnam-collection> (last accessed 10 January 2020); Bruce Palmer Jr's 'US Intelligence and Vietnam' at <https://www.cia.gov/library/reading room/docs/DOC_0001433692.pdf> (last accessed 10 January 2020); and Harold P. Ford, *The CIA and the Vietnam Policymakers: Three Episodes, 1962–1968* (Washington, DC: CIA, 2007), at <https://www.cia.gov/library/center-for-the-study-of-intelligence/csi-publications/books-and-monographs/cia-and-the-vietnam-policymakers-three-episodes-1962-1968> (last accessed 10 January 2020).
10. See Warner, 'US Intelligence and Vietnam', p. 615.

11. See Dixee Bartholomew-Feis, *The OSS and Ho Chi Minh: Unexpected Allies in the War Against Japan* (Lawrence: University Press of Kansas, 2006).
12. Warner, 'US Intelligence and Vietnam', p. 616.
13. One can identify several instances of CIA officers offering such an analysis. One potent example is a memorandum DCI John McCone sent to President Johnson upon his resignation in 1965; see Christopher Andrew, *For the President's Eyes Only: Secret Intelligence and the American Presidency from Washington to Bush* (New York: Harper Perennial, 1996), pp. 321–2.
14. Weiner, *Legacy of Ashes*, p. 243.
15. Prados, *Safe for Democracy*, pp. 339–40.
16. Ibid. p. 341.
17. Ibid. p. 339.
18. Ibid. p. 343.
19. See commentary on both specific programmes in Prados, *Safe for Democracy*, pp. 339–41.
20. See Kurlantzick, *A Great Place to Have a War*.
21. Prados, *Safe for Democracy*, pp. 363–4. The CIA's paramilitary and covert action programmes are discussed extensively in Thomas Ahern's internal histories, specifically the volume on *Undercover Armies: CIA and Surrogate Warfare in Laos*, and *CIA and Rural Pacification in South Vietnam*, <https://www.cia.gov/library/readingroom/collection/vietnam-histories> (last accessed 10 January 2020).
22. These difficulties are outlined in Warner, 'US Intelligence and Vietnam', pp. 616–18.
23. Richard Helms, *A Look Over My Shoulder: A Life in the Central Intelligence Agency* (New York: Ballantine Books, 2003), pp. 309, 317–18.
24. The more conservative or pessimistic thrust of the CIA's reporting is visible in several instances. See for example Andrew, *For the President's Eyes Only*, pp. 315–16, 321–2, 328–32, 336–7, 339, 345–6; Weiner, *Legacy of Ashes*, pp. 273–4, 281, 284, 285–6, 306–10, 332–3; Warner, 'US Intelligence and Vietnam', pp. 631–3; and Helms, *A Look Over My Shoulder*, pp. 311–12, 316.
25. Andrew, *For the President's Eyes Only*, pp. 328–32.
26. See James J. Wirtz, 'Intelligence to Please? The Order of Battle Controversy During the Vietnam War', *Political Science Quarterly*, 106.2 (1991), pp. 239–63.
27. See the full transcript at <https://www.npr.org/templates/story/story.php?storyId=106775685&t=1533573652294> (last accessed 10 January 2020).
28. See 'Milestones: 1961–1968', at <https://history.state.gov/milestones/1961-1968/tet> (last accessed 10 January 2020).
29. Andrew, *For the President's Eyes Only*, p. 341.
30. Helms, *A Look Over My Shoulder*, pp. 316–17.
31. Ibid. pp. 317–18.
32. See James J. Wirtz, *The Tet Offensive: Intelligence Failure in War* (Ithaca: Cornell University Press, 1991), pp. 172–9.

33. Helms, *A Look Over My Shoulder*, pp. 329.
34. See Wirtz, *The Tet Offensive*.
35. See the background to the report, and Maxwell Taylor's comments in Bromley Smith, 'Memorandum for the Director of Central Intelligence, Evaluation of the Quality of US Intelligence Bearing on the TET Offensive, January 1968', 29 July 1968, <https://www.cia.gov/library/readingroom/docs/CIA-RDP79B01737A000400020002-4.pdf> (last accessed 10 January 2020).
36. Ibid.

9   The CIA and Arms Control

Securing insight into foreign scientific and technical developments has always been a significant priority for spies – just as important as protecting a home nation's own engineering developments. Intelligence, weapons proliferation and counter-proliferation have historically been closely related. Intelligence was, in several senses, crucial to the development of the Cold War superpower nuclear arms race. The relentless intelligence effort of the USSR's intelligence services yielded the secrets of the Manhattan Project, easing Stalin's development of his first atomic bomb. Thereafter, all sides expended tremendous effort to understand the adversary's nuclear infrastructure and gauge their capabilities and intentions.[1] But as the twentieth century progressed and the superpowers shifted, incrementally and stutteringly, from arms races to a degree of arms control, the intelligence machinery found another role beyond espionage and counter-intelligence: namely, monitoring and verification.[2]

For at least the first twenty years of the Cold War, the US enjoyed a marked strategic advantage over the USSR. Despite certain key instances where the Soviets had stolen a march in developing strategic systems, such as developing versions of intercontinental bombers in the 1950s, or testing their first ICBM before the US in August 1957, these gains were soon offset. The US, with its NATO allies, compensated for any lag in long-range strategic capability by deploying shorter-range assets in Europe, closer to the USSR; and they soon developed their own ICBMs and intercontinental bombers and proceeded to build more of them more quickly than the USSR. Despite fears of a strategic imbalance in favour of the Soviets in the 1950s, most notably manifested in the bomber and missile 'gap' controversies as discussed in Chapter 6, by the 1960s the US retained this lead. US intelligence could, essentially, prove this beyond reasonable doubt owing to the rapid development of overhead reconnaissance technology: first the U-2 high-altitude aircraft from 1956, and then the CORONA reconnaissance satellite programme after 1961.[3] This intelligence was supplemented by human sources, the most significant being GRU Colonel Oleg Penkovsky (introduced in Chapter 7), who was recruited by SIS and run in partnership with the CIA. Penkovsky provided detailed information on the Soviet strategic rocket programme, before being identified and executed.[4] Stalin's spies may have stolen the blueprints for the bomb, but the CIA's work determined that at the turn of the 1960s, the US was demonstrably more capable and powerful than the Soviet Union.

This superiority generated the impetus for the Soviets to take significant and sometimes risky measures to attempt to achieve parity. As noted in Chapter 7, one of the motivations behind the deployment of intermediate- and medium-range missiles in Cuba in 1962 was to remedy the strategic imbalance: the Soviets had precious few ICBMs at this point, but an MRBM in Cuba served a similar deterrent purpose.[5] To paraphrase the cover of *Time* magazine: IRBM + Cuba = ICBM.[6] But the gambit failed. Far from redressing the balance and producing stability, the deployment precipitated a crisis so serious that some US officials believed that a nuclear war, and the end of civilisation, was nigh. The Soviets withdrew their missiles, their relative weakness and vulnerability on show for the whole world to see. Following the crisis, certain measures were implemented to manage such events in the future, such as the establishment of a 'hotline' between Moscow and Washington.[7] But the USSR also redoubled its efforts to gain strategic parity, with a significant development in its ICBM and SLBM programmes.[8] This, they judged, would allow them to negotiate with the US on security issues from a position of parity.[9] They were, in certain senses, successful. One of the key factors in driving the superpowers towards discussing arms control, rather than focusing exclusively on the arms race, was that by the 1970s the USSR was gaining parity with the US in certain systems and was even developing a numerical lead in others, including ICBMs and SLBMs – developments that the CIA monitored carefully.[10]

The key development in establishing a system of arms control was the negotiating and signing of the Strategic Arms Limitation Talks (SALT) agreement in 1972. This agreement, signed by President Richard Nixon and Secretary Leonid Brezhnev in Helsinki on 17 November, limited for the first time the number of delivery vehicles in the US and USSR's arsenals. It was not the first agreement between the superpowers concerning arms limitations. Previous accords included, for example, the Partial Test Ban Treaty, the agreement to limit nuclear tests in the atmosphere, outer space and under water, in 1963; the Outer Space Treaty limited the militarisation of space in 1967; the Non-Proliferation Treaty was signed in 1968; and the Biological Weapons Convention was agreed to in April 1972.[11] Nor was SALT I the final word on arms control – negotiations concerning SALT II began almost immediately after the signing of the original agreement. This agreement was not signed until June 1979. But following concerns in the US senate about the constraints it imposed on the US, and the Soviet invasion of Afghanistan, it was never ratified by the US. Nevertheless, both Moscow and Washington agreed to comply with its terms. SALT eventually gave way to the Strategic Arms Reduction Talks (START) under President Ronald Reagan. Arms control was a long-term process. Nevertheless, SALT I stands out as a significant milestone: the US State Department's Office of the Historian considers this agreement the 'crowning achievement of the Nixon-Kissinger strategy of détente'.[12]

The agreement, in effect, froze elements of the arms race, with the Soviets maintaining a numerical lead in ICBMs and SLBMs. It allowed for additional weapons to be constructed only after an equivalent number of older weapons had been removed from service. The most significant element was an agreement by both sides to limit the deployment of Anti-Ballistic Missile (ABM) systems and thus not develop technology that could fundamentally undermine the principle of mutual deterrence. Each was permitted two distinct ABM systems: one to protect the national capital, the other to protect an element of the national deterrent.[13] However, the agreement did not apply to bombers or shorter-range ballistic missiles. Nor did it limit Multiple Independently targetable Re-entry Vehicles (MIRVs), where the US maintained a quantitative and qualitative lead over the Soviets. The agreement froze elements of each side's strategic arsenals in time but did not end the arms race, which moved into a competition to develop more technologically advanced systems.[14]

The agreement could set limits, but it could not generate mutual trust. This much was clear to both sides during the negotiations. Monitoring and verification were key. But the Soviets would not agree to on-site inspectors, assuming (probably rightly) that such inspection teams would be heavily infiltrated by intelligence officers tasked with acquiring scientific and technical intelligence.[15] The solution was found in agreeing that both sides would use their technical intelligence capabilities, specifically imint and elint, to monitor the other side's developments and compliance. Article 5 of the SALT I treaty stated that each party would monitor with 'national technical means', that neither party would interfere with the 'national technical means' of the other, nor would they use deliberate concealment methods to hamper monitoring efforts.[16] Thus, both sides admitted that they had the capacity to spy on the other's strategic systems and in so doing underlined the importance of intelligence to strategic policy. Indeed, the provisions of the agreement arguably created an imperative to redouble intelligence efforts. Intelligence was now vital in order to verify whether or not each side was complying with the agreement's provisions, but also to develop forewarning of any secretive technological developments not covered by the agreement that could alter the strategic balance.

The CIA remained a central actor in the process. Indeed, the US intelligence community's input was vital for establishing the baseline assumptions on Soviet strength for negotiations: a Steering Group on Monitoring Strategic Arms Reductions had been formed under CIA chairmanship in June 1972 to establish this fundamental issue. Thereafter, the Steering Group was responsible for 'guidance to and supervision of all intelligence monitoring activities required under the strategic arms limitations agreements with the USSR'.[17] This was but part of a broader intelligence effort. The all-source intelligence capabilities of the US were put to work on questions concerning Soviet motives for arms control, their evolving capabilities and intentions, and monitoring for compliance. The technical intelligence derived from satellites, from radar monitoring stations in Iran and Turkey was of course vital (indeed, it is argued that the loss of the radar station in Iran after the 1979 revolution was a factor in undermining support for SALT II).[18] But the CIA also strove to develop and run more humint assets in the Soviet Union, to replace Penkovsky and the insights he provided; the crown jewel in this regard was perhaps the GRU officer Dimitri Polyakov.[19] The sum total of these activities was that the DCI was able to advise the NSC with a high degree of confidence on Soviet activities as they pertained to SALT.

The chapter reference document displays how this level of insight allowed the DCI to support the NSC in its efforts to verify Soviet compliance with the provisions of SALT. The question of how quickly the Soviets were decommissioning old ICBMs before building new SLBMs had been ongoing in the mid-1970s. The judgement of the SALT Monitoring Working Group was that the Soviets should be dismantling more sites more quickly. The handwritten notes on the paper indicate the confidence in the intelligence community's reporting and how it was used to challenge the Soviets:

> On 29 Oct – same date as this item, by coincidence – STAT2 sent Nodis [sic] to SALT delegation instructing US commissioner to inform Soviet counterpart that US, by National Technical Means, has confirmed Soviets were in technical violation on dismantling in Sept; US expects this will not happen in future.[20]

This level of insight and support underlines how significantly the CIA and the broader intelligence community had developed their capabilities over the previous decades. The challenge set in the late 1940s and early 1950s – how to penetrate Soviet secrecy to gather intelligence on the Soviets' strategic weaponry – had been answered by several ingenious projects, robust and productive cooperation with allies and a degree of good fortune. The outcome was, in essence, a clear demonstration of what good intelligence is ultimately for: to facilitate more coherent policymaking. Without the CIA's work, it is hard to imagine that enough mutual assurance could have been developed to sustain a robust arms control agreement. Knowledge, in this case, equalled confidence.

DIRECTOR OF CENTRAL INTELLIGENCE
**Steering Group on Monitoring Strategic Arms
Limitations**
TS 763130/76/b
29 October 1976
Copy /
MEMORANDUM FOR : Director of Central Intelligence
FROM   : E. Henry Knoche
Chairman, DCI Steering Group on
Monitoring Strategic Arms Limitations
SUBJECT   : Report of DCI SAL Steering Group on
                   Soviet Dismantling and Destruction
                   of Older ICBM Launchers

1. The attached memorandum was prepared by the SALT Monitoring Working Group and approved by the DCI Steering Group on Monitoring Strategic Arms Limitations. It reports that the Soviets are continuing their efforts to <u>dismantle older ICBM, launchers</u>. Of the 67 ICBM launchers which should have been completely dismantled or destroyed by early October 1976, at least 39 can be considered fully dismantled in accordance with procedures. At launch sites containing an additional 20 launchers dismantling or destruction has been essentially completed, but some equipment and dismantled components have not been removed from the sites as required by the agreed procedures.

2. To compensate for SLBM launchers on submarines on sea trials, dismantling should be initiated on 56 ICBM launchers by late October 1976 in addition to the 67 which should have been fully dismantled or destroyed. At present, we have identified dismantling activity at sites with 49 launchers in addition to the 59 launchers above on which dismantling or destruction has been fully or essentially completed.

SUBJECT: Report of DCI SAL Streeing Group on
            Soviet Dismantling and Destruction of
            Older ICBM Launchers

3. In accordance with established procedures, I rec-
ommend that the Chairman and all members of the NSC
Verification Panel receive copies of this report.
NOTE: transmuted in your observer by D/DCI to NSC
ALSO NOTE CLIPPED PARAS ON FUTURE SOVIET DISMANTLING
OBLIGATIONS.
ON 29 OCT – SAME DATE AT THIS ITEM, BY COINCIDENCE
– STATE SENT NO DIS TO SALT DOLOCATION INSTRUCTING
US COMMISSIONER TO INFORM SOVIET COUNTER PART THAT
U.S, 67 NAT.TECH.MEANS, HAS CONFIRMES SECTORS WERE
IN TECHNICAL VIOLATION ON DISMANTLING IN SOPT; U.S.
EXPEERS THIS WILL NOT HAPPEN IN FUTURE.

E. Henry Knoche

Attachment:
As Stated
Distribution:
Cy 1 – DCI
    2 – DDCI
    3 – Executive Registry
    4-5 – DDI
    6 – SALT Support Staff

CENTRAL INTELLIGENCY AGENCY
WASHINGTON.D.C. 20505

TS 763130/76/a
29 October 1976
Copy 14

MEMORANDUM FOR : Chairman
                 NSC Verification Panel
FROM   : George Bush
                 Director
SUBJECT   : Transmittal of DCI SAL Steering Group
                  Report on Soviet Dismantling and
                  Destruction of Older ICBM Launchers
1. Attached is a memorandum approved by the DCI Steering
Group on Monitoring Strategic Arms Limitations. The
memorandum reports that the Soviets are continuing
their efforts to dismantle older ICBM launchers. Of
the 67 ICBM launchers which should have been completely dismantled or destroyed by early October
1976, at least 39 can be considered fully dismantled

in accordance with procedures. At launch sites containing an additional 20 launchers dismantling or
destruction has been essentially completed, but some
equipment and dismantled components have not been
removed from the sites as required by the agreed
procedures.

2. To compensate for SLBM launchers on submarines
on sea trials, dismantling should be initiated on
56 ICBM launchers by late October 1976 in addition
to the 67 which should have been fully dismantled or
destroyed.

SUBJECT: Transmittal of DCI SAL Steering Group
             Report   on   Soviet   Dismantling   and
             Destruction of Older ICBM Lanunchers
3. Copies of this memorandum are also being furnished
to members of the Verification Panel.

                                        George Bush
Attachment:
As Stated

                                    TS 763130/76/a
                             (W/attach TS 763130/76)
MEMO: To Chairman, NSC Verification Panel re
        Transmittal of DCI SAL Steering Group Report
        on Soviet Dismantling and Destruction of Older
        ICBM Launchers
CONCURRED:

                                       29 Oct 76

_____   _____
Deputy Director for Intelligence   Date

DISTRIBUTION:
CY 1-2 - Chairman, NSC VP (w/Cy 1-2 of attach)
     3 - Mr. Rumsfeld   ("   3   "   "   )
     4 - LTGEN Scowcroft   ("   4   "   "   )
     5 - Mr. Clements   ("   5   "   "   )
     6 - Mr. Ellsworth   ("   6   "   "   )
     7 - Mr. Robinson   ("   7   "   "   )
     8 - Gen. Brown   ("   8   "   "   )

```
 9 - Dr. Ikle            ( "    9    "   "   )
10 - Gen. Wilson         ( "   10    "   "   )
11 - Mr. Saunders        ( "   11    "   "   )
12 - Mr. Graybeal        ( "   12    "   "   )
13 - Gen. Faurer         ( "   13    "   "   )
   - Mr. Hyland          ( "   14    "   "   )
   - Mr. Marcum          ( "   15    "   "   )
   - BGEN Serio          ( "   16    "   "   )
   - Mr. Sauerwein       ( "   17    "   "   )
   - Dr. Timbie          ( "   18    "   "   )
   - Mr. Finch           ( "   19    "   "   )
   - Mr. Fuerth          ( "   20    "   "   )
14 - DCI                 ( "   21    "   "   )
15 - DDCI                ( "   22    "   "   )
16 - ER                  ( "   23    "   "   )
17-18 - DDI              ( "   24/25  "   "   )
19 - L. Dirks            ( "   26    "   "   )
20 - N. Firth            ( "   27    "   "   )
21 - E. Hineman          ( "   28    "   "   )
22 - H. Stoertz          ( "   29    "   "   )
23 -                     ( "   30    "   "   )
24 -                     ( "   31    "   "   )
25 -                     ( "   34    "   "   )
26 - G. Allen            ( "   32    "   "   )
27 -                     ( "   33    "   "   )
28 - SALT Support St.    ( "   35    "   "   )
```

MEMORANDUM FOR: The Honorable Donald Rumsfeld
                 Secretary of Defense

The attached memorandum presents the results of our most recent review of Soviet progress in meeting their obligation to dismantle older ICBM launchers.

George Bush
Director

Attachment

Date 29 October 1976

IDENTICAL BLUE NOTE SENT TO:
Dep. Sec. of Defense (Ellsworth)

MEMORANDUM FOR Major General Lincoln D. Faurer
Defense Intelligence Agency

The attached memorandum presents the results of our most recent review of Soviet progress in meeting their obligation to dismantle older ICBM launchers.

Paul v. Walsh
Associate Deputy Director
for Intelligence

Attachment

Date

MEMORANDUM FOR LTGEN Brent Scowcroft
Assistant to the President for National Security
Affairs

Attached is a copy of the report on Soviet dismantling and destruction of older ICBM launchers sent to the Chairman of the NSC Verification Panel by the Director of Central Intelligence.

Sayre Stevens
Deputy Director for Intelligence

Attachment

Date

IDENTICAL BLUE NOTES SENT TO:
Deputy Secretary of State (Robinson)
Chairman, Joint Chiefs of Staff (Gen. Brown)
Director, ACDA (1kle)
Director, DIA (LTGEN Wilson)
Director, INR/State (Saunders)
US SCC Commissioner (Graybeal)
Deputy Secretary of Defense (Clements)

29 October 1976

MEMORANDUM
SUBJECT: Dismantling of SS-7 and SS-8 Launchers

Summary
The latest satellite photography ████████████ shows that Soviet dismantling or destruction of older ICBM launchers is continuing. There are still some deficiencies, however, in fulfilling all the detailed Standing Consultative Commission (SCC) procedures at some sites.

Based on our estimate of the number of SSBNs operational and on sea trials, dismantling of 123 older launchers should be complete or under way by late October to compensate for replacement SLBM launchers on submarines – including one unit which began sea trials in September and two which we believe began sea trials in October. Of these 123, 67 launchers should have been completely dismantled or destroyed by early October.

Dismantling or destruction activities are now visible at sites with 108 launchers.

TS 763130/76

Copy No. 21

Soviet Claims and Dismantling Requirements
Article IV of the Interim Agreement established that both parties may modernize and replace strategic offensive ballistic missiles and launchers covered by the Agreement. Agreed Statement K reviews which systems may be replaced and when dismantling of these systems should begin, and states that the SCC will determine the procedures for dismantling and destruction as well as for timely notification of such actions.* In July 1974, the SCC completed agreed procedures to be used in dismantling older ICBM and SLBM launchers. Thus far, the Soviets have dismantled only older ICBM launchers.

Dismantling or destruction of replaced ICBM launchers shall be completed no later than four months after the replacement submarine begins sea trials. (From SCC Procedures, Section II/5).

---

* *Appropriate sections from the SCC protocol and from the attachment to the SCC protocol are presented in italics in this memorandum*

To be in accord with the dismantling procedures of the SCC, the Soviets should have had 51 launchers fully dismantled by about 1 March. Only eight launchers were completely dismantled by that date, however. In early April, the Soviets after acknowledging that they had failed to meet the schedule, stated that they would have the additional launchers dismantled by 1 June. On 1 June, they notified the US that all 51 launchers were dismantled or destroyed in accordance with agreed procedures.

By late September, in addition to the 51 launchers which were required to be completely dismantled, another 44 were to be in process.

At the SCC meeting on 28 September, the Soviets claimed that 61 launchers were completely dismantled and that 34 were in the process.

By early October we believe the Soviets should have dismantled 67 older launchers and by late October have an additional 56 under way.

Dismantling or destruction of replaced launchers shall be initiated no later than the date of the beginning of sea trials of a replacement submarine. (SCC Procedures, Section II/5).

In the last six months the number of launchers on which dismantling should be complete or in process has risen from 51 to 123.* Five new submarines with 72 launchers have begun sea trials. Two of the new submarines were D-I class units, each with 12 launchers, which probably began sea trials in late July and mid-October. In early June a D-class unit with 16 launchers initiated sea trials. Another D-class with 16 tubes apparently began sea trials in September, based on the amount of time that has elapsed since it was launched and on the Soviet notification to the SCC. One more submarine of this type was photographed in one of the last stages of outfitting in

---

* Between 2 and 19 September, the Y-class submarine modified to carry 12 rather than its original complement of 16 launchers probably began sea trials which could reduce the total SLBM count by four tubes. The Soviets, however, did not reflect this reduction in their notification to the SCC on 28 September.

late September and it should have started sea trials
by the end of October.

Soviet Dismantling Actions

*Dismantling or destruction procedures for ICBM
launchers and associated facilities and for ballistic
missile submarines and SLBM launchers shall ensure
that they would be put in a condition that precludes
the possibility of their use for launching ICBMs or
SLBMs, respectively; shall ensure that reactivation of
units dismantled or destroyed would be detectable by
national technical means; shall be such that reactivation time of those units would not be substantially
less than the time required for new construction; and
shall preclude unreasonable delays in dismantling
or destruction.* (From SCC Protocol on Procedures
Governing Replacement, Dismantling or Destruction and
Notification Thereof for Strategic Offensive Arms).

*In all cases the following actions shall be accom-
plished in carrying out dismantling or destruction:
(a) removal from the launch site of the supply of
missiles and their components, warheads, and mobile
equipment; (b) dismantling of fixed launch equipment,
erecting and handling equipment, and propellant-
handling equipment from the launch site. Launch
equipment is understood to be systems, components,
and instruments required to launch a missile.* (SCC
Procedures, Section II/1).

*In the case of soft launch sites, in addition to
the actions specified in paragraph 1, the following
actions shall be performed: (a) areas of the launch
pads centered on the launch stand and at least 20
meters in diameter and missile launch control posts
(bunkers) shall be made unusable by dismantling or
destruction.* (SCC Procedures, Section II/2).

*(b) Fuel storage tanks shall be dismantled and
removed from the launch site; and (a) debris of
destroyed areas of launch pads and of missile launch
control posts (bunkers), and the fuel storage tank
foundations may be removed, and, after six months,
the places where they were located may be covered
with earth...* (SCC Procedure Section II/2).

167

> In the case of silo launch sites, in addition to the actions specified in paragraph 1, the following actions shall be performed: (a) silo doors, silo door rails, exhaust gas ducting, launch tubes and silo headworks shall be dismantled or destroyed, and dismantled components shall be removed from the launch site; and (b) after the actions provided for in sub-paragraph (a) above, have been accomplished, the silos shall remain open for a period of six months, after which they may be filled with earth. (SCC Procedures, Section II/3).

Notes

1. There are a number of studies of the Cold War atomic intelligence game. See Western efforts outlined in Michael S. Goodman, *Spying on the Nuclear Bear: Anglo-American Intelligence and the Soviet Bomb* (Stanford: Stanford University Press, 2007) and Jeffrey T. Richelson, *Spying on the Bomb: American Nuclear Intelligence from Nazi Germany to Iran and North Korea* (London: W. W. Norton, 2006). Soviet efforts are chronicled in Christopher Andrew and Vasili Mitrokhin, *The Mitrokhin Archive: The KGB in Europe and the West* (London: Penguin, 1999); and a glimpse into Soviet nuclear security is available in Olek Bukharin's works, 'US Atomic Energy Intelligence Against the Soviet Target, 1945–1970', *Intelligence and National Security*, 19.4, and 'The Cold War Atomic Intelligence Game, 1945–1970: From a Russian Perspective', *Studies in Intelligence*, 48.2 (2004), <https://www.cia.gov/library/center-for-the-study-of-intelligence/csi-publications/csi-studies/studies/vol48no2/article01.html> (last accessed 10 January 2020).
2. See for instance Henry D. Sokolski, *Best of Intentions: America's Campaign against Strategic Weapons Proliferation* (London: Prager, 2001).
3. For the CIA's history of the U-2 programme, see Gregory W. Pedlow and Donald E. Welzenbach, *The CIA and the U-2 Program, 1954–1974* (Washington, DC: CIA, 1998), <https://www.cia.gov/library/center-for-the-study-of-intelligence/csi-publications/books-and-monographs/the-cia-and-the-u-2-program-1954-1974/u2.pdf> (last accessed 10 January 2020). For the CORONA programme, see Kevin Ruffner (ed.), *CORONA: America's First Satellite Program*, CIA Cold War Records Series (Washington, DC: CIA, 1995), <https://www.cia.gov/library/center-for-the-study-of-intelligence/csi-publications/books-and-monographs/corona.pdf> (last accessed 10 January 2020).
4. On Penkovsky see, *inter alia*, Len Scott, 'Espionage and the Cold War: Oleg Penkovsky and the Cuban Missile Crisis', *Intelligence and National Security*, 14.3 (1999), pp. 23–47; and David Gioe, Len Scott and Christopher

Andrew (eds), *An International History of the Cuban Missile Crisis: A 50-year Retrospective* (Abingdon: Routledge, 2014), particularly Gioe's chapter, 'Handling HERO: Joint Anglo-American Tradecraft in the Case of Oleg Penkovsky'.

5. Several factors contributed to Khrushchev's decision; see Gioe et al., *An International History of the Cuban Missile Crisis*.

6. Len Scott and Huw Dylan, 'Cover for Thor: Divine Deception Planning for Cold War Missiles', *Journal of Strategic Studies*, 33.5 (2010), p. 762.

7. For a narrative history of the discussions concerning the hotline, see 'Memorandum of Understanding Between the United States of America and the Union of Soviet Socialist Republics Regarding the Establishment of a Direct Communications Link', June 1963, <https://www.state.gov/t/isn/4785.htm> (last accessed 10 January 2020).

8. T. E. Vadney, *The World Since 1945* (London: Penguin, 1998), p. 420.

9. Ibid. p. 420.

10. See the CIA's memorandum on 'Soviet Defence Policy, 1962–72', 28 April 1972, <https://www.cia.gov/library/center-for-the-study-of-intelligence/csi-publications/books-and-monographs/cias-analysis-of-the-soviet-union-1947-1991/memo_4_72.pdf> (last accessed 10 January 2020), and a retrospective comment on this development, 'The Development of Soviet Military Power: Trends Since 1965 and Prospects for the 1980s', CIA Directorate of Intelligence, April 1981, <https://www.cia.gov/library/center-for-the-study-of-intelligence/csi-publications/books-and-monographs/cias-analysis-of-the-soviet-union-1947-1991/sr_81_10035x.pdf> (last accessed 10 January 2020).

11. See Raymond L. Garthoff, 'Negotiating SALT', *The Wilson Quarterly*, 1.5 (1977), p. 83.

12. See the note on 'Strategic Arms Limitations Talks/Treaty (SALT) I and II', <https://history.state.gov/milestones/1969-1976/salt> (last accessed 10 January 2020).

13. Mason Willrich and John B. Rhinelander, 'An Overview of SALT 1', *The American Journal of International Law*, 67.5 (1973), pp. 28–35.

14. Vadney, *The World Since 1945*, p. 423.

15. Christopher Andrew, *For the President's Eyes Only: Secret Intelligence and the American Presidency from Washington to Bush* (New York: Harper Perennial, 1996), p. 384.

16. See text of SALT I at <https://fas.org/nuke/control/salt1/text/salt1.htm> (last accessed 10 January 2020).

17. 'Terms of Reference of USIB Steering Group on Monitoring of Strategic Arms Limitations', USIB-D-27. 5/5, 27 June 1972, <https://www.cia.gov/library/readingroom/docs/CIA-RDP79B01709A000200020018-0.pdf> (last accessed 10 January 2020).

18. Andrew, *For the President's Eyes Only*, p. 342.

19. See, *inter alia*, Sandra Grimes and Jeanne Vertefeuille, *Circle of Treason: A CIA Account of Traitor Aldrich Ames and the Men He Betrayed* (Annapolis: Naval Institute Press, 2013).

20. 'Report of DCI SAL Steering Group on Soviet Dismantling and Destruction of Older ICBM Launchers', TS 763130/76/b, memorandum from E. Henry Knoche to the DCI, 29 October 1976, <https://www.cia.gov/library/read-ingroom/docs/CIA-RDP79M00467A002400050008-3.pdf> (last accessed 10 January 2020).

10 The CIA's Counter-Intelligence Conundrum: The Case of Yuri Nosenko

Whilst all intelligence work is, by its very nature, somewhat uncertain, the world of counter-intelligence is even more fraught with complications. In the words of one US journalist, it is the 'wilderness of mirrors', where facts can be interpreted in various, often contrasting ways, depending on the starting assumption.[1] Frequently conflated with counter-espionage in the academic literature, the art of counter-intelligence is to protect the integrity of your intelligence from counter-measures by the adversary: domestically, therefore, it focuses on those inside your own service who are surreptitiously working for the other side. Sometimes this can refer to your own nationals; sometimes it refers to foreigners who offer their services but whose loyalty might be questionable. The 1947 National Security Act provided a starting point in the US for such endeavours:

> The term 'counterintelligence' means information gathered, and activities conducted to protect against espionage, other intelligence activities, sabotage, or assassinations conducted by or on behalf of foreign governments or elements thereof, foreign organizations, or foreign persons or international terrorist activities.
>
> – National Security Act of 1947, as amended (50 USC 401a)[2]

Counter-espionage has been described by one former CIA officer in a practical way: 'Successful counterespionage brings with it new or enhanced knowledge of the adversary. When a spy is found, a service may observe his activities and learn how the other side runs him, or may double him and begin gathering information that way. When a spy is arrested and confesses (as most do), his interrogations will yield a wealth of information about the other side, as well as lessons for his own.'[3] Verifying authenticity is often based on a very simple principle: what is already known about the subject and can therefore be checked. Following this, a variety of other factors come into play, often based on psychology. The CIA has historically also relied upon the polygraph test as a means of assessing the veracity of subjects, though it is not foolproof.[4] Counter-intelligence and counter-espionage work, history shows, can breed paranoia.

Within the annals of counter-intelligence there is no figure more notorious than the long-serving head of CIA's counter-intelligence staff, James Jesus Angleton. Angleton was an immensely complex and controversial figure, yet despite his idiosyncrasies and paranoia he remained in his post from 1954 to 1974.[5] Above all else, he is remembered for instigating a massive molehunt within the CIA, a search for traitors within its ranks that would not only cost the careers of scores of honest, patriotic officers, but would also affect the CIA's abilities to operate in and against the Soviet Union. One victim of his obsessive molehunting was Yuri Nosenko.

The case against Nosenko had its roots long before he personally had any interaction with the CIA in 1962; it would begin with the defection of a KGB officer in December 1961. A few weeks before Christmas, Major Anatoly Golitsyn knocked on the door of the CIA station chief in Helsinki, Finland. It was an unexpected approach, not only in the manner in which he contacted the CIA, but also in his background and role. Golitsyn, the KGB *rezident* in Finland, was immediately whisked off to the US via Sweden, where he was welcomed enthusiastically. Golitsyn was, at that time, the highest-ranking KGB officer ever to defect to the US. He had been born in 1926 in Ukraine and had joined the KGB following military service during the war. He was assigned to the First Chief Directorate, responsible for collecting foreign intelligence, and he personally was involved in running intelligence operations against the US. Much of his career was spent in counter-intelligence work, though he was also involved with some of the thinking behind reorganising Soviet intelligence in the early 1950s.[6]

Golitsyn's debriefing by the CIA began shortly after his arrival in the US. Given Angleton's position within the CIA, it is unsurprising that he was told about Golitsyn. From the outset, Golitsyn's background and personality aroused interest. As the doctor who examined his early interviews noted, 'The Subject himself is a very alert, perceptive and shrewd individual. Part of this may stem from his intelligence training and experience.' Yet, more ominously for what was to follow: 'There are indications of rather grandiose and omnipotent ideas as well as some paranoid feelings about his own intelligence service.'[7]

Golitsyn began by revealing details of the KGB's attempts to infiltrate NATO, but his most startling information referred to 'Sasha'. To someone like Angleton, who was already searching for an explanation as to how some earlier KGB officers working for the US had been betrayed, Sasha was the missing answer. According to Golitsyn, 'Sasha' was a CIA officer who had been recruited by the KGB in 1950 and who had risen up the ranks to a senior position. Tantalisingly, Golitsyn did not know Sasha's real identity but, from what he had learnt in the Soviet Union prior to his defection, the KGB spy inside the CIA had been stationed in Germany, had experience in working on electronic eavesdropping, and his name began with a 'K' and ended with either 'ski' or 'sky'. Almost immediately attention turned towards a Technical Services officer in the CIA called Peter Karlow, who had worked in Germany and been born Peter Klibansky before changing his name. Karlow would eventually be cleared by the CIA and awarded a significant financial settlement, but not before his career was terminated early under a cloud of suspicion.[8]

The CIA occasionally relied upon tried and tested former defectors to verify what it was being told. In this case they used Peter Deriabin, a former KGB officer who had defected in the mid-1950s. Deriabin had the advantage of having previously met Golitsyn whilst both were working in the KGB in the early 1950s. His view was that Golitsyn 'tended to invent stories which would make him look important'.[9] Such a view highlights the central issue around Golitsyn, both at the time and in the myriad writing that has appeared afterwards. There is no question that Golitsyn was a bona fide defector, one who had planned his departure from the Soviet system for some years beforehand; but the extent to which he embellished, misconstrued information or deceived in order to keep his stock high within CIA is still a matter of debate.[10]

The claims about 'Sasha' sent Angleton, the Counterintelligence Staff, and more broadly the CIA, into a headlong spin. Tying itself into knots, concern grew, assisted undoubtedly by Golitsyn's continued testimony and access to CIA operational files, that Sasha was just the tip of the KGB penetration. Golitsyn revealed that not only was the CIA riddled with Soviet spies, but so too were the French and British intelligence and security services. Angleton was utterly convinced by this, not least because it could be used to explain previous losses of CIA assets in the Soviet Union and abroad; so, too, were a number of British officers in MI5, the domestic Security Service.[11] But Golitsyn was not finished there. So concerned were the KGB by the defection of such a senior officer, Golitsyn confidently asserted that in his wake further KGB officers would offer their services to the US – but, he warned, these would be 'phonies', deliberate Soviet plants designed to sow confusion and discord, and therefore not to be trusted. A year later, as Golitsyn predicted, a new KGB officer appeared, one offering his services to the CIA.[12]

Whilst at a diplomatic event in Geneva, a mid-ranking KGB officer of the Seventh Directorate (surveillance) offered to reveal information to the US. Claiming that he had been robbed of $900 by a prostitute, he requested financial help in exchange for information; CIA agreed. Having initially claimed to have no desire to defect, he surprised his CIA handlers two years later by stating that he had to be immediately evacuated from Switzerland as he had been instructed to return to Moscow, making him deeply suspicious. The CIA, concerned at the prospect of losing such a significant asset, agreed, and he was flown to the US.

Nosenko was no ordinary KGB officer. The son of a high-ranking Soviet official (the former Minister of Shipbuilding), Nosenko had led a charmed life. By all accounts he was an average student, failing his final exams in Marxism, and his eventual entry into the KGB was eased by virtue of his family connections. He briefly served in Naval Intelligence before joining the KGB in the early 1950s where he served, amongst other positions, in the American Department of the Second Chief Directorate, focusing specifically on American journalists and attachés in Moscow.

Assessing his initial information provided in Geneva in mid-1962, his case officers thought he had great potential; by contrast, those back in Langley concluded that Nosenko was a fabrication, a deliberate provocation by the KGB, as Golitsyn had suggested, to deceive the Americans. Nosenko refused to be controlled and run in Moscow, but given that he was to travel regularly to the West, he agreed to be debriefed at subsequent meetings. In the short space between his initial contact and early 1964, when he surprised his CIA handlers with a request to defect, Nosenko's position had become more complicated.

A number of factors explained the degree of suspicion that accompanied Nosenko and his defection. The first was the revelation that two senior members of SIS, Britain's foreign intelligence service, had been secretly spying for the Russians for years. In January 1963 Kim Philby, the former SIS liaison officer in the US and a close confidante of Angleton, defected from Beirut, Lebanon. This followed the conviction of SIS officer George Blake as a Soviet spy, responsible for scores of agent deaths and revealing the Berlin Tunnel. These two defections caused considerable personal angst in Angleton, who had worked with and respected them. In addition, in November 1961 a senior German BND officer was arrested for spying for the KGB, whilst a former Polish intelligence officer, who had defected to the CIA shortly before, revealed that he had been told about KGB efforts to penetrate the CIA's Soviet operations. These episodes supported Golitsyn's thesis of a prolonged KGB effort to penetrate the West and served to strengthen the other accusations he made. The second great change was the assassination of President John F. Kennedy in Dallas, Texas, in November 1963 and the lingering question of whether the KGB had been somehow complicit.

Into this maelstrom of uncertainty and hypothesis waded Nosenko, who claimed to have two significant pieces of information. The first related to how Oleg Penkovsky, the most successful CIA (and SIS) spy, had been caught by the KGB. Nosenko claimed to have first-hand knowledge. The second and far more significant piece of information concerned Kennedy's assassination and the possible role played by Lee Harvey Oswald, the man suspected of pulling the trigger. Nosenko said that he had not only personally handled Oswald's attempted defection to the Soviet Union while living there a few years before, but that he had also read Oswald's KGB file. The timing was opportune, and upon Nosenko's surprising request for defection he was rushed back to the US for debriefing.[13]

In February 1964, Nosenko began to be debriefed. Initial discussions were complicated because there was lingering doubt over his authenticity, partly fuelled by Golitsyn's testimony, but increasingly by the questioning itself. It became clear that Nosenko's answers contained inconsistencies, and there grew a belief that instead of trying to play along with his fabrication, instead he should be broken and forced to confess to being a Soviet plant. Thus, two months later in April 1964, Nosenko was placed in solitary confinement and subjected to hostile interrogation.[14]

This was to last for over three and a half years, and had been signed off by the US Attorney General. Nosenko was placed in a specially constructed concrete bunker, was refused outside contact, cigarettes, any form of exercise or natural light. All the while he continued to be questioned, sometimes following periods of sleep or sensory deprivation, and always conducted in less than polite circumstances. At no point did Nosenko tell his interrogators that he was a Soviet plant, and he maintained the stance that he was a genuine defector. Nevertheless, his answers only served to convince those involved that he was inauthentic. To try and find an answer to his bona fides a number of different inquiries were conducted, amounting to many thousands of pages. Perhaps unsurprisingly, these came up with completely contrasting conclusions as the inconsistencies and ambiguity over Nosenko's answers and background could be used to justify both positions.[15]

In late 1967, responsibility for Nosenko passed to the CIA's Office of Security, which commissioned its own survey and interrogation. The subsequent report, by Bruce Solie, exonerated Nosenko and declared that he was genuine.[16] Nosenko was released from confinement, and in March 1969 became a paid consultant to the CIA. He would subsequently be awarded substantial financial compensation. Nonetheless, the debate did not end there. Angleton remained convinced by Golitsyn's claims and Nosenko's falsehood, and secretly and unofficially briefed journalists about it.[17] Others who had been directly involved, such as CIA officer Tennent 'Pete' Bagley, Nosenko's erstwhile case officer, wrote a stinging critique of Nosenko.[18]

What is the truth? The prevailing view taken by the CIA and most writers is that Nosenko was genuine. The best writing on the subject is a perceptive evaluation by Richards Heuer. A long-time CIA veteran, Heuer had served in the operations and analytical divisions; he had some first-hand experience of the case but was also permitted to consult some of the internal files. In his review, originally written as a classified article for the CIA's in-house journal, Heuer demonstrates how both sides of the Nosenko debate sought to use similar evidence to prove their thesis. The question, simply put, is whether Nosenko was innocent until proven guilty – or guilty until proven innocent? On balance, Heuer, who concedes that he was originally certain that Nosenko was a fake, concludes that he was genuine, and offers a variety of explanations as to why.[19]

Golitsyn figures prominently throughout. Although Angleton was a keen proponent of his information, Golitsyn himself was tremendously difficult during his own debriefing.[20] Much later, he would publish a series of books in which he made increasingly outlandish claims. Not only was he instrumental in setting the context for Nosenko's defection, but he was also intimately involved in it. The chapter reference document highlights this role: just as Deriabin had been brought in to review Golitsyn's testimony, so Golitsyn was brought in by Angleton to review what Nosenko revealed. This was, in the words of the CIA's chief historian David Robarge, a 'blunder'.[21]

The document itself was only released in mid-2017 as part of the final release of material related to the Kennedy assassination. It is a summary written by David Murphy, then Chief of the Soviet Russia (SR) Division, to Angleton. Murphy had a long and distinguished history in the CIA and was one of those who doubted Nosenko. Ironically, perhaps, he would be caught up in the Angleton-inspired molehunt later on. As the document makes clear, Golitsyn's role was fundamental to evaluating Nosenko's testimony, even though the former's involvement was often not as illuminating as might have been hoped. The document not only provides further detail into this, including the vast array of other intelligence the CIA provided to Golitsyn to assess, but also highlights the starting assumption of Nosenko's hostile interrogation: not to discover the truth, but to 'break him'. The Nosenko affair is easily characterised as a dark chapter in the CIA's history, but it is an open question if Angleton or Golitsyn contributed more to make it so.

```
                                              5 August 1964
MEMORANDUM FOR:  Chief, CI Staff
SUBJECT:         GOLITSYN's comments on the NOSENKO
                 Case
Introduction and General Assessment
1. In reviewing the value and validity of GOLITSYN's
comments on the NOSENKO case, it must be borne in
```

mind that although his current comments do not provide much that is new GOLITSYN himself has always been a key to our understanding of the NOSENKO case. In 1962 NOSENKO's information was closely keyed to what we could presume to be a KGB damage assessment of GOLITSYN's defection, a fact which we only noticed on comparison of NOSENKO's information with GOLITSYN's. Similarly, what GOLITSYN had told us about Department "D" enabled us to see how such a high-level provocation could be run. Furthermore, his most recent comments do in fact provide useful support to our analysis which had already been completed. We do need now to assess how much GOLITSYN may be in a position to help in our assessment and future handling of NOSENKO and other ramifications of this KGB provocation. His value and future contribution can be assessed on several levels:

a. How much new hard information can he contribute?

b. How much new insight can he provide us through his own knowledge of KGB procedures and personnel applied to the materials of this case?

c. How much guidance can he provide in our future manipulation of these operations and in breaking KROTKOV and NOSENKO?

2. Point "a" is discussed in paragraph 5 below. While there are several useful items, the total of new hard facts is not great. On point "b", his insight, as reflected in his oral comments and analysis, is disappointing as one would have expected him to provide a more penetrating analysis than that which we completed earlier. And in point "c" he himself admits to having no idea about how to break NOSENKO and KROTKOV, other than to point out that it will be most difficult, that we need to do some more groundwork and preparation before proceeding to an active attempt to do so (including perhaps uncovering a penetration of the U. S. Embassy, Moscow first), and that we should use well qualified interrogators.

3. We are faced at this point with the eminently complicated task of breaking NOSENKO. (While preparing to do so we are keeping him productive and examining the ramifications of the operation.) Our great need

now is for hard, incontrovertible facts with which we can confront NOSENKO, to prove to him that our conviction about his guilt is based on something more than analysis, which is what he now evidently thinks it is. For this, our only immediate asset is GOLITSYN, who looms so importantly as a factor in this operation. We therefore hope, despite GOLITSYN's relative lack of contribution thus far, to exhaust all possibilities and get from him every possible detail. Therefore, since there are many loose ends and unclear bits from his 29 June report, we are preparing followup questions for GOLITSYN which might assist our task. Some of these questions are attached hereto as Attachment A.

4. GOLITSYN's principal report on the NOSENKO case was contained in the oral presentation of 28 June 1964. As background for his study of the case, GOLITSYN was given a wide range of materials on NOSENKO including 113 pages of responses to specific questions GOLITSYN wanted put to NOSENKO (see attachment B for a listing of all materials pertaining to NOSENKO which were shown to GOLITSYN). In addition, GOLITSYN was given the CHEREPANOV papers with supporting documentation, as well as the KROTKOV case and manuscript, the BELITSKIY, the UNACUTE and POPOV cases. In general, this was nearly everything available to us in our analysis of 25 March, 11 May and 8 July, with the exception of the SCOTCH case.

What GOLITSYN said

5. Statements of fact: What GOLITSYN could contribute in the form of personal knowledge, as against supposition, is summarized in the subparagraphs below. Comments on each point are appended where appropriate. Several of these points are of real assistance, but certain aspects of their content or presentation weakens their impact or opens them and the source's accuracy to some question.

a. This man is the person he says he is, Yuriy Ivanovich NOSENKO, the son of former Minister NOSENKO, and he really was a KGB officer.

Comments:

(1) GOLITSYN knows this because he says he knew
NOSENKO personally, having met him two or three
times in II/1/1 in 1953 when GOLITSYN was there
on other business. GOLITSYN also met NOSENKO occasionally at work in 1958-1959. In 1959, GOLITSYN
asked NOSENKO where he worked, and NOSENKO said
in the Tourist Department. GOLITSYN asked him
about CHURANOV. In addition, NOSENKO and GOLITSYN
know one another indirectly through their common
friends CHURANOV, GUK, KASHEYEV, etc.

(2) NOSENKO, however, could not identify the photo
of GOLITSYN and, when told who it was, repeated
his earlier statements that he had never met
GOLITSYN and would of course remember if he had.
He had once been shown a group photo of him. (It is
difficult to see why NOSENKO would lie about this,
since we clearly could check through GOLITSYN and
a contrary statement would throw immediate doubt
on NOSENKO's bona fides, and there would apparently be nothing for him to lose merely admitting
it. This raises the question of why GOLITSYN might
lie about this point, similarly not very easy to
answer.)

b. NOSENKO served in II/1/1 from 1953 until 1957 or
1958, and was specifically responsible during the
period 1953-54 for American military personnel in
the Embassy. In 1955-57-58 he may have had the same
responsibilities, or may have been working against
other Embassy personnel or correspondents, but was
definitely in II/1/1.

Comments:

(1) NOSENKO says he was in II/1/1, working first
against correspondents and then against military
personnel, from March 1953 until mid-1955, and
claims then to have transferred to the 7th (Tourist)
Department of the Second Chief Directorate (II/7).

(2) In our own analysis of NOSENKO's story (11
May report) we had expressed doubts that NOSENKO
actually even served in the American Department
at all, since he was so vague about details
he should have known, since he was suspiciously

self-contradictory about when he entered and what he did, and since his later period in that Department (1960–62) is clearly a complete fabrication.

　c. NOSENKO served from 1957 or 1958 in the Tourist Department (II/7), where in 1959 he was a senior case officer.

Comments:

　(1) As noted above, this contradicts NOSENKO's story of having made this transfer in mid-1955, thus creating a period of two to three years which NOSENKO's legend is trying to cover up. This suggests to GOLITSYN that there was some success in the Embassy during this period, which is supported by other observations (see below).

　(2) There is reason to doubt the validity of GOLITSYN's statement, since NOSENKO is independently known to have been involved in at least one, and perhaps two, strictly tourist-type operations involving U. S. citizens in the period 1956–1958. One was Richard BURGI, whom NOSENKO recruited in June 1956 in the company of Anatoliy KOZLOV, Chief of II/7, who has confirmed NOSENKO's story and identified his picture. There was possibly one other American, Gisella Harris, in 1957 (she tentatively but uncertainly identified his photo) and he claims to have worked on three foreigners, one of whom, Sir Alan Lane, British, has confirmed the story and recognized NOSENKO's photo. The two others (Hans GERKENS, a German and Fnu SUENDER, a Norwegian) have not yet been identified.

　(3) Supporting GOLITSYN's statement, however, are the following points:

　(a) DERIABIN considers it quite possible that an American Department man might be used in a Tourist Department operation, if he had qualifications needed and others were not available at the time. There is an outside chance that this is what happened here.

　(b) In the 1962 meetings with CIA, NOSENKO claimed to have personally participated in the recruitment operation in 1956 against U.S. Embassy security officer, Edward Smith. When confronted

in 1964 with this earlier statement, NOSENKO vigorously denied it. His earlier claim could thus
have been a slip, or perhaps merely a gratuitous
boast (paralleling his 1962 claim to have been
involved in the October 1959 attempt against Russ
Langelle).

(c) NOSENKO has reported personal participation in only a few checkable tourist-line activities during the years 1955-58 although his year
1959 is replete with them, almost all confirmed
independently.

(d) The only other independently known activity
of NOSENKO during this period was two trips to
England in August 1957 and October 1958. These,
he claims, were merely to serve as watchdog for
two Soviet sporting groups (and to give him some
flavor of the West). They could presumably have
taken him from II/1 just as well as from II/7.

d. NOSENKO did not work in II/1 at any time in 1960,
and therefore it is unthinkable that he was there for
the one year 1961 either.
Comments:
(1) This confirms oar finding, as reported in 11
May report.
(2) GOLITSYN claims to know this because he was
aware in detail of who served in II/1/1 until his
departure for Helsinki in July 1960, and because
he visited Moscow and II/1 in December 1960 and
talked with the then head of II/1/1, KOVSHUK. He
would have known if NOSENKO were in the section
then at all, much less as deputy chief.
However:
- NOSENKO was away in Cuba until 13 December 1960
and thus may not have been there at the time.
Nonetheless, the fact that he had become Deputy
would presumably have come out of GOLITSYN's talks
with KOVSHUK, anyway.
- GOLITSYN had earlier said that PETROV was chief
of II/1/1, GRYAZNOV the deputy. Insofar as SR
records show, GOLITSYN had never named KOVSHUK in
this position, as far as we know, until he saw the
NOSENKO materials. KOVSHUK was, of course, named

by GOLITSYN many times as an active case officer in II/1/1.

e. Contrary to NOSENKO's statement that GORBATENKO remained as chief of II/1 until 1959, GOLITSYN knew that GORBATENKO was sent as senior KGB advisor to Hungary shortly after the Hungarian Revolution, probably about January 1957.

Comments:

(1) Since this is a high-powered job and represented a promotion, GOLITSYN thinks it may well have been given to GORBATENKO as a result of success in operations against the American Embassy, specifically a recruitment. GOLITSYN thinks NOSENKO may be covering this up by changing the dates of GORBATENKO's transfer, and associates this with KOVSHUK's trip to the U. S. in early 1957, presumably to follow up or complete a Moscow Embassy recruitment (about which trip NOSENKO also gave apparent disinformation, linking it to the "ANDREY" case, which we all agree is unlikely, especially since "ANDREY" left Moscow in the spring of 1954). Since the period involved here is the same one GOLITSYN thinks NOSENKO is covering up in his own biography (1955-57), this might indeed be a clue to an important penetration.

(2) We are examining U. S. Embassy departees from Moscow during 1956, and are preparing a paper presenting the circumstances of one possible theory.

f. NOSENKO did, in fact, have the woman trouble he claims, but GOLITSYN "recalls" that this took place in 1957 or 1958, not in 1954, and this was the reason he was transferred out of the more sensitive American Department to the Tourist Department.

Comment:

(1) GOLITSYN also said that the events "must have happened" after NOSENKO became a CP member (in 1956-57), suggesting GOLITSYN is not stating a fact but making a supposition. It is not clear, in fact, whether GOLITSYN knows or supposes that this caused NOSENKO's transfer out of II/1 into II/7.

g. The post of Assistant Section Chief - which GOLITSYN says NOSENKO claimed to occupy in 1960-62 - was abolished in 1959, those holding this title being made senior case officers.

Note: GOLITSYN is apparently confusing POMNACH (Assistant to the Chief) with ZAMNACH (Deputy Chief). NOSENKO also reported that Pomnaches were abolished and made senior case officers, while Zamnaches continue to this day. GOLITSYN must also believe this, since he has reported GRYAZNOV as Zamnach II/1/1.

6. Statements of opinion: In addition to the opinions connected with the facts summarized above, GOLITSYN provided a number of opinions, theories and suppositions on various detailed aspects of this case. By and large, these merely provide additional support for opinions already presented in our earlier reports on this operation. GOLITSYN concluded without doubt that NOSENKO is a KGB provocateur, that the operation could only have been run with KHRUSHCHEV's personal approval, and that it is designed among other things to hide various penetrations, one perhaps related to the POPOV compromise, and some of them threatened by leads provided by GOLITSYN. He considered that the NOSENKO operation is being run in close coordination with the KROTKOV and CHEREPANOV provocations, and that in order to carry out his mission properly NOSENKO must know many of the significant truths the KGB is trying to hide or protect. He believes that much of what NOSENKO has said is keyed to KGB knowledge, rather than supposition, about what GOLITSYN had reported to Western intelligence authorities. Since all of this has already been dealt with in detail in our earlier analysis, it is not repeated in the body of this memorandum.

David E. Murphy
Chief, SR Division

Attachments A and B

Questions for GOLITSYN based on 29 June Interview
What is your opinion of the general accuracy of what
NOSENKO has reported on KGB organization and person-
nel assignments? (Aside from ops and special inci-
dents connected with provocation)
Any contradictions between your present knowledge and
the information he provided re who was where when?
(Aside from GORBATENKO's departure date)

In your opinion, would the KGB give NOSENKO carte
blanche to tell the truth re organization, personnel
(including photo idens) and procedures? Would it feel
safe enough to permit him to make major lies on this,
especially general organization (such as Sluzhba,
Directorate of II, etc.)?

What are the specific points you think NOSENKO is
lying about re personnel?

You reported earlier that PETROV was chief of the
1st (Embassy) Section of the American Department,
and GRYAZNOV the deputy, as of 1960. NOSENKO reports
KOVSHUK had long been the chief, PETROV never had
been, and GRYAZNOV only became deputy after NOSENKO
left in January 1962. How do you explain NOSENKO's
statement?

What is your opinion about the general information NOSENKO gave on Tourist Department ops, i.e.,
the totals he reported (about 34 tourist agency
owners and employees, about 25 non-American tourists
recruited, and a few miscellaneous others), plus
about 19 American tourists - practically all already
identified, known or useless - and 5 American tourist
company personnel?

Do you know anything about the relative success in
recruiting tourists prior to 1961? Any considered
solid or important?

Did you have direct, earlier, knowledge of NOSENKO's
career and activity? Had you heard about his trouble

with women, the flap he reports as having occurred in 1954? (The transcript leaves it unclear whether it was your belief that it happened in 1957-58 or whether it was hard fact.)

Could you provide details of the approximate date, location, circumstances under which you met NOSENKO each time?

Do you know for a fact (or did you hear from KGB personnel) that NOSENKO <u>entered the KGB</u> in 1953? Or is that merely the first year you personally saw or heard about him? Had you ever heard of him before 1953?

Did you ever hear anything about Nosenko's background other than his father, i.e., his GRU service, schooling (especially Institute of Foreign Relations), residences (including dacha), neighbors?

Can you describe the Obzor you saw on the POPOV case, particularly its format and length? (NOSENKO has described it as hard-cardboard covered, only about five inches wide by eight high, and about 20-25 pages long.) Are all obzors produced in this or other standard format?

You have reported that a KGB officer named KOTOV, formerly in Yugoslav ops in Austria, suspected POPOV and was sent in 1958 to Germany on the POPOV investigation. We know of no KOTOV in Vienna in the period concerned. Did you mean Mikhail ZHUKOV? Another? Could you give us more details on KOTOV, such as full name, description, career?

Do you have any knowledge of direct contact between NOSENKO and PREISFREUND? NOSENKO claims not only to have been a case officer for PREISFREUND, but to have been his close friend, even prior to the time you left Helsinki. Can you comment?

What can you say about the selection of NOSENKO for the trips to England in August 1957 and October

1958? Would this be likely for Tourist or American Department officer? How about the Cuba trip, 1960, and Bulgaria 1961?

Why, in your opinion, might he have changed his "traveling" name from Nikolayev, which he used in England trips, to NOSENKO, which he used for Cuba trip and for application for U. S. visa earlier in 1960?

Materials made available to GOLITSYN listed in chronological order of passing to GOLITSYN, with dates passed.

1. Copies of first four substantive cables from Geneva relating circumstances of his contact with us in June 1962, including first meeting with MARK and first meeting with BAGLEY. (2 March 1964)
2. Copies of transcripts of all meetings between CIA and NOSENKO in 1962 (3 March 1964)
3. Copies of all transcripts of Geneva meetings, January-February 1964. (All passed to GOLITSYN by 13 March 1964)
4. Report of biographic information provided prior to hostile interrogation. (17 April 1964)
5. Final chronology, with our notations, of NOSENKO's life and KGB career, prepared after hostile interrogation. (Attachment A to 11 May 1964 report) (Passed 11 May 1964)
6. Copy of NOSENKO's handwritten notes and documents he brought out with him in 1964. (Passed in mid-April)
7. Resume of first week's hostile interrogation.
8. NOSENKO's comments on KROTKOV's manuscript "Fear". (Passed in mid-April)
9. Complete collection of photo identifications made by NOSENKO to date, with explanatory note re method of notation.
10. Questions re NOSENKO for GOLITSYN (passed in mid-April). Special questions passed on 15 June and 22 June.

11. CHEREPANOV papers. (22 April 1964)
12. Information on American personnel named in CHEREPANOV papers and otherwise of interest re Moscow Embassy security (WINTERS, including his ops activity; BOWDEN; LANGELLE; LIEBERMAN; Edward SMITH; WASHENKO; Leonid GRAN). 4 May 1964.
13. List of questions KROTKOV suggested be put to NOSENKO in order to confirm and clarify info given by KR0TKOV.
14. Copies of two reports prepared on KGB audio technical operations, one prepared on basis of GOLITSYN information in 1962, another based on NOSENKO information 1964.
15. KOZLOV case (AEFOSDICK) 4 May.
16. Case summaries: REPNIKOV, SIDOROVICH, AGAFONOV, IZHBOLDIN, RAFALOVICH, REPNIKOV, MARYUTIN (4 and 11 May). JUNG, PRIBYTKOVA (15 June).
17. Transcripts and chronology with background sketch on BELITSKIY.
18. File summary on FEDOROV aka RAZIN. (11 May and 12 June)
19. Charts re NOSENKO CI production (leads). (11 May)
20. Chronologies on KOVSHUK, GUK, FOMIN and IVANOV.
21. Outline of information on KGB structure and personnel assignments as reported by NOSENKO. (11 May)
22. ARTAMONOV case. (November 1963)
23. PENKOVSKIY case. (November 1963)
24. POPOV case. (November 1963)
25. Answers to special questions posed by GOLITSYN and asked of NOSENKO in interrogations in May 1964. Total 113 pages; all questions answered and Passed by 12 June.

Notes

1. David C. Martin, *Wilderness of Mirrors: Intrigue, Deception, and the Secrets that Destroyed Two of the Cold War's Most Important Agents* (London: Lyons Press, 2003). The title originally comes from a T. S. Eliot poem.
2. Available at <https://www.gpo.gov/fdsys/pkg/USCODE-2011-title50/pdf/USCODE-2011-title50-chap15-sec401a.pdf> (last accessed 10 January 2020).

3. J. Ehrman, 'Towards a Theory of CI: What Are We Talking About When We Talk About Counterintelligence?', *Studies in Intelligence*, 53.2 (June 2009), <https://www.cia.gov/library/center-for-the-study-of-intelligence/csi-publications/csi-studies/studies/vol53no2/toward-a-theory-of-ci.html> (last accessed 10 January 2020).

4. M. Varouhakis, 'An Institution-Level Theoretical Approach for Counter-intelligence', *International Journal of Intelligence and Counterintelligence*, 24.3 (2011), pp. 494–509.

5. Angleton has been the subject of a variety of articles and books, the most recent of which is Jefferson Morley, *The Ghost: The Secret Life of CIA Spymaster James Jesus Angleton* (London: Scribe, 2017).

6. See the brief biographical note in the foreword to his first book: Anatoliy Golitsyn, *New Lies for Old: The Communist Strategy of Deception and Disinformation* (London: G. S. G. & Associates, 1990).

7. 'Memorandum: Anatoliy Mikhaylovich Klimov, AKA Anatoliy Mikhaylovich Golitzyn', NARA: 104-10263-10004, <https://maryferrell.org/showDoc.html?docId=38159#relPageId=4&tab=page> (last accessed 10 January 2020).

8. David Wise, *Molehunt: The Secret Search for Traitors that Shattered the CIA* (London: Random House, 1992). On the actual identity of 'Sasha', see Barry G. Royden, 'James J Angleton, Anatoliy Golitsyn, and the "Monster Plot": Their Impact on CIA Personnel and Operations', *Studies in Intelligence*, 55.4 (December 2011), p. 45.

9. For more, see J. D. Ennis, 'Anatoli Golitsyn: Long-time CIA Agent?', *Intelligence and National Security*, 21.1 (2006), pp. 26–45.

10. This is a problem of all defectors, whose usefulness quickly evaporates once fully debriefed. On Golitsyn's long-term plan to defect, see J. D. Ennis, 'What Did Angleton Say about Golitsyn?', *Intelligence and National Security*, 22.6 (2007), pp. 905–9.

11. For the best account see Wise, *Molehunt*. The most vocal and active MI5 proponent of this theory was Peter Wright of *Spycatcher* fame.

12. Tom Mangold, *Cold Warrior: James Jesus Angleton: The CIA's Master Spy Hunter* (London: Simon & Schuster, 1991).

13. Nosenko claimed that Oswald had been rejected by the KGB and it had had nothing to do with Kennedy's assassination.

14. On the role of Angleton in this see S. Halpern and H. Peake, 'Did Angleton Jail Nosenko?' *International Journal of Intelligence and Counterintelligence*, 3.4 (1989), pp. 451–64.

15. For details, see R. J. Heuer, 'Nosenko: Five Paths to Judgment', in H. Bradfield Westerfield (ed.), *Inside CIA's Private World* (Ann Arbor: Edwards Brothers, 1987), pp. 379–414.

16. A copy of the report can be found here: <https://ia801906.us.archive.org/33/items/YuriNosenko/Nosenko%2C%20Yuri.pdf> (last accessed 10 January 2020).

17. For an early example see Edward J. Epstein, *Legend: The Secret World of Lee Harvey Oswald* (London: McGraw-Hill, 1978).

18. Tennent H. Bagley, *Spy Wars: Moles, Mysteries, and Deadly Games* (London: Yale University Press, 2008).
19. Heuer, 'Nosenko: Five Paths to Judgment'.
20. See Royden, 'Monster Plot', p. 46.
21. D. Robarge, 'Moles, Defectors, and Deceptions: James Angleton and CIA Counterintelligence', *Journal of Intelligence History*, 3.2 (2003), p. 39.

11   1975: The Year of the 'Intelligence Wars'

One could easily imagine a CIA officer who cut his or her teeth during the 'golden era' of the early years of the CIA looking back in 1975 on those heady, sometimes swashbuckling days with a fair degree of nostalgia. The fledgling agency had set a strong pace in intelligence collection and analysis, in cutting-edge technological development and in covert action, in Europe, Latin America, Asia and beyond. It had achieved notable successes; even its failures had resulted in policymakers' concluding that it needed more money, resources and support, not less.[1] The agency enjoyed a curious relationship with Congress and the public during those early decades. On the one hand, certainly compared to its sister services in the UK, MI5 and SIS, it enjoyed a much higher public profile. Its creation had, after all, been the culmination of a long public debate, and had been set in stone in the 1947 National Security Act. Certain issues, such as the failed operation at the Bay of Pigs in 1961, ensured that its profile never dropped too far. But, on the other hand, it had managed to sustain a cloak of secrecy over the scale of its operations and had enjoyed a significant degree of latitude from lawmakers who approved its budgets. Successive presidents had seen the agency as a tool at their disposal when dealing with all manner of issues; there had been very little pressure to create a more democratically robust system of oversight. That changed after 1975, and the fallout of 'the year of intelligence', when a series of revelations about the agency's activities was made public. The fallout and the attacks endured by the agency were judged by CIA officer Ray Cline to have 'nearly destroyed its effectiveness at home and abroad'.[2] The revelations gave rise to the infamous, though inaccurate, charge that the CIA 'may have been behaving like a rogue elephant on rampage.'[3]

Tolerable though the light-touch oversight of intelligence activities may have been throughout the first decades of the Cold War, by the 1970s the political, media and public mood was beginning to shift towards control, transparency and investigation. Several factors accounted for this shift, including disillusionment with the war in Vietnam, the (linked) leaking of the Pentagon Papers in 1971 and, of course, the Watergate affair, which unfolded from 1972 until President Nixon's resignation in August 1974. Unchecked power was no longer tolerable. It was perhaps inevitable that the secretive operations of the CIA would not remain exempt from this season of openness and inquiry, as indeed transpired to be the case. In 1974 the national press began publishing a series of exposés concerning the CIA's operations: abroad, in Chile; and, more seriously, at home, with the agency's surveillance of elements of the anti-war movement.[4] The Ford administration was forced to publicly discuss the procedures for authorising covert operations, in an attempt to assuage the agency's critics by reassuring them that procedures ensured a form of democratic control.[5] But the critics' voices grew louder with each revelation and the press smelled blood: as CIA chronicler Rhodri Jeffreys-Jones noted, intelligence 'had taken over from Watergate as the stick with which to beat the allegedly power-mad White House'.[6] The relative political weakness of Gerald Ford, Nixon's unelected successor, made it very difficult for him to withstand the pressure for more congressional control over US intelligence operations, or, indeed, for investigations.

The *New York Times* and *Washington Post* articles revealed but a tiny vignette of the CIA's operations. The agency had good reason to be concerned that further revelations could bring yet more unwelcome scrutiny. In a move almost presaging the congressional investigations of 1975, the CIA had been chronicling its own history. The outcome of this investigation was a document that became known as 'The Family Jewels'. It had been commissioned by James R. Schlesinger, who had succeeded Richard Helms as DCI in February 1973, determined to implement reforms in the agency. The spark that ignited the investigation was the revelation that two agency veterans, E. Howard Hunt and James McCord, had been involved in the Watergate burglary. In response, Schlesinger commanded William Colby, then Deputy Director for Operations and a future DCI, to report on 'any current or past Agency matters that might fall outside CIA authority'.[7] The result was a 693-page document of reports and allegations from staff at all levels of the CIA, covering a period of some twenty-five years.[8] The misdeeds chronicled in the document included covert postal interception at JFK airport, and that Watergate burglar E. Howard Hunt had requested a lock-picking device from the agency's External Employment Assistance Branch.[9] Colby did not inform President Nixon of the document's existence; nor was President Ford, who was well briefed on intelligence matters in general, informed until the Christmas holidays of 1974, when the scandal following Seymour Hersh's story had broken in the *New York Times*.[10] So sensitive was the document that the CIA resisted releasing it until 2007; indeed, the public version remains heavily redacted.[11] But for those who had read it in

1974, it was clear that any external investigations could unearth several skeletons once considered safely tucked away in the agency's closet.

The immediate outcome of the 1974 scandals on the governance of the CIA's activities was tighter control on the approval of covert actions in the form of the so-called Hughes-Ryan amendment. It required the President to produce a 'finding' that a covert activity was in pursuit of the national security of the US, and to inform the appropriate committees in Congress in a timely manner.[12] This was the first serious break with the traditionally lenient approach the Congress had taken to regulating CIA covert action since 1947, but it would not be the last. Hot on its heels came three investigations which, ultimately, led to significantly tighter control on the agency's activities. The first is often regarded as the White House's attempt to investigate the extent of CIA domestic operations whilst protecting the agency and the presidency from other, future investigations. President Ford established the Commission on CIA Activities within the United Sates in January 1975. It soon became synonymous with its chairman, Vice President Nelson Rockefeller, and remains generally known as the Rockefeller Commission.[13] The second investigation soon followed, with the Senate voting on 27 January to create a Select Committee to Study Governmental Operations with Respect to Intelligence Activities. Its remit was broader, including domestic operations, executive and congressional management and foreign operations. It was chaired by Senator Frank Church (D-ID), and is generally known as the Church Committee. The House of Representatives followed suit on 19 February, establishing a Select Committee on Intelligence, initially chaired by Lucien Nedzi and later by Otis Pike (D-NY), whose name is most generally associated with the probe. The dramas and the revelations associated with the three investigations ensured that intelligence was never far from the headlines in 1975, earning it the moniker 'the year of intelligence'.

Of the three inquiries, it was the Church Committee that had the greatest impact. The Rockefeller Committee reported in June 1975 and pulled few punches in criticising domestic surveillance and recommending a congressional oversight committee. Its investigation into assassinations, contained in an annex delivered to the President, remained unpublished.[14] The Pike Committee's investigation ebbed and flowed. Its investigations revealed a number of key features of US intelligence operations, particularly concerning the authorisation of operations. Henry Kissinger, then Secretary of State, noted that every operation was approved by the President, in a clear repudiation of the earlier 'rogue elephant' charge.[15] But the Committee's probing was increasingly frustrating to the White House, which accused it of releasing significant classified information, and ultimately the final report was supressed (only to be leaked in January 1976).[16] The Church

Committee's enquiries progressed, not without controversy or friction. It benefited significantly from DCI William Colby's decision – not entirely endorsed across CIA's senior ranks – to cooperate with an unprecedented degree of openness. Indeed, Colby's policy irked some elements of the intelligence establishment, who believed that Colby's cooperation undermined secrecy to an extent that it imperilled the operations of the agency. Richard Helms noted in his autobiography that Colby's behaviour gave the Soviets ample material to pore over, and that the 'DCI's unilateral actions effectively smashed the existing system of checks and balances protecting the national intelligence service.'[17] Regardless, the investigation amassed a wealth of evidence, which was presented in six substantial volumes to Congress and the public on 26 April 1976.

Both in terms of scope and detail, the volumes of the Church report were unprecedented. A huge number of the US intelligence community's controversial operations were laid bare before the public. Perhaps the most explosive revelations concerned not the CIA, but the FBI. Book three, examining intelligence activities and the rights of Americans, presented the FBI's COINTELPRO operations which had targeted several counterculture and civil rights organisations, including a sustained campaign against Dr Martin Luther King, intended 'to "neutralize" him as an effective civil rights leader'.[18] The testimony of William Sullivan, the leading officer in the 'war' against Dr King, was quoted verbatim at the outset of the chapter dedicated to the case. He noted 'No holds were barred. We have used [similar] techniques against Soviet agents.'[19]

Whereas the most controversial operations were attributed to the FBI, some of the most interesting revelations concerned the hitherto exceptionally secretive NSA. Much to the chagrin of the White House and security officials, the reports offered a glimpse at its operations, and therefore its capabilities, in its discussion of domestic surveillance in books two and three. But the CIA did not escape controversy. The reports detailed its domestic operations, including mail opening and investigations into foreign support for anti-war and radical organisations in the US, most famously Operation MHCHAOS.[20] The most sensational revelations concerned the CIA's (unsuccessful) assassination operations in Cuba and Congo, and operation MKULTRA, where unsuspecting Americans were given LSD as part of an Agency mind-control research programme. The report presented, in detail, the intricacies of Operation Mongoose, and how the CIA had co-opted underworld figures in its plots against Castro and his regime.[21] These operations remain staple elements of CIA folklore in the public imagination but, perhaps curiously, the CIA emerged with the key charge against it roundly refuted: the agency may have been involved in questionable operations, but it was not rogue in the sense that had been implied, these operations were undertaken at the instruction of successive presidents of the United States.

Indeed, many argue that the CIA emerged from the trials of 'the year of intelligence' with a 'refurbished reputation'.[22] Despite the tribulations of the investigations, the nation could be said to have benefited from a robust discussion over the uses and limits of intelligence, and the role of covert action in statecraft. Very few people concluded that there was no need for the CIA and the work it did; rather, the thrust of the debate concerned regulation and oversight. After all, how could a nation like the US wage the Cold War against the totalitarian Soviet Union if its intelligence agencies operated outside a legal framework and were, generally, unaccountable to the electorate? Thus, in the wake of the three investigations came the biggest shift in the oversight regime since the creation of the CIA in 1947. In May 1976 the Senate voted to create the Senate Select Committee on Intelligence (SSCI); the House followed suit the following year, establishing the House Permanent Select Committee on Intelligence (HPSCI). With the establishment of these committees, the intelligence community, and how it was used by the Executive, was subject to much tighter supervision than at any previous point in their history.[23]

The chapter reference document concerns the agency's first step towards compiling a record of its misdeeds, actual or alleged. The product of this investigation eventually became the 'Family Jewels' and the subject of so much sustained historical comment and controversy. Notable, perhaps, was the insistence of its author, DCI James R. Schlesinger, that the CIA needed to operate within its charter and, by extension, in accordance with the rule of US law. This was considered vital for retaining the legitimacy of the CIA and its activities in the minds of the US public. Arguably, the fallout that followed this document and the subsequent investigations, for all the controversy they caused, led to a far more democratically account-able and legitimate system.

```
              CENTRAL INTELLIGENCE AGENCY
                 WASHINGTON.D.C, 20505
                 OFFICE OF THE DIRECTOR
                     9 May 1973


MEMORANDUM FOR ALL CIA EMPLOYEES
1.  Recent  press  reports  outline  in  detail  certain
alleged  CIA  activities  with  respect  to  Mr.  Howard
Hunt  and  other  parties.  The  presently  known  facts
```

behind these stories are those stated in the attached draft of a statement I will be making to the Senate Committee on Appropriations on 9 May. As can be seen, the Agency provided limited assistance in response to a request by senior officials. The Agency has cooperated with and made available to the appropriate law enforcement bodies information about these activities and will continue to do so.

2. All CIA employees should understand my attitude on this type of issue. I shall do everything in my power to confine CIA activities to those which fall within a strict interpretation of its legislative charter. I take this position because I am determined that the law shall be respected and because this is the best way to foster the legitimate and necessary contributions we in CIA can make to the national security of the United States.

3. I am taking several actions to implement this objective:

- I have ordered all the senior operating officials of this Agency to report to me immediately on any activities now going on, or that have gone on in the past, which might be construed to be outside the legislative charter of this Agency.

- I hereby direct every person presently employed by CIA to report to me on any such activities of which he has knowledge. I invite all ex-employees to do the same. Anyone who has such information should call my secretary (extension 6363) and say that he wishes to talk to me about "activities outside CIA's charter."

4. To ensure that Agency activities are proper in the future, I hereby promulgate the following standing order for all CIA employees:

Any CIA employee who believes that he has received instructions which in any way appear inconsistent with the CIA legislative charter shall inform the Director of Central Intelligence immediately.

James R. Schlesinger
Director

Notes

1. Rhodri Jeffreys-Jones, *The CIA and American Democracy* (London: Yale, 2003); see chapter 3, 'The Mists of Bogota'.
2. Ibid. p. 195.
3. Michael Warner, *The Rise and Fall of Intelligence: An International Security History* (Washington, DC: Georgetown University Press, 2014), p. 212.
4. Christopher Andrew, *For the President's Eyes Only: Secret Intelligence and the American Presidency from Washington to Bush* (New York: Harper Perennial, 1996), p. 399–402.
5. Ibid. p. 400.
6. Jeffreys-Jones, *The CIA and American Democracy*, p. 199.
7. See National Security Archive, 'The CIA's Family Jewels', available at <https://nsarchive2.gwu.edu/NSAEBB/NSAEBB222/> (last accessed 10 January 2020).
8. Richard Helms, *A Look Over My Shoulder: A Life in the Central Intelligence Agency* (New York: Ballantine Books, 2003), pp. 426–7.
9. See 'The CIA's Family Jewels'.
10. Andrew, *For the President's Eyes Only*, p. 402–3.
11. See 'The Family Jewels', <https://www.cia.gov/library/readingroom/collection/family-jewels> (last accessed 10 January 2020).
12. Andrew, *For the President's Eyes Only*, p. 403.
13. Jeffreys-Jones, *The CIA and American Democracy*, p. 199.
14. Rhodri Jeffreys-Jones, *Cloak and Dollar: A History of American Secret Intelligence* (New Haven: Yale University Press, 2002), p. 214.
15. Ibid. p. 219.
16. Ibid. p. 220.
17. Helms, *A Look Over My Shoulder*, p. 429.
18. Final report of the Select Committee to Study Governmental Operations with Respect to Intelligence Activities, *Supplementary Detailed Staff Reports on Intelligence Activities and the Rights of Americans: Book 3*, p. 79, <https://www.intelligence.senate.gov/sites/default/files/94755_III.pdf> (last accessed 10 January 2020).
19. Ibid.
20. Ibid. p. 681.
21. See *Alleged Assassination Plots Involving Foreign Leaders*, <https://www.intelligence.senate.gov/sites/default/files/94465.pdf> (last accessed 10 January 2020).
22. Jeffreys-Jones, *The CIA and American Democracy*, p. 215.
23. For a discussion of how effective the Committees have been in practice see Loch K. Johnson, 'The Church Committee Investigation of 1975 and the Evolution of Modern Intelligence Accountability', *Intelligence and National Security*, 23.2 (2008).

12　Watching Khomeini

The fall of the Shah of Iran in January 1979 was a momentous event. Not only had the Iranian royal family ruled for 2,500 years, but the ushering in of an Islamic Republic irrevocably altered regional politics. For the CIA the revolution came as a great surprise, and almost instantly questions arose as to why it had not been foreseen. Many accounts have concentrated on the 1979 revolution in Iran as an intelligence failure, pondering the reasons behind it.[1] This chapter will take a different tack and will focus more squarely on CIA assessments of the main protagonist, Ayatollah Ruhollah Khomeini, rather than the revolution itself.

Khomeini was no stranger to the CIA, nor indeed to the Iranian political establishment. In fact, the Shah, who had been returned to power in 1953 following a coup, engineered in the West and orchestrated by the CIA, had long been a critic of, and target for, Iranian religious leaders. While Khomeini would not be the first Iranian religious leader to speak out against the ruling leadership, his vitriol would become one of the most vocal and prolific. For CIA analysts, writing sometime afterwards but looking at this early period (albeit with the benefit of hindsight), 'the emergence of a strong religious leader on a national level was inevitable'.[2] But it would be difficult to have made such a judgement at the time. A major factor behind this is contained in a post-mortem that the CIA conducted in the immediate aftermath of the revolution: collecting intelligence on domestic Iranian issues was a low priority.

The CIA post-mortem was explicit in its findings: 'most NFAC [the CIA's National Foreign Assessment Center] analysts began with the belief that the Shah and his regime were strong and the opposition weak and divided'.[3] Just like a badly shaped snowball at the top of the hill, once such an erroneous assumption was used as the starting position, the process quickly moved off track and lost its shape and direction. So what was known about Khomeini and why was his trajectory misjudged?

Khomeini was born in 1902 and developed a religious identity from an early age. His first book, written in his late thirties, was as much a religious tract as a political one. Yet it would be another two decades before he became significant as a political figure.[4] In 1963 Khomeini, together with other religious figures, formed a group to coordinate a campaign against the Shah. The vocal attacks were specific and personal and the Shah responded that summer by arresting a number of leading clergy, including Khomeini. This, in turn, led to rioting in Iran and, while not leading to any significant change, it did result in Khomeini becoming a nationally recognised figure and a hero to many. Within a few years Khomeini was in trouble again: interjecting in domestic politics, and publicly calling for the army to overthrow the government. In response he was arrested, and then exiled to Turkey.

A year later he moved to Iraq and from there tried to ensure that the moderate (and, at that time, only effective) opposition to the Shah was not ignored or allowed to whither. Throughout the late 1960s and into the early 1970s, relations between Khomeini and his followers and the Iranian government were strained, but he did not relent from his political opposition to the Shah. Quite how much attention the CIA paid to Khomeini during this period is uncertain, but at the very least one CIA report stated that 'there is little detail available on his activities during this period [late 1960s to early 1970s]'.[5]

Although Khomeini was still exiled abroad and residing in Iraq, his support in Iran had grown and in late 1972 several hundred were arrested following a demonstration and scuffle with government forces. Although the impact of this was almost certainly not appreciated by the CIA at the time, in hindsight 'politically and religiously the ground was being prepared for the events of 1978–9'.[6]

The CIA, at least in the period after the 1979 Iranian Revolution, did not know why Khomeini became so politically involved and so vocal in his rhetoric against the Shah. The only conclusion that analysts could reach was that it was 'based entirely in Khomeini's interpretation of religious principles', and that importantly, 'no early personal experience can be found that might have influenced him'. Even a few months after the 1979 revolution it was conceded that 'a detailed analysis of Khomeini's thought is not yet possible'.[7]

While the source of Khomeini's grievance and his thinking, aside from his written work, might have been something of a mystery to analysts in Langley, there was ample evidence of what was happening and the impact of his words within Iran. There are a multitude of reasons why the Iranian revolution occurred at the time it did, why it was so popular, and how a religious cleric currently then in France could engineer such widespread support as to topple the monarch and ruling elite.[8]

Whilst the seeds of revolution were sowed much earlier, the first physical evidence was rioting that broke out in early 1978, largely involving

Khomeini's supporters and designed to repudiate the slurs on his reputation seemingly engineered by the government. Clashes with the police led to a number of deaths, and a month later the mourning of those deceased led to a greater number of demonstrators in a larger number of cities. By the end of March demonstrations on behalf of Khomeini and against the government had broken out in over fifty different cities across Iran.[9]

The Shah, in response, dithered. He promised free elections for 1979 and a relaxation of censorship. Although this was greeted with a mixture of enthusiasm and scepticism, it did at least quell the rioters, and by the summer of 1978 the tension had eased somewhat. In early August the CIA produced an updated assessment of the situation. The CIA did not seem surprised by the call for elections; indeed, it was noted that this was in line with the Shah's thinking and actions, but it did question just how 'free' the elections would be and whether the more liberal approach would work. It was, therefore, considered to be a 'calculated risk'. For the CIA, most problems would be caused by 'nationalists' and 'religious groups', but the risk was mitigated by the fact that 'neither has a coherent program'. Finishing ominously, the report concluded that 'the next year in Iran could be . . . a turning point in Iranian history'.[10]

As it was, no one had to wait that long. Just ten days after the CIA report was disseminated a cinema in the south of Iran was burned down, killing over 400 people who had become trapped inside. The incident was used by Khomeini to blame the Shah and the feared Iranian secret police, sentiments taken up and amplified by his supporters. The temporary respite was broken by mass protests, escalating in number and location in the weeks following the fire. A much-fabled CIA assessment from the time concluded that Iran was 'not in a revolutionary or even prerevolutionary situation'.[11] Just under a month later, the discontent had reached such a crescendo that the Shah declared martial law in a number of major cities across Iran, including Tehran. Violence also began to spread, including the deaths of both protestors and soldiers on a day that became referred to as 'Black Friday'. Once more Khomeini extracted full influence value from the events, relocating to Paris in an attempt to further disseminate his speeches.

A CIA assessment, written shortly after his move, described Khomeini as a 'guide' to the demonstrators. His message was simple: 'the Shah must go and be replaced by an "Islamic Republic"'. Khomeini was described as a 'hardliner' who had a 'strong following'. The CIA's report did not speculate on what might happen next, nor on just how popular Khomeini was in Iran; instead it considered a variety of other opposition groups, including nationalist and communist parties.[12] The CIA's post-mortem highlighted that this was one of the greatest errors that had been made, namely that 'a misreading of the appeal of the religious opposition was one of the major problems with NFAC's analysis'. Indeed,

> ... although NFAC was alert to the importance of the religious groups for years before the start of the crisis, retrospect has allowed us to detect aspects of the religious-based opposition that strongly contributed to its powerful role in the overthrow of the Shah ... the problem was not the missing of one or two vital clues to the nature of the religious groups; rather it appears to have been a general outlook which did not give credence to the links between the religious leaders and the grievance of wide ranges of the general population.[13]

Just over a fortnight later, the CIA produced another assessment (the chapter reference document), this time looking specifically at 'The Politics of Ayatollah Ruhollah Khomeini'. Whilst the CIA might have missed the links between his rhetoric and its mass appeal in Iran, there was certainly nothing wrong with its interpretation of Khomeini's views or his objectives. The analysis concluded that Khomeini was an 'influential decisionmaker', but one who would 'probably find it difficult to reconcile his Shiite principles with the needs of a modern state – there is no precedent in Iran's modern history for what Khomeini proposes'.[14]

In Iran the Shah urged calm; in Paris Khomeini urged action. By mid-December 1978 the numbers protesting against the Shah reached more than six million. Persuaded by US president Jimmy Carter, in January the Shah decided to leave the country and move to Egypt; he would never set foot on Iranian soil again. Khomeini, in the meantime, secretly began a discussion with the White House, reassuring Carter that he would be an ally and despite his public rhetoric, would not exhibit 'any particular animosity with the Americans'. In fact, this was not the first time that Khomeini had covertly made contact with the US; indeed, in 1963 at the time he rose to prominence in Iran he attempted to calm any US concerns, writing that 'he thought that the American presence [in Iran] was necessary'. The CIA certainly knew of the 1963 contact, but there is no evidence that it knew of the January 1979 correspondence.[15]

With the Shah now exiled in Egypt, the US Secretary of State contacted his embassies in Paris and Tehran, informing them that 'we have decided that it is desirable to establish a direct American channel to Khomeini's entourage'. A number of meetings took place between US officials and Khomeini's inner circle, essentially paving the way for him to return to Iran and assume power. On an eventful morning, Khomeini returned to Iran on 1 February 1979, where he was greeted by thousands of supporters. The CIA, cognisant of developments and discussions, recorded at the time that the Iranian military would not oppose a change of government. The Iranian revolution was under way, and there was no longer anything the CIA or the US government could do to stop it.[16]

CENTRAL INTELLIGENCE AGENCY
National Foreign Assessment Center
20 November 1978

INTELLIGENCE MEMORANDUM

THE POLITICS OF AYATOLLAH RUHOLLAH KHOMEINI
KEY POINTS

- Ayatollah Khomeini has long been the central figure in the conservative Shia clerical opposition to the Shah. His influence is now so strong that neither other clerics nor civilian opposition leaders will take actions he opposes.
- Khomeini is determined to overthrow the Shah and is unlikely to accept any compromise. He considers the Pahlavi regime to be corrupt, anti-Islamic and controlled by the US.
- Khomeini's power base is composed of the Shia clergy, bazaar merchants, the urban lower classes and students. Senior military officers generally oppose and feel threatened by Khomeini, but junior officers and enlisted men presumably are more responsive to his Shia message.
- Khomeini is anti-communist but his following may be susceptible to communist and radical penetration. He has cooperated in the past with an Islamic terrorist group in Iran.

████████████████

This memorandum was coordinated within the Central Intelligence Agency. Comments and queries are welcome and may be addressed to the author, ████████████ *Iran Analytical Center, Office of Regional and Political Analysis, (Phone:* ████████ *with support from the Office of Central Reference.*

- An Iranian regime under Khomeini's influence would be xenophobic and probably prone to instability. It would probably not be aligned with either the US or USSR.
- Dependent on oil sales for the preponderant share of its revenues, a Khomeini-influenced regime would continue to sell oil to the US and its allies, perhaps with the exception of Israel. It might find it ideologically attractive, however, to slow the rate of industrialization and therefore institute more conservative petroleum extraction practices.

Ruhollah Khomeini has emerged this year as the leading figure in the opposition to the Shah of Iran. Khomeini, who holds the title of Ayatollah, meaning a prominent leader of Iran's Shia Muslims, is determined to see the Shah and the Pahlavi monarchy abolished even at the cost of throwing Iran into chaos and anarchy. In place of the Shah, Khomeini advocates the creation of a vaguely defined "Islamic Republic" to be guided only by the principles of Shia Islam. This concept is not Khomeini's alone; it is a doctrine firmly embedded in Shiism.

The eloquent and charismatic Khomeini has amassed wide support among Iran's 35 million people, and has so intimidated the moderate opponents of the Shah that they have accepted his veto over their activities. He does not control the opposition to the Shah, however. Although he has become its foremost spokesman and symbol, the opposition remains an amorphous and disunited movement.

Khomeini seems supremely confident that he has unleashed the forces that will destroy the Shah. He recently boasted that the "latest riots herald the start of a gigantic explosion which will have incalculable effects."

Shia Islam - Khomeini's Base
Shiites constitute about 70 million of Islam's 500 million believers, and Iran is the center of Shia Islam, with 93 percent of its population belonging to the sect. Shiism is a heterodox sect - the orthodox

are the Sunnis - which split from the rest of the community in a quarrel in the 7th century over who should succeed Muhammad as leader of the Muslim world. The Shia espoused the cause of Muhammad's son-in-law Ali.

In part because of its minority status in the Muslim world and in part because of its role as the "out" part in Islamic history, Shiism has a tradition of support for revolutionary dissidence against the established order. In Iran the conservative Shia religious leadership has played a major role in promoting dissent in all of the major historical turning points during this century, including the 1906 revolution and the 1953 crisis.

Islam is general does not grant formal religious authority to an institutionalized clergy. A clergy (known collectively as the ulema) exists, and the laity willingly grants them considerable authority, but since theological doctrine denies to any man religious preeminence over his brother, there is virtually no hierarchical structure. The ulema does interpret Islamic law, however, and the Shiite clergy in particular has traditionally had great influence in day-to-day secular matters.

What hierarchy does exist in the ulema is determined on an ad hoc basis. When a clerical leader achieves a certain status and eminence, based on the writings, reputation, and the quality of advice he gives, his followers may refer to him as "ayatollah," and if enough of the respected theologicans and the community accept the title, it sticks. Shia Islam's foremost leader is called the "pishva-ye-moslemin" (leader of the Muslims) and is chosen by a consensus of the Shia community as expressed through the ulema. Such a consensus is hard to achieve. Since the death of the last pishva in 1971, the post has been vacant. Khomeini is widely regarded as the leading candidate, but the Iranian Government has maneuvered to block any attempt to give him the title. The "mojtahed" - almost invariable an ayatollah as well, is the legal specialist with the right of independent interpretation. At the other end of the hierarchy are the "mullahs" or lesser clergy, prayer leaders, and Koran chanters.

Several holy cities are of importance to the Shia. Qom, Mashad, and Esfahan in Iran are centers of Shia learning. Najaf and Karbala in Iraq, scenes of the deaths of early martyrs in the Shia tradition, are important pilgrimage sites.

Shia Islam has several important religious holidays. The most significant is the mourning month of Moharram, which commemorates the death in Kerbala of Ali's second son, Hussein. Moharram – and especially the day of Ashura, which this year falls on 11 December – is always a time of high tension in Iran.

Ayatollah Khomeini – Early Activities
Khomeini was born in 1901 in a clerical family in Golpayegan. His father, a mullah, was murdered by the local governor for his participation in the 1906 revolution. Khomeini studied at Qom and Esfahan and later at Najaf and Karbala. He taught Islamic law and theological doctrine in Qom until the early 1960s.

Khomeini has always been closely identified with the conservative dissident views of the ulema in the holy cities. Much of the Iranian clergy has been alienated from the Pahlavi dynasty when the Shah's father Reza Shah began to impose a rapid modernization program on the country in the 1930s. The religious leadership's opposition to the Shah (led at the time by Ayatollah Kashani) at least initially supported those forces backing Prime Minister Mossadegh in the early 1950s.

Khomeini began to preach and issue leaflets critical of the regime in 1962. By January 1963, Khomeini's violent attacks on the Shah's land reform program and women's rights brought him nation-wide attention and he emerged as the symbol of Shia opposition to the Shah. In June 1963, during the mourning month of Moharram and following several inflammatory anti-Shah sermons, Khomeini was arrested. The arrest led to rioting in Tehran, Qom, and other cities. Martial law was imposed in some areas. Released from jail in April 1964, Khomeini almost immediately returned to the attack against the Shah with more inflammatory blasts.

██

████████ ████████████████████████ In November 1964 he was
again arrested and was exiled to Turkey.

The Years in Exile

Khomeini continued his anti-Shah activities from his
exile in Turkey, bitterly attacking the Shah as a
pawn of the United States and Israel. In return, the
Shah labeled Khomeini a tool of the radical Arabs led
by Egyptian President Nasir.

In 1965 the Turkish Government requested the Iranian
Government to remove him from Turkey. Khomeini rejected
an Iranian Government offer to return home on condi-
tion that he not engage in any political activity.
Instead he went to Iraq, where he was accepted by an
Iraqi Government eager to support dissidence in Iran.

Khomeini's Platform

Khomeini's views have not changed significantly since
he first led the mobs against the Shah in 1963. As
a fundamentalist Shia, he is opposed to the social
reforms that the Shah has enacted in the last 15
years. Khomeini argues that the Shah is anti-Islamic
and that the monarchy as an institution has become
inherently opposed to Shia Islam. He often gives as
an example the Shah's abortive effort to change the
Iranian calendar from its Islamic base to one dating
from the first Imperial dynasty in Persian history.

An examination of Khomeini's speeches and pham-
phlets between 1963 and the present reveals these
persistent themes:

— Opposition to the Shah's efforts to give equal
rights to women. This issue is symbolized by Khomeini's
insistence that the Shah has forced Iranian women to
give up the veil.

— Opposition to the Shah's land reform policy.
Khomeini claims that it is the Shah's land reform
efforts that are the cause of Iran's inability since
the early 1970s to produce enough food to feed itself.*

* The Shah's land reform program was the centerpiece of the White
  Revolution launched in 1963. Land was taken from the landlords and
  distributed to the peasantry, who were then organized into rural
  co-ops. Much land was also taken from the control of the ulema. The

— The Shah's regime is dictatorial and corrupt. It has wasted Iran's wealth on expensive weapons and grandeoise economic projects to keep itself in power.
— General xenophobia, particularly anti-American-ism. Khomeini appeals to the deepseated Iranian belief that the Shah's government was imposed on the country by the US, that it does the bidding of the US, and that the Shah has "subjugated Iran to foreign powers."
— Opposition to the Shah's cooperation with Israel. An anti-Zionist, Khomeini charges that the Israelis are helping to keep the Shah in power.
— A negative attitude toward religious minor-ity groups. Besides the Jews who are associ-ated with Israel, Khomeini has attacked the Bahai sect. This is a traditional rallying cry for Shia fanatics because the Bahai have long been over-represented at the highest levels of Iranian society.

To replace the Pahlavis, Khomeini suggests the establishment of an Islamic Republic. Khomeini has been vague as to what this would mean in practice. He rejects any comparison with Saudi Arabia or Libya and claims that "the only reference point (would be) the time of the Prophet Muhammad and the Imam Ali."

Khomeini's ambiguity reflects a lack of interest in a specific political program. For him Shia Islam is a total social/political/economic system that needs no further explanation. In addition, he would risk losing support from some elements of the opposi-tion if he tried to spell out a detailed program of action. The widely based and badly divided opposition movement probably would not support any platform that went beyond simple opposition to the Shah remaining in power.

Khomeini claims that he is not an opponent of mod-ernizing Iran, but that Islam provides a sufficient

government's bureaucracy has taken the place of the former landlords, and many farmers are no more enamored of their new rulers than they were of their previous masters.

206

guide. He argues that the Shah has concentrated on grandiose projects that do not benefit the masses of Iranians, and has failed to move the country ahead because he has allowed "foreigners" to steal Iran's wealth. Khomeini promises social equality and political democracy in his new Iran. Khomeini has labeled President Carter's human rights policy a propaganda move and in at least one clandestine pamphlet attacked the President by name.

Khomeini's Constituency

The ulema have always been able to rally wide support for their position in Iran. A traditional bedrock of this support has been the small shopkeepers and merchants of the bazaars in the cities. They provide much of the "khums" – a religious tithe the pious give to the ulema. This close alliance between the bazaars and the clergy continues today, and much of the recent unrest in the major cities has originated in the bazaars.

Khomeini also can count on the support of many of his fellow clergymen. The mullahs support his appeals to Islamic law and tradition, and most seem to back him for the post of pishva. There are moderate religious leaders in Iran who have disagreed with Khomeini in the past, but increasingly they have lost the will and the ability to stand up to him.

The ulema is not a monolithic bloc in Iran. There are rivalries, and differences. But these seem to work against the Shah, as each faction tries to outdo the other in appealing to the mobs.

Khomeini draws his greatest popular support from the lower classes in the urban centers. In the last several years, and especially since the oil boom began in 1973, Tehran and other Iranian cities have grown enormously.* In this milieu of rapid change and social upheaval, many illiterate and often unemployed workers have turned to the traditional values of their religion. A miserable existence, with difficulty in

---

* The population of Tehran has risen from 200,000 in 1900, to 540,000 in 1945, to 2,720,000 in 1966, and to 4,400,000 in 1976.

securing justice from the state, has festered in this group. In Khomeini they see the symbol of Shia purity and orthodoxy.

Khomeini also seems to be developing more and more support among the university students. Traditionally a source of dissidence against the Shah, the student population is divided between leftists and supporters of the religious right.

Khomeini appears to have little support among senior officers of the Iranian military. Most of the leading commanders of the military regard Khomeini as a threat to their privileged status in the country and are worried that if Khomeini should establish his Islamic republic in Iran they would lose power.

Khomeini may have more support among junior officers and rank and file soldiers. ███████████████ ████████████████████ ███████████████████████ ████████████████████ Khomeini has publicly called upon "the soldiers and younger officers" to "join the people's struggle."

Attitude Toward Communism

Publicly Khomeini is opposed to any collaboration with Iran's communists, the Tudeh Party. Last October he explicitly critized the Tudeh for anti-Islamic beliefs and materialistic tendencies. Khomeini also blasted the Soviet Union for meddling in Iran's internal affairs in the past. In May he told Le Monde that "we will not collaborate with the Marxists even to overthrow the Shah."

There is little reason to doubt that Khomeini is philosophically opposed to communism as an atheistic force. Although the Tudeh has endorsed Khomeini's opposition to the Shah, there is little clear evidence to indicate the scope of the role the Tudeh Party has played in the disturbances that have beset Iran this year.

Khomeini in Power - Implications

Khomeini claims to have no interest in holding power himself. Nonetheless, a new regime in Tehran led by the civilian opposition would obviously be greatly influenced by his beliefs.* Any regime that replaces the Shah will have to deal with Khomeini and will come under great pressure to allow him to return to Iran and have a voice in policymaking.

If Khomeini is successful in unseating the Shah and comes to play an important, role in a future regime in Iran there would be serious policy implications for the United States. We would expect a regime under his influence to be xenophobic. Khomeini might:

- Move Iran away from its alignment with the US. While it is unlikely that Khomeini would put Iran in the Soviet orbit, he probably would like to see the country adopt a non-aligned posture.
- Cut off Iran's ties with Israel. Iran sells Israel most of its oil ████████████████████
- Curtail Iran's support for pro-Western regimes in the Persian Gulf like Oman. A radical Shia state might in time even try to support dissidence in the conservative Sunni dominated states like Saudi Arabia and Qatar which have Shia minorities.
- Renege on business deals with the US. Khomeini has stated that all of Iran's agreements with foreign states – including arms purchases from the US – will have to be renegotiated in Iran's favor if the Shah is removed. Khomeini might not feel restrained by Iran's dependence on foreign technology in the pursuit of a xenophobic foreign policy.
- Dependent on oil sales for the preponderant share of its revenues, a Khomeini-influenced regime would continue to sell oil to the US and its allies, perhaps with the exception of Israel. It might find it ideologically attractive, however, to slow the rate of industrialization and therefore institute more conservative petroleum extration practices.

The most significant implication for the US of a regime under the influence of Khomeini, however, is likely to be instability in Iran itself. In fact he is unlikely to be able to contain the revolutionary

---

* A devout Shiite is expected to choose a living Mojtahed to whom he will turn and whose advice he will follow in all matters. If strictly followed, this would place a clergyman at the elbow of every government official.

209

impetus he has helped to spark and might be preempted by a leftist regime or a military dictatorship.

Khomeini as an influential decisionmaker would probably find it difficult to reconcile his Shiite principles with the needs of a modern state - there is no precedent in Iran's modern history for what Khomeini proposes.

Notes

1. The best is Robert Jervis, *Why Intelligence Fails: Lessons from the Iranian Revolution and the Iraq War* (Ithaca: Cornell University Press, 2011).
2. 'Islam in Iran', CIA National Foreign Assessment Center [NFAC], March 1980, <https://www.cia.gov/library/readingroom/docs/CIA-RDP81B00401R000400110013-5.pdf> (last accessed 10 January 2020).
3. John F. Devlin and Robert L. Jervis, 'Analysis of NFAC's Performance on Iran's Domestic Crisis, Mid-1977 – 7 November 1978', 15 June 1979, <https://www.cia.gov/library/readingroom/docs/DOC_0001259322.pdf> (last accessed 10 January 2020).
4. Moin Bager, *Khomeini: Life of the Ayatollah* (London: I. B. Tauris, 2009).
5. 'Islam in Iran'.
6. Ibid.
7. Ibid.
8. For a good overview, see Charles Kurzman, *The Unthinkable Revolution in Iran* (Cambridge, MA: Harvard University Press, 2004).
9. Michael Axworthy, *Revolutionary Iran: A History of the Islamic Republic* (Oxford: Oxford University Press, 2013).
10. 'Iran: A Political Assessment', memorandum for D/ORPA, 9 August 1978, <https://www.cia.gov/library/readingroom/docs/CIA-RDP80T00634A000400010058-9.pdf> (last accessed 10 January 2020).
11. Cited in W. J. Daugherty, 'Behind the Intelligence Failure in Iran', *International Journal of Intelligence and Counterintelligence*, 14.4 (2001), p. 461.
12. 'The Opposition to the Shah', memorandum for Deputy Director for National Foreign Assessment, 30 October 1978, <https://www.cia.gov/library/readingroom/docs/CIA-RDP81B00401R002000120002-8.pdf> (last accessed 10 January 2020).
13. Devlin and Jervis, 'Analysis of NFAC's Performance'.
14. 'The Politics of Ayatollah Ruhollah Khomeini', CIA NFAC, 20 November 1978, <https://www.cia.gov/library/readingroom/docs/CIA-RDP80T00634A000500010002-9.pdf> (last accessed 10 January 2020).
15. For more, see 'Two Weeks in January: America's Secret Engagement with Khomeini', *BBC Persia*, 3 June 2016, <www.bbc.co.uk/news/world-us-canada-36431160> (last accessed 10 January 2020).
16. Details in 'Two Weeks in January'.

13   The CIA and the Soviet Invasion of Afghanistan

In December 1979, the Soviet Union launched a major offensive inside Afghanistan. What was, on paper, a one-sided military conflict would rage on for ten years, becoming for the Russians what Vietnam had been to the Americans. The Soviet army fought to maintain communist control of Afghanistan, suppress dissent and improve the Soviet Union's geopolitical standing. For the West, the war for Afghanistan was seen as that of a minor power resisting a superpower aggressor – and an opportunity.

It would soon become much more than a fight for one country, with the mountains of Afghanistan becoming the battleground for a significant Cold War proxy conflict. Propped up by American (and in particular CIA) support, the religious warriors of the Afghan Mujahedin took the fight to the Soviet forces. Armed with an internationally supplied armoury of the most basic but also, eventually, sophisticated weaponry, as well as other forms of equipment, medical supplies and military training, the Mujahedin were able to hold the Soviets at bay for a decade. For the United States, this was an opportunity to embarrass and weaken the Soviet Union and its communist cause; yet no significant attention was paid to what a generation of fighters, emboldened and trained, might do once the conflict was over.

The Soviet intervention in December 1979 came at a critical juncture in the evolution of the Cold War. Just as the era of détente was coming to an end, attention was temporarily diverted elsewhere. The news of the Ayatollah Khomeini's Islamic Republic in Iran (see Chapter 12) had been greeted enthusiastically in Moscow, with the Soviet leadership encouraging its anti-Western sentiments. Despite the fact that the Tudeh Party, Iran's communist movement, was its most natural ally, for the Soviet Union the maxim of 'my enemy's enemy is my friend' was a powerful one. Yet it would be support for another communist party that would trigger the intervention in Afghanistan.

The People's Democratic Party of Afghanistan had been created in 1965 with the support and encouragement of Moscow. It quickly splintered into warring offshoots, with the Khalq faction eventually consolidating power in April 1978. On 30 April the new communist government formed the Democratic Republic of Afghanistan, which was recognised a few hours later by the Soviet Union. The new regime was brutal, conducting a purge of the armed forces and executing thousands in its pursuit of land reform. A number of disputes arose over the reform agenda between the Khalq faction, other communists (particularly the Parcham faction) and the Afghan Islamic fundamentalists. By late 1978 many parts of Afghanistan had, as a result, descended into civil war.[1] In December 1978, largely as a result, the Afghan and Soviet governments signed a Friendship Treaty, a component of which was a Soviet guarantee to offer military assistance when requested.

The situation remained tense throughout the first half of 1979. Premier Brezhnev sent military advisors and a limited detachment to guard the main airports in April, but it soon become clear that this was far from sufficient. In Moscow, the Politburo debated whether or not to accede to Afghan demands to send troops to supplement and strengthen the position of the Khalq. Brezhnev wavered and avoided a full-scale military commitment. By the autumn of 1979, however, it had become apparent that the Afghan government had lost control of almost all the territory outside the cities, and that its leadership was detested by the majority of the population. Once more, Brezhnev was reluctant to authorise a military intervention. By December the situation in Afghanistan had reached a critical juncture, and the decision was finally taken to act: the Soviet Union began to concentrate significant forces around several strategic positions on the Afghan periphery. Finally, on 25 December 1979, the first Soviet airborne forces landed on Afghan territory.[2]

The CIA had been monitoring the situation for quite some time. In the months and weeks prior to the Soviet invasion the CIA was able to furnish policymakers with impressively accurate forecasts on what was going to happen. In the period immediately prior to the December attack the White House was warned that not only was a large-scale intervention possible, but that some small Soviet combat units were already in the country. In fact, so pleased was the CIA with its reporting that within a fortnight of the invasion the DCI, Stansfield Turner, wrote to relevant staff to congratulate them on their performance. The first chapter reference document attached provides Turner's note, as well as a brief chronology of the warning assessments that the CIA had provided.[3] Related to this is the second chapter reference document: an assessment written in early January 1980, which accurately reveals the Soviet intentions behind the invasion.[4]

Within two days of the attack Soviet troops had taken control of most of the major governmental, military and media headquarters, including the Presidential Palace. In a coup in the capital Kabul, the Afghan President,

Amin, was assassinated and the existing government replaced. For the Soviet Union it had been inconceivable that communism could be maintained and secured without replacing the current, universally unpopular leadership. At the same time, elements of the Red Army crossed into Afghanistan from the north. Further reinforcements arrived over the following hours, and within a week of the start of operations there were over 60,000 military personnel in the country.[5]

From the outset, Afghanistan presented problems for the Soviets. The terrain was inhospitable, making it difficult to manoeuvre, and there arose a significant resistance movement. Indeed, the Afghan resistance was different to anything the Soviet Union had previously faced. Not only did it vehemently oppose the indigenous communist government and the imperialist Soviet Union, but it was equally fuelled by religious ideology. Very quickly an opportunity presented itself: the large-scale arming of the resistance fighters, the Mujahedin, was a means to embarrass the Soviet Union and its global political brand as well as ruining the morale of its military.

The opportunity was not lost on the United States. By the time the Soviet Union invaded in December 1979, the US had already been arming the Mujahedin for six months.[6] These efforts were, however, on the small side, certainly in comparison to what would follow. It would not be until late 1982 that the intelligence community would grasp just how ill-prepared and armed the Mujahedin were and, from that point onwards, the flow of weapons increased significantly.

The Soviet Army enjoyed early successes. By the early summer of 1980 it had taken control of many major cities and access routes. The Mujahedin had split into various different groups, dispersed across the country but, importantly for their cause, their numbers were swelled by a steady and significant influx of foreign fighters, amassed to combat the Soviet forces. As the number of Mujahedin grew, so too did the flow of arms from the US. By late 1983, as the third attached CIA assessment makes clear, the US policy had shown signs of success. 'The resistance', it began, 'is an effective guerrilla force that controls much of the country.' Indeed, barring any significant change in Soviet policy, 'the resistance will continue at a high enough level to prevent a significant improvement in the Soviet position'.[7]

The Russians were forced to respond. A few months later they increased their own troop contingent in the country, but this was not significant enough to turn the tide decisively in their favour. Two years later, in late 1986, the CIA sought to increase the pressure on Soviet troops by denying them airborne mobility through delivering to the resistance the modern anti-aircraft 'Stinger' missile. They employed these new tools to great operational and tactical success. The simple outcome of all this was a relative stalemate: the Russians could not be forced out militarily, but

213

equally there could be no hope of destroying the Mujahedin without a huge increase in forces. This quandary came at a time of change in Moscow: the ailing leaderships of Brezhnev, Andropov and Chernenko had passed and the new man in power, Mikhail Gorbachev, sought a new strategy for the conflict.[8]

In 1986, responsibility for the conduct of the war passed to the Afghan armed forces, thereby offering Gorbachev a possible exit strategy for Soviet involvement. Beginning in 1988 the Soviet Union gradually began to withdraw its forces, with the final troops leaving in February 1989.[9] Despite the new strategy that Gorbachev instigated upon coming to power, the US continued to send arms, increasing in volume and technical sophistication throughout the conflict. The end of the war in 1989 marked a decade of involvement for the Soviet Union.

What had begun as a militarily straightforward question had turned into an intense political and military embarrassment: the might of the Soviet army could not overcome groups of resistance fighters, while the communist leadership it fought to maintain singularly failed to be accepted. In Afghanistan the CIA continued to support the Afghan rebels beyond the Soviet withdrawal, though this would not be for long.[10] Kabul, for instance, finally fell to the Mujahedin in April 1992. With the war over, the majority of those who had flocked to Afghanistan to fight the Soviets fell silent; but many would resurface a few years later, when war broke out in the Balkans and once more a political skirmish became enmeshed with religious overtones.[11] The skills learnt amongst the mountains of Afghanistan, armed and trained by the CIA, would again be used over a decade later against another invading force – this time the US, in the aftermath of the 9/11 attacks.

```
        THE DIRECTOR OF CENTRAL INTELLIGENCE
              WASHINGTON, D. C. 20505
National Intelligence Officers          3 January 1980

MEMORANDUM FOR: Director of Central Intelligence
               Deputy Director of Central
               Intelligence
THROUGH        : Deputy Director for National Foreign
               Assessment
FROM           : Richard Lehman
               National Intelligence Officer for
               Warning
SUBJECT        : Strategic Warning Staff's
               Performance
```

214

1. <u>Action Requested</u>: That you sign the attached memorandum to Director for Strategic Warning Staff.

2. <u>Background</u>: The Strategic Warning Staff was the prime mover, and at times the sole voice of dissent, during the period leading up to massive Soviet intervention in Afghanistan. Starting in August, the Staff attended meetings, wrote memoranda to the National Intelligence Officer for Warning, requested additional collection, and generally kept the pot boiling when the conventional view of the community was one of complacency. A brief summary of the Staff's memoranda is attached.

3. As a direct result of the Staff's analysis and constant attention to the more ominous alternatives, the Intelligence Community's performance can only be termed a success: we issued Alert Memoranda on 14 September, 19 December, and 25 December. Our policy-makers were well warned.

4. In view of the amount of attention devoted to "intelligence failures," it seems appropriate to recognize a resounding success. To that end, I recommend you sign the accompanying memorandum.

Richard Lehman

Attachments:

A.   Summary of Staff's Memoranda

B.   Letter for DCI Signature

All Portions of this Memorandum are classified <u>SECRET</u>

SUBJECT: Strategic Warning Staff's Performance (NFAC #0027/80)
Distribution:
1 - Addressee
1 - DCI
1 - DDCI
1 - ER
1 - NIO/W Chrono
1 - A/NIO/W
1 - NFAC Registry

SUMMARY
USSR-Afghanistan Memoranda from Strategic Warning
Staff

10 August :   There is a strong likelihood that the Soviets will commit a limited amount of combat forces, and are likely to find themselves being drawn into a larger operation.
(to NIO/W)

24 August :   A number of events in recent days point to an impending increase in Soviet military aid - suggesting that the decision to increase support has in fact already been made.
(to NIO/W)

28 August :   A request that attaché tasking for Kabul be expanded to include Soviet air activity was submitted to DIA when the Strategic Warning Staff discovered that Soviet flights were not being detected by technical means.
(to DIA)

6 September : We are not arguing that the Soviets have made a decision to commit combat troops (although they may have) but that they have made decisions which indicate they are <u>prepared</u> to introduce forces if that is what it takes to preserve their position.
(to NIO/W)

14 September : On balance, taking into account the evidence available to us, we believe there is a better than even chance that the report of Soviet troop movement to Afghanistan is accurate.
(to NIO/W)

21 September : Following is a chronology of Soviet military activities in the week which we view as indications of possible Soviet intentions to introduce combat forces into Afghanistan.
(to NIO/W)

26 October : We are concerned that in the month that has been elapsed since the USSR-Afghanistan Alert Memorandum (14 September), the Soviets appear to have put themselves in position to move a larger ground combat force into Afghanistan in less time with less advance warning.
(to NIO/W, readdressed to Warning Working Group on 29 October)

12 December: Continuing analysis leads me to believe we should immediately produce a follow-up to the 14 September Alert Memorandum. The Soviets appear to be preparing to introduce sizeable combat forces into Afghanistan.
(to NIO/W)

13 December: I left the meeting yesterday with the feeling that we had not accomplished much. Most of those present seemed to continue to hold the view that the Soviets are moving tentatively. By their actions, the Soviets have indicated they are willing to take the large political step of putting their own combat units into a foreign country.
(to NIO/W)

14 December: We believe the additional indications we have detected in recent days are

particularly significant in that they suggest that the forces to be committed come from units other than just the 105th Guards Airborne Division.
(to NIO/W)

MEMORANDUM FOR : Director, Strategic Warning Staff
SUBJECT   : USSR-Afghanistan

The performance of your Staff during the period preceding massive Soviet intervention in Afghanistan was exemplary. Through your attendance at various meetings and your memoranda to the National Intelligence Officer for Warning, you caused the Intelligence Community to consider alternate, more ominous, hypotheses. As a result, our policymakers were warned as early as 14 September of the possibility that Soviet troops would be employed in Afghanistan. It is encouraging to witness such a resounding intelligence success, for which you deserve a large share of the credit. Well done.

STANSFIELD TURNER

All Portions of this memorandum
are classified SECRET

The Soviet Invasion of Afghanistan

On 27 December the Soviet Union toppled the government of President Hafizullah Amin and installed a new regime headed by Babrak Karmal. The coup was supported by a major Soviet military operation designed to ensure that the new regime retains power. The open-ended nature of the USSR's commitment to control Afghanistan in the face of what is likely to be protracted insurgency means that Soviet military forces will be involved there for the foreseeable future. This in turn will have profound implications for southwest Asia and could substantially influence the future course of Soviet foreign policy as well.

Soviet Motivations

The Soviet invasion followed almost two years of gradually increasing Soviet military support for the Marxist Afghan regime that took power as a result of the April 1978 revolution. But the instability of Marxist Afghan politics, the ineffectiveness of the new leadership and its counterproductive policies, and a growing tribal-based insurgency threatened the pro-Soviet regime's control over the country.

Moscow was deeply concerned throughout 1979 with the regime's ability to hold onto power. Moscow recognized that the Afghanistan military was becoming increasingly ineffective and that the insurgents were extending their operations throughout the country.

Throughout the year, the Soviets tried to get an effective government in Kabul that could deal with the growing problems. The Soviets wanted a regime better able to win military and tribal support. Moscow was involved in intrigues with former President Taraki to oust Amin in the summer of 1979. But Amin turned the tables on Moscow and, in a bloody coup in mid-September, ousted Taraki and his supporters. Amin's move - only days after Soviet President Brezhnev met with and personally endorsed Taraki - may have added a personal dimension to Moscow's interest in removing him.

The Soviets thought Amin was alienating the military, was failing to establish broader political support, and was unresponsive to Soviet counsel. Moscow probably thought his government was losing ground against the insurgents.

The Soviets probably considered installing a non-Marxist government in Kabul. But Moscow must have decided that it needed greater control over Afghanistan than reliance on such elements would have allowed.

Soviet Security Concerns

In the first instance, the Soviets probably were motivated to move into Afghanistan less by the positive benefits to them of maintaining a Marxist regime in power, than by the negative costs if it had been defeated. They probably perceived that the continued

219

deterioration of the security situation would at best have led to prolonged fighting, further coups, and political chaos. At worst, they may have thought it would have led to the installation of an anti-Soviet regime that might have sought to develop ties with Iran, the United States and China.

Such a development would have been a blow to Soviet prestige and could have damaged Soviet credibility with other client regimes, which might reassess their ties with Moscow if the USSR failed to save a revolutionary government on its very borders. Coming at a time when the United States was beginning to reassert its presence in the Indian Ocean, the Soviets might have seen it as creating an image of Soviet weakness.

Moscow has claimed that it intervened in response to foreign intervention in Afghanistan and because the country might have become a "bridgehead" for activities by Soviet "enemies" against the USSR itself. While the Soviets probably do not believe such hyperbole, an unfriendly government in Afghanistan would have put another hostile or unstable regime along the USSR's southern border. The prospect of an unstable regime alongside Iran probably particularly troubled Moscow. The political disarray that has accompanied the hostage crisis in Tehran may have intensified these fears.

Finally, Moscow may have been concerned by long-term implications for Russian domination of Soviet Central Asia. Although Moscow is not now confronted with significant unrest among its own Muslim population, the predominantly Russian leadership may have been troubled by the possibility of having yet another militantly Islamic state on its border.

Potential Benefits

Moscow probably also saw geopolitical benefits from dramatic, forceful action. It would be a clear demonstration of Soviet power – and willingness to use it – that would have a positive impact on neighboring states and on Soviet clients. It would contribute to Moscow's strategy of encircling China.

Moscow may have thought Soviet control over Afghanistan

would pressure Iran and Pakistan to accommodate to Soviet policies. It would leave Pakistan isolated between a pro-Soviet India and a Soviet-controlled Afghanistan. In the event that either Iran or Pakistan fragmented or deteriorated into political chaos, it would provide Moscow with a potential bridgehead for extending its influence in such areas as Baluchcestan. Over the longer run, Moscow may have thought control of Afghanistan could contribute to Moscow's longstanding attempts to improve its position in the Persian Gulf and Indian Ocean.

Opportune Timing
The Soviets undoubtedly saw almost no risk of outside military reaction. For one thing, Tehran and Washington were preoccupied with the hostage problem.

Indeed, Moscow might have thought the United States could be induced to acquiesce in the Soviet invasion in return for Soviet nonobstruction of US pressure on Iran. Furthermore, the West was occupied with the Christmas season. This would lead to a less intense foreign reaction. Moscow's Czech experience – when the sharp Western reaction soon led to business as usual – probably also comforted the USSR.

The Soviets probably thought the negative trends in Soviet relations with the West made this as good a time as any for its move. The Soviet action came at a low point in US-Soviet relations. The Soviets saw the SALT treaty in deep trouble and probably expected few new initiatives from the United States during an election year. Moscow said the NATO theater nuclear force decision had "destroyed the basis" for serious negotiations in West Europe on Brezhnev's arms proposals. Relations with China were already bad, and Moscow had no expectation that the negotiations with Beijing set to resume in early 1980 were going anywhere.

In the subcontinent, Moscow probably recognized that Pakistan would be apprehensive, but may have thought the strains in US-Pakistan ties over nuclear proliferation and the Embassy burning made a US-Pakistani rapproachement unlikely. The Soviets may have reasoned that Islamabad would eventually come to terms with the Soviet action. In any event, India has long been the focus of Soviet interest on the subcontinent. The increasingly good prospects for Indira Gandhi's return to power made it likely that the next Indian government would be more pro-Soviet than either the Desai or Charan Singh regimes.

The Soviet Operation

The Soviets have undoubtedly been examining their military options in Afghanistan for some time. During his stay in Afghanistan in late summer and early fall, Soviet Army Chief Pavlovskiy probably had as one of his tasks contingincy planning for a military occupation of Afghanistan.

The final Soviet Politburo-level decision to invade was probably made in late November or early December. This would have been around the time of the 28 November Central Committee Plenum and the return to Moscow on 6 December of Ambassador Dobrynin – who probably was asked to assess likely US reactions. Increased urban violence in Kabul, rumors of military disaffection and continued insurgent activity during the period may have helped push the Soviet leaders toward their decision.

Military Preparations

Soviet military preparations for the move entered into high gear in early December. The Soviets made carefully and systematically to plan and prepare the operation.

In early December some 1,500 Soviet troops were sent to Bagram Airfield north of Kabul to join 400 lightly armed troops that had been there since summer. We suspect that Moscow obtained Amin's approval on the grounds that these troops were to protect Soviet advisers and to ensure the security of his regime.

Additional Soviet airborne forces apparently began to prepare for the operation in mid-December. Ground and tactical air combat forces were assembled. Motorized rifle divisions at Termez and Kushka were mobilized

222

and moved to forward staging areas near the Afghan-Soviet border. Soviet reservists were recalled; some interviewed in Kabul at year's end had been activated within the previous 20 days. Tactical aviation forces opposite Afghanistan were reinforced.

The Coup

The massive airlift of troops and equipment into Afghanistan began on 24 December. The operation provides a vivid example of Moscow's ability to organize and rapidly move an intervention force, and underscores the growth in the Soviet airlift capability during the 1970s.

Airborne units in the western and south central USSR flew to Afghanistan and airborne units already in Turkestan also moved into Afghanistan. At least two regiments – about 4,000 troops equipped with armored vehicles – went to Kabul, while smaller units went to Shindand and Qandahar.

The Soviets continued to mislead Amin about the nature of their movements. On 23 December, Pravda, possibly for Amin's benefit, denied there were Soviet "combat troops" in Afghanistan. Amin may have accepted Kremlin assurances that the Soviet forces were there to guarantee the security of his regime and that some of the flights carried new equipment for his forces. The Soviets apparently got Amin to move to the Darulaman Palace, a residence on the outskirts of Kabul. Some reports indicate they did so on the pretext that this would give Amin better security, but actually to make it easier to eliminate him. Furthermore, on the afternoon of the coup, the Soviet communications minister met with Amin, apparently to indicate that it was business as usual. The Soviets also tricked Afghan army units by taking away their weapons under the pretense that they would give them new ones.

With airborne forces in Kabul, the Soviets moved quickly on 27 December to topple Amin and replace him with Babrak Karmal. An airborne unit went to the People's Place – the Afghan seat of government. Airborne troops along with some Babrak partisans

223

went to the Darulaman Palace and battled loyal Afghan forces. Amin was apparently executed on the spot. Heavy fighting broke out near the Kabul radio station and in other sections of the city, but Soviet troops quickly got the upper hand. By 28 December, fighting was sporadic and the Soviets had control. They manned most strategic points and encircled some recalcitrant Afghan garrisons.

Babrak Karmal – who had earlier been in exile in Eastern Europe – apparently arrived in Kabul by plane from the USSR soon after the coup. His initial broadcasts appear to have been tape recordings carried by radio stations in the USSR. His supporters, as well as other Marxist enemies of Amin, some of whom may have been in hiding at the Soviet Embassy, moved quickly to take over government administration.

In coordination with events in Kabul, the Soviets moved two Ground Forces divisions into Afghanistan on 28 and 29 December. The Termez division drove south into the Kabul area. Prior to the movement of this division, Soviet troops secured the difficult Termez-Kabul road, including the Salang Pass. The division from Kushka drove south to Heart – some of its elements also moved into Shindand and other areas.

Some Afghan forces apparently offered limited resistance that cost the Soviets several hundred casualties, especially in the street fighting in Kabul. The number two man in the Soviet MVD (the internal police), Lt. Gen. Paputin, apparently was killed in the fighting. Paputin had been in Kabul in early December, probably to survey the scene for the coup. He may have had the job of getting Amin. Aside from some relatively minor incidents, insurgent tribal forces did not attempt to tackle the heavily armed Soviet troops.

By 1 December, the Soviets had seized control of key cities, airfields and communications routes. But they will face the hard task of subduing the fiercely independent Afghans and considerable additional fighting against the tribal based and Islamic insurgency is in store.

Notes

1. For more, see Henry S. Bradsher, *Afghan Communism and Soviet Intervention* (Oxford: Oxford University Press, 1999). See also M. Hassan Kakar, *Afghanistan: The Soviet Invasion and the Afghan Response, 1979–1982* (London: University of California Press, 1995).
2. M. W. Wolf, 'Stumbling Towards War: The Soviet Decision to Invade Afghanistan', *Past Imperfect*, 12 (2006), pp. 1–19.
3. 'The Soviet Invasion of Afghanistan', CIA report, 16 January 1980.
4. Memorandum for the Director of Central Intelligence, 3 January 1980.
5. For the best overview see Rodric Braithwaite, *Afgantsy: The Russians in Afghanistan, 1979–89* (Oxford: Oxford University Press, 2011).
6. The best account of this arming, as well as the impact it would have in the decades after the decision, is Steve Coll, *Ghost Wars: The Secret History of the CIA, Afghanistan and Bin Laden from the Soviet Invasion to September 10, 2001* (London: Penguin, 2005).
7. 'Afghanistan: Prospects for the Resistance', NIE 37-83, 4 October 1983, <https://www.cia.gov/library/readingroom/docs/CIA-RDP86T00302R000400 570001-8.pdf> (last accessed 10 January 2020).
8. For more detail, see C. F. Ostermann, 'New Evidence on the War in Afghanistan', *Cold War International History Project*, 14.15 (2011), pp. 139–272.
9. For more, see Gregory Feifer, *The Great Gamble: The Soviet War in Afghanistan* (New York: HarperCollins, 2009).
10. Tim Weiner, *Legacy of Ashes: The History of the CIA* (Penguin: London, 2007), p. 421.
11. Evan F. Kohlmann, *Al-Qaida's Jihad in Europe: The Afghan-Bosnian Network* (London: Berg, 2004).

14   Martial Law in Poland

There is perhaps no greater value that an intelligence agency can provide than a well-placed, reliable source at a time of unrest and uncertainty. For an agency focused primarily on human intelligence (humint) like the CIA, having an agent in place, one who can be hurriedly tasked and has a rapid means of passing information, as a crisis develops, provides the best example of why it is invaluable to US policymaking. The events in Poland in early 1980 were a classic example of this. The episode is important not only as a case study in humint, but also because of how it presaged the growing nationalist sentiments and discontent within the Soviet Union that would come to mark the 1980s.

Poland had been one of the original and more involved nations within the communist, Soviet bloc. Throughout the 1970s food supplies in Poland, like many other places within Eastern Europe, became more and more stretched and so prices began to rise. Quite unrelated to this a movement began to grow within one of the main dockyards which, in late 1980, was crystallised into the first non-communist union, Solidarity. Amongst its major objectives was not to replace communism *per se*, but rather to foster support for the growing discontent at rising food prices, growing unemployment and the shrinking economy. As its membership swelled its focus began to shift, and increasingly it became a mouthpiece for anti-Soviet sentiments.[1]

In Moscow the reaction was one of indecision and uncertainty, much as it had been with previous signs of discontent in the past. The leaders of the more hardline Satellite states urged a forceful response while Brezhnev dithered. Ultimately the answer came from within Poland itself: in late October 1980 the government began plans for imposing martial law. In Moscow there was general support for the Polish government and its decision. Unlike the previous instances in Hungary (1956), Czechoslovakia (1968) and Afghanistan (1979), this time around the government in question worked closely with the Kremlin in coordinating a response. The assurances provided by the government in Warsaw – that matters could be controlled without recourse to military intervention – persuaded Brezhnev to allow martial law to proceed.[2]

However, government control was only partial, and in February 1981, following fresh strikes, the Polish prime minister was replaced by the more hardline General Wojciech Jaruzelski, who had been Minister of National Defence since 1968. Almost immediately a series of raids and arrests were made, including some of the leading members of Solidarity. A general strike that had been threatened for the end of March 1981 was called off, while in Moscow, renewed plans for an intervention force, masquerading as a Warsaw Pact exercise, were suspended. Once more the expectation was that the Polish leadership, under President Stanislaw Kania and then Jaruzelski, could contain matters and could be relied upon to request Russian assistance should the need arise.

A few months beforehand, in November 1980, Ronald Reagan had been elected as the next president of the United States. His inauguration in January 1981 would signify a change to the tempo and rhetoric of the Cold War. Reagan's predecessor, Jimmy Carter, had issued a few statements in late 1980 decrying the potential likelihood of Soviet aggression, but these had achieved little. Reagan's initial moves echoed these and throughout the spring and summer of 1981 attention was focused on what the Polish government, and by association the Soviet Union, might do.

Assisting the US position were a variety of different sources, the most important of whom was Colonel Ryszard Kuklinski. Kuklinski first volunteered to work for the CIA in the early 1970s. In a letter to the US Embassy in Bonn, West Germany, in which he volunteered his services, Kuklinski claimed that his motivation was the Russian suppression of the Czechoslovakian uprising in 1968 and the crushing of protests in Poland in 1970.[3] Over an espionage career that spanned a decade, Kuklinski passed across an estimated 35,000 pages of sensitive and restricted documents. Unquestionably his greatest contribution was during the ongoing crisis in Poland, and as a senior staff officer he had access not only to Polish military planning, but also political and technical information. Kuklinski was able to communicate with his CIA case officers via a specially constructed encrypted communications device, and this would prove to be invaluable when he got wind of what was being planned.[4]

Some of the most recent material released shows what a cunning operator Kuklinski was. Files declassified in 2017 in Poland focus on the counterintelligence efforts of Polish intelligence. Nine of these files in particular detail the measures taken to monitor and follow a known CIA officer in the US Embassy in Warsaw, Sue Burggraf. Burggraf was the first full-time CIA operational officer to work in Poland, and she was given the role of being Kuklinski's case officer. What is remarkable about these new files is not the extent to which the Polish secret police had Burggraf under surveillance, but the simple fact that it never got wind of who she might be running.[5]

Material provided by Kuklinski showed that in the summer of 1981 the Soviet leadership was exerting great pressure on the Polish government to use force to crush members of the Solidarity movement. Other information revealed the measures that the Soviet military machine was putting into place to get ready for a possible armed intervention. Taken together, Kuklinski's reporting made it abundantly clear that the Polish leadership was under severe pressure to impose martial law.[6] That this was a possible outcome was certainly not lost on the CIA. An assessment towards the end of August 1981, reproduced as a chapter reference document, has this subject as its title.

Some of Kuklinski's most interesting information was on Jaruzelski and the demons tearing him apart: on the one hand, he informed the CIA, Jaruzelski agreed with those in the Kremlin that Solidarity had to be crushed, but on the other he did not think that martial law would achieve this objective.[7] With growing discontent within Poland, in October 1981 President Kania resigned and was replaced by Jaruzelski. This was a significant change, for Kania had been consistently against using force. Jaruzelski initially attempted to work with Solidarity to improve the economic conditions within Poland, but it soon became clear that the movement's demands were undeliverable. With increasing calls from some members for political reform, and with internal discontent within the Party on the rise, Jaruzelski was left in a precarious position. In late November, desperate to stem the economic decline, the government adopted a tougher new stance that could only realistically be employed through force. To achieve this, in mid-December 1981, with Soviet support, the Polish government announced the imposition of martial law.

The response was immediate. The Solidarity movement was declared illegal and its leaders were arrested. Security forces forcibly squashed many of the opposition groups distributed throughout Poland, with riot police deployed to prevent strikes. Large numbers were arrested and there were various skirmishes, resulting in scores of deaths. For Kuklinski, this was the ultimate Polish betrayal to the Soviets. The martial law plans themselves had been worked out in great detail in advance, and had almost entirely been revealed to the CIA courtesy of Kuklinski. The first chapter reference document makes this clear, though it obfuscates the provenance of the source. On the other hand, it does suggest something of the quality of the reporting in saying that it has been assigned a 'codeword', given the 'extremely sensitive agent sources of CIA's Directorate of Operations'.

Despite its foreknowledge of the plans for martial law and the suggestions of its actual instigation, the US intelligence community was still caught off guard by its announcement in December 1981. The analytical reasoning behind this has been explored in great depth elsewhere, but the logic concerns the fact that it was assumed by the Poles that martial law would not achieve the desired aims, and it was therefore considered unlikely to be pursued by analysts in Langley.[8] There are hints of this in the second chapter reference document, which is a special report by the CIA's 'Strategic Warning Staff' on events in Poland. It was written in November 1980 and raised the very real prospect of martial law whilst also discussing how little advance notice might be provided.

As it was, the Reagan administration did little, and was largely a passive observer as events unfolded. In Poland, Kuklinski, fearing that a Polish counter-intelligence investigation had identified him as a CIA agent, escaped. His defection to the United States, where he resided until his death in 2004, and his role in passing information has been the source of much controversy: was he a Polish patriot, seeking the best for his country and attempting to achieve this by getting the US to assist in the demise of communism? Or was he a traitor to his homeland for conspiring with a foreign power? The consensus is the former, but to many he remains a polarising figure. Kuklinski's role became known surprisingly quickly, and prompted debate both in the US and in Poland.[9] The episode is interesting for a number of reasons, not least because it underlines that the product of first-rate human agents does not always translate to first-rate assessments. It also raises questions about the legacy of agents and their reputation, as well as the impact of intelligence on policy.

Martial law itself remained in place until July 1983. Quite what it achieved in the longer term is debatable, and certainly it did little to slow down the rise of nationalism, anti-Soviet sentiments or the eventual collapse of communism. The third chapter reference document, entitled simply 'Poland: Prospects for Solidarity', is a CIA assessment produced at around this time. It considers the impact of martial law and the future of the Solidarity movement, assessing that in many ways it did achieve its aim in the sense that Solidarity 'cannot be resurrected'. At the same time, importantly, it concluded that a 'younger generation' of Poles have become influenced by the events and would 'become permanent additions to the Polish political spectrum'. Prescient words indeed.

229

```
             CENTRAL INTELLIGENCE AGENCY
               WASHINGTON, D.C. 20505
```

┌─────────────────────────────┐
│ RELEASE IN PART   │
│ EXEMPTION: HR70-14   │
│ DATE: 08-19-2008   │
└─────────────────────────────┘

                                        25 AUG 1981

MEMORANDUM FOR: The Director of Central
                 Intelligence
                 The Deputy Director of Central
                 Intelligence
FROM: ████████████
                 Chief, ████████████████ OSR
SUBJECT: Martial Law in Poland

1. The attached memorandum prepared by the _____ of
the Office of Strategic Research describes the major
facets of Poland's proposed martial law program and
discusses the Polish leadership's feelings toward its
implementation. It also describes possible Soviet
reactions to the program. The Polish government,
reluctant to impose such an extensive and pervasive
program because of the program because of the risks
involved, may be leaning toward the implementation
of only parts of it, or of less stringent versions.
Polish Armed Forces, considered effective if used
early enough in a crisis and in a positive manner, may
not be able to counter an on-going violent outbreak.
The Soviets probably feel that martial law in Poland
would increase the chances that their forces might be
called upon to assist, or ultimately to restore order
unilaterally.
2. This is a ████████ report. For convenience of reference by NFIB agencies, the codeword ████ has been
assigned to the product of certain extremely sensitive agent source of CIA's Directorate of Operations.
The word ████████ is classified ████████ and is to be
used only among persons authorized to read and handle
this material.

3. This memorandum must be handled in accordance with established security procedures. It may not be reproduced for any purpose. Queries regarding the substance of this memorandum may be addressed to the Chief, ██████████. Requests for extra copies or for utilization of any part of this report in any other form should be addressed to the Deputy Director for Operations.

SUBJECT: Marital Law in Poland
Distribution:
   The Secretary of State
   The Secretary of Defense
   Director of Central Intelligence
   Director of Intelligence and Research Department of State
   Director, Defense Intelligence Agency
   Director, National Security Agency
   Deputy Director of Central Intelligence
   Director, National Foreign Assessment Center

CENTRAL INTELLIGENCY AGENT
WASHINGTON, D.C. 20505

25 AUG 1981

MEMORANDUM
SUBJECT: Martial Law 1n Poland
1. Over the past year, the Polish government has been concerned that it might have to take strong measures to maintain its authority. Sensitive documents reveal that the Polish government has engaged in extensive contingency planning for the imposition of a severe martial law program in Poland. Enacted in full, this program would impose military authority over large sectors of the populace through military duty, "special work obligations," and changes in basic Polish law. Because of the risks involved, the government has been reluctant to impose the program except as a last resort. Recent information indicates that the Jaruzelski regime might now be prepared

to impose emergency measures that could include parts of the program. The Soviets would welcome the Polish government's using strong repressive efforts to restore its authority, but in doing so, must recognize that failure of the program could require them to intervene at a time other than that of their own choosing.

NOTE: This memorandum was prepared 1n the Office of Strategic Research, National Foreign Assessment Center by ▮▮▮▮▮▮▮.

The Martial Law Plan

2. Martial law would include a callup of reserves and a nationwide conscription of unlimited duration for both military and civil defense duty. In addition, specified sectors of the economy would become "militarized units." Workers in such units would be obligated to continue their assigned labor and be subject to involuntary reassignments, while losing any right to strike or quit. Under some conditions, they could also be forced to remain in billets at the unit. Severe penalties, including death, could be imposed for noncompliance.

3. There would also be many changes in the application of Polish law, including: legal authority to prohibit internal movement; censorship and monitoring of all forms of communication; provisions for obligatory deliveries of agricultural products; and the suspension of the activities of existing legitimate associations (including trade unions but specifically excepting churches and religious organizations). Provision would be made for criminal matters to be dealt with by summary proceedings, which would have the authority to deal with crimes committed prior to the imposition of martial law but whose "effects or consequences" are felt during the period. Irrespective of the type of crime or any existing statutory limitations on punishment, such courts could impose severe penalties, including death sentences.

4. Plans also call for the execution of an intern-

ment program called "Operation Spring." Selected individuals would be rounded up "during the night hours after the decree goes into effect but before it is made public. . . ." In addition, "threatening citizens" could be arrested for up to 48 hours by administrative decision alone.

Can It Work?
5. The effectiveness of such a program is dependent upon the acquiescence of large portions of the populace and the support military and police units. It is likely, therefore, that the conditions which might provoke the program's implementation would be precisely those which would ensure its failure.
6. The effective use of propaganda is emphasized to explain the reasons for and objectives of the measures to the populace. Concern with popular support was also reflected in the specific exceptions provided for church and religious affairs. All mobilization and conscription plans also call for formal "soldier's assemblies" and similar civil meetings to prepare those affected.
7. The martial law program was inspired and approved by the Soviets. It was designed to destroy Solidarity and to take back the government's concessions of the past year. This program has been viewed by the polish leadership as a last resort, and has been regarded by many as unworkable.
8. The program would be dependent upon the coordinated implementation of broadly defined repressive measures by local authorities. Excesses, even within the context of these plans, could occur in some jurisdictions, while in others implementation might be half-hearted. If so, the resultant confusion and exacerbation of the already critical situation could result in complete breakdown of order. To reduce its risks, the government might impose elements of the program "piece-meal," with each step implemented and evaluated before another is taken. This might allow the government to reimpose some degree of control over certain sectors of Polish life while avoiding the risks attending all-out martial law. The poten-

tial for confrontation would be reduced or at least faced incrementally, and the chances of ultimate success increased.

<u>Attitudes of the Polish Leadership</u>
9. The Polish leadership has been reluctant to impose the full martial law program. Recent evidence, however, suggests greater willingness to implement something less draconian, and therefore less risky. Measures at this end of the spectrum of possibilities may be designed to create the necessary context for broad-scale economic reform. Recent government actions such as the formation of a special commission to combat speculation and black marketeering, the stated intent to involve the military in that process, and the appointment of some generals to governmental posts, may represent first steps at the more benign end of this spectrum. The incremental involvement of the military in these measures serves to include them at an early stage, in actions to which they find it easy to accede.
10. The evolution of confrontation between Solidarity and the government would determine the government's choice of additional action for the immediate future. The government could tailor its actions to the degree of danger. If the security situation deteriorates only moderately, the government could implement limited emergency measures. Should the situation worsen dramatically, the government might impose more restrictive emergency measures, though perhaps still short of a national declaration of martial law. Government actions toward Solidarity's leaders probably would depend on the actions and posture of those leaders and the regime's assessments of public reactions.
11. In either of these cases, the military – still a respected national institution – could be used effectively. The cooperation of the military might best be assured by their early introduction in an unobtrusive manner, before any outbreak of violence, and particularly if their contribution included not just police functions, but positive activities, such as managing the distribution of foodstuffs.

12. If the situation deteriorated more rapidly, and some event were to spark widespread street violence, the government might see no other choice but to turn to its "last resort," and impose the full program of martial law. The military, if thrust abruptly into this deteriorated situation and required to confront violence already under way, probably would not be able to muster the collective will necessary to establish effective control. Of the 60,000 men conscripted by the Polish Armed Forces in April, 50 percent were members of Solidarity. The figure for the fall 1980 conscription was 30 percent. These figures suggest that up to 15 percent of the Polish Armed Forces are already members of Solidarity.

13. The greatest risk of a Polish effort to impose martial law is that its failure would lead to a Soviet military intervention. We believe that the Soviets would applaud any attempt by the Polish leadership to reassert Party authority in Poland. At the same time, although not eager to intervene militarily, the Soviets would recognize that Polish failure would almost certainly require such action. A failed martial law effort could provide propitious circumstances for the Soviets to adopt a posture of restoring order from chaos and of ending rather than inciting bloodshed.

Strategic Warning Staff
Washington, D.C. 20301

14 November 1980

MEMORANDUM FOR: See Distribution List

SUBJECT: Strategic Warning Staff

Attached is a draft Special Report prepared by the Strategic Warning Staff. This draft is circulated for comment. Your formal coordination, however, is not solicited. Direct contact with the analysts is encouraged. The Gray phone number is ███████████. Recipients are requested to respond as early as possible and no later than 1200 17 November 1980.

235

Director /SWS

1 Attachment

DISTRIBUTION LIST

<u>CIA</u>
D/National Foreign Assessments
NIO/W
NIO/USSR
NIO/GPF
Director/OSR
Director/OPA

<u>STATE</u>
INR (ATTN: Robert Baraz)

<u>NSA</u>
ATTN: ███████████████
<u>DIA</u>

JS ███████████ for distribution within DIA as you see appropriate

Regular reporting on the political situation in Poland and the Alert Memoranda concerning the crisis have already alerted US policymakers to be prepared for a possible Soviet intervention. The following discussion is intended to inform readers that they may no longer be able to depend on seeing a full range of warning indicators spanning the one to two week period prior to an actual Soviet invasion. As Soviet leaders lose confidence in the Polish regime and armed forces, Moscow may feel pressured to react rapidly and forcefully. The Soviets are likely to place heavy emphasis on the need for complete tactical surprise if an invasion under these circumstances is to be launched at all. In that event, we may have only a day or two of advance warning of the crossing of the Polish frontier by Soviet forces.

1. The unrest in Poland is of intense interest and importance to the Soviet Union and its leading East European clients. Since late summer, the USSR has carefully maintained a full range of options in response to the upsurge of the free trade union movement throughout Poland, from upgrading its military posture in the region to professing full confidence in the new Kania regime in Warsaw.

2. There is a variety of indications, however, that the USSR and its allies may be losing confidence that the present Polish leadership is either able or willing to take needed steps to reverse the "antisocialist" tide. At the same time, there are signs that the Polish government and armed forces are preparing for a possible national emergency resulting from renewed large-scale strike activity. In Soviet eyes this might constitute evidence that the prospects for a satisfactory outcome are worsening rather than improving, and that the chances are increasing that "disloyal" Polish troops will heavily resist any Soviet intervention in the crisis.

3. According to one recent report detailing Kania's visit to Moscow at the end of October, Soviet leaders insisted on a detailed description of Polish policy if, despite Kania's predictions to the contrary, a general strike were to be declared during November 1980. Kania told the Soviets that he would then immediately declare a state of emergency, would mobilize Polish military and security forces, and would order the arrest of any union or dissident leader who continued to express opposition. Yet at the same time, Kania reportedly acknowledged doubts as to the willingness of the average Polish soldier to use force against the strikers. In this regard, he claimed that plans were ready for loyal units made up of officer trainees to occupy key industrial areas. According to this report, the Soviets, while expressing satisfaction with this plan, offered "help" if it were needed.

4. There are recent signs as well that Moscow's European allies view the Polish situation with growing unease. Exchanges among East European leaders have picked up, with the Czechs apparently taking the lead. Following

237

a trip to East Germany by Czech foreign minister Chnoupek on 4 November and a visit to Bulgaria by Czech Premier Strougal on 10–11 November, Hungarian party first secretary Kadar arrived in Bratislava on 12 November for an unscheduled meeting with Czech party chief Husak. The joint communique issued after their talks stressed the theme of solidarity with "Polish Communists" now facing not only an "onslaught of antisocialist forces" but "attempts by international imperialism to interfere in Poland's internal affairs." Romania is reportedly Strougal's next stop, with arrival set for 21 November. As for East Germany, an SED Central Committee official recently stated privately that the situation in Poland was regarded by his party as more dangerous than that of Czechoslovakia in 1968.

5. All-source reporting continues to reveal no firm indications of increased military readiness or unusual military preparations suggestive of immediate military actions by any of the participants. Several anomalies worthy of attention have been noted recently, however, and these are outlined in an annex to this report.

6. At the same time, there are continuing indications of strenuous effort to stabilize the situation in Poland. Foremost among these is the decision issued by the Polish Supreme Court on 10 November allowing the registration of the free trade union organization "Solidarnosc" on terms acceptable to the movement's leaders. Soviet media coverage of the latest developments has remained unemotional and largely upbeat. For their part, the Poles seemingly remain unconvinced that the worst is behind them. An unusual recall of Polish military attaches from embassies abroad is now under way, while Polish diplomats speculate over such possibilities as actual Soviet intervention or the introduction of martial law within the country. One novel measure of the situation, a public opinion survey in Poland recently conducted for a French magazine, reportedly suggested that only three percent of the populace would vote for the Communist Party in a free election.

7. Looking to the weeks and months ahead, it is clear that the continuing downspin of the Polish economy makes the satisfaction of many of the basic grievances voiced by the union movement increasingly unlikely. A national congress of Solidarnosc is scheduled to convene in mid-December with the formal task of assessing the regime's compliance with the accords reached last September. If the government's performance at that point is found wanting, renewed resort to large-scale strike threats may be the result. The Polish Communist Party, for its part, will soon be deeply embroiled in preparations for its "extraordinary" Ninth Congress, with numerous political careers as well as concrete issues at stake. An already floundering party will hardly be capable of reasserting its role in resolving basic social and economic conflicts if it remains unable to master itself. Worst of all, the responsiveness of the Polish armed forces to the regime's commands evidently can no longer be taken for granted.

8. Knowledge of these symptoms of decay almost certainly affects Soviet confidence that the Polish leadership is capable of resolving the current conflict on terms compatible with Moscow's interests. This perception may put Soviet leaders under increased pressure to reach a final decision over how to deal with the Polish challenge in the near term, apart from any new turn of events in Poland.

9. Increasingly suspecting that personnel and perhaps entire units of the Polish armed forces would not support the regime against the strikers and might even resist a Soviet invasion, Moscow may be putting heavy emphasis on the need for complete tactical surprise if a military intervention is to be launched at all. In practical terms, this would lead to a conscious effort to minimize such political indicators as "heavy message" propaganda and protracted consultations among Warsaw Pact leaders. It would also lead the Soviets to make concrete preparations for a "standing start" invasion with little or no interval following mobilization. In such a move, Moscow would rely on the demoralizing and disorganizing effect of

a blitzkrieg-style operation. Using mobility and the shock effect of the sudden appearance of an invading army to compensate for any lack of overwhelming troop strength.

10. An intelligence judgment regarding overall Soviet intentions toward Poland remains difficult. If the USSR is already well past the decision point on the Polish question – having determined that a military solution is unavoidable and that only the timing of such a move remains a question – awareness that the resistance is gathering strength would surely advance Moscow's plans considerably. If, on the other hand, the Soviets have not yet agreed among themselves that an invasion of Poland is the only alternative, indications of likely Polish resistance would almost certainly have a galvanizing effect on the Politburo, creating a strong sense that a fundamental decision must be made sooner rather than later.

11. The Soviets would almost certainly be confident that they could meet the diplomatic costs of a Polish invasion, including massive but perhaps temporary disruption of European detente. They may be less certain about accepting the military costs of the operation, including the possibility that a bloody invasion followed by imposition of an occupation-style regime might significantly curtail Soviet military options elsewhere. Soviet leaders must also be aware that an invasion of Poland would cause massive economic disruption throughout Eastern Europe and would even affect the USSR. Yet none of these factors would be likely to deter the Soviets from invading once they had concluded that the situation in Poland had gotten out of control.

12. The possibility that a situation may arise in Poland that the Soviets viewed as so serious that immediate action must be taken carries implications for warning related to the reduced preparation time for invading Soviet forces. Mobilization and assembly of Soviet divisions for the three armies in the western USSR stationed near the Polish border seems likely to take two to three days regardless of the circumstances. Our ability to provide warning of

this mobilization process will be less than we would expect for a larger scale, more deliberate Soviet move into Poland. We may be able to supply warning of the preparations some one to two days in advance of the crossing of the Polish frontier. If the Soviet decision to carry out the invasion is made as a result of some conspicuous event in Poland, we may be able to see signs of Soviet intervention somewhat earlier.

ANNEX
For the last two months or so we have had evidence of Soviet activities almost certainly related to preparations for a contingency requiring an invasion of Poland. It is clear that the preparations have not been completed but the Soviets almost certainly have reduced the time it would take to complete them. There is still no evidence of the broad scale mobilization and movement necessary prior to an invasion but there have been some disquieting events reported, in addition to those in the text, that might be indicative of a movement toward a more serious situation. ████████████

EAST GERMANY
- Unofficial travel to and through Poland by all members of the East German Army has been prohibited until further notice, except in special cases, by a decree issued by the East German National Peoples Army Chief of Staff. Official duty travel, however, is still allowed.
- military reserve doctors and other reservists with medical experience were called up around 25 October 1980. ████████████ the East German armed forces are at a state of alert similar to that maintained during the Czech crisis in 1968.

CZECHOSLOVAKIA
- ████████████ in September 1980 ████████████ acquaintances and co-workers were called up without prior notice to participate in a military exercise. This call up was supposedly in preparation for actions concerning Poland.

- ▮▮▮▮▮▮▮▮▮▮▮▮▮ ˙on 4 November that the military compound in Bruntal, Czechoslovakia, which includes the headquarters of the Soviet 31st Tank Division, was empty. ▮▮▮▮▮▮▮ the troops ordinarily stationed there had been transfered to the Czech-Polish border and that the woods along the border were "crawling with" Soviet soldiers and tanks. ▮▮▮▮▮ the Soviet "tent city" formerly located outside of Prague was now located at an unidentified point along the Polish border.

USSR
- ON 11-12 November, while passing through Brest – a major transportation junction in the Belorussian Military District – ▮▮▮▮▮▮▮▮▮▮▮▮▮ an esti-mated 2000 Soviet military personnel, of mixed ser-vices and branches and clearly not recent draftees, apparently headed for East Germany by rail.

Poland: Prospects
for Solidarity

An Intelligence Assessment

State Dept. review
completed

Poland: Prospects
for Solidarity

An Intelligence Assessment

This paper was prepared by ▮▮▮▮▮ the Office of European Analysis. It was coordinated with the National Intelligence Council. Comments and queries are welcome and may be directed to the Chief Eastern Europe Division, EURA, ▮▮▮▮▮▮▮▮

Poland: Prospects
for Solidarity

Key Judgments
Information available
as of 11 March 1983
was used in this report.

The suspension of martial law and the release of most internees reflect a regime calculation that Solidarity no longer poses a serious near-term threat. We believe the authorities' assessment is correct, but, in failing to satisfy demands for reform, they have ensured that social tensions, as well as the possibility of spontaneous outbursts of unrest, will remain high.

The union never recovered from the initial shock of martial law largely because of relentless regime pressure that denied it effective leadership, communications, and organization. The underground's failure to organize widespread strikes in November 1982 protesting the union's dissolution virtually destroyed the hope of most activists that they could force concessions from the regime.

The release of Walesa and other union leaders from their internment camps has brought on what we believe will be an extended and difficult discussion of what their strategy should now be. Some may argue that any resistance activity is futile against a regime so determined and able to put down protests, especially when the workers who gave the union its clout are despondent and tired. But many union activists, in our view, probably are not willing to quit.

Some militants probably will continue to argue for and seek to organize strikes and protests, while others may try to subvert regime-created trade unions or self-management organizations. ███████████████████████ Solidarity supporters believe they should concentrate on building underground self-help organizations – a so-called parallel society. We believe underground activity will proceed without the direct participation of Walesa and other

prominent leaders released from internment camps,
who instead probably will limit their opposition to
speaking out in favor of union "pluralism," worker
self-management in factories, and freedom of speech.

We have no reason to believe that, having achieved
a victory over Solidarity, the authorities will ease
up in their efforts to root out the underground
and intimidate would-be protesters, no matter what
tactics Solidarity adopts. The low-level and fragmented resistance will be troublesome to the authorities, but will not, in our opinion, endanger their
control. We believe that Premier Jaruzelski may, with
the support of many regime moderates, try to co-opt
the reformist spirit that Solidarity represented
by giving new emphasis to the economic and bureaucratic reforms he has said are necessary if Poland
is to avoid another crisis. Even if he does try, his
efforts to fill the void left by Solidarity by creating a new mass movement, new trade unions, and new
self-management organs are likely to fall far short
of satisfying the demands of workers or Solidarity
activists - including Walesa and other moderates.
The pace and extent of changes he can make will be
constrained by opposition within the Polish party and
by Soviet concern that he maintain full control over
labor activity.

Many senior Church leaders have accepted the dissolution of Solidarity as a fait accompli and see
its residual resistance activities as impediments
to addressing Poland's serious problems. But some
younger priests and several bishops, dissatisfied
with Jozef Cardinal Glemp's leadership, are more
willing to provide moral and material support to
Solidarity supporters and underground activity. The
divisions within the Church - which will enhance the
centrifugal forces at work within opposition circles
- will persist because the authorities will look
to the Church hierarchy to play a moderating role
and Solidarity activists will seek Church aid. But
Church unity will, in our view, remain largely intact
because of the traditional stress on presenting a
united front to the authorities.

Solidarity as a legal actor cannot be resurrected, but we believe that the people who supported its reforms will long affect Polish political behavior. Opponents of reform will use continuing low-level resistance activity - and the occasional dramatic flareups caused by the more militant activists - to keep alive the fear of Solidarity and to prevent changes in Poland's inefficient bureaucracies. They are likely to succeed, if only because regime moderates share the hardliners' fear of a revived Solidarity. The resulting immobility almost guarantees an extended period of elevated tensions in which the authorities have to continue to rely on repression to maintain control.

The lack of reform could ensure that the young people who were Solidarity's driving force remain deeply estranged from the corrupt, inefficient political system they tried to change. These young people, with the practical experience of the Solidarity period behind them, will pose a serious, long-term challenge to the regime. In any future confrontations with the authorities, they will be better organized and more radical than before; many Poles fear that the possibility of violence and wide-scale bloodshed will be significantly higher the next time around.

Poland: Prospects
for Solidarity

A Time for Reassessment

The release of Lech Walesa and most other Solidarity leaders in conjunction with the suspension of martial law has brought on what we believe promises to be a difficult period of stocktaking by union activists. Although some will drop out of the political struggle, many others remain determined to persevere because they feel the need to preserve their personal dignity and because they believe the authorities are not able to resolve Poland's difficult political and economic problems - that is, they lost the battle, but the war is yet to come. Decisions on tactics and

245

goals are likely to proceed, however, from what we believe will be a near unanimous assessment that the underground is in no position to challenge immediately the security-conscious regime.

Initial Shock of Martial Law

Solidarity never recovered from the initial shock of martial law, largely because of relentless regime pressure that deprived the union of leaders, communications, and organizational structure. The regime's total blackout of internal and international communications on 13 December 1981 and its well-executed internment of 6,000 key Solidarity leaders and supporters prevented the union from mounting any significant immediate counterattack. According to numerous Solidarity activists, the regime quickly came to be feared as it used threats of physical abuse, imprisonment, and loss of jobs or pay to discourage participation in strikes or demonstrations. The occasional use of excessive force by the increasingly confident regime reinforced the sense of fear.

During the initial four months of martial law, union leaders who remained at large, according to their own published statements, were able to do little more than assess their options and try to establish contacts. Solidarity activists sustained themselves with dreams of resurgence and revenge, reflected in the slogan, "The winter is yours, but the spring will be ours." The primary clandestine activity was the publication of underground leaflets and newsletters - involving almost 1,700 different titles by mid-March, according to the US Embassy - that passed word of planned protests, initiated discussion of strategy and tactics, and sought to lift morale by creating an impression that the union was on the road to recovery. But this activity, as with most other resistance efforts, relied largely on spontaneous actions by a small number of people. The severe difficulties the activists faced in reestablishing quickly an organizational base stemmed, in our view, from Solidarity's nature as a massive, loosely organized, and totally open organization that had never prepared seriously to work underground.

Union leaders were able finally to set up a national Temporary Coordinating Committee (TKK) in April, but only after two previous efforts to constitute a national leadership had failed. Primarily under the guiding influence of moderate Zbigniew Bujak, the articulate leader of the union's Warsaw chapter, the TKK tried to restrain the emotions and actions of the rank and file; more often than not, it followed rather than led. This was because of Bujak's rejection of the concept of a highly centralized underground, difficulties in communications, and differences among the leaders - especially between Bujak and Bogdan Lis, the radical leader from Gdansk.

Solidarity national leaders had only limited success in creating a nationwide network of underground organizations. In early August, the weekly of the Warsaw underground claimed that 14 regional coordination centers had been created, but admitted that contacts had not been established with smaller cities and factories. Many small groups - variously called Committees of Social Defense, interfactory committees, or provisional factory committees - did spring up, but they tended to be inward looking and defensive. They published papers and leaflets, polled union members, collected contributions, helped the families of internees, arranged occasional small protests, put up posters, and boycotted collaborators. They did not, however, prove to be effective in getting large numbers of people into the streets or in leading strikes.

The failure to organize in factories was clearly demonstrated in October, when two-day strikes in the Lenin Shipyards to protest the delegalization of Solidarity collapsed largely because no leaders came forward to take command, as Walesa had in 1980. ████████████████████████ workers realized that anyone who assumed a leadership role would expose himself to direct and immediate retribution from the security services and the plant management. Solidarity activists in Krakow believed in early November that the union had virtually no organization left in that region.

Obstacles to a Counterattack

We believe that a key reason the underground could not organize well was penetration by the security services. ███████████████ the person responsible for disseminating documents drafted by the national leadership was found to be working for the police. The secret police extensively circulated fake underground literature, which caused such confusion among the rank and file ███████████████ that some activists could not decide what to believe. Workers increasingly distrusted leaflets urging them to strike or demonstrate.

The security services also succeeded in arresting numerous underground leaders. Radio Solidarity broadcasts, which boosted morale from April through June, were almost completely halted by late November through arrests of key personnel. The detention on 31 August of underground activist Janusz Romaszewski ███████████████ caused particular consternation among Solidarity activists because he knew all the communications arrangements of the underground. ███████████████ the arrest of the Wroclaw leader, Wladyslaw Frasyniuk, on 10 October had plunged his fellow activists into despair and prompted them to go into hiding. By November, police raids had put much of the underground press out of business.

In our assessment, divisions among union leaders also hindered underground activity. Debate over goals and tactics – initiated some time in March – revealed serious differences on how the resistance movement should be organized and what sort of struggle it should carry on. Writing from an internment camp, Jacek Kuron, a prominent activist, argued in the underground press for a highly centralized, well-organized resistance movement to prepare "a simultaneous offensive against all centers of power and information throughout the country." On the other hand, Bujak argued that a social outburst was not inevitable, that underground resistance was futile because of police penetration, and that a strongly centralized movement would only galvanize the authorities. He advocated a decentralized underground move-

ment that would try to establish a "parallel society"
of committees to help those out of work, operate
presses, and create schools. He admitted, however,
that this "struggle for position" was not the path to
achieving fast and spectacular success.

Debate over whether the union should attempt a
general strike to force the regime's hand became a
key issue dividing moderates and radicals. Pressure
for such a strike arose in late spring from militant
workers who ███████████████████ had tired of the
go-slow approach. According to a poll of workers
conducted by the underground in Wroclaw in early May,
75 percent supported either a general strike or armed
insurrection, with almost nine out of 10 pledging to
participate.

Bogdan Lis argued in the underground press for
such a strike, asserting first that the union would
lose support if workers believed no "decisive steps"
were being planned and later claiming that careful
preparation of a general strike was necessary to
prevent an uncontrolled outburst of worker resentment. As debate about a general strike raged in the
underground press, such prominent Solidarity leaders
as Adam Michnik and Janus Onyszkiewicz - still in
internment camps - supported Bujak's opposition to a
strike.

They argued that Jaruzelski would refuse to negotiate under pressure and would not hesitate to suppress
strikes. A general strike, they added, would radical-
ize the movement and could get out of control.

At no time during the debate laid out in the underground press did any of the senior leaders advocate
violence or terror. Solidarity leaders had prided
themselves on their ability to prevent bloodshed and
saw it as one of their tasks to calm the hotheads.
In fact, union militants persistently defended their
strategy as the only way to force the regime to compromise and to prevent an explosion that would lead
to widespread deaths, civil war, and a Soviet military intervention.

The argument over a general strike subsided in the
early summer when Solidarity leaders called for a

moratorium on strikes and demonstrations in order not to jeopardize a possible Papal visit and in hope that the regime would announce concessions on 22 July, Poland's national day. Even when these hopes proved groundless, the response of the moderates was to channel worker anger into street demonstrations at the end of August and not toward a general strike. They labeled the August demonstrations a "moral victory," and they again tried to avoid confrontation by encouraging activists to build the underground society as the primary means of defense. And, even when it became clear that the government was moving quickly to abolish the union, the underground leadership hesitated, realizing that its previous efforts to organize protests had failed and fearing that a more confrontational stand could bring bloodshed.

One factor, we believe, that fostered moderation in the leadership was the realization that workers – despite the enthusiasm shown by the underground polls – had not turned out in large numbers for strikes or demonstrations. Even during the demonstrations in August – the apparent high point of protests – only 100,000 to 120,000 people participated. Workers openly expressed the sentiment that nothing short of an all-out general strike would have a chance of success.

The abolition of Solidarity in early October was a provocative act that, according to Solidarity activists, gave new momentum to union militants, even though it provoked only limited spontaneous strikes, mainly in the Lenin shipyards where Solidarity had been born. The underground leadership laid out a plan of action that included a nationwide eight-hour strike and street demonstrations on 10 November, additional demonstrations on 11 November, a wave of protests from 13-17 December, and a general strike some time in the spring. Little happened, however, on 10 November ███████████████████████ as a result of the failure of the union to make good on the first phase of its plan, the top leadership descended into "savage bickering" over the failure and about how to proceed in the future.

The release of Lech Walesa on 13 November from his private internment prompted the TKK to signal a return to a more moderate course. Claiming that a "completely new" political situation had been created by the release and by the government's agreement to a Papal visit, the underground leadership called off the demonstrations planned for December. Walesa's statements and behavior after his release probably reinforced the position of the moderates in the underground. Walesa reaffirmed a cautious determination to pursue the "spirit" of the Gdansk agreements of 1980 – especially the provisions for pluralism in the union movement – but called for a long-term struggle. ████████████████ he remains an "idealist" who believes that the regime can never destroy Solidarity and that he still has a role to play in changing Poland's fate.

Walesa and the Underground
Walesa has admitted the continuing need for an underground, ████████████████████████████ He is gradually reestablishing contact with some former advisers who were released from internment camps as a result of the suspension of martial law, but appears to have no specific ideas on how to bring pressure on the authorities other than by issuing public statements. In late January, he signed an appeal with 13 former Solidarity leaders for the release of still-imprisoned union leaders and in defense of workers' rights.

Meanwhile, underground leaders have shown no signs of concluding that Walesa's release obviates the need for their continuing activities or that their activities conflict with the more limited and open role chosen by Walesa in his circumstances. Moderate underground leader Bujak commented in early January in an interview with a Western journalist that his work would complement that of Walesa. He conceded that the union underground must develop ways to allow activists to work in the open, but argued that clandestine activity continues to be necessary to help prepare for eventual overt action. ████████████████████████ only a small number of people are actively involved in the underground; Bujak allegedly estimated during conversations with other underground activists in December that there might be as few as 200 activists in 10 different centers. This number, which presumably refers to individuals who are working full-time on resistance activities, probably has since dwindled because of continuing arrests and because some have given themselves up. Bujak's estimate probably does not include, however, a much larger number of workers who are carrying out clandestine propaganda and organizational activities while holding down factory jobs.

The difficulties in establishing and maintaining contact between the underground and those working above ground have on occasion dramatized longstanding personal and philosophical differences in the movement. ▓▓▓▓▓▓▓▓▓▓▓▓▓▓▓▓▓▓ Walesa responded to the underground leadership's call in January for an eventual general strike by noting that such a strike is not in his program.

We believe that, largely because of continuing regime pressure, union activists will move in increasingly different directions. Walesa and other former Solidarity leaders - both in the underground and among those released from internment camps - will try to devise a coherent set of goals and tactics but, in our view, will agree only on some basic principles. In its prime, Solidarity could not agree on a program; in the current environment agreement must be even more difficult. Walesa will be shown again to have only limited ability to guide debate and action, and the main challenge for him and other leaders may be to preserve a sense of unity as activists both above and underground pursue markedly different activities. Their arguments for and against five different courses of action are listed below. These courses are not, of course, mutually exclusive and several could be pursued simultaneously or sequentially depending on domestic conditions.

Lying Low. The arguments for doing nothing are compelling. Moderates such as Walesa and Bujak, as

well as militants such as Lis, have publicly admitted that the overwhelming majority of workers who
gave the union its political muscle are tired of
confrontation, see no benefit to symbolic acts of
defiance, and are unwilling to take chances that
might worsen their already difficult economic situation. This sense of despair reaches into the ranks
of former union officials and advisers, and a steady
trickle of underground activists in hiding since the
declaration of martial law are giving themselves
up to the police. In addition, a growing number of
former activists have opted for the ultimate form
of resignation - emigration. According to a government spokesman, as of mid-January 5,000 persons had
applied to emigrate for political reasons and 1,070
activists had already left, including 37 members
of Solidarity's National Commission and 233 of its
provincial leaders. ███████████████████████
██ in
their first weeks of liberty, former Walesa advisers
lost a great deal of their belief in the continued
effectiveness of resistance activity. They had been
struck by the extent of public apathy as well as the
efficiency of the security apparatus.

Nonetheless, Walesa and many other recently released
internees - as well as remaining underground activists
- believe, in our view, that the regime is not capable
of resolving its economic or political problems and
eventually will be forced to make concessions. They
seem convinced that they must do something - if only
building an underground infrastructure and pressing
workers' rights through regime-controlled organs - to
keep alive the spirit of Solidarity and be prepared
to exploit future regime weaknesses. Writers in the
underground press have tried to play down the union's
loss of its mass base by arguing that only a small
number of dedicated people are needed to spearhead
revolutionary movements.

Sporadic Protests. Walesa and other recently
released Solidarity leaders are unlikely to put much
effort into organizing active resistance, realizing

that the risk of arrest is too great and the chances of success too limited and perhaps calculating that enough spontaneous resistance will continue to keep pressure on the regime. Although large-scale and coordinated opposition activity has disappeared, harassment of party and government officials continues, some workers openly show support for Solidarity, and leaflets still appear. In addition, there continue to be sporadic incidents of what appears to be politically motivated sabotage, and reporting in the Polish press and from Embassy sources indicates that some underground groups have small caches of weapons. We believe that calls for strikes or demonstrations, however, will not attract significant worker support as long as the regime continues to show its determination and ability to contain and punish such resistance.

A General Strike. Failure of the planned eight-hour strike on 10 November 1982 will not dissuade radical militants from pursuing efforts to organize a general strike, even though would-be organizers probably realize, in our estimation, that it would be an uphill struggle. ▄▄▄▄▄▄▄   ▄▄▄▄▄▄▄▄▄▄
▄▄▄▄▄▄▄▄▄▄ In the program which it released in late January, the TKK asserted that a general strike is "inevitable," but Bujak later emphasized in an interview published in a Spanish journal that he considers a general strike an extreme measure that could succeed only under very favorable conditions. Walesa is unlikely, judging from his public comments since being released, to support the staging of a general strike any time soon, largely because of doubts about its feasibility.

Building the Underground Society. This option, which now appears to have Walesa's support as well as that of some of the regional and local underground organizations, involves a long-term effort to build a network of underground, self-help organizations, and appeals to many, we believe, because it allows for low-level resistance activities while people wait for a better time to press the regime more directly. We believe that at least some Solidarity underground activists with whom Embassy officers have talked are exaggerating the possibility of building such a "parallel society," just as they previously overestimated their ability to force concessions through strikes and demonstrations.

Subversion of Regime Institutions. Both Walesa and the TKK want workers to use every opportunity – and some regime-sponsored organizations – to press for their full legal rights, but the workers do not seem prepared to end the boycott of the official trade unions that began spontaneously after the regime dissolved Solidarity. Some union activists argued in October and November ▮▮▮▮▮▮▮▮▮▮▮▮▮▮▮▮▮ that, barring any other legal alternatives, workers should try to gain control of the new regime-sponsored unions; the TKK has urged continuation of the boycott. ▮▮▮▮▮▮▮▮▮▮▮▮▮▮ most reports from Western journalists, in fact, indicate continuing great reluctance among workers to join the new regime-sponsored unions. For many, joining amounts to capitulation and lends legitimacy to a regime endeavor that, judging by their experience, is unlikely to represent their interests. Workers' suspicions in this regard have been fueled by the heavyhanded presence of party stalwarts at union organizing sessions and the exaggerated claims of support for the new bodies. As of mid-February the regime claimed that more than 1 million workers had joined. Over the next several years, several million more probably will join – if only because the unions will take over their traditional role of providing vacations, medical care, and other economic benefits – but this will comprise only a small part of the industrial labor force of about 13 million.

Judging from his public statements, we believe Walesa seems more interested in seeking to take advantage of the regime-sponsored self-management organizations than of the new unions. Factory self-management was a key Solidarity demand, and Walesa may believe that

the new self-management councils will be less easily
manipulated by the regime. The councils are slated to
begin functioning by the end of March, although the
regime has restricted the council's powers to ensure
they are not "abused."

More generally, the TKK has urged workers to
take advantage of the labor code to defend their
interests. Specifically, workers have been advised
to demand information about production decisions
and to expose mismanagement. If plant management
balks, they are urged to organize group protests
and refuse to work overtime. ████████████
████████████ some Solidarity factory commissions
are trying to collect and publicize workers' economic
grievances.

The Regime
The Polish authorities clearly have demonstrated
that they have the will and ability to put down any
direct challenge from workers, whether it be sporadic demonstrations or work actions. We doubt that,
having achieved their victory over the underground,
they will soon ease up in their efforts to throttle
the underground press, arrest fugitive leaders, or
generally prevent underground organizational work.
During the first two months of 1983, the security
services arrested additional activists involved in
underground publishing work. Jaruzelski in his speech
on 12 December emphatically stated that "anarchy will
not be allowed to enter Poland." Subsequently, other
senior officials reaffirmed in public speeches their
concern over the threat from the underground and the
need to be on guard.

The regime probably will continue to rely heavily
on the use of force, threats of imprisonment, and
economic reprisal to silence would-be dissenters
or to make life very uncomfortable for them. The
authorities cannot stop all protests, especially if
they want to convey some sense of normality by relaxing controls, but they will break up protests that
promise to encourage increased dissent. The regime
will use harassment to thwart efforts to build an

"underground society."* Finally, the authorities are well aware of the discussion about subverting the unions or self-management organizations and have provided themselves with legal and physical powers to stop such efforts.

As Solidarity leaders try to regroup their forces, Jaruzelski may finally get a chance to refocus his attention from emasculating Solidarity to introducing the economic and administrative reforms that he has said are necessary for Poland's recovery. Jaruzelski's publicly stated, long-term goal is to create a strong, efficient state bureaucracy that will be able to manage the country and improve living conditions, thus preventing yet another explosion of public anger. His initial efforts to reform the economy or to fill the void left by the dissolution of Solidarity have not, however, been far reaching or effective.

The national patriotic movement (Patriotic Movement for National Rebirth), in which Jaruzelski has appeared to place some hope as a vehicle for creating "national accord," has failed to attract support, especially from the young. According to Embassy contacts, this is largely because it has been staffed and promoted by discredited party and government officials. The new trade unions, as mentioned earlier, face similar credibility problems.

In fact, a considerable gap probably exists between the maximum that Jaruzelski is willing to offer in search of social accord and the minimum that Polish society could find acceptable. We believe Jaruzelski will remain opposed to the creation of any institutions with substantial autonomy; certainly, his goal of creating an effective centralized administration does not allow for meaningful inputs from society or restraints on the regime's freedom of action.

Whatever his personal intentions or desires, we believe that Jaruzelski does not have a free hand. He

---

* Jarek Kuron, the prominent dissident from pre-Solidarity days who helped popularize this concept in the late 1970s, has said the effort cannot succeed because the current authorities will not be as lenient as was then-party leader Gierek.

continues to rely heavily on existing party and government bureaucracies that prefer the old and often ineffective methods. Although Jaruzelski appears to doubt the competence of many in the party apparatus, the need to respect the "leading role of the party" limits the extent and pace of changes he can make. Party members, meanwhile, may become more quarrelsome as they see the military continue to wield considerable power.

Jaruzelski must also take into account Moscow's consistent opposition to any form of labor organization that could become a political rival to the party. In the months preceding Solidarity's delegalization, the Soviets made it clear that they were impatient for decisive action; their subsequent commentary has indicated general satisfaction with Jaruzelski's stern handling of Solidarity's remnants. Moscow appears to recognize that future Polish trade unions will differ from the Soviet model, but Jaruzelski will have to maintain firm control over labor activity in order to avoid renewed Soviet criticism.

The Church

Officials of the Catholic Church publicly expressed deep regred at the summary dissolution of Solidarity, but most accept the action as a fait accompli. ▮▮▮▮▮▮▮▮▮▮▮ ▮▮▮▮▮▮▮▮▮▮▮

▮▮▮▮▮▮ The Church, generally, probably considers pursuit of any of residual Solidarity's options as an impediment to the nation's getting on with its formidable tasks. As part of its continuing effort to prevent bloodshed, the Church will seek, we believe, to guide Walesa away from provoking the regime. ▮▮▮▮▮▮▮▮▮ ▮▮▮▮▮▮▮▮▮

▮▮▮▮▮▮▮▮ In any case, the regime would not, in our estimation, allow him to occupy any position – Church-related or otherwise – that he could use to criticize or challenge the authorities.

Some local priests are likely to continue helping Solidarity supporters and to bitterly criticize the regime. Solidarity activists will continue to use Church events as meeting places and, occasionally, as the starting point for demonstrations. The higher echelons of the Church probably will try to set limits on such help, however, because they do not want to give the regime an excuse to rescind Church privileges or to endanger the Papal visit now slated to begin in June. The Church Episcopate will probably limit itself to periodic critiques of regime policy and to efforts behind the scenes to get the regime to adopt more conciliatory policies.

The schizophrenia in the Church's attitude toward resistance activities – with Glemp and the Episcopate supporting moderation and the lower levels of the clergy sometimes giving moral and physical support to more militant positions – seems likely to rein-force the centrifugal forces at work within oppo-sition forces. The moderate Bujak has complained ████████████████████ that the Church leadership has not been aggressive in its criticism of the regime. Also, Walesa has been sharply criticized, ████████████ for being too much under Glemp's influence.

The official stance of the Church regarding Solidarity has generated some internal criticism that Glemp has been too weak and conciliatory toward the regime. Such beliefs apparently are shared by a few bishops but seem to come predominantly from younger parish priests, who are closer to the suffering of their people. ███████████████████████ ██████████████ ██████████████████████ Glemp's actions have reflected the gradualist philosophy he learned from his prede-cessor, Carinal Wyszynski, and which, we believe, is basically shared by Pope John Paul II. Polish Church leader believe that the Church has remained strong because it has remained unified against the Communist authorities, and we believe concerns about main-taining unity will limit disagreement over current tactics.

Prospects
Solidarity as a legal actor cannot be resurrected, but we believe that the political and organizational skills of the younger generation who supported it and the ideas it fostered have become permanent

259

additions to the Polish political spectrum. Polish workers have long memories, and the betrayal they felt at the imposition of martial law will condition their attitudes toward the authorities for years to come.* Moreover, the problems which led to the rise of Solidarity have not been resolved.

In its weakened state Solidarity cannot generate widespread strikes or demonstrations. The most serious protests from the regime's point of view will be spontaneous strikes and demonstrations that take both the underground and the security services by surprise. We believe prospects for political or economic improvement in the next few years are so dismal, and popular anger and resentment so deep, that serious disturbances cannot be prevented. The incidents triggering such explosions could be as trivial as the firing of a crane operator at the Lenin Shipyards (which sparked the strikes there in 1980) or the raising of prices on scarce consumer goods.

Alternatively, the initiative for a confrontation could come from the small groups of extremist Solidarity militants who might resort to terrorism. Although the probability of an act such as the assassination of Jaruzelski or some other official is not high, such a thing could happen and would lead to retribution from the security forces that would provoke widespread protests.†

Such an event, if it caught the security services unprepared and led to an initial victory by protesting workers, could provoke a rapidly accelerating series of strikes. The situation might become particularly serious if former union leaders, including Walesa, joined the workers. They would provide the leadership and inspiration that have been missing

---

* Walesa cut his teeth on oppositional activity in the shipyard strike in Gdansk in 1970. and he persisted until his efforts bore fruit.

† One of the most radical underground organizations – "Combatant Solidarity" in Wroclaw – advocated in 1982 the employment of "revolutionary means" to advance its interests ███████████████ ████████████████ This group may have been responsible for some of the scattered sabotage reported in the press.

since the imposition of martial law. There is little prospect, however, that workers could "win" in such circumstances as they did with the signing of the Gdansk accords in August of 1980. The current authorities are determined to avoid making concessions under pressure and, we believe, clearly are willing to use force to show their resolve. The realization by most Poles that the regime would carry out its threats limited resistance under martial law and seems likely to dampen the will to resist openly in the near future.

Solidarity's greatest impact over the next several years, in our view, will not be in what it can force the regime to do, but in the ways its specter may prevent the regime from adopting conciliatory policies. The ongoing but low-level resistance activity will be a constant reminder to the authorities of their security concerns and, we believe, will be used by security forces and party hardliners to reinforce their demands for political power. The "spirit of Solidarity past" certainly will play a key role in discussions within the party and government on future economic and political policies ███████████ the party has been so traumatized by the experience with Solidarity between August 1980 and December 1981 that no compromise is possible. At the 10th Central Committee plenum in October 1982, party hardliners attacked some of the regime's economic reforms – which Solidarity had supported – and implicitly criticized persons in the party who backed them, including Jaruzelski. Even though Jaruzelski easily turned back the criticism, the episode illustrates that political and economic changes will be attacked and resisted because, it will be claimed, they threaten to allow Solidarity to regain its former influence. The most determined and effective resistance to change may not come from Warsaw, however, but from intermediate and lower level bureaucrats intent on seeking revenge for what they suffered during the Solidarity era and on reestablishing unquestioned power.

We believe that the combination of Jaruzelski's determination to restore the essential elements of a centralized "socialist" system, combined with political resistance by hardliners to changes that he does not consider threatening to the system, will lead to a high degree of immobility. It seems unlikely that the regime can create much legitimacy without first making concessions to union pluralism that Jaruzelski neither could nor would make. And, on the economic side, while some marginal improvement is possible, we believe worker alienation combined with an inefficient economic system highly resistant to reform and little additional help from East or West will ensure that the economy can at best limp along. Thus, in the coming years the authorities will probably be compelled to rely heavily on their repressive apparatus, directly or indirectly, to maintain control.

Over the longer term some Poles, especially moderates in the regime, appear to believe that Poland might be able to make use of the Hungarian experience to create trust of the authorities and a more efficient bureaucracy. Their interest is evident from the number of official visits between Warsaw and Budapest and the periodic positive assessments of Hungarian accomplishments. There are, however, several factors that will work against Jaruzelski's being able to import a solution to his problem. The Hungarian authorities thoroughly broke the spirit of resistance during five years of often-brutal repression after 1956. The spirit of passive resistance is still strong in Poland, and it is unlikely that Jaruzelski or any successor can exterminate it. Secondly, as mentioned above, the party and government bureaucracies will continue to pose strong resistance to concessions. Thus, although the trappings are different, the political dynamics operating in Jaruzelski's Poland are essentially the same as those in Gomulka's or Gierek's. This means, we believe, that the next Polish crisis is only awaiting some new catalyst to spark it and that residual Solidarity, despite its divisions and weaknesses, will indeed have the opportunity for another round.

Notes

1. For more detail, see Michael Szporer, *Solidarity: The Great Workers Strike of 1980* (Kentucky: Lexington Books, 2012).
2. M. Kramer, 'Soviet Deliberations during the Polish Crisis, 1980–1981', *Cold War International History Project*, Special Working Paper No 1 (2011), <https://www.wilsoncenter.org/sites/default/files/ACF56F.pdf> (last accessed 10 January 2020).
3. R. Cornwell, 'Ryszard Kuklinski: Cold War Spy for the West', *The Independent*, 13 February 2004. The letter itself can be seen here: <http://digitalarchive.wilsoncenter.org/document/165266> (last accessed 10 January 2020).
4. For more see Benjamin Weiser, *A Secret Life: The Polish Officer, His Covert Mission, and the Price He Paid to Save His Country* (New York: Public Affairs, 2004).
5. See 'In the IPN Registered Collection, Among Others Case "Aneta-79/II" Regarding the CIA in Poland', 25 January 2017, <http://dzieje.pl/aktualnosci/w-zbiorze-zastrzezonym-ipn-min-sprawa-aneta-79ii-dot-cia-w-polsce> (last accessed 10 January 2020).
6. M. Kramer, 'The Kuklinski Files and the Polish Crisis of 1980–1981: An Analysis of the Newly Released CIA Documents on Ryszard Kuklinski', *Cold War International History Project*, Working Paper #59 (March 2009), <https://www.wilsoncenter.org/sites/default/files/WP59_Kramer_webfinal1.pdf> (last accessed 10 January 2020).
7. Cited in Kramer, 'The Kuklinski Files'.
8. Douglas J. MacEachin, *US Intelligence and the Polish Crisis, 1980–1981* (Washington, DC: CIA Center for the Study of Intelligence, 2000), <https://www.cia.gov/library/readingroom/docs/2000-01-01.pdf> (last accessed 10 January 2020). See also M. Kramer, 'US Intelligence Performance and US Policy during the Polish Crisis of 1980–81: Revelations from Kuklinkski Files', *Intelligence and National Security*, 26.2–3 (2011), pp. 313–29.
9. For instance, B. Woodward and M. Dobbs, 'CIA Had Secret Agent on Polish General Staff', *The Washington Post*, 4 June 1986, <https://www.cia.gov/library/readingroom/docs/CIA-RDP90-00965R000807560045-0.pdf> (last accessed 10 January 2020).

15   Able Archer and the NATO War Scare

Few events have earned the dubious honour of being described as 'the closest the world came to nuclear war'. The Cuban Missile Crisis of 1962 is one; the 1983 Able Archer war scare is another. The episode has produced a vast amount of literature, focusing on the US and Russian sides and, to a lesser extent, the British perspective.[1] The episode has all the hallmarks of a great spy film: a paranoid, aging dictator in the Kremlin; a military exercise that almost ended in disaster; and a disillusioned spy providing intelligence that was pivotal in attempting to understand the complicated cycles of reaction and overreaction, perception and misperception.

On 2 November 1983 NATO forces began the latest in a series of scheduled military exercises. Able Archer-83 was a command post exercise designed to include senior officials from across the US government, the movement of 40,000 NATO troops, and hundreds of different missions. Importantly, it also included a component designed to simulate the release of 'tactical' nuclear weapons against a variety of Soviet and Warsaw Pact targets. From a Western perspective this was simply another in a regular series of war games and as far as the military was concerned, it ultimately passed off without incident and little more attention was paid to it.[2]

That feeling did not last long, though, and there was some initial concern that the Russians had reacted in a peculiar and unconventional manner, particularly that the Soviet Air Force in East Germany had moved to a heightened state of alert.[3] This fact had been noted but was not interpreted, initially at least, as being especially significant.[4] What limited analysis there was at this stage suggested that the Soviet reaction could be attributed to the paranoia of the ailing Soviet leader, Yuri Andropov, in the Kremlin.[5] This view would soon change, though.

As Andropov lay dying in a hospital bed in the last weeks of 1983 and start of 1984, his KGB *rezident* in London was busy providing snippets of high-value intelligence to the British Secret Intelligence Service. Oleg Gordievsky had volunteered to work for SIS whilst stationed in Copenhagen, Denmark, in 1974. He claimed to have become disenchanted with the Soviet system following the violent crushing of the 1968 uprising in Czechoslovakia. His foreign postings confirmed his unease, revealing the lies and untruths inherent in the Soviet system. He continued to pass extraordinary intelligence to SIS, which shared it (though not his identity) with counterparts in the CIA. In 1982 Gordievsky was posted to London to act as *rezident* for the KGB.[6]

Over the course of the first few months of 1984 Gordievsky was tasked with providing information on Able Archer and the peculiar Soviet reaction.[7] This complemented information that the CIA was able to procure via one of its own sources within the Czechoslovak intelligence organisation.[8] Gordievsky revealed that a few years before, in 1981, a new plan had been instigated by Brezhnev (then Soviet leader) and Andropov (then Chairman of the KGB) called 'RYaN', designed to provide forewarning of any US plan for war. Within a short period of time instructions had been passed to KGB stations worldwide to look out for any signs of preparations, though the focus inevitably was on London and Washington.[9] Indeed, in February 1983 RYaN had taken on greater prominence when a fresh instruction declared that it was of 'particularly grave importance' to monitor for signs. This became ever more important when, a month later, President Reagan announced the Strategic Defense Initiative (SDI), colloquially known as 'Star Wars', which intended to develop a space-based anti-ballistic missile system in order to prevent a successful Soviet nuclear first strike. This challenge to the existing deterrence framework of mutually assured destruction (MAD) raised alarming questions in Moscow. The revised RYaN instruction requested all potential intelligence be provided 'at a very early stage' and 'without delay'.[10]

In the United States the CIA concluded, on the basis of all this information, that if the Soviet Union really had, genuinely, believed that the NATO exercise Able Archer had been a real event, then the reaction would have been different.[11] As CIA historian Ben Fischer has noted, the US intelligence community continued to maintain that this was not evidence of the Russians believing that they were about to be attacked.[12] Gordievsky eventually defected in dramatic fashion in 1985.[13] Once in London, British intelligence apprised the US of his identity and provided additional intelligence on the views of those in the Kremlin and military. On the basis of this intelligence there was consensus in the UK that the Russians had reacted genuinely; that they had believed that they were under attack, yet even still the US community was reluctant to change its opinion.[14] It is this erroneous assessment, as much as the episode itself, that has prompted debate in the literature.

As we now know, Gordievsky's reporting was accurate. The Soviet leadership, in contrast to the majority of the Soviet political, military and intelligence machinery, saw the US threat as real and genuinely believed in the possibility of a pre-emptive Western nuclear strike. Recent evidence from Russian sources suggests that the Kremlin's reaction to Able Archer was based on more than just paranoia:

1. The exercise was seen from Moscow as unusually broad and encompassing.
2. The format deviated from common practice in the transition from the conventional to nuclear phase of the exercise.
3. The exercise would include all the phases of alert up to those for an actual nuclear launch.
4. Before the exercise, the Soviets allegedly spotted that the US bases surrounding the Soviet Union had moved to a higher level of combat readiness.
5. Communications were in a new top-secret message format.

It was the combination of these, it has been argued, rather than traditional accounts of Soviet paranoia, which explained the abnormal Soviet reaction in November 1983.[15]

So why had the CIA and US intelligence community got it so wrong? In 1990 the President's Foreign Intelligence Advisory Board (PFIAB) produced a lengthy post-mortem report into what had happened. The report was scathing: the US intelligence community was admonished for not taking the Soviet reaction, and therefore the possibility of a war scare, seriously enough. It cited a number of analytical failures that had taken place despite strong sources of intelligence collection and it highlighted the potentially catastrophic significance of these mistakes: the fact that the Soviet reaction and genuine belief that this might be a Western nuclear strike might well have prompted those in the Kremlin to authorise its own use of nuclear weapons to pre-empt the perceived Western attack.[16]

In the UK, Prime Minister Margaret Thatcher used Gordievsky and his reporting about the Soviet fears of a Western nuclear first strike to persuade President Reagan to tone down his anti-Soviet rhetoric, which he did in his second term, and Gordievsky himself was flown across the Atlantic to meet Reagan personally in the Oval Office at the White House. By the time this was happening there was a new man in the Kremlin, a younger (by Soviet standards) leader with great ambitions for reform called Mikhail Gorbachev. Although the Soviet fears greatly dissipated with Gorbachev's arrival, RYaN was not cancelled as a standing Soviet intelligence collection requirement until 1991.[17]

For this chapter there are two reference documents. The first is a translated KGB report despatched to stations abroad after the Able Archer incident, but very much representative of the sort of instruction circulated as part of RYaN. It is a large list of indicators, the presence of a sufficient number of which would have been taken, in aggregate, to suggest that US plans for a pre-emptive nuclear war had begun. The other document is a CIA Special National Intelligence Estimate from May 1984. Despite noting the presence of a number of unusual Soviet activities, it was categorically assessed that 'we believe strongly that Soviet actions are not inspired by, and Soviet leaders do not perceive, a genuine danger of imminent conflict or confrontation with the United States'. The remainder of the report attempts to justify this confident, and as we now know, entirely erroneous analytical conclusion. In simple terms, the episode highlights that good intelligence does not necessarily lead to good analysis.

```
Main Department III


Berlin, 26 November 1984
Copy Nr.:
(40 pages)


Strictly confidential!
Indicators  to  recognize  adversarial  preparations
for  a  surprise  nuclear  missile  attack  (summarizing
catalogue)
(This material is to be kept safe only with Head of
Department III in person)


                              Berlin, 27 August 1984


Main Directorate A [HV A]
Deputy Head
EYES ONLY!
Head Main Department III
Comrade Major General Männchen


Indicator catalogue of the KGB
Attached you receive a summarizing catalogue prepared
by the 1st Main Directorate of the KGB about indica-
tors  to  recognize  adversarial  preparations  for  a
surprise nuclear missile attack.


   You are requested to use this document as a basis
for input to the HV A catalogue of indicators coming
```

up for review in October 1984. In particular those
hostile measures and indicators are to be considered which are not covered by methods of signal
intelligence.
[signed]
G e y e r
Major General

Appendix
Strictly confidential

Translation from Russian

**Indicators to recognize adversarial preparations
for a surprise nuclear missile attack (summarizing
catalogue)**

Moscow, 1984
The summarizing catalogue of indicators to recognize
a nuclear missile attack is divided into the following areas: political and military, activities of
intelligence services, civil defense, economic.

With regard to each mentioned area, listed below are,
with support of mutually coordinated indexation,
- the main tasks to uncover immediate preparations
for a nuclear missile attack in the respective area;
- the main measures/indicators of immediate preparations for a nuclear missile attack in the respective
area;
- special indicators of immediate preparations for a
nuclear missile attack in the respective area.

Political Area
Main tasks to uncover immediate preparations for a
nuclear missile attack in the political area
1. Uncovering measures of preparation and adoption of
political decisions for a surprise nuclear missile
attack.
2. Uncovering the implementation of mobilization
measures to secure operations of the US leadership
under conditions of a nuclear war.

268

3. Notice of consultations with allied partners about implementation of a nuclear attack.

4. Uncovering measures to guarantee the operation of NATO states' governments under conditions of a nuclear war.

5. Noticing the fact of the order forwarded to troops to launch missiles.

Main measures/indicators of immediate preparations for a nuclear missile attack in the political area

1.1. Holding of extraordinary meetings by the National Security Council of the United States and of special crisis groups (White House "situation room").

1.2. Activation of work of US government institutions involved in especially important decisions (State Department, Department of Defense, CIA, and others).

1.3. Increase in protection for leading US politicians and government institutions.

2.1. US President and people in charge at the White House relocate to protected command centers to continue the government.

2.2. Evacuation of people close to the highest political leadership of the United States from areas of increased risk on US territory and in foreign countries.

2.3. Information to the US National Archives to guarantee preservation of most important government documents.

2.4. Activation of operations by FEMA representatives in leading US government institutions.

2.5. Relocation of the most important people from leading US government agencies to places especially equipped for their work under war conditions.

3.1. Holding of extraordinary consultations by the US political leadership and the NATO states.

3.2. Activation of the mechanism of "nuclear consultations" of NATO.

3.3. Changes in political activities of US embassies in the NATO states.

4.1. Activation of work by government institutions of NATO states in charge of adoption of particularly important decisions and contacts with the United States and the other NATO allies.

4.2. Increase in protection for leading politicians and government institutions of NATO states.

4.3. Relocation of the highest political leadership and leading people from government institutions of the NATO states to protected command centers to continue government.

4.4. Relocation of the most important people from NATO Headquarters to places especially equipped for its work under war conditions.

5.1. Forwarding of the order to the troops to launch missiles.

Special indicators of immediate preparations for a nuclear missile attack in the political area

1.1.1. Formation of special operative groups of government agencies to prepare material for the President and the National Security Council on the issue of a military attack.

1.1.2. Holding of consultations between the President and leading US politicians and military, people close to him, leading Senators, former Presidents, and influential members of business circles on the issue of a military attack.

1.1.3. Arrival of former US Presidents in Washington.

1.1.4. Frequent visits to the White House by leading US politicians and military.

1.1.5. Simultaneous presence of most members from the National Security Council and special crisis groups in Washington.

1.1.6. Parking of a large number of vehicles used by official people at the parking lot of the White House (at the area adjacent to the White House).

1.1.7. Reduction of meetings by the US President and the Secretary of State with representatives of the mass media.

1.2.1. Surprise cancellations of travel, speeches, and meetings by representatives of the military-political leadership of the country.

1.2.2. Turndowns by high-ranking official people to attend receptions and earlier planned business meetings.

1.2.3. Simultaneous unexpected leaves from receptions, dinners, balls, and business meetings by official people.

1.2.4. Early unexpected returns by leading government representatives and their family members from vacation.

1.2.5. Intensification of work in government agencies involved in preparations for decisions about the nuclear missile attack. Work by according institutions (by a large number of employees) in evening hours and on Sundays and holidays. Parking by a larger number of vehicles as usual near administrative buildings.

1.2.6. Violation of existing protocol for meetings by high-ranking US government people. Arrival of Secretaries in their respective departments at unusual times.

1.2.7. Significant increase in anti-Soviet propaganda, unleashing of a war hysteria.

1.2.8. Statements in the press, radio, and on TV about an increase of aggressiveness in USSR policy, and the subsequent need to take countermeasures in this context.

1.3.1. Limitation of access to the White House.

1.3.2. Increased security for the White House. Deployment of police posts on the White House yards, and on the roofs of buildings adjacent to the White House. Increased police car patrol rides around the White House.

1.3.3. Providing employees of the White House with security.

1.3.4. Increased security for leading members of the State Department and the federal departments.

1.3.5. Introduction of a special secrecy routine regarding rides by the President and the Vice President, keeping their driving routes secret.

2.1.1. Surprising departure by the US President, his family, the Vice President, and the President's close advisers from Washington and their accommodation in the especially equipped nuclear shelter (Fort Ritzi) [sic, Fort Ritchie].

2.1.2. Unexpected departure by the family members of the President from their permanent residences (outside the White House).

2.4.1. Holding of extraordinary FEMA meetings.

2.4.2. Activation of operations by FEMA coordinators in government institutions.

2.4.3. Activation of operations by FEMA in the 10 regional headquarters.

2.5.1. Preparation of potential evacuation routes. Increase of police activities on roads where evacuation is supposed to occur.

3.1.1. Information of the highest military-political leadership of the NATO bloc, and the leading member countries of the bloc, about the preparation of a surprise nuclear missile attack.

3.1.2. Unexpected appearances by US government leaders in capitals of NATO states, without announcement in the press or after advance information.

3.1.3. Unplanned and unexpected visits by leading politicians from NATO states in Washington.

3.1.4. Intensive exchange of opinions between governments of the United States and the NATO countries through utilization of additional information channels.

3.2.1. Transfer of national centers on assessment of the situation to a working routine around the clock. Adding more personnel to national situation rooms and the NATO situation room (Ever, Belgium) [sic, Evere].

3.2.2. Increase of operative centers in the staffs of the Supreme Headquarters Allied Powers Europe (Casteaux) [sic, Casteau], the Supreme Allied Commander Atlantic (Norfolk, United States), and the NATO Allied Maritime Command (Northwood, Great Britain) by additional personnel.

3.2.3. Announcement of alert condition "Bravo" or "Charly" [sic, Charlie] for bloc headquarters by the NATO Secretary General.

3.2.4. Deployment of military representatives of national delegations at NATO headquarters, among else the French military mission, to guarantee communication between the situation room of the bloc, the national situation rooms, and the governments of the member countries.

3.2.5. Organization of a 24-hour-duty by representatives of national delegations at NATO headquarters in the meeting rooms of the Council, respectively the Defense Planning Committee of NATO.

3.2.6. Establishment of special working groups with representatives from the international military staff to support the NATO situation room.

3.2.7. Convening of a joint meeting of Council/Defense Planning Committee and NATO Military Committee.

3.2.8. Sending of urgent messages of type "Whisky" by the most important military leaderships of NATO to the Council/Defense Planning Committee of the bloc, and to the governments of the member countries, in case of a decision by most important leaderships to ask for permission of the use of nuclear weapons.

3.2.9. Replenishing personnel of the data evaluation unit on nuclear issues at the NATO situation room to analyze requests and information concerning the use of nuclear weapons.

3.2.10. Arrival of the request about use of nuclear weapons, or information about the intention to use nuclear weapons, at NATO headquarters.

3.3.1. Activation of operations of US embassies, exit of employees from US institutions under various pre-texts, destroying of documents at the embassy.

3.3.2. Simultaneous arrival of US ambassadors from the capitals of NATO states for consultations in Washington.

4.1.1. Unusual activities in the residence of a head of the executive of a country. Frequent visits to the residence by leading politicians and military of the country, and by representatives of the United States and the NATO bloc.

4.1.2. Intensification of work by the most important government institutions. Work by a large number of employees on evenings and at night hours, as well as on non-workdays.

4.1.3. Early and surprising return by politicians from vacations, bans on taking leave for individual categories of government employees.

4.1.4. Cancellations of planned meetings, events, visits, and travel abroad by leading politicians of the country.

4.1.5. Turndowns by high-ranking official people

to attend receptions and earlier planned business meetings.

4.1.6. Simultaneous unexpected leaves from receptions and business meetings by official people.

4.1.7. Unusual activity in the work of staffs of NATO military leaderships which are not in a context of implementing large command staff exercises of the bloc. Instructions to members of the staff to work at unusual times.

4.1.8. Organization of frequent personal meetings, unplanned in advance, between the Supreme Commander or the Chief of Staff of the Supreme Command of the Allied Joint Forces Europe with the NATO Secretary General, especially at unusual times.

4.1.9. Organization of meetings by the leadership of the NATO states with leading politicians and military, as well as with people close to them.

4.1.10. Establishment of special crisis groups consisting of government members and representatives of military and political circles.

4.1.11. Formation of special operative groups of agencies to prepare material for reporting to the political leadership of the country and members of the crisis groups.

Military Area

Main tasks to uncover immediate preparations for a nuclear missile attack in the military area

1. Uncovering measures of immediate preparation by the US forces for a surprise nuclear missile attack.

2. Uncovering measures of immediate preparation by NATO forces for a surprise nuclear missile attack.

3. Noticing the fact of the order forwarded to troops to launch missiles.

Main measures/indicators of immediate preparations for a nuclear missile attack in the military area

1.1. Activation of command and leadership centers of United States and NATO forces.

1.2. Raising of the level of combat readiness for the strategic offensive forces of the United States (intercontinental ballistic missiles, nuclear subma-

rines with ballistic missiles, self-propelled artillery), preparation and implementation of extensive
exercises.
1.3. Raising the level of combat readiness for the
forward-deployed nuclear forces of the United States
in Europe.
1.4. Moving American military objects abroad to
higher level of combat readiness.
1.5. Organization of extensive relocations of US
forces.
2.1. Significant modifications in operation of military communication networks of the United States and
NATO (putting reserve channels into operation; launch
of the mode "Minimize").
2.2. Increase of the level of combat readiness for
England's nuclear forces.
2.3. Increase of the level of combat readiness for
France's nuclear forces.
2.4. Putting the military objects of armies from NATO
states into higher combat readiness, launch of the
NATO alarm system.
3.1. Forwarding the order to the troops to launch the
missiles, preparing the weapons systems for launch.
Special indicators of immediate preparations for a
nuclear missile attack in the military area
1.1.1. Replenishing of war staffs and reserve command
centers, increase of duty in the staff and command
centers.
1.1.2. Review and clarification of alarm, mobilization, and operative planning, and of alert systems
for personnel, staffs, and units.
1.1.3. Relocation of staffs of battlefield armies,
and those of the army corps, divisions, and brigades
to the main, forward, and reserve command centers.
1.2.1. Accelerated completion of scheduled work and
technical maintenance at launching pads of intercontinental ballistic missiles; extraordinary launch of
their combat readiness; removal of technical maintenance crews in intercontinental ballistic missile
squadrons from launching pads and missile command
centers.
1.2.2. Termination of regular technical maintenance

and scheduled work at launching pads and missile command centers.

1.2.3. Termination of scheduled exercises and test missile launches at launching pads of the 1st Training Division and missile test launching sites; extensive work at those sites to prepare combat missiles for launch.

1.2.4. Conducting of work by flying and technical personnel to incorporate those planes into the alert system which are not part of alert forces.

1.2.5. Distribution of nuclear ammunition (aircraft bombs and cruise missiles) from stocks of the Air Force bases of the Strategic Air Command to fighter aircraft which are not part of alert forces; transport of this ammunition to the aircraft and its installation.

1.2.6. Introduction of flights by the strategic Air Force to flight routes of combat patrol units with nuclear weapons on board.

1.2.7. Rushed preparations and departure of nuclear missile submarines from rearward bases and into forward deployment areas (in this context: working intensity increases concerning these aspects, daily routines are changing, and security gets tightened).

1.2.8. Rushed withdrawal of nuclear submarines not ready for combat, as well as of floating bases, transporters, docks, and other swimming devices from rearward bases and their de-centralization at war anchoring locations.

1.2.9. Transfer of alert nuclear submarines with ballistic missiles from daily patrol areas to patrol areas for extraordinary situations.

1.2.10. In case of alert, assembly of the entire personnel of units, groups, and institutions of the Strategic Air Command.

1.2.11. Termination of discharges of personnel from the Strategic Air Command that had completed its fixed terms in the armed forces.

1.2.12. Provision of means for collective protection from weapons of mass destruction, and for conducting exercises with personnel on airfields and bases.

1.3.1. Withdrawal of nuclear units in armed ground

forces from their permanent areas of deployment and their transfer to areas of de-centralization, as well as preparation for manning, or the actual manning, of the firing positions to launch the attack.

1.3.2. Take-off by a part of Strategic Air Force for combat patrol flights with nuclear weapons on board.

1.3.3. Removal of nuclear weapons from stocks and distribution of nuclear ammunition to the units.

1.3.4. Increase in protection and defense of nuclear ammunition stocks, as well as of units in possession of nuclear weapons.

1.3.5. Advance of all batteries from guided missiles of types "Pershing" and "Lance", as well as of supply units for nuclear ammunition, into their areas of operation.

1.3.6. Alerting of all units with surface-to-air missiles of type "Nike Hercules" to combat readiness.

1.3.7. Appearance (numerical increase) of aircraft from Strategic Air Force (reconnaissance aircraft, tanker aircraft), as well as of aircraft carriers from tactical Air Force, at Air Force bases where they had not been observed previously.

1.3.8. Inclusion of aircraft not part of alert forces into the alert system, by flying and technical personnel.

1.3.9. Mass delivery of conventional aerial bombs and guided missiles, as well as delivery of fuels and lubricants, from inventories to the airbases.

1.3.10. Start of nuclear ballistic missile submarines from their base Holy Loch in Great Britain - 2 to 3 nuclear submarines with ballistic missiles.

1.3.11. Transfer of a part of American nuclear submarines with ballistic missiles to operative command of the Supreme Allied Commander of NATO Forces in Europe.

1.3.12. Early arrival of second crews in forward deployment positions for potential replenishment, or substitution of crews from nuclear submarines with ballistic missiles.

1.3.13. Increase in numbers of patrolling relay station aircraft to communicate with nuclear submarines with ballistic missiles.

1.3.14. Replenishing of stocks in submarines for material and technical supply norms for wartimes (for 90 days).
1.3.15. Preparation of warships for going to sea.
1.3.16. Activation of airborne air forces.
1.3.17. Start of 24-hour-work to complete repair of warships in marine bases.
1.3.18. Towing of ships to the sea that cannot be repaired in time.
1.4.1. Increase of security for bases, staffs, units, and objects through higher numbers of guards, deployment of additional posts, sending out of patrols, and increase in readiness for units on alert; application of stricter rules for entries [to bases and objects].
1.4.2. Intensive activities of military transportation in the area of military objects.
1.4.3. Preparations for distribution of mobilization supply of ammunition and food, complete refueling of vehicles with fuels and lubricants.
1.4.4. Concentration of a higher number than usual of military supplies and military technology in train stations, ports, and bases.
1.4.5. Leave restrictions or leave bans for personnel; no permission to leave unit or garrison.
1.4.6. Distribution of individual protective chemicals to personnel, and of protective gear against weapons of mass destruction.
1.5.1. Take-off by tanker aircraft from airbases on the US continent and their landing on stopover air force bases along air routes of the tactical air force (Bermuda, Azores, and others).
1.5.2. Beginning of mass transports of forces by air from the United States to Europe in North Atlantic direction (USA, Newfoundland Islands, Great Britain, FRG) and in Central Atlantic direction (United States, Azores, Spain, FRG, Greece, Turkey), to Asia in central direction (USA, Hawai'i Islands, Marianas, Southeast Asia), and in Northern direction (USA, Alaska, Japan). Those routes are flown by strategic military transport aircraft of types C-5A and C-141.
1.5.3. Work to prepare foreign airbases for landing of aircraft from the tactical Air Force, arriving

from the United States according to double-base status.

1.5.4. Arrival of special transport ships in ports to transport personnel and ammunition to designated areas.

2.1.1. Installation and activation of a reserve system to guide forces and material of the US Strategic Air Command.

2.1.2. Increase of radiation due to a check of means of communication of the main and to-be-installed reserve system to guide forces of the US Strategic Air Command.

2.1.3. Increase of traffic in communication systems "Alpha", "Bravo", "Green Pine", and others.

2.1.4. Alerting personnel of the command post and communication center of the Strategic Air Command, that lives in residences of their units as well as in cities nearby, or where command centers and staff are deployed.

2.1.5. Restriction of work with means of communication and introduction of "Minimize" mode in national communication networks and in NATO communication networks.

2.1.6. Review of national civilian plans of the NATO states to guarantee secrecy of the means of communication operations.

2.1.7. Preparation by national agencies of NATO states to reduce some civilian services in order to transfer signal frequencies used for the purposes of NATO.

2.1.8. Starting the system of recognition and call signals by the Supreme Allied Commander of NATO forces.

2.1.9.Starting the system of telecommunication and covered voice communication between NATO headquarters, the capitals of member states, and the bloc's most important military leaderships.

2.1.10. National control and takeover of commercial communication networks.

2.4.1. Military units and forces in the state of increased readiness are kept in garrisons or military training areas under the pretext to conduct exercises.

2.4.2. Preparation for distribution of mobilization supplies of ammunition and iron food rations, complete refueling of vehicles with fuels and lubricants.

2.4.3. Leave restrictions or leave bans, as well as no permission to leave units, for the personnel.

2.4.4. Preparation for application of ECM [Electronic Countermeasures] and ECCM [Electronic Counter-Countermeasures].

2.4.5. Distribution of individual protective chemicals and protective gear against weapons of mass destruction to personnel.

2.4.6. Exercise of stricter control over electromagnetic radiation in bases of their troops and in objects in the hinterland.

2.4.7. Increase of security for bases, staffs, units, and objects through higher numbers of guards, deployment of additional posts, sending out patrols, and increase in readiness for units on-duty; application of stricter rules for entries.

Area of Activities of Intelligence Services
Main tasks to uncover immediate preparations for a nuclear missile attack in the area of activities of intelligence services

1. Notice of intelligence measures immediately preceding a nuclear missile attack.

2. Notice of counterintelligence measures immediately preceding a nuclear missile attack.

Main measures/indicators of immediate preparations for a nuclear missile attack in the area of activities of intelligence services

1.1. Activation of operations by intelligence services of the United States and NATO on territory of the socialist states, intensification of gathering intelligence information about objects against which a nuclear attack is directed.

1.2. Activation of efforts by intelligence services of the United States and NATO to pin down exact locations of the highest USSR party and state leadership.

1.3. Activation of the adversary's technological intelligence operations.

2.1. Blocking of actions of Soviet foreign intelligence on the territory of the United States and other NATO states.

2.2. Relocation of personnel from central units of intelligence services and documentation in rearward positions.

2.3. Increase in security routines at military objects of the United States on its own territory and abroad.

2.4. Increased countermeasures against Soviet technological intelligence.

2.5. Tightening of the administrative and police routines on US territory and in other NATO states.

2.6. Increased measures to guarantee security of abroad institutions of the United States in socialist states, destroying of secret documents.

2.7. Increase in security routines at military objects of the armies of the NATO states.

Special indicators of immediate preparations for a nuclear missile attack in the area of activities of intelligence services

1.1.1. Incoming instructions from foreign intelligence leadership for immediate gathering of information on the final decision about a nuclear missile attack, which is going to show in a change of work routine by the adversary's legal foreign resident agents.

1.1.2. Increase in number of cadres of US legal foreign resident agents. and the residents of the NATO states on USSR territory; their extensive quantitative equipment with most recent operative technology, allocation of additional financial funds, removal of agents.

1.1.3. Activation of efforts by Western intelligence services to gather and obtain precise information about objects against which a nuclear missile attack is supposedly directed on the territory of the USSR; about centers of government and military leadership, and the means of communication; about locations of deployment of strategic nuclear fores, and most important industry, transportation, and energy supply objects.

1.1.4. Significant changes in the structure of foreign military intelligence organs of the United States and the NATO states.

1.1.5. Activation of operations by special units from intelligence services of the United States and NATO states which are designated for acts of diversion on USSR territory.

1.1.6. Significant activation of foreign intelligence operations of the United States and the NATO states in the border regions of the USSR.

1.1.7. Establishment of new centers of espionage near the borders with socialist states, and reduction of the training period in espionage training of the US and NATO states.

1.1.8. Increase in numbers of personnel of American foreign military intelligence centers in Western Europe, especially of the operative foreign intelligence center of the US Air Force in Europe (Rammstein Airbase, FRG [sic, Ramstein]), the American group for generalization of information with the Staff of the Supreme Command of Allied Forces Central Europe (located in a bunker of the war staff of the according Supreme Command in Berfink, Netherlands [sic, Börfink, West Germany], and the center for assessment of intelligence information in conflict situations with the Staff of the US European Command (Stuttgart, FRG).

1.1.9. Activation of information exchange between the center for assessment of intelligence information in conflict situations with the Staff of the US European Command and foreign intelligence organs of the NATO states about bilateral communication links between the center and various capitals of the bloc's member countries. Organization of an intensive information exchange between civilian and military foreign intelligence organs of the bloc's countries and national delegations at NATO headquarters, between the headquarters itself and these organs, as well as directly between the intelligence services of the NATO states.

1.1.10. Chance in procedure of distributing foreign intelligence information within NATO. (Usually, foreign intelligence organs of the bloc's member countries send their information to the NATO situation room, which then distributes it to the Secretariat, the international military staff, the most important military leadership organs, and the delegations of member countries at headquarters and their governments. In an unusual situation, national foreign intelligence organs have permission to send urgent information straight to recipients).

1.1.11. More frequent than usual (once within 24 hours) distribution by the NATO situation room of intelligence overviews that are unrelated to the bloc's large command staff exercises.

1.3.1. Additional starts of artificial space satellites, space apparatuses, and space transportation ships of the Shuttle type (from Cape Canaveral and the testing site of the Vandernberg base [sic, Vandenberg]).

1.3.2. Surveillance aircraft and unmanned intelligence devices are moved to a status guaranteeing their immediate operation.

1.3.3. Application of mobile means of technological intelligence on the ground.

1.3.4. Moving ground units for space technological intelligence towards working in increased shifts.

1.3.5. Arrival of the war contingent of specialists at the ground units of NASA.

1.3.6. Arrival of specialists from higher-ranking organizations at the main units and means of technological intelligence.

1.3.7. Increased delivery of additional material and devices to the units and means of technological intelligence.

1.3.8. Additional equipment of civilian and warships with devices for technological intelligence.

1.3.9. In objects of technological intelligence: installation of stations and allocation of equipment for decontamination, and for protection of personnel and technology against chemical and bacteriological agents.

2.1.1. Grave deterioration of the operative situation for foreign intelligence organs of the USSR and the other socialist states, application of signal intelligence as well as of operative technology. Implementation of operative measures to gather data about the USSR's status of information concerning plans of the United States for the execution of a nuclear missile attack.

2.1.2. Activation of actions by the US propaganda apparatus to create inside the country, and in allied states, a situation of chauvinism and of undermining the international reputation of the USSR.

2.1.3. Surprising changes in work routines of the adversary's foreign intelligences services and their units, with simultaneous tightening of the security regime.

Analogous changes in working routines of legislative and government organs in charge of controlling operations of foreign intelligence.

2.1.4. Increase in observation operations against employees of Soviet institutions. Moving of observation service to different news frequencies.

2.1.5. Intensification of monitoring of Soviet citizens.

2.1.6. Extensive application of operative technology against Soviet institutions and citizens.

2.1.7. Introduction of additional travel restrictions in the country for USSR representatives.

2.1.8. Reduction of the number of Soviet institutions and expulsion of individual employees.

2.1.9. Massive numbers of declines of diplomatic visa for representatives of the USSR and other member countries of the Warsaw Treaty.

2.1.10. Creating a tense situation near Soviet institutions, threat of physical violence against Soviet representatives, organization of demonstrations and manifestations as well as other provocations, among else approaches for recruitment and similar things.

2.1.11. Organization of repressive measures by counterintelligence and police against progressive organizations and individual people, among else against those who maintain contacts with the Soviet embassy.

2.3.1. Strong activation of operations of military counterintelligence, transfer of employees of these organs to a 24-hour work mode, introduction of a tight security regime in military objects.

2.3.2. Declines of permissions for foreign diplomats

and journalists to travel to areas where military objects are located.

2.3.3. Introduction of a tight security regime in individual areas of the country, especially where most important mobilization measures are implemented. Setting up of street checkpoints.

2.4.1. Change of secret codes and ciphers of government and military institutions, in NATO staff, and in the armed forces; introduction of additional measures to protect communication lines from eavesdropping.

2.5.1. Increase of security for government institutions and restriction of access to administrative buildings.

2.5.2. Tightening of security and guarding of buildings of intelligence services and their offices, as well as of adjacent areas.

2.5.3. Increase in security for government officials and high-ranking people.

2.5.4. Increase of border and customs control at state borders, airports, and in sea ports.

2.5.5. Tightening of security to guard airports, river and sea ports, train stations and hubs, main roads, and bridges.

2.5.6. Introduction of censorship of the press and other mass media. Increase in mail censorship and imposing of restrictions for phone and telex connections to foreign countries.

2.5.7. Cancellation of radio amateur licenses for the territory of the United States.

2.6.1. Increased coordination of diplomatic activities between representations of the United States and NATO states within the USSR.

2.6.2. Transmission of instructions from the capitals of the United States and the other NATO countries to their representations in Moscow and in other cities of the USSR.

2.6.3. Unexpected and unmotivated departures from the USSR by heads of diplomatic and other representations of the United States and other NATO states.

2.6.4. Surprising mass destruction of documents in representations of the United States and other NATO states in the USSR.

2.6.5. Surprising leave from exercises of the USSR and its allies within the Warsaw Treaty by observers from the United States and other NATO countries.

Area of Civil Defense
Main tasks to uncover immediate preparations for a nuclear missile attack in the area of activities of civil defense
1. Notice of measures to increase mobilization readiness in organs of civil defense in the context of an immediate preparation for a nuclear missile attack.
2. Notice of measures to prepare shelters to accommodate the population, to replenish food and water reserves in the context of an immediate preparation for a nuclear missile attack.
3. Notice of measures to secure medical care of the population under conditions of a nuclear counterattack.
4. Notice of preparations to evacuate specialists (from the overall population);
5. Notice of measures to bring important material valuables and national cultural treasures to safety from a nuclear attack.
Main measures/indicators of immediate preparations for a nuclear missile attack in the area of activities of civil defense
1.1. Activation of operations by the Federal Emergency Management Agency (FEMA) and its regional staffs.
1.2. Activation of operations of government institutions of Western European states in charge of organizing the civil defense systems of those countries.
1.3. Preparation and implementation of extensive exercises of the civil defense systems of the United States and NATO.
2.1. Testing of communication and information means of the civil defense systems of the Western states.
2.2. Installation of shelter and camouflaged accommodations of the civil defense system.
2.3. Replenishment of food and water reserves.
3.1. Expansion of the network of medical institutions.
3.2. Activation of blood donations.
3.3. Replenishment and distribution of inventories of special medications.

4.1. Mobilization preparation of personnel from a limited circle of most important companies, institutions, local and mail services.

4.2. Preparation of roads for mass evacuations of population from large cities, and establishment of decentralized areas for the population.

4.3. Bringing to safety especially important material valuables, national culture monuments, and pieces of art.

Special indicators of immediate preparations for a nuclear missile attack in the area of activities of civil defense

1.1.1. Significant changes in operations of FEMA. FEMA Headquarters: 1725 I Street, Washington D.C. 20472

The FEMA has regional staff in 10 regions on United States territory, in particular in:

- 26 Federal Plaza, Room 1349, New York, NY 10007.

- 211 Main Street, Room 220, San Francisco, CA 94105.

1.1.2. Transfer of FEMA and its regional staff to work under war mode.

2.1.1. Transfer of means of information and communication to permanent working routines. Introduction of 24-hour-duty in signal center.

2.2.1. Removal of unnecessary items from shelters and radiation protection rooms.

2.2.2. Removal of nuclear radiation observation posts.

2.2.3. Checking of filter ventilation systems and electricity supply for hermetic tightness and functioning.

3.1.1. Creating additional hospital space in existing military clinics.

3.1.2. Establishment of mobile military clinics and hospitals.

3.1.3. Additional delegations to courses for training medical personnel.

3.1.4. Establishment of additional medical installations at potential evacuation routes.

3.1.5. Maximum release of sick people from hospitals and increase in capacities of military clinics.

3.2.1. Conducting a mass campaign to donate blood,

with an expansion of the number of pure blood donors, plasma donors, and paid donors.

3.2.2. Activation of measures to propagate blood donations on radio, television, in the press, and the like.

3.2.3. Collecting donations not just in large cities, but especially in suburbs and rural areas, and in places with probable locations of military hospitals and evacuated population.

3.2.4. Decentralization of blood banks and stocking up of installations, equipment, standard serum, blood preparations, and blood substitutes in relatively safe areas, activation of operations of private blood banks.

3.2.5. Expanding the pool of autonomous mobile stations with blood supplies.

3.2.6. Additional recruitment and training of personnel to work in mobile stations with blood supplies and in blood donation centers.

4.1.1. Conducting prophylactic vaccinations (especially in factories and institutions with priority relevance in the period of rebuilding).

4.1.2. Distribution of individual protective gear to units in factories and institutions.

4.1.3. Implementation of evacuation plans for families of military employees and civilian personnel from staffs and troops of the United States and NATO.

4.2.1. Removal of means of transportation designated for evacuation purposes from potential areas of destruction.

4.2.2. Preparation and partial implementation of plans to evacuate the civilian population (especially from the endangered areas).

5.1.1. Closing of the largest museums and exhibition sites (maybe under the pretext of repair work, testing of civil defense systems, and the like).

Economic Area
Main tasks to uncover immediate preparations for a nuclear missile attack in the economic area
1. Notice of mobilization measures to guarantee security for the leadership and for assets of large

corporations and banks under conditions of a nuclear war.

2. Notice of mobilization measures to guarantee operations of the most important industrial objects under conditions of a nuclear war.

3. Notice of measures to mobilize means of transportation and their complete allocation to operate under conditions of a nuclear war.

Main measures/indicators of immediate preparations for a nuclear missile attack in the economic area

1.1 Relocation of personnel from central administrations, and from the most important employees of large factories, banks, companies, and academic centers to protected shelters and accommodations.

1.2. Restrictions of operations, and transfer of assets of the largest banks of the United States and other NATO countries to neutral states.

1.3. Implementation of additional measures for physical protection of the most important industrial sites.

2.2. Replenishing and decentralization of raw material and fuel supplies (on a national level, in individual factories and warehouses).

2.3. Selection of additional workers for most important armament factories by job placement centers.

3.1. Activation of operations in US government institutions in charge of mobilization of transportation in emergency situations.

3.2. Mobilization of civilian aviation.

3.3. Decentralization of ships of civilian navigation.

3.4. Mobilization of train and vehicle transportation.

Special indicators of immediate preparations for a nuclear missile attack in the economic area

1.1.1. Evacuation of headquarters of leading US banks and corporations in areas designated for use under war conditions. In particular relocation of headquarters of the telecommunication branch of AT&T (American Telephone & Telegraph Corporation) from Badminister [sic, Bedminster] (State of New Jersey) to the underground shelter in Netkong [sic, Netcong] (State of New Jersey).

1.2.1. Transfer of financial and currency assets of

the largest banks of the US and other NATO states to foreign banks (especially to Swiss banks).

1.2.2. Significant changes in policies of banks and insurance companies from the US and other NATO states, in particular the FRG, with regard to crediting and insurance of trade agreements with the socialist states.

2.1.1. Evacuation of equipment and products of certain factories, especially from the border areas.

2.2.1. Increase of raw material and fuel supplies to a maximum, not caused by current production but depending on capacities of warehouses and company sites.

2.2.2. Mass slaughter of livestock and storage of meat for a long period.

3.1.1. Intensive preparations to transfer transportation services of United States and NATO states to a state of war.

3.2.1. Handover of aircraft from civilian airlines to the Allied Air Forces, in particular to the Danish airline SAS.

3.3.1. Confidential information to shipping agencies and ship owners about the rise of international tensions, and recommendation to reduce maritime traffic of NATO states and their allies in respective regions.

3.3.2. Takeover of ships from merchant and passenger fleets for deployment for military purposes.

3.3.3. Changes in customs and immigration procedures of required arrival formalities for Soviet passenger and trade ships in ports of those countries.

3.3.4. Unexpected departure by civilian ships from the US and NATO states from ports and territorial waters of Warsaw Treaty member countries.

3.4.1. Mobilization of means of transportation to evacuate civilian factories and the population from large cities.

3.4.2. Intensive relocation of military and civilian vehicle transportation means from the depths of NATO countries in areas close to border districts and troop concentration of the Warsaw Treaty armed forces.

Implications of Recent
Soviet Military-Political
Activities

APPROVED FOR RELEASED DATE: 13-Apr-2010

SNIE 11-10-84
IMPLICATIONS OF
RECENT SOVIET MILITARY-POLITICAL ACTIVITIES

THIS ESTIMATE IS ISSUED BY THE DIRECTOR OF CENTRAL
INTELLIGENCE.

THE NATIONAL FOREIGN INTELLIGENCE BOARD CONCURS,
EXCEPT AS NOTED IN THE TEXT.
*The following intelligence organizations partici-
pated in the preparation of the Estimate:*
    The Central Intelligence Agency, the Defense
    Intelligence Agency, the National Security Agency,
    and the intelligence organization of the Department
    of State.

Also Participating:
    The Assistant Chief of Staff for Intelligence,
    Department of the Army
    The Director of Naval Intelligence, Department of
    the Navy
    The Assistant Chief of Staff, Intelligence,
    Department of the Air Force
    The Director of Intelligence, Headquarters, Marine
    Corps

KEY JUDGMENTS
During the past several months, a number of coin-
cident Soviet activities have created concern that
they reflect abnormal Soviet fear of conflict with
the United States, belligerent intent that might risk
conflict, or some other underlying Soviet purpose.
These activities have included large-scale military

exercises (among them a major naval exercise in the Norwegian Sea, unprecedented SS-20 launch activity, and large-scale SSBN dispersal); preparations for air operations against Afghanistan; attempts to change the air corridor regime in Berlin; new military measures termed responsive to NATO INF deployments; and shrill propaganda attributing a heightened danger of war to US behavior.

Examining these developments in terms of several hypotheses, we reach the following conclusions:

- We believe strongly that Soviet actions are not inspired by, and Soviet leaders do not perceive, a genuine danger of imminent conflict or confrontation with the United States. This judgment is based on the absence of forcewide combat readiness or other war preparation moves in the USSR, and the absence of a tone of fear or belligerence in Soviet diplomatic communications, although the latter remain uncompromising on many issues. There have also been instances where the Soviets appear to have avoided belligerent propaganda or actions. Recent Soviet "war scare" propaganda, of declining intensity over the period examined, is aimed primarily at discrediting US policies and mobilizing "peace" pressures among various audiences abroad. This war scare propaganda has reverberated in Soviet security bureaucracies and emanated through other channels such as human sources. We do not believe it reflects authentic leadership fears of imminent conflict.

- We do not believe that Soviet war talk and other actions "mask" Soviet preparations for an imminent move toward confrontation on the part of the USSR, although they have an incentive to take initiatives that discredit US policies even at some risk. Were the Soviets preparing an initiative they believed carried a real risk of military confrontation with the United States, we would see preparatory signs which the Soviets could not mask.

- The Soviet actions examined are influenced to

some extent by Soviet perceptions of a mounting challenge from US foreign and defense policy. However, these activities do not all fit into an integrated pattern of current Soviet foreign policy tactics.

- Each Soviet action has its own military or political purpose sufficient to explain it. Soviet military exercises are designed to meet long-term requirements for force development and training which have become ever more complex with the growth of Soviet military capabilities.

- In specific cases, Soviet military exercises are probably intended to have the ancillary effect of signaling Soviet power and resolve to some audience. For instance, maneuvers in the Tonkin Gulf were aimed at backing Vietnam against China; Soviet airpower use in Afghanistan could have been partly aimed at intimidating Pakistan; and Soviet action on Berlin has the effect of reminding the West of its vulnerable access, but very low-key Soviet handling has muted this effect.

Taken in their totality, Soviet talk about the increased likelihood of nuclear war and Soviet military actions do suggest a political intention of speaking with a louder voice and showing firmness through a controlled display of military muscle. The apprehensive outlook we believe the Soviet leadership has toward the longer term US arms buildup could in the future increase its willingness to consider actions - even at some heightened risk - that recapture the initiative and neutralize the challenge posed by the United States.

These judgments are tempered by some uncertainty as to current Soviet leadership perceptions of the United States, by continued uncertainty about Politburo decision making processes, and by our inability at this point to conduct a detailed examination of how the Soviets might have assessed recent US/NATO military exercises and reconnaissance operations. Notwithstanding these uncertainties, however, we are confident that, as of now, the Soviets see not an imminent military clash but a costly and - to some extent – more perilous strategic and political struggle over the rest of the decade.

DISCUSSION

Introduction

1. There has been much Soviet talk about the increased danger of nuclear war. This theme has appeared in public pronouncements by Soviet political and military leaders, in statements by high officials targeted at both domestic and foreign audiences, in internal communications, and in other channels. Soviet authorities have declared that Washington is preparing for war, and have issued dire warnings that the USSR will not give in to nuclear blackmail or other military pressure. The articulation of this theme has paralleled the Soviet campaign to derail US INF deployment. It continues to this day, although at a somewhat lower intensity in recent months than in late 1983.

2. Since November 1983 there has been a high level of Soviet military activity, with new deployments of weapons and strike forces, large-scale military exercises, and several other noteworthy events:

- *INF response:* Start of construction of additional SS-20 bases following Andropov's announcement on 24 November 1983 of termination of the 20-month moratorium on SS-20 deployments opposite NATO; initiation in late December of patrols by E-II nuclear-powered cruise missile submarines off the US coast; first-ever forward deployment in mid-January 1984 of long-range missile-carrying D-class SSBNs; and the start of deployment also in mid-January of 925-km range SS-12/22 missiles in East Germany and Czechoslovakia, and continued propaganda and active measures against INF deployment.

- *Response to NATO exercise:* Assumption by Soviet air units in Germany and Poland from ▇▇▇▇ November 1983 of high alert status with readying of nuclear strike forces as NATO conducted "Able Archer-83," a nuclear release command post exercise.

- *Soviet exercises:* Large-scale exercise activity during spring 1984 which has stressed integrated strategic strike operations, featuring the multiple launches of SS-20s and SLBMs; survivability training including the dispersal of ▮▮▮▮ operational Northern Fleet SSBNs supported by a large number of ships; and the use of survivable command, control, and communications platforms, possibly in a transattack scenario.

- *Berlin air corridors:* Periodic Soviet imposition beginning 20 February 1984 of minimum flight altitudes for the entire length of one or more of the Berlin air corridors - a unilateral change in the rules governing air access to Berlin.
- *Afghanistan:* Deployment in mid-April of several airborne units to Afghanistan, launching of a major spring offensive into the Panjsher Valley, and initiation on 21 April for the first time of high-intensity bombing of Afghanistan by over 105 TU-16 and SU-24 bombers based in the USSR.
- *East Asia:* Deployment in mid-November 1983 of naval TU-16 strike aircraft to Vietnam for the first time; positioning of both Soviet operational aircraft carriers for the first time simultaneously in Asian waters in March 1984; and the first joint Soviet/Vietnamese amphibious assault exercises on the coast of Vietnam in April.
- *Caribbean:* A small combined Soviet/Cuban naval exercise in the Gulf of Mexico, with the first-ever visit of a Soviet helicopter carrier in April/May, and Soviet/Cuban antisubmarine drills.
- *Troop rotation:* Initiation of the airlift portion of Soviet troop rotation in Eastern Europe 10 days later in April than this has occurred for the past five years.

This Estimate explores whether the Soviet talk about the increasing likelihood of nuclear war and the Soviet military activities listed above constitute a pattern of behavior intended either to alarm or intimidate the United States and its allies or to achieve other goals.

Possible Explanations

3. Specifically, in examining the facts we address five explanatory hypotheses:

295

a. Both the Soviet talk about war and the military activities have been consciously orchestrated across the board to achieve political effects through posturing and propaganda. The object has been to discredit US defense and foreign policies; to put Washington on notice that the USSR will pursue a hard – perhaps even dangerous – line, unless US concessions are forthcoming; to maintain an atmosphere of tension conducive to pressure by "peace" groups on Western governments; and, if possible, to undercut President Reagan's reelection prospects.

b. Soviet behavior is a response to Washington's rhetoric, US military procurement and R&D goals, and US military exercises and reconnaissance activities near Soviet territory – which have excited Soviet concerns and caused Moscow to flex its own military responsiveness, signaling to Washington that it is prepared for any eventuality.

c. Moscow itself is preparing for threatening military action in the future requiring a degree of surprise. The real aim behind its recent actions is not to alarm, but to desensitize the United States to higher levels of Soviet military activity – thus masking intended future moves and reducing US warning time.

d. A weak General Secretary and political jockeying in the Soviet leadership have lessened policy control at the top and permitted a hardline faction, under abnormally high military influence, to pursue its own agenda, which – intentionally or not – looks more confrontational to the observer.

e. The Soviet military actions at issue are not linked with the talk about war and are basically unrelated events, each with its own rationale.

Soviet Talk About Nuclear War

4. Our assessment of the meaning of alarmist statements and propaganda about the danger of nuclear war provides a starting point for evaluating recent Soviet military activities.

5. Soviet talk about the war danger is unquestionably highly orchestrated. It has obvious external aims:
- To create a tense international climate that fosters "peace" activism in the West and public pressure on Western governments to backtrack on INF deployment, reduce commitments to NATO, and distance themselves from US foreign policy objectives.
- To elicit concessions in arms control negotiations by manipulating the anxieties of Western political leaders about Soviet thinking.
- To strengthen cohesion within the Warsaw Pact and reinforce Soviet pressure for higher military outlays by non-Soviet member states.

The overall propaganda campaign against the United States has recently been supplemented with the boycott of the Olympic Games.

6. The talk about the danger of nuclear war also has a clear domestic propaganda function: to rationalize demands on the Soviet labor force, continued consumer deprivation, and ideological vigilance in the society. This message is also being disseminated ▇▇▇▇▇ within the Soviet and East European ▇▇▇▇▇ bureaucracies, ▇▇▇▇▇

7. The central question remains: what are the real perceptions at top decisionmaking levels of the regime? Our information about such leadership perceptions is largely inferential. Nevertheless, we have confidence in several broad conclusions.

8. First, we believe that there is a serious concern with US defense and foreign policy trends. There is a large measure of agreement among both political and military leaders that the United States has undertaken a global offensive against Soviet interests. Central to this perception is the overall scope and momentum of the US military buildup. Fundamentally, the Soviets are concerned that US programs will undercut overall Soviet military strategy and force posture. Seen in this context, Moscow condemns INF deployment as a telling - but subordinate - element in a more far-reaching and comprehensive US effort aimed at "regaining military superiority." *The threat here is not immediate, but longer term.* However, the

297

ability of the United States to carry out its longer term plans is questioned by Soviet leaders not only to reassure domestic audiences but also because they genuinely see some uncertainty in the ability of the United States to sustain its military effort.

9. Secondly, in our judgment *the nature of the concern is as much political as it is military.* There is a healthy respect for US technological prowess and anxiety that this could in due course be used against the USSR. The Soviets are thus concerned that the United States might pursue an arms competition that could over time strain the Soviet economy and disrupt the regime's ability to manage competing military and civilian requirements. More immediately, the Soviets are concerned that the United States could achieve a shift in the overall balance of military power which, through more interventionist foreign policies, could effectively thwart the extension of Soviet influence in world affairs and even roll back past Soviet gains. From this perspective, the United States' actions in Central America, Lebanon, Grenada, and southern Africa are seen as a token of what could be expected on a broader scale in the future.

10. Third, and most important for this assessment, we do not believe the Soviet leadership sees an imminent threat of war with the United States. It is conceivable that the stridency of Soviet "war scare" propaganda reflects a genuine Soviet worry about a near-future attack on them. This concern could be inspired by Soviet views about the depth of anti-Soviet intentions in Washington combined with elements of their own military doctrine projected onto the United States, such as the virtues of surprise, striking first, and masking hostile initiatives in exercises. Some political and military leaders have stressed the danger of war more forcefully than others, suggesting that there may have been differences on this score – or at least how to talk about the issue – over the past half year.

11. However, on the basis of what we believe to be very strong evidence, we judge that the Soviet leadership does not perceive an imminent danger of war.

Our reasons are the following:
- The Soviets have not initiated the military readiness moves they would have made if they believed a US attack were imminent.
- In private US diplomatic exchanges with Moscow over the past six months the Soviets have neither made any direct threats connected with regional or other issues nor betrayed any fear of a US attack.
- Obligatory public assertions of the viability of the Soviet nuclear deterrent have been paralleled by private assertions within regime circles by Soviet experts that there is currently a stable nuclear balance in which the United States does not have sufficient strength for a first strike.
- In recent months top leaders, including the Minister of Defense and Politburo member Dmitriy Ustinov, have somewhat downplayed the nuclear war danger, noting that it should not be "over-dramatized" (although Ustinov's recent Victory Day speech returned to a somewhat shriller tone). At the same time, high foreign affairs officials have challenged the thesis that the United States can unleash nuclear war and have emphasized constraints on such a course of action.

Moreover, the Soviets know that the United States is at present far from having accomplished all of its force buildup objectives.

Recent Soviet Military Activities

12. *Intimidation?* It is possible that some of the Soviet military activities listed above were intended, as ancillary to their military objectives, to intimidate selected audiences:
- The East Asian naval maneuvers, deployment of strike aircraft to Vietnam, and amphibious exercises have displayed military muscle to China.
- The bombing campaign in Afghanistan could be seen not only as an operation against the insurgency but also as an implicit threat to neighboring countries - Pakistan and perhaps Iran.
- In mounting large-scale and visible exercises (such as the March-April Northern and Baltic Fleet

exercise in the Norwegian Sea) Moscow would understand that they could be perceived as threatening by NATO audiences.

13. Soviet INF-related military activities have also been designed to convey an impression to the West that the world *is* a more dangerous place following US INF deployment and that the USSR is making good on its predeployment threats to counter with deployments of its own.

14. There is uncertainty within the Intelligence Community on the origins of Soviet behavior with respect to the Berlin air corridors. It is possible that Soviet action was a deliberate reminder of Western vulnerability. Alternatively, airspace requirements for exercises may have motivated this move. The low-key manner in which the Soviets have handled the issue does not suggest that they have been interested in squeezing access to Berlin for intimidation purposes. Nevertheless, the Soviets have been in the process of unilaterally changing the corridor flight rules and thereby reminding the West of their ultimate power to control access to Berlin. After a short hiatus in late April and early May, the Soviets declared new air corridor restrictions, indicating that this effort continues. In a possibly related, very recent development, the Soviets declared tight new restrictions on travel in East Germany by allied missions located in Potsdam.

15. In a number of instances we have observed the Soviets avoiding threatening behavior or propaganda when they might have acted otherwise, perhaps in some cases to avoid embarrassment or overcommitment. For example, they:

- Never publicly acknowledged the incident in November 1983 in which a Soviet attack submarine was disabled off the US coast as it attempted to evade a US ASW ship, and moved the sub quickly out of Cuba where it had come for emergency repairs.
- Warned Soviet ships in late January to stay away from US ships in the eastern Mediterranean.
- Took no tangible action in March when one of their merchant tankers hit a mine off Nicaragua.

– Notified Washington of multiple missile launches in early April as a gesture of "good will."

16. ***Reaction to US actions?*** The new Soviet deployments of nuclear-armed submarines off US coasts and the forward deployment of SS-12/22 missiles in Eastern Europe are a Soviet reaction to NATO INF deployment, which the Soviets claim is very threatening to them – although the threat perceived here by Moscow is certainly not one of imminent nuclear attack.

17. Soviet military exercises themselves sometimes embody a "reactive" element. They frequently incorporate Western operational concepts and weapon systems into exercise scenarios, including projected US/NATO weapons and systems well before these systems are actually deployed. On occasion there is real- or near-real-time counterexercising, in which US/NATO exercise activity is incorporated into "Red" scenarios, thereby sensitizing Soviet forces to the US/NATO opponent. A key issue is whether this counterexercising takes on the character of actual preparation for response to a perceived threat of possible US attack.

18. A case in point is the Soviet reaction to "Able Archer-83." This was a NATO command post exercise held in November 1983 that was larger than previous "Able Archer" exercises and included new command, control, and communications procedures for authorizing use of nuclear weapons. The elaborate Soviet reaction to this recent exercise included ▮▮▮▮▮▮▮ increased intelligence collection flights, and the placing of Soviet air units in East Germany and Poland in heightened readiness in what was declared to be a threat of possible aggression against the USSR and Warsaw Pact countries. Alert measures included increasing the number of fighter-interceptors on strip alert, ▮▮▮▮▮ Although the Soviet reaction was somewhat greater than usual, by confining heightened readiness to selected air units Moscow clearly revealed that it did not in fact think there was a possibility at this time of a NATO attack.

19. How the Soviets choose to respond to ongoing US military activities, such as exercises and reconnaissance operations, depends on how they assess their

scope, the trends they may display, and above all the hostile intent that might be read into them. We are at present uncertain as to what novelty or possible military objectives the Soviets may have read into recent US and NATO exercises and reconnaissance operations because a detailed comparison of simultaneous "Red" and "Blue" actions has not been accomplished. The Soviets have, as in the past, ascribed the same threatening character to these activities as to US military buildup plans, that is, calling them preparations for war. But they have not charged a US intent to prepare for imminent war.

20. ***Preparation for surprise military action?*** There is one case in our set of military activities that might conceivably be ascribed to the "masking" of threatening Soviet initiatives. For the first time in five years, the airlift portion of the troop rotation in Eastern Europe began on 25 April rather than 15 April. This may have reflected a change in training and manning practices or the introduction of new airlift procedures. The change of timing of the airlift portion of the annual troop rotation could also be a step toward blurring a warning indicator – a comprehensive delay of annual Soviet troop rotations which would prevent degradation of the forces by withdrawing trained men. But the rail portion of the rotation began ahead of schedule and, in any event, the pattern of rotation was within broad historical norms.

21. In early April, when the Soviets began to assemble a bomber strike force in the Turkestan Military District, there was some concern that it might represent masking of preparations for operations against Pakistan, or even Iran, rather than against the most obvious target, Afghanistan. At this point the force is clearly occupied against Afghanistan. It was never suitably deployed for use against Iran. We believe that, although the force could be used against Pakistan, a major air offensive against Pakistan without forewarning or precursor political pressure would serve no Soviet purpose and is extremely unlikely.

22. Soviet military exercises display and contribute to steadily growing Soviet force capabilities. These exercises have become increasingly complex as Moscow has deployed more capable and sophisticated weapons and command and control systems. The exercises have stressed the ability to assume a wartime posture rapidly and respond flexibly to a variety of contingencies. We know that this activity ████████ is planned and scheduled months or years in advance. Typically, these plans have not been significantly affected by concurrent US or NATO exercise activity. We see no evidence that this program is now being driven by some sort of target date or deadline. Rather, it appears to respond – in annual and five-year plan increments – to new problems and operational considerations that constantly arise with ongoing force modernization. Thus, we interpret the accelerated tempo of Soviet live exercise activity as a reflection of the learning curve inherent in the exercise process itself and of long-term Soviet military objectives, rather than of preparations for, or masking of, surprise Soviet military actions.

23. *Policy impact of leadership weakness or factionalism?* The Soviet Union has had three General Secretaries in as many years and, given the age and frail health of Chernenko, yet another change can be expected in a few years. This uncertain political environment could be conducive to increased maneuvering within the leadership and magnification of policy disagreements. Some have argued that either the Soviet military or a hardline foreign policy faction led by Gromyko and Ustinov exerts more influence than it could were Chernenko a stronger figure. Although individual Soviet military leaders enjoy great authority in the regime and military priorities remain high for the whole leadership, we do not believe that the Soviet military, as an institution, is exerting unusually heavy influence on Soviet policy. Nor do we believe that any faction is exerting influence other than through Politburo consensus. Consequently we reject the hypothesis that weak central leadership accounts for the Soviet actions examined here.

24. *A comprehensive pattern?* In our view, the military activities under examination here do tend to have their own military rationales and the exercises are integrated by long-term Soviet force development plans. However, these activities do not all fit into an integrated pattern of current Soviet foreign policy tactics. The different leadtimes involved in initiating various activities argue against orchestration for a political purpose. A number of the activities represent routine training or simply refine previous exercises. In other cases, the activities respond to circumstances that could not have been predicted ahead of time.

Conclusions
25. Taken in their totality, Soviet talk about the increased likelihood of nuclear war and Soviet military actions do suggest a political intention of speaking with a louder voice and showing firmness through a controlled display of military muscle. At the same time, Moscow has given little sign of desiring to escalate tensions sharply or to provoke possible armed confrontation with the United States.
26. Soviet talk of nuclear war has been deliberately manipulated to rationalize military efforts with domestic audiences and to influence Western electorates and political elites. Some Soviet military activities have also been designed to have an alarming or intimidating effect on various audiences (notably INF "counterdeployments," the naval exercise in the Norwegian Sea, and naval and air activities in Asia).
27. Our assessment of both Soviet talk about nuclear war and Soviet military activities indicates a very low probability that the top Soviet leadership is seriously worried about the imminent outbreak of nuclear war, although it is quite possible that official propaganda and vigilance campaigning have generated an atmosphere of anxiety throughout the military and security apparatus. The available evidence suggests that none of the military activities discussed in this Estimate have been generated by a real fear of imminent US attack.

28. Although recent Soviet military exercises combine with other ongoing Soviet programs to heighten overall military capabilities, we believe it unlikely that they are intended to mask current or near-future preparations by the USSR for some directly hostile military initiative. Moreover, we are confident that the activities we have examined in this Estimate would not successfully mask all the extensive logistic and other military preparations the Soviets would have to commence well before a realistic offensive initiative against any major regional security target.

29. Both the talk of nuclear war and the military activities address the concerns of a longer time horizon. Moscow's inability to elicit major concessions in the arms talks, successful US INF deployment, and – most important by far – the long-term prospect of a buildup of US strategic and conventional military forces, have created serious concern in the Kremlin. We judge that the Soviet leadership does indeed believe that the United States is attempting to restore a military posture that severely undercuts the Soviet power position in the world.

30. The apprehensive outlook we believe the Soviet leadership has toward the longer term Western arms buildup could in the future increase its willingness to consider actions – even at some heightened risk – that recapture the initiative and neutralize the military challenge posed by the United States. Warning of such actions could be ambiguous.

31. Our judgments in this Estimate are subject to three main sources of uncertainty. We have inadequate information about:

a. The current mind-set of the Soviet political leadership, which has seen some of its optimistic international expectations from the Brezhnev era disappointed.

b. The ways in which military operations and foreign policy tactics may be influenced by political differences and the policy process in the Kremlin.

c. The Soviet reading of our own military operations, that is, current reconnaissance and exercises.

d. Notwithstanding these uncertainties, however, we

> are confident that, as of now, the Soviets see not
> an imminent military clash but a costly and – to some
> extent – more perilous strategic and political
> struggle over the rest of the decade.

Notes

1. The most recent account is Nate Jones, *Able Archer 83: The Secret History of the NATO Exercise That Almost Triggered Nuclear War* (London: The New Press, 2016).
2. In fact the timing coincided with a number of other unrelated incidents, including the US invasion of Grenada and the hostile activities of a Soviet submarine near the American coast. See A. Manchanda, 'When Truth is Stranger than Fiction: The Able Archer Incident', *Cold War History*, 9.1 (February 2009).
3. See Don Oberdorfer, *From the Cold War to a New Era: The United States and the Soviet Union, 1983–1991* (London: Johns Hopkins Press, 1998); and also B. B. Fischer, 'Anglo-American Intelligence and the Soviet War Scare: The Untold Story', *Intelligence and National Security*, 27.1 (February 2012).
4. L. V. Scott, 'Intelligence and the Risk of Nuclear War: *Able Archer-83* Revisited', *Intelligence and National Security*, 26.4 (2011).
5. Gordon S. Barrass, *The Great Cold War: A Journey Through the Hall of Mirrors* (Stanford: Stanford University Press, 2009).
6. Oleg Gordievsky, *Next Stop Execution* (Basingstoke: Macmillan, 1995). See also Ben MacIntyre, *The Spy and the Traitor: The Greatest Espionage Story of the Cold War* (London: Penguin, 2018).
7. Barrass, *Great Cold War*, pp. 297–301. Andropov passed away on 9 February 1984.
8. B. B. Fischer, 'The 1983 War Scare in US–Soviet Relations', *Studies in Intelligence* (1996), <https://www.cia.gov/library/readingroom/docs/DOC_0006122556.pdf> (last accessed 10 January 2020).
9. For details, see *The Soviet 'War Scare': President's Foreign Intelligence Advisory Board Report, February 15, 1990*, <https://nsarchive2.gwu.edu//nukevault/ebb533-The-Able-Archer-War-Scare-Declassified-PFIAB-Report-Released/2012-0238-MR.pdf> (last accessed 10 January 2020).
10. Christopher Andrew and Oleg Gordievsky, *Instructions from the Centre: Top Secret Files on KGB Operations, 1975–1985* (London: Frank Cass, 1992).
11. Scott, 'Intelligence and the Risk of Nuclear War'.
12. Fischer, 'The 1983 War Scare'.
13. Gordievsky, *Next Stop Execution*.
14. G. S. Barrass, '*Able Archer 83*: What Were the Soviets Thinking?', *Survival*, 58:6 (December 2016 – January 2017).
15. D. D. Adamsky, '"Not Crying Wolf": Soviet Intelligence and the 1983 War Scare', in Leopoldo Nuti et al. (eds), *The Euromissile Crisis and the End of the Cold War* (Stanford: Stanford University Press, 2015), pp. 49–65.

16. B. B. Fischer, 'Scolding Intelligence: The PFIAB Report on the Soviet War Scare', *International Journal of Intelligence and Counterintelligence*, 31.1 (2018). The PFIAB report itself is available at <https://nsarchive2.gwu.edu/ nukevault/ebb533-The-Able-Archer-War-Scare-Declassified-PFIAB-Report-Released/2012-0238-MR.pdf> (last accessed 10 January 2020).

17. Mikhail A. Alexeev, *Without Warning: Threat Assessment, Intelligence, and Global Struggle* (London: St Martin's Press, 1997).

16 The Soviet Leadership and Kremlinology in the 1980s

Most academic attention on the Soviet system in the 1980s has focused on General Secretary Mikhail Gorbachev's dual policies of *perestroika* (reforms) and *glasnost* (openness) and how the Soviet system imploded. Far less studied, and certainly no less important, is the precise focus on the leaders of the Soviet Union and how their different approaches affected the political, economic and military course the country followed. By the early 1980s the Soviet leadership of the worldwide communist movement appeared to be running out of ideas. In the Kremlin was the aging and increasingly paranoid leader Leonid Brezhnev. He had ruled since 1964, but his involvement at a senior level extended to the period of Stalin's rule. His tenure had seen an increase in military expenditure but this had been coupled with a growth in economic and industrial stagnation. The CIA keenly monitored his health and well-being, just as they had with his predecessors, and there was little surprise in late 1982 when he died.[1]

A common aspect of the CIA's work was 'Kremlinology': the precise watching of individuals within the Soviet system, looking at the movers and shakers, studying those rising and falling politically and pondering what it all meant.[2] With Brezhnev having been ill for so long there had been lots of attention and discussion about who might replace him. Brezhnev had surrounded himself with other aging, old Soviet hands. Would one of these be the successor, or might someone younger take the helm? Such questions were consequential not only for the Soviet Union itself, but also for the CIA and the policymakers it informed.

The debate cannot have lasted long. Within twenty-four hours of Brezhnev's death, his replacement had been chosen: Yuri Andropov. Andropov was no stranger to power, having risen up through the Soviet system. He was ambassador to Hungary in 1956 at the time of the uprising and forcibly urged a swift and brutal Soviet military response. This experience persuaded him that any opposition to Soviet rule should be dealt with in the harshest possible manner, and a year after taking over as head of the KGB in 1968, he urged that the Czechoslovak liberalisation movement under Alexander Dubček be crushed. He remained the head of the KGB until his appointment to replace Brezhnev in 1982.[3]

Within a week of his announcement the CIA had produced an analysis of Andropov's character and how his background and experiences would characterise his rule: speed, certainty and decisiveness would be key traits.[4] A month later the CIA had produced a long and detailed assessment of Andropov, describing that he had 'demonstrated impressive political power' and had 'more strength than Brezhnev', and noting his 'decisiveness'. Perhaps just as importantly, it was observed that because he had come to power relatively easily and without the customary 'major political bloodbath', it implied that he had 'new momentum to leadership decisionmaking'. The Kremlinologists in the CIA were clearly quite impressed by the new Soviet leader and his control over the Kremlin, but Andropov faced some serious problems. The full assessment is reproduced as the first chapter reference document and provides a sense not only of how important the single figure of the leader was in the Soviet (or any authoritarian) system, but also the level of detail and attention of analysts.[5]

The major issue was the economy and the question of how to reverse the trend of decline. Andropov was no economist – his expertise was in foreign affairs and domestic security – and so the CIA's Kremlinologists closely watched who might be appointed as advisors. A CIA assessment in mid-1983 highlighted that while Andropov was only too well aware of the problems, he faced a dilemma:

> Andropov is dissatisfied with the poor performance of the economy. He is aware of the resulting tensions that declining economic growth and inefficiency are generating in Soviet society, and he is convinced of the need to combine regime firmness toward the population with significant change in the economic mechanism. The key constraint upon change . . . is that Andropov and the rest of the leadership . . . will not dismantle the command economy and replace it with some kind of market socialism.[6]

For the Kremlinologists at Langley there was an equally important consideration: how long would Andropov last? Four months into his tenure the CIA produced a paper entitled 'A USSR without Andropov?' It began by explaining that it would be 'prudent to consider what the consequences might be if he departed the political scene'. Two main candidates existed: the Defence Minister Dmitri Ustinov, and the man Andropov had defeated, the Second Secretary of the Communist Party, Konstantin Chernenko. Although the assessment did not predict how long Andropov might last, it did consider the different policies and approaches both men would likely take, concluding that Ustinov was the likeliest choice.[7]

Andropov's ailing health was clear to those in West, and from early 1983 evidence of his enduring kidney problems was correctly identified. In February 1984, Andropov died. Although Andropov had not favoured him, Chernenko was rapidly appointed as the next general secretary of the Communist Party. He had long been on the CIA's radar. A 1980 assessment, written whilst Brezhnev was still alive, described Chernenko's rise as 'spectacular'. The main factor behind this was Brezhnev himself, who promoted Chernenko four times between 1976 and 1978.[8] An assessment written during Andropov's brief tenure had commented that Chernenko was not an ideal candidate for leader: 'having spent most of his career as a staff man, he lacks any significant experience in line party leadership or in supervising the economy . . . key figures . . . are said to have misgivings about his leadership ability'.[9]

As it was, Chernenko was elected as successor by the Politburo, a slightly odd move given how ill he already was at the time of his appointment. Chernenko had enduring health problems too, mainly to do with the smoking habit he had had since early childhood. Nonetheless the CIA's Kremlin watchers wasted no time in producing a variety of assessments. A month into his new tenure the CIA's Directorate of Intelligence produced a lengthy paper on the new man in the Kremlin. It focused on Chernenko's rise, his personal nature, his grasp on power, policies towards various national and international events, and prospects for the future.[10]

The assessment began candidly: 'we still do not know what political tradeoffs have been struck that enabled Chernenko to get the top job'. In spite of this, it was acknowledged that he had 'staged a remarkable political comeback' but that he would need to spend the coming months strengthening his support. The surprise at his ascent to the top job is implicit in much of the report, for instance in commenting that 'we are uncertain about the nature of the new regime'. To complicate matters further, what little was known about Chernenko's views was likely to become 'modified as he attempts to gain more support'. There was no great sense that this was going to be a long-term choice, though, for as the Kremlinologists confirmed, 'age' and 'health problems' were 'important liabilities of the new General Secretary'.[11]

Six months later an updated assessment was issued. Importantly it not only commented on Chernenko's position and status, but also on what had happened to Andropov's heir apparent, Mikhail Gorbachev. The report was passed to the Director of Central Intelligence with a cover note confirming that it was written to be shared with 'other Kremlin watchers around town'.[12] Although stamped 'Top Secret', it is not obvious what sources the Kremlinologists had at their disposal. Certainly a significant component of their thinking was Gorbachev's failure to address the October 1984 Central

Committee Plenum, a move interpreted as suggesting that his 'status as heir apparent . . . has come into question'. Other open-source evidence – coverage of several events in *Pravda* and Gorbachev's involvement, or lack thereof, in several recent ceremonies – supported this contention. Several scenarios were cited as possible explanations: a voluntary retreat, punishment for poor economic performance (Gorbachev was then responsible for agricultural matters), or a political move by Chernenko to increase his own grasp of power. Whichever was most likely, the CIA's analysts concluded that Gorbachev's 'setback may only be temporary'.

The assessment finished with a note on Chernenko himself. It reiterated the March 1984 view and went further: 'Chernenko's age, health and dependence on his colleagues will likely prevent him from ever really consolidating power.' No firm prediction was provided, though the possibility that nothing significant would really change for the best part of a decade was aired.[13] This would be far from the mark for a number of reasons. The first significant change was Chernenko's death in March 1985, less than a year after taking office. His successor was the relatively young Gorbachev.

One hundred days into his new role, the Kremlinologists produced a significant survey, a copy of which is included as the second chapter reference document. The report described him as a 'new broom', a remarkably good metaphor given what would transpire, and revealing as to what the seasoned Kremlin watchers in Langley thought of the new man. Without a doubt he made a number of swift and brave policy moves, blowing away the cobwebs from the previous regimes that had been run by anachronistic Soviet leaders. There is certainly a sense of this in the CIA's assessment, but the sober language of intelligence reports does not reveal what unfiltered opinions or hunches those analysts might have held.

A canny politician, Gorbachev knew that big changes were required if the Soviet Union was to escape the economic malaise from which it suffered. Not only was a new political direction required, but so too was a new sort of leader. He attacked the corruption endemic in the Soviet system, changing the way that officials could be chosen while also publicly criticising various senior leaders. At the same time, he made more public appearances, utilised his wife for political engagements and was far more populist in outlook. For those in the CIA these were significant changes to be noted, thus: 'he is the most aggressive and activist Soviet leader since Khrushchev . . . the very insistence of his rhetoric allows little room for compromise or retreat'.[14]

His new politics and style aside, it was assumed that Gorbachev's future was intimately tied to the fate of the Soviet economy. Within six months of taking office he had publicly criticised previous Russian planning approaches and had hinted at sweeping economic changes. In addition, a number of the important old Soviet economic guard had been replaced. Accurately reporting these significant developments as they unfolded, the CIA predicted that future details would be forthcoming the following February.[15]

At the end of February 1986, as predicted, the 27th Congress of the Communist Party of the Soviet Union began. Ending in early March, the proceedings were brought to a close with a speech by Mikhail Gorbachev. He discussed the economic plight of the Soviet Union and outlined his twin policies of *perestroika* and *glasnost* – the two phrases or approaches that would characterise his tenure. Once more the Kremlinologists were quick to grasp the novelty and significance of these words, though they would not fully appreciate the consequences that would be set in train by them.[16] Gorbachev's other great achievement at this time was in changing those around him. In a series of swift and bloodless moves he removed a number of the old guard and replaced them with his loyal followers, thereby significantly strengthening his grip on power and, by extension, the ability to pass and implement his new policies.[17]

Subsequent analytical reports focused on every aspect of Gorbachev's policies. Of note was the manner in which he was prepared to change policy or approach when previous tactics did not work or were too slow in producing results. An assessment in early 1987 commented that he was 'off to a strong start' and that he had 'consolidated power with unprecedented speed', but cautioned that his 'greatest challenge lies ahead', in terms of achieving the optimistic economic goals he had set.[18] As Gorbachev pursued these goals, other significant problems began to arise. An April 1989 assessment captured some of them, though it did not quite grasp the urgency behind them:

> The Soviet Union is less stable today than at any time since Stalin's great purges in the 1930s. General Secretary Gorbachev clearly hopes that, by shaking up the Soviet system, he can rouse the population out of its lethargy and channel the forces he is releasing in a constructive direction. Even Gorbachev realises, however, that it is far from certain that he will be able to control the process he has set in motion.

The assessment recorded various 'incidents of political unrest', placing Gorbachev and his policies as the root cause not of the discontent, but the manner in which such grievances could be displayed.[19] Another paper, two months later, placed ownership of the current problems squarely at Gorbachev's feet: 'General Secretary Mikhail Gorbachev has launched a major reorganisation of the party's bureaucracy that has changed the decisionmaking structure and could result in a historic redefinition of the party's place in Soviet society.'[20]

Even if the seeds had been planted earlier and by others, these reforms and their impact constitute Gorbachev's legacy. Langley's Kremlinologists were, to some extent, well informed of significant developments, but repeatedly surprised to some degree about what they, in aggregate, foretold. Spending a career watching those thousands of miles away, monitoring their every move, assessing the significance of who stood next to whom and who attended which event, was a serious and important undertaking. The CIA's Kremlinologists, like those in London, watched their prey closely, but by dint of their familiarity were perhaps the worst placed to spot some of the novel developments percolating through the Soviet system. When the Soviet system imploded Kremlinology became a dying art form – only to be resurrected in the twenty-first century when another strongman took up residence in the Kremlin.

```
              Central Intelligence Agency
      Office of the Deputy Director for Intelligence


                  14 December 1982
NOTE TO: MajGen Richard Boverie
         National Security Council Staff
         Rm. 386 OEOB
FROM    : Deputy Director for Intelligence


Attached are the papers requested on Andropov and
the Soviet economy. Let me know if there is anything
further we can do.



                                    Robert M. Gates



          Central Intelligence Agency Office
       of the Deputy Director for Intelligence


                              14 December 1982

NOTE TO: Hugh Montgomery
         Director, state/INR
         Rm. 6531 New State
FROM    : Deputy Director for Intelligence
```

Attached are copies of the papers on Andropov and the Soviet economy we have submitted to Dick Boverie at the NSC staff.

Robert M. Gates

DIRECTORATE OF INTELLIGENCE[*]
13 December 1982
ASSESSMENT OF ANDROPOV'S POWER

Andropov's Power

General Secretary Yuriy Andropov is the most authoritative leader in the Politburo and has demonstrated impressive political power from the outset. He certainly has more strength than Brezhnev had at the beginning of his long tenure (in 1964). Andropov's status as top leader was most visible in his meetings with foreign leaders only days after he had become General Secretary. Moreover, Andropov has already been given pride of place in protocol rankings and in leadership listings, and a few officials have begun to refer to him as the "head of the Politburo," an accolade given to Brezhnev several years after he was named General Secretary.

The Politburo's decision to promote Andropov almost certainly reflected an informal understanding at least among a core group of members that the country needed a strong leader, that Andropov was best qualified to assume the post, and, more importantly, that Chernenko – his chief rival and Brezhnev's choice – was weak and unacceptable. Andropov undoubtedly exploited such negative views of Chernenko in his successful efforts in May to maneuver his way back into the Secretariat in order to become a major contender in the succession sweepstakes. While Brezhnev's

* This paper was prepared by the Policy Analysis Division, Office of Soviet Analysis. Comments and queries are welcome and may be directed to the Chief, Policy Analysis Division, _____

314

patronage gave Chernenko some obvious advantages in this contest, this strength was not institutionalized and evaporated with Brezhnev's death. The speed of Andropov's ascendancy reflected a leadership desire to project an image of decisiveness abroad and avoid any signal of conflict and political paralysis, not a prearranged decision made last May when Andropov entered the Secretariat. Chernenko's own visibility and activity in recent months suggest that the contest remained open while Brezhnev was alive.

The Lineup

We do not know how various Politburo members actually voted in the Andropov-Chernenko contest or even whether a formal vote was taken, but Moscow rumors, ██████████████████████ leadership status indicators, and informed speculation provide the basis for a reconstruction of the likely lineup. At a minimum Andropov seems to have had strong backing from Defense Minister Ustinov, Foreign Minister Gromyko, and Ukrainian party boss Shcherbitskiy. With their political fortunes still ahead of them, the two youngest Politburo members – party secretary Gorbachev and Leningrad First Secretary Romanov – may have joined this strong coalition as well, at least on this vote. Chernenko probably received support from the two Brezhnev loyalists – Prime Minister Tikhonov and Kazakhstan First Secretary Kunayev. Grishin, the Moscow party chief, may have joined this group possibly in hopes of becoming a compromise choice. Octogenarian Arvid Pelshe was very likely too sick to play a role in the decision. For his part Chernenko apparently did not fight the decision to the bitter end, opting instead to close ranks behind Andropov and preserve his position as "second" secretary, a strategy that for the present has been successful. Only Grishin – to judge from his slippage in protocol – seems to have fought excessively and suffered for it.

Andropov, thus, has institutional support where it counts. The national security apparatus, particularly the military-industrial complex and the KGB, is behind him. Such backing gives him added room for maneuver but, at least in the case of the military, cannot be taken for granted. He will, in addition, need to strengthen his position within the party apparatus. He lacks a strong regional base and must depend on officials whose careers he has had little influence in shaping.

Opportunities and Flexibility

Andropov, nonetheless, has come to power with what seems to be solid backing and without resorting to a major political bloodbath. This situation has allowed him to assume a more authoritative stance in the leadership than Stalin, Khrushchev, or Brezhnev did at a comparable point in these successions. His promotion has given a new momentum to leadership decisionmaking. Indeed, for the first time in years the Soviets have a leader who puts in a full day ████████ From what we can tell, his colleagues recognize and value his ability and perceive him to be intelligent. They know from his tenure as KGB chief that he can be counted on to be decisive in preserving the party's legitimacy and social order. They probably expect him – within limits – to be a bold, forceful leader, and they are likely to give him some room to be such. As a result, he is probably in a strong position to influence and lead the Politburo consensus.

Andropov seems to be in a particularly good position to chart the course of Soviet foreign policy. He has considerable experience and knowledge in this area and is obviously inclined to take an active role. Foreign policy initiatives, moreover, have the potential for producing beneficial results more quickly than changes in domestic policy, a matter of considerable importance for a leader who wants to build his power. He is not as likely, in addition, to encounter the sharp factional infighting and debate that occurs over proposals for domestic shifts, particularly in economic management.

This situation effectively means that the Soviet Union will not be paralyzed in the foreign policy arena. Andropov has room for maneuver here and can be expected to propose initiatives and respond to those from abroad he deems serious. In doing so, however, Andropov will rely heavily on two of his colleagues on the Defense Council, Defense Minister Ustinov and Foreign Minister Gromyko, for advice. He would certainly need their support to get the Politburo's assent to a major shift in Soviet foreign policy or to make major modifications in arms control negotiations with the US. Andropov will probably count on his personal and political alliance with Ustinov and apparently good working relationship with Gromyko to help create the Politburo consensus required for important departures.

It seems likely that the three have been key figures in the Soviet foreign policy line pursued in Brezhnev's last years. ██████████████████████ As long as they remain united the politburo is likely to follow their lead. If, on the other hand, there are significant disagreements between them on future foreign policy steps or tactics, Andropov would not be likely to force the issue at least in the near term.

Constraints

This flexibility on foreign policy, nonetheless, does not mean that he has carte blanche from the Politburo. While he can lead and shape the consensus, he is still bound by it. The Politburo remains a collegial body and its current membership is not beholden to Andropov nor under his thumb. Andropov is indebted to many of his Politburo colleagues, particularly Ustinov, and is dependent on their collusion and support until he can reshape the Politburo, a process that could take several years.

Andropov's colleagues are evidently trying to hold back his advance. The failure to name a replacement for Brezhnev as Chairman of the Presidium of the Supreme Soviet indicates conflict. The personnel changes (Aliyev, Komsomol, progaganda organs, Council of ministers) made since Andropov became party chief while almost certainly endorsed by him, seem to have served many interests within the leadership (Ustinov, Chernenko) as well. Even if Andropov is named Soviet President at a scheduled session of the Supreme Soviet on 21 December (a better than even possibility), he must still push through even more politically important personnel shifts in the Politburo and Secretariat to fully consolidate his position and to dominate policy.

The collective restraint on Andropov is likely to be particularly evident in domestic policy. While the entire leadership is undoubtedly committed to solving Soviet economic problems as a top priority, consensus on what the solution should be has not been reached. Economic issues are inherently political, complex, and controversial. The bureaucratic obstacles to significant changes in economic management are immense. Andropov is probably generally knowledgeable about the economy and is certainly well informed about issues affecting internal security, but he has little personal experience in economic management and his closest supporters are more concerned with foreign and security policy. No one, moreover, as Andropov emphasized to the Central Committee, has all the solutions to the country's economic difficulties. As a result, he is likely to move cautiously in this area - a strategy he said was needed in his plenum speech.

Domestic and Foreign Policy Linkage
Significant movement toward resolving the nation's economic problems might, in fact, require Andropov to achieve some relaxation of tensions with the US on China or both. Only by doing so can he justify to his colleagues and the military some reallocation of resources from defense to investment, an essential step in any plan to address the country's economic problems. In this regard, the next two years are particularly crucial for Andropov and the Politburo. The planning cycle for the 12th Five Year Plan - 1986-1990 - is already underway. ▮▮▮▮▮▮ the Soviet military's assessment of the external threat is an essential element in this cycle and will be formally developed during 1983. The Politburo in 1984 will act on this military assessment in allocating resources

for the next five year defense plan. This will be the new Politburo's first formal and comprehensive ordering of internal priorities between economic investment and defense procurement. Without reduction in international tensions, which some in the military such as Chief of the General Staff Ogarkov, contend are exceedingly high, the rate of defense growth will be politically hard to reduce. Failure to reduce defense spending, nonetheless, will make it very difficult to solve Soviet economic problems and will over the long run erode the economic base of the military industrial complex itself.

Advisers

Andropov will also get advice from his own staff of foreign and domestic aides. He is now assembling his team, and a few have already been publicly identified.

In addition to the formally identified group of personal aides to Andropov, the new party leader will likely tap three old associates on an ad hoc basis: Georgiy Arbatov, director of the Institute of the USA and Canada, Aleksandr Bovin, a Brezhnev speech writer, and Fedor Burlatskiy, an expert on China and public opinion. All three worked for Andropov in the 1960s when he was the party secretary responsible for Communist Bloc relations. These men are knowledgeable, sophisticated observers of US policy and have been identified with Brezhnev's detente strategy, but their actual influence on Andropov is not known.

Prospects

On balance, the speed with which the new General Secretary was appointed, his assertion of a leading role in foreign policy, and the self confident statements of Andropov and Ustinov on international issues reflect real strengths and potential flexibility on Soviet policy that were not present in Brezhnev's final days. While there are bureaucratic obstacles to significant changes in economic management, there does seem to be general agreement on the need for action and this will provide some receptivity to specific proposals as long as they preserve party power. Additionally, the improved leadership ranking of the key actors in national security affairs (i.e., Andropov, Ustinov, and Gromyko) and the clouds on the international horizon for the USSR provide the necessary consensus and incentive for change and flexibility in foreign affairs.

During previous succession periods in the 1950s and 1960s, for example, there were definite new departures in foreign policy. In the fifties, the Soviets ended the Korean War, signed a peace treaty accepting Austrian neutrality, reopened diplomatic relations with Israel, called off disputes with Greece and Turkey, and moved towards summitry with President Eisenhower. They also made their first moves to counter Western influence in the Third World. In the sixties, the Soviets developed a policy of selective detente with France, then slowly did the same with West Germany, before turning to improved relations with the US. Partly in response to worsening relations with China, the Soviets also pressed for a series of arms control measures that led to the nonproliferation treaty and SALT I. At the same time, they began the buildup on the Sino-Soviet border, gave impetus to a massive Soviet arms program, and began aiding North Vietnam's effort to take over the South.

The new leadership has already taken pains to reaffirm the broad outlines of Brezhnev's foreign policy and to signal the importance of improved ties with the US. Andropov's decision to meet with Vice President Bush and Secretary of State Shultz within hours after Brezhnev's funeral indicated the Kremlin's interest in some normalization of US–Soviet relations. In view of the prospect of an enhanced US strategic challenge in this decade, there appears to be ample incentive for Andropov to try to curb new US arms program and particularly to prevent or at least delay the deployment of INF. The specter of Pershing-II in the FRG and the attendant threat to Soviet strategic forces and command and control capabilities could lead to new initiatives in the INF negotiations as well as to build European opposition to INF deployment.

Gromyko's visit to Bonn next month - would provide a convenient forum for such an initiative.

The Gromyko visit provides an opportunity not only to put the US on the defensive but to increase divisions between the US and its NATO allies. Gromyko will lobby for increased Soviet-West European cooperation and trade, which provide political as well as economic benefits for the Soviets. The removal of US sanctions imposed after Afghanistan and the steady return to normalcy in Poland will add to the credibility of Gromyko's brief in Bonn.

The inability to effect some visible reduction of tensions with the US will generate even greater interest in Moscow to improve Sino-Soviet relations and to exploit differences between Washington and Beijing. The Soviets clearly do not want continued antagonism on "two fronts" at a time of more assertive US policies, a mounting US defense effort, and ever increasing economic problems at home. For these reasons, the Soviets have sufficient incentive to entertain a unilateral move that would include withdrawing a division or two from the Sino-Soviet border or Mongolia in addition to thinning out various units in the area.

Although the reduction of force in any area would be highly controversial within the Soviet military, it would probably create the greatest geopolitical payoff if Moscow were able to do so in Afghanistan. Any significant diminishing of the Soviet military role there would offer considerable potential rewards:
- removal of a key obstacle to improved relations with both the US and China,
- termination of a source of embarrassment in the entire Islamic community,
- earlier dealings with key European actors as well as India, and
- savings in both lives and treasure at home.

Elsewhere, continuity appears to be the order of the day. Continued fighting between Iran and Iraq as well as the loss of credibility in the wake of the Israeli invasion of Lebanon add up to rather bleak short-term options in the Middle East. There are no likely targets of opportunity in South America at this juncture, and the Soviets will probably be content to pursue their gradual and incremental strategy in Central America. In Africa, the Soviets will concentrate on complicating the Namibean talks in which the Soviets also find themselves as odd man out. They also will be alert to opportunities in southern Africa – such as in Mozambique – to expand their (and especially the Cuban) presence. Senior Politburo member Grishin's anniversary speech earlier this month, which reaffirmed Soviet support for Cuba and Vietnam, argues for continued activism on behalf of Moscow's most important clients in the Third World.

These Soviet priorities suggest areas for US pressure and/or blandishment that could have an impact on Soviet ability to improve their international position. Indeed, Andropov must realize that the US is well placed in certain respects to challenge the international position of the USSR and to exploit Moscow's fear of the specter of encirclement.

– The US could play the role of spoiler in the Sino-Soviet-US triangle by holding out to the Chinese the promise of increased defense cooperation, expanded technological ties, and a more equivocal position on Taiwan.

– US willingness to modify the "zero option" at INF would preempt Soviet initiatives in this area and might help sustain support for US deployments in Western Europe (although such modifications might have other, less desirable consequences).

– The mere perception of US pressure on Israeli and South Africa to become more conciliatory would enhance Washington's prestige and leverage in the Middle East and Southern Africa and commensurately reduce Soviet influences.

Conversely, the US is in a position to offer to Moscow some restoration of the centrality of Soviet-American relations that would enhance Moscow's international position and ameliorate Moscow's economic problems.

– There are several economic initiatives open to the US, particularly some easing up of limits on credits and technology transfer.

- Notwithstanding recent Soviet references to strengthening defense, Moscow would like to prevent a major US arms buildup, which they would be hard-pressed to match right now and sees arms control as the best way to achieve this.
- Less acrimonious atmospherics and a dialogue with the US on Third World trouble spots would also be attractive to Moscow, although past experience strongly suggests they would not alter their behavior.

The Soviets have already suggested that they are looking for ways to restore the notion of the cen-trality of Soviet–American relations in international affairs, and presumably realize that some relaxation of tensions would ease the problems of making their own choices on future allocation of resources as well as the pressure from the national security apparatus for increased military spending. The rise in stature for Andropov, Ustinov, and Gromyko suggests the emergence of a consensus on national security issues in general and the prospect of some flexibility on specific issues. Such putative critics of Andropov as Chernenko and Grishin would probably support the triumvirate's efforts to improve relations with the US in view of their earlier support for Brezhnev's detente and arms control initiatives. The key role will be played by Ustinov who appears to be in a posi-tion to block those initiatives that do not protect the equity of the military.

DIRECTORATE OF INTELLIGENCE*
JUNE 1985
Gorbachev, the New Broom

Summary
Gorbachev has demonstrated in his first 100 days that he is the most aggressive and activist Soviet leader since Khrushchev. He is willing to take controversial

---

* This paper was prepared by ████████████████ the Office of Soviet Analysis. comments and questions may be directed to the Chief, Domestic Policy Division, ████████████

and even unpopular decisions - like the antialcohol
campaign - and to break with recent precedent by
criticizing the actions of his colleagues on the
Politburo.

He has thrown down the gauntlet on issues as controversial as the allocation of investment, broadgauged
management reform, and purging the system of incom-
petent and corrupt officials. The very insistence of
his rhetoric allows little room for compromise or
retreat.

Gorbachev is gambling that an attack on corruption
and inefficiency, not radical reform, will turn the
domestic situation around. While a risky course, his
prospects for success should not be underestimated.
Although his approach is controversial, his near term
prospects look good. Unlike his immediate predecessors, he has already managed to firm up his base of
support in the Politburo and Secretariat. He can also
count on some support from middle level officials of
the bureaucracy who were frustrated by the stagnation
of the Brezhnev era. The public as well has responded
favorably to his style, judging by initial reaction
filtering back through Western sources. His aggressiveness has placed the opposition on the defensive.
His opponents are probably biding their time hoping
he makes a major misstep.

Gorbachev's Style

Gorbachev has moved to draw a sharp contrast in style
to his recent predecessors, who treated the bureaucracy gingerly and approached change cautiously.
Brezhnev and Chernenko voiced concern about the deep-
ening economic and morale problems in the country,
but they were not prepared to confront the bureaucracies standing in the way of solutions. Brezhnev's
solicitous attitude toward the bureaucracy limited
the power of his office as officials came to believe
they had lifetime tenure. Andropov moved to break
this mold, but he was handicapped by his poor health
and the lingering presence of Brezhnevites, including Chernenko and Premier Tikhonov. Learning from
Andropov's experience, Gorbachev has consciously

created an environment of urgency and made clear he intends to confront problems.

Gorbachev's populist style has not been seen since Khrushchev's frequent forays among the public and bare knuckles approach to dealing with the bureaucracy:

- He has visited factories in Moscow and Leningrad and found other opportunities to rub shoulders with workers in an effort to burnish his image as a man of the people. Soviet television has highlighted his easy give-and-take with ordinary citizens.
- He is carefully managing public relations.
- Gorbachev has also moved his wife Raisa into the spotlight. She has appeared in the Soviet press and on television, and a protocol officer reportedly has been assigned to handle her activities. The wife of Politburo member Vorotnikov, who recently visited Canada, was overheard to say that all wives of Politburo members must now accompany their husbands on foreign trips.

While these traits mark Gorbachev as an unconventional Soviet politician, it is his no-holds-barred approach to confronting chronic domestic problems that underscores his new style as a leader. Gorbachev may feel that an aggressive approach is essential if he is to avoid getting bogged down like Andropov. A wide spectrum of Soviet officials complained of drift and corruption under Brezhnev and became discouraged when Andropov's ill health caused his initiatives to lose momentum. They provide a well-spring of potential support for Gorbachev's approach:

- He has instituted a sweeping crackdown on the deep-rooted problem of alcoholism, reportedly even denying a request from Foreign Minister Gromyko to exempt diplomatic functions.
- He criticized his Politburo colleagues in public during his visit to Leningrad, terming their recent decision on the allocation of land for private plots inadequate and dismissing objections apparently raised by his colleagues.
- He has assailed ministers by name for lack of innovation, laziness, and poor management and has

strongly implied that they will be removed. He has attacked the complacent attitude toward corruption within the party bureaucracy and called for promotion of younger and more competent officials at all levels. While such rhetoric is not new in itself, he has already underscored his intention to back up his tough rhetoric with dismissals by sacking some middle-level officials.

- ████████████████████████ claims that Gorbachev has begun to boss around high officials with a "wave of his hand," asking for information and then issuing orders without consultation. ████████████████ Gorbachev will systematically replace old guard holdovers both in Moscow and the provinces with young and technically competent officials.

Gorbachev has made it clear that he believes his policies are justified by the growing foreign and domestic problems facing the USSR:

- He has studded his speeches with language that evokes the image of a crisis, and suggested that the USSR is now at a turning point. ██████████████████████████ he has decided to raise Russian national consciousness and to impose "super-enforcement" of order and discipline.
- At the April Central Committee plenum, he was sharply critical of the economic laxity under Brezhnev and the failure to follow through on decisions which had been taken by the leadership.
- In his speech to the S&T conference in early June, he warned that accelerated economic growth was an imperative due to the need to sustain current levels of consumption while making the investments in defense required by current international tensions.

Consolidating Power
Gorbachev is using time honored methods for building his power, advancing his allies into key leadership positions, but he is off to a faster start than any of his recent predecessors. More changes are likely soon:

- By advancing three allies to full Politburo membership in April he has probably achieved a working majority on most issues.
- The designation of Yegor Ligachev – one of the three promoted – as unofficial "second secretary" isolated his major rival, Secretary Grigoriy Romanov, who has been nearly invisible politically. ███████████████ Ligachev – who is Gorbachev's close friend – has now eclipsed Foreign Minister Gromyko and Premier Tikhonov in political importance
- KGB boss Chebrikov – who was also promoted – appears to be another close ally, giving the General Secretary an important advantage in exerting political pressure against would-be Politburo opponents, most of whom are tainted by corruption.
- Gorbachev also placed a younger protege in charge of the department that oversees personnel appointments, further consolidating his control over personnel policy and setting the groundwork for potentially sweeping personnel changes preceding next February's party congress. He is off to a fast pace in replacing his opponents in the bureaucracy. He has retired one deputy premier and three ministers, and named nine new regional party bosses and three new Central Committee department heads.

Domestic Strategy
Using his strong political position, Gorbachev's first priority is to push his domestic economic program. While some Soviet officials have indicated he is sympathetic to the use of pragmatic methods, including tapping private initiative, his statements and actions underscore his overall commitment to the current economic system and his determination to make it work better. Having acknowledged the gravity of the economic problem, Gorbachev exudes an optimism that he and his team can eliminate waste, tighten discipline, increase the quality and quantit of production, and accelerate economic growth. While expressing great pride in the historical acomplishments of central planning, he has sharply criticized

its recent performance, and called for "revolutionary" changes in the way the system works.

His first priority fix is to reduce waste and
tighten discipline, particularly among managers:

- Gorbachev has cited cases of such waste, such
  as the 20 percent loss of the harvest. Figures
  published in the Soviet press indicate Andropov's
  discipline campaign has reduced losses in working
  time about 20 percent, and Ukrainian party boss
  Shcherbitskiy recently announced that the campaign had saved several hundred million rubles.
  Gorbachev probably hopes to squeeze out similar
  resources.
- ███████████████████████ Gorbachev has reinvigorated
  Andropov's discipline campaign. ██████████████
  Gorbachev has reinitiated document checks
  and crackdowns on drunks and deadbeats, and
  ███████████████████████ he is even threatening to fire
  managers who have filled to correct such problem
  among their workers.
- His speeches indicate he will extend earlier
  efforts to tie pay more closely to productivity
  both for workers and managers, not only reward-
  ing good workers but penalizing - perhaps even
  docking the salaries - of poor performers.

Building from a base of improved worker discipline
and management effectivness, Gorbachev's hopes to
further boost long-term growth entail a modernization of the capital base by increased investment in
machine-building and retooling existing factories.
While the effects of this approach will not be
felt for some time, he has remanded the draft Five-
Year Plan for 1986-90 to redirect it toward growth
based on increased productivity rather than expanded
resources. More specifically:

- He has called for investment in modernizing factories to be increased from 1/3 to 1/2 of investment,*

---

* Soviet bureaucrats, both ministerial and party, have traditionally
called for new construction. Such projects have been doled out to
satisfy local lobbies like pork barrel projects. In his S&T conference
speech, Gorbachev condemned this approach and insisted on focusing
investment on where it was needed most.

and demanded that investment and output in civilian machine-building be doubled. He even called for "mothballing" some new construction projects, as an unusually candid admission of a major Soviet problem in the construction sector. His stress on conservation rather than increased output of raw materials also indicates a heightened emphasis in this area.

Beyond this, he has been less specific on other economic initiatives, but his statements suggests he may intend to press even more controversial policies touching on the powers of the bureaucracy:

- His public statements suggest he wants to amalgamate ministries and redirect them and the State Planning Committee (Gosplan) away from day-to-day management decisions.
- He would like to see greater autonomy for plant managers and will probably push for reduction of centrally dictated indicators.
- He has criticized intermediate management bodies that choke off initiative, hinting that they should be streamlined or eliminated. His aim is to eliminate some of the massive bureaucratic apparatus that, as he complained in his speech to the S&T conference, implements Central Committee decisions in such a manner that after they are finished "nothing is left of these principles."
- He may advocate legalizing some parts of the "second economy" and allow a limited expansion of the role of private agriculture, despite potential ideological opposition. He hinted at this in his Leningrad speech in May. Gorbachev may feel some limited concessions – like tolerating private repairmen or allowing greater access to summer gardens for urban dwellers – could help improve the quality of life without undermining the system or forcing a showdown with ideological purists in the elite who traditionally have resisted such steps.

<u>Foreign Policy</u>

Gorbachev's impact on foreign policy has so far been mostly stylistic. He has revealed no urgent agenda to match his determination to accelerate economic growth at home. Some of his gambits – like the INF moratorium – are stale leftovers from his predecessor. His immediate goal has apparently been to demonstrate to both allies and adversaries that there is now a strong and active leader in the Kremlin. Despite the press of domestic business, Gorbachev has received a steady stream of European and Third World leaders. He has been more activist than his immediate predecessors and will reportedly embark soon on a vigorous shedule of personal diplomacy and foreign trips. He is slated to travel to Paris in October for meetings with Mitterrand and he may visit India later this year.

Although he has not yet made any serious new initiative toward the US, he has already made his presence felt on Soviet policy. He reportedly ratified the return to the bargaining table in Geneva even before Chernenko's death in March. He softened Soviet conditions for a summit with President Reagan soon after entering office. Since then, he has apparently sanctioned the recent expansion of bilateral exchanges and met with several US delegations.

In public statements ████████████████████ however, Gorbachev is clearly intent on presenting ███████ a tough hardline image abroad and convincing American policymakers that bilateral relations will improve only if US policy changes. He and his colleagues evidently do not believe an early improvement in relations is likely:

- ██████████████ Gorbachev will concentrate on cultivating an image of strength, not conciliation.
- ██████████████ Gorbachev's chief foreign policy adviser believes he is not disposed to concessions, in part because he does not believe arms control can significantly reduce domestic economic problems.
- In talks with American visitors he has bristled at efforts to raise human rights issues,

    demanded that the US not take a "carrot and stick"
    approach, and insisted that Soviet leaders will
    be ready to deal only when the US starts treating
    the USSR as an equal.
- Moscow's more recent decision to play hard to
    get on a summit dovetails with this strategy.
    ████████████

He has already spoken publicly of a "community or
interest" between the USSR and Western Europe, met
with a series of European leaders, and indicated that
Moscow is now prepared to establish political relations with the European Community:

Gorbachev has also taken a tough line within the <u>Warsaw
Pact</u>, reportedly sending ripples of concern through
the more Brezhnevite regimes, such as Czechoslovakia.
His public statements have stressed the need for bloc
unity and closer economic integration. Despite his
reported sympathy for East European economic reform,
he allegedly told party leaders at their summit in
April that "something is rotten in Denmark," which
they took to signal his dissatisfaction with corruption and economic laxity in this region.

Gorbachev's early actions have also signaled strong
support for allies in Afghanistan and Central America:
- Soviet forces in Afghanistan continue to pursue
    the more aggressive military approach that we
    began to see last year.
- He met Nicaraguan leader Ortega only days after
    the US Congress turned down the President's orig-
    inal request for aid to the Contras and pledged
    increased oil deliveries to bolster the regime.

<u>Opposition to Gorbachev's Juggernaut?</u>
Opposition to Gorbachev for now appears disorganized.
The old guard in the Politburo – such as Premier
Tikhonov, Moscow party boss Grishin or republic
bosses Shcherbitskiy and Kunayev – are probably on
the defensive due to charges of mismanagement or corruption in their organizations. Secretary Romanov, a
potential focus for opposition, has been outflanked
by Gorbachev's personnel moves and probably is no
longer an effective rallying point.

As a result, those threatened by Gorbachev at the Central Committee level lack an effective spokesman. While they can resist by footdragging on his policies, he can probably remove them if they don't appear to be falling into line. Many elderly Brezhnev-era holdovers may well find it easier to retire than fight.

Despite his strong position, Gorbachev does not have an entirely free hand. Other Politburo members can still slow up his initiatives. Independents or even allies might balk at some aspects of Gorbachev's freewheeling style. There are some signs, moreover, that Gorbachev's initiatives have already been watered down or met resistance:

- Judging from his remarks in Leningrad, the Politburo rejected his more far reaching proposals for expansion of garden plots, evidently on the grounds that this amounts to encouraging private enterprise.
- Some evidence suggests that the timing of a US-Soviet summit has became entangled in leadership politics.
- ▮▮▮▮▮▮▮▮▮ Gorbachev's bold domestic strategy is also controversial at the lower levels, and he will have to contend with thousands of local party officials who are unwilling to accede to the wishes of the central party leadership. Many rank-and-file workers will probably also resent the increased demands for productivity and be fearful that they might lose their job security.
- ▮▮▮▮▮▮▮▮▮ Gorbachev's edicts on alcoholiam, if carried out to the letter, will create serious problems among the working class. ▮▮▮▮▮▮ his campaign against corruption will not win him any friends.

Soviet media treatment of Gorbachev's speeches suggests that his policy agenda is meeting some high-level resistance:

- Press versions of Gorbachev's speech in Leningrad toned down his criticism of the Politburo decison on extending the private plots.
- Published versions also eliminated references to

Gorbachev's personal sponsorship or support of economic reform initiatives.
- On some occasions, the media have published full accounts of his speeches only after a delay of several days.

Nonetheless, the strength of Gorbachev's position suggest that his detractors will have to wait until he makes a major misstep or overreaches on a controversial issue in order to give them an opportunity to coalesce. The real test may come when evidence begins to roll in on the success or failure of his program.

Can Gorbachev Succeed Where Khrushchev Failed?
Gorbachev's efforts to force greater efficiency out of the system is still a risky gamble, despite the disorganized state of resistance. Khrushchev, for instance, succeeded for nearly ten years in keeping the opposition on the defensive through endless reorganizations and campaigns, but eventually he alienated his own supporters. Khrushchev's approach was so helter skelter that the bureaucrats often could not discern what he really wanted them to do.

Having witnessed Khrushchev's mistakes, Gorbachev's signals are likely to be much clearer and more consistent. Yet, a number of these clear signals are likely to produce resistance. Gorbachev's investment strategy may cause him the most problems with the bureaucracy. The allocation of investment is closely tied to the power of officialdom, who can dole out "pork barrel" projects as a kind of political payment for loyalty. By sharply reducing investment funds in some sectors and requiring a new approach to management, moreover, Gorbachev's approach is bound to alienate many in the bureaucracy upon whom he must depend for policy implementation. While he can use the power of hiring and firing to discipline this group, such an approach - as Khrushchev discovered - potentially has its cost in terms of production and political support.

Gorbachev's call for faster economic growth may also come back to haunt him. Efforts to reconstruct existing factories may lead to declining output at a time when he is proposing a return to higher economic growth rates. While his four percent growth prediction for the next Five Year Plan may not be entirely out of reach, it forces managers into the position of choosing between increasing output and reequipping their factories. Massive shifts in investment priorities could also create bottlenecks and disruptions in the economy. For instance, shifting resouces from energy extraction - at a time when both coal and oil output is declining - to the production of more energy efficient machinery might exacerbate the energy balance in the short term.

Gorbachev will have to carefully calibrate his policies in order to avoid pitfalls in a system where emphasizing specific priorities at the top frequently translates into slackened effort on other areas. The prospects for a radical reorientation of Soviet managers toward quality rather than quantity are also not good - it runs counter to the approach of the last 55 years. But, Andropov's experience demonstrated that a concerted effort on management discipline - backed by the threat of firing - can probably have beneficial effects.

Looking Ahead

With the urgent rhetoric and ambitious agenda he has set so far, Gorbachev will be under the gun to show continuing evidence of momentum or else risk allowing potential opponents to draw together and work against him.

Consolidating power. Gorbachev is likely to be elected President at next week's Supreme Soviet session. He might also advance other allies into junior slots in the leadership at a plenum preceding the Supreme Soviet. Gorbachev will almost certainly use the party elections campaign before the party congress next year to replace many Brezhnev holdovers among regional party and government leaders. Party Secretary Romanov, once Gorbachev's major rival, is already in decline, and a recent smear campaign linking him to Gorbachev's opponents may be intended to pave the way for his removal.

Gorbachev will continue to oust symbols of the Brezhnev old guard in the economic bureaucracy. The ministers he named at the S&T conference are almost certain to go. Gorbachev's attacks on the ministries have made Premier Tikhonov's position increasingly untenable, and he could be gracefully eased out even before the party congress. The retirement of Gosplan chief Baybakov, a symbol of resistance to change since the Brezhnev era, would send a strong message to the bureaucracy.

Domestic Agenda. If Gorbachev wants to signal a new tone, he could defer the traditional summer vacation and work on getting the draft Five Year Plan and party program in shape for the congress. The draft program might be unveiled at the next plenum and should certainly echo his themes of increased discipline and technological progress. When the draft of the economic plan is made public, it should reflect his demands for increased economic growth rates and a new investment strategy.

He could also make additional forays outside of Moscow to demonstrate his leadership and activism. He has just returned from a visit to the Ukraine and might undertake a visit to somewhere in Siberia to further increase his exposure. He could use these trips to keep up the rhetorical pressure on the economic bureaucrats.

Foreign Policy. We will probably begin to see a growing Gorbachev Impact on foreign policy. Gromyko's influence will decline further from its high point in the Chernenko regime. A meeting with President Reagan would also burnish his image as a statesman, and an early move by Moscow to arrange a summit cannot be ruled out.

His activism may also be reflected in bolder efforts to put pressure on current US policy. We could, for example, see more skillful attempts to woo Tokyo by exploiting trade frictions between the US and Japan, or a symbolic gesture toward Beijing designed to disrupt Sino-US relations. New initiatives to undermine NATO cooperation on SDI and COCOM restrictions are also likely.

335

Signals of Setback for Gorbachev

Opponents will be looking for opportunities to slow Gorbachev's momentum. An early indicator of political difficulties would be his failure to get the Presidency. While there may be reasons for a General Secretary to delay assumption of the Presidency – Andropov may have for instance – Gorbachev would have to consider the cost of losing political momentum, especially when he so clearly linked the offices of General Secretary and President in nominating Chernenko as chief of state last year.

- ███████████████ Gromyko might be in line for the job, and Gorbachev might prefer him in this ceremonial post instead of being Foreign Minister. On balance, however, Gorbachev would probably still benefit more from holding both posts, and it would facilitate his enagement in personal summitry with foreign heads of state.

Another sign of resistance would be delays in the publication of the draft Five Year Plan or party program or the failure of the drafts to show new approaches to economic and social policy. If Gorbachev fails to follow up on his tough rhetoric by firing the ministers he has criticized, it would be widely read in the USSR as a setback. He has made personnel turnover a major issue, and failure to make changes in the top echelon of the party and ministries would signify that his Politburo colleagues are unwilling to go along.

Internal Distribution
1 - DCI
2 - DDCI
3 - SA/DCI
4 - ED/DCI
5 - Executive Registry
6 - DDI
7 - Senior Review Panel
8 - 13 OCPAS/IMD/CB
14 - Chairman NIC
15 - NIO/USSR-EE

```
16 - NIO/SP
17 - C/DDO/SE Reports
18 - C/DCD/PES
19 - D/SOVA
20 - DD/SOVA
21 - C/SOVA/NIG
22 - C/SOVA/NIG/EPD
23 - C/SOVA/NIG/DPD
24 - C/SOVA/NIG/DPD/LP
25 - C/SOVA/NIG/DPD/BF
26 - C/SOVA/NIG/DPD/SI
27 - C/SOVA/RIG
28 - C/RIG/EAD
29 - C/RIG/TWAD
30 - C/SOVA/SIG
31 - C/SOVA/SIG/SFD
32 - C/SOVA/SIG/SPD
33 - C/SOVA/DEIG
34 - C/SOVA/DEIG/DEA
35 - C/SOVA/DEIG/DID
36 - PDB Staff
```

```
EXTERNAL DISTRIBUTION
1   Admiral Poindexter
    Deputy Assistant to the President
    National Security Affairs
    White House
2   Ambassador Matlock, Jr.
    Special Assistant To the President
    Senior Director, European and Soviet Affairs
    National Security Council
    Rm 368, EOB
3   Mr. Fred C. Ikle
    Undersecretary of Defense for Policy
    Rm 4E812
    The Pentagon
4   Mr. Richard L. Armitage
    Assistant Secretary of Defense
    Rm 4E817
    The Pentagon
5   The Honorable Michael H. Armacost
    Undersecretary for Political Affairs
```

```
      Rm 7240
      Department of State
 6    Mr. Richard Burt
      Assistant Secretary
      Bureau of European Affairs
      Rm 6226
      Department of State
 7    Mr. Mark Palmer
      Deputy Assistant Secretary for
      Bureau of European Affairs
      Rm 6219
      Department of State
 8    Mr. Donald Gregg
      Assistant to the Vice President
      for National Security Affairs
      Rm 298
      The White House
 9    Lt. Gen William Odom
      Direcotr, NSA
      T532/CDB
      Fort Meade Md
10    Mr. Richard E. Combs, Jr.
      Director, Office of Eastern European Affairs
      Bureau of European Affairs
      Rm 6226
      Department of State
11    Mr. Robert Dean
      Deputy Director, Politico-Military Affairs
      Rm 7327
      Department of State
12    Morton I. Abramowitz
      Director, INR
      Department of State
13    Mr. Robert Baraz
      Director, Office of Analysis for the Soviet Union
      and Western Europe INR
      Department of State
14    Linda Wetzel
      Policy Assistant for USSR/Eastern Europe Affairs
      OASD/ISP/EUR/NATO Regional Policy
      Rm 1D469, Pentagon
```

15 Jay Kalner
    ACDA/SP
    Rm 4495
    Department of State
16 Col Tyrus Cobb
    Staff Member NSC
    Rm 373, EOB
17 Don Graves
    INR/SEE/ST
    Department of State
    Rm 4844
18 John Danylyk
    Chief INR/EC/USSR
    Department of State
    Rm 8662 New State
19 Bill Courtney
    Special Assistant, Office of Under Secretary
    of State
Rm 7240 New State

Notes

1. For an overview of this aspect of the CIA's work see J. D. Clemente, 'CIA's Medical and Psychological Analysis Center (MPAC) and the Health of Foreign Leaders', *International Journal of Intelligence and Counterintelligence*, 19.3 (2006), pp. 385–423.
2. A certain type of person fulfilled such a role. For a fascinating glimpse of the minutiae involved see R. W. Shryock, 'For an Eclectic Sovietology', *Studies in Intelligence*, 8.1 (1995).
3. Christopher Andrew and Vasili Mitrokhin, *The Mitrokhin Archive: The KGB in Europe and the West* (London: Penguin, 1999).
4. 'Andropov: His Power and Program', Deputy Director for Intelligence to Director of Central Intelligence, 17 November 1982, <https://www.cia.gov/library/readingroom/docs/CIA-RDP84B01072R000200110011-4.pdf> (last accessed 10 January 2020).
5. 'Assessment of Andropov's Power', CIA Directorate of Intelligence, 13 December 1982.
6. 'Andropov's Likely Strategy for Economic Change', CIA Directorate of Intelligence, 1 July 1983, <https://www.cia.gov/library/readingroom/docs/DOC_0000498531.pdf> (last accessed 10 January 2020).
7. 'A USSR Without Andropov?', CIA Directorate of Intelligence, 28 March 1983, <https://www.cia.gov/library/readingroom/docs/CIA-RDP85T00153R000100060026-7.pdf> (last accessed 10 January 2020).

8. For far more detail see 'Konstantin Chernenko: His Role in the Brezhnev Succession', CIA National Foreign Assessment Center, 13 March 1980, <https://www.cia.gov/library/readingroom/docs/DOC_0000972979.pdf> (last accessed 10 January 2020).

9. 'A USSR Without Andropov?'

10. 'Chernenko: A Preliminary Assessment of the Man and His Policy Agenda', CIA Directorate of Intelligence, 16 March 1984, <https://www.cia.gov/library/readingroom/docs/CIA-RDP85T00287R001400410001-3.pdf> (last accessed 10 January 2020).

11. Ibid.

12. 'Political Maneuvering in the Soviet Leadership', Director of Soviet Analysis to Director of Central Intelligence, 31 October 1984, <https://www.cia.gov/library/readingroom/docs/CIA-RDP86B00420R000500950008-5.pdf> (last accessed 10 January 2020).

13. Ibid.

14. 'Gorbachev, the New Broom', CIA Directorate of Intelligence, June 1985, <https://www.cia.gov/library/readingroom/docs/CIA-RDP85T01058R00050 7710001-6.pdf> (last accessed 10 January 2020).

15. 'Gorbachev's Economic Agenda: Promises, Potentials, and Pitfalls', CIA Directorate of Intelligence, September 1985, <https://www.cia.gov/library/readingroom/docs/19850901.pdf> (last accessed 10 January 2020).

16. 'The Soviet Economy under a New Leader', joint report by CIA and DIA, 19 March 1986, <https://www.cia.gov/library/readingroom/docs/19860319.pdf> (last accessed 10 January 2020).

17. 'The 27th CPSU Congress: Gorbachev's Unfinished Business', CIA Directorate of Intelligence, April 1986, <https://www.cia.gov/library/readingroom/docs/19860401A.pdf> (last accessed 10 January 2020).

18. 'Gorbachev's Domestic Challenge: The Looming Problems', CIA Directorate of Intelligence, February 1987, <https://www.cia.gov/library/readingroom/docs/19870201.pdf> (last accessed 10 January 2020).

19. 'Rising Political Instability Under Gorbachev: Understanding the Problems and Prospects for Resolution', CIA Directorate of Intelligence, April 1989, <https://www.cia.gov/library/readingroom/docs/19890401A.pdf> (last accessed 10 January 2020).

20. 'Gorbachev's Reorganization of the Party: Breaking the Stranglehold of the Apparatus', CIA Directorate of Intelligence, June 1989, <https://www.cia.gov/library/readingroom/docs/19890601.pdf> (last accessed 10 January 2020).

17 The CIA and the (First) Persian Gulf War

Iraq has proven to be a crucible in which US intelligence, and the CIA in particular, was tested over and again. The operations of the CIA and its sister services in and concerning Iraq have demonstrated their impressive capabilities, but also the limits of their reach. The high points include the detail with which the US intelligence community (USIC) profiled the Iraqi army before and during Operation Desert Storm, in 1991. The USIC's satellites and technical sensors, combined with the all-source intelligence fusion of CIA and other agency analysts, provided allied forces with a hitherto unprecedented level of insight into the locations, disposition and strength of the opposing forces, the difficulty encountered in disseminating this information down to tactical commanders notwithstanding.[1] The low points included the long-term weakness in gathering intelligence on, and correctly assessing the nature of, erstwhile Iraqi dictator Saddam Hussein's weapons of mass destruction programmes. This was clearly underlined both in the assessments of Saddam's nuclear capabilities in the late 1980s and before the Persian Gulf War, which underestimated the progress and strength of his programme, and a decade later in the intelligence estimates preceding the 2003 Iraq War, which overestimated his capabilities.[2] The second Gulf War (2003) and the subsequent investigations into the intelligence failures that surrounded it have resonated as one of the most significant and painful episodes in the CIA's history.

Both successes and failures relate to the struggle US intelligence grappled with over the years of the Cold War, namely the challenge of spying on closed, secure and secretive authoritarian and police states, and the solutions it found to the problem. These solutions were often based on technical means of peeking in from the outside. A variety of sensors – including aircraft, satellites, radar stations and even submarines – intercepted and collected all manner of communications, telemetry, signature and imagery intelligence from behind the Iron Curtain. This was melded with the more limited volume of human intelligence and open-source reporting that was available to allow the US to gauge the strength, readiness and leadership of the Soviet military. The results were not always perfect. But technical sources offered the West a competent understanding of Soviet military capabilities from fairly early in the Cold War.[3] Later, as discussed in previous chapters, they became so developed that presidents were confident in relying upon them to monitor Soviet compliance with strategic arms control agreements without the need for intrusive and problematic on-site inspections.

Yet there were crucial intelligence challenges with standoff sources. One concerned their capacity to identify new or discreet weapons systems before they were tested and deployed (for instance, the extent of the Soviets' biological weapons programme remained hidden for decades, as did aspects of its nuclear weapons research and development infrastructure.)[4] Another concerned the limited amount of insight they could provide into a target's intentions. During the Reagan presidency and the time of 'the second Cold War' in the early 1980s, technical sources could outline the contours of the Soviet military machine; what it could not do was highlight how the Soviet leadership, under Andropov, believed they might have to use it pre-emptively, based on their incorrect belief that the US was planning to use a NATO exercise as a surprise attack (see Chapter 15 on Exercise Able Archer 1983). That insight only came with the recruitment and reporting of a well-placed source inside the KGB, Oleg Gordievsky.[5] A similar dynamic was visible in Saddam's Iraq, with its ruthless, brutal and highly effective secret police. Deployed capabilities, on the open desert plains of Iraq, were visible to the USIC's myriad technical collection platforms, notwithstanding Iraq's creative denial and deception operations. Its secret programmes, the research institutes that housed hitherto untested weapons, were not as susceptible to technical collection. Observing Saddam Hussein's bellicose political rhetoric, military machinations and oppressive rule was relatively straightforward. Recruiting a spy who could give accurate insight into his intentions was not. If Moscow was CIA's archetypal denied area challenge, Baghdad was not far behind.

The documentary evidence released concerning the CIA's work in the Persian Gulf War of 1991 and the crisis leading up to the war is relatively sparse, certainly when compared to the volumes that have been released in the wake of the 2003 Iraq War. Likewise, the amount of scholarship devoted to examining the role of intelligence in 1990 and 1991 is comparatively limited.[6] However, the record reveals that the agency was closely engaged with both monitoring and attempting to influence developments in the Gulf. Through the 1980s and earlier, monitoring the Soviet Union's influence in the region was a pressing concern for successive US administrations, of course. But the long and brutal Iran–Iraq war that ignited in 1980 and culminated, eventually, in an Iraqi victory in August 1988 was also a key factor in focusing the CIA and the broader intelligence community's attention on the region. The US was drawn into the conflict, supporting secular Iraq as a bulwark against theocratic Iranian influence in the Middle East. But any notions that the Iraqi dictator could be moderated or used as a regional tool to promote US interests were soon dashed.[7] Saddam's ruthless use of chemical weapons against military and civilian targets in March 1988 was noted with concern by the CIA's National Intelligence Officer (NIO) for Warning, who also issued a judgement that Saddam would probably be willing to use chemical weapons offensively in a future conflict.[8] Saddam's belligerence concerning Israel, his continued pursuit of weapons of mass destruction, and his disinclination to demobilise after his victory also prompted concerns (the CIA considered, for instance, Iraq's purchasing of Soviet T-72 tanks to be a potentially destabilising development in Arab–Israeli relations).[9] By January 1990 the National Warning Staff was monitoring and reviewing indicators concerning the threat Saddam posed not only to Israel, but also to his neighbours Saudi Arabia and Kuwait, both key US allies.[10]

As well as monitoring Iraq's military, the CIA worked to understand the regime and its political power base. Saddam had been a figure of some interest to the agency as his influence grew in Baghdad and in the Baath party. By the 1970s the CIA understood him as a powerful and significant figure, describing him as 'tough opportunist ... a former Baathist street fighter who helped plan the Baathist coup that toppled the government in July 1968'.[11] In 1976, it read the various promotions Saddam received from the ailing President Ahmad Hasan al-Bakr as, potentially, a strategy for bolstering his legitimacy and easing his path to the presidency. By October 1978, agency analysts had a detailed profile of his background and career and were carefully observing his growing power in Iraq. They described him as 'pragmatic' but also 'opportunistic and vengeful'. It was clear that his pursuit of 'enemies of the state' was 'relentless', and that he was the dominant force in Iraqi politics.[12]

Saddam seized power in 1979. Thereafter the CIA carefully studied the foundations of his rule, assessing that his domestic security and power base was partly a product of his appointment of fellow Tikritis to key positions.[13] This foundation and his grip on internal security made any internal challenges unlikely, even during the difficult years of the Iran–Iraq war. CIA analysts judged that the war had rendered his regime 'more brittle', but 'more dependent on fear as an instrument of control than it was when the war began'.[14] Reports confirmed that the Iraqi dictator was strengthening his position by strategically blunting threats from the Iraqi Shia community, with a combination of co-option and repression.[15] By 1990, therefore, the years of patient study had ensured that the key features of Saddam's regime and his personality were well documented. In early May 1990, the CIA issued a warning that his regime might have set its sights on Kuwait.[16]

Although George H. W. Bush was a savvy consumer of intelligence – having the distinction of being the only former DCI to occupy the Oval Office – the initial warning was met with a degree of scepticism in his administration. But over the following months satellite imagery and sigint analysis offered a clear indication of a troop build-up and underscored the possibility that an invasion was being contemplated. As May turned to June, and June to July, it became harder for the CIA analysts to conclude that Saddam was merely engaged in a show of force to extract political and economic concessions; rather, they judged, the troops were likely there to invade Kuwait. The NIO for Warning assessed that the movement of elite Republican Guard units as well as a long logistical tail merited a 'Warning of War' memorandum, circulated on 25 July, assessing that even if Kuwait conceded to Baghdad's demands there remained a considerable chance of war.[17] Meanwhile, the military developments remained a priority concern for the US intelligence community – particularly among combat support agencies – with myriad technical sources devoted to the matter and showing that preparations for the invasion were proceeding apace. On 1 August the NIO for Warning issued a 'warning of attack', noting that the invasion was imminent, a few short hours before Iraqi troops crossed the border and annexed oil-rich Kuwait, precipitating a new phase of the crisis.[18]

The immediate repercussions of Iraq's actions were significant. The CIA judged that, should he decide to do so, Saddam was capable of launching a further attack against US ally Saudi Arabia.[19] US help to protect the Kingdom was offered and eventually accepted, leading to the deployment of US forces to the Saudi hinterland as part of Operation Desert Shield. Meanwhile, Iraq's actions were roundly condemned at the United Nations, which on 6 August demanded an unconditional withdrawal from Kuwait, and following months of Iraqi intransigence authorised the use of 'all necessary means' to eject Iraq if it failed to comply with the UN's will.[20] US and allied troops poured into the region, and President Bush stated repeatedly that he would be willing to use force.[21] Essentially, the US and international community placed the ball in Saddam's court: leave, or face an attack.

The chapter reference document concerns US assessments of Saddam's intentions during the aftermath of the invasion, before Operation Desert Storm, when the Iraqi dictator had to decide what to do. The document presents an astute analysis of Saddam's strategy concerning his attempts to split the coalition by playing the Israel card, and the judgement that regime survival is the highest priority. The judgement that Saddam could probably survive a withdrawal from Kuwait in the face of the threat of attack was in all likelihood sound; Saddam survived a devastating military defeat in 1991. As the document illustrates, however, a key element of ambiguity remained over Saddam's perceptions and intentions, to the extent that even Saddam himself had a knowable strategy to achieve his regional hegemonic ambitions. The question of whether or not he believed that the US possessed the will to go to war remained unresolved. This underlines first, the difficulty the CIA and Western intelligence had in penetrating the ruling clique in Iraq; and, second, the difficulty that authoritarian leaders like Saddam Hussein often have in accepting information or analyses that contradict their preconceptions, such as the resolve of President Bush. It was a mistake the Iraqi dictator would repeat in 2003.

```
Iraq's Saddam Husayn:
The Next Six Weeks


Special National Intelligence Estimate


This Special National Intelligence Estimate represents
the views of the Director of Central Intelligence
with    the    advice    and    assistance    of    the
US Intelligence Community



                   SNIE 36.2-90
      Iraq's Saddam Husayn: The Next Six Weeks

Information available as of 17 December 1990 was used
in the preparation of this Special National Intelligence
Estimate.

The following intelligence organizations participated
in the preparation of this Estimate:
The Central Intelligence Agency
The Defense Intelligence Agency
The National Security Agency
The Bureau of Intelligence and Research,
Department of State
The Office of Intelligence Support,
Department of the Treasury
```

The Office of the Deputy Assistant Secretary
for Intelligence, Department of Energy

also participating:
The Office of the Deputy Chief of Staff
for Intelligence, Department of the Army
The Office of the Director of Naval
Intelligence, Department of the Navy
The Office of the Assistant Chief of Staff,
Intelligence, Department of the Air Force
The Director of Intelligence, Headquarters, Marine
Corps

---

*This Estimate was approved for publication by the
National Foreign Intelligence Board.*

Key Judgments
Iraq's Saddam Husayn: The Next Six Weeks

During the critical weeks ahead, Saddam Husayn will
attempt to defy the United States, mixing propaganda
with diplomacy to avert a military assault, to pry
apart the US-led coalition, to exploit antiwar sentiment in Congress, and to shift attention from Kuwait
to the Palestinian issue. This represents a continuation of his strategy to stand fast and play for
time. The danger for Saddam of misreading signals and
misinterpreting intentions will remain high.

We believe Saddam is also developing alternative
options and has not foreclosed any of them to date.
The key to his behavior in coming weeks will be
whether he becomes fully convinced that he faces a
devastating war if he does not pull out of Kuwait.
All agencies agree that he is not yet convinced and
that convincing him will be difficult. Several agencies believe that he cannot be convinced short of war
itself.

We judge that, if Saddam becomes convinced that a
coalition attack on him not only would be certain
but also would be devastating, quick, and decisive,
he would take bold action to emerge from the crisis

with his regime and military intact. His most likely option under such conditions would be to announce a withdrawal from Kuwait.* Exploiting this move as his principal weapon to divide the coalition, he would try to implement such a withdrawal over a lengthy period and only partially. We believe he could survive a withdrawal from Kuwait. At the moment, however, he continues to question US resolve, despite the increase in US forces in Saudi Arabia. He will stay in Kuwait so long as doubts about US resolve persist. Should Saddam withdraw from Kuwait, in whole or in part, coalition military options could be severely constrained and the coalition significantly weakened. Partial withdrawal would be widely perceived among coalition members as a positive move toward implementing the UN resolution. As a consequence, support for a hard line toward Iraq would erode.

As long as Saddam is not convinced of the coalition's determination to attack if he does not withdraw from Kuwait, and even as he becomes fully aware of the risks he is taking, Saddam will try other ploys to divide the coalition:

- He may propose an easing of sanctions as an incentive for further Iraqi concessions, holding an international conference on Middle East issues, pursuing an "Arab solution" to the Gulf crisis, and allowing more frequent nuclear inspections.
- Saddam will try to play the "Israel card" to rally Arab popular support, force Arab governments to abandon the coalition, and reinforce his credentials as an Arab leader. Saddam defines the Israel card as a policy that portrays his Arab adversaries as "stooges" of Israel and its American patron. He will also try to link the Palestinian problem to resolution of the Gulf crisis.

---

* The Director, Defense intelligence Agency, the Director of Naval Intelligence; the Assistant Chief of Staff Intelligence, Department of the Air Force; the Director of intelligence. Headquarters, Marine Corps; and the Deputy Chief of Staff for Intelligence, Department of the Army, believe that, in the absence of any prospect for negotiations or an Arab brokered solution following withdrawal, Iraq is likely to stay and fight in Kuwait.

- These diversionary steps are unlikely to work. They will not materially improve Saddam's position.

Despite Saddam's current unwillingness to agree to dates for the Baker–Aziz visits, we judge that he regards the US proposal as an opportunity to begin a protracted process of negotiations. He hopes that this process will lead to movement toward a political solution of the crisis that leaves him with some of his Kuwaiti gains.

Simultaneously, he will continue to strengthen his military defenses in the Kuwait Theater of Operations to reinforce his diplomatic strategy and to prepare for its possible failure. We estimate that over the next six weeks he will improve his barrier and obstacle system and upgrade the survivability of his forces. Reinforcements will consist primarily of more infantry divisions, but a few additional heavy brigades probably will be added to the theater. These defensive improvements and reinforcements are likely to be, concentrated in the western sector of the theater.

If Saddam concludes – rightly or wrongly – that he is about to be attacked and decides to stand and fight, he may conduct a preemptive strike by air or missile attacks to disrupt perceived coalition operational plans. We consider an all-out ground attack less likely because it would move Iraqi forces out of their favored defensive positions and expose them to the full effect of coalition airpower.

Despite US and international actions, there is a good chance* that Saddam over the next six weeks will remain unconvinced that the United States will attack Iraq. He might also overestimate his own military capabilities. In this situation, he would probably stick to his basic tactic of playing for time. This "standfast" option could result either from an Iraqi miscalculation of US intentions, military, capabil-

---

* *The Director, Defense Intelligence Agency; the Director of Naval Intelligence; the Assistant Chief of Staff, Intelligence, Department of the Air Force; the Director of Intelligence Headquarters, Marine Corps; and the Deputy Chief of Staff for Intelligence, Department of the Army believe that over the next six weeks it is likely that Saadam will remain unconvinced.*

ity or resolve, or from Saddam's judgment that Iraq's postwar political position were seen in the Arab world as the victim rather than the initiator of hostilities.*

If Saddam decides to stand firm and endure a US attack, he would try to undermine US national will by using his formidable defensive position to cause maximum casualties, stop the coalition short of its objective, and seek a stalemate on the ground to force the United States to negotiate a settlement.

Contents

Page

Key Judgments

Discussion

Saddam's Goals and Objectives

Saddam's Actions

Saddam May Offer a Surprise

Effectiveness of Saddam's Actions

Implications of an Iraqi Withdrawal

Discussion

The US announcement in mid-November doubling US troop deployments in the Persian Gulf, the UN resolution approving military action after 15 January, and President Bush's offer of direct talks are apparently prompting Baghdad to adjust its tactics, although Saddam's strategy is still to stand fast and play for time. He has adapted to the fluid environment by showing a willingness to take bold steps. Nevertheless, for Saddam the danger of misreading

---

* The Director, Defense Intelligence Agency; the Director of Naval Intelligence; the Assistant Chief of Staff, Intelligence, Department of the Air Force; the Director of Intelligence Headquarters, Marine Corps; and the Deputy Chief of Staff for Intelligence, Department of the Army believe that Saadam will not abandon this option without some level of US military action.

349

signals and misinterpreting intentions will remain high over the next several weeks.

We believe Saddam is developing alternative options and has not foreclosed any of them. His actions reflect both worry over US military intentions and his perception that opposition to war is growing in the United States and is subject to manipulation. His initial acceptance of the President's proposal was quickly followed by the test-firing of Scud-type missiles and the appointment of a more effective defense minister, intended as signals of Iraq's military capability and resolve. His recent decision to release all hostages held in Iraq and Kuwait is designed to show flexibility on an issue important to the United States and the world community but of declining value to him.

Saddam's Goals and Objectives

Saddam's basic goals are to emerge from the crisis with his regime and military forces intact and to retain as many of his gains in Kuwait as he can. Between now and 15 January, he will try to:

- Make that deadline irrelevant through efforts to buy time by creating conditions in which it would be progressively more difficult for the coalition to launch an offensive after mid-January.
- Drive a wedge between the United States and its coalition partners by exploiting what he sees as the latters' "softness" on the use of force against Iraq, especially with respect to some European and Arab countries.
- Exploit antiwar sentiment in Congress and among the American public, thus weakening US resolve to pursue the military option.
- Continue extensive military preparations to deter military action and underscore the possibility of a heavy toll in American lives if war breaks out.
- Divert attention from Iraq's occupation and dismantling of Kuwait by emphasizing the importance of the Palestinian question.
- Seek relief from economic sanctions.

These short-term objectives are directly related to Saddam's longer term goals of surviving, keeping intact his military capabilities, retaining his capacity to exert Arab leadership and intimidate his wealthy neighbors, increasing oil revenues needed for economic development and continued military modernization, and avoiding reparations

Saddam's Actions*
Over the next month or so, Saddam will pursue political and military courses of action. He will continue extensive military preparations in the Kuwait Theater of Operations both to extend his defenses and as a political signal of staying power. Simultaneously, he will offer diplomatic initiatives to gain international support for a political solution.

This dual strategy-extending defenses and offering diplomatic initiatives - reflects Saddam's continued doubts about US resolve. It remains uncertain at this point whether Saddam understands his own vulnerabilities and sees them as foreclosing his ability to win or even survive a war with the United States. He probably believes the US Administration would be prepared to use military force against him, but he thinks it is under increasing public and Congressional pressure to avoid war. Saddam has often voiced his belief that the US experience in Vietnam left it with no will to fight or to risk the kind of casualties he believes the Iraqi people have proved they can absorb. He probably hopes to exploit President Bush's offer of talks to make gains with those in the United States opposed to war, but Saddam also suspects that the administration is going through the motions of seeking a peaceful solution before it attacks.

Indicators of an Iraqi Decision
To Withdraw From Kuwait
If Saddam contemplating withdrawal from Kuwait, we might see several signs in advance.

---

* The Intelligence Community is preparing a Memorandum to Holders of SNIE 36.2-5-90 *Iraq as a Military Adversary, this* Memorandum will address current Iraqi military preparations and perceptions of a possible war with the coalition.

- *A toning down of reference to Kuwait as Iraq's 19th province.*
- *Street demonstrations clearly organised by the Iraq's in Kuwait City or Baghdad noting support for Saddam and approving withdrawal.*
- *Stories in the Iraqi media focusing on the possibility of withdrawal following Kuwait's "liberation."*
- *Reports that Iraqi security forces in Kuwait have stopped security searches and are not enforcing regulations that Kuwaitis be re-registered as Iraqi citizens.*
- *Saddam's use of Arab intermediaries to obtain guarantees that his force would not be attacked during or after a withdrawal.*
- *An Iraqi press barrage about how much Saddam has done to dramatise the Palestinian cause coupled with thinly veiled hints that Iraq will "sacrifice" Kuwait for the PLO. Military indicators of an intent to withdraw are unlikely. Iraqi ground forces probably would continue preparations to defend Kuwait until Saddam received assurances that they would not be attacked. We cannot rule out that Iraqi border before announcing an intention to withdraw. Baghdad, however, is aware of US imagery capabilities and might not want to tip its hand by providing such an obvious indicator.*

Saddam will probe for diplomatic and economic avenues to divide or distract our European and Arab partners in the coalition:
- He will continue efforts to woo Paris and Moscow by urging that an international conference be held to resolve broader Middle Eastern issues, including an Israeli withdrawal from "Palestine," a term he does not define.
- He will continue to pursue an "Arab solution" by suggesting talks with Saudi Arabia and Egypt. He will also play upon a perception in the Middle East that the US-Iraqi talks imply negotiations over Kuwait. He will urge Arab intermediaries to contact King Fand and President Mubarak to encourage them to enter into direct negotiations with him.

- He will intensify his efforts to get relief from sanctions as a reward for his decision to release the hostages and to encourage further Iraqi "flexibility." He will also continue to exaggerate the impact of sanctions in an effort to strengthen US domestic opinion against early resort to military action. The impact of sanctions is being felt in Baghdad, but Saddam probably thinks he can continue to cope. We believe that economic hardships alone will not compel him to rethink his policy toward Kuwait over the next several weeks.
- Baghdad apparently is willing to allow the International Atomic Energy Agency (IAEA) to step up inspection and verification of the only weapons-grade uranium known to be in Iraq, possibly in January or February. The safeguarded uranium in question is not relevant to the achievement of Iraq's long-term nuclear aims. But he is probably aware that the issue of a near-term Iraqi nuclear explosive capability is on the "short list" of rationales garnering public support for coalition military action. By removing the hostage and nuclear issues, Saddam would challenge the United States to rebuild domestic and international support.

Despite Saddam's current unwillingness to agree to dates for the Baker–Aziz visits, we judge that he regards the US proposal for talks as an opportunity to begin a protracted process of negotiations leading to movement toward a political solution of the crisis that leaves him with some of his Kuwaiti gains.

Such a process, in Saddam's view, would greatly complicate the use of force by the coalition at an early date. He will try to engage the United States in negotiations about negotiations, calculating that Washington would not be able to stop its diplomatic initiative without looking as though it had no interest in a process short of war.

Saddam's current delaying tactics signal his intent to try to string out the talks beyond mid-January. He will expect no US attack as long as the talks continue. To supplement his strategy, he will use forthcoming visits of high-level officials from Europe and the Middle East to show that he is not diplomatically isolated and that he desires peace.

Saddam May Offer a Surprise

Saddam is likely to take bold steps to emerge from the crisis with his regime and military intact. He will change direction in response to US initiatives. At the moment, however, he continues to question US resolve, despite the increase in US forces in Saudi Arabia. Most dramatically, he could announce a partial or total withdrawal from Kuwait as his principal weapon against the coalition. He would try to implement such a withdrawal over a lengthy period and only partially. If Saddam becomes fully convinced that he faces the prospect of a devastating war if he does not pull out of Kuwait, a partial or even a total withdrawal from Kuwait, in our view, would be his most likely course.* Such an action might also result if he comes to believe that he would retain significant political or territorial advantages as a result of a withdrawal. We believe he could survive a withdrawal from Kuwait.

An offer to withdraw probably would be accompanied by a request for a buffer of Arab troops while the withdrawal took place and thus be part of the "Arab solution" that Saddam has talked about for several weeks. He probably would also announce a willing-ness to abide by a plebiscite to decide the fate of "free" Kuwait; he would hope that he had created a new population base that would accept de facto Iraqi hegemony.

On the diplomatic front, Saddam could propose to meet President Bush one-on-one in Geneva. He would remind the United States of his perception that it faces two choices: a war it cannot win without

---

* *The Director, Defense Intelligence Agency, the Director of Naval Intelligence, the Assistant Chief of Staff, Intelligence, Department-of the Air Force, the Director of Intelligence, Headquarters, Marine Corps, and the Deputy Chief of Staff for Intelligence, Department of the Army believe that in the absence of any prospect for negotiations or an Arab brokered solution following withdrawal, Iraq is likely to stay and fight in Kuwait.*

massive casualties or a negotiated settlement that
would allow him some gains. He might offer to compromise on his linkage proposal by accepting a vague
declaration or agreement in principle to resolve the
Arab-Israeli conflict.

*Saddam will try to play the "Israel card" to rally
Arab popular support, force Arab governments to
abandon the coalition, and bolster his credentials
as an Arab leader.* Saddam defines the Israel card
as encompassing a portrayal of his Arab adversaries
as "stooges" of Israel and its American patrons. He
almost certainly assumes that Israel wants the crisis
to be resolved by military action. As part of a settlement, therefore, he may ask for US assurances that
Israel will not attack him. He will also try to link
the Palestinian problem to resolution of the Gulf
crisis.

*We believe that Iraq will not authorize terror-
ist action against Western targets over the next
few weeks because such attacks would run counter
to Saddam's strategy of presenting himself as a
peacemaker and because of the risk of retaliation
by the coalition.* Incidents staged by Iraqi agents
and Palestinian collaborators cannot be ruled out
if Saddam believed he could avoid retaliation and
maintain deniability. Such actions probably would
be targeted primarily against Arab governments that
support the coalition. Some extremist Palestinian
groups, acting independently of Baghdad, may use terrorism in efforts to provoke a Middle Eastern war if
it appears that a diplomatic solution that does not
address the Palestinian problem is likely.

*To reinforce his diplomatic strategy and to prepare
for its possible failure, Saddam will continue to
beef up his defenses in Kuwait.* Over the next several
weeks, the Iraqis will strengthen the main obstacle
belt and add more maneuver units. The additional soldiers Saddam is calling up probably will be used in
units that replace those guarding the Iranian border
area, thus freeing those troops for duty in Kuwait.
These units, however, will vary widely in training,
personnel, and equipment. Because all of Iraq's heavy

divisions are already in Kuwait, future reinforcements, consisting of a few additional heavy brigades,
will represent smaller increments of combat power.
Iraq's overall combat potential will be increased
primarily by reinforcing and extending the western
portion of Iraqi forward defenses in the Kuwait
Theater. The additional troops, however, will impose
a heavier burden on an already strained logistic
system.

*Saddam is more likely to withdraw from Kuwait
unilaterally than to launch a preemptive attack on
coalition forces.* At a minimum, such an attack would
be unlikely while the talks remain active. Should
Saddam believe, particularly in January, that coalition military operations are imminent, and should he
make the decision to fight, a preemptive attack would
become more likely. Its purpose would be to disrupt
coalition plans. It probably would take the form
of air and missile attacks and could involve up to
brigade-size spoiling attacks.

We consider an all-out ground attack less likely.
Such an attack would move Iraqi forces out of their
carefully prepared and favored defensive positions
and expose them to the full effects of coalition airpower. A large-scale ground offensive would involve
extensive preparations, and thus would provide additional warning to the coalition, and it would also
severely tax the Iraqi logistic system.

Despite US and international actions, there is
a good chance* that Saddam over the next six weeks
will remain unconvinced that the United States would
attack Iraq. He might also overestimate his own military capabilities. In this situation, he would probably stick to his basic tactic of playing for time,
choosing neither to withdraw nor to preempt. This

---

* *The Director, Defense Intelligence Agency, the Director of Naval
Intelligence, the Assistant Chief of Staff, Intelligence, Department
of the Air Force, the Director of Intelligence, Headquarters, Marine
Corps, and the Deputy Chief of Staff for Intelligence, Department of the
Army believe that over the next six weeks. It is likely that Saddam
will remain unconvinced.*

course of action – a standfast option* – could result either from an Iraqi miscalculation of US intentions and military capability or resolve or from Saddam's judgment that Iraq's postwar political position would be stronger if it were seen in the Arab world as the victim rather than the initiator of hostilities. If Saddam decides to stand firm and endure a US attack, he would try to undermine US national will by using his formidable defensive position to cause maximum casualties, stop the coalition short of its objective, and seek a stalemate on the ground to force the United States to negotiate a settlement.

Effectiveness of Saddam's Actions
The Iraqi withdrawal scenario would be the most effective Iraqi option for disrupting the coalition. Other actions, including efforts to sow suspicion among the Arabs about US intentions are not likely to have significant impact among key coalition governments. His various ploys undoubtedly, will receive considerable media attention and indirectly will heighten concern that sanctions have not been given enough time to work and that all avenues toward a diplomatic solution have not been fully explored.

Saddam probably would like to extend the timetable for talks with Washington. He may calculate that Arab resolve will wane, domestic pressures in the United States and Europe will grow, and religious and political factors will force the Saudis to seek a drawdown of US forces. This calculation would depend on stretching the talks through mid-March, when the Islamic holy month of Ramadan begins, and June, when the annual pilgrimage to Mecca (Hajj) begins.

---

* *The Director, Defense Intelligence Agency, the Director of Naval Intelligence, the Assistant Chief of Staff, Intelligence, Department of the Air Force, the Director of Intelligence, Headquarters, Marine Corps, and the Deputy Chief of Staff for Intelligence. Department of the Army believe that Saddam will not abandon this option without some level of US military action.*

Implications of an Iraqi Withdrawal

Should Saddam withdraw from Kuwait, in whole or in part, coalition military options could be severely constrained and the coalition significantly weakened. A partial withdrawal would place a heavier burden on the sanctions regime to achieve remaining coalition goals. Total withdrawal, however, could lead to the lifting of sanctions. In addition, the availability of economic assistance to adversely affected states would become more critical to the maintenance of sanctions against Iraq. If Saddam succeeded in using his withdrawal ploy to craft an "Arab solution," he could emerge with territorial and economic gains, as well as enhanced regional influence. He would continue to strive for regional leadership and would be tempted again to exert his will through force in the future.

On the other hand, a peaceful solution to the crisis could reduce the regional instability that would result from major hostilities between Iraq and the coalition. If, as is likely, Gulf Arabs request some form of US military presence, Saddam might be further constrained by the knowledge that the international community had demonstrated its ability to take action against him.

A resolution of the crisis that allowed Saddam to keep his military establishment intact would increase the danger of an Israeli military attack aimed at eliminating Iraq's missile, chemical, biological, and nuclear capabilities. Such an attack would generate a broad-based and adverse reaction against the United States in the Arab world.

Notes

1. Loch K. Johnson, *Bombs, Bugs, Drugs, and Thugs: Intelligence and America's Quest for Security* (London: New York University Press, 2000), p. 6. See also the challenges recorded in the House Committee on Armed Services report, 'Intelligence Successes and Failures in Operations Desert Shield/Storm', <http://www.dtic.mil/dtic/tr/fulltext/u2/a338886.pdf> (last accessed 10 January 2020).

2. See Richard L. Russell, 'CIA's Strategic Intelligence in Iraq', *Political Science Quarterly*, 117.2 (2002), p. 201. For the post-war analyses of the CIA's performance see 'Report on the US Intelligence Community's Prewar Intelligence Assessments on Iraq', <https://nsarchive2.gwu.edu/NSAEBB/NSAEBB254/doc12.pdf> (last accessed 10 January 2020).
3. See Matthew Aid, 'The National Security Agency and the Cold War', *Intelligence and National Security*, 16.1 (2001).
4. See Oleg Bukharin, 'US Atomic Energy Intelligence against the Soviet Target, 1945–1970', *Intelligence and National Security*, 19.4 (2004), pp. 655–79.
5. See *inter alia* Ben Macintyre, *The Spy and the Traitor* (Milton Keynes: Viking, 2018), pp. 144–62.
6. See for example the Digital National Security Archive's project on Iraq: 'Iraqgate: Saddam Hussein, US Policy, and the Prelude to the Persian Gulf War, 1980–1994', <https://nsarchive.gwu.edu/project/iraq-project> (last accessed 10 January 2020).
7. Tim Weiner, *Legacy of Ashes: The History of the CIA* (Penguin: London, 2007), p. 491.
8. Charles E. Allen, 'Warning and Iraq's Invasion of Kuwait: A Retrospective Look', *Defence Intelligence Journal*, 7.2 (1998), pp. 33–44.
9. See 'Monthly Warning Assessment: Near East and South Asia', memorandum from Robert C. Ames to the DCI, 24 July 1979, <https://www.cia.gov/library/readingroom/docs/CIA-RDP83B01027R000300110006-0.pdf> (last accessed 10 January 2020).
10. Allen, 'Warning and Iraq's Invasion of Kuwait', pp. 33–44.
11. See 'Iraq: Saddam Husayn Appointed General', 13 January 1976, <https://www.cia.gov/library/readingroom/docs/DOC_0005388899.pdf> (last accessed 10 January 2020).
12. 'Government in Iraq', CIA intelligence memorandum, 31 October 1978, <https://www.cia.gov/library/readingroom/docs/CIA-RDP80T00634A000400010048-0.pdf> (last accessed 10 January 2020).
13. See 'Iraq's Tikritis: Power Base of Saddam Husayn', CIA Directorate of Intelligence, February 1987, <https://www.cia.gov/library/readingroom/docs/CIA-RDP88T00096R000400540002-8.pdf> (last accessed 10 January 2020).
14. See 'Prospects for Iraq', SNIE 36.2-83, 19 July 1983 <https://www.cia.gov/library/readingroom/docs/CIA-RDP86T00302R000901440012-4.pdf> (last accessed 10 January 2020).
15. See 'Iraq's Shias: Saddam Blunts a Potential Threat', CIA Directorate of Intelligence, 1 November 1984, <https://www.cia.gov/library/readingroom/docs/CIA-RDP85T00314R000300110003-5.pdf> (last accessed 10 January 2020).
16. Christopher Andrew, *For the President's Eyes Only: Secret Intelligence and the American Presidency from Washington to Bush* (New York: Harper Perennial, 1996), p. 515.
17. Allen, 'Warning and Iraq's Invasion of Kuwait', pp. 33–44.
18. Ibid. pp. 33–44.

19. Andrew, *For the President's Eyes Only*, p. 519.
20. Several timelines of the Kuwait crisis are available. See for instance BBC News, <http://news.bbc.co.uk/1/hi/world/middle_east/861164.stm> (last accessed 10 January 2020).
21. Andrew, *For the President's Eyes Only*, p. 520.

18   A Mole in Their Midst: The CIA and Aldrich Ames

Committing espionage is always a unique and deeply personal calculation, but there are several common factors. Some people spy because they are coerced into a corner and they feel that revealing secrets to a hostile intelligence service is the only choice left to them (commonly known as compromise or blackmail); others spy for egotistical reasons or to get revenge for a perceived wrong; many of the most damaging historical spies have cited ideological reasons as the root cause of their treachery. But for some, betrayal is purely and simply down to financial greed. For Aldrich 'Rick' Ames, money was the prime motivator for a betrayal that lasted nearly a decade. He was probably the most destructive Soviet mole in the CIA, crippling agency operations against the hardest intelligence topic through the end of the Cold War and beyond.[1]

Ames was born in May 1941 in River Falls, Wisconsin. Spying was in his blood: his father, a nondescript and part-time academic, spent a three-year tour as a CIA operations officer in Rangoon, Burma in the early 1950s. By all accounts this did not go well, and when he returned to the CIA Ames senior found it difficult to find a Division that would have him, eventually – and somewhat ironically – ending up working with James Angleton (see Chapter 10) in the Counterintelligence Staff. The rest of his CIA career was uneventful and he became more and more dependent on alcohol. Following in his father's footsteps, Ames junior interned in the CIA in the late 1950s whilst at university, and joined the agency full time in 1962.

Aldrich Ames spent just over three decades in the CIA, though he never broke into its senior ranks. The vast majority of his career was spent in the Directorate of Operations with a focus on the Soviet Union. His first and relatively unremarkable posting was to Ankara, Turkey, in the late 1960s. As various publications cite, his annual appraisals were underwhelming and upon return to headquarters he took up a desk job within the Soviet–East European (SE) Division. Although his performance evaluations from this period were competitive with his peers, by this point his marriage was breaking down and he was drinking more and more. Still, he was a capable and trusted insider. According to the Senate intelligence committee report on Ames, he was sent to a domestic CIA station in New York where he 'handled two important Soviet assets for the CIA' and received the highest evaluations of his career.[2] This was a high-pressure role, and although he had risen to the occasion professionally, it was the simultaneous disintegration of his personal life that would sow the seeds of his subsequent betrayal.

Ames' next posting was to Mexico, where he reported without his wife, who did not wish to accompany him. He received lukewarm appraisals and his fondness for alcohol did not go unnoticed. Whilst in Mexico Ames met Maria del Rosario Casas, a Colombian cultural attaché with whom he fell in love. She agreed to move with him to Washington when he returned in late 1983. Despite his mediocre professional performance, his new post was exceptionally sensitive: he was to be responsible for counter-intelligence within the SE division. Ames therefore had access to the files of every Russian, worldwide, who had decided to work for the CIA. Complicating his work was his personal life: he had agreed to an expensive divorce settlement that was financially prohibitive, and coupled with that was the fact that his new partner, Rosario, spent considerable amounts of money on phone calls to her family in Colombia as well as on clothes and shoes.

The consequence was immediate: Ames was in spiralling amounts of debt. To get himself out of this financial predicament, he had a solution: he would sell secrets of limited utility to the Russians. To some extent Ames' thinking must have been eased by his working role, in which he not only had access to a number of important files, but was also able to meet Soviet officers under the pretence of liaison meetings. Thus, in mid-April 1985 Ames arranged to meet a KGB officer based in the US. When the latter failed to show Ames brazenly walked to the Soviet Embassy, demanded to speak to the KGB *rezident*, and deposited a letter revealing his intent. In it he asked for $50,000 in exchange for revealing the identity of several Soviet spies whom, he later alleged, he suspected were plants anyway, i.e. not real spies but agents intentionally dangled by the Russians to confuse the CIA with misinformation.

Far more important and interesting to the KGB was Ames himself, who did not reveal his name, but did reveal that he was the head of the Soviet counter-intelligence branch of the CIA. Unsurprisingly, not only were the Russians keen, but they wanted more – and Ames, increasingly, was happy to provide it. Although his next assignment took him to Rome, Italy, he continued to provide classified documents, both originals and copies, to his handlers. Not only did he offer those relevant to his own role, but he also supplied whatever other operational material he could access. Within two years of starting his espionage career Ames was awash with cash, so much so that he had to open new Swiss bank accounts. His earlier convictions about passing information of limited value had been forgotten; indeed, the volume of material he had provided was so extensive that the KGB asked him to slow down, as they could not process it all.

By 1989 Ames had crossed another threshold: he allowed himself to be tasked by the KGB. This was perhaps not remarkable in intelligence terms, but it highlighted how far Ames, the financially driven spy, had sunk for money. The quantity of material he passed to the Russians was staggering: while in Rome, with more limited access to documents, he was still passing over 1,000 documents each year. To get around this problem Ames began to save files onto computer discs, which he would dutifully deliver to various pre-defined drops or in person at pre-arranged meetings. In this case, the digital age had come to CIA as the insider threat.

Unsurprisingly, the CIA was not immune to what was happening. In late 1985 it had become aware that a number of key sources within the Soviet system had disappeared. Initial investigations suggested that the cases could have become compromised via technical vulnerabilities or poor operational tradecraft, as opposed to anything more sinister. In fact, it was not until almost a year later that the CIA realised that it had an unthinkable problem of tremendous magnitude; it concluded that an astonishing forty-five different cases had been compromised.[3] Meanwhile, Ames, who had avoided any suspicion, was thriving. Ironically, with parallel shades of Kim Philby's assignment to Soviet counter-intelligence, Ames was appointed to the counter-intelligence mole taskforce – the very one trying to find him – and in the context of a broader reorganisation of SE division, was able to maintain his extensive access to files and secrets for years. Even the collapse of the Soviet Union had no significant effect on him or his espionage. The Russians wanted his material as much as the Soviets had, and they continued to reward him handsomely for it.

The undermining of US intelligence sources and networks became increasingly apparent – and alarming. In both the CIA and the FBI, taskforces were created to discover the source of the leaks. After years of false starts, suppositions, accusations and debate, there was little in the way of hard evidence to definitively confirm anyone's guilt. In the end, it was a joint CIA–FBI taskforce from which Sandy Grimes, a mild-mannered and unprepossessing female veteran of the CIA, found the answer. Perhaps appropriately (and with hindsight, obviously), it was all about the money. Ames' expenditure far outweighed his income, and once this was realised and no explanation was forthcoming, substantial evidence of his guilt was found.

Ames and Rosario were both arrested in February 1994. Although he initially professed his innocence, the pretence did not last long and Ames quickly confessed, revealing all. His wife was sentenced to five years for conspiracy to commit espionage and tax evasion, while Ames himself received a life sentence. More than two decades on, he remains in prison for his crimes, presumably never to be released.

In the aftermath of his arrest and conviction, three main questions emerged: why did he do it? What did he pass to the Russians? And how did he get away with it for so long? In the first interviews following his arrest, Ames claimed that finding a solution to his debt was the sole motivation: he would provide a one-off delivery to the Russians for $50,000, and this would alleviate his position. But was this the reality? Within a short space of time Ames changed his tune. Money possibly was the primary motive, but it was by no means the only reason, even though Ames became a very wealthy man following his fateful decision. During his trial Ames explained that in fact it had not been money but politics that had prompted his decision: he objected to the shift to the 'extreme right', which he claimed had been a gradual move over several decades in US foreign policy; and he also 'had come to believe that the espionage business, as carried out by the CIA ... was and is a self-serving sham, carried out by careerist bureaucrats who have managed to deceive several generations of American policymakers and the public about both the necessity and value of their work'.[4] It was this more righteous argument, rather than money, which Ames repeated in various interviews following his incarceration. But why the Russians? In a newspaper report shortly after his conviction, Ames was recorded as having said, like some of the atom spies decades before, that he wanted to 'level the playing field' between a 'decaying Moscow and a dominant Washington', thereby bringing the Cold War to an earlier end.[5] In fact, in one message which the FBI intercepted whilst investigating Ames, he referred to the Russians as his 'colleagues'[6] – which was true, in a manner of speaking. Together they had conspired to end the lives of perhaps a dozen CIA sources in Russia and decimated the agency's Russia programme. Only FBI Special Agent Robert Hanssen, arrested seven years hence, would have as much Russian blood on his conscience.

Quite whether Ames was naive or conceited enough to actually believe this is one thing, but the damage he caused was undeniably considerable. The CIA's Directorate of Operations, and especially the SE Division, were the most sensitive parts of a highly secret organisation. Remarkably, whilst documents were tightly controlled and compartmentalised throughout the agency, where Ames worked these measures were relaxed somewhat, so he was able to access and pass to the Russians a broad variety of documents, not just those with which he was involved. By all accounts, even the Russians were surprised at the level of his access.[7] In addition to current files, Ames was also permitted to access historical files of Russians who had volunteered to work for the CIA, many of whom were no longer active but who had avoided compromise.[8] Towards the end of his time in the CIA

Ames was transferred to the Crime and Narcotics Center, a joint analytical and operational unit. From this vantage point he was able to access the intranet system and download over three hundred documents from across the Directorate of Operations, files that he could not have accessed previously.[9] All of this made its way to the Lubyanka.

From this treasure trove of information, the Russians were able to identify a number of their nationals who were covertly providing intelligence to the US and other allied countries. One estimate suggests that three dozen CIA agents alone were compromised, of whom at least ten were executed. Hundreds of CIA operations were disclosed too, and while the loss of human life is perhaps the greatest of Ames' betrayals, he also disclosed information on US (and allied) political and military matters. In addition, he caused a significant breach of technical data, both from the CIA and NSA, including details of technical operations against the Soviet Union.[10]

All of which begs the question: how did Ames get away with it for so long? In the aftermath of his arrest and conviction this became the key aspect to tackle, and a number of formal inquiries took place. What became clear very quickly was not only that Ames had no great difficulties in either obtaining or passing the information to the Russians, but that in many of his positions he was encouraged to meet and attempt to recruit the very people to whom he was covertly passing secrets. But worse was to come once the practical details emerged and the realisation dawned that Ames should have been spotted and stopped far earlier.

The initial concern in 1985 over the sudden and unexplained disappearance of a number of US assets in the Soviet Union did not manifest itself in any sort of serious or concerted effort to uncover the source. Moscow was, admittedly and understandably, clever in the way it attempted to divert attention away from the actual source, using the known identity of another turncoat CIA officer, Edward Lee Howard, who had spied and defected to the Soviet Union as the source of the leaks.[11] When no obvious lead was uncovered the CIA's efforts to locate the source dwindled and effort was diverted to other matters, a move that was mirrored by renewed deception efforts by Moscow to conceal Ames' role, as described in the chapter reference document.[12]

With the benefit of hindsight, a number of other mistakes were made and opportunities missed. Perhaps the greatest of these was the manner in which Ames was able to placate anyone interested in his newfound lavish lifestyle, one that outmatched his income. The CIA was well aware that he could not afford everything on his salary alone, and although limited enquiries were made into Ames' claim that his wife's family in Colombia was the source of the new wealth, nobody followed up on the inconsistencies in this story. Even when attention was, finally, focused on Ames, other mistakes were made. For instance, FBI surveillance vehicles managed to miss his Jaguar car leaving the CIA and the tracker placed within the car did not work properly, so they did not see him making a dead letter box drop. The CIA, too, was not without blame: inexplicably, whilst under investigation Ames was allowed to travel to Moscow on a work trip; the CIA was very slow to inform the FBI about its suspicions, once attention was focused on him; it was known that Ames had held meetings with Russian intelligence officers that he had not declared to the CIA, and that he often asked lots of probing questions of colleagues, far more than his assigned work should have required him to do.[13]

In total there were three official investigations into the Ames case and what mistakes were made on the path to identifying him. The most thorough was that conducted by Frederick Hitz, the CIA's Inspector General, a copy of which is the chapter reference document. The role of the 'Inspector General' dated back to the 1940s, but changes in 1989 had created a degree of separation from the CIA itself by providing 'independent oversight', with the postholder being nominated by the president and confirmed by the Senate.[14] Hitz himself was a former CIA operations officer who had moved around various departments of the US government. His report was very critical of the CIA, identifying a number of individuals for criticism, and was followed by both the Senate and House reports. Just as the US intelligence community was adjusting to the details of lessons from the Ames case, another spy, this time the FBI's Robert Hanssen, was revealed as working for the Russians. He certainly will not be the last.

UNCLASSIFIED ABSTRACT OF THE
CIA INSPECTOR GENERAL'S REPORT
ON THE ALDRICH H. AMES CASE
PREFACE TO THE REPORT FROM THE IG
Procedurally, this has been an unusual report for the CIA IG to write. In the first instance, our inquiry was directly requested by the Chairman and Vice-Chairman of the Select Committee on Intelligence of the U.S. Senate in late February 1994 – shortly after Aldrich H. Ames was arrested. Normally, our congressional oversight committees ask the Director of Central Intelligence to request an IG investigation. On this occasion their request was directed to the IG.
Second, the DCI chose to ask us to look into the Ames matter in phases after Ames's arrest for fear of

disrupting the Ames prosecution. We were requested to inquire into the circumstances surrounding the CI investigation of the Ames betrayal – what procedures were in place respecting CIA counterespionage investigations at the time Ames volunteered to the Soviets in 1985; how well did they work; and what was the nature of CIA's cooperation with the FBI in this case. On March 10, 1994, the DCI asked us to seek to determine if individuals in Ames's supervisory chain discharged their responsibilities in the manner expected of them and directed the Executive Director of CIA to prepare a list of Ames's supervisors during the relevant periods. The DCI also directed that awards and promotions for the individuals on the Executive Director's list be held in escrow pending the outcome of the IG investigation. I wish to state at this point that neither I nor any member of the team investigating the Ames case have viewed the DCI's escrow list. We wanted to be as completely unaffected by the names on the list as we could be in order to discharge our responsibility to advise the DCI objectively of possible disciplinary recommendations. As a precautionary measure, I did ask my Deputy for Inspections, who is otherwise uninvolved in the Ames investigation, to view the escrow list to advise of any individuals on it whom we might have failed to interview through inadvertence. That has been our only involvement with the escrow list.

Third, there was an unusual limitation placed on our inquiry at the outset caused by a desire on the part of the DCI, the Department of Justice and the U.S. Attorney in the Eastern District of Virginia to do nothing that would complicate the Ames trial. We willingly complied with these constraints, confining ourselves to background file reviews and interviews of non-witnesses until the Ameses pled guilty on April 28, 1994. The consequence has been that we have had to cover a great deal of ground in a short period of time to conduct this investigation in order to have a report ready for the DCI and the congressional

SUMMARY

1. In the spring and summer of 1985, Aldrich H. Ames began his espionage activities on behalf of the Soviet Union. In 1985 and 1986, it became increasingly clear to officials within CIA that the Agency was faced with a major CI problem. A significant number of CIA Soviet sources began to be compromised, recalled to the Soviet Union and, in many cases, executed. A number of these cases were believed to have been exposed by Edward Lee Howard, who fled the United States in September 1985 to avoid prosecution for disclosures he made earlier that year. However, it was evident by fall of 1985 that not all of the compromised sources could be attributed to him.

2. Later in 1985, the first Agency efforts were initiated to ascertain whether the unexplained compromises could be the result of a) faulty practices by the sources or the CIA officers who were assigned to handle them (i.e., whether the cases each contained "seeds of their own destruction"), b) a physical or electronic intrusion into the Agency's Moscow Station or Agency communications, or c) a human penetration within the Agency (a "mole"). Although they were never discounted altogether, the first two theories diminished in favor over the years as possible explanations for the losses. A "molehunt" – an effort to determine whether there was a human penetration, a spy, within CIA's ranks – was pursued more or less continuously and with varying degrees of intensity until Ames was convicted of espionage in 1994, nine years after the compromises began to occur.

3. The 1985-1986 compromises were first discussed in late 1985 with DCI William Casey, who directed that the Deputy Director for Operations (DDO) make every effort to determine the reason for them. In January 1986, SE Division* instituted new and extraordinary compartmentation measures to prevent further compromises. In the fall of 1986, a small Special

* Soviet East European Division, later renamed Central Eurasia Division, directed operations related to the Soviet Union and its successor states.

Task Force (STF) of four officers operating under the direction of the Counterintelligence Staff (CI Staff) was directed to begin an effort to determine the cause of the compromises. This effort, which was primarily analytic in nature, paralleled a separate FBI task force to determine whether the FBI had been penetrated. The FBI task force ended, and the CIA STF effort diminished significantly in 1988 as its participants became caught up in the creation of the Counterintelligence Center (CIC). Between 1988 and 1990, the CIA molehunt came to a low ebb as the officers involved concentrated on other CI matters that were believed to have higher priority.

4. In late 1989, after his return from Rome, Ames's lifestyle and spending habits had changed as a result of the large amounts of money he had received from the KGB in return for the information he provided. Ames made no special efforts to conceal his newly acquired wealth and, for example, paid cash for a $540,000 home. This unexplained affluence was brought to the attention of the molehunt team by a CIA employee in late 1989, and a CIC officer began a financial inquiry. The preliminary results of the financial inquiry indicated several large cash transactions but were not considered particularly significant at the time.

5. Nevertheless, information regarding Ames's finances was provided to the Office of Security (OS) by CIC in 1990. A background investigation (BI) was conducted and a polygraph examination was scheduled. The BI was very thorough and produced information that indicated further questions about Ames and his spending habits. However, this information was not made available to the polygraph examiners who tested him, and CIC did not take steps to ensure that the examiners would have full knowledge of all it knew about Ames at the time. In April 1991, OS determined that Ames had successfully completed the reinvestigation polygraph with no indications of deception, just as he had five years previously.

6. In 1991, CIA's molehunt was revitalized and rejuvenated. Two counterintelligence officers were

assigned full-time to find the cause of the 1985-86 compromises. The FBI provided two officers to work as part of the molehunt team.

7. During this phase, attention was redirected at Ames and a number of other possible suspects. In March 1992, a decision was made to complete the financial inquiry of Ames that had been initiated in 1989. In August 1992, a correlation was made between bank deposits by Ames that were identified by the financial inquiry and meetings between Ames and a Soviet official that the Agency and FBI had authorized in 1985. The joint CIA/FBI analytic effort resulted in a report written in March 1993, which concluded that, among other things, there was a penetration of the CIA. It was expected by CIA and FBI officials that the report, which included lists of CIA employees who had access to the compromised cases, would be reviewed by the FBI in consideration of further investigative steps.

8. The totality of the information available to CIC and the FBI prompted the FBI to launch an intensive CI investigation of Ames. During this phase, the FBI attempted to gather sufficient information to determine whether Ames was in fact engaged in espionage, and the Agency molehunt team was relegated to a supporting role. Every effort was made to avoid alerting Ames to the FBI CI investigation. According to FBI and Agency officials, it was not until a search of Ames's residential trash in September 1993, which produced a copy of an operational note from Ames to the Russians, that they were certain Ames was a spy. After the FBI had gathered additional information, Ames was arrested on February 21, 1994 and pled guilty to espionage on April 28, 1994.

9. The two CIA officers and the two FBI officers who began working in earnest on the possibility of an Agency penetration in 1991 under the auspices of the Agency's CIC, deserve credit for the ultimate identification of Ames as a hostile intelligence penetration of CIA. Without their efforts, it is possible that Ames might never have been successfully identified and prosecuted. Although proof of his espionage activi-

ties was not obtained until after the FBI began its CI investigation of Ames in 1993, the CIA molehunt team played a critical role in providing a context for the opening of an intensive investigation by the FBI. Moreover, although the CIA and the FBI have had disagreements and difficulties with coordination in other cases in the past, there is ample evidence to support the statements by both FBI and CIA senior management that the Ames case was a model of CI cooperation between the two agencies.

10. From its beginnings in 1986, however, the management of CIA's molehunt effort was deficient in several respects. These management deficiencies contributed to the delay in identifying Ames as a possible penetration, even though he was a careless spy who was sloppy and inattentive to measures that would conceal his activities. Despite the persistence of the individuals who played a part in the molehunt, it suffered from insufficient senior management attention, a lack of proper resources, and an array of immediate and extended distractions. The existence and toleration of these deficiencies is difficult to understand in light of the seriousness of the 1985-86 compromises and especially when considered in the context of the series of other CI failures that the Agency suffered in the 1980s and the decade-long history of external attention to the weaknesses in the Agency's CI and security programs. The deficiencies reflect a CIA CI function that has not recovered its legitimacy since the excesses of James Angleton, which resulted in his involuntary retirement from CIA in 1974. Furthermore, to some extent, the "Angleton Syndrome" has become a canard that is used to downplay the role of CI in the Agency.

11. Even in this context, it is difficult to understand the repeated failure to focus more attention on Ames earlier when his name continued to come up throughout the investigation. He had access to all the compromised cases; his financial resources improved substantially for unestablished reasons; and his laziness and poor performance were rather widely known. All of these are CI indicators that should

have drawn attention to Ames. Combined, they should have made him stand out. Arguably, these indicators played a role in the fact that Ames was often named as a prime suspect by those involved in the molehunt.

12. One result of management inattention was the failure of CIA to bring a full range of potential resources to bear on this counterespionage investigation. There was an over-emphasis on operational analysis and the qualifications thought necessary to engage in such analysis, and a failure to employ fully such investigative techniques as financial analysis, the polygraph, behavioral analysis interviews, and the review of public and governmental records. These problems were exacerbated by the ambiguous division of the counterespionage function between CIC and OS and the continuing subordination by the Directorate of Operations (DO) of CI concerns to foreign intelligence collection interests. Excessive compartmentation has broadened the gap in communications between CIC and OS, and this problem has not been overcome despite efforts to improve coordination. CIC did not share information fully with OS or properly coordinate the OS investigation process.

13. These defects in the Agency's capability to conduct counterespionage investigations have been accompanied by a degradation of the security function within the Agency due to management policies and resource decisions during the past decade. These management policies emphasize generalization over expertise, quantity over quality, and accommodation rather than professionalism in the security field. This degradation of the security function has manifested itself in the reinvestigation and polygraph programs and appears to have contributed to Ames's ability to complete polygraphs successfully in 1986 and 1991 after he began his espionage activities.

14. Beyond defects in counterespionage investigations and related security programs, the Ames case reflects significant deficiencies in the Agency's personnel management policies. No evidence has been found that any Agency manager knowingly and willfully aided Ames in his espionage activities. However, Ames continued

to be selected for positions in SE Division, CIC and the Counternarcotics Center that gave him significant access to highly sensitive information despite strong evidence of performance and suitability problems and, in the last few years of his career, substantial suspicion regarding his trustworthiness. A psychological profile of Ames that was prepared as part of this investigation indicates a troubled employee with a significant potential to engage in harmful activities.

15. Although information regarding Ames's professional and personal failings may not have been available in the aggregate to all of his managers or in any complete and official record, little effort was made by those managers who were aware of Ames's poor performance and behavioral problems to identify the problems officially and deal with them. If Agency management had acted more responsibly and responsively as these problems arose, it is possible that the Ames case could have been avoided in that he might not have been placed in a position where he could give away such sensitive source information.

16. The principal deficiency in the Ames case was the failure to ensure that the Agency employed its best efforts and adequate resources in determining on a timely basis the cause, including the possibility of a human penetration, of the compromises in 1985-86 of essentially its entire cadre of Soviet sources. The individual officers who deserve recognition for their roles in the eventual identification of Ames were forced to overcome what appears to have been significant inattentiveness on the part of senior Agency management. As time wore on and other priorities intervened, the 1985-86 compromises received less and less senior management attention. The compromises were not addressed resolutely until the spring of 1991 when it was decided that a concerted effort was required to resolve them. Even then, it took nearly three years to identify and arrest Ames, not because he was careful and crafty, but because the Agency effort was inadequate.

17. Senior Agency management, including several DDOs,

DO Division Chiefs, CIC and DO officials, should be held accountable for permitting an officer with obvious problems such as Ames to continue to be placed in sensitive positions where he was able to engage in activities that have caused great harm to the United States. Senior Agency management, including at least several DCIs, Deputy Directors, DO Division Chiefs, and senior CI and security officials, should also be held accountable for not ensuring that the Agency made a maximum effort to resolve the compromises quickly through the conduct of a focused investigation conducted by adequate numbers of qualified personnel.

WHAT WAS AMES'S CAREER HISTORY WITH CIA?

18. In June 1962, Ames completed full processing for staff employment with the Agency and entered on duty as a GS-4 document analyst in the Records Integration Division (RID) of the DO. Within RID, Ames read, coded, filed, and retrieved documents related to clandestine operations against an East European target. He remained in this position for five years while attending George Washington University, on a part-time or full-time basis. In September 1967, Ames received his Bachelor of Arts degree in history with an average grade of B-.

19. Ames originally viewed his work with RID as a stopgap measure to finance his way through college. However, he grew increasingly fascinated by intelligence operations against Communist countries, and, influenced by other RID colleagues who were entering the Career Trainee (CT) program, he applied and was accepted as a CT in December 1967. When Ames completed this training nearly a year later, he was assigned to an SE Division branch. He remained there for several months before beginning Turkish language studies.

20. Ames's first overseas posting took place between 1969 and 1972. It was not a successful tour, and the last Performance Appraisal Report (PAR) of his tour stated, in effect, that Ames as unsuited for field work and should spend the remainder of his career at Headquarters. The PAR noted that Ames preferred "assignments that do not involve face-to-face situations with relatively unknown personalities who must

be manipulated." Such a comment was devastating for an operations officer, and Ames was discouraged enough to consider leaving the Agency.

21. Ames spent the next four years, 1972-76, at Headquarters in SE Division. Managing the paperwork and planning associated with field operations at a distance was more comfortable for Ames than trying to recruit in the field himself, and he won generally enthusiastic reviews from his supervisors. One payoff from this improved performance was the decision in September 1974 to name Ames as both the Headquarters and field case officer to manage a highly valued Agency asset.

22. Ames's opportunity to expand his field experience came with his assignment to the New York Base of the DO's Foreign Resources Division from 1976 to 1981. The PARs that Ames received during the last four of his five years in New York were the strongest of his career. These PARs led Ames to be ranked in the top 10% of GS-13 DO operations officers ranked for promotion in early 1982. He was promoted to GS-14 in May 1982.

23. The career momentum Ames established in New York was not maintained during his 1981-83 tour in Mexico City. This assignment, like his earlier tour and his later tour in Rome, failed to play to Ames's strengths as a handler of established sources and emphasized instead an area where he was weak – the development and recruitment of new assets. In Mexico City, Ames spent little time working outside the Embassy, developed few assets, and was chronically late with his financial accountings. Further, Ames developed problems with alcohol abuse that worsened to the point that he often was able to accomplish little work after long, liquid lunches. His PARs focused heavily, and negatively, on his failure to maintain proper accountings and were generally unenthusiastic. In Mexico City, Ames also became involved in an intimate relationship with the Colombian cultural attaché, Maria del Rosario Casas Dupuy.

24. Despite his lackluster performance in Mexico City, Ames returned to Headquarters in 1983 to a position

that he valued highly. His appointment as Chief of a branch in an SE Division Group was recommended by the officer who had supervised Ames in New York and approved by Chief, SE Division and the DDO. This position gave him access to the Agency's worldwide Soviet operations. Ames completed this tour with SE Division by being selected by the SE Division Chief as one of the primary debriefers for the defector Vitaly Yurchenko from August to September 1985. For his work in the SE Division Group, Ames was ranked very near the lower quarter of DO operations officers at his grade at this time.

25. By early 1984, Ames was thinking ahead to his next field assignment and asked to go to Rome as Chief of a branch where he had access to information regarding many operations run or supported from that post. He left for Rome in 1986. He once again began to drink heavily, particularly at lunch, did little work, sometimes slept at his desk in the afternoons, rarely initiated developmental activity, and often fell behind in accountings, reporting and other administrative matters. Ames was successful in managing liaison relations with U.S. military intelligence units in Italy, but he registered few other achievements.

26. Ames's mediocre performance for the Agency in Rome did not prevent his assignment upon his return to Headquarters in mid-1989 to head a branch of an SE Division Group. Here again he had access to many sensitive cases. When that position was eliminated in a December 1989 reorganization of SE Division, Ames became Chief of another SE Division branch, where he remained until late 1990. At this time, Ames was ranked in the bottom 10% of DO GS-14 operations officers. He appears to have been a weak manager who focused only on what interested him.

27. Ames moved to a position in the Counterintelligence Center in October 1990. In the CIC, where he remained until August 1991, he prepared analytical papers on issues relating to the KGB but also had access to sensitive data bases. Discussions between Ames and the Deputy Chief, SE Division, resulted in Ames's

temporary return to SE Division as head of a small KGB Working Group between August and November 1991.

28. In 1991, Chief SE Division requested that a counternarcotics program be established through liaison with the states of the former Soviet Union. Thereafter, Ames began a rotation to the Counternarcotics Center (CNC) in December 1991. At CNC, where Ames remained until his arrest, he worked primarily on developing a program for intelligence sharing between the United States and cooperating countries.

29. Ames was arrested on February 21, 1994. On that date, DCI Woolsey terminated his employment with the Agency.

WHAT WERE AMES'S STRENGTHS, WEAKNESSES AND VULNERABILITIES?

Performance Problems

30. Ames appears to have been most successful and productive in assignments that drew on his:

• Analytical skills, particularly collating myriad bits of information into coherent patterns;

• Writing skills, both in drafting operational cables and crafting more intuitive thought pieces;

• Intellectual curiosity and willingness to educate himself on issues that were beyond the scope of his immediate assignment; and

• Creativity in conceiving and implementing sometimes complex operational schemes and liaison programs.

31. Ames was far less successful – and indeed was generally judged a failure – in overseas assignments where the development and recruitment of assets was the key measure of his performance. For most of his career, moreover, a number of work habits also had a dampening impact on his performance. These included:

• Inattention to personal hygiene and a sometimes overbearing manner that aggravated the perception that he was a poor performer;

• A lack of enthusiasm for handling routine administrative matters. By the late 1970s, when Ames was assigned to New York, this pattern of behavior was evident in his tardy filing of financial accountings and failure to document all of his meetings in contact reports. Ames's disdain for detail also

manifested itself in his pack-rat amassing of paper
and his failure, especially in Rome, to handle action
cables appropriately and expeditiously; and
• Selective enthusiasm. With the passage of time,
Ames increasingly demonstrated zeal only for those
few tasks that captured his imagination while ignor-
ing elements of his job that were of little personal
interest to him.

Sleeping on the Job

32. A significant number of individuals who have
worked with Ames in both domestic and foreign assignments state that it was not uncommon for Ames to be
seen asleep at his desk during working hours. This
behavior often coincided, especially in Rome and at
Headquarters in the 1990s, with Ames having returned
from lunch where he consumed alcohol.

Failure to File Required Reports

33. The Agency has an established system of reports
of various kinds that serve administrative, operational, security, and counterintelligence purposes.
Ames paid very little attention to a variety of these
reporting requirements. His inattention to these
matters was by and large ignored, to the extent it
was known by Agency management.

Foreign Travel

34. Over the course of several years, Ames failed to
report foreign travel to OS as required by Headquarters
Regulation. It is difficult to determine whether and
to what extent management was aware of his unreported
travel. The official record includes no mention, but
fellow employees appear to have had some knowledge of
his travels, especially in Rome.

Contact Reports

35. Ames also failed to file timely contact reports
regarding many of his meetings with foreign officials. While this failure originally may have been
related to his laziness and disdain for regulations,
it became more calculated and had serious CI implications once he had volunteered to the Soviets in
1985. Ames states that he deliberately avoided filing
complete and timely reports of his contacts with
Soviet officials in Washington. If he had done so, he

believes, Agency and FBI officials might have identified contradictions. Moreover, he believes they would
have seen no operational advantage to the meetings,
ceased the operation, and removed the ready pretext
for his espionage activities. This also was true of
his meetings with Soviets in Rome.

Financial Accountings

36. Throughout the course of Ames's career, managers reported that they frequently counseled and
reprimanded him, or cited in his PAR Ames's refusal
to provide timely accountings and properly maintain
his revolving operational funds. This is more than a
question of financial responsibility for DO officers.
It also provides DO managers with another means of
monitoring and verifying the activities of the operations officers they supervise.

Foreign National Contacts and Marriage

37. Ames also did not fully comply with Agency
requirements in documenting his relationship with
Rosario. He never reported his intimate relationship
with her as a "close and continuing" one while he was
in Mexico City. Management was aware generally of a
relationship but not its intimate nature and did not
pursue the reporting. He did follow proper procedures
in obtaining approval for their marriage. However,
Agency management did not accept or implement properly the CI Staff Chief's recommendation at the time
that Ames be placed in less sensitive positions until
Rosario became a U.S. citizen.

Security Problems

38. Ames also seemed predisposed to ignore and
violate Agency security rules and regulations. In New
York in 1976, he committed a potentially very serious
security violation when he left a briefcase full of
classified information on a New York subway train.
In 1984, Ames brought Rosario to an Agency-provided
apartment; a clear violation that compromised the
cover of other operations officers. Ames also committed a breach of security by leaving a sensitive
secure communications system unsecured at the FR/New
York office. On July 2, 1985, Ames received the only
official security violation that was issued to him

when he left his office safe open and unlocked upon departure for the evening. Ames admits to using his home computer occasionally when in Rome between 1986 and 1989 to draft classified memoranda and cables that he would print out and take into the office the next day. In the most extreme example of his disregard for physical security regulations, of course, Ames wrapped up five to seven pounds of cable traffic in plastic bags in June 1985 and carried it out of Headquarters to deliver to the KGB.

Alcohol Abuse

39. Much has been made since his arrest of Ames's drinking habits. While it is clear that he drank too much too often and there is some basis to believe this may have clouded his judgment over time, he does not appear to have been an acute alcoholic who was constantly inebriated. Ames acknowledges the presence of a variety of symptoms of alcohol addiction. The term "alcoholic" often conjures up images of broken individuals who spend their days helplessly craving a drink, becoming intoxicated beyond any self-control, and only breaking out of their intoxication with severe withdrawal symptoms. As explained in the psychological profile prepared by the psychologist detailed to the IG, alcohol addiction is, in reality, a more subtle, insidious process. This accounts for the fact that many of Ames's colleagues and a few supervisors were able to work with Ames without noticing his substance abuse problem.

40. In regard to why they did not deal with problems associated with Ames's alcohol abuse, several Agency managers say that alcohol abuse was not uncommon in the DO during the mid- to late-1980s and that Ames's drinking did not stand out since there were employees with much more serious alcohol cases. Other managers cite a lack of support from Headquarters in dealing with problem employees abroad.

41. Medical experts believe that alcohol, because it diminishes judgment, inhibitions, and long-term thinking ability, may play some role in the decision to commit espionage. At the same time, because the number of spies is so small relative to the frac-

tion of the US population that has an alcohol abuse problem, statistical correlations cannot be made. As a result, alcohol abuse cannot be said to have a predictive connection to espionage and, in and of itself, cannot be used as an indicator of any real CI significance.

Financial Problems

42. In 1983-85, Ames became exceedingly vulnerable to potential espionage as a result of his perception that he was facing severe financial problems. According to Ames, once Rosario moved in with him in December 1983 he had begun to feel a financial pinch. Ames describes being faced with a credit squeeze that included a new car loan, a signature loan that had been "tapped to the max," mounting credit card payments, and, finally, a divorce settlement that he believed threatened to bankrupt him.

43. Ames claims to have first contemplated espionage between December 1984 and February 1985 as a way out of his mounting financial dilemma. Confronting a divorce that he knew by that time was going to be financially draining, and facing added expenses connected with his imminent marriage to someone with already established extravagant spending habits, Ames claims that his financial predicament caused him to commit espionage for financial relief.

WHY DID AMES COMMIT ESPIONAGE?

44. Ames states that the primary motivating factor for his decision to commit espionage was his desperation regarding financial indebtedness he incurred at the time of his separation from his first wife, their divorce settlement and his cohabitation with Rosario. He also says that several otherwise inhibiting "barriers" had been lowered by a) the opportunity to meet Soviet officials under Agency sanction, b) the lack of concern that he would soon be subject to a reinvestigation polygraph, c) his fading respect for the value of his Agency work as a result of lengthy discussions with Soviet officials, and d) his belief that the rules that governed others did not apply to him. Ames claims he conceived of a one-time "scam" directed against the Soviets to obtain the $50,000

he believed he needed to satisfy his outstanding debt in return for information about Agency operations he believed were actually controlled by the Soviets. He recognized subsequently that there was no turning back and acted to protect himself from the Soviet intelligence services by compromising Agency sources first in the June 1985 "big dump."

HOW WERE INDICATIONS OF SUBSTANTIAL CHANGES IN AMES'S FINANCIAL SITUATION HANDLED?

45. The financial inquiry regarding Ames began in November 1989 with the receipt of information from at least one Agency employee that Ames's financial situation had changed and he was living rather extravagantly. Upon his return from Rome, Ames purchased a home in Arlington for more than a half million dollars in cash and made plans to remodel the kitchen and landscape the yard, sparing no expense. Ames was also known to have purchased a Jaguar automobile and to have Filipino servants whom he had flown to and from the Philippines. Ames's lifestyle change was apparent to others as well and several employees state that they noticed at that time a marked improvement in Ames's physical appearance, including capped teeth and expensive Italian suits and shoes.

46. The financial inquiry faltered over resource limitations and priority conflicts, was reinvigorated in March 1992 and was not completed until mid-1993. The information obtained as a result of the Ames financial review, especially the correlation between deposits made by the Ameses and the operational meetings, was an essential element in shifting the focus of the molehunt toward Ames and paving the way, both psychologically and factually, for the further investigation that resulted in his arrest. Yet the financial review was permitted to stall for almost a year while other matters consumed the time and effort of the single CIC officer who possessed the interest and ability necessary to conduct it. Technical management expertise to oversee the investigator's activities and help guide him was lacking. Given the responsibility that was placed on the investigator and his relative inexperience in conducting and analyzing

financial information, he did a remarkable job. But there was clearly a lack of adequate resources and expertise available in CIC for this purpose.

47. If the financial inquiry had been pursued more rapidly and without interruption, significant information about Ames's finances would have been acquired earlier.

WAS THE COUNTERESPIONAGE INVESTIGATION COORDINATED PROPERLY WITH THE FBI?

48. Under Executive Order 12333, CIA is authorized to conduct counterintelligence activities abroad and to coordinate the counterintelligence activities of other agencies abroad. The Order also authorizes CIA to conduct counterintelligence activities in the United States, provided these activities are coordinated with the FBI. Under a 1988 CIA-FBI Memorandum of Understanding (MOU) the FBI must be notified immediately when there is a reasonable belief that an individual may engage in activities harmful to the national security of the United States.

49. CIA-FBI cooperation in the Ames case after the spring of 1991 generally exceeded the coordination requirements under the 1988 MOU. The FBI could have taken over the Ames case completely in 1991 but apparently concluded that it did not have sufficient cause to open an intensive CI investigation directed specifically at Ames. The FBI officers who were part of the team were provided unprecedented access to CIA information related to Ames and to other CIA cases. These FBI officers indicate that they had full access to all of the CIA information they needed and requested. Once the FBI did take over the case in 1993, CIA cooperation with the Bureau was excellent, according to FBI and CIA accounts.

WERE SUFFICIENT RESOURCES AND MANAGEMENT ATTENTION DEVOTED TO THE AMES INVESTIGATION?

50. In considering whether the resources that were applied to the molehunt were sufficient, it is necessary to evaluate the need for secrecy and compartmentation. If alerting a potential mole to the investigation was to be avoided at all costs, then concerns about the size and discretion of any group

undertaking the investigation would be paramount. Nevertheless there must be some balance between secrecy and progress. Despite the arguments for the small size of the molehunt team, many officers concede that more resources could have been brought to bear earlier on the Ames investigation.

51. Even accepting the argument that the team had to be small to maintain compartmentation and to manage a complex CI investigative process, the resource issue remains because the molehunt team members who were made available were not focused exclusively on the task, but were frequently diverted to other requirements. The limited size and diffused focus of the molehunt team does not support DO management's assertions that the 1985-86 compromised Soviet cases were "the biggest failure a spy Agency could have." Rather, the resources applied to the task force indicate lack of management attention to this most serious of intelligence failures.

52. The resources that the Agency devoted to the molehunt were inadequate from the outset, especially when considered in light of the fact that the 1985-86 compromises were the worst intelligence losses in CIA history.

HAS AGENCY USE OF POLYGRAPHS AND BACKGROUND INVESTIGATIONS BEEN SUFFICIENT TO DETECT POSSIBLE AGENCY COUNTERINTELLIGENCE PROBLEMS AT THE EARLIEST TIME?

53. The fact that Ames conceived, executed and sustained an espionage enterprise for almost nine years makes it difficult to argue that Agency screening techniques functioned adequately to detect a CI problem at the earliest possible time. The question then becomes whether the screening techniques, particularly the periodic polygraph examination, were adequate and why they did not detect Ames. The available evidence indicates that there were weaknesses in the polygraph methods that were used. However, it is difficult to conclude that the techniques themselves are inadequate since the major failing in the Ames case appears to be traceable to non-coordination and non-sharing of derogatory information concerning Ames.

54. Although this IG investigation necessarily focused on the Ames polygraph and background investigations, many employees of the Office of Security also raised more generic problems in these programs. At a minimum, these expressions of concern about the Agency's polygraph program reflect a significant morale problem.

55. In light of the dominant role that the polygraph plays in the reinvestigation process, OS management came to be interested in production. For most of the time since 1986 – when the five-year periodic reinvestigation program was begun – until the present, the reinvestigation program has been behind schedule. As a result, OS managers have stressed the successful completion of polygraph examinations. Many examiners believe that this requirement implicitly stressed quantity over quality. In addition to the pressures of production, the lack of experience in the polygraph corps has detrimentally affected the Agency's polygraph program. The 1988 IG reinspection of the polygraph program noted this loss of experience. Many current and former OS polygraphers say that the OS policy of promoting generalists has caused the loss of experience. Many individuals also cite the lack of complete information on testing subjects as a defect in the Agency's polygraph program.

56. The 1986 polygraph of Ames was deficient and the 1991 polygraph sessions were not properly coordinated by CIC after they were requested. The Office of Security (OS) conducted a background investigation (BI) prior to Ames's polygraph examination in 1991. This 1991 BI is deemed by OS personnel to be a very professional and in-depth investigation of Ames's personal and professional activities. The investigator who conducted this BI deserves great credit for the competency and thoroughness of her efforts. Unfortunately, the results of this 1991 BI were not available to the polygraph examiners at the time they tested Ames nor was financial information that had been developed by CIC. Ultimately, the miscommunication between the CIC and OS components that were involved led the individual examiners

to conduct standard reinvestigation polygraph tests that Ames passed. Both examiners say that having such detailed information available could have significantly altered their approach to testing Ames.

TO WHAT EXTENT DID AMES USE COMPUTER ACCESS AND CAPABILITIES TO ENGAGE IN ESPIONAGE ACTIVITIES?

57. Ames reports that he bought his first computer in the late winter or early spring of 1986 just prior to leaving for Rome. Ames's interest, however, was limited to computer applications rather than the technical aspects of computer science or programming. Ames admits to using his home computer occasionally when in Rome to draft classified memoranda and cables that he would print out and take into the office the next day. Ames admits to writing all his notes to the Soviets on his home computer using *WordPerfect* word processing software while in Rome. These notes, however, were passed only in paper form. Ames began preparing at home and passing computer disks to the Soviets after returning to Washington. These disks had been password-protected by the Russians. The information contained on the disks, according to Ames, consisted only of one or two-page messages from him to his handler. All other information he passed was in the form of paper copies of documents. The intent was for Ames to leave a disk at a drop site and have the same disk returned later at his pick-up site.

58. Ames says that passing disks and using passwords was entirely his idea. Although Ames admits to discussing Agency computer systems with the Soviets, he says it was obvious that his handlers had little or no expertise in basic computer skills. Ames describes his handlers as being "rather proud of their having been able to turn a machine on, crank up *WordPerfect* and get my message on it."

59. Ames states consistently that he did not use or abuse computer access as a means for enhancing his espionage capabilities. He explains that the computer systems to which he had access in CIC, SE/CE Division and Rome Station were "really no more than bona fide electric typewriters." He does say, however,

that this changed after he was given access to the CNC Local Area Network (LAN). That LAN featured the DO's message delivery system (MDS). However, the CNC terminals differed from DO LANs in that the capability to download information to floppy disks had not been disabled in the CNC LAN. The combination of having the MDS system available on terminals that had floppy disk capabilities represented a serious system vulnerability.

60. Ames clearly viewed his access to the CNC LAN as a very significant event in his ability to conduct espionage. The broadened access, combined with the compactness of disks, greatly enhanced the volume of data he could carry out of Agency facilities with significantly reduced risk. Fortunately, he was arrested before he could take full advantage of this system vulnerability.

61. No specific precautions were taken by Agency officials to minimize Ames's computer access to information within the scope of his official duties. In fact, there is one instance where Ames was granted expanded computer access despite expressions of concern by CIC and SE Division management at the time about his trustworthiness. Ames states he was surprised when he signed on and found that he had access to information about double agent cases. This allowed him to compromise a significant amount of sensitive data from the CIC to which he did not have an established need-to-know.

IS THERE ANY MERIT TO THE ALLEGATIONS IN THE "POISON FAX?"

62. In April 1994, an anonymous memorandum was faxed to the Senate Select Committee on Intelligence criticizing CIA counterintelligence policies and practices. That memorandum, which came to be known as the "poison fax," also alleged that an SE Division manager had warned Ames he was suspected of being a KGB mole and that a message from the field confirmed this. These allegations were featured in the press and raised questions in the Congress. No evidence has been found to substantiate these allegations.

HAS CIA BEEN EFFECTIVELY ORGANIZED TO DETECT PENETRATIONS SUCH AS AMES?

63. During the period of the Agency molehunt that led to Ames, the CI function and its counterespionage element was divided between the DO and OS. This division created problems that adversely affected the Agency's ability to focus on Ames. Although attempts were made to overcome these problems by written understandings and the assignment of OS officers to CIC, these attempts were not altogether successful.

64. Senior security officials have pointed out that there always has been a "fault line" in communications between the CIC, and its predecessors, and the OS. This division has created a number of problems, given the disparate cultures of the two organizations. Attempts are being made to employ CIC-OS teams to overcome these problems, but the problems are inherent to the division of CI responsibilities. The division of responsibility for CI between CIC and OS interfered with a comprehensive approach to the molehunt. When financial leads were obtained in 1989 and 1990, CIC essentially turned the matter over to OS for Ames's reinvestigation but failed to communicate all the relevant facts effectively with the OS personnel who were involved in the reinvestigation.

65. Many senior managers and other officers have strong opinions regarding whether the Agency's CI element, at least the portion that handles possible penetrations of the Agency, should report through the DDO. A number of officers believe that taking the CI function out of the DO would permit the addition of personnel who are not subject to the limitations of the DO culture and mindset. Other officers view the prospect of taking counterespionage outside the DO as impossible and potentially disastrous. Doing so, they argue, would never work because access to DO information would become more difficult. Some officers also argue that reporting directly to the DCI would be copying the KGB approach, which proved over the years to be unworkable. As a counter argument, however, former DCI Webster believes, in retrospect, that the CIC he created in 1988 should have reported

to him directly with an informational reporting role to the DDO.

WERE CIA COUNTERINTELLIGENCE PERSONNEL WHO CONDUCTED THE MOLEHUNT PROPERLY QUALIFIED BY TRAINING AND EXPERIENCE?

66. Of the four officers who were assigned to the STF in 1986, one remained when the molehunt team was established by CIC in 1991 to continue to pursue the cause of the 1985-86 compromises. That officer was chosen to head the effort primarily because she was an experienced SE Division officer, was familiar with the KGB and wanted to pursue the compromises. According to her supervisor, there were not many other employees who had the years of experience, the operational knowledge, the interest, the temperament, and the personality to persist in this effort. She was joined by another officer who had headed the Moscow Task Force inquiry charged with doing the DO damage assessment concerning the Lonetree/Bracy allegations. A third officer, who had been on rotation to CIC from the Office of Security was chosen to assist the team because of his background and CI experience, although he was not actually made a team member until June 1993. While this investigator was certainly not the only person in CIA who was capable of performing a financial analysis, he was the only one who was known to, and trusted by, the team leader. He was ideal in her view because of his previous work with her on other CI cases. In addition, two FBI officers were assigned to the effort.

67. Put most simply, the consensus view of those in CIC who were directly involved in the molehunt seems to be that good CI officers have both innate and learned characteristics that make them effective. In addition to innate CI ability, a good CI analyst needs a great deal of general and particular knowledge to make the mental connections necessary to conduct a CI investigation. General knowledge in the molehunt context refers to knowledge of the KGB, while particular knowledge refers to knowledge of the 1985-86 compromised cases. In addition, many CIC employees say that operational experience is essential to CI

work. Although this general and particular knowledge can be acquired through study, for the most part it is obtained over years of experience actually working on foreign intelligence operations and CI cases in a particular subject area.

68. In the judgment of the IG, these criteria for qualification as a CI analyst and for the process of conducting a CI investigation reflect a very narrow view of the scope and nature of CI investigations. In the Ames case, it was unduly cramped and justified an unfortunate resistance to adding more personnel to the molehunt unless they were deemed by the team leader to be qualified. Further, this view of counterespionage presents significant risks both to the Agency and successful prosecutions in the future. In the Ames investigation, the equities of any future prosecution were protected by the fact of FBI participation. Law enforcement officers bring an understanding of investigation procedure critical to building a successful prosecution. Without FBI participation, the risk of the narrow CIC view is that prosecutions may be jeopardized in future CI investigations. In addition to protecting Agency and prosecutive equities, training in law enforcement and other investigative techniques would expand the scope of information and techniques available to the Agency's CI investigators.

69. Despite these general shortcomings in CI training and methodology, the molehunters performed admirably. Their work included useful analysis that helped advance the resolution of the 1985-86 compromises significantly. On occasion, their work also went beyond the scope of what had been considered an adequate CI investigation to that point. Thus, they advanced the art form of CI investigations within CIA. In the final analysis, they contributed substantially to catching a spy.

WAS THE MOLEHUNT THAT LED TO AMES MANAGED PROPERLY, AND WHO WAS RESPONSIBLE?

70. Supervisory responsibility for the molehunt that eventually led to Ames shifted over time as managers, organizations and circumstances changed.

71. The primary responsibility for the molehunt within the Agency rested with officials in the CI Staff, later the CIC, as well as senior DO management. Management of the molehunt during the initial, analytic phase was inconsistent and sporadic. Although keen interest was expressed from time to time in determining what went wrong, the resources devoted to the molehunt were quite modest, especially considering the significance to the DO and the Agency of the rapid compromise of essentially all major Soviet sources. Those directly engaged in the molehunt also had to contend with competing assignments and were distracted from the molehunt by other possible explanations for the compromises, such as technical penetrations and the Lonetree/Bracy case, that eventually proved not to be fruitful. Senior CI managers at the time admit that they could, and probably should, have devoted more resources to the effort.

72. In the CI Staff, the early years of the molehunt were primarily analytical and episodic, rather than investigative and comprehensive. Although information gathering and file review are important, little else appears to have been done during this time. A number of CI cases concerning Agency employees were opened based on suspicious activity, but none were brought to resolution. No comprehensive list of Agency officers with the requisite access was created and analyzed during this stage in an attempt to narrow the focus of the molehunt.

73. SE Division management must also assume some responsibility, given the fact that the 1985-86 compromises involved major SE Division assets. SE Division management should have insisted upon an extensive effort and added its own resources if necessary to determine the cause of the compromises. It is not sufficient to say, as these and many other officials now do, that they did not more closely monitor or encourage the molehunt effort because they knew they were suspects themselves and did not wish to appear to be attempting to influence the matter in an undue fashion. The distinction between encouraging a responsible effort and improperly interfering in

the progress of that effort is considerable. In any event, another senior SE official who was not on the list could have been given the necessary authority and responsibility.

74. Given the importance of the compromises and the need to determine their cause, the DDOs during this phase also must bear responsibility for not paying more attention to and better managing the molehunt.

75. Beyond those in the DO and CIC who had direct responsibility for the molehunt during this phase, OS should have done a better job of developing leads that would have assisted the molehunt team in focusing its attention on Ames as early as 1986. In the mid-1980s, OS had fallen behind in its reinvestigation poly-graphs, and many officers had not been repolygraphed for periods much longer than the required five-year intervals. Ames had not been polygraphed for almost ten years when he was scheduled for a reinvestiga-tion polygraph in 1986. That polygraph raised several questions but failed to reveal any problems despite the fact he had begun spying for the Soviets a year earlier and he reports he was very apprehensive at the time about being exposed.

76. The reorganization of OS in 1986 was followed in 1988 by the creation of the CIC which included a large OS contingent operating as an integral part of CIC. While one of the purposes of CIC was to consolidate all of the Agency's CI resources in a single compo-nent, the result was an overlap of missions, juris-dictional struggles at the highest levels of OS and CIC, and a failure to share information. According to a May 1991 Office of Inspector General Report of Inspection concerning OS, these problems were caused by the failure of Agency management to define the relative responsibilities of the two components, to provide a mechanism for a smooth flow of information between them, and to establish policy for managing cases of common interest.

77. CIC and the FBI can be credited for initiating a collaborative effort to revitalize the molehunt in April 1991. However, CIC management must also bear responsibility for not allocating sufficient dedi-

cated resources to ensure that the effort was carried out thoroughly, professionally and expeditiously. The delay in the financial inquiry can be attributed largely to the lack of investigative resources allocated to the effort. The CIC investigator deserves a great deal of credit for his initiative and interest in financial analysis and it appears clear that an inquiry into Ames's finances would not have occurred to anyone else in CIC had he not been available to suggest it and carry it out. However, the failure to either dedicate the investigator fully to this inquiry before 1992, or to bring in other officers who would have been able to conduct a similar or more thorough financial analysis of Ames, represents one of the most glaring shortcomings of the molehunt. This failure alone appears to have delayed the identification of Ames by at least two years.

78. In 1993, when the FBI opened an intensive CI investigation of Ames, the Agency was fully cooperative and provided excellent support to the FBI's investigation. CIA deferred to the FBI's decisions regarding the investigation and allowed Ames continued access to classified information in order to avoid alerting him and to assist in developing evidence of his espionage. The common goal was to apprehend Ames, while safeguarding evidence for a successful prosecution. As has been stated earlier, the CIA/FBI working relationship during the FBI phase appears to have been a model of cooperation.

Notes

1. Unless otherwise indicated, the factual account is drawn from a series of books and reports: Pete Earley, *Confessions of a Spy: The Real Story of Aldrich Ames* (London: Putnam's Sons, 1997); Peter Maas, *Killer Spy: The Inside Story of the FBI's Pursuit and Capture of Aldrich Ames, America's Deadliest Spy* (London: Warner, 1995); Tim Weiner et al., *Betrayal: The Story of Aldrich Ames – An American Spy* (London: Richard Cohen Books, 1996); David Wise, *Nightmover: How Aldrich Ames Sold the CIA to the KGB for $4.6 Million* (London: HarperCollins, 1995).
2. *An Assessment of the Aldrich H. Ames Espionage Case and its Implications for US Intelligence*, Senate Select Committee on Intelligence, US Senate,

1 November 1994, p. 6, <https://www.intelligence.senate.gov/sites/default/files/publications/10390.pdf> (last accessed 10 January 2020).

3. Sandra Grimes and Jeanne Vertefeuille, *Circle of Treason: A CIA Account of Traitor Aldrich Ames and the Men He Betrayed* (Annapolis: Naval Institute Press, 2013).

4. 'Excerpts from Statement by CIA Officer Guilty in Spy Case', *The New York Times*, 29 April 1994, <https://www.nytimes.com/1994/04/29/us/excerpts-from-statement-by-cia-officer-guilty-in-spy-case.html> (last accessed 10 January 2020).

5. 'Betrayer's Tale: A Special Report: A Decade as a Turncoat: Aldrich Ames's Own Story', *The New York Times*, 28 July 1994, <https://www.nytimes.com/1994/07/28/us/betrayer-s-tale-a-special-report-a-decade-as-a-turncoat-aldrich-ames-s-own-story.html> (last accessed 10 January 2020).

6. 'Prosecutors Say Official at CIA Spied for Russia', *The New York Times*, 23 February 1994, <https://www.nytimes.com/1994/02/23/us/prosecutors-say-official-at-cia-spied-for-russia.html> (last accessed 10 January 2020).

7. Cited in Wise, *Nightmover*, p. 151.

8. Wise, *Nightmover*, p. 189.

9. Details in *Report of Investigation: The Aldrich Ames Espionage Case*, Permanent Select Committee on Intelligence, US House of Representatives, 30 November 1994.

10. Wise, *Nightmover*, p. 326.

11. David Wise, *The Spy Who Got Away: The Inside Story of Edward Lee Howard, the CIA Agent Who Betrayed His Country's Sections and Escaped to Moscow* (London: Random House, 1988).

12. See *Unclassified Abstract of the CIA Inspector General's Report on the Aldrich H. Ames Case*. This document is appended to this chapter.

13. Details in Wise, *Nightmover*.

14. See the relevant page on the CIA's website: <https://www.cia.gov/offices-of-cia/inspector-general>. For background, see A. J. Radsan, 'One Lantern in the Darkest Night – The CIA's Inspector General', *Journal of National Security Law and Policy*, 247 (2010), <https://open.mitchellhamline.edu/cgi/viewcontent.cgi?article=1201&context=facsch> (last accessed 10 January 2020).

19 'The System was Blinking Red': The Peace Dividend and the Road to 9/11

That the Cold War had ended peacefully with America's subsequent uni-polar moment did not translate into re-election for George H. W. Bush, the only president to be a former Director of Central Intelligence. The election of 1992 would sweep Arkansas Governor William J. Clinton into the Oval Office, and the difference between his relations with the CIA and those of his predecessor could not have been starker. For those working in Langley, the Potomac River separating them from the White House seemed to have broadened into a gulf. 'It wasn't that I had a bad relationship with the President. It just didn't exist,' recollected Clinton's first DCI, R. James Woolsey. 'Remember the guy who in 1994 crashed his plane onto the White House lawn? That was me trying to get an appointment to see President Clinton.'[1] Perhaps it stood to reason. The Soviet Bear menaced its Cold War foe no longer, and Clinton had run on a domestic agenda. Many wondered, sometimes aloud, what the CIA was for. As late as 1997, newly appointed DCI George J. Tenet appeared on a panel which sought to answer the question, 'Does America Need the CIA?'[2]

Perhaps inevitably, the demise of the Soviet Union led to a 'peace dividend'; the great enemy was no more. Like the rest of the national security apparatus, CIA's budget was shrunk and its staff recruiting efforts dwindled to approximate those of a rural fire department, at times not even keeping pace with retirements. As Tenet recalled: 'We lost nearly one in four of our positions. This loss of manpower was devastating, particularly in our two most manpower intensive activities: all-source analysis and human source collection. By the mid-1990s, recruitment of new CIA analysts and case officers had come to a virtual halt.'[3]

If the White House seemed distant, Capitol Hill was outright hostile. In his proposed legislation, the 'End of the Cold War Act of 1991',[4] Senator Daniel Patrick Moynihan (D-NY) suggested CIA should be shuttered, the superfluous vestige of a bygone era. Given the apparent hostility in the legislative chamber to CIA as a relevant tool in the post-Cold War world, CIA attempted to reground itself firmly under the executive branch in its mission statement for 1991: 'Secret Intelligence aims to further our knowledge and foreknowledge of the world around us – the prelude to *Presidential* decision and action' (emphasis added).[5] It was a troubling time for an agency that had for decades been at the centre of power, needed and – sometimes – heeded by the White House and the Hill. Morale plummeted.

Although some people in Washington with the purse strings, like Moynihan, felt that CIA had outlived its usefulness, CIA itself saw no reason to have such a sanguine view of international developments. As James Woolsey described the precarious post-Cold War environment to Congress,

> It's as if we were fighting a dragon for some 45 years and slew the dragon and then found ourselves in a jungle full of a number of poisonous snakes. And in many ways, the snakes are a lot harder to keep track of than the dragon ever was. The snakes are rogue states and terrorists and the like. We have now six or eight major issues we have to watch instead of just the workings of the Soviet Union and its various manifestations in the world. And that has meant that on these crucial issues for US intelligence, rogue states, weapons of mass destruction, terrorism, narcotics smuggling, the community has found itself very strapped.[6]

Many did not heed this prescient warning, and Woolsey was not the only intelligence chief trying to do more with less. The peace divided would not just shrink CIA, but would impact its closest liaison partner as well. The British SIS suffered an overall staff strength reduction of 25 per cent, and shuttered some stations in the Far East and Africa.[7] Former Chief ('C') of SIS, Sir Richard Dearlove, captured the mood in London: 'I cannot really exaggerate the extent to which our preoccupations of national security, hitherto so very firmly anchored, were cut adrift when the Cold War ended.'[8] The cuts in the British intelligence community would have transatlantic repercussions a decade hence.

The immediate post-Cold War era did nothing to halt international drug traffickers, stem the breeding grounds of Islamist terror, bring peace to the Korean peninsula, dampen Beijing's claims over Taiwan or contain Iraq, Iran or their terrorist proxies. Additionally, the end of the Cold War exacerbated problems such as the emergence of Russian organised crime and concomitant weakening of their nuclear, biological and chemical weapons safeguards. Indeed, from Langley's vantage point this was no time to rest on Cold War laurels. The optimistic sentiments voiced from inside American and British think tanks and universities about the 'end of history'[9] were, in the eyes of many, misplaced. Many saw far more ominous omens portending a clash of civilisations.[10]

Notwithstanding the cuts in resources and personnel, the CIA sought to adapt to the new environment. It identified an increasing number of transnational and issue-specific threats in addition to the customary state-based threats, prompting a reorganisation to create cross-functional and cross-regional centres to address them. As part of this new approach, counterterrorism emerged as a core focus for CIA. From an organisational standpoint, at least, CIA was prepared to meet the challenge, having created the DCI's Counterterrorist Center (CTC) in 1986, during the twilight of the Cold War, with Duane 'Dewey' Clarridge as its first chief. Although a senior officer in the Directorate of Operations, Clarridge presided over a fiefdom that included clandestine service officers, analysts and other specialists working together side by side. This was a far cry from the days when a wall in CIA's cafeteria separated the analysts from those who were undercover. CTC was not only notable because of the close coordination between operations and analysis, but also because its resources were not slashed as severely as other divisions, and even enjoyed a modest fillip on occasion.

Although CTC tried to keep tabs on largely Iranian-backed Shia terror groups, such as Hizballah, through the 1980s, the 1990s belonged to Sunni groups which not only became the agency's quarry but also targeted it directly. During morning rush hour, on 25 January 1993, Pakistani national Amal Kasi killed two CIA officers and wounded three more with an assault rifle as they waited at a red traffic light to turn left into the entrance of what, six years hence, would be christened the George Bush Center for Intelligence.[11] When news of the killings arrived in Pakistan, some hailed him as a hero.[12] A joint CIA–FBI team finally caught up with him in 1997 in Pakistan from whence he was extradited to the United States, tried and executed in 2002 for the murder of Dr Lansing Bennett, a CIA medical officer, and Frank Darling, a CIA communications officer. Bennett and Darling would become the 69th and 70th stars on CIA's memorial wall.[13] Upon repatriation, Kasi's remains were heralded as those of a martyr in some parts of Pakistan, presaging CIA's fraught relationship with Pakistan in the coming War on Terror.[14]

The murders of Bennett and Darling would not be the only bloodshed caused by terrorism on US soil in 1993. A month and a day later, the embryonic elements of what would soon become al-Qa'ida attempted to bring down the twin towers of the World Trade Center in New York by detonating a truck bomb in the basement parking garage. They intended to knock the north tower into the south tower, destroying both. Miraculously, the attack failed to inflict the mass casualties it could have; the bomb killed six people. But it brought Islamist terror into the consciousness of American citizens and lawmakers alike. The world had not become a truly safe place after all. The perpetrator, Ramzi Yousef, nephew of 9/11 plotter Khalid

Shaykh Muhammad (KSM), the 'terrorist entrepreneur' who would go on to mastermind the 9/11 attacks, was arrested in 1995 in Pakistan, where Amal Kasi had also fled. He was convicted and given a life sentence, but the 1993 plot was not his only interest. Along with his uncle, KSM, Yousef also planned the 1995 Bojinka plot, which sought to assassinate Pope John Paul II and blow up eleven jumbo jets over the Pacific Ocean as they transited from Asia to the United States. The Bojinka plot was foiled,[15] but al-Qa'ida's fascination with aircraft as weapons of terror endured.[16] The 1993 domestic attack was a harbinger of things to come, but not recognised as such at time, and other connections would be developed only years later. For instance, October of 1993 also saw the Battle of Mogadishu, Somalia, which pitted US Army Rangers and special operations forces against loosely organised Somali fighters with tenuous connections to nascent al-Qa'ida leadership figures.[17] The tide was beginning to swell.

The year after the Bojinka plot, CIA created a unit specifically tasked to monitor al-Qa'ida: the Bin Ladin Station, codenamed Alec. Career analyst Michael Scheuer, who was a veritable walking encyclopaedia on bin Ladin and his group, led it. CIA had broken the mould in creating a 'field station' inside its own headquarters to deal with a single issue, and would further pioneer all-source intelligence fusion against their target. Not only did Alec Station combine various intelligence disciplines, it also combined liaison officers (or 'detailees') from around the intelligence community under its umbrella. Despite pioneering methodologies and being lavished with resources during lean budget years, Alec Station's reputation for an insular staff culture and external alarmism about the al-Qa'ida threat was growing, at times derisively described by those outside the ring of trust as 'the Manson family',[18] or more derisively as 'the coven' due to the group's high percentage of senior female analysts, who developed a reputation for being brusque with those outside their close-knit cadre.[19]

Despite al-Qa'ida's continued interest in aeroplanes as weapons of terror, the air was not al-Qa'ida's only vector of attack; plots were afoot on land and sea as well. In June of 1998, CIA collected intelligence that foiled a bomb plot against the US Embassy in Tirana, Albania, but the other undetected plotting continued throughout the summer with deadly results.[20] On 7 August 1998, al-Qa'ida operatives executed a near simultaneous truck bomb attack on the US Embassies in Dar es Salaam, Tanzania, and Nairobi, Kenya, leaving 225 people dead. According to press accounts, the victims were mostly locals but forty-four were Americans, including two CIA officers, Tom Shah and Molly Hardy.[21] DCI Tenet had had enough, declaring 'war' on al-Qa'ida by December.[22]

The man to lead Tenet's War on Terror was his newly installed Chief of CTC, an experienced operations officer named J. Cofer Black, who set about collecting actionable intelligence on al-Qa'ida as well as developing disruption operations. Black had cut his teeth in CIA's Africa Division and was no stranger to the world of international terrorism, having been Chief of Station in Khartoum, Sudan when Ilich Ramírez Sánchez (better known as Carlos the Jackal) was arrested in 1994. Given this proven track record against terrorism, Tenet knew Black was the right man for the job. Notably, al-Qa'ida's leadership agreed with Tenet's assessment of Black's counterterrorism effectiveness, and mounted an assassination attempt on Black in Khartoum the following year.[23] As it happened, although Black's team foiled the attempt, both sides were hatching assassination plots.

After the 1998 East Africa bombings, President Clinton signed a presidential finding authorising CIA to kill bin Ladin.[24] The CIA had developed actionable intelligence that bin Ladin would be at a terrorist training camp near Khost, Afghanistan, on 20 August 1998, and Clinton authorised the US military to rain down Tomahawk cruise missiles targeting bin Ladin and several lieutenants in Operation Infinite Reach – which also destroyed a pharmaceutical plant in Sudan that was accused, with much subsequent controversy, of making chemical weapons for al-Qa'ida.[25] It is not clear if bin Ladin departed the camp earlier than expected or if he was never there at all, but he escaped this attempt on his life. Ever attentive to the information warfare dimension, bin Ladin's supporters announced he had survived, thumbing their nose at the technology-driven military might of the US. As one journalist put it, the event elevated bin Ladin as a 'symbolic figure of resistance'.[26] Such frustrations over being a proverbial day late and a dollar short in the hunt for bin Ladin were a primary driver for CIA to seek real-time intelligence and surveillance feeds through a partnership with the US Air Force to fly stealthy reconnaissance drones over al-Qa'ida strongholds.[27] These remotely piloted operations would mature years later, over Afghanistan, Iraq, Somalia and others, but for the late 1990s the gap between real-time intelligence and action proved difficult to bridge.

The game of cat and mouse continued with increasing tempo and urgency in Langley as the millennium approached. The bevy of al-Qa'ida plots to ring in the year 2000 were disrupted – most famously, the plot to bomb Los Angeles International Airport (LAX)[28] – but, on 12 October 2000, al-Qa'ida proved its naval prowess with a waterborne suicide attack on the destroyer USS Cole in the port of Aden, Yemen, killing seventeen American sailors. Most analysts working on counterterrorism issues instinctively knew the attack had the hallmarks of al-Qa'ida, but as early reports of the incident came into the US intelligence and law enforcement community, some still felt attacking a warship was beyond their reach. Naval analysts scoured Cold War-era military armament reference books about naval weapons, trying to discern what sort of mine might breach a destroyer at

399

its midpoint along the waterline.[29] Counterterrorism analysts, on the other hand, pointed out that al-Qa'ida's Yemen branch had actually plotted to attack the USS *The Sullivans* in the same manner in January 2000, as part of the millennium plots; but on that occasion they had overloaded the small attack craft with explosives, and it had sunk.[30] Al-Qa'ida remained determined to attack a warship, and modified its unsuccessful attack on *The Sullivans* to successfully breach the *Cole*. It was increasingly clear that al-Qa'ida would return to its highest-priority targets, having adjusted its methods with care. Given al-Qa'ida's effectiveness on land and in the water, it was no surprise that they returned to a spectacular air attack for their finale. They were ambitious, well resourced, and driven.

That al-Qa'ida was building towards a finale seemed clear in 2001; the drumbeat of disconcerting intelligence climbed from *forte* to *fortissimo*. According to former DCI George Tenet, as Washington's temperature rose in July, so did the heat of the warnings. CIA warned the Bush White House of 'multiple' and 'simultaneous' attacks that would be 'spectacular' in nature. Most alarming, they would be 'coming here'.[31] Past experience and institutional focus had initially conditioned CIA analysts to believe that attacks occurred abroad, but several indicators suggested that this pattern would be broken. By August, the warnings were as close as the humidity. One such warning looms above the rest – the first explicit warning from CIA that the US homeland was in jeopardy.

On 6 August 2001, the CIA document known as the President's Daily Brief (PDB) carried an article entitled 'Bin Ladin Determined to Strike in US', reproduced as this chapter's reference document. As is clear from the document, bin Ladin had a longstanding wish to 'bring the fighting to America'. The document also notes bin Ladin's abiding interest in aeroplanes, but for hijacking to secure concessions like the release of fellow terrorists, not as giant missiles. CIA officials have occasionally pointed to this document, declassified on 10 April 2004, to show that they had discharged their duty to warn policymakers of imminent danger; in this case, strategic warning. However, a careful reading of the document from the perspective of the policymaker would not generate much satisfaction, due to sparse tactical intelligence. From an executive optic, it does not give any indications of actionable intelligence such as targets selected for attack, a mode of attack, a time frame, or any hint as to who specifically might be involved in carrying it out. This was, of course, related to the fact that al-Qa'ida was a hard target to penetrate. But it was not impossible.

The PDB is the most important single document produced by CIA, and analysts writing PDB articles relied upon the best information generated by the disparate collection elements across the US intelligence community. The PDB product is all-source intelligence fusion, so it is in this method that it can best be analysed to discern what kinds of intelligence the PDB article authors had to work with to craft their piece. Given that CIA analysts would use their strongest evidence up front, it is revealing that CIA opted to lead with open-source intelligence (osint) that was already at least three years old. The PDB also incorporates community input, in this case FBI information, which is a customarily a strength of the PDB; but the misleading – though reassuring – figure of seventy full field investigations was subsequently characterised by the 9/11 Commission Report as a 'generous calculation', including irrelevant cases and double-counting others.[32] Indeed, the FBI's shortcomings in international counterterrorism would be highlighted in vivid colour in several post-9/11 reports and investigations.

However, a careful reading of the document also reveals the CIA's own inadequate intelligence collection posture with respect to the imminent attack. For an organisation that exists to provide cutting-edge intelligence collected by its clandestine service, no such clandestinely acquired human intelligence is referenced until nearly the end of the document, and that humint was also three years old. Further, although it was mostly unredacted, the three redactions that remained in the text all start with 'a' or 'an' and are immediately followed by the word 'service', suggesting that the sources of these pieces of information are liaison services. For a spy organisation that prizes unilateral clandestine collection above other collection methods, forcing analysts to rely on intelligence actually collected by foreign intelligence agencies or freely available in the media would not inspire confidence in the CIA's ability to generate critical intelligence. Indeed, the CIA's own Inspector General concluded that 'CIA's reliance on foreign services to develop human sources meant that CIA had insufficient focus on unilateral operations.'[33] Many would point to the relentless cutting of the agency's staff and budget in the 1990s as a root cause of this fundamental weakness, and it explains why CIA went on a hiring binge after 9/11.

Nevertheless, looking beyond the 6 August PDB, CIA was correct about the urgent strategic nature of the threat as provided in the course of briefings to various sub-cabinet level committees over 2001. In fact, CIA provided more than forty PDB articles on bin Ladin and al-Qa'ida between 20 January 2001 (the inauguration of George W. Bush) and 10 September 2001.[34] Other CIA analytical products, such as its Senior Executive Intelligence Brief (SEIB), over the spring and summer included headlines such as 'Bin Ladin Planning Multiple Operations', 'Bin Ladin Public Profile May Presage Attack', 'Bin Ladin Network's Plans Advancing', 'Bin Ladin Attacks May Be Imminent', 'Bin Ladin and Associates Making Near-Term Threats' and 'Bin Ladin Threats Are Real'.[35] Although CIA did not provide the tactical warning that would have been welcomed by busy national security staffers, it was also true that it faced an uphill political battle for policymaker attention in the young Bush administration, which had campaigned on a conception of national security as defense from hostile regimes with advanced ballistic missiles that could strike American cities.[36]

Over the summer of 2001, the entire US intelligence community was offering briefings and warning memos, and trying to coordinate disruption operations for any al-Qa'ida plots. The State Department and the Department of Defense increased their security posture at overseas locations; some military exercises were cancelled; troops were moved; Tenet asked CIA station chiefs to brief ambassadors on the threat; some embassies were closed and others put on alert. CIA and FBI were, in their parlance, 'shaking trees' and 'rattling cages' to pry loose any shred of information that could open up further investigative avenues. As DCI Tenet said, 'the system was blinking red'. But the window of warning had closed.

Bin Ladin Determined To Strike in US

Clandestine, foreign government, and media reports indicate Bin Ladin since 1997 has wanted to conduct terrorist attacks in the US. Bin Ladin implied in US television interviews in 1997 and 1998 that his followers would follow the example of World Trade Center bomber Ramzi Yousef and "bring the fighting to America."

> After US missile strikes on his base in Afghanistan in 1998, Bin Ladin told followers he wanted to retaliate in Washington, according to a ███████ service.

> An Egyptian Islamic Jihad (EIJ) operative told an ███████ service at the same time that Bin Ladin was planning to exploit the operative's access to the US to mount a terrorist strike.

The millennium plotting in Canada in 1999 may have been part of Bin Ladin's first serious attempt to implement a terrorist strike in the US. Convicted plotter Ahmed Ressam has told the FBI that he conceived the idea to attack Los Angeles International

Airport himself, but that Bin Ladin lieutenant Abu Zubaydah encouraged him and helped facilitate the operation. Ressam also said that in 1998 Abu Zubaydah was planning his own US attack.

Ressam says Bin Ladin was aware of the Los Angeles operation.

Although Bin Ladin has not succeeded, his attacks against the US Embassies in Kenya and Tanzania in 1998 demonstrate that he prepares operations years in advance and is not deterred by setbacks. Bin Ladin associates surveilled our Embassies in Nairobi and Dar es Salaam as early as 1993, and some members of the Nairobi cell planning the bombings were arrested and deported in 1997.

Al-Qa'ida members – including some who are US citizens – have resided in or travelled to the US for years, and the group apparently maintains a support structure that could aid attacks. Two al-Qa'ida members found guilty in the conspiracy to bomb our Embassies in East Africa were US citizens, and a senior EIJ member lived in California in the mid-1990s.

A clandestine source said in 1998 that a Bin Ladin cell in New York was recruiting Muslim–American youth for attacks.

We have not been able to corroborate some of the more sensational threat reporting, such as that from a ▓▓▓▓▓▓▓ *service in 1998 saying that Bin Ladin wanted to hijack a US aircraft to gain the release of "Blind Shaykh" 'Umar' Abd al-Rahman and other US-held extremists.*

continued

- Nevertheless, FBI information since that time indicates patterns of suspicious activity in this country consistent with preparations for hijackings or other types of attacks, including recent surveillance of federal buildings in New York.

The FBI is conducting approximately 70 full field investigations throughout the US that it considers Bin Ladin-related. CIA and the FBI are investigating a call to our Embassy in the UAE in May saying that a group of Bin Ladin supporters was in the US planning attacks with explosives.

Notes

1. As quoted in Michael Warner, *The Rise and Fall of Intelligence: An International Security History* (Washington, DC: Georgetown University Press, 2014), p. 260.
2. Steve Coll, *Ghost Wars: The Secret History of the CIA, Afghanistan, and Bin Laden, from the Soviet Invasion to September 10, 2001* (New York: Penguin, 2004), p. 359.
3. As quoted by Bill Powell, 'How George Tenet Brought the CIA Back from the Dead', *Fortune International (Europe)*, 148.8, 13 October 2003, p. 84.
4. 'Moynihan Bill Would Abolish CIA, Shift Functions to State', *The Washington Post*, 23 January 1991, <https://www.washingtonpost.com/archive/politics/1991/01/23/moynihan-bill-would-abolish-cia-shift-functions-to-state/> (last accessed 10 January 2020).
5. *Central Intelligence Agency Factbook on Intelligence* (Washington, DC: Office of Public Affairs, 1991).
6. 'Former CIA Director Woolsey Delivers Remarks aAt Foreign Press Center', 7 March 2000, *Cryptome*, <https://cryptome.org/echelon-cia.htm> (last accessed 10 January 2020).
7. Gordon Corera, *The Art of Betrayal: The Secret History of MI6* (New York: Pegasus Books, 2012), p. 316.
8. Richard Dearlove, 'Our Changing Perceptions of National Security', transcript of lecture to Gresham College, 25 November 2009, <https://www.gresham.ac.uk/lectures-and-events/our-changing-perceptions-of-national-security> (last accessed 10 January 2020).
9. Francis Fukuyama, *The End of History and the Last Man* (New York: Free Press, 1992).
10. Samuel Huntington, 'The Clash of Civilizations', *Foreign Affairs*, 72.3 (1993).
11. A. H. Cordesman, *Terrorism, Asymmetric Warfare, and Weapons of Mass Destruction: Defending the US Homeland* (Westport, CT: Greenwood Publishing Group, 2002), p. 84.
12. Patricia Davis and Maria Glod, 'CIA Shooter Kasi, Harbinger of Terror, Set to Die Tonight', *The Washington Post*, 14 November 2002, <https://www.washingtonpost.com/archive/politics/2002/11/14/cia-shooter-kasi-harbinger-of-terror-set-to-die-tonight/f5010a86-a29d-4481-a339-6b51eddf3ee4/> (last accessed 10 January 2020).

13. Ted Gup, *The Book of Honor* (New York: Doubleday, 2000), p. 373.
14. 'Thousands at Stadium Funeral of Pakistani Martyr', *The Telegraph*, 19 November 2002.
15. Erik J. Dahl, 'The Plots That Failed: Intelligence Lessons Learned from Unsuccessful Terrorist Attacks Against the United States', *Studies in Conflict & Terrorism*, 34.8 (2011), pp. 621–48.
16. Coll, *Ghost Wars*, p. 420.
17. Peter Bergen, *Holy War Inc.: Inside the Secret World of Osama bin Laden* (New York: Simon and Schuster, 2002), p. 22.
18. Coll, *Ghost Wars*, p. 454.
19. Author recollection.
20. Testimony of Cofer Black to the Congressional Joint Investigation Committee, 26 September 2002, <https://fas.org/irp/congress/2002_hr/092602black.html> (last accessed 10 January 2020).
21. Matt Apuzzo and Adam Goldman, 'Raid on bin Laden Compound Avenged CIA Deaths in 1998', *The Salt Lake Tribune*, 19 May 2011.
22. Testimony of George J. Tenet to the Congressional Joint Investigation Committee, 17 October 2002, <https://www.intelligence.senate.gov/hearings/joint-inquiry-intelligence-community-activities-and-after-terrorist-attacks-september-11-0#> (last accessed 10 January 2020).
23. Testimony of Cofer Black to the Congressional Joint Investigation Committee, 26 September 2002, <https://fas.org/irp/congress/2002_hr/092602black.html> (last accessed 10 January 2020).
24. Jane Mayer, 'The Search for Osama', *The New Yorker*, 4 August 2003, p. 26.
25. Eric Croddy, 'Dealing with Al Shifa: Intelligence and Counterproliferation', *International Journal of Intelligence & Counterintelligence*, 15.1 (January 2002), pp. 52–60.
26. Lawrence Wright, *The Looming Tower: al-Qaeda and the Road to 9/11* (New York: Alfred A. Knopf, 2006), p. 285.
27. Chris Woods, 'The Story of America's Very First Drone Strike', *The Atlantic*, 30 May 2015, <https://www.theatlantic.com/international/archive/2015/05/america-first-drone-strike-afghanistan/394463/> (last accessed 10 January 2020).
28. FBI, 'Millennium Plot/Ahmed Ressam', <https://www.fbi.gov/history/famous-cases/millennium-plot-ahmed-ressam> (last accessed 10 January 2020).
29. Author recollection.
30. FBI, 'Terrorism 2000/2001', Publication #0308, p. 8, <https://www.fbi.gov/file-repository/stats-services-publications-terror-terror00_01.pdf/view> (last accessed 10 January 2020).
31. George J. Tenet, *At the Center of the Storm: My Years at the CIA* (New York: Harper Collins, 2007), pp. 133–58; and *Final Report of the National Commission on Terrorist Attacks upon the United States* (New York: W. W. Norton and Company, 2004), p. 259. Hereafter, '9/11 Commission Report'.
32. 9/11 Commission Report, p. 535.

33. Office of [CIA] Inspector General (OIG) Report on CIA Accountability with Respect to the 9/11 Attacks, June 2005 (approved for release 19 March 2015), p. 324.
34. 9/11 Commission Report, p. 254.
35. 9/11 Commission Report, pp. 255, 534.
36. Coll, *Ghost Wars*, p. 541.

20 Reckoning and Redemption: The 9/11 Commission, the Director of National Intelligence and the CIA at War

On the morning of 11 September 2001, nineteen al-Qa'ida terrorists hijacked four commercial airliners. Two slammed into the north and south towers of lower Manhattan's World Trade Center complex, causing the twin towers to crumble; one plane smashed into the Pentagon in Arlington, Virginia; and one crashed in a field in Shanksville, Pennsylvania, after passengers heroically fought back against the hijackers. Nearly 3,000 people, from many countries, were killed that morning after eighteen Saudi Arabian citizens and one Lebanese, having identified security weaknesses in America's civil aviation sector, caused ten billion dollars' worth of property damage and changed the course of history.[1] The reverberations of the attacks and the international response to them are still felt today.

CIA headquarters itself was evacuated due to the fear that it might have been the target of one of the hijacked airliners. For those who worked counterterrorism accounts in the American intelligence community there was no need to wait for claims of responsibility; several of them stayed at their desks in Langley to keep information flowing despite the general evacuation order. The attack had all the hallmarks of al-Qa'ida – a spectacular simultaneous mass casualty event on a symbolic target, echoing both the 1993 World Trade Center attack and also 1998 twin East Africa embassy bombings on a much larger scale.

As CIA's analytical cadre worked overtime to unravel details of the plot, its paramilitary Special Activities Division (SAD) began recontacting sources from the 1980s, when they had fought together against the Soviet invasion of Afghanistan. A few weeks after 9/11, CIA's paramilitary 'Jawbreaker' team was on the ground and ready to aid the primary resistance to the Taliban regime in Afghanistan, a loosely coordinated coalition generally known as the Northern Alliance. CIA set to work with US military Special Forces troops to dismantle al-Qa'ida's support structure and training camps. This was dangerous work; very few Americans were on the ground in Afghanistan during the early phase of the operation, and some of those that were had been literally pulled out of the retirement process.[2]

In late November, CIA suffered its first post-9/11 casualty when paramilitary officer Johnny 'Mike' Spann was killed during a prisoner uprising at the Qala-i-Jangi prison near Mazar-i-Sharif, Afghanistan. Spann, a former Marine captain, was interrogating prisoners and attempting to discover bin Ladin's whereabouts.[3] In a rare public display for a fallen undercover operative, DCI George Tenet followed the funeral procession with Spann's widow and children at Arlington National Cemetery. The 79th star on CIA's memorial wall represents Mike Spann; but Spann would not be the last CIA officer to die in Afghanistan.[4] Seven CIA officers perished as victims of a double-agent suicide bomber on 30 December 2009 at Camp Chapman in Khost, Afghanistan, CIA's deadliest day since the 1983 Beirut Embassy bombing which claimed several agency officers' lives.

The scale of the task in Afghanistan meant that the CIA's relatively small cadre of paramilitary operations officers were joined by traditional case officers in bases dotted around Afghanistan and Pakistan. The pressure on officer numbers was also compounded by the evolution of political priorities. As this chapter will explore, the Bush administration considered there to be a link between al-Qa'ida and Iraq, meaning that Afghanistan would have to compete with Iraq for CIA resources and attention. It was the rare case officer who was not directed for an assignment in some country related to the war on terrorism. But, owing to the pull from Iraq, the agency team hunting bin Ladin 'lost at least half of its original strength', according to former CTC official Vincent Cannistraro, who pointed out in 2003 that 'Arabic speakers are in short supply. You still have some intelligence-collection assets in Afghanistan, but mostly it's just small teams looking for signals. That's because of Iraq.'[5]

While CIA was going on the offense in Afghanistan it was fighting a rear-guard action in Washington concerning culpability for the greatest strategic surprise to face the US since Pearl Harbor.[6] Of all US agencies, CIA bore the brunt of the blame in the finger-pointing that ensued. This was inevitable given CIA's elevated position in the USIC, but also because CIA claimed the job for itself, routinely characterising itself as 'the nation's first line of defense' and the agency that could get the hardest tasks done. Its claim to the public was: 'We accomplish what others cannot accomplish and go where others cannot go.'[7] However, in the view of influential senators, CIA failed to accomplish its mission as the nation's first line of defense precisely because it was going to the same places it always went, and was therefore not postured to collect the counterterrorism intelligence that would have yielded insight into the 9/11 plot. In the estimation of SSCI Vice Chairman Richard Shelby, CIA had been 'too reluctant to develop nontraditional Humint platforms, and has stuck too much and for too long with the comparatively easy work of operating under diplomatic cover from US embassies. This approach is patently unsuited to Humint collection against nontraditional threats such as terrorism or proliferation targets.'[8]

If Shelby's criticism was blunt, Richard Clarke, the National Security Council Coordinator for Counterterrorism in the Clinton administration, was even more strident, stating that 'the capability of the CIA's Directorate of Operations was far less than advertised. The Directorate of Operations would like people to think it's a great James Bond operation, but for years it essentially assigned officers undercover as diplomats to attend cocktail parties.'[9] Unsurprisingly, Clarke's criticism of CIA's collection platforms being misaligned with the requirement was unwelcome at CIA, where a senior officer characterised Clarke's position as 'bullshit'.[10] The CIA's Inspector General report, this chapter's reference document, found that CTC 'had made a number of creative efforts to unilaterally penetrate al-Qa'ida especially after the East Africa bombings in 1998', but these did not generate sufficient intelligence; and, echoing Shelby's diagnosis, that the Directorate of Operations 'made little use of nonofficial cover (NOC) officers or nontraditional platforms to address the al-Qa'ida target . . .'.[11]

A senior CIA official countered that the problem was not one of collection posture, but one of attitude. He said the CIA had wanted to be more aggressive during Clinton's second term, but was not given the legal authorities to execute. Thus, from Langley, the matter was not one of operational capability, but of political will: 'Risk-taking depends on political will allowing you to take the risk. It wasn't until after September 11th that people wanted the gloves to come off.'[12] There was not only the matter of risk from a staff safety perspective, but also the matter of institutional risk – that of CIA being seen overlooking human rights abuses, in a pure 'ends justify the means' moral calculus. In 1995, after an incident in Guatemala, DCI John Deutch decreed that the CIA would not recruit agents with human rights violations without senior approval. This led to a chilling effect on agent recruitment, thanks to a widespread perception among case officers that well-intentioned human rights concerns limited the sorts of assets that CIA managers would permit line officers to recruit. Although there was a path to such recruitments, case officers felt the legal challenges and extra paperwork were not worth the opportunity cost in terms of their time. One case officer captured the frustrations of his colleagues: 'The message was clear. Do not take risks. Do not deal with unsavory characters. Do not put yourself through the hassle of all that paperwork. . . . How do you expect us to penetrate terrorist organizations, narcotics trafficking organizations, and organized crime if we can only recruit choirboys?'[13] The ghosts of case officers hung out to dry over human rights concerns still stalked the hallways of CIA, and likely impacted CIA's stable of counterterrorism assets before 9/11.

409

Operational managers were not the only ones to bristle at charges of intelligence failure. Paul Pillar, a senior analytical manager in CTC, argued: 'September 11 revealed nothing new about the intentions of general capabilities of al-Qa'ida. The size and scope of the group's presence in Afghanistan, its relationship with the Taliban, its global reach, and most of all its intention to do the United States deadly harm were the subjects of repeated – and accurate – production by the intelligence community.'[14] As Cofer Black testified, 'We provided strategic warning. Despite our intense efforts, we were unable to provide tactical warning on 9/11.'[15] The question of what level of warning a government should *reasonably expect* from its intelligence services remains a point of debate. During the Clinton administration, CIA forwarded too many highly unlikely threat reports, and some argued it did so to insulate itself from inevitable claims of failure to warn. This was scaled back under the Bush administration, which perhaps would have benefited from a more robust threat matrix as a corrective to their focus on conventional security threats. In either case, omnipotence was neither then, nor is it now, an option for the CIA.

Although Pillar in particular rejected much of the blame heaped on CIA after 9/11, a glance at the transatlantic dimension reveals that there were also failures on Britain's side of the Atlantic. One prominent British think-tank paper observed: 'By the mid-1990s the UK's intelligence agencies were well aware that London was increasingly being used as a base by individuals involved in promoting, funding and planning terrorism in the Middle East and elsewhere.'[16] Despite an awareness of these developments, 'these individuals were not viewed as a threat to the UK's national security, and so they were left to continue their activities with relative impunity, a policy which caused much anger amongst foreign governments concerned.' Indeed, one of the most fraught aspects of the special relationship of the 1990s was the American perception that British officials were permitting their country to be infiltrated by Islamic extremists who were plotting against US interests, and one could hardly discuss British counterterrorism in Langley without a derisive dig at the capitol as 'Londonistan'.[17]

The report continued: 'As a result of giving lower priority to international terrorism [presumably compared to Irish Republican terrorism], the British authorities did not fully appreciate the threat from al-Qa'ida' – although the much tougher Terrorism Act 2000[18] was viewed in Langley as an important piece of legislation to help its closest liaison partner address the problem. The Terrorism Act enabled the British intelligence and security services to redress the deficiencies over the preceding decade, but the rot had penetrated deeply in Britain; new laws alone could not stem the tide, and neither did they help to uncover any clues about 9/11. British academics concluded: 'The failure to gain any warning from existing information of the 9/11 attacks on the United States was an intelligence failure of the entire Western alliance, not only of the US intelligence community.'[19] However, it should be noted that in the estimation of MI5's official historian, Christopher Andrew, despite earlier lapses, the 9/11 attacks 'immediately gave a new intensity to the intelligence Special Relationship'. Thus, on 12 September 2001, one aircraft was permitted to enter US airspace. On its flight manifest were the leaders of the British intelligence community and the promise of closer cooperation for the challenges ahead.[20] George Tenet characterised the visit as 'an affirmation of the special relationship' and recalled that it was 'as touching an event as I experienced during my seven years as DCI'.[21] Tenet would receive no such succour or support from the 9/11 Commission.

If Chatham House found fault with the entire Western alliance, the 9/11 Commission found fault with the structure and organisation of America's sprawling intelligence community. Its report suggested, amongst other far-reaching recommendations, that the position of the DCI be replaced by a Director of National Intelligence (DNI) to oversee and coordinate the varied, extensive and expensive intelligence community. This was not the first time that a question mark had been raised over the DCI's twin roles as Director of the CIA and titular but nominal chief of the intelligence community. As before, the intent was to smooth over rivalries, eliminate duplication of effort and establish clear chains of command. This time, the political will was irresistible. Many at CIA felt it was being singled out for punishment for the 9/11 attacks; others on the periphery saw it as a new mode of accountability, and a way to increase efficiency in a sprawling and labyrinthine series of bureaucracies. Most agreed that some aspects of the DCI's community management authority could be strengthened, particularly as concerned budgetary controls, but the radical change proposed would be the most sweeping change in CIA's history. Since its creation in 1947, CIA was *primus inter pares* in the intelligence community. It housed the office and staff of the DCI, and enjoyed having no bureaucratic layer between it and the White House (unlike the Department of Defense combat support agencies such as NSA, DIA, NGA and others). In Washington, access to the Oval Office is a key element of power and the DCI usually enjoyed daily access to the president to deliver the President's Daily Brief, which was overwhelmingly authored by CIA analysts. The new arrangements would, in the opinion of many, degrade the agency's standing.

Although the 9/11 Commission's recommendations were modified somewhat over the course of subsequent political wrangling, CIA's position as first among equals ended on 17 December 2004 when President George W. Bush signed the Intelligence Reform and Terrorism Prevention Act, which abolished the positions of Director of Central Intelligence and Deputy

Director of Central Intelligence and created the position of Director, Central Intelligence Agency (D/CIA). This development gave Porter J. Goss the dubious distinction of being both the last DCI and also the first D/CIA, having his empire shorn of all but his Langley fiefdom. His new boss, veteran diplomat John Negroponte, was appointed as Director of National Intelligence to coordinate and oversee the sprawling intelligence community of seventeen agencies and departments through his Office of the Director of National Intelligence (ODNI). On 22 April 2005, Negroponte personally delivered the President's Daily Brief – thus ending CIA's tenure, since 1947, as the link between the president and his intelligence community.[22]

While the DNI took some of the erstwhile DCI's authority in legal terms, the reality in practice was often at odds with the lines of authority as represented on organisational wire diagrams. In perhaps the most notable case of a CIA/DNI turf war, in May 2009 DNI Dennis C. Blair, a retired four-star Navy admiral, asserted the authority in 'rare circumstances' to name someone other than the CIA chief of station (COS) as the senior intelligence representative in a foreign capital.[23] Blair's language was measured, and he claimed this would only be done in cases where it might make sense to designate a senior official from another USIC agency – such as cases where sigint cooperation, and not humint, might be the most important liaison issue.

If Blair viewed the move as a litmus test for the remit of the DNI, CIA Director Leon Panetta viewed it as the thin edge of the wedge, and he could not let such a precedent be set. Removing the designation authority for the coveted and powerful title of COS would be tantamount to cutting Samson's hair, and Panetta crossed swords with Blair over it, with Panetta countermanding Blair's order the following day. Blair won the first round in the Senate, which ruled that 'the DNI, exercising his authority under the law, has made the decision that the directive is the right choice for the Intelligence Community. The Committee supports the DNI in that choice and looks forward to the CIA's prompt adherence to his decision.'[24]

However powerful a former combatant commander might be – and more so with the power of law and the SSCI bolstering his position – it was not enough to win the fight. The White House ultimately sided with Panetta, and the CIA Director retained the responsibility to manage intelligence collection and liaison relationships, though the title of DNI representative was added to the COS portfolio. The line and block charts that were, in theory, settled with the creation of the DNI had confusing ripple effects once put into practice. Even with good faith on the part of the intelligence community members, restructuring during a moment of crisis and rapid response seemed to cause as much confusion as it solved. A popular quip in the halls of Langley was that reorganising the US intelligence community after 9/11 was like changing the tyres on a car while driving at sixty miles per hour.[25]

If the external turf wars that bubbled up from time to time were hard-fought affairs, the internal ones were completely one-sided; and, cumulatively, they skewed the agency's focus and expertise towards the high-tempo work of international counterterrorism. Financial and personnel resources that had formerly belonged to CIA Cold War baronets in Europe and Central Eurasia divisions surged to the Near East division and the Counterterrorist Center, whose ranks ballooned. It rapidly became clear that not only did the chiefs of NE and CTC wear the largest Stetsons in the saloon of the DCI's conference room, they also had the sharpest spurs. But several noted that these changes were having unintended and potentially negative consequences. Senior managers with responsibility for staffing the most challenging operational assignments in hard-target countries complained that the War on Terror was developing bad habits in their junior case officers, such as using the telephone to communicate with contacts or employing surveillance detection routes that emphasised physical security over clandestinity – Mosul rules, rather than Moscow. More traditional managers wondered whether their officers – off on assignment in CTC or NE divisions – would be able to readjust to the more deliberate pace of traditional tradecraft. Would junior case officers be able to trade their rollercoaster ride for a game of chess on their next assignment? As former CIA inspector general Frederick Hitz described it, 'CIA became predator-centric and paramilitary focused.'[26] The War on Terror was affecting traditional humint tradecraft and the next generation of case officers. Likewise, the CIA's analytical cadre tried not to compete with cable news for scoops, but strategic level analysis often lost out to tactical analysis, in part because consumers wanted headlines and action.

The paramilitary focus that Hitz described in the period since 9/11 shaped the agency profoundly, from both the bottom up and the top down. Before CIA's total engagement in the War on Terror, historically, those with deep language and cultural expertise would be promoted, especially after service in hard-target and 'denied area' countries where they demonstrated excellence in classic espionage. After 9/11 CIA took on a more paramilitary complexion, with paramilitary officers taking high-profile assignments in the field and then correspondingly senior jobs back at Langley. Those officers who often came from elite military units, and who spent more time in combat boots than wingtips, quickly pushed out more traditional operations officers from senior positions. Those with decades of operational experience in traditional CIA postings, but outside of warzones, found themselves elbowed out by the 'cowboys'. Perhaps it is understandable that CIA wanted to be respected by the military's general officers in places like

Iraq and Afghanistan and therefore wanted their own Chiefs of Station to have the resume and swagger of combat-hardened warriors – especially those steeped in the special units where intelligence, reconnaissance, raids and similar advise and assist operations melded together in the new form of warfare. Even outside of the senior ranks, it became clear to CIA clandestine service officers that promotion prospects would be markedly enhanced with a warzone tour (or several) under their belt. It was therefore important to give clandestine service recruits at least a modicum of military bearing and familiarity with weapons and battlefield conditions: not only so they could survive, but also at some level so its officers would not embarrass CIA when they were working beside military colleagues, as most would in short order.

This was both wholly understandable in the circumstances, and disruptive to the traditional character of the agency. That not all operational recruits were prepared for such immediate immersion into the world of paramilitary culture became clear, often in humorous ways. During the paramilitary training phase of the field tradecraft course, one recruit, a former accountant, was chastised by a member of the instructor cadre, a moustachioed, grizzled paramilitary veteran, because his 'ranger ropes' – stray uniform threads – were left uncut. That this small bit of military protocol was never explained to recruits was beside the point; the culture clash was disorienting for all involved.[27]

Most recruits took to the paramilitary emphasis swimmingly (and eagerly), and in the decade following the 9/11 attacks, CIA, NSA, FBI and Special Forces operators systematically dismembered al-Qa'ida's operational leadership, killing or capturing group members with such alacrity that its operational planners hardly had time to settle into their new roles before they were targeted and removed. Bin Ladin was a rare exception. He had escaped from near encirclement in the Tora Bora Mountains in the closing weeks of 2001. In the meantime, CIA turned over every stone, chased every lead and grasped at every straw to identify his whereabouts, ever taunted by videotaped messages emerging to confirm that 'UBL' was still alive. CIA analysts would scrutinise each tape for hints as to UBL's well-being, state of mind, operational nexus to his terror group, and even the slightest indication of where he might be hiding. Finding him unified the CIA's paramilitary operators, the analysts and support staff at Langley, and the rest of the DNI's new community, who brought other intelligence disciplines to the hunt. The reforms that his most spectacular attack had set in motion would ultimately lead to his death in Abbottabad, Pakistan, nearly ten years after the attacks of September 11th.

The key development was the ability of the CIA and, indeed, the US intelligence community more broadly, to quickly turn intelligence into

414

action. Alongside the increasingly paramilitary complexion of CIA in the post-9/11 era, the most notable development was the near seamless relationship between CIA and the Pentagon's Joint Special Operations Command (JSOC). Nowhere was this partnership more on display than during Operation Neptune Spear, when a CIA-driven Navy SEAL raid killed bin Ladin in his compound in Abbottabad after one of history's longest manhunts. As a CIA account put it, the raid was a 'team effort, the product of increased integration within the IC and of close collaboration with our military partners. The CIA was at the center of it all, driving the collection of vital information, assessing each piece of data, and analyzing all sources to produce the compelling intelligence case that led US forces to Abbottabad.'[28] From one point of view, the bin Ladin raid was the apotheosis of linkage between CIA and JSOC. Yet from another perspective, there was nothing particularly remarkable about the raid itself, other than the celebrity of its target. Operators trained for the mission and executed it with professionalism and daring that, in a way, have become routine for them, and the intelligence collection and analysis that drove the raid was the same careful and focused process used hundreds of times before and since against less famous targets. This machine continued to operate relentlessly after bin Ladin's death: following and targeting al-Qa'ida, its myriad spin-off regional franchises in Africa and South East Asia and, of course, the Islamic State in Iraq and the Levant, wherever they appeared.

While the 9/11 Commission felt that Presidents Clinton and Bush were not 'well served' by CIA in the lead up to 9/11, the subsequent years have seen CIA transition from reckoning to redemption. After 9/11, CIA determinedly and relentlessly adapted to support America's War on Terror. Whereas the Soviet threat dominated the agency's Cold War, spying on and fighting terrorists have been the defining feature of CIA's mission for the twenty-first century. This was, perhaps, inevitable, given the devastation of 9/11. But in the view of an increasing number of intelligence professionals, CIA ought to break with its recent experience with paramilitary operations and should return to its roots and refocus on core tradecraft against traditional state-based threats. As Frederick Hitz advised, 'The US needs to return to the regular, pre-war order in intelligence collection and analysis. It needs to pay attention to those foreign policy and intelligence questions that have traditionally concerned us regarding both our closest allies and our fiercest rivals: future prospects for the euro and European unity; relations with Russia, China and North Korea; America's role in the Pacific.'[29] The US and its allies continue to exist in a dangerous world, and threats come in many guises. Some will require decisive immediate action, others patient monitoring and management. Policymakers might not be best served by an overly militarised CIA.

As this chapter has explored, in addition to forever changing America, 9/11 had a profound impact on the development of CIA itself. In its post-9/11 years, CIA mirrored the Department of Defense in that counterterrorism became its primary focus, arguably to the exclusion of other state-based threats. However, America's National Security Strategy for 2018 has re-emphasised state-based priorities and softened the existential alarm concerning threat posed by terrorism. It would not be surprising for CIA to recalibrate itself yet again to suit the policymakers' newest concerns.

Central Intelligence Agency
Inspector General
IG 2003-0005-IN

(U) OFFICE OF INSPECTOR GENERAL REPORT ON CENTRAL INTELLIGENCE AGENCY ACCOUNTABILITY REGARDING FINDINGS AND CONCLUSIONS OF THE REPORT OF THE JOINT INQUIRY INTO INTELLIGENCE COMMUNITY ACTIVITIES BEFORE AND AFTER THE TERRORIST ATTACKS OF SEPTEMBER 11, 2001

JUNE 2005

(U) SYSTEMIC FINDING 11: HUMINT OPERATIONS AGAINST AL-QA'IDA

(S//NF) Systemic Finding 11 of the Joint Inquiry (JI) report states that, "Prior to September 11, 2001, the Intelligence Community did not effectively develop and use human sources to penetrate the al-Qa'ida inner circle. This lack of reliable and knowledgeable human sources significantly limited the Community's ability to acquire intelligence that could be acted upon before the September 11 attacks. In part, at least, the lack of unilateral (i.e., US-recruited) counterterrorism sources was a product of an excessive reliance on foreign liaison services."

(U) Joint Inquiry Discussion

(S//NF) The JI acknowledges that the Counterterrorist Center (CTC) made a number of creative efforts to unilaterally penetrate al-Qa'ida especially after the East Africa embassy bombings in August 1998. ████████████

(S//NF) CTC interviewees told the JI staff that the Center at various times had ████████████ outside the al-Qa'ida inner circle who were reporting on the terrorist organization and ████████████ who were being developed for recruitment prior to 11 September 2001 (9/11). The CIA and Federal Bureau of Investigation (FBI) handled the best source jointly. In addition, the report notes that the CIA managed a network of ████████████ in Afghanistan that reported information on Bin Ladin-related security details, personalities, logistics, foreign visitors, movements, and relations with the Taliban. These sources occasionally provided threat information as well but had no access to the al-Qa'ida inner circle. Moreover, these and other sources never provided any intelligence relevant to the 9/11 operation that anyone could act upon prior to September 11.

(S//NF) The JI acknowledges that CIA faced a number of external impediments that made al-Qa'ida a hard target to penetrate:

- Members of the inner circle of Usama Bin Ladin (UBL) had close bonds established by kinship, wartime experience, and long-term association.
- Information about major terrorist plots was not widely shared within al-Qa'ida.
- Many of UBL's closest associates lived in war-torn Afghanistan, where the United States had no official presence.
- Pakistan provided the principal access to al-Qa'ida's main operating area in southern Afghanistan, but US-Pakistani relations were strained.

(S//NF) The JI implies that CIA had a flawed human intelligence (HUMINT) operations strategy and identifies several self-created impediments that limited the Agency's success in obtaining unilateral penetrations of al-Qa'ida. These impediments included:

- **Reliance on liaison.** While acknowledging that most disruptions of al-Qa'ida activities abroad before

9/11 resulted from foreign government operations, the JI report concludes that CIA's reliance on foreign services to develop human sources meant that CIA had insufficient focus on unilateral operations.

- **Focus on disruption and capture.** The report indicates that, per the National Security Council's direction, CIA's HUMINT emphasis was on pinpointing the location of UBL and his principal lieutenants in Afghanistan so as to capture and render them to law enforcement authorities. As a consequence, the report suggests that CIA did not focus as heavily as it could have on recruiting relevant sources in other locations. ████████████

- **Value of walk-ins.**[*]
  ████████████

- **Dirty asset rules.**[†] CTC personnel told the JI that they did not view guidelines issued by former Director of Central Intelligence (DCI) John Deutch in 1996 concerning CIA recruitment of human sources with poor human rights records or who had committed proscribed acts as an impediment to pursuit of terrorist recruitments in al-Qa'ida. Nonetheless, the JI was skeptical, noting that a July 2002 report of the House Permanent Select Committee on Intelligence Subcommittee on Terrorism and Homeland Security found that CIA officers in the field did feel constrained by these guidelines.[‡]

(U) Assessment of Joint Inquiry Finding

(S//NF) The Office of Inspector General (OIG) 9/11 Review Team concurs with the JI's conclusion that CIA HUMINT operations were unable to penetrate al-Qa'ida's inner circle and that both external and

---

[*] (U) For simplicity, we use the term walk-ins to refer to volunteers who walk in, call in, or write in offering to provide information of value.

[†] (S//NF) Dirty asset rules is the shorthand description for regulations that govern the operational use of agents tainted by criminal acts or involvement in human rights abuses. [redacted]

[‡] (U) US House of Representatives, Permanent Select Committee on Intelligence, Subcommittee on Terrorism and Homeland Security, *Counterterrorism Intelligence Capabilities and Performance Prior to 9-11,* dated 17 July 2002, pp. 27-29.

internal factors limited CIA's ability to be more effective. However, the Team differs to some degree with the JI's analysis and conclusions about the various flaws in CIA's operational strategy. The 9/11 Team:

- Does not concur that CIA reliance on liaison was excessive but agrees that it was not balanced with a strong focus on unilateral operations until after mid-1999. The Team addresses this issue in detail in Systemic Finding 15.
- Agrees that CIA's operational focus was on Afghanistan, although not just to capture UBL but also to gain HUMINT access to the plans and intentions of his inner circle there. This strategy did reduce the focus on HUMINT operations elsewhere, however.
- Concurs that the CIA relied on walk-ins as its principal unilateral sources but disagrees that these afforded little value as counterterrorism sources.
- Agrees that bureaucratic rules may have impeded recruitment operations – but cannot evaluate the extent of the negative impact.

(S//NF) The 9/11 Team also assessed two additional HUMINT collection issues that were not addressed in the JI findings:

- In their additional views to the JI Report, Senators Shelby and Dewine charged that the CIA had been negligent in failing to adjust its posture away from official cover to nontraditional platforms more suited to the terrorist target.* The Team found that the Directorate of Operations (DO) made little use of nonofficial cover (NOC) officers or nontraditional platforms to address the al-Qa'ida target because these platforms were indeed too weak to offer much potential.
- ███████████

---

* (U) "September 11 and Imperative of Reform in the US Intelligence Community, Additional Views of Senator Richard C. Shelby, Vice Chairman, Senate Select Committee on Intelligence," JI Final Report, Appendix – Additional Views of Members of the Joint Inquiry, 10 December 2002.

(U) The Balance Between Collection and Disruption
~~(S//NF)~~ CTC's HUMINT strategy regarding UBL evolved over the years from one focused on disruptions and capture ███████████ CTC never achieved access to UBL's inner circle.

(U) Early Focus on Disruption
~~(S//NF)~~ Prior to mid-1999, CTC's main focus was disruption ███████████ well aware that CIA had been unsuccessful at penetrating the inner core of ███████████ necessary for CIA to use the information it was collecting to take action to disrupt the terrorist infrastructure before it could be used to attack the United States. ███████████ told the Team that ███████████ considered CTC's balance between collection and disruption to be appropriate.*

███████████

(U) Renewed Focus on Recruitments
~~(S//NF)~~ In mid-1999, the new Chief/CTC determined that the Center's al-Qa'ida effort was weighted too heavily toward disruptions and that CTC needed to focus its efforts on recruiting ███████████ told the Team that the earlier double-tap strategy was too heavily focused on liaison and the FBI and that the new Chief had put renewed focus on unilateral operations.

~~(S//NF)~~ The Team found that the increased focus on unilateral operations resulted in increased recruitment of unilateral assets and an increase in unilateral reporting ███████████ Figure S11-1 shows ███████████

Figure S11-1

███████████

Figure S11-3

███████████

---

* ~~(C//NF)~~ Double-tap refers to the shooting tactic of firing two rounds quickly (tapping the trigger twice) to neutralize a threatening aggressor. However, in this context, it refers to law enforcement action against terrorists including monitoring, questioning, and arresting suspected terrorists under whatever criminal statutes possible, thereby accomplishing two goals: disrupting potential terrorist attacks and obtaining intelligence information on terrorist activities.

Figure S11-4

███████████

(S//NF) In interviews conducted during the OIG's inspection of CTC in 2000-2001, customers evaluated counterterrorism reporting positively. Most ███████████ field customers of CTC's reports termed the reporting useful, good, or meeting their needs. The few Washington customers who commented on CTC reporting also called it important and valuable. The 9/11 Team did not contact CTC customers for this current review.

(S//NF) A memorandum from an AIG manager in May 2000 shows that CTC was fully aware it had significant collection gaps. This memorandum stated that, among other key issues, the Intelligence Community lacked information on:

███████████

(U) Value of Walk-ins

███████████

(S//NF) ███████████ walk-ins was a former ███████████ officer in UBL's organization ███████████ and walked in to the US Embassy ███████████ This walk-in ███████████ which defined UBL as head of a worldwide terrorist organization. His reporting helped establish Bin Ladin's intent to target the United States on its own soil and his interest in obtaining weapons of mass destruction-related materials. ███████████ Intelligence Community build a case against UBL and understand the al-Qa'ida organization.

███████████

(U) Dirty Asset Rules

(S//NF) Although the 9/11 Review Team believes that the weight of evidence tilts to the conclusion that the dirty asset rules hampered the effectiveness of unilateral operations, the Team's *review* of this issue surfaced contradictory information.

(S//NF) On the one hand, most CIA officers the Team interviewed said the rules had no impact, since senior Agency leadership approved every case that officers put forward:

██████████

(S//NF) On the other hand, a number of senior CIA officers and CTC managers admitted their concern that the guidelines did have a negative impact on the willingness of field officers to pursue problem cases:

- A former Deputy Director of Central Intelligence felt that senior Agency leaders were never able to convince DO working-level officers that these guidelines were to protect the Station and case officers and not to hinder their efforts.

- Another ████████ identified one terrorist case that led to an oral reprimand of the ████████ The reprimand came after Congress learned that a for a terrorist group. ████████ added that the DCI's handling of this incident helped send the message to the DO that the DCI would not protect anyone.

- ████████ said that ████████ found that it was a common misperception in CTC before 9/11 that any potential asset with human rights baggage was an automatic nonstarter ████████ spent time explaining to CTC officers that this was not so.

(S//NF) Several senior DO managers and CTC officers acknowledged that these guidelines affected how case officers approached operations. ████████ said it had the effect of steering case officers to targets no less important, but unlikely to involve "dirty asset" issues. ████████ acknowledged that the guidelines served as another bureaucratic hoop that made recruitments more difficult, and another officer who served ████████ said that it was a general complaint in the Station that they felt handcuffed by these rules.

██████████

(U) Insufficient Use of Nonofficial Cover Platforms

(U) The JI report did not address the issue of NOC utilization, but, as noted earlier, US Senators Shelby and Dewine cited it as a significant Agency shortcoming in addressing the terrorist threat. Senator Shelby sums up these views: "The CIA's Directorate of Operations (DO) has been too reluctant to develop nontraditional HUMINT platforms, and has stuck too much and for too long with the comparatively easy work of operating under diplomatic cover from US embassies. This approach is patently unsuited to HUMINT collection against nontraditional threats such as terrorism or proliferation targets, and the CIA must move emphatically to develop an entirely new collection paradigm involving greater use of nonofficial cover (NOC) officers.*

(U) Implications
(S//NF) The Chief of CTC prior to 1999 made reasonable choices in implementing a collection strategy he believed had the best potential to achieve results based on his understanding of the target at the time, the meager operational tools he had available, and the difficult natural impediments he faced. If this Chief had not discounted the potential of unilateral operations, CIA would have had two more years to achieve results. However, if an earlier focus on unilateral operations had been at the expense of work with liaison on disruptions and renditions, an unintended consequence might have been the failure to thwart a terrorist attack against the United States.

(S//NF) Armed with the knowledge that liaison operations were not achieving the needed access to al-Qa'ida plans and intentions, the CTC Chief who took over in 1999 made a logical adjustment toward more unilateral operations and a focus on Afghanistan, since that was where the inner core of al-Qa'ida resided. The JI report suggests that other countries may have had more benign operating environments where CTC could have achieved better results in penetrating al-Qa'ida. The Team cannot judge whether the operational potential to acquire an agent with access to al-Qa'ida plans and intentions would have justified

---

* (U) "September 11 and Imperative of Reform in the US Intelligence Community, Additional Views of Senator Richard C. Shelby, Vice Chairman, Senate Select Committee on Intelligence," JI Final Report, Appendix – Additional Views of Members of the Joint inquiry. December 10, 2002, page 12.

the costs of pursuing such an agent in other countries far removed from the al-Qa'ida leadership in
Afghanistan. Nonetheless, by not casting the Center's
net wider, the Chief may have lost opportunities to
penetrate al-Qa'ida.

(U) Accountability

(C//NF) CTC officers were extremely committed and
did their best, but HUMINT operations were of only
limited effectiveness against the hard al-Qa'ida
and UBL targets. CTC may have missed opportunities
to improve its results because of the operational
choices it made and those it discarded, such as more
active engagement with ██████████ so that all possible
HUMINT platforms were engaged in the effort to target
al-Qa'ida. Nonetheless, the 9/11 Team believes that
Center management made reasonable choices in implementing the HUMINT collection strategy it believed
had the best potential to achieve results against al-
Qa'ida. Given the inherent and systemic impediments
it faced, CTC continually adapted its HUMINT operations to try to penetrate the al-Qa'ida target and
disrupt its activities. Accordingly, the Team makes
no recommendations with respect to accountability for
these decisions.

Notes

1. Aside from the 9/11 Commission Report, a primary source document, there
   is a rich literature of secondary sources on the lead up to the 9/11 attacks.
   Some of the better treatments include Lawrence Wright, *The Looming Tower:
   al-Qaeda and the Road to 9/11* (New York: Alfred A. Knopf, 2006) and Steve
   Coll, *Ghost Wars: The Secret History of the CIA, Afghanistan, and Bin Laden,
   from the Soviet Invasion to September 10, 2001* (New York: Penguin, 2004).
2. On the activities of the Jawbreaker team, see Gary Berntsen, *Jawbreaker* (New
   York: Crown Publishers, 2005). On early CIA operations in Afghanistan see
   Gary C. Schroen, *First In* (New York: Presidio Press, 2005).
3. 'Remembering CIA's Heroes: Johnny Micheal Spann', CIA website: *News
   & Information*, 25 November 2009, <https://www.cia.gov/news-information/
   featured-story-archive/johnny-micheal-spann.html> (last accessed 10 January
   2020).
4. CIA's contribution to the War on Terror, of course, went well beyond

Afghanistan, with operations and sacrifice in many countries around the world. For instance, Jeffrey R. Patneau lost his life in Yemen in 2008, and will be remembered fondly.

5. As quoted in Jane Mayer, 'The Search for Osama', *The New Yorker*, 4 August 2003, p. 26.
6. For a comparison between Pearl Harbor and 9/11, see F. L. Borch, 'Comparing Pearl Harbor and "9/11": Intelligence Failure? American Unpreparedness? Military Responsibility?' *The Journal of Military History*, 67.3 (2003), p. 845.
7. CIA, Office of Public Affairs brochure, <https://www.cia.gov/library/publica tions/resources/central-intelligence-agency-brochure/CleanedOPA%20Broch ure%20final.pdf> (last accessed 10 January 2020).
8. As quoted in CIA IG Report, p. 342, originally found in 'September 11 and Imperative of Reform in the US Intelligence Community, Additional Views of Senator Richard C. Shelby, Vice Chairman, Senate Select Committee on Intelligence', Joint Inquiry Final Report, Appendix – Additional Views of Members of the Joint Inquiry. 10 December 2002, p. 12.
9. As quoted in Mayer, 'The Search for Osama', p. 26.
10. Ibid.
11. CIA Inspector General Report, pp. 323, 324.
12. As quoted in Mayer, 'The Search for Osama', p. 26.
13. James M. Olson, *Fair Play: The Moral Dilemmas of Spying* (Washington: Potomac Books, 2006), p. 84.
14. Paul Pillar, 'Intelligence', in Audrey Kurth Cronin and James M. Ludes (eds), *Attacking Terrorism: Elements of a Grand Strategy* (Washington: Georgetown University Press, 2004), p. 126.
15. Congressional testimony of Cofer Black.
16. Frank Gregory and Paul Wilkinson, *International Security Programme New Security Challenges Briefing Paper 05/01*, 18 July 2005, Chatham House, p. 2.
17. Although we cannot discern who coined the phrase 'Londonistan', it was popularised in Melanie Phillips, *Londonistan* (New York: Encounter Books, 2006).
18. For full details of the Terrorism Act 2000, see <https://www.legislation.gov. uk/ukpga/2000/11/contents> (last accessed 10 January 2020).
19. Gregory and Wilkinson, *International Security Programme New Security Challenges Briefing Paper*, p. 2.
20. Christopher Andrew, *Defend the Realm* (New York: Vintage Books, 2010), p. 810.
21. George Tenet, *At the Center of the Storm* (New York: HarperCollins, 2007), p. 174.
22. Alfred Rolington, 'Objective Intelligence or Plausible Denial: An Open Source Review of Intelligence Method and Process Since 9/11', in Len Scott and R. Gerald Hughes (eds.) *Intelligence, Crises and Security: Prospects and Retrospects* (Abingdon: Routledge, 2008), p. 105.
23. Walter Pincus, 'Senate Committee Sides With DNI in Its Bureaucratic Turf War With CIA', *The Washington Post*, 23 July 2009, <http://www.washing

tonpost.com/wp-dyn/content/article/2009/07/22/AR2009072202979.html> (last accessed 10 January 2020).

24. Senate Report 111-55, 'Report to Accompany S. 1494, the Intelligence Authorization Act for Fiscal Year 2010', 22 July 2009, <https://www.intel ligence.senate.gov/publications/report-accompany-s-1494-intelligence-auth orization-act-fiscal-year-2010-july-22-2009> (last accessed 10 January 2020).
25. Author recollection.
26. Frederick P. Hitz, 'US Intelligence after the War on Terror', *World Politics Review*, 5 June 2012, <https://www.worldpoliticsreview.com/articles/12019/u-s-intelligence-after-the-war-on-terror> (last accessed 10 January 2020).
27. Author recollection.
28. 'Minutes and Years: The Bin Ladin Operation', CIA website: *News & Information*, 29 April 2016, <https://www.cia.gov/news-information/featured-story-archive/2016-featured-story-archive/minutes-and-years-the-bin-ladin-operation.html>. For further detail on the hunt for bin Ladin and the raid that took his life, see Peter L. Bergen, *Manhunt: The Ten-Year Search for bin Ladin from 9/11 to Abbottabad* (New York: Crown Publishing Group, 2012).
29. Hitz, 'US Intelligence after the War on Terror'.

21 The 'Slam Dunk':
The CIA and the Invasion of Iraq

There are few worse sins for an intelligence agency than getting dragged into a political battle where it is seen to lose objectivity, integrity and, consequently, reputation. On the heels of what was seen as the CIA's largest intelligence failure since its inception, the agency's reputation and capability were soon to be again in question. On 20 March 2003 the combined forces of the US, UK, Australia and Poland invaded Iraq. The US military contingent was the largest, comprising roughly 150,000 troops. For President George W. Bush, 'Operation Iraqi Freedom' was designed to 'disarm Iraq of weapons of mass destruction, to end Saddam Hussein's support for terrorism, and to free the Iraqi people'.[1] Although the war was initially supported by many Americans, it was also fiercely opposed – particularly internationally. Many felt that a diplomatic solution was a more viable option, and this view was endorsed by the governments of Germany, France and New Zealand.

The primary factor for debate concerning the cause for war centred around Iraq's supposed possession of weapons of mass destruction (WMD). Did it possess any? If so, what threat did they pose, and would Saddam use them? Prior to the invasion, significant efforts took place in public and behind the scenes to convince the world that Iraq had such weapons. Multinational diplomatic efforts took place through the prism of the UN and the on-site inspections undertaken by the UN Monitoring, Verification and Inspection Commission (UNMOVIC), led by Hans Blix.

A fortnight before the invasion took place, Blix informed the UN that no such weapons had been found so far.[2] Proponents of an invasion argued that it would only be possible to find the weapons once Saddam's government had been toppled and proper searches conducted, without Iraqi obfuscation. Meanwhile, high-profile presentations were designed and delivered with the objective of convincing those who were unsure or wavering that Iraq did indeed possess prohibited weapons. These included what would become the most infamous public defence of the case for war: Secretary of State Colin Powell's presentation to the UN in February 2003, when he held aloft illustrations of mobile biological warfare laboratories. For the general population as well as foreign governments alike, the intended message was clear: the US government was in possession of specific and accurate intelligence that revealed Iraqi WMD, and the only way to rid the world of this threat was invasion and forcible disarmament.

History, of course, disproved such a thesis. Iraq was invaded, the government of Saddam Hussein toppled, and no weapons of mass destruction were discovered (other than some prohibited missiles). Quite understandably, very serious questions began to be raised – not only about the political decision to go to war and what really lay behind such an enterprise, but about what the role of the intelligence community had been. The former of these, the political aspects, have been written about in great detail.[3] The intelligence aspects, too, have been heavily dissected, with focus varying between the politicisation of the intelligence process and the raising of serious questions about analytical errors of judgement within the US, and several allied, intelligence communities.[4] Many commentators conflate the issues, but where possible it is worthwhile separating the issues of intelligence production from the political decision to go to war. In the case of Iraq this is, admittedly, tremendously difficult. From the focus of collection requirements, through the political pressure put upon analysts to find evidence (implicit or otherwise), to the manner in which secret intelligence was used in a public environment to prove the case for a political decision, the intelligence machinery was abused.[5] Nonetheless, the case of Iraqi WMD raises a related set of interesting questions: it is one thing to find evidence that a country possesses weapons, but is it possible to prove the negative – that it does not? And, related to which, is it possible to produce the wrong intelligence assessment but for the correct reasons? It is these questions that this chapter and the related chapter reference document address.

The sub-field of scientific and technical intelligence developed during the Second World War with the work of R. V. Jones, the first head of scientific intelligence for the British government.[6] Since that point it has become more important as monitoring target states' weapons' capabilities has grown as a requirement. One of the fascinating areas it poses is the issue of capabilities versus intentions, and the precise relationship between the two.[7] Can, for instance, knowledge of capabilities be used to impute intentions? This aspect becomes clearer when the second question is considered: producing the wrong forecast but having done so for the correct reasons. As the chapter reference document makes clear, an argument can be made that the CIA analysts correctly produced an assessment on the basis of their grasp of Iraqi intentions and capabilities – and on what the USIC was able to collect on these issues – even though it would ultimately turn out to be wrong.

Sherman Kent, the father of strategic intelligence in the CIA, once wrote of how assessments of the Cuban Missile Crisis had been incorrect, despite all the intelligence having been assessed correctly.[8] It could be argued that a similar mistake was made with Iraqi WMD. The chapter reference document presents evidence for this, though this is not the conclusion it reaches. It is an internal post-mortem written by the CIA on why its analysts got it so wrong regarding Iraq's WMD.[9] The underlying conclusion is significant: that analysts looked at the situation from their own perspective rather than that of someone inside a dictatorship sitting in Baghdad, an 'Iraqi prism'.[10] In the words of one author, it represents a 'mea culpa' for the CIA.[11] So what went wrong?

The simple conclusion is this: Iraq intentionally gave the misleading impression that it possessed weapons of mass destruction. This was evident in a number of different ways, all of which complemented what little intelligence the CIA actually possessed. In terms of gauging capabilities and intentions, there were tangible signs of both. 'Proof' was provided by human sources, like the Iraqi engineer codenamed Curveball, that Iraq was in possession of WMD. These sources turned out to be unreliable, and the CIA was too willing to believe them. As the CIA report makes clear, this evidence was reinforced by the actions of the Iraqi government, where its repeated obfuscation, denial and deception regarding weapons inspections gave the impression that they had something to hide, thereby 'reinvigorat[ing] the hunt for concealed WMD'.

Related to this, the Iraqi tradition of employing deception was sufficient to force analysts to assume that they were deliberately hiding something. The lack of a converse was also telling – i.e., the fact that leading Iraqis did nothing to overturn this historic practice of deception and be especially helpful merely served to reinforce the belief that they were violating international rules. But worse than this, there was further evidence of deception. On this point the CIA document provides examples, but much of the information has been redacted. Suffice it to say, the impression was certainly that the Iraqis were intentionally trying to hide something.

With the benefit of hindsight the CIA was able to reflect upon its processes and its assessments, and to question why the Iraqi leadership gave the impression that it had prohibited weapons, or, at least, was unwilling to let anyone prove decisively that it did not have them. Could it have been simply a show of force? Could it have been, as the paper surmised, that Saddam never realistically expected the US-led coalition to invade and that, therefore, it was designed as a show of strength to intimidate the main regional enemies of Iran and Israel?

A more interesting conclusion of the report is the one that Iraqi deception was so pervasive and the fear of internal retribution so great, that there is some evidence to suggest that Saddam and senior generals were under the assumption that Iraqi actually possessed WMD. Thus, 'Iraqi leaders may have made decisions and projected an image of strength on the basis of inaccurate and inflated capabilities ... many generals were not necessarily aware that Iraq did not have WMD.'[12]

This assessment was given the benefit of the doubt in light of the previously ambiguous picture regarding Iraqi possession of WMD, which would certainly have lurked in the backs of analysts' minds. Since the first Gulf War in 1990, assessments of Iraq's WMD programme had waxed and waned: sometimes the picture had been too gloomy, at other times it had been too rosy. Thus, following the 1990 confrontation, the CIA had come to over-appreciate how developed and significant the WMD programme was, so assessments were revised downwards. In 1995, assessments of how developed and significant the Iraqi WMD programme was were revised upwards following the defection of Saddam's son-in-law, Hussein Kamel, who had previously been responsible for them.[13] This sine wave pattern of over- and underestimation certainly led to confusion in assessing possible capabilities.

CIA analysts, then, had to contend with producing assessments on what are traditionally some of the most secret aspects of a closed regime, in an environment where there was little concrete intelligence to go on, but where the prior practice of deception was still in evidence, Iraqi obfuscation was taken to mean something was intentionally being concealed, and the leadership gave the appearance that they had WMD.[14] The summation of this was that weight of intelligence on both intentions and capabilities pointed towards illicit possession. Whether or not this level of confidence warranted the political decision to go to war is a policy question for the Bush administration. While we do not really know the probabilistic language in which assessments would have been couched, certainly it is difficult to argue against the contention that the wrong assessment (in retrospect) was produced on correct judgements and the information analysts had before them.[15]

The greatest problem, as the CIA post-mortem makes clear, was that the CIA's analysts were too stuck in a Washington-centric mindset and did not review the evidence from the perspective of those in Baghdad. Had they done so, the implication is that a different conclusion would have been reached: 'Analysts tended to focus on what was most important to us [i.e. the CIA and US] – the hunt for WMD – and less on what would be most important for a paranoid dictatorship to protect. Viewed through an Iraqi prism, their reputation, their security, their overall technological capabilities, and their status needed to be preserved.' The proverbial 'slam dunk' conclusion, voiced by DCI George Tenet, that Iraq had WMD and the *casus belli* was airtight was to be the final straw breaking Tenet's long tenure in the CIA's director's suite.

```
EO 13526 1.4(b)<25Yrs
EO 13526 1.4(c)<25Yrs
EO 13526 1.4(d)<25Yrs
EO 13526 3.5(c)
```

> 5 January 2006
> Misreading Intentions: Iraq's
> Reaction to Inspections
> Created Picture of Deception
> Iraq WMD Retrospective Series

APPROVED
FOR RELEASE
05-Jun-2012

Misreading Intentions: Iraq's Reaction to Inspections Created Picture of Deception
Iraq WMD Retrospective Series _____

Key Findings ▮ Iraq's intransigence and deceptive practices during the periods of UN inspections between 1991 and 2003 deepened suspicions among many world governments and intelligence services that Baghdad had ongoing WMD programs. Ironically, even at key junctures when the regime attempted to partially or fully comply with UN resolutions, its suspicious behavior and destruction of authenticating documentation only reinforced the perception that Iraq was being deceptive.

Key events and Iraqi behaviors that shaped Western perceptions include:

- An early established pattern of "cheat and retreat." Iraq concealed items and activities in the early 1990s, and when detected, attempted to rectify the shortcomings, usually secretly and without documentation. Those coverups were

431

seen to validate analytic assessments that Iraq intended to deny, deceive, and maintain forbidden capabilities.

- Shocked by the unexpected aggressiveness of early UN Special Commission (UNSCOM) inspections in 1991, Iraq secretly destroyed or dismantled most undeclared items and records that could have been used to validate the unilateral destruction, leaving Baghdad unable to provide convincing proof when it later tried to demonstrate compliance.

- We now judge that the 1995 defection of Saddam's son-in-law Husayn Kamil – a critical figure in Iraq's WMD and denial and deception (D&D) activities – prompted Iraq to change strategic direction and cease efforts to retain WMD programs. Iraqi attempts that year to find face-saving means to disclose previously hidden information, however, reinforced the idea that Baghdad was deceptive and unreliable. Instead of helping to close the books, Iraq's actions reinvigorated the hunt for concealed WMD, as analysts perceived that Iraq had both the intent and capability to continue WMD efforts during inspections.

- When Iraq's revelations were met by added UN scrutiny and distrust, frustrated Iraqi leaders deepened their belief that inspections were politically motivated and would not lead to the end of sanctions. As Iraq turned its political focus to illicit economic efforts to end its isolation, eliminate sanctions, and protect its dual-use infrastructure, these actions increased suspicions that Iraq continued to hide WMD.

- Other Iraqi actions that fueled the perception of WMD-related deceptions included Special Security Organization (SSO) and other efforts to hide non-WMD secrets to protect Saddam and the regime ███████████ Iraq also continued to provide inaccuracies in UN declarations ████████ for a variety of reasons, not the least of which was an inability to document these statements.

- Iraq did not accurately interpret US and international policy drivers; in 2003, it assessed that the United States would not invade Iraq.

- Several people claimed that Iraqi officials did not believe that all of Iraq's WMD had been destroyed. These officials may in good faith have conveyed the message to others that Iraq retained WMD. ██████████

Early 1990s concealment activity combined with unexpected revelations following Husayn Kamil's defection led analysts to view Iraq as a sophisticated D&D practitioner. Faced with inconclusive or uncertain data, analysts made judgments with conviction that Iraq could successfully conceal damaging data. ██████ We recognize that portions of our data were supplied by the same people who were responsible for the deception campaign and provided insight in captivity. Captured documentary evidence exploited to date so far supports the conclusions of this paper. ██████████

Contents
Key Findings
Scope Note
Overview

Other Factors Reinforce Deceptive Image ▮▮▮▮
   Security State
   Corrupt Science Projects
   Internal Self-Deception
Analytic Liabilities ▮▮
Insets
Overall Pattern of 'Cheat and Retreat'
Officials Recount Chaotic Document Movements
▮▮▮▮

Baghdad's Threat Perception ▮▮▮

The Analysts' Retrospective ▮▮▮

Scope Note   This is one in a series of intelligence assessments (IAs) in the CIA's *Iraq WMD Retrospective Series** that addresses our post-Operation Iraqi Freedom (OIF) understanding of Iraq's weapons of mass destruction (WMD), delivery system, and denial and deception (D&D) programs. These IAs reevaluate past assessments and reporting in light of the investigations carried out by the Iraq Survey Group (ISG). ▮▮▮

This assessment addresses how the Iraqis perceived and reacted to the international inspection process and the effect these actions had on analyst perceptions. This IA is not intended to be a comprehensive review of all CIA analysis or the analytical process on Iraqi WMD issues. The conclusions of this IA are generally consistent with ISG's findings as reflected in the *Comprehensive Report of the Special Advisor to the DCI on Iraq's WMD* issued on 30 September 2004 and other products. This review of histori-

* More comprehensive papers on the individual Iraqi WMD programs, including comparisons of prewar estimates and postwar conclusions, are to be published elsewhere in this *Retrospective Series*. ▮▮

cal reporting and assessments helps to provide additional context on the interplay between Iraqi actions and intelligence judgments. ██████████████

Misreading Intentions: Iraq's Reaction to Inspections Created Picture of Deception
Iraq WMD Retrospective Series

Overview

Iraqi leadership reactions to UN resolutions on weapons inspections between 1991 and 2003 fostered an atmosphere of distrust with the world community. Analysts interpreted Iraq's intransigence and ongoing deceptive practices as indicators of continued WMD programs or an intent to preserve WMD capabilities, reinforcing intelligence we were receiving at the time that Saddam Husayn continued to pursue WMD. A combination of poorly and hastily considered Iraqi actions, regime assumptions and beliefs that did not reflect an accurate understanding of the world outside Iraq, and the typical paranoia of a security state led to Baghdad's inability to extricate itself from what it viewed as oppressive sanctions and outside suspicion. Instead, Iraq continued to exhibit obstructive and inconsistent behaviors that perpetuated the belief by ███████████ that Baghdad was not fully complying with UN resolutions and was concealing ongoing WMD programs. ██████

1991: Initial Approach to Inspections ... (U)

Iraq initially tried to end sanctions without fully revealing WMD programs as required by UN resolutions, believing that appearing to comply would be sufficient. Iraqi leaders were optimistic that inspections and sanctions would end quickly.* Their approach to

---

* This assessment was prepared by the Office of Iraq Analysis. Comments and queries are welcome and may be directed to ████

inspections was to make sure that nothing was found to contradict their initial false declarations while they destroyed contradictory evidence:

- Several officials stated after the fall of the regime that Iraq's original belief was that it would not have to comply with the inspections, which would be cursory and only last a few weeks.
- ███████████ initially believed that it would not have to follow any UN mandates, because in its view no one had ever followed a UN mandate ███████████

Iraq planned to gather declared items for presentation, hide other materials in place, disperse and conceal nuclear materials, and deny the existence of pre-1991 WMD efforts: ███████████

Overall Pattern of 'Cheat and Retreat' ███████
The reactions of both sides to the inspection process formed a pattern; Iraq would start to rectify an uncovered shortcoming, usually in secret. The West viewed the discoveries as validation that Iraq had a continued intent to deny, deceive, and maintain forbidden capabilities, especially because Iraqis usually begrudgingly revealed that they had given up those capabilities after being caught with discrepancies. ████
International weapons inspectors often detected Iraq's concealment activities and discrepancies in WMD-related information, triggering investigations that delayed the lifting of sanctions, thus forming a pattern that deepened mutual suspicion:

- *In interviews conducted after the fall of the regime, senior officials indicated that Saddam sought to avoid involvement in a drawn-out process with UNSCOM and the IAEA to investigate every new issue.*
- *In April 1991, for example, Iraq declared that it had neither a nuclear weapons program nor an enrichment program. Inspections in June and September 1991 proved that Iraq had lied on both counts, had explored multiple enrichment paths,*

and had a well-developed nuclear weapons program.
███████████

Baghdad destroyed rather than revealed items, attempting to make its inaccurate assertions of no programs correct in a legalistic sense. ██████████ *Decisions to destroy much of the paperwork that could have verified the destruction exacerbated Iraq's inability to later extricate itself from being viewed in the "cheat and retreat" paradigm:*
████████████ *March 1992, Iraq decided to declare the unilateral destruction of certain prohibited items to the Security Council, while continuing to conceal its biological warfare (BW) program and important aspects of the nuclear, chemical, and missile programs* ████████
Saddam Husayn ordered Husayn Kamil to hide the weapons in 1991, but gave them up once cornered. He said that Saddam destroyed all WMD in secret after pressure from the UN and inspectors, after initially thinking he could hide weapons █████████ *also acknowledged the 1991 unilateral destruction.*
███████████ *said that the 1991 order to destroy all documents related to the BW program caused problems later, when Iraq did not have the documentation to support revised declarations in the late 1990s admitting to an offensive program* ████████
███████████ wondered why he was ordered to destroy the paperwork for the missile destruction in 1991, forcing Iraqis to rely upon personal recollection in later years when trying to prove that destruction had actually taken place ████████

... Leads to Decision on Unilateral Destruction

When the inspections proved more intrusive than expected, the Iraqi leadership appears to have panicked and made a fateful decision to secretly destroy much of the remaining nondeclared items, and eliminate the evidence. According to several officials, Iraq decided to surreptitiously destroy many items and hide others, rather than contradict earlier declarations. Many officials described the regime's shock over inspectors' aggressiveness, citing examples like the June 1991 discovery by IAEA ███████████ that Iraqis were moving nuclear electromagnetic isotope separation (EMIS) components away from an inspection:

- ████████ even after the IAEA inspectors tracked down EMIS components, the regime did not fully understand the implications of its initial false declarations, and Baghdad decided to unilaterally destroy much of the hidden material rather than declare it.
- ██████████ likened this decision to Iraq's fateful 1990 decision to invade Kuwait in terms of having negative consequences for Iraq.

█████████ July 1991, after consulting with Saddam, to destroy items, although some allegedly were hidden without ██████████ The bulk of the materials were destroyed in this initial period:

- ██████████ the destruction order for the BW program came in June 1991 ██████████ recalls getting 48 hours to get rid of everything ████████████████████ time, was their primary BW agent production and storage facility prior to the Gulf War. As with the other programs, orders were given to destroy documentation of the destruction and to retain no copies of other documents. WMD-related organizations received orders to turn over key "know-how" documents to the Special Security Organization (SSO) for safe-keeping ████████
- ████████ said Iraq retained two Scud-type ballistic missiles after the initial unilateral destruction in the summer of 1991 that were destroyed later that year ██████
- Iraq unilaterally destroyed 25 biological al-Husayn warheads and approximately 134 biological R-400 aerial bombs in 1991 ██████████ noted the destruction of 20 concealed al-Husayn chemical warfare (CW) warheads in the summer of 1991.

Weapons Deceptions Maintained After 1992

██████████████ at the time Iraq still did not admit to having destroyed biological bombs and warheads and represented BW warheads as being CW warheads.

• Iraq officials did not admit to weaponized BW agent until after the defection of Husayn Kamil the next month.

Diplomacy 1992-95: Iraq Tries To Break Free (U)

Frustration with continued sanctions led Baghdad to alternate between challenging the UN and talking diplomatic steps during this period that the regime thought would alleviate Iraq's isolation. Saddam's regime also experienced intense economic and security pressure, with the Iraqi dinar falling to its lowest level ever in November 1995 and several notable security threats, including a 1995 coup plot and associated unrest with the Dulaym tribe:

• Baghdad refused to allow a July 1992 inspection of the Ministry of Agriculture, saying it would violate Iraq's sovereignty and was intended for intelligence collection.

• In November 1993, Iraq accepted UNSCR 715 that allowed for long-term UN monitoring of its weapons programs following two years of Iraqi objections that such monitoring constituted an unacceptable infringement of sovereignty. Baghdad expressed its hope that this step would lead to the immediate lifting of sanctions.

• In October 1994, the regime threatened to end cooperation with the UN and moved forces to the Kuwaiti border after dashed expectations of a positive UNSCOM report in September. Baghdad defused the crisis by agreeing to recognize the Kuwait border ██████████████

By the summer of 1995, international will to sustain sanctions and inspections was dwindling ████████ and an emboldened Iraq in June had issued an ultimatum to the UN to lift sanctions ████████

Turning Point - August 1995: Iraq 'Scared (Mostly) Straight ▮▮

Iraq's reaction to the defection of Husayn Kamil - a former Minister of Industry and Military Industrialization, Minister of Defense, and Minister of Oil, among other positions - in August 1995 appears to be the key turning point in Iraq's decision to cooperate more with inspections, but it also strengthened the West's perception of Iraq as a successful and efficient deceiver. Clumsy but genuine Iraqi moves toward transparency - significant alterations to their "cheat and retreat" pattern - not only went undetected but instead seemed to confirm that Iraq could and would conceal evidence of proscribed programs. ▮▮▮▮
We had previously assessed that Iraq used Kamil's defection as an opportunity to disclose additional WMD documentation. ▮▮▮▮▮ We now judge that the Iraqis feared that Kamil - a critical figure in Iraq's WMD and D&D activities - would reveal additional undisclosed information. Iraq decided that further widespread deception and attempts to hold onto extensive WMD programs while under UN sanctions was untenable and changed strategic direction by adopting a policy of disclosure and improved cooperation:

- ▮▮▮▮▮ states that Iraq tried to conceal everything from the UN prior to 1992, but after Kamil's 1995 defection he was told to release information to the UN without restrictions ▮▮▮▮
- Iraq's attempts to find face-saving means to reveal previously concealed information and extricate itself from sanctions appeared deceptive and reinforced the idea that it was still hiding important elements of its programs. ▮▮▮▮

Confusion at the Top
Several high-ranking detained Iraqi officials described the chain of events surrounding the defection and the resulting panic. Even the highest levels of leadership were unsure what Kamil could reveal, what WMD information was still retained, and what actions to take. ▮▮▮▮▮▮▮

- ██████████ contained elements of an Iraqi damage assessment, laying out what Kamil knew and might not know, and what was still hidden, all of which Iraq later declared. ████
- Multiple high-level security and government officials affirmed receiving orders to move WMD documents to Kamil's farm, where they were presented to the UN, and Kamil received blame for their concealment. ████████

We now believe the movement of documents to Husayn Kamil's chicken farm and their turnover to the UN represented a genuine attempt to come clean on programs albeit while saving face. Baghdad blamed the previous concealment of aspects of Iraq's WMD programs and the resulting complications with inspectors on an untrustworthy traitor. Captured documentary evidence and interviews support the idea that major concealment operations ended in 1995. Iraqis publicly continued to attribute all WMD and concealment activity to Husayn Kamil – a trend that continued even after the fall of the regime.

Officials Recount Chaotic Document Movements

████████ *officials provided first-hand accounts of the confusion and competing orders, and they admitted their roles in the movement, destruction, concealment, and deliberate misrepresentation of the nature of the cache of documents:*

██

██

Iraq's firmly established "cheat and retreat" pattern made it difficult for UN inspectors and Western analysts to accept new Iraqi assertions at face value, especially when there was evidence at the time that the chicken farm documents were placed there by the regime after the defection. ████████████████████

██

██

Proven Deception Underscores Analytic Mindset

Iraqi revelations after Husayn Kamil's flight to Jordan led to an irrevocable loss of trust by the West. Iraq was again judged dishonest and deceptive in its dealings with the UN and determined to retain WMD capabilities. The new declarations ███████████ effectively sidelined previous attempts to accurately account for material balances of CW agent production and weaponization:

- Some of the information revealed in 1995, such as a more extensive weaponization effort for BW aerial bombs, missile warheads, and spray tanks, was not previously suspected and surprised the UN, provoking deep suspicion of future Iraqi behaviors and declarations.
- The defection exposed the previously unknown 1991 crash program to develop nuclear weapons, ████████████████

The 1995 events reinforced the prevailing analytical paradigm that the Iraqis had been successful in hiding evidence of significant WMD programs, proved that they had not intended to cooperate with the UN, and would only reveal or dismantle programs after being caught in a lie. Iraq attained the veneer of competence as a D&D practitioner, and future activities were viewed through the prism:

- The turnover of an incomplete set of documents, rather than being viewed as a sign of Iraqi cooperation, opened new issues for UNSCOM and the IAEA to investigate.
- Instead of helping close the books on Iraqi WMD programs, Iraq's actions reinvigorated the hunt for concealed WMD _____

Mutual Suspicion Grows: 1996-98 _____

After the revelations following the defection, UNSCOM began a series of inspections of Iraq's security apparatus and concealment mechanisms. Iraq viewed this new investigation as proof that WMD was being used as

a pretense to bring about regime change. ████████████
███████████████████████████ ██████████████████
passage of the Iraq Liberation Act by the US Congress
enhanced Iraqi suspicions. Iraq also accepted UNSCR
986 (Oil-For-Food), which led to growing external trade and decreased international isolation, as
well as an increased Iraqi willingness to push back
against inspections. A series of standoffs with the
UN over inspections culminated in Operation Desert
Fox in December 1998 and the expulsion of the inspectors. ███████████

Concerns About Never-Ending Inspections and US, UN Motives

After 1995, Iraqi leaders solidified their belief
that inspections would not end and sanctions would
not be lifted, especially when Iraq's new disclosures did not lead to any relief of restrictions.
Iraq's focus turned to protecting its technological
infrastructure.

███████████████████ the highest level of Iraqi command
believed that the US ██████ knew that Iraq's programs
were dormant, it could account for some of Iraq's
subsequent behaviors:

- It is possible that Baghdad decided to pursue
  a more aggressive strategy toward inspections,
  convinced that Washington lacked the proof to
  convince the rest of the world.
- ██████████████████████████ believed" that the
  United States thought that Iraq had nothing
  ██████ Enough officials recounted this story to
  suggest that Iraq understood it to be true, and
  ███████████████

Many officials expressed the belief that the inspectors wanted to prolong their high UN salaries and did
not want to resolve technical issues. Such exchanges
support idea that the Iraqi regime did not understand the West's position on weapons and sanctions,
and they sought other reasons to explain continued
inspections:

- ███████████████ believed that Iraq would never get a clean bill of health from the UN ██████ This was one factor that prompted them to cease cooperation with the UN in August 1998.
- After the fall of the regime ██████████ expressed surprise when a former US inspector came into the room to try to resolve old material balance issues, because they felt it had been a ruse for US policy goals and not a legitimate concern. ████████████ told debriefers that certain UN inspectors did not want to solve any problems because they were making salaries "100 times higher" than their families back home.

Saddam Resented Inspections, Distrusted Motives. Available reporting suggests that Saddam resented the inspections and thought they infringed upon Iraq's sovereignty and viability. Saddam personally expressed his dissatisfaction with the inspection process on several occasions:

███████████████████████████████████
███████████████████████████████████

Baghdad's Threat Perception ████████

████████████████████ *Iraqis viewed Iran and Israel, rather than the United States, as the primary threat to the regime. This could explain why Iraq might have continued to give the impression that it was concealing WMD — to instill fear or at least uncertainty in their neighbors:*

- ████████████ *emphatically believed in Iran as Iraq's principal enemy — "past, present, and future," asserting the United States was oceans away and did not have long-term designs on Iraq* ██████

- ████████████████ *said that Iraq did not want to come clean about the final destruction of Scuds following the defection of Husayn Kamil, thinking that belief in retained Scuds would deter Iran from invading* ██████████

444

Inspections Resume With UNMOVIC 2002-03 ███████

By the summer of 2002, it became apparent that Iraq would be willing to accept another round of inspections, this time under the banner of the United Nations Monitoring, Verification and Inspection Commission (UNMOVIC). Iraq again began preparations for active inspections inside its borders.

Leaders Convinced US Would Not Invade

Officials said that the Iraqi leadership in 2002 and 2003 assessed that the United States would not invade Iraq and would at worst institute an air-strike campaign along the lines of Operation Desert Fox:
- ███████████████ Saddam still believed that there would be no war, as the United States had achieved its goal of domination in the Gulf and Red Sea area.
- ███████████████ and said that the leadership believed the United States did not have the forces to invade Iraq, and press reports said that Washington was not willing to sacrifice US lives. ████████

Iraq's Own Actions Compound Problems

Top regime officials have conceded since Operation Iraqi Freedom (OIF) that past Iraqi deception led to suspicion of Iraq's motives. Iraqi leaders, however, did not understand that they would have had to take specific steps with UNMOVIC to overcome perceptions of dishonesty. Several officials reported that they believed that just presenting the truth would be enough to rectify past problems:

- ███████████ puzzlement at the idea that Iraq needed to do something beyond allowing inspectors access to sites to establish trust with the UN.
- ███████████ felt that if the inspections had only been allowed to continue for seven more months in 2003, all outstanding issues would have been resolved, equating successful inspections with the number of sites visited. ████████

Most senior leaders admitted that the UN and United

States could have perceived Iraq's behaviors as suspicious, and offered unprompted examples:

- ███████████████ decisions like Iraq's development of missiles with ranges only 20 or 30 km beyond the allowed 150-km range gave the impression that Iraq was defying the UN.
- ███████████ claimed that even though WMD had been destroyed in 1991, not letting inspectors into palaces aroused suspicions.
- ███████████ whether important information had been concealed. He found that people moved "unimportant things," such as furniture, and felt that "what those stupid people did gave the inspectors the right to suspect all kinds of things. ████████"

Over-Preparation for Inspections

From many accounts, Iraqis tried hard to make sure the final round of UN inspections went smoothly, conducting their own investigations into potential anomalies. ████████████ actions taken by the Iraqi side, however, caused them to continue to give the appearance of deception, especially as Iraq continued to hide some information on lesser points:

- ████████████ official who had hidden missile documents in his house, even though this person had attested to the UN that he had nothing. The investigation concluded that the official had taken the papers to bolster his scientific credentials and to use in a private business. ████████ Iraqi leadership worried that these items would affect the content of its 2002 declaration.
- █████████ 1994 hid documentation related to the consumption and unilateral destruction of Scud propellant because it would show that Iraq had produced its own oxidizer for its Scud-type ballistic missiles before 1991. This contributed to UNSCOM's and UNMOVICs inability to account for Iraq's Scud propellant, a gap that suggested Iraq retained a covert Scud-variant SRBM force ████████

Many high-ranking officials did not want to give the appearance of obstructing the UN, and they tried to ensure smooth cooperation. They ordered working-level Iraqi security officers to cooperate with the UN and not cause problems. Steps were taken to make sure that sites and documentation would endure inspectors' scrutiny, but some of the moves were heavyhanded, and seemed more suspicious to the West. The question of intent is still unclear - senior-level officials insist that their motives were benign, but many of their actions are still ambiguous as to whether cooperation or sanitization was intended:

███████████████████████████████████████

███████████████████████████████████████

Other Factors Reinforce Deceptive Image

Throughout the 1990s and beyond, other ongoing Iraqi activities, policies, and societal norms reinforced UN and international suspicion that Baghdad continued WMD denial and deception. These internal policies and mindsets - especially the importance of regime security - now appear to be even stronger drivers than earlier assessed, and caused the Iraqi leadership to present an aggressive and unrepentant image ████████████

Security State
The Iraqi regime had an extreme distrust of outsiders combined with a fanatical devotion to security that in many cases led to actions that sabotaged efforts to demonstrate that it wanted cooperation. The presence of SSO minders was interpreted as concealment and evasion activity, when their purpose was to warn Saddam of inspections and to handle "sensitive site" inspections as part of their Presidential protection function:

███████████████████████████████████████

Internal Self-Deception

Fear of retribution and delivering bad news meant that the highest levels of leadership might not have known the true limits of Iraq's technical and military capabilities. Iraqi leaders may have made decisions and projected an image of strength on the basis of inaccurate and inflated capabilities:

███

Several people claimed that many Iraqi officials did not believe that they had destroyed all of Iraq's WMD. They may have in good faith conveyed the message to others that Iraq retained WMD:

- ███████████████ many generals were not necessarily aware that Iraq did not have WMD ██████████

Analytic Liabilities (U)

The example of pre-2003 US analysis on Iraq's WMD programs highlights the problem of how to assess ambiguous data in light of past practices. Given Iraq's extensive history of deception and only small changes in outward behavior, analysts did not spend adequate time examining the premise that the Iraqis had undergone a change in their behavior, and that what Iraq was saying by the end of 1995 was, for the most part, accurate. This was combined with the analysts' knowledge that they had underestimated Iraq's programs prior to Operation Desert Storm. A liability of intelligence analysis is that once a party has been proven to be an effective deceiver, that knowledge becomes a heavy factor in the calculations of the analytical observer. In the Iraqi example, this impression was based on a series of undocumented revelations of unilateral destruction combined with unexpected revelations from a high-level, well-placed defector, leading analysts to be more likely predisposed to interpret similar but unrelated behaviors observed after 1996 as proof of continued forbidden activity ██████████████

The Analysts' Retrospective
The concept for this paper was generated by analysts who had worked Iraq WMD and D&D for several years, including many with experience going back to Operation Desert Storm ▮▮▮▮▮▮▮▮▮▮
Several general themes emerged from our investigation:

- *Analysts tended to focus on what was most important to us – the hunt for WMD – and less on what would be most important for a paranoid dictatorship to protect. Viewed through an Iraqi prism, their reputation, their security, their overall technological capabilities, and their status needed to be preserved. Deceptions were perpetrated and detected, but the reasons for those deceptions were misread.*
- *We were surprised to discover just how broken and ineffective the Iraqi regime was.* ▮▮▮▮▮▮▮▮▮
- *Analysts understood that the Iraqis were working with a different logic system, but did not go far enough in accounting for how greatly Iraqi and Western thought differs.* ▮▮▮▮▮▮▮▮

Notes

1. This is taken from the President's Radio Address that accompanied the invasion. Details are available at <https://georgewbush-whitehouse.archives.gov/news/releases/2003/03/20030322.html> (last accessed 10 January 2020).
2. 'United Nations Weapons Inspectors Report to Security Council on Progress in Disarmament of Iraq', 7 March 2003, <https://www.un.org/press/en/2003/sc7682.doc.htm> (last accessed 10 January 2020).
3. For a good overview see Michael R. Gordon and Bernard E. Trainor, *Cobra II: The Inside Story of the Invasion and Occupation of Iraq* (New York: Pantheon, 2006).
4. For example, *The Commission on the Intelligence Capabilities of the United States Regarding Weapons of Mass Destruction, Report to the President of the United States, March 31, 2005* (Washington, DC: CIA, 2005). Also Bob Drogin, *Curveball: Spies, Lies and the Man Behind Them – The Real Reason America Went to War in Iraq* (London: Ebury Press, 2008).
5. For example, see R. Jervis, 'Reports: Politics and Intelligence Failures: The Case of Iraq', *Journal of Strategic Studies*, 29.1 (2006), pp. 3–52; James Bamford, *A Pretext for War: 9/11, Iraq, and the Abuse of America's Intelligence Agencies* (London: Anchor, 2005); A. Glees and P. H. J. Davies, 'Intelligence, Iraq and

the Limits of Legislative Accountability During Political Crisis', *Intelligence and National Security*, 21.5 (2006), pp. 848–83.

6. James A. Goodchild, *Most Enigmatic War: R. V. Jones and the Genesis of British Scientific Intelligence, 1939–45* (London: Helion and Company, 2017).

7. Michael S. Goodman, 'Jones' Paradigm: The How, Why, and Wherefore of Scientific Intelligence', *Intelligence and National Security*, 24.2 (2009).

8. Sherman Kent, 'A Crucial Estimate Relived', *Studies in Intelligence*, 36.5 (Spring 1964), pp. 111–19, <https://www.cia.gov/library/center-for-the-study-of-intelligence/csi-publications/books-and-monographs/sherman-kent-and-the-board-of-national-estimates-collected-essays/9crucial.html> (last accessed 10 January 2020).

9. 'Misreading Intentions: Iraq's Reaction to Inspections Created Picture of Deception', 5 January 2006, <https://nsarchive2.gwu.edu/news/20120905/CIA-Iraq.pdf> (last accessed 10 January 2020).

10. The document was initially obtained by the National Security Archive and the phrase belongs to it; <https://nsarchive2.gwu.edu/news/20120905/> (last accessed 10 January 2020).

11. T. Blanton, 'A Classified CIA Mea Culpa on Iraq', *Foreign Policy*, 5 September 2012, <https://foreignpolicy.com/2012/09/05/a-classified-cia-mea-culpa-on-iraq/> (last accessed 10 January 2020).

12. 'Misreading Intentions: Iraq's Reaction to Inspections Created Picture of Deception'.

13. K. M. Pollack, 'Spies, Lies and Weapons: What Went Wrong', *The Atlantic Monthly*, 293.1 (2004), pp. 78–92.

14. 'Misreading Intentions: Iraq's Reaction to Inspections Created Picture of Deception'.

15. For more, see Robert Jervis, *Why Intelligence Fails: Lessons from the Iranian Revolution and the Iraq War* (Ithaca: Cornell University Press, 2011).

22 The Terrorist Hunters Become Political Quarry: The CIA and Rendition, Detention and Interrogation

After the national trauma of the attacks of September 11th, 2001, there was alarm in the intelligence community that al-Qa'ida was not done terrorising Americans with high-profile mass-casualty attacks in the homeland. In response, CIA requested that the George W. Bush administration provide it with expanded funding and authorities, in a focused mission to prevent follow-on attacks. As former Director of the National Clandestine Service (D/NCS) Jose Rodriguez memorably phrased the request: 'We needed to get everybody in government to put their big boy pants on and provide the authorities that we needed.'[1] With smoke still billowing from lower Manhattan, the Bush administration was eager to oblige. In time, however, as this chapter will explore, the authorities granted to CIA – or CIA's interpretation and exercise of those authorities – would stretch CIA's relations with its political masters to the breaking point.

After the post-Cold War malaise, CIA had a new mission – one it would follow relentlessly – and a mandate to find the masterminds of 9/11 'dead or alive', as President Bush put it. CIA wasted no time in retooling for a new fight. Working with military, interagency and law enforcement partners, CIA foiled several post-9/11 attacks by collecting, analysing and disseminating threat intelligence.[2] Beyond refocusing on interagency partnerships with other elements of the US government, CIA also worked jointly with international partners, some of whom it had theretofore been unwilling to have deeper liaison relations with given other concerns, such as their human rights records. These 'nontraditional liaison partners' provided capabilities, resources and access to people and places that CIA did not have before 9/11, but also came with moral hazard that would prove difficult to navigate in practical and political terms.[3]

To say that 9/11 changed the agency would be an understatement. As voiced by Cofer Black, a well-regarded career agency officer who served as Chief of the DCI Counterterrorist Center (C/CTC) between 1999 and 2002, 'there was before 9/11 and after 9/11'.[4] Indeed, the agency was placed on a war footing, and that meant new partners, new technologies (such as drones armed with precision missiles) and new rules for how to deal with what then-Defense Secretary Donald Rumsfeld called 'the worst of the worst' terrorists. These included indefinite detention at Guantanamo Bay Naval Base, Cuba, as well as other aggressive CIA activities – unapologetically termed 'hard measures' by Jose Rodriguez[5] – such as 'extraordinary renditions' and 'enhanced interrogation techniques' (EITs), which were added to the CIA playbook under the collective nomenclature of Rendition, Detention and Interrogation (RDI).[6] If the CIA was accused of being risk-averse[7] in the lead up to 9/11, agency leaders, especially those charged with counterterrorism operations, were willing, in Cofer Black's words, to 'take the gloves off'[8] to prevent another 9/11 – which, as CIA was reminded by academics, pundits and politicians, was an 'intelligence failure'[9] only matched in scale by the Japanese surprise attack on Pearl Harbor.

Taking the gloves off, to CIA, meant aggressively pursuing al-Qa'ida as far the law allowed and using the authorities granted by the Department of Justice 'to the edge' of the playing field, while still remaining in bounds (to use General Michael Hayden's metaphor).[10] As CIA began to systematically dismantle central or 'core' al-Qa'ida, questions about how best to interrogate captured senior al-Qa'ida operational figures – and where best to do this – quickly came to the fore.

At so-called 'black sites'[11] – secret prisons hidden from the press, the public and even other governmental arms – certain high-value detainees were subject to enhanced interrogation techniques, the most notorious of which was the simulated drowning known as waterboarding. Zayn al-Abidin Muhammed Hussein (*nom de guerre* Abu Zubaydah), a close associate of Usama bin Ladin, was captured in March 2002. He already had a reputation as one of al-Qa'ida's most lethal terrorists due to his involvement in the simultaneous 1998 US Embassy bombings in East Africa that had left over 200 people dead, including several US diplomats and CIA officers. Once in captivity, Zubaydah was reportedly uncooperative and was therefore subjected to waterboarding, as would be the 9/11 mastermind, Khalid Shaykh Muhammad (KSM), sparking the greatest accusations of moral turpitude since the agency's reckoning with its 'family jewels' in the 1970s.

Even in the context of these authorised measures, at times those conducting the interrogations exceeded even the wide legal berth extended by the Department of Justice. There were episodes in which interrogators went beyond waterboarding, using the whirring of live power drills and brandishing of (unloaded) firearms as threats against detainee Abd al-Rahim al-Nashiri, the mastermind of the suicide attack on the destroyer USS *Cole* that killed 17 US sailors on 12 October 2000 in the port of Aden, Yemen. CIA did not condone practices that exceeded the legal authorities. 'The

CIA in no way endorsed behaviour – no matter how infrequent – that went beyond formal guidance,' explained a spokesman.[12] In a declassified but heavily redacted eighteen-page memo issued by the Department of Justice's [DOJ] Office of Legal Counsel on 1 August 2002 regarding the interpretation of laws forbidding torture, Assistant Attorney General Jay S. Bybee seemed to make a legal distinction between mental and physical anguish with respect to what might be permitted during interrogation, explaining: 'we will consider physical pain and mental pain separately'.[13] Still, some observers saw little fundamental difference between authorised mock drowning and forbidden mock executions.

Even within CIA there was a forceful exchange of views on the necessity of EITs on Nashiri in particular, and whether such measures would eventually be counterproductive. In the first chapter reference document, a draft 'Immediate' precedence cable entitled 'Concerns over revised interrogation plan for Nashiri', a CIA staff officer provided the following guidance to a field station, likely a black site:

> We have serious reservations with the continued use of enhanced techniques with Nashiri (Subject) and its long term impact on him. Subject has been held for three months in very difficult conditions, both physically and mentally. It is the assessment of prior interrogators that Nashiri has been mainly truthful and is not withholding significant information. To continue to use enhanced technique without clear indications that he [is] withholding important info is excessive and may cause him to cease cooperation on any level. Subject may come to the conclusion that whether he cooperates or not, he will continually be subjected to enhanced techniques, therefore, what is the incentive for continued cooperation[?] Also, [experts] believe continued enhanced methods may push subject over the edge psychologically.[14]

It is unclear whether this cable was ever formally released, as it appears from the declassified but redacted record that the author emailed the draft cable to a colleague (possibly legal counsel), commenting, 'Below is a cable that I drafted which I don't expect to go anywhere but I want it entered for the record.'[15] It was thus clear even by January 2003 that CIA personnel were rejecting a one-size-fits-all approach to even the most loathsome detainees.

Over time, however, the feeling of a national emergency subsided; the American public regained a feeling of security, at least on American soil, and the political winds eventually shifted. Nearly a decade removed from 9/11, Congress sought to investigate CIA activities on what Vice President Dick Cheney ominously termed 'the dark side'.[16] Almost impossible to foresee in the immediate aftermath of 9/11, critics of CIA's post-9/11 counterterrorism programmes ascended the moral high ground, and such harsh measures appeared increasingly unjustified years hence. The Senate Select Committee on Intelligence (SSCI) seized the moment and undertook a multi-year-long review of CIA's activities. The SSCI staffers were granted access to millions of pages of CIA records relating to the rendition, detention and interrogation programme. From this immense document source pool, they drafted a classified 6,700-page report. Of those, 528 pages were selected for declassification and public release as the executive summary.

On 9 December 2014, the SSCI released its several-hundred-page 'Committee Study of the Central Intelligence Agency's Detention and Interrogation Program' (popularly known in the media as the 'CIA torture report').[17] Hoping to draw a line under such unpleasant activities, President Barack Obama heralded the release of the report: 'I hope that today's report can help us leave these techniques where they belong – in the past.'[18] According to Obama administration White House spokesman Josh Earnest, 'The president believes that on principle, it's important to release that report, so that people around the world and people here at home understand exactly what transpired.'[19] As would become clear, CIA felt thrown under the bus. And indeed, it was a curious argument to suggest that the government itself was unable to abandon such methods independently without global publicity, but transparency and accountability were in the wind.

Senator Dianne Feinstein wrote in the foreword to the Executive Summary, 'As the Chairman of the Committee since 2009, I write to offer some additional views, context, and history.' Feinstein went on to state her horror at the national trauma that occurred on 9/11 and acknowledged, 'it is against that backdrop . . . that the events described in this report were undertaken'. She concluded, 'It is easy to forget the context in which the program began.'[20] This was certainly true, as many Americans had already done so, and younger citizens had no memory of 9/11. Still, if it was charitable of her to offer this context in the foreword, she hastened to add that context could not excuse the programmes, concluding they were 'a stain on our values and our history'.[21]

In the initial phases of the investigation, senior agency officials responded with equanimity, reassuring junior colleagues that it was customary to occasionally expiate the sins of the CIA through public flailing reminiscent of the Church and Pike Committees of the mid-1970s, and there was nothing but to bear it. As the lopsided conclusions became evident, however, senior officials from retired and active ranks broke with historical precedent to condemn them.

The SSCI report was more than accusatory in tone – it literally accused CIA of wrongdoing. Not simply an accounting of CIA's post-9/11 counterterrorism practices, it was an indictment. Not merely a catalogue of sins – like the 'family jewels' from the previous CIA reckoning with ethics and oversight – the SSCI report set out a thesis that, in CIA's view, used selective evidence (and wilfully neglected collection of other evidence) to bolster its core proposition: principally, that the techniques used by CIA had no meaningful intelligence gains, thus debunking CIA's claims to the contrary. At a time when, perhaps, controlling the narrative had never been more important, the SSCI report moved beyond a chronicle of alleged abuses to weaving those abuses into a larger narrative, depicting an out-of-control and deceitful intelligence community. When CIA officials vigorously protested that the agency was neither deceitful in misleading Congress nor avoiding oversight, going so far as to release documents showing dates and content of oversight briefings to congressional leaders as evidence,[22] House Speaker Nancy Pelosi replied that CIA lies to Congress 'all the time'.[23] The atmosphere had become toxic, and it was unclear how to bridge the lack of trust between the overseers and the overseen. The SSCI majority report implied malice that the CIA had intentionally withheld information, and on this point the CIA could not budge. The agency admitted that it could have done more and briefings at times should have been more complete, but the CIA argued that it had acted in good faith.

The report split the SSCI membership along party lines, with the Republican minority writing separately from the Democratic majority – a symptom of the polarisation and politicisation that had finally come to affect the last bastions of bipartisanship in American politics. The Republican SSCI minority observed that the research process and product would impress any historian, but the historical interpretation of that evidence was wrong:

> The Study has all the appearances of an authoritative history of CIA's [Rendition, Detention and Interrogation] effort. As Chairman Feinstein announced to the press the day it was approved by the Committee, its authors had access to 6 million pages of records – most provided by CIA – and they cite more than 35,000 footnotes. However, although the Study contains an impressive amount of detail, it fails in significant and consequential ways to correctly portray and analyze that detail. Simply put, the Study tells part of the story of CIA's experience with RDI, but there are too many flaws for it to stand as the official record of the program.[24]

The report not only cleaved the SSCI in two, it also split the overseers from the overseen and caused a nasty public spat between then-CIA Director John Brennan and SSCI Chair Feinstein. This was perhaps the most public – and most personal – disagreement between a CIA Director (or DCI) and a Senator since the agency's founding in 1947.

Predictably, the spat between CIA and the SSCI majority emerged onto the pages of newspapers, blogs and the Twittersphere, with (mostly former) CIA officers accusing the SSCI of wilful ignorance and selection bias and the SSCI accusing CIA leadership of not having actually read their report. In an unprecedented move in CIA's history, former senior CIA officials struck back publicly at the report's conclusions using social media by establishing a website (www.ciasavedlives.com) where their side of the story was told. If the 'gloves came off' initially in CIA's counterterrorism operations in pursuit of American national security, it remained a bare-knuckled brawl in defence of both institutional and personal reputations.

Former agency officials, such as former CTC chief Robert Grenier, reacted with some of the most strongly worded public editorials that have ever emanated from those who spent their lives in the shadows. For instance, Grenier vociferously alleged: 'Senator Feinstein and her minions on the committee have produced a set of conclusions which reflect a blatant carica-ture of reality' and concluded that the report's findings were 'cartoonish'.[25] Even before the findings were released, Senators Feinstein and Rockefeller wrote an opinion piece in the *Washington Post* in which they argued: 'The full committee was not briefed on the CIA's detention and interrogation program until September 2006 – more than four years after the program had begun.'[26] Grenier called such an assertion 'studied mendacity', turning on the senators' use of the word 'full' – because in operations of 'extraor-dinary sensitivity', CIA can, under provisions of the National Security Act, brief 'the Gang of Eight' (congressional leadership plus intelligence com-mittee chairs and vice chairs), which was done in 2002.[27] Not satisfied with using only a website to counter the 2014 report, a year later eight former senior CIA officials published a book to rebut the SSCI majority's view.[28] The battle over the narrative was waged as publicly as the black sites had been private, with both sides asking the American people to umpire this sorry state of affairs.

Retired former directors and senior officers were not the only ones to enter the political fracas. In response to what was perceived in Langley as an unfair and out-of-context hit job on the agency, the CIA, under Brennan's hand, released its own 136-page 'CIA Comments on the Senate Select Committee on Intelligence Report on the Rendition, Detention, and Interrogation Program', taking issue with the central tenets of the SSCI report. CIA maintained that such programmes did yield critical intelligence that thwarted terrorist plots and led to the capture of other high-value targets. As Director Brennan averred in a public statement on the same day that the SSCI report was released, 'Our review indicates that interrogations of detainees on whom EITs were used did produce intelligence that helped thwart attack plans, capture terrorists, and save lives. The intelligence gained from the program was critical to our understanding of al-Qa'ida and continues to inform our counterterrorism efforts to this day.'[29] The staunch official response to the report offered by CIA, reproduced as chapter reference document 2, was a strong indicator that these matters remained far from settled, and probably never would be. As Director Brennan suggests in the chapter reference document, some of the conclusions about the efficacy of harsh interrogation methods were 'unknowable'. As it would be a counterfactual to posit whether such information could have been gleaned through other methods, the CIA did not speculate on this possibility. While defensive in tone, the CIA rebuttal included a number of statements that were critical of its operations. For instance, it was clear that the CIA – an agency skilled in the elicitation and debriefing of intelligence – had strayed from its core competencies and did not have the expertise to run such programmes. The agency subsequently admitted mistakes in this regard.

If CIA acknowledged sins of commission, John Rizzo, CIA's former acting general counsel and the person perhaps most closely identified with CIA's legal basis for EITs, identified a sin of omission that he continued to rue in his memoir, writing that only briefing the Gang of Eight instead of the full committees on the EITs was 'one of the biggest strategic blunders' of the time.[30] Rizzo judged that CIA leaders (and the White House to a degree), were

> naïve to expect that a handful of politicians would remain stalwart forever after being forced to sit and listen to the dicey and disagreeable details of the EIT program in sporadic, off the record sessions. The decision in 2002 to limit congressional knowledge of the EITs to the Gang of 8 and to stick to that position for four long years – as the prevailing political winds were increasingly howling in the other direction – was foolish and feckless. For our part, we in the CIA leadership should have insisted at the outset that all members of the intelligence committees be apprised of all the gory details all along the way, on the record in closed congressional proceedings. To allow all of our congressional overseers – to compel them, really – to take a stand and either endorse the program or stop it in its tracks.[31]

Finally, one politician did. President Obama formally ended the CIA's interrogation programme via Executive Order 13491 in 2009, although CIA had terminated its use of enhanced interrogation techniques by 2007. CIA was restricted to interrogation techniques authorised by the US Army Field Manual, and was no longer authorised to operate detention facilities.

The question of efficacy is raised throughout the SSCI report, and has been argued vociferously on both sides, by both former CIA senior officials and former administration officials on one hand, and with equal passion by the SSCI majority and human rights activists. The question of whether the measures identified in the SSCI report amount to torture is beyond the scope of this chapter, save simply to mention that language has meaning and word choices can colour the interpretation of the past. The question of whether such measures were warranted and whether they were effective are difficult ones as well. Ultimately very few people truly know the answer to these questions, and the extent to which they are knowable is also debatable. Were such measures warranted? Perhaps, and perhaps not, but the importance of context cannot be overstated.

One way to gain greater context would include oral accounts of those who were involved in the programme. Such testimonies are often the key to unlocking meaningful interpretation from troves of documents. In this saga, the SSCI majority did not interview any of the key players involved, a point repeatedly made by those whose reputations fare the worst in the report. The SSCI staffers argued that they were legally barred from interviewing responsible CIA officers, a claim that those CIA officers rejected. In the words of Robert Grenier:

> Some of my former colleagues have expressed genuine wonderment as to why neither they nor any of their currently-serving colleagues were interviewed as part of the Senate study. The lame explanation from Senator Feinstein is that, in view of the criminal investigation ongoing at the time, CIA persons' testimony could not be compelled. But in many, and perhaps most cases, no compulsion was necessary. Many of my former colleagues, myself included, would have been more than happy to testify, legal jeopardy or not. Again, we were not invited.[32]

The historian may not be best placed to interpret the legal complexities of whether or not several senior officials could have been interviewed, but hundreds of other working-level case officers, collection managers, staff operations officers, medical personnel and analysts were privy to the interview techniques and their product. Interviews with them, perhaps anonymously or in exchange for legal protections, would have added important texture to the report. The senior CIA officers who were not legally available for interviews, in the SSCI majority's view, were not the ones collecting, disseminating or fusing the intelligence product into all-source analysis. They were not the analysts in the Directorate of Intelligence trying to make sense of these intelligence reports or trying to fit them into other finished intelligence reports or other operations leads. Senior managers aside, the working-level officers involved would have had a substantial oral history contribution to make to this report, and this was a key oversight by oversight officials. Moreover, and curiously for such a report, there were no recommendations for improvement or changes.

Although Senator Feinstein stated in 2014: 'History will judge us by our commitment to a just society governed by law and the willingness to face an ugly truth and say "never again" ',[33] only two years later, during a campaign event in February 2016, then-presidential candidate Donald Trump argued that 'torture works', doubling down on an earlier promise: 'I would absolutely authorize something beyond waterboarding.'[34] Former DCIA Michael Hayden replied that if Trump wanted somebody waterboarded, he should 'bring his own bucket'.[35] Notably, Hayden was not rejecting so-called 'enhanced interrogation' methods, but instead recalling that criminal probes for actions that had been deemed legal during a preceding administration had had a chilling effect on CIA officers, who saw what happened when the political winds changed. As Hayden referenced, the continuing odyssey of legal jeopardy for CIA officers was one of the most significant aspects of the fallout from the investigation of the RDI programme.

The debate about whether CIA acted legally seems to have been settled with an acknowledgment, however grudging, that CIA's actions with respect to the RDI programme were legal. However, the public political debate about whether the agency's actions were moral remained contentious, and it was reignited in May 2018 when President Trump nominated Acting DCIA Gina Haspel for the top job. During her public Senate confirmation hearing to be CIA Director, she stated that CIA had acted legally, but senators grilled her about whether CIA had acted morally. She argued that she had a firm moral compass and would never return the agency to those times, but she would not disavow what had happened in the aftermath of 9/11.

Ultimately, the RDI programme was a problematic policy decision that CIA carried out imperfectly, but the characterisation of CIA officials as deceitful sadists was unjustified. As the draft cable over the Nashiri interrogation plan showed, CIA's application of EITs was not wanton, and officials were trying to honourably play a rotten hand. If not illegal, the application of EITs in the early years of the war on terrorism may have been unwise; but it may have saved lives, too. Readers can judge for themselves whether the CIA or the SSCI majority won the battle over the political narrative. As John Brennan said, the net result of the programme may be unknowable with respect to CIA's corporate work product, but as Hayden observed, no longer would any CIA officer jeopardise his or her own freedom undertaking 'hard measures' following the sordid history of the detention programme. Perhaps that is a good thing, but all Americans will have to live with those consequences. It seems likely that this debate will resurface with renewed acrimony should America ever suffer another attack similar to 9/11. Such an event, like many aspects of this chapter, may be unknowable – but it is certain that CIA will keep the SSCI report in its institutional memory, and it will shape CIA's relations with its political masters for generations to come.

                                                           █████████

                                                  22 January 2003

MEMORANDUM FOR: ██████████

FROM: ██████████

OFFICE: ██████████

SUBJECT: CONCERNS OVER REVISED INTERROGATION PLAN FOR NASHIRI

REFERENCE: ████████████ Below is a cable that I drafted which I don't expect to go anywhere but I want it entered for the record. ██████████

Originator	Previous Reviewer(s)	Current Reviewer	Future Reviewer(s)
████████ →	████████ →	████████ →	████████

STAFF

TO: IMMEDIATE ██████████

FROM: ██████████

SUBJECT: CONCERNS OVER REVISED INTERROGATION PLAN FOR NASHIRI

REF: ██████████

TEXT:

1. ACTION REQUIRED: NONE, FYI.

2. APPRECIATE REF DETAILED INTERROGATION PLAN FOR NASHIRI, HOWEVER, WE HAVE SERIOUS RESERVATIONS WITH THE CONTINUED USE OF ENHANCED TECHNIQUES WITH NASHIRI (SUBJECT) AND ITS LONG TERM IMPACT ON HIM. SUBJECT HAS BEEN HELD FOR THREE MONTHS IN VERY DIFFICULT CONDITIONS, BOTH PHYSICALLY AND MENTALLY. IT IS THE ASSESSMENT OF PRIOR INTERROGATORS THAT NASHIRI HAS BEEN MAINLY TRUTHFUL AND IS NOT WITHHOLDING SIGNIFICANT INFORMATION. TO CONTINUE TO USE ENHANCED TECHNIQUE WITHOUT CLEAR INDICATIONS THAT HE WITHOLDING IMPORTANT INFO IS EXCESSIVE AND MAY CAUSE HIM TO CEASE COOPERATION ON ANY LEVEL. SUBJECT MAY COME TO THE CONCLUSION THAT WHETHER HE COOPERATES OR NOT, HE WILL CONTINUALLY BE SUBJECTED TO ENHANCED TECHNIQUES, THEREFORE, WHAT

IS THE INCENTIVE FOR CONTINUED COOPERATION. ALSO, BOTH C/CTC/RG AND HVT INTERROGATOR ███████ WHO DEPARTED ███████ IN ███████ JANUARY, BELIEVE CONTINUED ENHANCED METHODS MAY PUSH SUBJECT OVER THE EDGE PSYCHOLOGICALLY.

3. ANOTHER AREA OF CONCERN IS THE USE OF THE PSYCHOLOGIST AS AN INTERROGATOR. THE ROLE OF THE OPS PSYCHOLOGIST IS TO BE A DETACHED OBSERVER AND SERVE AS A CHECK ON THE INTERROGATOR TO PREVENT THE INTERROGATOR FROM ANY UNINTENTIONAL EXCESS OF PRESSURE WHICH MIGHT CAUSE PERMANENT PSYCHOLOGICAL HARM TO THE SUBJECT. THE MEDICAL OFFICER IS ON HAND TO PROVIDE THE SAME PROTECTION FROM PHYSICAL ACTIONS THAT MIGHT HARM THE SUBJECT. THEREFORE, THE MEDICAL OFFICER AND THE PSYCHOLOGIST SHOULD NOT SERVE AS AN INTERROGATOR, WHICH IS A CONFLICT OF RESPONSIBILITY. WE NOTE THAT REF CONTAINS A PSYCHOLOGICAL INTERROGATION ASSESSMENT BY ███████ PSYCHOLOGIST ███████ WHICH IS TO BE CARRIED OUT BY INTERROGATOR ███████ WE HAVE A PROBLEM WITH HIM CONDUCTING BOTH ROLES SIMULTANEOUSLY.

███████

CC:
Sent on 22 January 2003 at 11:25:11 AM

THE DIRECTOR
CENTRAL INTELLIGENCE AGENCY
WASHINGTON, D.C. 20505

27 June 2013

MEMORANDUM FOR: The Honorable Dianne Feinstein
                  The Honorable Saxby Chambliss
SUBJECT: (S) CIA Comments on the Senate
                  Select Committee on Intelligence
                  Report on the Rendition, Detention,
                  and Interrogation Program

Chairman Feinstein,

1. (S) I appreciate the opportunity for the Central intelligence Agency to comment on the Senate Select Committee on Intelligence's Study of the Agency's long-terminated Rendition, Detention,

and Interrogation Program (hereafter referred
to as the "Study"). As I noted during my confirmation hearing and in subsequent discussions
with you and with Committee members, the lengthy
Study deserved careful review by the Agency in
light of the significance and sensitivity of
the subject matter and, of particular concern,
the serious charges made.in the Study about the
Agency's performance and record.

2. (S) As you know, one of the President's first
acts in office more than four years ago was to
sign Executive Order 13491, which brought to
an end the program that is the subject of the
Committee's work. In particular, the President
directed that the CIA no longer operate detention
facilities and banned the use of all interrogation techniques not in the Army Field Manual.
Thus, before getting into the substance of the
CIA's review of the Study, I want to reaffirm
what I said during my confirmation hearing: I
agree with the President's decision, and, while
I am the Director of the CIA, this program will
not under any circumstances be reinitiated. I
personally remain firm in my belief that enhanced
interrogation techniques are not an appropriate
method to obtain intelligence and that their use
impairs our ability to continue to play a leadership role in the world.

3. (S) Nevertheless, as Director of the CIA, it
is not my role to engage in a debate about
the appropriateness of the decisions that were
made in a previous Administration to conduct a
detention and enhanced interrogation program of
suspected terrorists following the attacks on 11
September 2001. Rather, it is my responsibility to review the performance of the CIA with
regard to the program and to take whatever steps
necessary to strengthen the conduct as well as
the institutional oversight of CIA covert action
programs. This is the perspective I took when
reviewing CIA's comments on the Study.

4. (S) The CIA's comments on the Study were the

result of a comprehensive and thorough review of the Study's 20 conclusions and 20 case studies. In fulfilling my pledge to you, I want you to have the full benefit of the overall findings and recommendations of the Agency review team (TAB A) as well as the team's analysis of each of the Study's 20 conclusions and 20 case studies (TABS B and C, respectively). I strongly encourage you as well as all Committee Members and Staff to read the entirety of the Agency's comments.

5. (S) I have carefully reviewed and concur with the Agency's comments, which I would like to summarize briefly. First of all, we agree with a number of the Study's conclusions. In particular, we agree that the Agency:

- Was unprepared and lacked core competencies to respond effectively to the decision made in the aftermath of the 9/11 attacks that the Agency undertake what would be an unprecedented program of detaining and interrogating suspected Al Qa'ida and affiliated terrorists. This lack of preparation and competencies resulted in significant lapses in the Agency's ability to develop and monitor its initial detention and interrogation activities. These initial lapses, most of which were corrected by 2003 and have been the subject of multiple internal and external investigations, were the result of a failure of management at multiple levels, albeit at a time when CIA management was stretched to the limit as the CIA led the U.S. Government's counterterrorism response to the 9/11 attacks against the Homeland;
- Struggled to formulate and gain policy approval for a viable plan to move detainees out of Agency-run detention facilities;
- Failed to perform a comprehensive and independent analysis on the effectiveness of enhanced interrogation techniques;
- Allowed a conflict of interest to exist wherein the contractors who helped design and employ

463

the enhanced interrogation techniques also were involved in assessing the fitness of detainees to be subjected to such techniques and the effectiveness of those same techniques;

- Detained some individuals under a flawed interpretation of the authorities granted to CIA, and;
- Fell short when it came to holding individuals accountable for poor performance and management failures.

6. (S) Notwithstanding the above areas of agreement, there are several areas of disagreement as well. In particular, the Agency disagrees with the Study's unqualified assertions that the overall detention and interrogation program did not produce unique intelligence that led terrorist plots to be disrupted, terrorists to be captured, or lives to be saved. The Study's claims on this score are inconsistent with the factual record, and we provide detailed comments in TAB C on where and why the Study's assertions and representations are wrong.

- The Agency takes no position on whether intelligence obtained from detainees who were subjected to enhanced interrogation techniques could have been obtained through other means or from other individuals. The answer to this question is and will forever remain unknowable.
- After reviewing the Committee Study and the comments of the Agency review team, and as I indicated at the outset of this memorandum, I personally remain firm in my belief that enhanced interrogation techniques are an inappropriate method for obtaining intelligence. Moreover, it is my resolute intention never to allow any Agency officer to participate in any interrogation activity in which enhanced interrogation techniques would be employed.

7. (S) Regarding the Study's claim that the Agency resisted internal and external oversight and deliberately misrepresented the program to Congress, the Executive Branch, the media, and the American people, the factual record maintained by the

Agency does not support such conclusions. In addition, the Study's conclusion regarding CIA's misrepresentations of the program rely heavily on its flawed conclusion regarding the lack of any intelligence that flowed from the program. Nevertheless, we do agree with the Study that there were instances where representations about the program that were used or approved by Agency officers were inaccurate, imprecise, or fell short of Agency tradecraft standards. Those limited number of misrepresentations and instances of imprecision never should have happened.

8. (S) As a result of the Committee's Study and our review, I have approved and the CIA has started to implement eight recommendations made by the Agency review team, which are included in TAB A. It is critically important that the Agency leadership team take immediate steps to prevent any shortcomings in Agency covert action programs, as flawed performance - on the part of the Agency as an institution or by individual Agency officers - can have devastating consequences. In addition, our review team is ready to brief Committee members as well as meet with Committee staff at any time to walk through our comments.

9. (U) I sincerely hope that, as a result of the Committee's work and our subsequent review and comments, we can take steps to enhance the Agency's ability to meet successfully the ever-growing array of intelligence and national security challenges that face our Nation. By learning from the past while focusing on the future, we will be able to best meet our mutual responsibility to protect and advance the national security interests of the American people. As always, I look forward to working with you and the entire Committee on these important matters.

JOHN O. BRENNAN

Notes

1. As quoted in Amy Davidson Sorkin, 'Jose Rodriguez and the Ninety-Two Tapes', *The New Yorker*, 30 April 2012, <https://www.newyorker.com/news/amy-davidson/jose-rodriguez-and-the-ninety-two-tapes> (last accessed 10 January 2020).

2. Jena Baker McNeill, James Jay Carafano and Jessica Zuckerman, '30 Terrorist Plots Foiled: How the System Worked', *Heritage Foundation Backgrounder*, No. 2405, 29 April 2010.

3. Jeremy Scahill, *Dirty Wars: The World is a Battlefield* (New York: Nation Books, 2013), p. 121.

4. Congressional testimony of Cofer Black, 26 September 2002, <https://fas.org/irp/congress/2002_hr/092602black.html> (last accessed 10 January 2020).

5. Jose A. Rodriguez, Jr, *Hard Measures: How Aggressive CIA Actions after 9/11 Saved American Lives* (Threshold Editions: New York, 2012).

6. John Rizzo, *Company Man: Thirty Years of Controversy and Crisis in the CIA* (New York: Scribner, 2014).

7. James Risen, 'Report Faults CIA's Recruitment Rules', *The New York Times*, 18 July 2002, <https://www.nytimes.com/2002/07/18/us/report-faults-cia-s-recruitment-rules.html> (last accessed 10 January 2020).

8. Congressional testimony of Cofer Black, 26 September 2002.

9. Anthony Glees, '9/11: An Intelligence Failure and Its Consequences', London School of Economics blog, 11 September 2011, <http://eprints.lse.ac.uk/81287/1/blogs.lse.ac.uk-911%20an%20intelligence%20failure%20and%20its%20consequences.pdf> (last accessed 10 January 2020).

10. Michael Hayden, *Playing to the Edge: American Intelligence in the Age of Terror* (New York: Penguin Press, 2016).

11. Rizzo, *Company Man*, p. 3.

12. Joby Warrick and R. Jeffrey Smith, 'CIA Used Gun, Drill in Interrogation of Alleged Cole Mastermind', *The Washington Post*, 22 August 2009, <http://www.washingtonpost.com/wp-dyn/content/article/2009/08/22/AR2009082200045.html> (last accessed 10 January 2020).

13. Jay S. Bybee, 'Memorandum for [redacted], Interrogation of [redacted], 1 August 2002.

14. Email [sender redacted] to [recipient redacted] of draft cable 'Concerns over Revised Interrogation Plan for Nashiri', 22 January 2003, declassified 10 June 2016.

15. Ibid.

16. Dick Cheney on 'Meet the Press', 16 September 2001, transcript available at <http://www.washingtonpost.com/wp-srv/nation/specials/attacked/transcripts/cheney091601.html> (last accessed 10 January 2020).

17. Senate Report number 113-288, <https://www.intelligence.senate.gov/sites/default/files/documents/CRPT-113srpt288.pdf>

18. David Jackson, 'Obama Condemns Past Interrogation Techniques', *USA Today*, 9 December 2014.

19. Felicia Schwartz, 'US Takes Security Precautions Overseas Ahead of CIA Report', *Wall Street Journal*, 8 December 2014, <http://www.wsj.com/articles/u-s-takes-security-precautions-overseas-ahead-of-cia-report-1418073261> (last accessed 10 January 2020).

20. Senator Feinstein's foreword is pp. 1–6 of the declassified report, which is available in full at <https://fas.org/irp/congress/2014_rpt/ssci-rdi.pdf> (last accessed 10 January 2020).

21. Ibid.

22. Paul Kane, 'CIA Says Pelosi Was Briefed on Use of "Enhanced Interrogations"', *The Washington Post*, 7 May 2009, <http://voices.washingtonpost.com/capitol-briefing/2009/05/cia_says_pelosi_was_briefed_on.html> (last accessed 10 January 2020).

23. Glenn Thrush, 'Elder Bush: Pelosi "paying a price" for CIA crack', *Politico*, 15 June 2009, <https://www.politico.com/blogs/on-congress/2009/06/elder-bush-pelosi-paying-a-price-for-cia-crack-019098> (last accessed 10 January 2020).

24. 'Minority Views' appendix of the Senate report.

25. Robert Grenier, 'From Truth and Reconciliation to Lies and Obfuscation: The Senate RDI Report', *Huffington Post*, 10 August 2014, <https://www.huffingtonpost.com/robert-l-grenier/senate-rdi-report-lies-obfuscation_b_5663595.html> (last accessed 10 January 2020).

26. Dianne Feinstein and Jay Rockefeller, 'The Senate Report on the CIA's Interrogation Program Should Be Made Public', *The Washington Post*, 10 April 2014, <https://www.washingtonpost.com/opinions/the-senate-report-on-the-cias-interrogation-program-should-be-made-public/2014/04/10/eeeb237a-c0c3-11e3-bcec-b71ee10e9bc3_story.html?utm_term=.71b74c4f33ef> (last accessed 10 January 2020).

27. Rizzo, *Company Man*, p. 200.

28. Bill Harlow (ed.), *Rebuttal: The CIA Responds to the Senate Intelligence Committee's Study of Its Detention and Interrogation Program* (Annapolis: Naval Institute Press, 2015).

29. 'Statement from Director Brennan on the SSCI Study on the Former Detention and Interrogation Program', CIA website: *News & Information*, 9 December 2014, <https://www.cia.gov/news-information/press-releases-statements/2014-press-releases-statements/statement-from-director-brennan-on-ssci-study-on-detention-interrogation-program.html> (last accessed 10 January 2020).

30. Rizzo, *Company Man*, p. 200.

31. Ibid.

32. Grenier, 'From Truth and Reconciliation to Lies and Obfuscation'.

33. As quoted in Mark Mazetti, 'Panel Faults CIA over Brutality and Deceit in Terrorism Interrogations', *The New York Times*, 9 December 2014, <https://www.nytimes.com/2014/12/10/world/senate-intelligence-committee-cia-torture-report.html> (last accessed 10 January 2020).

34. As quoted in Jenna Johnson, 'Donald Trump on waterboarding: "Torture works"', *The Washington Post*, 17 February 2017, <https://www.wash ingtonpost.com/news/post-politics/wp/2016/02/17/donald-trump-on-water boarding-torture-works/> (last accessed 10 January 2020).
35. As quoted in Christopher Woolf, 'Ex-CIA director to Trump: "Bring your own bucket" if you want to waterboard', *Public Radio International*, 29 February 2016.

23 Innovation at the CIA: From Sputnik to Silicon Valley and Venona to Vault 7

On 4 October 1957 the Soviet Union successfully launched its Sputnik satellite into low earth orbit. This achievement of the Soviet space programme was not a surprise to US intelligence officials or policymakers; actually, the CIA had been reporting on it for years.[1] But Sputnik was a wake-up call for US science and engineering nationwide. Foreign scientific and technological developments had constituted a key target set for the CIA since its creation, and while the CIA was keeping tabs, America was not keeping up. It has always been crucial to know what capabilities potential enemies are developing; often, the pressure to gather such intelligence has been the catalyst for the agency's own technological intelligence gathering capacity, from the U-2 to imint satellites to micro listening devices. Today, foreign rocket and aircraft capabilities remain vital collection targets, but the leading edge of scientific and technical intelligence concerns exploiting – and defending against – information technology and code. Innovating in this space is as crucial now as the space race was during the Cold War.[2]

New technologies can be both invaluable and disruptive. The development of high-altitude imint capabilities allowed CIA to gain insights into Soviet 'ground truth' that were unprecedented, allowing it to support US policymakers and war fighters far more effectively than before. The contributions of the U-2 during the Cuban Missile Crisis are a testimony to the value of technological innovation, complemented by high-level humint, for intelligence.[3] But it also proved disruptive, creating new avenues of risk for the agency and US policy, manifested most notably in the fallout from downing Francis Gary Powers' U-2 over Soviet airspace on 1 May 1960,[4] which cast a pall over the Paris summit that month and cancelled Eisenhower's planned visit to Moscow the following month.

The shift to the digital realm has not altered the double-edged sword of technological promise and pitfalls: CIA and the broader US intelligence community have developed significant capability in the cyber domain,[5] but with this come new risks in myriad forms, many more complex and intractable than those faced in the analogue age. Although it may be expected that the National Security Agency might be considered the US intelligence community member most interested and invested in technology, actually CIA's interest in cutting-edge technology should not be surprising: as Jeffrey Richelson has shown, a history of CIA is also a history of innovation.[6] Innovation-driven adaptability has been one of the agency's hallmarks.

The digital revolution has transformed societies as well as their intelligence bureaucracies. It was inevitable that CIA would enter this domain. After all, a key element of remaining a global leader in the craft of intelligence is keeping pace with, and mastering, the potential of disruptive technological developments and the various ways they will impact operations and counter-intelligence vulnerabilities.[7] Such technical vulnerabilities were on full display even before CIA was established, when Soviet code clerks in Washington, DC (and several other capitals) re-used one-time pads to encrypt Soviet diplomatic and intelligence messages before transmitting them to Moscow, allowing successful American cryptanalytical attacks against them. The Venona project, pioneered by the US Army's Signals Intelligence Service (subsequently overtaken by the National Security Agency and joined by CIA as a partner in 1952) collected and decrypted enough messages to begin to unravel the Cambridge spy ring and also revealed the extent of Soviet espionage against the Manhattan Project.[8] Thus, as with the space race and a myriad of other technologies, US intelligence was both a victim and an exploiter of innovation.

This chapter is concerned with CIA's efforts to adapt to, and structure itself for, the information age. This has been an iterative process. In 1963, sixteen years after CIA was established, DCI John McCone created the Directorate of Science and Technology (DS&T) and placed it under the leadership of Albert 'Bud' Wheelon, a physicist with the remit to develop aerial reconnaissance systems. Wheelon incorporated several different existing offices into his new directorate, including computer services and scientific intelligence, providing a central locus for science and technology at CIA.[9] Even before the DS&T was established, however, Joseph Becker, a senior officer in computer services and CIA's leading expert on information storage and retrieval, foresaw that 'Computers and auxiliary machines for the electronic processing of data are emerging as potentially revolutionary intelligence tools to extend and multiply the human skills of the community ... [this] is certain to produce radical changes in the ways intelligence information is collected, transmitted, stored, and utilized.'[10] He was correct.

As Becker predicted, CIA harnessed technology in profound ways that fundamentally changed the way CIA approached its core functions. Over time, CIA moved from developing and deploying 'traditional' stand-off espionage technologies, such as satellite technology or tiny listening devices, and moved into Silicon Valley.[11] It has done so because the intelligence community is now, unlike during the Cold War, not necessarily where the most cutting-edge developments occur. The CIA has calculated that it cannot set the pace of innovation in-house, or even keep up, and therefore has emerged slightly from the shadows to closer partnerships with private sector innovation and expertise. More than this, CIA aimed to harness and direct the innovative power of the US technology industry by providing seed capital for intelligence-specific requirements, the most notable example being CIA's venture capital start-up in Silicon Valley, In-Q-Tel.[12]

In-Q-Tel represents CIA's long-term bet that operationally relevant innovation may best be accomplished through partnerships outside of the traditional government bureaucracy, but that the benefits can, nonetheless, be brought inside for secret application. Established in 1999 as a not-for-profit venture capital firm to provide US intelligence agencies with cutting-edge technology, In-Q-Tel is a combination of the word 'intelligence' and the James Bond character 'Q', who reliably supplied 007 with ingenious gadgets to be deployed at precisely the right operational moment. In-Q-Tel was formed not only in an effort to bridge the gap between the CIA and emerging technology, but also because the CIA faced a significant challenge in data processing; it had an overload of potentially significant data, and did not have the resources or network infrastructure to sift through it efficiently.[13] In-Q-Tel is unique in that the CIA is its only major investor, thereby taxpayer funded at approximately \$120 million per year. Instead of being focused on profit maximisation and return on capital investments, however, it is focused on providing CIA with access to 'cutting edge technology being developed in the private sector'.[14] This represents a new innovation model for the twenty-first century, and a departure from the CIA's standard practices since its inception.

The focus on emerging technological risks and opportunities has left its mark on the architecture of the agency. Separate from the DS&T, since at least May 2004, CIA's Directorate of Operations has had an Information Operations Center (IOC) as a functional centre (equivalent to other DO divisions), the purpose of which was to bring technology to bear on intelligence collection and analysis. As of 2016, it became known as the Center for Cyber Intelligence, under an agency-wide reorganisation (internally referred to as 'modernisation'). Indeed, by 2015, CIA had elevated digital innovation beyond a component part of the Directorate of Operations and, for the first time in fifty years, created a new directorate (versus a division or centre within the Directorate of Operations). The objective of this reorganisation was to bring technology and innovation to the mainstream across operations. Aptly, the fledgling section was named the Directorate for Digital Innovation (DDI) – its abbreviated form, confusingly, previously having referred to the Deputy Director for Intelligence, who has since become the Deputy Director for Analysis – and the magnitude of this change was a clear indication that the digital revolution was now integral to the mission of the agency.

The DDI has been active since 1 October 2015, seeking to 'streamline and integrate digital and cybersecurity capabilities into the CIA's espionage, counter-intelligence, all-source analysis, open-source intelligence collection and covert action operations'.[15] Or, as explained by the CIA's then deputy director David Cohen, to assist the agency's personnel with 'approaching the digital domain in a well-coordinated, determined, and assertive fashion to develop and adopt digital solutions in aspects of our work from collection to analysis and our internal business practices'.[16] Unsurprisingly vague on the particulars of the mission, Cohen's statement clearly underlined the determination of CIA's management that their traditional roles can be supplemented by, occasionally supplanted by, and almost certainly generally augmented by actions undertaken in cyberspace or by exploitation of the open-source record. As this chapter describes, media reports suggest that the CIA has embraced its increasing focus on digital intelligence capabilities and techniques with considerable energy and capacity.

Many discussions of the adaptation and exploitation of digital technologies focus on the potential contributions of open-source intelligence to the national intelligence mission.[17] And, indeed, the World Wide Web has generated significant potential to exploit openly available data. It would be wise to remember that this is neither a new challenge nor a new collection typology. Indeed, since its founding in 1947 CIA has overseen the work of the semi-autonomous Foreign Broadcast Information Service (FBIS), which monitored global media for its customers. In 2005, FBIS became known as the Open Source Center (OSC)[18] and then the Open Source Enterprise (OSE), once it became part of the DDI in 2016.[19] Between name changes, however, one of the most profound worldwide shifts occurred when social media became as important as foreign media.[20] The OSE's mandate now includes 'collecting, analyzing, and disseminating publicly available information of intelligence value on foreign web sites and social media.'[21] Osint may be an age-old discipline, but digital technology facilitates its exploitation in powerful ways.

But to limit the potential of digital innovation to osint would be to think small. The CIA is primarily a humint agency, and in the modern world being effective in humint operations against sophisticated adversaries requires a robust capacity in cyberspace. As one scholar put it: 'The CIA's job, after all, is to collect intelligence, and while its primary purview is human intelligence, hacking systems interacts synergistically with that collection.'[22] It has been frequently observed that the internet has acted as an enabler on a key element of the CIA's core tasks: identifying potential agents. Source identification and targeting is a painstaking process often entailing months of work, but it can be substantially accelerated with the prevalence of social media profiles that freely advertise one's placement and access (often including job responsibilities and security clearances). Initiating contact online can be as effective as it is convenient. Further, the ease of digital communication means that aspects of the recruitment process can take place online, reducing the number of dangerous face-to-face meetings.

Operating in cyberspace is a significant tradecraft advantage when considering denied or dangerous areas that are not cut off from the internet. Likewise, the clandestine handling of recruited agents has benefited from the widespread online penetration of publicly available encryption used by many secure communication platforms.[23] And the digital space not only offers opportunities in terms of remote recruitment and handling. More traditional human assets can, depending on their natural access, exploit adversaries' networks and systems in a number of ways. Agents might fulfil any number of intelligence activities using digital means, such as extracting information from computer or implanting technical tools. With such rapid advancements in espionage technology, the only limits on the range and scope of these collection operations seem to be the access and placement of the agent and the imagination of the case officer, who might employ any number of techniques to produce fruitful human-enabled cyber operations (facilitating digital collection by CIA through means of a human source) or source-driven cyber operations (digital collection done on behalf of CIA by sources recruited for that purpose, either physically or remotely). CIA officials also believe that cyber capabilities will have other uses as well, such as 'penetrating Internet savvy adversaries such as the Islamic State'.[24]

While the hype surrounding cyber capabilities may imply that intelligence has been revolutionised, that would be an overstatement.[25] Cyber espionage will no more replace traditional humint than will cyber operations replace traditional military operations. The future will be characterised by continuity as well as change. Technological innovation adds new capabilities but also new challenges. Considering the matter beyond humint, there are clearly trade-offs to consider in the adoption of digital technology. A significant challenge is information overload. Once information or data is collected it often requires processing to refine the material into intelligence useful to analysts as they create and disseminate products for decision-makers. Vast amounts of data must be parsed, filtered, tagged, archived and made readily accessible to be useful. The sheer volume of collected material can outstrip the capacity of analysts to process it. This problem was grasped by late 1960, when CIA began to consider the wide application of computerised technology to the intelligence business. Joseph Becker articulated areas to be considered for evaluation of machine-enhanced analysis and production. He considered the potential of ingesting large amounts of media that was digitised for increased speed of consumption and process-ing.[26] Becker's recommendation to automate elements of the intelligence cycle to alleviate the labour-hours required by human analysts to sort the data and correlate substantial linkages warranting further scrutiny is on the cusp of realisation.

There is also significant potential regarding data categorisation, moving beyond the traditional scrapers and crawlers that currently scour the web for relevant data. Robert Cardillo, a former Director of the National Geospatial-Intelligence Agency (NGA), suggested that 'bots will perform 75% of the tasks currently being done by employees to analyze and interpret images beamed in from around the globe'.[27] Images, surely, constitute the bread and butter of an imint agency like NGA, but CIA's innovation goals seek to move beyond images and to include the wide swathe of material that risks overwhelming analysts. This would not be possible without applica-tion of artificial intelligence and machine learning. According to Dawn Meyerriecks, Deputy Director for Science and Technology, as of late 2017 CIA was pursuing over 137 separate initiatives related to artificial intelli-gence. Whether these programmes are more accurately described as artificial intelligence or machine learning is unclear, but they certainly vary widely; examples range from 'automatically tagging objects in video (so analysts can pay attention to what's important) to better predicting future events based on big data and correlational evidence'.[28] As with previous technological developments, the digital age is pregnant with potential, but is no panacea.

To build a communications architecture sophisticated and robust enough to handle these heavy data requirements, CIA invested in human capital with the necessary technical expertise required for automation on an agency-wide scale. As outlined by Cohen, 'The DDI will be responsible for a cadre of data scientists who will develop and deploy customised IT tools to help analysts make connections in the data. This will require sophisticated and cutting-edge big data analysis.'[29] There is a certain Orwellian tint as more technology and technologists is viewed as the answer to the problems generated by too much data. The key question remains whether the DDI and any technology it develops will be able to overcome traditional cultural or bureaucratic resistance to information-sharing across the intelligence community, and thus make the technology as effective as its potential.

Digital innovations have the potential to alter core CIA disciplines such as targeting, assessment, recruitment and agent handling on the operational side, and also processing, analysis and dissemination of intelligence for analysts. But they also have the potential to undermine a key element of CIA tradecraft, namely cover. Maintaining the cover of CIA personnel has become more difficult in the digital age; after all, cameras and microphones are ubiquitous. Biometrics are collected at many international border crossings, and databases storing such unique records are increasingly net-worked.[30] Maintaining cover identities is becoming increasingly difficult, as is maintaining anonymity in the digital age.

If maintaining one's cover in reality were not hard enough, it is not difficult to use the internet to delve into someone's digital history (or lack thereof) to challenge a cover legend. Maintaining cover requires evading adversaries' counter-intelligence methods, not just constant scrutiny in reality, but often involving computer forensics. Defeating an adversarial surveillance team has been the gold standard in field tradecraft since CIA's founding, but defeating an algorithm is another challenge. A key element of maintaining a plausible cover story is a sufficiently detailed cyber persona (an identity used to interact online), but the linkages between a cyber persona and physical identity may be discovered through technical means. The discovery of 'digital footprints' may reveal real-world information compromised by the cyber persona.[31] This cyber counter-intelligence aspect of modern humint is a challenge for CIA to master if it is to continue to operate effectively against sophisticated adversaries.

Not limited to field tradecraft, data processing or protecting cover, the issue of cybersecurity pervades everything the agency does. The double-edged sword of computerised networks is enhanced efficiency on the one hand, set against the increased risk posed by vulnerabilities in operating and maintaining an information technology architecture that carries and stores classified national security data on the scale that CIA requires. Maintaining a global architecture of this size requires administrators constantly chal-lenged with maintaining peak efficiency, maximum availability and high levels of security.

The contemporary challenge presented to CIA is much larger than mere information security required to protect its secrets. The agency must be prepared to defend itself against the possibility of cyber-attack from a hostile service. Defending the agency's interests against hostile cyber actors appears to have fallen to the Directorate of Digital Innovation. According to the CIA, 'One of the DDI's key responsibilities is developing the poli-cies, technologies, and protocols to better defend the Agency against these attacks. Its cyber threat analysts work with highly classified intelligence on the plans, intentions, and capabilities of an ever-expanding assortment of malicious cyber actors. These analysts defend our networks, and protect our highly sensitive data from exploitation.'[32] But as recent history has shown, securing the agency's databases, networks and even its tools is no easy task. CIA has not been immune to digital leakage.

While CIA's cyber threat analysts were scanning foreign horizons they fell victim to an insider threat. On 7 March 2017, the self-described transparency website WikiLeaks announced it had obtained a significant portion of the CIA's own computer hacking tools, allegedly from a former CIA employee, and began posting information online about the files, which it called 'Vault 7', according to media reports. As one cybersecurity expert noted, 'there is nothing particularly surprising about an intelligence agency being involved in such surveillance tactics', but the compromise of operational security was staggering: 'someone apparently managed to compromise a Top Secret CIA development environment, exfiltrate a whole host of material, and is now releasing it to the world'.[33] That this insider betrayal happened several years after Army Private Chelsea (then Bradley) Manning and contractor Edward Snowden exfiltrated troves of classified intelligence from across the US intelligence community and defence establishment was shocking, but perhaps not surprising. Even secret institutions are not immune to the danger posed by the ease of transfer and transport of digital materials.

While often silent on scandals swirling around it, in this most serious breach the CIA apparently felt compelled to come to its own defence and place a public statement on its website as reproduced in the chapter reference document, 'CIA Statement on Claims by Wikileaks'. While the CIA would not comment on the authenticity of the documents or any steps it was taking to investigate or remediate the breach, it offered its own full-throated defence of its collection tools and activities. CIA asserted that its mission was to be 'innovative' and 'cutting-edge' in pursuit of American national security, and indeed, the historical record is consistent on that claim, as this chapter has shown. CIA emphasised that its activities are subject to 'rigorous oversight' (a more recent historical development) and any hacking or cyber tools that it may have would not be legally used 'here at home' against 'fellow Americans'. In closing, CIA argued from a counter-intelligence perspective that such leaks not only jeopardised CIA personnel and operations, but also reminded the public that such tools were powerful and that revealing them 'equip[s] our adversaries with tools and information to do us harm'.[34] Perhaps put another way, CIA was arguing that they would be in dereliction of duty in not developing and exploiting such techniques.

It is unclear whether the releases could be reverse-engineered by adversaries to attack American interests or citizens, but it is beyond doubt that the compromise of CIA's tools hurts its operational capabilities by informing potential targets of the vector of attack, enabling them to shore up their own cyber defences. It also echoes earlier narratives that US intelligence is careless with respect to privacy concerns and unaccountable, although that is not in fact the case – certainly when compared to its major adversaries. It does, however, remind potential clandestine agents that CIA has been unable to secure some of its most sensitive data, a message that cannot be reassuring. The critical intelligence that will never be collected from agents who are never recruited due to security concerns is the real enduring damage and cost of such leaks.[35]

When viewed in long-term historical perspective, contemporary innovation at CIA is more evolutionary than revolutionary. These efforts, given renewed vigour under Director Brennan, range from development of nascent technologies in partnership with commercial industry to development of machine learning algorithms that perform complex functions within the intelligence cycle at machine speed. Staffed with a growing number of computer programmers and cyber-threat analysts, nearly every aspect of traditional espionage now encompasses a cyber angle, which creates opportunity and vulnerability simultaneously. With traditional rivals such as China and Russia pursuing cyber initiatives, CIA feels a pressing need to maintain its willingness to develop advanced cyber capabilities that can be exercised independently through remote means or in concert with human intelligence operations in the field. The modern CIA has organised around the proposition that rapid adoption of new technologies keeps the agency at the forefront of spycraft in an increasingly digitised world.

CIA Statement on Claims by Wikileaks
8 March 2017

We have no comment on the authenticity of purported intelligence documents released by Wikileaks or on the status of any investigation into the source of the documents. However, there are several critical points we would like to make.

CIA's mission is to aggressively collect foreign intelligence overseas to protect America from terrorists, hostile nation states and other adversaries. It is CIA's job to be innovative, cutting-edge, and the first line of defense in protecting this country from enemies abroad. America deserves nothing less.

It is also important to note that CIA is legally prohibited from conducting electronic surveillance targeting individuals here at home, including our fellow Americans, and CIA does not do so. CIA's activities are subject to rigorous oversight to ensure that they comply fully with U.S. law and the Constitution.

The American public should be deeply troubled by any Wikileaks disclosure designed to damage the Intelligence Community's ability to protect America against terrorists and other adversaries. Such disclosures not only jeopardize U.S. personnel and operations, but also equip our adversaries with tools and information to do us harm.

Notes

1. Amy Ryan and Gary Keeley, 'Sputnik and US Intelligence: The Warning Record', *Studies in Intelligence*, 61.3 (2017), pp. 1–16.
2. Stephen H. Campbell, 'Intelligence in the Post-Cold War Period: The Impact of Technology', *The Intelligencer*, 20.1 (2013), pp. 57–65.
3. David Gioe, 'Handling HERO: Joint Anglo-American Tradecraft in the Case of Oleg Penkovsky', in David Gioe, Len Scott and Christopher Andrew (eds), *An International History of the Cuban Missile Crisis: A 50-year Retrospective* (Abingdon: Routledge, 2014).
4. Scott Shane, Matthew Rosenberg and Andrew W. Lehren, 'WikiLeaks Releases Trove of Alleged CIA Hacking Documents', *The New York Times*, 7 March 2017, <https://www.nytimes.com/2017/03/07/world/europe/wikileaks-cia-hacking.html> (last accessed 10 January 2020).
5. Sean Lyngaas, 'How (And Why) the CIA Plans to Expand Cyber Capabilities', *Federal Computer Week*, 24 February 2015, <https://fcw.com/articles/2015/02/24/cia-expand-cyber.aspx> (last accessed 10 January 2020).
6. See Jeffrey T. Richelson, *The Wizards of Langley: Inside the CIA's Directorate of Science and Technology* (Boulder, CO: Westview Press, 2001).
7. D. V. Gioe, '"The More Things Change": HUMINT in the Cyber Age', in: R. Dover, H. Dylan and M. Goodman (eds), *The Palgrave Handbook of Security, Risk and Intelligence* (London: Palgrave Macmillan, 2017).
8. John Earl Haynes and Harvey Klehr, *Venona: Decoding Soviet Espionage in America* (New Haven: Yale University Press, 2000).
9. Douglas Martin, 'Albert D. Wheelon, Architect of Aerial Spying, Dies at 84', *The New York Times*, 2 October 2013, <https://www.nytimes.com/2013/10/03/us/albert-d-wheelon-architect-of-aerial-spying-dies-at-84.html> (last accessed 10 January 2020).
10. Joseph Becker, 'The Computer: Capabilities, Prospects and Implications', *Studies in Intelligence*, 4.4 (Fall 1960), p. 63, <https://www.cia.gov/library/center-for-the-study-of-intelligence/kent-csi/vol4no4/html/v04i4a04p_0001.htm> (last accessed 10 January 2020).
11. For a comprehensive review of CIA gadgets and technology, see Robert Wallace, Keith H. Melton and Henry R. Schlesinger (eds), *Spycraft: The Secret*

History of the CIA's Spytechs, from Communism to Al-Qaeda (Basingstoke: Penguin, 2009).

12. Steve Henn, 'In-Q-Tel: The CIA's Tax Funded Player in Silicon Valley', *National Public Radio*, 16 July 2012, <https://www.npr.org/sections/alltechconsidered/2012/07/16/156839153/in-q-tel-the-cias-tax-funded-player-in-silicon-valley> (last accessed 10 January 2020). See also Jason D. Rowley, 'In-Q-Tel: The CIA's VC Arm, Has Had A Busy Few Years', *Mattermark* blog, 1 December 2016, <https://mattermark.com/q-tel-cias-vc-arm-busy-years/> (last accessed 10 January 2020).

13. Henn, 'In-Q-Tel: The CIA's Tax Funded Player in Silicon Valley'.

14. Rowley, 'In-Q-Tel: The CIA's VC Arm'.

15. Chris Bing, 'New CIA Director Inherits an Agency That Is Quickly Developing Cyber Capabilities', *fedscoop*, 27 January 2017, <https://www.fedscoop.com/new-cia-director-inherits-agency-quickly-developing-cyber-capabilities/> (last accessed 10 January 2020).

16. David S. Cohen, 'Deputy Director Cohen Delivers Remarks on CIA of the Future at Cornell University', CIA website: *News & Information*, 17 September 2015, <https://www.cia.gov/news-information/speeches-testimony/2015-speeches-testimony/deputy-director-cohen-delivers-remarks-on-cia-of-the-future-at-cornell-university.html> (last accessed 10 January 2020).

17. John Gannon, 'The Strategic Use of Open-Source Information', *Studies in Intelligence*, 45.3 (2001), pp. 67–71. See also Stephen C. Mercado, 'Sailing the Sea of OSINT in the Information Age', *Studies in Intelligence*, 48.3 (2004), pp. 45–55.

18. Susan B. Glasser, 'Probing Galaxies of Data for Nuggets', *The Washington Post*, 25 November 2005, <http://www.washingtonpost.com/wp-dyn/content/article/2005/11/24/AR2005112400848.html> (last accessed 10 January 2020).

19. 'From Pearl Harbor to the Digital Age: Open Source Enterprise Celebrates 75th Anniversary', CIA website: *News & Information*, 7 December 2016, <https://www.cia.gov/news-information/featured-story-archive/2016-featured-story-archive/ose-pearl-harbor-to-digital-age.html> (last accessed 10 January 2020).

20. David Omand, Jamie Bartlett and Carl Miller, 'Introducing Social Media Intelligence (SOCMINT)', *Intelligence and National Security*, 27.6 (2012), pp. 1–23.

21. Cohen, 'Deputy Director Cohen Delivers Remarks'.

22. Nicholas Weaver, 'The CIA's No Good, Very Bad, Totally Awful Tuesday', *Lawfare* blog, 7 March 2017, <https://www.lawfareblog.com/cias-no-good-very-bad-totally-awful-tuesday> (last accessed 10 January 2020).

23. Gioe, '"The More Things Change"'.

24. Greg Miller, 'CIA Looks to Expand Its Cyber Espionage Capabilities', *The Washington Post*, 23 February 2015, <https://www.washingtonpost.com/world/national-security/cia-looks-to-expand-its-cyber-espionage-capabilities/2015/02/23.html> (last accessed 10 January 2020).

25. David V. Gioe, Michael S. Goodman and Tim Stevens, 'Intelligence in the Cyber Age: Evolution or Revolution?' *Political Science Quarterly* (forthcoming).

26. Becker, 'The Computer', pp. 63ff.
27. Jenna McLaughlin, 'The Robots will Run the CIA, Too', *Foreign Policy*, 7 September 2017, <https://foreignpolicy.com/2017/09/07/the-robots-will-run-the-cia-too/> (last accessed 10 January 2020).
28. Patrick Tucker, 'What the CIA's Tech Director Wants from AI', *Defense One*, 6 September 2017, <https://www.defenseone.com/technology/2017/09/cia-technology-director-artificial-intelligence/140801/> (last accessed 10 January 2020).
29. Cohen, 'Deputy Director Cohen Delivers Remarks'.
30. Colin Clark, 'Biometrics May Mean the End of a Spy's Disguise', *Breaking Defense*, 20 October 2014, <http://breakingdefense.com/2014/10/biometrics-may-mean-end-of-the-spys-disguise/> (last accessed 10 January 2020).
31. Ibid.
32. 'Deputy Director Cohen Delivers Remarks'.
33. Weaver, 'The CIA's No Good, Very Bad, Totally Awful Tuesday'.
34. 'CIA Statement on Claims by Wikileaks', CIA website: *News & Information*, 8 March 2017, <https://www.cia.gov/news-information/press-releases-statements/2017-press-releases-statements/cia-statement-on-claims-by-wikileaks.html> (last accessed 10 January 2020).
35. David V. Gioe, 'Tinker, Tailor, Leaker, Spy: The Future Costs of Mass Leaks', *The National Interest*, 129 (2014), pp. 51–9.

24 Entering the Electoral Fray: The CIA and Russian Meddling in the 2016 Election

As the leaves began to turn in the cool October air, the Kremlin's electoral rhetoric was heating up in the final weeks leading to the hotly contested American presidential election. With an economic recession eight years in the rear-view mirror, America's economy was again booming, even if its ill-conceived overseas military efforts were going badly in the face of a determined insurgent force hiding among a sympathetic populace. As the generals were complaining about dwindling force levels, politicians were again debating the proper scope of national health insurance legislation. But there was trouble afoot.

From his office overlooking the brilliant autumnal foliage, a worried senior CIA official decided to inform the Director, a registered Republican, 'In the last few months ... new elements in [Moscow's] attitude have become evident.' Specifically, since the nomination convention, Moscow's leaders 'have taken up a harsher propaganda line'. Speaking for the Board of National Estimates, its Chairman observed that this 'propaganda line reflects some genuine concern' along the Moskva river. Indeed, something was different this campaign season. 'This year', wrote the Chairman, the veteran intelligence officer Sherman Kent, Moscow had 'made it plain that there are sharp distinctions between the contending parties and policies' and that the Kremlin has made 'their preference' known.[1] It was 1964.

If Director of Central Intelligence John McCone was alarmed upon receipt of the Board's assessment of Soviet propaganda, he need not have been. Its impact was probably marginal. Lyndon Johnson certainly did not need Soviet Premier Nikita Khrushchev's assistance to secure his crushing victory over Barry Goldwater. This was not the last time, however, that the Director of Central Intelligence would receive an October memo warning about Soviet meddling in a presidential election. Nearly twenty years later, the Politburo would again discern marked policy differences between the White House incumbent and his challenger.

A politically attuned lawyer, Bill Casey served as Ronald Reagan's campaign manager before being named Director of Central Intelligence. Less than two years into the job, he received a memo proposing a 'study to determine the evidence, if any, of Soviet efforts to influence previous US elections . . . and to judge the prospects for such activity in 1984'. The memo warned that 'after years of intense efforts . . . the Soviet grasp of the US political system is better than ever. Hence the Soviet capacity for influencing votes is higher.' The memo's authorship remains redacted, but its drafter may have calculated that tickling Casey's nose for political intrigue would be the best way to secure his approval for such a study, noting: 'It won't be long before various Soviet activities and proposals are regarded, at least by some, as part of a scheme to tip the 1984 US elections.'[2] It is unknown whether Casey assented to the proposed study, but the premise behind the request was sound. The KGB had ordered a full court press, instructing its officers in America to penetrate the campaign staffs of both political parties. Further, it unleashed the KGB's propaganda arm to paint Reagan as a militarist and warmonger, popularising the slogan, 'Reagan Means War!' as ostensible help for the hapless Walter Mondale.[3] It was an ineffectual influence campaign, and Reagan handily secured another term. Mondale was beaten even more soundly than Goldwater had been, winning just his home state of Minnesota and the District of Columbia.[4]

Taking the long-term historical view, it is clear that the Soviets and subsequently the Russians have expressed preferences for candidates of both US political parties since at least 1964, and have used propaganda to manifest their preferences. But their operations before the 2016 elections have led to an unprecedented level of discussion and challenge from the US political and intelligence machinery. Former Director of National Intelligence James Clapper characterised the 2016 Russian efforts to shape American political discourse as a durable Russian effort that spanned both the Cold War and post-Cold war East–West relations: 'Russia's influence activities in the run up to the 2016 election constituted the high-water mark of their long-running efforts since the 1960s to disrupt and influence our elections.'[5] His statement underlines the fact that what many considered to be an extraordinary event, focused on the debate between Clinton and Trump, was in fact part of a historic pattern of behaviour of which CIA has been manifestly aware since at least the mid-Cold War.

However, this election in particular brought CIA closer to the hot stove of American politics than at any time since Watergate. The scope of Russian operations was broad, and the level of coordination across disparate strands was not evident at the surface level. Although the intent was entirely consistent with Russian practice and objectives, the cyber hacking and disinformation dimension was a new wineskin for an older vintage. Tracing each thread to its origin became the work of the intelligence community. Indeed, the Russian interference was undertaken at such a volume that in December 2016 the Obama administration tasked the intelligence community with conducting a review of Russian activity in the information environment. The following month, President Obama authorised release of a portion of the intelligence community's reporting on the topic, leading to a declassified version of an otherwise highly classified Intelligence Community Assessment (ICA) of Russian influence in the 2016 election. This is the chapter reference document, dated 6 January 2017.[6] Unsurprisingly, such tasks and the resulting reports have historically been uncomfortable ground for the US intelligence community – releasing intelligence material in public is frequently polarising, and leads to claims of a politicised intelligence community – and this time was no exception.

This ICA, plainly titled 'Assessing Russian Activities and Intentions in Recent US Elections', was jointly written by CIA, FBI and NSA under the coordination of the DNI. It explained the scope and degree of Russian interference in the elections, especially through the cyber domain with its utilisation of bots and trolls, placing cyber and information operations at the heart of its findings. This conclusion ought not to have been such a surprise to the US political class. In fact, a cyber vector of attack was already in the public sphere, but it gained little traction outside cybersecurity circles. Even before the release of the ICA, the USIC and Department of Homeland Security publicly fingered brazen Russian hacking during the presidential campaign in an unclassified October 2016 report, stating it was 'confident that the Russian Government directed the recent compromises of e-mails from US persons and institutions, including from US political organisations. The recent disclosures of alleged hacked e-mails on sites like DCLeaks. com and WikiLeaks and by the Guccifer2.0 online persona are consistent with the methods and motivations of Russian-directed efforts. These thefts and disclosures are intended to interfere with the US election process.'[7] The operations did not abate even after the initial public warning, and the following month a celebrity real-estate mogul captured the White House.

The Russian operations loomed like a dark cloud over President-elect Trump. Two weeks before his inauguration, the USIC increased its certainty regarding Russian electoral interference, this time assessing 'with high confidence that Russian military intelligence (General Staff Main Intelligence Directorate or GRU) used the Guccifer2.0 persona and DCLeaks.com to release US victim data obtained in cyber operations publicly and in exclusives to media outlets and relayed material to WikiLeaks'.[8] Wikileaks, of course, was the USIC's bête noire, an organisation described by former CIA Director Mike Pompeo as 'a non-state hostile intelligence service often abetted by state actors like Russia'.[9] President Trump would be parrying accusations concerning his campaign's links to the website for years following his election victory.

The investigations revealed that Russian influence operations did not only take place on the World Wide Web. The television station RT (formerly known as Russia Today) was also a compliant vector for Russian intelligence, according to the ICA. It characterised RT as 'the Kremlin's principal international propaganda outlet', and RT was given particular attention in the declassified sections of the ICA – although this may have been because it would not have required revealing the reporting of a clandestine agent to uncover RT's obvious role in Putin's regime. Indeed, over half of the report's main section dealt with RT's role as the Kremlin's bullhorn. From the intelligence community's perspective, however, this unvarnished explication of RT's activities caused some embarrassing self-reflection and cast an immediate spotlight on the questionable media decisions of retired Lieutenant General Michael Flynn, a former director of the Defense Intelligence Agency, who earned tens of thousands of dollars in speaking fees from Russian entities after his retirement.[10] He courted controversy when he helped legitimise RT by attending its tenth anniversary gala dinner in Moscow and sitting next to Putin, which was conveniently caught on camera.[11]

The trap set for the complaisant Lieutenant General Flynn, fired as national security advisor within twenty-one days of Trump's inauguration, was emblematic of the Russian approach: combining classic overt appeals to useful fools with cleverly weaponised information and social media narratives. As the ICA explained: 'Moscow's influence campaign followed a Russian messaging strategy that blends covert intelligence operations – such as cyber activity – with overt efforts by Russian Government agencies, state-funded media, third-party intermediaries, and paid social media users or "trolls".'[12] Variety is a hallmark of the Russian approach, as, in some instances, is brazenness. As Clapper testified, the Russian effort was a 'multifaceted influence campaign, including aggressive use of cyber capabilities', adding, 'Hacking was only one part of it . . . [the influence campaign] also entailed classical propaganda [and] disinformation.'[13] The shock many felt on learning of the Russian operations over 2015 and 2016 is attributable to the combination of breadth and specificity, combining the bludgeon with the scalpel.

The ICA, under the authority of DNI Clapper, was notable for its focus on blending the information warfare aspects into a larger mosaic of Russian intelligence activity. But it was unambiguous in its claim that the matter of the efficacy of the Russian interference campaign was beyond its remit: it 'did not make an assessment of the impact that Russian activities had on the outcome of the 2016 election', because an assessment of a domestic 'political process' is beyond the mandate of American intelligence. However, later, as a private citizen Clapper opined, 'I had no doubt they influenced at least some voters.'[14] In his memoir, Clapper recounted the Russian disinformation and fake news effort, concluding that 'of course the Russian effort affected the outcome. Surprising even themselves, they swung the election to a Trump win. To conclude otherwise stretches logic, common sense, and credulity to the breaking point.'[15] Given Clapper's long professional history in intelligence and his reputation for measured assessments, this assessment carries some weight. It should serve as a clear notice to the body politic, not only in the US, but in all democratic states, that dealing with the dangers posed to the integrity of its political process by malign actors must be considered an urgent priority.

Although the ICA explicitly made no assessment of its electoral impact, it made for uncomfortable reading in the White House. The response of the new administration was equivocal in some respects, and direct in others. The response seemed to indicate that the administration felt itself painted into a corner. It found it difficult to accept the ICA wholesale, because by acknowledging the validity of the report it would undermine the legitimacy of the 2016 election. Consistent with his customary use of social media, after the ICA was released the President tweeted: 'Intelligence stated very strongly there was absolutely no evidence that hacking affected the election results. Voting machines not touched!'[16] This type of response was of concern to many, as it indicated that the White House was not receptive to unwelcome news, and often the CIA's job is to deliver exactly that.

The unwelcome news in this case was manifest. In concurrence with Trump's tweet, as the report notes, the Department of Homeland Security concluded that there was no evidence to suggest actual votes were tampered with. But one of the ICA's key judgements was that not only was Putin intent on harming Democratic nominee Hillary Clinton's candidacy, but it actively promoted the Trump campaign, assessing that 'Russia's goals were to undermine public faith in the US democratic process, denigrate Secretary Clinton, and harm her electability and potential presidency.' Further, 'Putin and the Russian Government developed a clear preference for President-elect Trump.'[17]

This latter judgement was a bridge too far for the Republican members of the House Permanent Select Committee on Intelligence (HPSCI), which suffered near partisan paralysis under the controversial and theatrical leadership of California Republican Devin Nunes, who was widely seen to be carrying President Trump's water on Capitol Hill, especially when it came to the Russia investigation. The HPSCI released a separate report about the ICA in April 2017 that, unsurprisingly, largely validated the ICA, 'except with respect to Putin's supposed preference for candidate Trump'[18] – because, in Representative Mike Conaway's view, the Republicans 'believe[d] that the assessment of that issue by the few analysts who did it did not use the proper tradecraft'.[19] The following month, in May 2017, the Republican-controlled SSCI completed its own review of the ICA and, contrary to his fellow Republican Conaway, Chairman Richard Burr stated that he had 'no reason to dispute the [ICA's] conclusions'. Democratic SSCI Vice Chairman Mark Warner added that 'after a thorough review, our staff concluded that the ICA conclusions were accurate and on point. The Russian effort was extensive, sophisticated, and ordered by President Putin himself for the purpose of helping Donald Trump and hurting Hillary Clinton.'[20] Not only did the House and Senate intelligence committees take different views of the ICA, but it split the Republican caucus as well. The CIA, and the intelligence community in general, were uncomfortably set between them.

In addition to treading on political eggshells, the co-authors of the ICA had the particular challenge of balancing declassification with properly supporting their analytical judgements with releasable evidence. This challenge only further inflamed the political debate concerning the ICA and its conclusions. The declassified version did not go far enough for those who wished to see the 'smoking gun' evidence of Russian meddling. Indeed, as the report's header itself conceded, 'this version does not include the full supporting information on key elements of the influence campaign'. Given the sources and methods involved in collecting the supporting evidence, which, according to journalists Michael Shear and David Sanger, 'would include intercepts of conversations and the harvesting of computer data from "implants" that the United States and its allies have put in Russian computer networks', it is perhaps not surprising that they were removed from the published version of the report.[21] Nonetheless, CIA (and FBI) stated that they had 'high confidence' in their conclusions. Subsequently, a statement by the SSCI confirmed that the CIA was right to have such confidence, describing the report as a 'sound intelligence product' and further observing that 'analysts were under no politically motivated pressure to reach any conclusions', which were 'reached in a professional and transparent manner'.[22]

Indicative of a troubling dynamic between the President and his intelligence services, Trump was no more publicly receptive to this ICA produced by his intelligence community than in earlier statements dismissing their products. Despite the SSCI's endorsement of the integrity of the analytical tradecraft involved in the crafting of this ICA, Trump's reaction echoed his earlier scepticism when he noted that CIA had been wrong in their assessments before. Citing CIA's erroneous analysis regarding Saddam Hussein's weapons of mass destruction programme in the lead up to the invasion of Iraq, Trump averred CIA's incorrect judgement 'was one of the great mistakes of all time'.[23] However, upon his inauguration, his first stop was at

CIA headquarters to mend the relations after harsh accusations, claiming: 'There is nobody that feels stronger about the intelligence community and the CIA than Donald Trump.'[24]

The good feelings were short-lived. Subsequently the President suggested that beyond incompetence, the ICA was politically motivated to undermine his presidency. These attacks on CIA would be the nadir of the President's relationship with his foreign intelligence service. The FBI, however, a co-author of the ICA, would face even more strident criticism for securing a Foreign Intelligence Surveillance Act (FISA) warrant to surveil Trump campaign foreign policy advisor Carter Page and, in the spring of 2018, farcical allegations that FBI improperly 'spied on' the campaign with a confidential human source.[25] This, the president concluded, was evidence of a 'criminal deep state'.[26]

Faced with what many considered to be an unprecedented and unfounded charge, former senior CIA officials took exception to Trump's accusation of politicisation of intelligence – something they spent their careers trying to avoid. During and following the election, Michael Morell, former acting CIA director, expressed his deep concerns about Donald Trump's statements, believing they posed a threat to national (and international) security. He stated that the president's 'disparagement of American intelligence officers ... is likely to cause significant damage to the CIA'. Predicting damage especially in the realm of intelligence liaison, Morell asked, 'Why would a foreign intelligence service take the CIA seriously (and share important information with it) when the American president doesn't?'[27]

Morell's stand was not made alone. Several other former senior intelligence officers publicly defended the CIA from the president's broadsides. One of Morell's mentors, former CIA and NSA Director General Michael Hayden, described Russian meddling as 'the most successful covert influence campaign in recorded history'.[28] And the battle was waged beyond the ranks of retired senior CIA officers. Before his retirement, DNI Clapper testified that the Russians 'must be congratulating themselves for having exceeded their wildest expectations with a minimal expenditure of resources'.[29] Indeed, assuming that a key element of the Russian operation was to sow division, disillusionment and chaos in the US body politic, its impact has been highly effective, even impressive.[30] Given such apparent success in the election and resulting political maelstrom, Americans would be right to be deeply worried about future elections. The operation appears to have yielded gainful returns with minimal costs. As the ICA warned, 'Moscow will apply lessons learned from its Putin-ordered campaign aimed at the US presidential election to future influence efforts worldwide, including against US allies and their election processes.'[31] The stand made by former intelligence officers in defence of the ICA's judgement on the nature of the threat is indicative of a belief that in order to counter threats, they should be understood as well as possible.

The CIA's mantra is to speak truth to power, but this mostly happens in classified documents and briefings. The ICA represents a departure, not unique, but significant, in which the CIA, FBI and NSA sought to speak truth to people directly through a declassified report detailing the complex Russian attack recently visited upon voters. This report placed the intelligence community in the political limelight, uncomfortably as always. Perhaps unsurprisingly, given the polarised political climate, the intelligence community was again decried as being biased; the analytical tradecraft was also pilloried by some congressional overseers and, in a dramatic break with history, their First Customer, the president. It would not be the last time, however, that judgements by the CIA and its sister members of the USIC stirred up a political hornet's nest in the Trump administration.

```
Assessing Russian Activities and Intentions in Recent
US Elections
                              ICA 2017-01D 6 January 2017
Key Judgments
Russian efforts to influence the 2016 US presidential
election represent the most recent expression of
Moscow's longstanding desire to undermine the US-led
liberal democratic order, but these activities demon-
strated a significant escalation in directness, level
of activity, and scope of effort compared to previous
operations.

We assess Russian President Vladimir Putin ordered
an influence campaign in 2016 aimed at the US presi-
dential election. Russia's goals were to undermine
public faith in the US democratic process, denigrate
Secretary Clinton, and harm her electability and
potential presidency. We further assess Putin and
the Russian Government developed a clear preference
for President-elect Trump. We have high confidence in
these judgments.

• We also assess Putin and the Russian Government
  aspired to help President-elect Trump's election
  chances when possible by discrediting Secretary
  Clinton and publicly contrasting her unfavorably to
```

him. All three agencies agree with this judgment. CIA and FBI have high confidence in this judgment; NSA has moderate confidence.

- Moscow's approach evolved over the course of the campaign based on Russia's understanding of the electoral prospects of the two main candidates. When it appeared to Moscow that Secretary Clinton was likely to win the election, the Russian influence campaign began to focus more on undermining her future presidency.
- Further information has come to light since Election Day that, when combined with Russian behavior since early November 2016, increases our confidence in our assessments of Russian motivations and goals.

Moscow's influence campaign followed a Russian messaging strategy that blends covert intelligence operations – such as cyber activity – with overt efforts by Russian Government agencies, state-funded media, third-party intermediaries, and paid social media users or "trolls."

Russia, like its Soviet predecessor, has a history of conducting covert influence campaigns focused on US presidential elections that have used intelligence officers and agents and press placements to disparage candidates perceived as hostile to the Kremlin.

- Russia's intelligence services conducted cyber operations against targets associated with the 2016 US presidential election, including targets associated with both major US political parties.
- We assess with high confidence that Russian military intelligence (General Staff Main Intelligence Directorate or GRU) used the Guccifer 2.0 persona and DCLeaks.com to release US victim data obtained in cyber operations publicly and in exclusives to media outlets and relayed material to WikiLeaks.
- Russian intelligence obtained and maintained access to elements of multiple US state or local electoral boards. **DHS assesses that the types of systems**

Russian actors targeted or compromised were not involved in vote tallying.

- Russia's state-run propaganda machine contributed to the influence campaign by serving as a platform for Kremlin messaging to Russian and international audiences.

We assess Moscow will apply lessons learned from its Putin-ordered campaign aimed at the US presidential election to future influence efforts worldwide, including against US allies and their election processes.

Notes

1. Sherman Kent, 'Khrushchev and the American Election', memorandum from Sherman Kent to the DCI, 8 October 1964, <https://www.cia.gov/library/readingroom/docs/CIA-RDP79R00904A001100010022-4.pdf> (last accessed 10 January 2020).
2. 'The Soviets and the 1984 US Elections', memorandum for DCI (sender redacted), 28 October 1982, <https://www.cia.gov/library/readingroom/docs/CIA-RDP85T00153R000300020043-0.pdf> (last accessed 10 January 2020).
3. Christopher Andrew and Vasili Mitrokhin, *The Sword and the Shield: The Mitrokhin Archive and the Secret History of the KGB* (Basic Books: New York, 1999), p. 243.
4. This section taken from David V. Gioe, 'Cyber Operations and Useful Fools: The Approach of Russian Hybrid Intelligence', *Intelligence and National Security*, 33.7 (2018), pp. 954–73.
5. Congressional testimony of James Clapper, 8 May 2017.
6. Director of National Intelligence, 'Assessing Russian Activities and Intentions in Recent US Elections', 6 January 2017. Hereafter DNI, 'Assessment'.
7. Joint Statement from the Department of Homeland Security and Office of the Director of National Intelligence on Election Security, October 7, 2016.
8. DNI, 'Assessment', 6 January 2017.
9. Mike Pompeo, 'Director Pompeo Delivers Remarks at CSIS', transcript of speech, 13 April 2017, <https://www.cia.gov/news-information/speeches-testimony/2017-speeches-testimony/pompeo-delivers-remarks-at-csis.html> (last accessed 10 January 2020).
10. Ken Dilanian, 'Russians Paid Mike Flynn $45K for Moscow Speech, Documents Show', *NBCnews.com*, 6 March 2017.
11. As quoted in Damien Sharkov, 'Flynn-Putin Dinner: Russian Leader Had No Idea Who US General Was, Says RT Chief', *Newsweek*, 4 December 2017.

12. Office of the Director of National Intelligence, 'Assessing Russian Activities and Intentions in Recent US Elections', *Intelligence Community Assessment*, 6 January 2017.

13. United States Senate Committee on Armed Services hearing on Foreign Cyber Threats to the United States, 5 January 2017.

14. James R. Clapper, *Facts and Fears: Hard Truths from a Life in Intelligence* (New York: Viking, 2018), p. 395.

15. Ibid. p. 396.

16. <https://twitter.com/realDonaldTrump/status/817701436096126977?ref_src=twsrc%5Etfw> (last accessed 10 January 2020).

17. DNI 'Assessment'.

18. HPSCI Statement on Russia Investigation, <https://intelligence.house.gov/uploadedfiles/hpsci_russia_investigation_one_page_summary.pdf> (last accessed 10 January 2020).

19. As quoted in Betsy Woodruff, 'House Russia Probe Chief: Putin May Have Wanted Trump', *The Daily Beast*, 3 March 2018, <https://www.thedailybeast.com/house-russia-probe-chief-putin-may-have-wanted-trump> (last accessed 10 January 2020).

20. 'Senate Intel Completes Review of Intelligence Community Assessment on Russian Activities in the 2016 US Elections', press release by the office of Senator Richard Burr, 16 May 2018, <https://www.burr.senate.gov/press/releases/senate-intel-completes-review-of-intelligence-community-assessment-on-russian-activities-in-the-2016-us-elections> (last accessed 10 January 2020).

21. Michael D. Shear and David E. Sanger, 'Putin Led a Complex Cyberattack Scheme to Aid Trump, Report Finds', *The New York Times*, 6 January 2017, <https://www.nytimes.com/2017/01/06/us/politics/donald-trump-wall-hack-russia.html> (last accessed 10 January 2020).

22. 'Unclassified Summary of Initial Findings of 2017 Intelligence Community Assessment', Senate Select Committee on Intelligence, 3 July 2018, <https://www.burr.senate.gov/download/final-ssci-ica-assessment> (last accessed 10 January 2020).

23. Shear and Sanger, 'Putin Led a Complex Cyberattack Scheme'.

24. Philip Rucker and Greg Miller, 'Trump Visits CIA Headquarters after Sharply Criticizing the Intelligence Community', *The Washington Post*, 21 January 2017, <https://www.washingtonpost.com/news/post-politics/wp/2017/01/21/trump-to-visit-cia-headquarters-after-sharply-criticizing-the-intelligence-community/> (last accessed 10 January 2020).

25. Adam Goldman, Mark Mazetti and Matthew Rosenberg, 'FBI Used Informant to Investigate Russia Ties to Campaign, Not to Spy, as Trump Claims', *The New York Times*, 8 May 2018, <https://www.nytimes.com/2018/05/18/us/politics/trump-fbi-informant-russia-investigation.html> (last accessed 10 January 2020).

26. Brett Samuels, 'Trump: "Criminal deep state" caught up in "major spy scandal"', *The Hill*, 23 May 2018

27. Michael J. Morell, 'Trump's Dangerous Anti-CIA Crusade', *The New York*

Times, 6 January 2017, <https://www.nytimes.com/2017/01/06/opinion/trum ps-dangerous-anti-cia-crusade.html> (last accessed 10 January 2020).

28. *Cyberwar*, 'Who hacked the DNC?', Season 2, episode 2 (2016), transcript available at <https://www.springfieldspringfield.co.uk/view_episode_scripts. php?tv-show=cyberwar-2016&episode=s02e02> (last accessed 10 January 2020).

29. Statement of James R. Clapper concerning Russian interference in the 2016 United States election before the Committee on the Judiciary Subcommittee on Crime and Terrorism United States Senate, 8 May 2017, <https://www. judiciary.senate.gov/imo/media/doc/05-08-17%20Clapper%20Testimony. pdf> (last accessed 10 January 2020).

30. *Cyberwar*, 'Who hacked the DNC?'

31. Office of the Director of National Intelligence, 'Assessing Russian Activities and Intentions in Recent US Elections', *Intelligence Community Assessment*, 6 January 2017.

25 Flying Blind? The CIA and the Trump Administration

Historians are usually uncomfortable with the word 'unprecedented' for a few reasons. First, almost every development has historical drivers and antecedents that help explain the timing and manner of its emergence. Indeed, as historians often note, history is contingent on a multitude of interconnected linkages that build on or interact with what has come before. Some linkages are causal, others merely correlate – and discerning the difference is key for analysis and interpretation of the past. In all things, however, history is continuous, not episodic. Although this history of the CIA has been divided up into chapters for convenience and readability, it is worth remembering these points. Second, in our contemporary societal condition of what Christopher Andrew has termed 'Historical Attention Span Deficit Disorder',[1] many things are labelled 'unprecedented' only because the commenter did not bother to look to the past for reference. As we have tried to show, certain developments and circumstances in the history of the CIA have rhyming forebears. Still, some initially promising historical parallels from a distance become more mirage than oasis upon closer inspection, leading to a judgement that certain developments are actually unprecedented, even in considered historical perspective. Such is, in fact, the relationship between President Donald Trump and the CIA.

On 20 January 2017, Donald J. Trump was inaugurated as the 45th president of the United States and the US intelligence community received a new and very unusual First Customer. There can be little doubt that following a nasty campaign, generally accepted to have been marred by outside intervention, the new president's relationship with the CIA was beset by tension, distrust and even antipathy in some quarters. Many career officials felt it an ominous sign when the President-elect eschewed his daily intelligence briefing, explaining, 'I don't have to be told – you know, I'm, like, a smart person. . . . I don't have to be told the same thing and the same words every single day for the next eight years.'[2] While still the incumbent, President Obama inveighed against this view, making the case that for a president to go without daily analysis from the intelligence community is tantamount to 'flying blind'.[3] Traditionally, certainly, the President's Daily Brief (PDB) has been a staple for sitting presidents navigating a very dangerous world.

The apparent undervaluing of the PDB – symbolising, of course, an undervaluing of the general work of the analysts at Langley and the broader USIC – was not the only factor that contributed to a fraught early relationship. As Chapter 24 explored, then-candidate Trump had also dismissed CIA's finding that Russia played a role in the 2016 campaign that favoured him and, after assuming that the leak of a secret dossier from a former British intelligence officer must have come from deep inside the secret state, he tweeted, 'Intelligence agencies should never have allowed this fake news to "leak" into the public. One last shot at me. Are we living in Nazi Germany?' He added later: 'That's something that Nazi Germany would have done and did do.'[4] Outgoing CIA director John Brennan could not let a comparison to Nazi Germany go unanswered, stating that it was 'outrageous' and that he took 'great umbrage'.[5] Many others, no doubt, shared this sentiment, but Brennan's consistent criticism of Trump's low regard for intelligence has prompted Trump to revoke Brennan's security clearance. He has threatened to do the same to fellow former CIA Director Michael Hayden, former DNI Clapper and several former (and current) officials of the FBI and Department of Justice.[6]

The curious start to the relationship was reinforced almost immediately with the President's visit to CIA headquarters the day after his inauguration, where his apparent dismissal of the agency's analysts was supplanted by a resounding vote of confidence in the potential of its covert operations. There he spoke with a workforce whose analysis he had recently disparaged and whose apolitical character – perhaps its most precious asset – he had questioned. Standing in front of CIA's memorial wall and book of honour, he estimated that 'probably almost everybody in this room voted for me'. He then attempted to begin a new chapter with his premier intelligence service, proclaiming, 'I want to just let you know I am so behind you. And I know maybe sometimes you haven't gotten the backing that you've wanted, and you're going to get so much backing. Maybe you're going to say, please don't give us so much backing.'[7]

This 'backing', in Trump's vernacular, translated to relaxing what he considered to be the excessive restraint on the CIA's activities imposed by the Obama administration, harking back to President Reagan and his promise to 'unleash the CIA'. This sentiment has certainly been expressed, although perhaps not so openly, by several previous incumbents of the Oval Office. Turning to the hidden hand has often seemed an attractive 'quick fix' to intractable policy problems. Director Michael Hayden used to joke that he should bring appetite suppressant pills to National Security Council meetings to administer to political officials whose appetite for covert action as a panacea for global challenges seemed gluttonous. It has often also led to difficulty and controversy. As Chapter 22 explored, the CIA's more aggressive posture even while tethered to a legal leash led to unprecedented acrimony with Congress, echoing the serious controversy generated by covert activities in the 1960s and 1970s, explored in Chapters 7 and 11.

There is little indication that President Trump had considered the weight of this history when promising to relax the constraints on the CIA's operators, or that he had considered how CIA's capabilities might support his foreign policy or national security agenda. In fact, the issue may turn on what the term 'support' means in practice. For CIA, supporting their First Customer would mean informing him by providing unvarnished intelligence assessments and narrowing the cone of uncertainty on potential policies. For Trump, it seems that 'support' ought to mean echoing his talking points. For instance, CIA's measured assessments of Iran have not matched Trump's hawkish rhetoric, inviting withering rebukes. When leaders of the USIC testified to Congress in January 2019 that Iran was largely abiding by the terms of the Joint Comprehensive Plan of Action (JCPOA, the Iran nuclear deal) from which Trump had withdrawn, Trump tweeted: 'The Intelligence people seem to be extremely passive and naive when it comes to the dangers of Iran. They are wrong! . . . Perhaps Intelligence should go back to school!'[8] While it was unclear on what evidence Trump was contradicting the intelligence chiefs that he had nominated for their positions, these public attacks on the competence of his intelligence bureaucracy and the disposition of the leaders that he selected were unprecedented. As this book has shown, presidents have often been frustrated with their intelligence chiefs, and Chapter 7's examination of the Bay of Pigs fiasco reminds us that President Kennedy was furious with his DCI – but these frustrations and disagreements have always been handled privately.

The relationship between the CIA and its First Customer should be strong if the intelligence community is to effectively fulfil its primary function of supporting US policy. Whatever the CIA's misgivings about its First Customer, CIA's commitment to providing intelligence to the Executive Branch endured, although not without concern from the ranks of former officers. For example, before Trump was inaugurated, former Acting Director Michael Morell warned that disparagement of CIA hurts CIA itself as well as national security by extension. Further, publicly questioning CIA's competence and accusing it of political bias is a 'gut punch'.[9] Indeed, one of the characteristics of an effective relationship between an intelligence consumer and producer in a democratic society is the ability to disagree on matters of substance without questioning the other side's good faith or naiveté. The apparent lack of good faith in elements of President Trump's critique or dismissal of CIA assessments – visible with the intelligence community's conclusions over Russian activities in the 2016 election, the Iran deal, the defeat of Islamic State in Syria and, reportedly, again in November 2018 concerning the CIA's assessments of the involvement of senior elements of the Saudi ruling family in the gruesome murder of the journalist Jamal Khashoggi[10] – appears corrosive to a fruitful consumer–producer relationship; not to mention that, as Senator Mark Warner (D-VA) noted: 'People risk their lives for the intelligence he just tosses aside on Twitter.'[11]

Tailoring the worldwide threat assessment to suit Trump's public statements would be a form of politicisation of intelligence, and identifiable as such. The charge of politicisation is a serious one for any democratic intelligence service, particularly in the wake of Iraq. And given the importance of trying to provide policymakers with the best possible independent analysis, accusations of politicising intelligence are taken seriously. CIA officers have an ombudsman available, outside the chain of command, to hear complaints of politicisation if they arise. In a cynical world, it may seem quaint to believe that politics, agendas or worldviews do not drive intelligence analysis, but the CIA's overall record – with notable exceptions – has borne this out. This is not to say that politicisation has not been part of CIA's history or that it could never happen. As Chapter 21 explored, many outside observers felt that CIA bowed under political pressure to provide evidence to support the Iraq War. But the accusation of politicisation is very damaging to the CIA because even the taint of massaging intelligence to support a political narrative undermines the agency's relationship with its political consumers and, through oversight mechanisms, the American public as well.

Learning from its mistakes, especially in Iraq, the intelligence community has since added more explicit confidence levels for its analytical judgements as a way of improving the clarity of its judgements for its customers. There is little evidence in the public domain that President Trump will accept even 'high confidence' judgements that do not coincide with his worldview. The reaction to the assessment of Russian interference in 2016, as detailed in Chapter 24, and Khashoggi's murder bear this out. President Trump's reaction to these has been equivocal, as with his reaction to allegations of President Putin's culpability for interference in US elections: 'maybe he [knew] and maybe he didn't'.[12] It is, of course, the President's prerogative not to take advice, or to come to different conclusions. Indeed, intelligence agencies exist to uncover secret and hidden information and assessments are based on judgements of the interplay between the weight of evidence and probability.

Some have argued that the dynamic, very publicly visible, between the agency and its First Customer will damage its reputation and ultimately hamper its operations. Michael Morell warned that dismissing CIA's analysis will weaken its position both with its liaison partners and with its sensitive sources, who may wonder why they are risking arrest or even death to provide secrets if they are not valued: 'Knowing their information is making its way to the president is an important motivator for spies,' he claimed. Drawing on one of the most important cases in CIA's history, Morell asked: 'Would the modern-day Adolf Tolkachev, the CIA's most important agent within the Soviet Union – who was executed as a spy in 1986 – sign on to work for Donald Trump? I doubt it. The potential loss of critical information could be extraordinary.' It is impossible to know the opportunity cost of intelligence from spies who never spy, but surely connecting the dots for national security becomes harder when there are fewer dots. And for intelligence agencies, reputations that have taken decades to nurture can be burned quickly.

This is not the first time that the CIA has endured accusations of politicisation, or has had to weather a difficult or practically non-existent relationship between the director and the president. As we explored in Chapter 11, the CIA went through a period of profound political turmoil in the mid-1970s, famously (although inaccurately) being accused of operating as 'rogue elephants'. (Reportedly, some CIA officers took it in stride, and the CIA softball team had new uniforms made with their new mascot across the chest: The Rogue Elephants.) Neither is Trump's dismissal of CIA's analytical conclusions the first time CIA felt marginalised. As noted in Chapter 19, when a small plane landed on the White House lawn in 1994, DCI R. James Woolsey quipped that it was him trying to meet with President Clinton.

The reactions to these past storms have in several senses been reassuring for the American public. That the proverbial red carpet was not unfurled for Woolsey did not cause him to request that his analysts find welcome intelligence for Clinton to curry favour. Similarly, Chapter 8's consideration of CIA and the Vietnam War underscores that speaking truth to power is easier said than done, and that there is often a price to be paid. The CIA did not provide intelligence to justify political considerations, instead offering (relatively) clear-eyed analytical judgements concerning the likelihood of a victory in Vietnam, and its assessments of North Vietnamese military capability in particular were often at odds with the Pentagon. This was consistent with CIA's mandate of not seeking to please its First Customer, but to inform him, although it hardly endeared DCI John McCone to President Johnson. It is precisely because of the deviation from this rule that the matter of Iraq's weapons of mass destruction, discussed in Chapter 21, were so damaging to the CIA and its reputation.

An unwavering commitment to delivering unwelcome but accurate news is at the root of the CIA's credo. The visual metaphor of a verse from John's

Gospel, 'And ye shall know the truth, and the truth shall make you free,' being literally carved in stone in the lobby of the Old Headquarters Building in Langley is a not particularly subtle reminder of this for all employees and visitors.[13] Recruiting foreign spies and stealing secrets to inform policy decisions probably were not at the forefront of the Apostle John's mind, but Allen Dulles had those words chiselled as a literal touchstone of the incomparable value of insight and warning for US policymakers. The attack at Pearl Harbor was still relatively fresh in the collective memory of all Americans when the words were carved. Subsequent generations of officers will have read them with renewed resonance in the context of more recent attacks and surprises, 9/11 most notably. Preventing future surprises will depend not only on effective operations and assessment, but effective and functional relationships with the White House, which ought to be capable of listening to uncomfortable truths in formulating policy.

Baseball legend Yogi Berra famously observed that 'it's tough to make predictions, especially about the future'. No one knows that better than intelligence analysts, and being wrong is part of the work. Even senior analysts like Michael Morell make predictions from time to time that do not occur; one looms large for CIA in the age of Trump. Morell predicted that, if Trump continued to alternately disparage and dismiss his experts in Langley, from CIA there would come a 'wave of resignations' and that 'attrition will skyrocket'.[14] Trump has shown little appetite to moderate his behaviour, but, despite a few theatrical resignations, agency officers did not leave in droves. The overwhelming majority continued on without a hiccup, despite whatever private misgivings they might have about their agency's relationship with the White House or the occupant in general. This underlines, to many, the fact that the agency has developed the ability to weather political storms, and to continue to operate in the service of the Republic. Perhaps in these most polarised of times, this is a reminder that the lessons of the past concerning the ideal of a resolutely apolitical agency weigh heavily on the officers and the leadership of the agency, and their sense of mission.

A shared sense of mission seems important in binding the agency. Throughout the years chronicled in our twenty-five chapters, the CIA has enjoyed spectacularly low levels of attrition, and a significant number of its officers have stayed for a full career. Partly this is about duty and patriot- ism, no doubt. But one must also remember the allure of secrecy, the same secrecy that feeds the myths and misconceptions alluded to in the introduc- tion to this book. During hard days on the job, senior officers remind their juniors that it is a unique privilege to recruit spies, steal secrets and play in the great game. CIA officers understand that it is 'a very dangerous world'. And, as many state, they report to work every day because of that fact. The need for intelligence has rarely been more profound than it is today, with resurgent conventional threats complementing the potent threat posed by international terrorist organisations. Despite the turmoil in Washington, played out with an often dispiriting lack of courtesy on television and in print, the CIA will continue to attract recruits who are driven by a thirst for adventure, professional meaning and a determination that they too can make a difference. Retaining this flow will, however, require ensuring that the agency is managed with due regard and respect for democratic values and adherence to an ethical code.

As this book has explored, the CIA was created by politicians, has been used as a tool in international politics, has informed political masters of many stripes and has provided analysis that some believed was overly political, such as in the Iraq War or judgements about Russian activity in the 2016 election. It would therefore seem reasonable that CIA would be an inherently political creature itself. Certainly, a bureaucracy the size of CIA, which exists to support and inform policy, could never claim to be completely free of political considerations. To believe so would be naive. Bureaucracies compete for resources; bureaucracies are staffed by people; intelligence is concerned with politics; intelligence is political. The key question for the CIA is how to minimise the chance of becoming *politicised*.

Its geography is symbolic of this struggle. The CIA's splendid – and intentional – isolation, in a leafy compound across the Potomac River from Pennsylvania Avenue and Capitol Hill, symbolises the agency's drive to an apolitical ideal (no matter how imperfect in practice), as outlined in its charter and mandate. The verdant CIA grounds were originally intended to evoke studious feelings of a college campus where expert analysts and scholars could write intelligence estimates away from the policy process and political noise. Consistent with this geographical degree of separation from Washington is a longstanding tradition of analytical integrity and a training programme designed to identify and root out bias – aiming to ensure that it would be nearly impossible to discern an agency officer's political views in the intelligence they collect, or in their analytical work. As one senior manager recalled, new recruits were always told upon entering on duty: 'Leave your political views in your car in the parking lot. Don't bring them in the building.'[15] History shows that this ideal has been met far more frequently than not. It is a worthy aspiration: history also shows that overly politicised agencies are far more liable to corruption and failure.

Although CIA's work product is free of political considerations, its employees have their own political views. Over recent years there has been a growing tendency for former CIA officers to become public figures, either in the commentariat or as politicians. This should perhaps not be surprising; an agency like the CIA will inevitably attract those who are interested in politics and public service. Increasingly, former CIA employees have run for electoral office with success. Although former clandestine service operations officer Evan McMullin lost his independent bid for the presidency in 2016, a small handful of CIA veterans have been elected to the House of Representatives, including former operations officers Will Hurd from the 23rd district of Texas, Abigail Spanberger from Virginia's 7th district and former analyst Elissa Slotkin, representing Michigan's 8th district. Although divided by a political aisle, how this younger generation of agency veterans turned lawmakers interpret their shared intelligence past will be a critical question for the future relationship between Langley and Capitol Hill. Many would argue that having representatives familiar with the uses and limits of intelligence will be a boon for the intelligence community. Others may fear a slow seepage of overt politics back into the agency. Time will tell.

Gen-X CIA veterans being elected to Congress was not the only notable trail blazed on Capitol Hill in 2018. On 17 May, the Senate confirmed career clandestine service officer Gina Haspel as Director of the CIA, the first woman to hold the job. In turn, Haspel named Beth Kimber as the first female Deputy Director for Operations (another first) and Cynthia Rapp as Deputy Director for Analysis. They joined Dawn Meyerriecks, who was already the Deputy Director for Science and Technology, as noted in Chapter 23. In addition to a female director and three female deputy directors, the general counsel and director for diversity are female as well.[16] If intelligence was one of the last bastions of the 'men's club', times have changed.

Aside from the social progress reflected in having woman at the helm for the first time in CIA's history, it is also notable that Haspel is the first career employee to be promoted from within since Robert Gates became DCI in 1991.[17] Gates rose through the analytical ranks, serving in senior analytical jobs as well as at the coalface of intelligence support to policy-making, thanks to a stint on the National Security Council. The last DCI to come from the operational side of the house, like Haspel, was OSS veteran William Colby, who served a full career at CIA, culminating as DCI from 1973 until 1976. Haspel's clandestine service background will surely affect her leadership of the agency as it navigates what are clearly treacherous waters surrounding both domestic politics and international affairs.

As we observed in the introduction to this book, the CIA has become globally mythologised, the subject of vast quantities of infotainment and a sure route to movie ticket sales, TV ratings or clickbait articles that have little if any foundation in reality. Although the mystique of CIA may help recruitment efforts for both staff officers and their agents, the veneers of myth have obscured CIA's history and tendentious commentators, to include elected politicians, have hampered serious inquiry. What this study has attempted to reveal is that the CIA is neither saint nor villain. It has missed some significant developments and made its share of mistakes. It struggles with public relations, and the eternal question facing an intelligence service in a democracy: how to balance necessary operational secrecy with transparency and oversight. But for all of its imperfections, CIA has also served a vital purpose as America's clandestine outer perimeter, and its officers and agents have sacrificed much to deliver timely, relevant and accurate intelligence to decision-makers. The mission of the Central Intelligence Agency endures because it is 'a very dangerous world'. If history is any guide, CIA will continue to play a leading role in America's pursuit of security.

```
   Donald J. Trump ✳
   @realDonaldTrump                    🐦 Follow
Intelligence agencies should never have
allowed this fake news to "leak" into the
public. One last shot at me. Are we living in
Nazi Germany?
12:48 PM-11 Jan 2017
✚  ✚  30,252    ❤ 99,566
```

Notes

1. As quoted in David Omand, 'The Ethics of Digital Intelligence', speech to the Harkness Fellows Association, September 2018, <https://www.harknessfellows.org.uk/event-reports/sir-david-omand> (last accessed 10 January 2020).
2. As quoted in Don Gonyea, 'What Exactly Is The "President's Daily Brief" And Why Is It Important?' *NPR Politics*, 13 December 2016.
3. Greg Evans, 'Barack Obama On "Daily Show" Warns Against "Flying Blind" Without Intelligence Briefings', *Deadline*, 12 December 2016.
4. As quoted in Steve Benen, 'Revisiting an Old Trump Question: "Are we living in Nazi Germany?"', *The Maddow Blog*, 14 August 2017, <http://www.msnbc.com/rachel-maddow-show/revisiting-old-trump-question-are-we-living-nazi-germany> (last accessed 10 January 2020).
5. John Brennan interviewed by Chris Wallace on Fox News, 16 January 2017.
6. 'Press Briefing by Press Secretary Sarah Sanders', 15 August 2018, <https://www.whitehouse.gov/briefings-statements/press-briefing-press-secretary-sarah-sanders-081518/> (last accessed 10 January 2020).
7. Statement transcribed at <https://www.whitehouse.gov/briefings-statements/remarks-president-trump-vice-president-pence-cia-headquarters/> (last accessed 10 January 2020).
8. Eileen Sullivan, 'Trump Calls Intelligence Officials "Naive" After They

Contradict Him', *The New York Times*, 30 January 2019, <https://www.
nytimes.com/2019/01/30/us/politics/trump-intelligence.html> (last accessed
10 January 2020).

9. Morell, 'Trump's Dangerous Anti-CIA Crusade'.

10. Josh Dawsey, Shane Harris and Karen DeYoung, 'Trump calls Saudi Arabia
a "great ally," discounts crown prince's responsibility for Khashoggi's death',
The Washington Post, 20 November 2018, <https://www.washingtonpost.com/
politics/trump-defends-saudia-arabias-denial-about-the-planning-of-khash
oggis-death/2018/11/20/b64d2cc6-eceb-11e8-9236-bb94154151d2_story.
html?utm_term=.16974ddb252b> (last accessed 10 January 2020).

11. Sullivan, 'Trump Calls Intelligence Officials "Naive"'.

12. Greg Myre, '"Maybe He Did, Maybe He Didn't": Trump Defends Saudis,
Downplays US Intel', National Public Radio, 20 November 2018, <https://
www.npr.org/2018/11/20/669708254/maybe-he-did-maybe-he-didnt-trump-
defends-saudis-downplays-u-s-intel> (last accessed 10 January 2020).

13. See 'Headquarters Photo Tour', <https://www.cia.gov/about-cia/headquarters-
tour/headquarters-photo-tour> (last accessed 10 January 2020).

14. Morell, 'Trump's Dangerous Anti-CIA Crusade'.

15. As quoted in Adam Entous, 'John Brennan's Choice to Confront Trump', *The
New Yorker*, 20 August 2018, <https://www.newyorker.com/news/news-desk/
john-brennans-choice-to-confront-trump> (last accessed 10 January 2020).

16. Robert Windrem, 'Sisterhood of Spies: Women Now Hold the Top Positions
at the CIA', NBC News, 5 January 2019, <https://www.nbcnews.com/news/
us-news/all-three-cia-directorates-will-now-be-headed-women-n954956> (last
accessed 10 January 2020).

17. Former DCIA Porter Goss started his career at CIA, but served a brief period.

Bibliography

Print Sources

Aid, Matthew, 'The National Security Agency and the Cold War', *Intelligence and National Security*, 16.1 (2001).

Aid, Matthew, *The Secret Sentry: The Untold Story of the National Security Agency* (London: Bloomsbury, 2010).

Aid, Matthew, 'US Humint and Comint in the Korean War: From the Approach of War to the Chinese Intervention', *Intelligence and National Security*, 14.4 (1999).

Aldrich, Richard J., *The Hidden Hand: Britain, America, and Cold War Secret Intelligence* (London: Allen Lane, 2001).

Alexeev, Mikhail A., *Without Warning: Threat Assessment, Intelligence, and Global Struggle* (London: St Martin's Press, 1997).

Allen, Charles E., 'Warning and Iraq's Invasion of Kuwait: A Retrospective Look', *Defence Intelligence Journal*, 7.2 (1998).

Andrew, Christopher, *Defend the Realm* (New York: Vintage Books, 2010).

Andrew, Christopher, *For the President's Eyes Only: Secret Intelligence and the American Presidency from Washington to Bush* (New York: Harper Perennial, 1996).

Andrew, Christopher M., and David Dilks, *The Missing Dimension: Governments and Intelligence Communities in the Twentieth Century* (Urbana: University of Illinois Press, 1984).

Andrew, Christopher, and Oleg Gordievsky, *Instructions from the Centre: Top Secret Files on KGB Operations, 1975–1985* (London: Frank Cass, 1992).

Andrew, Christopher, and Oleg Gordievsky, *KGB: The Inside Story of its Foreign Operations from Lenin to Gorbachev* (New York: Harper Collins, 1990).

Andrew, Christopher, and Vasili Mitrokhin, *The Mitrokhin Archive: The KGB in Europe and the West* (London: Penguin, 2000).

Andrew, Christopher, and Vasili Mitrokhin, *The Sword and the Shield: The Mitrokhin Archive and the Secret History of the KGB* (Basic Books: New York, 1999).

Ashton, S. R. (ed.), *Documents on British Policy Overseas, Series I, Volume VIII: Britain and China, 1945–1950* (London: Frank Cass, 2002).

Axworthy, Michael, *Revolutionary Iran: A History of the Islamic Republic* (Oxford: Oxford University Press, 2013).

Bager, Moin, *Khomeini: Life of the Ayatollah* (London: I. B. Tauris, 2009).

Bagley, Tennent H., *Spy Wars: Moles, Mysteries, and Deadly Games* (London: Yale University Press, 2008).

Bamford, James, *A Pretext for War: 9/11, Iraq, and the Abuse of America's Intelligence Agencies* (London: Anchor, 2005).

Barrass, Gordon S., *The Great Cold War: A Journey Through the Hall of Mirrors* (Stanford: Stanford University Press, 2009).

Bartholomew-Feis, Dixee, *The OSS and Ho Chi Minh: Unexpected Allies in the War Against Japan* (Lawrence: University Press of Kansas, 2006).

Bergen, Peter L., *Manhunt: The Ten-Year Search for bin Ladin from 9/11 to Abbottabad* (New York: Crown Publishing Group, 2012).

Berntsen, Gary, *Jawbreaker* (New York: Crown Publishers, 2005).

Borch, F. L., 'Comparing Pearl Harbor and "9/11": Intelligence Failure? American Unpreparedness? Military Responsibility?' *The Journal of Military History*, 67.3 (2003).

Bradsher, Henry S., *Afghan Communism and Soviet Intervention* (Oxford: Oxford University Press, 1999).

Braithwaite, Rodric, *Afgantsy: The Russians in Afghanistan, 1979–89* (Oxford: Oxford University Press, 2011).

Bukharin, Oleg, 'US Atomic Energy Intelligence against the Soviet Target, 1945–1970', *Intelligence and National Security*, 19.4 (2004).

Campbell, Stephen H., 'Intelligence in the Post-Cold War Period: The Impact of Technology', *The Intelligencer*, 20.1 (2013).

Clapper, James R., *Facts and Fears: Hard Truths from a Life in Intelligence* (New York: Viking, 2018).

Clemente, J. D., 'CIA's Medical and Psychological Analysis Center (MPAC) and the Health of Foreign Leaders', *International Journal of Intelligence and Counterintelligence*, 19.3 (2006).

Coll, Steve, *Ghost Wars: The Secret History of the CIA, Afghanistan and Bin Laden from the Soviet Invasion to September 10, 2001* (London: Penguin, 2005).

Cooper, Chester L., *The Lion's Last Roar: Suez, 1956* (New York: Harper & Row, 1978).

Cordesman, A. H., *Terrorism, Asymmetric Warfare, and Weapons of Mass Destruction: Defending the US Homeland* (Westport, CT: Greenwood Publishing Group, 2002).

Corera, Gordon, *The Art of Betrayal: The Secret History of MI6* (New York: Pegasus Books, 2012).

Cullather, Nicholas, *Operation PBSUCCESS: The United States and Guatemala, 1952–1954* (Washington, DC: CIA, 1994).

Dahl, Erik J., 'The Plots That Failed: Intelligence Lessons Learned from Unsuccessful Terrorist Attacks against the United States', *Studies in Conflict & Terrorism*, 34.8 (2011).

Danchev, Alex, 'On Friendship: Anglo-America at fin de siècle,' *International Affairs*, 73.4 (1997).

Daugherty, W. J., 'Behind the Intelligence Failure in Iran', *International Journal of Intelligence and Counterintelligence*, 14.4 (2001).

Dockrill, M. L., 'The Foreign Office, Anglo-American Relations and the Korean War, June 1950–June 1951', *International Affairs*, 62.3 (1986).

Drea, Edward J., *MacArthur's Ultra: Codebreaking and the War against Japan* (Lawrence: University Press of Kansas, 1991).

Drogin, B., *Curveball: Spies, Lies and the Man Behind Them – The Real Reason America Went to War in Iraq* (London: Ebury Press, 2008).

Dulles, Allen, *The Craft of Intelligence* (Guilfort, CT: The Lyons Press, 2006).

Duns, Jeremy, *Dead Drop: The True Story of Oleg Penkovsky and the Cold War's Most Dangerous Operation* (London: Simon & Schuster, 2013).

Dylan, Huw, *Defence Intelligence and the Cold War: Britain's Joint Intelligence Bureau, 1946–1964* (Oxford: Oxford University Press, 2014).

Earley, Pete, *Confessions of a Spy: The Real Story of Aldrich Ames* (London: Putnam's Sons, 1997).

Ennis, J. D., 'Anatoli Golitsyn: Long-time CIA Agent?', *Intelligence and National Security*, 21.1 (2006).

Ennis, J. D., 'What Did Angleton Say about Golitsyn?', *Intelligence and National Security*, 22.6 (2007).

Epstein, Edward J., *Legend: The Secret World of Lee Harvey Oswald* (London: McGraw-Hill, 1978).

Feifer, Gregory, *The Great Gamble: The Soviet War in Afghanistan* (New York: HarperCollins, 2009).

Feklisov, Alexander, *The Man Behind the Rosenbergs: Memoirs of the KGB Spymaster Who Also Controlled Klaus Fuchs and Helped Resolve the Cuban Missile Crisis* (New York: Enigma Books, 2001).

Fennegan, John Patrick, and Romana Danysh, *Military Intelligence* (Washington, DC: Center of Military History, 1998).

Final Report of the National Commission on Terrorist Attacks upon the United States (New York: W. W. Norton and Company, 2004).

Fischer, B. B., 'Anglo-American Intelligence and the Soviet War Scare: The Untold Story', *Intelligence and National Security*, 27.1 (February 2012).

Fischer, B. B., 'Scolding Intelligence: The PFIAB Report on the Soviet War Scare', *International Journal of Intelligence and Counterintelligence*, 31.1 (2018).

Foreign Relations of the United States, 1949: The Far East: China, Volume IX (Washington, DC: CIA, 1974).

Freedman, Lawrence, *US Intelligence and the Soviet Strategic Threat* (Princeton: Princeton University Press, 1986).

Gaddis, John Lewis, *The Cold War* (London: Allen Lane, 2005).

Gannon, John, 'The Strategic Use of Open-Source Information', *Studies in Intelligence*, 45.3 (2001).

Garthoff, Raymond L., 'Negotiating SALT', *The Wilson Quarterly*, 1.5 (1977).

Gioe, David V., 'Tinker, Tailor, Leaker, Spy: The Future Costs of Mass Leaks', *The National Interest*, 129 (2014).

Gioe, David, Len Scott and Christopher Andrew, *An International History of the Cuban Missile Crisis* (Abingdon: Routledge, 2014).

Glees, A., and P. H. J. Davies, 'Intelligence, Iraq and the Limits of Legislative Accountability During Political Crisis', *Intelligence and National Security*, 21.5 (2006).

Gleijeses, Piero, 'Ships in the Night: The CIA, the White House and the Bay of Pigs', *Journal of Latin American Studies*, 27.1 (1995).

Golitsyn, Anatoliy, *New Lies for Old: The Communist Strategy of Deception and Disinformation* (London: G. S. G. & Associates, 1990).

Gordon, Michael R., and Bernard E. Trainor, *Cobra II: The Inside Story of the Invasion and Occupation of Iraq* (New York: Pantheon, 2006).

Gonzalez, Servando, *The Nuclear Deception: Nikita Khrushchev and the Cuban Missile Crisis* (Oakland, CA: Spooks Books, 2002).

Goodchild, J. A., *Most Enigmatic War: R. V. Jones and the Genesis of British Scientific Intelligence, 1939–45* (London: Helion and Company, 2017).

Goodman, Michael S., 'Jones' Paradigm: The How, Why, and Wherefore of Scientific Intelligence', *Intelligence and National Security*, 24.2 (2009).

Goodman, Michael S., *The Official History of the Joint Intelligence Committee, Volume I: From the Approach of the Second World War to the Suez Crisis* (London: Routledge, 2014).

Goodman, Michael S., *Spying on the Nuclear Bear: Anglo-American Intelligence and the Soviet Bomb* (Stanford: Stanford University Press, 2007).

Gordievsky, Oleg, *Next Stop Execution* (Basingstoke: Macmillan, 1995).

Gregory, Frank, and Paul Wilkinson, *International Security Programme New Security Challenges Briefing Paper 05/01*, Chatham House, 18 July 2005.

Gribkov, Anatoli I., William Y. Smith and Alfred Friendly, *Operation Anadyr: US and Soviet Generals Recount the Cuban Missile Crisis* (Chicago: Edition Q, 1994).

Grimes, Sandra, and Jeanne Vertefeuille, *Circle of Treason: A CIA Account of Traitor Aldrich Ames and the Men He Betrayed* (Annapolis: Naval Institute Press, 2013).

Halpern, S., and H. Peake, 'Did Angleton Jail Nosenko?', *International Journal of Intelligence and Counterintelligence*, 3.4 (1989).

Harlow, Bill (ed.), *Rebuttal: The CIA Responds to the Senate Intelligence Committee's Study of Its Detention and Interrogation Program* (Naval Institute Press: Annapolis, 2015).

Hayden, Michael, *Playing to the Edge: American Intelligence in the Age of Terror* (New York: Penguin Press, 2016).

Haynes, John Earl, and Harvey Klehr, *Venona: Decoding Soviet Espionage in America* (New Haven: Yale University Press, 2000).

Helms, Richard, *A Look Over My Shoulder: A Life in the Central Intelligence Agency* (New York: Ballantine Books, 2003).

Hennessy, Peter, *The Secret State: Whitehall and the Cold War* (London: Allen Lane, 2002).

Holloway, David, *Stalin and the Bomb: The Soviet Union and Atomic Energy, 1939–1956* (London: Yale University Press, 1994).

Jeffreys-Jones, Rhodri, *The CIA and American Democracy* (London: Yale, 2003).

Jeffreys-Jones, Rhodri, *Cloak and Dollar: A History of American Secret Intelligence* (New Haven: Yale University Press, 2002).

Jervis, R., 'Reports: Politics and Intelligence Failures: The Case of Iraq', *Journal of Strategic Studies*, 29.1 (2006).

Jervis, Robert, *Why Intelligence Fails: Lessons from the Iranian Revolution and the Iraq War* (Ithaca: Cornell University Press, 2011).

Johnson, Loch K., *Bombs, Bugs, Drugs, and Thugs: Intelligence and America's Quest for Security* (London: New York University Press, 2000).

Johnson, Loch K., 'The Church Committee Investigation of 1975 and the Evolution of Modern Intelligence Accountability', *Intelligence and National Security*, 23.2 (2008).

Jones, Howard, *Crucible of Power: A History of American Foreign Relations from 1897* (Lanham, MD: Rowan and Littlefield, 2008).

Jones, Nate, *Able Archer 83: The Secret History of the NATO Exercise that Almost Triggered Nuclear War* (London: The New Press, 2016).

Kakar, M. Hassan, *Afghanistan: The Soviet Invasion and the Afghan Response, 1979–1982* (London: University of California Press, 1995).

Kaplan, Fred, *The Wizards of Armageddon* (Stanford: Stanford University Press, 1983).

Karalekas, Anne, 'History of the Central Intelligence Agency', *Book IV, Final Report of the Select Committee to Study Governmental Operations with Respect to Intelligence Activities. United States Senate* (Washington, DC: CIA, 1976).

Kohlmann, Evan F., *Al-Qaida's Jihad in Europe: The Afghan-Bosnian Network* (London: Berg, 2004).

Kramer, M., 'US Intelligence Performance and US Policy during the Polish Crisis of 1980–81: Revelations from Kuklinkski Files', *Intelligence and National Security*, 26.2–3 (2011).

Kruh, Louis, 'Stimson, the Black Chamber, and the "Gentlemen's Mail" quote', *Cryptologia*, 12.2 (1988).

Kurlantzick, Joshua, *A Great Place to Have a War: America in Laos and the Birth of a Military CIA* (New York: Simon and Schuster, 2016).

Kurzman, Charles, *The Unthinkable Revolution in Iran* (Cambridge, MA: Harvard University Press, 2004).

Leffler, Melvyn P., and Odd Arne Westad (eds), *The Cambridge History of the Cold War, Vol 1: Origins* (Cambridge: Cambridge University Press, 2005).

Maas, Peter, *Killer Spy: The Inside Story of the FBI's Pursuit and Capture of Aldrich Ames, America's Deadliest Spy* (London: Warner, 1995).

Macintyre, Ben, *The Spy and the Traitor* (Milton Keynes: Viking, 2018).

Maddrell, Paul, *Spying on Science: Western Intelligence in Divided Germany, 1945–1961* (Oxford: Oxford University Press, 2006).

Manchanda, A., 'When Truth is Stranger Than Fiction: The Able Archer Incident', *Cold War History*, 9.1 (February 2009).

Mangold, Tom, *Cold Warrior: James Jesus Angleton: The CIA's Master Spy Hunter* (London: Simon & Schuster, 1991).

Martin, David C., *Wilderness of Mirrors: Intrigue, Deception, and the Secrets that Destroyed Two of the Cold War's Most Important Agents* (London: Lyons Press, 2003).

McNeill, Jena Baker, James Jay Carafano and Jessica Zuckerman, '30 Terrorist Plots Foiled: How the System Worked', *Heritage Foundation Backgrounder*, No. 2405 (29 April 2010).

Mercado, Stephen C., 'Sailing the Sea of OSINT in the Information Age', *Studies in Intelligence*, 48.3 (2004).

Morley, Jefferson, *The Ghost: The Secret Life of CIA Spymaster James Jesus Angleton* (London: Scribe, 2017).

Murphy, David E., Sergei A. Kondrashev and George Bailey, *Battleground Berlin: CIA vs. KGB in the Cold War* (New Haven: Yale University Press, 1997).

Nuti, Leopoldo, Frederic Bozo, Marie-Pierre Rey and Bernd Rother (eds), *The Euromissile Crisis and the End of the Cold War* (Stanford: Stanford University Press, 2015).

Nutting, Anthony, *No End of a Lesson: The Story of Suez* (New York: C. N. Potter, 1967).

Oberdorfer, Don, *From the Cold War to a New Era: The United States and the Soviet Union, 1983–1991* (London: Johns Hopkins Press, 1998).

Olson, James M., *Fair Play: The Moral Dilemmas of Spying* (Washington, DC: Potomac Books, 2006).

Omand, David, Jamie Bartlett and Carl Miller, 'Introducing Social Media Intelligence (SOCMINT)', *Intelligence and National Security*, 27.6 (2012).

Ostermann, C. F., 'New Evidence on the War in Afghanistan', *Cold War International History Project*, 14.15 (2011).

Ovendale, R., 'Britain, the United States, and the Recognition of Communist China', *The Historical Journal*, 26.1 (1983).

Ovodenko, A., '(Mis)interpreting Threats: A Case Study of the Korean War', *Security Studies*, 16.2 (2007).

Phillips, Melanie, *Londonistan* (New York: Encounter Books, 2006).

Pillar, Paul, 'Intelligence', in Audrey Kurth Cronin and James M. Ludes (eds), *Attacking Terrorism: Elements of a Grand Strategy* (Washington, DC: Georgetown University Press, 2004).

Pollack, K. M., 'Spies, Lies and Weapons: What Went Wrong', *The Atlantic Monthly*, 293.1 (2004).

Powell, Bill, 'How George Tenet Brought the CIA Back from the Dead', *Fortune International (Europe)*, 148.8 (13 October 2003).

Prados, John, *Combined Fleet Decoded: The Secret History of American Intelligence and the Japanese Navy in World War II* (New York: Random House, 1995).

Prados, John, *Safe for Democracy: The Secret Wars of the CIA* (Chicago: Ivan R. Dee, 2006).

Prados, John, *The Soviet Estimate: US Analyses of the Soviet Union, 1947–1991* (Princeton: Princeton University Press, 1982).

Prados, John, *Vietnam: A History of an Unwinnable War, 1945–1975* (Lawrence: University Press of Kansas, 2009).

Quirk, Robert E., *Fidel Castro* (New York: W. W. Norton and Co., 1993).

Radsan, A. J., 'One Lantern in the Darkest Night – The CIA's Inspector General', *Journal of National Security Law and Policy*, 247 (2010).

Richelson, Jeffrey T., *Spying on the Bomb: American Nuclear Intelligence form Nazi Germany to Iran and North Korea* (London: W. W. Norton, 2006).

Richelson, Jeffrey T., *The Wizards of Langley: Inside the CIA's Directorate of Science and Technology* (Boulder, CO: Westview Press, 2008).

Rizzo, John, *Company Man: Thirty Years of Controversy and Crisis in the CIA* (New York: Scribner, 2014).

Roadnight, Andrew, *United States Policy towards Indonesia in the Truman and Eisenhower Years* (Basingstoke: Palgrave Macmillan, 2002).

Robarge, D., 'Moles, Defectors, and Deceptions: James Angleton and CIA Counterintelligence', *Journal of Intelligence History*, 3.2 (2003).

Rodriguez, Jose A., Jr, *Hard Measures: How Aggressive CIA Actions After 9/11 Saved American Lives* (New York: Threshold Editions, 2012).

Roman, Peter J., *Eisenhower and the Missile Gap* (Ithaca: Cornell University Press, 1995).

Royden, Barry G., 'James J. Angleton, Anatoliy Golitsyn, and the "Monster Plot": Their Impact on CIA Personnel and Operations', *Studies in Intelligence*, 55.4 (December 2011).

Russell, Richard L., 'CIA's Strategic Intelligence in Iraq', *Political Science Quarterly*, 117.2 (2002).

Ryan, Amy, and Gary Keeley, 'Sputnik and US Intelligence: The Warning Record', *Studies in Intelligence*, 61.3 (2017).

Sacquety, Troy J., *The OSS in Burma: Jungle War against the Japanese* (Lawrence: University Press of Kansas, 2013).

Scahill, Jeremy, *Dirty Wars: The World is a Battlefield* (New York: Nation Books, 2013).

Schecter, Jerrold, and Peter Deriabin, *The Spy who Saved the World: How a Soviet Colonel Changed the Course of the Cold War* (New York: Scribner, 1992).

Schlesinger, Arthur M., Jr, *A Thousand Days: John F. Kennedy in the White House* (Boston: Houghton Mifflin, 1965).

Scott, L. V., 'Intelligence and the Risk of Nuclear War: *Able Archer-83* Revisited', *Intelligence and National Security*, 26.4 (2011).

Scott, Len, 'Espionage and the Cold War: Oleg Penkovsky and the Cuban Missile Crisis', *Intelligence and National Security*, 14.3 (1999).

Scott, Len, and Huw Dylan, 'Cover for Thor: Divine Deception Planning for Cold War Missiles', *Journal of Strategic Studies*, 33.5 (2010).

Sharkov, Damien, 'Flynn–Putin Dinner: Russian Leader Had No Idea Who US General Was, Says RT Chief', *Newsweek*, 4 December 2017.

Shryock, R. W., 'For an Eclectic Sovietology', *Studies in Intelligence*, 8.1 (1995).

Shuckburgh, Evelyn, and John Charmley, *Descent to Suez: Diaries, 1951–56* (New York: Norton, 1987).

Simpson, Paul, *A Brief History of the Spy: Modern Spying from the Cold War to the War on Terror* (Philadelphia: Running Press, 2013).

Sokolski, Henry D., *Best of Intentions: America's Campaign against Strategic Weapons Proliferation* (London: Prager, 2001).

Stafford, David, *Spies Beneath Berlin* (London: John Murray, 2002).

Steury, Donald P. (ed.), *On the Front Lines of the Cold War: Documents on the Intelligence War in Berlin, 1946 to 1961*, 2nd edn (Washington, DC: Center for the Study of Intelligence, 2000).

Stout, Mark, 'World War I and the Birth of American Intelligence Culture', *Intelligence and National Security*, 32.3 (2017).

Stuart, Douglas T., *Creating the National Security State: A History of the Law that Transformed America* (Woodstock: Princeton University Press, 2008).

Szporer, Michael, *Solidarity: The Great Workers Strike of 1980* (Lexington, KY: Lexington Books, 2014).

Tenet, George J., *At the Center of the Storm: My Years at the CIA* (New York: Harper Collins, 2007).

The Commission on the Intelligence Capabilities of the United States Regarding Weapons of Mass Destruction – Report to the President of the United States, March 31, 2005 (Washington, DC: CIA, 2005).

Vadney, T. E., *The World Since 1945* (London: Penguin, 1998).

Varouhakis, M., 'An Institution-Level Theoretical Approach for Counterintelligence', *International Journal of Intelligence and Counterintelligence*, 24.3 (2011).

Wallace, Robert H., Keith Melton and Henry R. Schlesinger, *Spycraft: The Secret History of the CIA's Spytechs, from Communism to Al-Qaeda* (London: Penguin, 2009).

Walton, Calder, *Empire of Secrets* (London: Harper Press, 2013).

Warner, Michael, 'Lessons Unlearned: The CIA's Internal Probe of the Bay of Pigs Affair', *Studies in Intelligence*, 42.5 (2007).

Warner, Michael, *The Rise and Fall of Intelligence: An International Security History* (Washington, DC: Georgetown University Press, 2014).

Warner, Michael, 'US Intelligence and Vietnam: The Official Versions(s)', *Intelligence and National Security*, 25.5 (2010).

Weiner, Tim, *Legacy of Ashes: The History of the CIA* (London: Penguin, 2007).

Weiner, Tim, David Johnston and Neil A. Lewis, *Betrayal: The Story of Aldrich Ames, An American Spy* (London: Richard Cohen Books, 1996).

Weiser, Benjamin, *A Secret Life: The Polish Officer, His Covert Mission, and the Price He Paid to Save His Country* (New York: Public Affairs, 2004).

Wells, Luke Benjamin, 'The "Bomber Gap": British Intelligence and an American Delusion', *Journal of Strategic Studies*, 40.7 (2017).

Westerfield, H. Bradfield (ed.), *Inside CIA's Private World* (Ann Arbor: Edwards Brothers, 1987).

Willrich, Mason, and John B. Rhinelander, 'An Overview of SALT 1', *The American Journal of International Law*, 67.5 (1973).

Wirtz, James J., 'Intelligence to Please? The Order of Battle Controversy during the Vietnam War', *Political Science Quarterly*, 106.2 (1991).

Wirtz, James J., *The Tet Offensive: Intelligence Failure in War* (Ithaca: Cornell University Press, 1991).

Wise, David, *Molehunt: The Secret Search for Traitors That Shattered the CIA* (London: Random House, 1992).

Wise, David, *Nightmover: How Aldrich Ames Sold the CIA to the KGB for $4.6 Million* (London: HarperCollins, 1995).

Wise, David, *The Spy Who Got Away: The Inside Story of Edward Lee Howard, the CIA Agent Who Betrayed His Country's Sections and Escaped to Moscow* (London: Random House, 1988).

Wolf, M. W., 'Stumbling Towards War: The Soviet Decision to Invade Afghanistan', *Past Imperfect*, 12 (2006).

Woods, Randall B., *Shadow Warrior: William Egan Colby and the CIA* (New York: Basic Books, 2018).

Wright, Lawrence, *The Looming Tower: Al-Qaeda and the Road to 9/11* (New York: Alfred A. Knopf, 2006).

Zaloga, Steven J., *The Kremlin's Nuclear Sword: The Rise and Fall of Russia's Strategic Nuclear Forces, 1945–2000* (Washington, DC: Smithsonian Books, 2002).

Online Sources and Documents by Organisation

All online documents last accessed 10 January 2020, unless otherwise noted.

The American Presidency Project
Kennedy, John F., 'Statement on Cuba by Senator John F. Kennedy', *The American Presidency Project*, <https://www.presidency.ucsb.edu/node/274373>.

The Atlantic
Woods, Chris, 'The Story of America's Very First Drone Strike', *The Atlantic*, 30 May 2015, <https://www.theatlantic.com/international/archive/2015/05/america-first-drone-strike-afghanistan/394463/>.

BBC
BBC News timeline of the Kuwait Crisis, <http://news.bbc.co.uk/1/hi/world/middle_east/861164.stm>.

'Two Weeks in January: America's Secret Engagement with Khomeini', *BBC Persia*, 3 June 2016, <www.bbc.co.uk/news/world-us-canada-36431160>.

Breaking Defense
Clark, Colin, 'Biometrics May Mean the End of a Spy's Disguise', *Breaking Defense*, 20 October 2014, <http://breakingdefense.com/2014/10/biometrics-may-mean-end-of-the-spys-disguise/>.

Central Intelligence Agency

'A USSR Without Andropov?', CIA Directorate of Intelligence, 28 March 1983, <https://www.cia.gov/library/readingroom/docs/CIA-RDP85T00153R000100 060026-7.pdf>.

'Afghanistan: Prospects for the Resistance', NIE 37-83, 4 October 1983, <https://www.cia.gov/library/readingroom/docs/CIA-RDP86T00302R000400570001-8.pdf>.

Ahern, Thomas L., Jr, *Vietnam Histories*, CIA website: *Library*, <https://www.cia.gov/library/readingroom/collection/vietnam-histories>.

'Andropov: His Power and Program', Deputy Director for Intelligence to Director of Central Intelligence, 17 November 1982, <https://www.cia.gov/library/readingroom/docs/CIA-RDP84B01072R000200110011-4.pdf>.

'Andropov's Likely Strategy for Economic Change', CIA Directorate of Intelligence, 1 July 1983, <https://www.cia.gov/library/readingroom/docs/DOC_0000498531.pdf>.

Becker, Joseph, 'The Computer: Capabilities, Prospects and Implications', *Studies in Intelligence*, 4.4 (Fall 1960), p. 63, <https://www.cia.gov/library/center-for-the-study-of-intelligence/kent-csi/vol4no4/html/v04i4a04p_0001.htm>.

Bukharin, Oleg, 'The Cold War Atomic Intelligence Game, 1945–1970: From a Russian Perspective', *Studies in Intelligence*, 48.2 (2004), <https://www.cia.gov/library/center-for-the-study-of-intelligence/csi-publications/csi-studies/studies/vol48no2/article01.html>.

Bundy, McGeorge, 'Memorandum for the President: Meeting on Cuba, 4:00 PM, March 15, 1961', declassified 24 October 2014, <https://www.cia.gov/library/readingroom/docs/CIA-RDP85-00664R000400050065-2.pdf>.

Cabell, C. P., 'The Inspector General's Survey of the Cuban Operation', 15 December 1961, <https://www.cia.gov/library/readingroom/docs/CIA-RDP80B01676R001 900160013-3.pdf>.

'Chernenko: A Preliminary Assessment of the Man and His Policy Agenda', CIA Directorate of Intelligence, 16 March 1984, <https://www.cia.gov/library/readingroom/docs/CIA-RDP85T00287R001400410001-3.pdf>.

CIA, Office of Public Affairs brochure, <https://www.cia.gov/library/publications/resources/central-intelligence-agency-brochure/CleanedOPA%20Brochure%20final.pdf>.

'CIA Statement on Claims by Wikileaks', CIA website: *News & Information*, 8 March 2017, <https://www.cia.gov/news-information/press-releases-statements/2017-press-releases-statements/cia-statement-on-claims-by-wikileaks.html>.

'Clandestine Services History: The Berlin Tunnel Operation 1952–1956', CS Historical Paper No. 150, published in classified form (internally) 25 August 1967, declassified and released 15 February 2007, <https://www.cia.gov/library/readingroom/docs/DOC_0001459120.pdf>.

Cohen, David S., 'Deputy Director Cohen Delivers Remarks on CIA of the Future at Cornell University', CIA website: *News & Information*, 17 September 2015, <https://www.cia.gov/news-information/speeches-testimony/2015-speeches-testimony/deputy-director-cohen-delivers-remarks-on-cia-of-the-future-at-cornell-university.html>.

Devlin, John F., and Robert L. Jervis, 'Analysis of NFAC's Performance on Iran's Domestic Crisis, Mid-1977 – 7 November 1978', 15 June 1979, <https://www.cia.gov/library/readingroom/docs/DOC_0001259322.pdf>.

Dujmovic, Nicholas, 'The Significance of Walter Bedell Smith as Director of Central Intelligence, 1950–1953', n.d., <https://www.cia.gov/library/readingroom/docs/Misc-009.pdf>.

Dulles, Allen W., William H. Jackson and Mathias F. Correa, *The Central Intelligence Agency and National Organization for Intelligence*, report to the NSC, 1 January 1949, <https://www.cia.gov/library/readingroom/docs/CIA-RDP86B00269R001100090002-8.pdf>.

Ehrman, J., 'Towards a Theory of CI: What Are We Talking About When We Talk About Counterintelligence?', *Studies in Intelligence*, 53.2 (June 2009), <https://www.cia.gov/library/center-for-the-study-of-intelligence/csi-publications/csi-studies/studies/vol53no2/toward-a-theory-of-ci.html>.

Fischer, B. B., 'The 1983 War Scare in US–Soviet Relations', *Studies in Intelligence* (1996), <https://www.cia.gov/library/readingroom/docs/DOC_0006122556.pdf>.

Ford, Harold P., *The CIA and the Vietnam Policymakers: Three Episodes, 1962–1968* (Washington, DC: CIA, 2007), <https://www.cia.gov/library/center-for-the-study-of-intelligence/csi-publications/books-and-monographs/cia-and-the-vietnam-policymakers-three-episodes-1962-1968>.

'From Pearl Harbor to the Digital Age: Open Source Enterprise Celebrates 75th Anniversary', CIA website: *News & Information*, 7 December 2016, <https://www.cia.gov/news-information/featured-story-archive/2016-featured-story-archive/ose-pearl-harbor-to-digital-age.html>.

'Gorbachev, the New Broom', CIA Directorate of Intelligence, June 1985, <https://www.cia.gov/library/readingroom/docs/CIA-RDP85T01058R000507710001-6.pdf>.

'Gorbachev's Domestic Challenge: The Looming Problems', CIA Directorate of Intelligence, February 1987, <https://www.cia.gov/library/readingroom/docs/19870201.pdf>.

'Gorbachev's Economic Agenda: Promises, Potentials, and Pitfalls', CIA Directorate of Intelligence, September 1985, <https://www.cia.gov/library/readingroom/docs/19850901.pdf>.

'Gorbachev's Reorganization of the Party: Breaking the Stranglehold of the Apparatus', CIA Directorate of Intelligence, June 1989, <https://www.cia.gov/library/readingroom/docs/19890601.pdf>.

'Government in Iraq', CIA intelligence memorandum, 31 October 1978, <https://www.cia.gov/library/readingroom/docs/CIA-RDP80T00634A000400010048-0.pdf>.

Haines, Gerald K., and Robert E. Legget, *CIA's Analysis of the Soviet Union, 1947–1991* (Washington, DC: CIA, 2001), <https://www.cia.gov/library/center-for-the-study-of-intelligence/csi-publications/books-and-monographs/cias-analysis-of-the-soviet-union-1947-1991/index.html>.

Haines, Gerald K., and Robert E. Legget, *Watching the Bear: Essays on CIA's*

Analysis of the Soviet Union (Washington, DC: CIA, 2003), <https://www.cia.gov/library/center-for-the-study-of-intelligence/csi-publications/books-and-monographs/watching-the-bear-essays-on-cias-analysis-of-the-soviet-union/>.

Haines, Gerald K., *At Cold War's End: US Intelligence on the Soviet Union and Eastern Europe, 1989–1991* (Washington, DC: CIA, 1999), <https://www.cia.gov/library/center-for-the-study-of-intelligence/csi-publications/books-and-monographs/at-cold-wars-end-us-intelligence-on-the-soviet-union-and-eastern-europe-1989-1991/art-1.html>.

'History of the CIA', CIA website: *About CIA*, 10 April 2007, <https://www.cia.gov/about-cia/history-of-the-cia>.

'Iran: A Political Assessment', memorandum for D/ORPA, 9 August 1978, <https://www.cia.gov/library/readingroom/docs/CIA-RDP80T00634A0004000 10058-9.pdf>.

'Iraq: Saddam Husayn Appointed General', 13 January 1976, <https://www.cia.gov/library/readingroom/docs/DOC_0005388899.pdf>.

'Iraq's Shias: Saddam Blunts a Potential Threat', CIA Directorate of Intelligence, 1 November 1984, <https://www.cia.gov/library/readingroom/docs/CIA-RDP85 T00314R000300110003-5.pdf>.

'Iraq's Tikritis: Power Base of Saddam Husayn', CIA Directorate of Intelligence, February 1987, <https://www.cia.gov/library/readingroom/docs/CIA-RDP88T0 0096R000400540002-8.pdf>.

'Islam in Iran', CIA National Foreign Assessment Center [NFAC], March 1980, <https://www.cia.gov/library/readingroom/docs/CIA-RDP81B00401R0004001 10013-5.pdf>.

Kent, Sherman, 'A Crucial Estimate Relived', *Studies in Intelligence*, 36.5 (Spring 1964), pp. 111–19, <https://www.cia.gov/library/center-for-the-study-of-intelli gence/csi-publications/books-and-monographs/sherman-kent-and-the-board-of-national-estimates-collected-essays/9crucial.html>.

Kent, Sherman, 'The First Year of the Office of National Estimates', 10 December 1970, <https://www.cia.gov/library/center-for-the-study-of-intelligence/csi-publi cations/books-and-monographs/sherman-kent-and-the-board-of-national-esti mates-collected-essays/7year.html>.

'Khrushchev and the American Election', memorandum from Sherman Kent to the DCI, 8 October 1964, <https://www.cia.gov/library/readingroom/docs/CIA-RDP79R00904A001100010022-4.pdf>.

'Konstantin Chernenko: His Role in the Brezhnev Succession', CIA National Foreign Assessment Center, 13 March 1980, <https://www.cia.gov/library/read ingroom/docs/DOC_0000972979.pdf>.

'Learning to Estimate', CIA website: *News & Information*, 12 March 2008, <https://www.cia.gov/news-information/featured-story-archive/2008-featured-story-archive/learning-to-estimate-1948.html>.

MacEachin, Douglas J., *US Intelligence and the Polish Crisis, 1980–1981* (Washington, DC: CIA Center for the Study of Intelligence, 2000), <https://www.cia.gov/library/readingroom/docs/2000-01-01.pdf>.

'Minutes and Years: The Bin Ladin Operation', CIA website: *News & Information*,

29 April 2016, <https://www.cia.gov/news-information/featured-story-archive/2016-featured-story-archive/minutes-and-years-the-bin-ladin-operation.html>.

Minutes of the Intelligence Advisory Committee, IAC-M-1, 20 October 1950, <https://www.cia.gov/library/readingroom/docs/CIA-RDP82-00400R000100010001-4.pdf>.

'Monthly Warning Assessment: Near East and South Asia', memorandum from Robert C. Ames to the DCI, 24 July 1979, <https://www.cia.gov/library/readingroom/docs/CIA-RDP83B01027R000300110006-0.pdf>.

Parkinson, Leonard F., and Logan H. Potter, 'Closing the Missile Gap', in Joan Bird and John Bird (eds), *Penetrating the Iron Curtain: Closing the Missile Gap With Technology* (Washington, DC: CIA, 2011), <https://www.cia.gov/library/publications/cold-war/resolving-the-missile-gap-with-technology/missile-gap.pdf>.

Pedlow, Gregory W., and Donald E. Welzenbach, *The CIA and the U-2 Program, 1954–1974* (Washington, DC: CIA, 1998), <https://www.cia.gov/library/center-for-the-study-of-intelligence/csi-publications/books-and-monographs/the-cia-and-the-u-2-program-1954-1974/u2.pdf>.

Pedlow, Gregory W., and Donald E. Welzenbach, *The Central Intelligence Agency and Overhead Reconnaissance: The U-2 and OXCART Programs, 1954–1974* (New York: Skyhorse Publishing, 2016), <https://www.cia.gov/library/readingroom/docs/DOC_0000190094.pdf>.

'Political Maneuvring in the Soviet Leadership', Director of Soviet Analysis to Director of Central Intelligence, 31 October 1984, <https://www.cia.gov/library/readingroom/docs/CIA-RDP86B00420R000500950008-5.pdf>.

Pompeo, Mike, 'Director Pompeo Delivers Remarks at CSIS', transcript of speech, 13 April 2017, <https://www.cia.gov/news-information/speeches-testimony/2017-speeches-testimony/pompeo-delivers-remarks-at-csis.html>.

'Prospects for Iraq', SNIE 36.2-83, 19 July 1983, <https://www.cia.gov/library/readingroom/docs/CIA-RDP86T00302R000901440012-4.pdf>.

'Remembering CIA's Heroes: Johnny Micheal Spann', CIA website: *News & Information*, 25 November 2009, <https://www.cia.gov/news-information/featured-story-archive/johnny-micheal-spann.html>.

'Report of DCI SAL Steering Group on Soviet Dismantling and Destruction of Older ICBM Launchers', TS 763130/76/b, memorandum from E. Henry Knoche to the DCI, 29 October 1976, <https://www.cia.gov/library/readingroom/docs/CIA-RDP79M00467A002400050008-3.pdf>.

'Rising Political Instability under Gorbachev: Understanding the Problems and Prospects for Resolution', CIA Directorate of Intelligence, April 1989, <https://www.cia.gov/library/readingroom/docs/19890401A.pdf>.

Ruffner, Kevin (ed.), *CORONA: America's First Satellite Program*, CIA Cold War Records Series (Washington, DC: CIA, 1995), <https://www.cia.gov/library/center-for-the-study-of-intelligence/csi-publications/books-and-monographs/corona.pdf>.

Smith, Bromley, 'Memorandum for the Director of Central Intelligence, Evaluation of the Quality of US Intelligence Bearing on the TET Offensive, January

1968', 29 July 1968, <https://www.cia.gov/library/readingroom/docs/CIA-RDP79B01737A000400020002-4.pdf>.

'Soviet Capabilities for Long Range Attack Through Mid-1965', NIE 11-8-60, 1 August 1960, <https://www.cia.gov/library/readingroom/docs/DOC_0000267734.pdf>.

'Soviet Defense Policy, 1962–72', CIA Directorate of Intelligence, 28 April 1972, <https://www.cia.gov/library/center-for-the-study-of-intelligence/csi-publications/books-and-monographs/cias-analysis-of-the-soviet-union-1947-1991/memo_4_72.pdf>.

'Statement from Director Brennan on the SSCI Study on the Former Detention and Interrogation Program', CIA website: *News & Information*, 9 December 2014, <https://www.cia.gov/news-information/press-releases-statements/2014-press-releases-statements/statement-from-director-brennan-on-ssci-study-on-detention-interrogation-program.html>.

Steury, Donald P., 'How the CIA Missed Stalin's Bomb', *Studies in Intelligence*, 49.1 (2005), <https://www.cia.gov/library/center-for-the-study-of-intelligence/csi-publications/csi-studies/studies/vol49no1/html_files/stalins_bomb_3.html>.

'Strength and Composition of the Soviet Long Range Bomber Force', SNIE 11-7-58, 5 June 1958, <https://www.cia.gov/library/readingroom/docs/DOC_0000267654.pdf>.

'Strength and Deployment of Soviet Long Range Ballistic Missile Forces', NIE 11-8/1-61, 4 August 1961, <https://www.cia.gov/library/readingroom/docs/DOC_0000267739.pdf>.

'Survey of the Central Intelligence Agency', Souers to Secretary of Defense, 27 February 1948, <https://www.cia.gov/library/readingroom/docs/CIA-RDP86B00269R000500030006-7.pdf>.

'Terms of Reference of USIB Steering Group on Monitoring of Strategic Arms Limitations', USIB-D-27. 5/5, 27 June 1972, <https://www.cia.gov/library/readingroom/docs/CIA-RDP79B01709A000200020018-0.pdf>.

'The 27th CPSU Congress: Gorbachev's Unfinished Business', CIA Directorate of Intelligence, April 1986, <https://www.cia.gov/library/readingroom/docs/19860401A.pdf>.

'The Development of Soviet Military Power: Trends Since 1965 and Prospects for the 1980s', CIA Directorate of Intelligence, April 1981, <https://www.cia.gov/library/center-for-the-study-of-intelligence/csi-publications/books-and-monographs/cias-analysis-of-the-soviet-union-1947-1991/sr_81_10035x.pdf>.

The National Security Act 1947, <https://www.cia.gov/library/readingroom/docs/1947-07-26.pdf>.

'The Office of Strategic Services Memorial: Honoring the Forerunner of Today's CIA', CIA website: *News & Information*, 21 January 2010, <https://www.cia.gov/news-information/featured-story-archive/2010-featured-story-archive/oss-memorial.html>.

'The Opposition to the Shah', memorandum for Deputy Director for National Foreign Assessment, 30 October 1978, <https://www.cia.gov/library/readingroom/docs/CIA-RDP81B00401R002000120002-8.pdf>.

'The Politics of Ayatollah Ruhollah Khomeini', CIA NFAC, 20 November 1978, <https://www.cia.gov/library/readingroom/docs/CIA-RDP80T00634A00 0500010002-9.pdf>.

'The Soviet Economy under a New Leader', joint report by CIA and DIA, 19 March 1986, <https://www.cia.gov/library/readingroom/docs/19860319.pdf>.

'The Soviets and the 1984 US Elections', memorandum for DCI (sender redacted), 28 October 1982, <https://www.cia.gov/library/readingroom/docs/CIA-RDP85 T00153R000300020043-0.pdf>.

Valero, Larry A., 'The American Joint Intelligence Committee and Estimates of the Soviet Union, 1945–1947', *Studies in Intelligence*, 9 (Summer 2000), pp. 65–80, <https://www.cia.gov/library/center-for-the-study-of-intelligence/csi-publications/csi-studies/studies/summer00/art06.html>.

Warner, Michael, 'Central Intelligence: Origin and Evolution', in *The Creation of the Intelligence Community: Founding Documents* (Washington, DC: CIA, 2012), <https://www.cia.gov/library/publications/intelligence-history/creation-of-ic-founding-documents/creation-of-the-intelligence-community.pdf>.

Warner, Michael, 'COI Came First', in *The Office of Strategic Services: America's First Intelligence Agency* (Washington, DC: CIA, 2007), <https://www.cia.gov/library/publications/intelligence-history/oss/art02.htm>.

Warner, Michael, *The Office of Strategic Services: America's First Intelligence Agency* (Washington, DC: CIA, 2007), <https://www.cia.gov/library/publica tions/intelligence-history/oss/art05.htm>.

Woodward, B., and M. Dobbs, 'CIA Had Secret Agent on Polish General Staff', *Washington Post*, 4 June 1986, <https://www.cia.gov/library/readingroom/docs/ CIA-RDP90-00965R000807560045-0.pdf>.

CNN

Browne, Ryan, 'McMaster: "We have failed to impose sufficient costs" on Russia', *CNN Politics*, 4 April 2018, <https://edition.cnn.com/2018/04/03/politics/mc master-russia-costs/index.html>.

McKirdy, Euan, 'WikiLeaks' Assange: Russia didn't give us emails', *CNN.com*, 4 January 2017, <https://edition.cnn.com/2017/01/04/politics/assange-wikileaks-hannity-intv/index.html>.

Cold War International History Project

Cornwell, R., 'Ryszard Kuklinski: Cold War Spy for the West', *The Independent*, 13 February 2004. The letter itself can be seen here: <http://digitalarchive.wil soncenter.org/document/165266>.

Kramer, M., 'Soviet Deliberations during the Polish Crisis, 1980–1981', *Cold War International History Project*, Special Working Paper No. 1 (2011), <https:// www.wilsoncenter.org/sites/default/files/ACF56F.PDF>.

Kramer, M., 'The Kuklinski Files and the Polish Crisis of 1980–1981: An Analysis of the Newly Released CIA Documents on Ryszard Kuklinski', *Cold War International History Project*, Working Paper #59 (March 2009), <https://www. wilsoncenter.org/sites/default/files/WP59_Kramer_webfinal1.pdf>.

Wilson Center, *Cold War International History Project* section on the Venona decrypts, <https://www.wilsoncenter.org/article/venona-project-and-vassiliev-notebooks-index-and-concordance>.

CrowdStrike

Alperovitch, Dmitri, 'Bears in the Midst: Intrusion into the Democratic National Committee', *CrowdStrike* blog, 15 June 2016, <https://www.crowdstrike.com/blog/bears-midst-intrusion-democratic-national-committee/>.

Crunchbase

Cherney, Max A., 'Here's What 20+ In-Q-Tel Investments Said,' *Crunchbase* blog, 17 July 2017, <https://news.crunchbase.com/news/heres-20-q-tel-investments-said-taking-cias-money/>.

Cryptome

'Former CIA Director Woolsey Delivers Remarks aAt Foreign Press Center', 7 March 2000, *Cryptome*, <https://cryptome.org/echelon-cia.htm> (last accessed 10 January 2020).

Deadline

Evans, Greg, 'Barack Obama On "Daily Show" Warns Against "Flying Blind" Without Intelligence Briefings', *Deadline*, 12 December 2016, <https://dead-line.com/2016/12/barack-obama-daily-show-intelligence-briefings-russian-hacking-1201869345/>.

Defense One

Tucker, Patrick, 'What the CIA's Tech Director Wants from AI', *Defense One*, 6 September 2017, <https://www.defenseone.com/technology/2017/09/cia-technology-director-artificial-intelligence/140801/>.

Digital National Security Archive

Digital National Security Archive's project on Iraq: 'Iraqgate: Saddam Hussein, US Policy, and the Prelude to the Persan Gulf War, 1980–1994', <https://nsarchive.gwu.edu/project/iraq-project>.

'Misreading Intentions: Iraq's Reaction to Inspections Created Picture of Deception', 5 January 2006, <https://nsarchive2.gwu.edu/news/20120905/CIA-Iraq.pdf>.

National Security Archive interview with Sidney Grayeal, 29 January 1998, <http://www.gwu.edu/~nsarchiv/coldwar/interviews/episode-21/graybeal1.html>.

National Security Archive, 'The CIA's Family Jewels', <https://nsarchive2.gwu.edu/NSAEBB/NSAEBB222/>.

Pfeiffer, Jack B., 'The Taylor Commission Investigation of the Bay of Pigs', 9 November 1984 (approved for public release 25 July 2011), <https://nsarchive2.gwu.edu/NSAEBB/NSAEBB355/bop-vol4.pdf>.

'Report on the US Intelligence Community's Prewar Intelligence Assessments on Iraq', <https://nsarchive2.gwu.edu/NSAEBB/NSAEBB254/doc12.pdf>.

'The Soviet "War Scare": President's Foreign Intelligence Advisory Board Report', 15 February 1990, <https://nsarchive2.gwu.edu//nukevault/ebb533-The-Able-Archer-War-Scare-Declassified-PFIAB-Report-Released/2012-0238-MR.pdf>.

DTIC

House Committee on Armed Services report, 'Intelligence Successes and Failures in Operations Desert Shield/Storm', <http://www.dtic.mil/dtic/tr/fulltext/u2/a3 38886.pdf>.

Dzieje

'In the IPN Registered Collection, Among Others Case "Aneta-79/II" Regarding the CIA in Poland', 25 January 2017, <http://dzieje.pl/aktualnosci/w-zbiorze-zastrzezonym-ipn-min-sprawa-aneta-79ii-dot-cia-w-polsce>.

Federal Bureau of Investigation

Federal Bureau of Investigation, 'Terrorism 2000/2001', Publication #0308, p. 8, <https://www.fbi.gov/file-repository/stats-services-publications-terror-terror00_01.pdf/view>.

Federal Computer Week

Lyngaas, Sean, 'How (And Why) the CIA Plans to Expand Cyber Capabilities', *Federal Computer Week*, 24 February 2015, <https://fcw.com/articles/2015/02/24/cia-expand-cyber.aspx>.

Federation of American Scientists

Report of Investigation: The Aldrich Ames Espionage Case, Permanent Select Committee on Intelligence, US House of Representatives, 30 November 1994, <https://fas.org/irp/congress/1994_rpt/ssci_ames.htm>. Senator Feinstein's fore word is pp. 1–6 of the declassified report, which is available in full at <https://fas.org/irp/congress/2014_rpt/ssci-rdi.pdf>.

SALT I, <https://fas.org/nuke/control/salt1/text/salt1.htm>.

Testimony of Cofer Black to the Congressional Joint Investigation Committee, 26 September 2002, <https://fas.org/irp/congress/2002_hr/092602black.html>.

Fedscoop

Bing, Chris, 'New CIA Director Inherits an Agency That Is Quickly Developing Cyber Capabilities', *Fedscoop*, 27 January 2017, <https://www.fedscoop.com/new-cia-director-inherits-agency-quickly-developing-cyber-capabilities/>.

Forbes

Hudson, Marianne, 'What the Heck Are Warrants? Answers to Questions Some Angels Are Afraid to Ask,' *Forbes*, 22 December 2016, <https://www.forbes.com/sites/mariannehudson/2016/12/22/what-the-heck-are-warrants-answers-to-questions-some-angels-are-afraid-to-ask/#3ec340e147e5>.

Foreign Policy

Blanton, T., 'A Classified CIA Mea Culpa on Iraq', *Foreign Policy*, 5 September 2012, <https://foreignpolicy.com/2012/09/05/a-classified-cia-mea-culpa-on-iraq/>.

McLaughlin, Jenna, 'The Robots will Run the CIA, Too', *Foreign Policy*, 7 September 2017, <https://foreignpolicy.com/2017/09/07/the-robots-will-run-the-cia-too/>.

Gresham College

Dearlove, Richard, 'Our Changing Perceptions of National Security', transcript of lecture at Gresham College, 25 November 2009, <https://www.gresham.ac.uk/lectures-and-events/our-changing-perceptions-of-national-security>.

The Hill

Samuels, Brett, 'Trump: "Criminal deep state" caught up in "major spy scandal"', *The Hill*, 23 May 2018, <https://thehill.com/homenews/administration/388933-trump-criminal-deep-state-caught-up-in-major-spy-scandal>.

Huffington Post

Grenier, Robert, 'From Truth and Reconciliation to Lies and Obfuscation: The Senate RDI Report', *Huffington Post*, 10 August 2014, <https://www.huffingtonpost.com/robert-l-grenier/senate-rdi-report-lies-obfuscation_b_5663595.html>.

Lawfare

Weaver, Nicholas, 'The CIA's No Good, Very Bad, Totally Awful Tuesday', *Lawfare* blog, 7 March 2017, <https://www.lawfareblog.com/cias-no-good-very-bad-totally-awful-tuesday>.

London School of Economics

Glees, Anthony, '9/11: An Intelligence Failure and Its Consequences', London School of Economics blog, 11 September 2011, <http://eprints.lse.ac.uk/81287/1/blogs.lse.ac.uk-911%20an%20intelligence%20failure%20and%20its%20consequences.pdf>.

The Maddow Blog

Benen, Steve, 'Revisiting an Old Trump Question: "Are we living in Nazi Germany?"', *The Maddow Blog*, 14 August 2017, <http://www.msnbc.com/rachel-maddow-show/revisiting-old-trump-question-are-we-living-nazi-germany>.

Mary Ferrell Foundation

'Memorandum: Anatoliy Mikhaylovich Klimov, AKA Anatoliy Mikhaylovich Golitzyn', NARA: 104-10263-10004, <https://maryferrell.org/showDoc.html?docId=38159#relPageId=4&tab=page>.

Mattermark

Rowley, Jason D., 'In-Q-Tel: The CIA's VC Arm, Has Had a Busy Few Years,' *Mattermark* blog, 1 December 2016, <https://mattermark.com/q-tel-cias-vc-arm-busy-years/>.

Medium.com

O'Connell, Kevin, and Alice Chang, 'Biohacking Isn't Just for Biology Anymore?' *B.Next* blog, 18 September 2017 <https://medium.com/bioquest/biohacking-isnt-just-for-biology-anymore-fe074f90b65f>.

O'Connell, Kevin, 'The Galloping Horse GIF is Just the Trailer', *B.Next* blog, 8 August 2017, <https://medium.com/bioquest/the-galloping-horse-gif-is-just-the-trailer-ab85e7cd7bb>.

Shermeyer, Jake, 'Comet Time Series (CometTS: A New Tool for Analyzing a Time-Series of Satellite Imagery', 7 March 2018, <https://medium.com/the-downlinq/comet-time-series-cometts-a-new-tool-for-analyzing-a-time-series-of-satellite-imagery-f00c859499c7>.

National Public Radio

Gonyea, Don, 'What Exactly Is The "President's Daily Brief" And Why Is It Important?', *NPR Politics*, 13 December 2016, <https://www.npr.org/2016/12/13/505348507/what-exactly-is-the-presidents-daily-brief-and-why-is-it-important>.

Henn, Steve, 'In-Q-Tel: The CIA's Tax Funded Player in Silicon Valley,' *National Public Radio*, 16 July 2012, <https://www.npr.org/sections/alltechconsidered/2012/07/16/156839153/in-q-tel-the-cias-tax-funded-player-in-silicon-valley.>.

National Security Agency

Hanyok, Robert J., *Spartans in Darkness: American SIGINT and the Indochina War, 1945–1975*, <https://www.nsa.gov/news-features/declassified-documents/cryptologic-histories/assets/files/spartans_in_darkness.pdf>.

The National Security Agency has published a significant amount of material concerning the Venona Programme; see <https://www.nsa.gov/news-features/declassified-documents/venona/>.

NBC News

Dilanian, Ken, 'Russians Paid Mike Flynn $45K for Moscow Speech, Documents Show', *NBCnews.com*, 6 March 2017, <https://www.nbcnews.com/news/us-news/russians-paid-mike-flynn-45k-moscow-speech-documents-show-n734506>.

The New York Times

'Betrayer's Tale: A Special Report: A Decade as a Turncoat: Aldrich Ames's Own Story', *The New York Times*, 28 July 1994, <https://www.nytimes.com/1994/07/28/us/betrayer-s-tale-a-special-report-a-decade-as-a-turncoat-aldrich-ames-s-own-story.html>.

'Excerpts from Statement by CIA Officer Guilt in Spy Case', *The New York Times*, 29 April 1994, <https://www.nytimes.com/1994/04/29/us/excerpts-from-statement-by-cia-officer-guilty-in-spy-case.html>.

Goldman, Adam, Mark Mazetti and Matthew Rosenberg, 'FBI Used Informant to Investigate Russia Ties to Campaign, Not to Spy, as Trump Claims', *The New York Times*, 8 May 2018, <https://www.nytimes.com/2018/05/18/us/politics/trump-fbi-informant-russia-investigation.html>.

Landler, Mark, and David E. Sanger, 'Obama Says He Told Putin: "Cut It Out" on Hacking', *The New York Times*, 16 December 2016, <https://www.nytimes.com/2016/12/16/us/politics/obama-putin-hacking-news-conference.html>.

Martin, Douglas, 'Albert D. Wheelon, Architect of Aerial Spying, Dies at 84', *The New York Times*, 2 October 2013, <https://www.nytimes.com/2013/10/03/us/albert-d-wheelon-architect-of-aerial-spying-dies-at-84.html>.

Mazetti, Mark, 'Panel Faults CIA Over Brutality and Deceit in Terrorism Interrogations', *The New York Times*, 9 December 2014, <http://www.nytimes.com/2014/12/10/world/senate-intelligence-committee-cia-torture-report.html>.

Morell, Michael J., 'Trump's Dangerous Anti-CIA Crusade', *The New York Times*, 6 January 2017, <https://www.nytimes.com/2017/01/06/opinion/trumps-dangerous-anti-cia-crusade.html>.

'Prosecutors Say Official at CIA Spied for Russia', *The New York Times*, 23 February 1994, <https://www.nytimes.com/1994/02/23/us/prosecutors-say-official-at-cia-spied-for-russia.html>.

Risen, James, 'Report Faults CIA's Recruitment Rules', *The New York Times*, 18 July 2002, <https://www.nytimes.com/2002/07/18/us/report-faults-cia-s-recruitment-rules.html>.

Shane, Scott, Matthew Rosenberg and Andrew W. Lehren, 'WikiLeaks Releases Trove of Alleged CIA Hacking Documents', *The New York Times*, 7 March 2017, <https://www.nytimes.com/2017/03/07/world/europe/wikileaks-cia-hacking.html>.

Shear, Michael D., and David E. Sanger, 'Putin Led a Complex Cyberattack Scheme to Aid Trump, Report Finds', *The New York Times*, 6 January 2017, <https://www.nytimes.com/2017/01/06/us/politics/donald-trump-wall-hack-russia.html>.

The New Yorker

Entous, Adam, 'John Brennan's Choice to Confront Trump', *The New Yorker*, 20 August 2018, <https://www.newyorker.com/news/news-desk/john-brennans-choice-to-confront-trump>.

Mayer, Jane, 'The Search for Osama', *The New Yorker*, 4 August 2003, <https://www.newyorker.com/magazine/2003/08/04/the-search-for-osama>.

Sorkin, Amy Davidson, 'Jose Rodriguez and the Ninety-Two Tapes', *The New Yorker*, 30 April 2012, <https://www.newyorker.com/news/amy-davidson/jose-rodriguez-and-the-ninety-two-tapes>.

Office of the Director of National intelligence
National Security Act 1947, <https://www.dni.gov/index.php/ic-legal-reference-book/national-security-act-of-1947>.
'Appropriations', in 'CIA Act of 1949', 20 June 1949, <https://www.dni.gov/index.php/ic-legal-reference-book/central-intelligence-agency-act-of-1949>.

Politico
Thrush, Glenn, 'Elder Bush: Pelosi "paying a price" for CIA crack', *Politico*, 15 June 2009, <https://www.politico.com/blogs/on-congress/2009/06/elder-bush-pelosi-paying-a-price-for-cia-crack-019098>.

Public Radio International
Woolf, Christopher, 'Ex-CIA director to Trump: "Bring your own bucket" if you want to waterboard', *Public Radio International*, 29 February 2016, <https://www.pri.org/stories/2016-02-29/ex-cia-director-trump-bring-your-own-bucket-if-you-want-waterboard>.

Salt Lake Tribune
Apuzzo, Matt, and Adam Goldman, 'Raid on Bin Laden Compound Avenged CIA Deaths in 1998', *The Salt Lake Tribune*, 19 May 2011.

Springfield! Springfield!
Cyberwar, 'Who Hacked the DNC?', season 2, episode 2 (2016), transcript <https://www.springfieldspringfield.co.uk/view_episode_scripts.php?tv-show=cyberwar-2016&episode=s02e02>.

The State Department of the United States
'Doolittle Report', 'Report on the Covert Activities of the Central Intelligence Agency', 30 September 1954, <https://history.state.gov/historicaldocuments/frus1950-55Intel/d192>.
Foreign Relations of the United States, 1964–1968, Volume XII, Western Europe – Note on US Covert Actions, <https://history.state.gov/historicaldocuments/frus1964-68v12/actionsstatement>.
'Memorandum of Understanding Between the United States of America and the Union of Soviet Socialist Republics Regarding the Establishment of a Direct Communications Link', June 1963, <https://www.state.gov/t/isn/4785.htm>.
'National Security Council Directive on Office of Special Projects', NSC 10/2, 18 June 1948, <https://history.state.gov/historicaldocuments/frus1945-50Intel/d292>.
'NSC-50 Comments and Recommendations to the National Security Council on the Report of The Dulles-Jackson-Correa Committee Prepared by the Secretary of State and Secretary of Defense', 1 July 1949, <https://history.state.gov/historicaldocuments/frus1945-50Intel/d384>.
Office of the Historian, <https://history.state.gov/historicaldocuments/guide-to-sources-on-vietnam-1969-1975>.

'Strategic Arms Limitations Talks/Treaty (SALT) I and II', <https://history.state.gov/milestones/1969-1976/salt>.
US Department of State Office of the Historian, 'The Cuban Missile Crisis, October 1962', <https://history.state.gov/milestones/1961-1968/cuban-missile-crisis>.

The Times
'Retired SIS Officer Says He "Averted War in Cuba",' letter from Baroness Park of Monmouth to *The Times*, 8 February 2004.

Truman Library
'Long Telegram', <https://www.trumanlibrary.gov/library/research-files/telegram-george-kennan-james-byrnes-long-telegram>.

The Wall Street Journal
Schwartz, Felicia, 'US Takes Security Precautions Overseas Ahead of CIA Report', *Wall Street Journal*, 8 December 2014, <http://www.wsj.com/articles/u-s-takes-security-precautions-overseas-ahead-of-cia-report-1418073261>.

War on the Rocks
Waller, Douglas, 'How the OSS Shaped the CIA and American Special Ops', *War on the Rocks*, 2015 <https://warontherocks.com/2015/09/how-the-oss-shaped-the-cia-and-american-special-ops/>.

The Washington Post
Dawsey, Josh, Shane Harris and Karen DeYoung, 'Trump Calls Saudi Arabia a "Great Ally", Discounts Crown Prince's Responsibility for Khashoggi's Death', *Washington Post*, 20 November 2018, <https://www.washingtonpost.com/politics/trump-defends-saudia-arabias-denial-about-the-planning-of-khashoggis-death/2018/11/20/b64d2cc6-eceb-11e8-9236-bb94154151d2_story.html?utm_term=.16974ddb252b>.
Davis, Patricia, and Maria Glod, 'CIA Shooter Kasi, Harbinger of Terror, Set to Die Tonight', *The Washington Post*, 14 November 2002, <https://www.washingtonpost.com/archive/politics/2002/11/14/cia-shooter-kasi-harbinger-of-terror-set-to-die-tonight/f5010a86-a29d-4481-a339-6b51eddf3ee4/>.
Entous, Adam, Ellen Nakashima and Greg Jaffe, 'Kremlin Trolls Burned across the Internet as Washington Debated Options', *Washington Post*, 25 December 2017, <https://www.washingtonpost.com/world/national-security/kremlin-trolls-burned-across-the-internet-as-washington-debated-options/2017/12/23/e7b9dc92-e403-11e7-ab50-621fe0588340_story.html>.
Feinstein, Dianne, and Jay Rockefeller, 'The Senate Report on the CIA's Interrogation Program Should Be Made Public', *Washington Post*, 10 April 2014, <https://www.washingtonpost.com/opinions/the-senate-report-on-the-cias-interrogation-program-should-be-made-public/2014/04/10/eeeb237a-c0c3-11e3-bcec-b71ee10e9bc3_story.html?utm_term=.71b74c4f33ef>.
Glasser, Susan B., 'Probing Galaxies of Data for Nuggets', *The Washington Post*,

25 November 2005, <http://www.washingtonpost.com/wp-dyn/content/article/2005/11/24/AR2005112400848.html>.

Johnson, Jenna, 'Donald Trump on Waterboarding: "Torture works" ', *Washington Post*, 17 February 2017, <https://www.washingtonpost.com/news/post-politics/wp/2016/02/17/donald-trump-on-waterboarding-torture-works/>.

Kane, Paul, 'CIA Says Pelosi Was Briefed on Use of "Enhanced Interrogations" ', *Washington Post*, 7 May 2009, <http://voices.washingtonpost.com/capitol-briefing/2009/05/cia_says_pelosi_was_briefed_on.html>.

'Meet the Press' interview with Dick Cheney transcribed in *Washington Post*, 16 September 2001, <http://www.washingtonpost.com/wp-srv/nation/specials/attacked/transcripts/cheney091601.html>.

Miller, Greg, 'CIA Looks to Expand its Cyber Espionage Capabilities', *Washington Post*, 23 February 2015, <https://www.washingtonpost.com/world/national-security/cia-looks-to-expand-its-cyber-espionage-capabilities/2015/02/23/a028e80c-b94d-11e4-9423-f3d0a1ec335c_story.html>.

'Moynihan Bill Would Abolish CIA, Shift Functions to State', *Washington Post*, 23 January 1991, <https://www.washingtonpost.com/archive/politics/1991/01/23/moynihan-bill-would-abolish-cia-shift-functions-to-state/>.

Pincus, Walter, 'Senate Committee Sides With DNI in Its Bureaucratic Turf War With CIA', *Washington Post*, 23 July 2009, <http://www.washingtonpost.com/wp-dyn/content/article/2009/07/22/AR2009072202979.html>.

Rucker, Philip, and Greg Miller, 'Trump Visits CIA Headquarters after Sharply Criticizing the Intelligence Community', *Washington Post*, 21 January 2017, <https://www.washingtonpost.com/news/post-politics/wp/2017/01/21/trump-to-visit-cia-headquarters-after-sharply-criticizing-the-intelligence-community/>.

Taylor, Adam, 'Trump Said He Would "Take Out" the Families of ISIS Fighters', *Washington Post*, 27 May 2017, <https://www.washingtonpost.com/news/worldviews/wp/2017/05/27/trump-said-he-would-take-out-the-families-of-isis-fighters-did-an-airstrike-in-syria-do-just-that/>.

Warrick, Joby, and R. Jeffrey Smith, 'CIA Used Gun, Drill in Interrogation of Alleged Cole Mastermind', *Washington Post*, 22 August 2009, <http://www.washingtonpost.com/wp-dyn/content/article/2009/08/22/AR2009082200045.html>.

The White House

'President Discusses Beginning of Operation Iraqi Freedom', <https://georgewbush-whitehouse.archives.gov/news/releases/2003/03/20030322.html>.

'Remarks by President Trump and Vice President Pence at CIA Headquarters', <https://www.whitehouse.gov/briefings-statements/remarks-president-trump-vice-president-pence-cia-headquarters/>.

World Politics Review

Hitz, Frederick P. (5 June 2012), 'US Intelligence after the War on Terror', *World Politics Review*, <https://www.worldpoliticsreview.com/articles/12019/u-s-intelligence-after-the-war-on-terror>.

USA Today
Jackson, David, 'Obama Condemns Past Interrogation Techniques', *USA Today*, 9 December 2014, <https://eu.usatoday.com/story/theoval/2014/12/09/obama-senate-torture-report-enhanced-interrogation-techniques/20137941/>.

United Nations
'United Nations Weapons Inspectors Report to Security Council on Progress in Disarmament of Iraq', 7 March 2003, <https://www.un.org/press/en/2003/sc 7682.doc.htm>.

United States Computer Readiness Response Team
US Department of Homeland Security, 'GRIZZLY STEPPE – Russian Malicious Cyber Activity', Joint Analysis Report, 29 December 2016, <https://www.us-cert.gov/sites/default/files/publications/JAR_16-20296A_GRIZZLY%20STEPPE-2016-1229.pdf>.

United States Department of Justice
DOJ Indictment, United States of America v. Internet Research Agency, et.al., filed 16 February 2018 in the US District Court for the District of Columbia. Case 1:18-cr-00032-DLF, <https://www.justice.gov/file/1035477/download>.

United States National Archives, College Park
CIA investigation into Nosenko conducted by Bruce Solie, Office of Security, <https://ia801906.us.archive.org/33/items/YuriNosenko/Nosenko%2C%20Yuri.pdf>.
US National Archives, College Park, ORE 1, 'Soviet Foreign and Military Policy', 23 July 1946, <https://catalog.archives.gov/id/6924242>.
US National Archives, 'List of ORE Documents by Number', 14 September 1993, <https://catalog.archives.gov/id/6924241>.

United States Senate
Final report of the Select Committee to Study Governmental Operations with Respect to Intelligence Activities, *Alleged Assassination Plots Involving Foreign Leaders*, <https://www.intelligence.senate.gov/sites/default/files/94465.pdf>.
Final report of the Select Committee to Study Governmental Operations with Respect to Intelligence Activities, *Supplementary Detailed Staff Reports on Intelligence Activities and the Rights of Americans: Book 3*, <https://www.intelligence.senate.gov/sites/default/files/94755_III.pdf>.
Senate Report 111-55, 'Report to Accompany S. 1494, the Intelligence Authorization Act for Fiscal Year 2010', 22 July 2009, <https://www.intelligence.senate.gov/publications/report-accompany-s-1494-intelligence-authorization-act-fiscal-year-2010-july-22-2009>.
Senate Report 113-288, 'Report of the Senate Select Committee on Intelligence Committee Study of the CIA's Detention and Interrogation Program', 9 December 2014, <https://www.intelligence.senate.gov/sites/default/files/documents/CRPT-113srpt288.pdf>.

Statement of James R. Clapper, former Director of National Intelligence, concerning Russian interference in the 2016 United States election before the Committee on the Judiciary Subcommittee on Crime and Terrorism, United States Senate, 8 May 2017, <https://www.judiciary.senate.gov/imo/media/doc/05-08-17%20 Clapper%20Testimony.pdf>.

Index

CPSIA information can be obtained
at www.ICGtesting.com
Printed in the USA
JSHW051619280222
23433JS00004B/10

9 781474 428859